Gendered Intersections

An Introduction to Women's and Gender Studies

2nd edition

edited by
C. Lesley Biggs, Susan Gingell and Pamela J. Downe

D0761715

Fernwood Publishing • Halifax & Winnipeg

Editing: Eileen Young
Cover design: John van der Woude
Printed and bound in Canada by Hignell Book Printing

Published in Canada by Fernwood Publishing
32 Oceanvista Lane
Black Point, Nova Scotia, B0J 1B0
and 748 Broadway Avenue, Winnipeg, Manitoba, R3G 0X3
www.fernwoodpublishing.ca

Fernwood Publishing Company Limited gratefully acknowledges the financial support of the Government
of Canada through the Canada Book Fund, the Canada Council for the Arts, the Nova Scotia Department
of Tourism and Culture, the Manitoba Department of Culture, Heritage and Tourism under the Manitoba
Publishers Marketing Assistance Program and the Province of Manitoba, through the Book Publishing Tax
Credit, for our publishing program.

Library and Archives Canada Cataloguing in Publication

Gendered intersections: an introduction to women's and gender studies
/ edited by C. Lesley Biggs, Susan Gingell & Pamela Downe. — 2nd ed.

ISBN 978-1-55266-429-2 (bound).—ISBN 978-1-55266-413-1 (pbk.)

1. Sex role. 2. Women. 3. Women—Sociological aspects. 4. Women—Literary collections. I. Biggs, Lesley
II. Gingell, Susan, 1951- III. Downe, Pamela, 1964-

HQ1233.G465 2011   305.3   C2010-908038-6

Contents

SECTION I
SETTING THE STAGE: WHAT DOES IT MEAN
TO BE A WOMAN OR A MAN? C. Lesley Biggs / 28

Section I A: Setting the Stage – Pedagogy

Section I B: Setting the Stage – History

Section I B: Setting the Stage – Gender and Difference

SECTION II
FORGING FEMININITIES AND MASCULINITIES THROUGH MEDIA
AND MATERIAL CULTURES C. Lesley Biggs / 123

SECTION III
SEXUALIZING WOMEN AND MEN
Pamela J. Downe, C. Lesley Biggs and Susan Gingell / 155

SECTION IV
BODY AND SOUL: SPIRITUALITY, HEALTH AND VIOLENCE
C. Lesley Biggs and Pamela J. Downe / 205

Section IV A: Body and Soul – Religion, Spirituality and Identity

SECTION V
CARING FOR THE GENERATIONS: A LABOUR OF LOVE
C. Lesley Biggs and Pamela Downe / 311

SECTION VI
GENDERED ECONOMIES AND WAGED WORK
C. Lesley Biggs / 364

SECTION VII
LAW, GOVERNANCE, POLITICS AND PUBLIC POLICY
C. Lesley Biggs / 424

SECTION VIII
CHANGING THE WORLD: ACTIVISM FOR EQUITY
C. Lesley Biggs / 477

Online Resources

As you're reading through this text you'll note that there are references to accompanying online resources. On the partner website for this text, you'll find a number of helpful materials, including those specific to this book's chapters—images, audio of the poetry being read by the authors and the women's history quiz—as well as extras, including links to further reading, related videos and other useful resources.

Please visit the Gendered Intersections website at:
fernwoodpublishing.ca/gi2
to access these helpful resources as you read through this text.

Acknowledgements

A book of this complexity would not have been possible without the assistance of many people. We thank our Women's and Gender Studies students, who inspire us to keep (re) thinking feminism's legacy and future possibilities, and to find new ways of teaching in creative and innovative ways. We are all learners in this process! We also thank our contributors who have made this book possible through their thoughtful and imaginative work. Thanks to Jolene Beckmann for her careful review of the transcriptions of the previously published work, and to Kathleen James-Cavan who directed us to the work of poets writing about disability. A heartfelt thanks to the staff of Fernwood Publishing, to Eileen Young for her scrupulous copyediting, Curran Farris for collecting some of the biographical material and the reprint permissions, Beverley Rach for production coordination, Debbie Mathers for pre-production, Brenda Conroy for page design, Sarah Michaelson for proofreading and John van der Woude for cover design. Finally, we thank Wayne Antony, our publisher, for his unwavering support of this book, his meticulous feedback and his good humour; the book wouldn't have happened without him. Lesley dedicates this book to her dad, Bill Biggs, who helped make her the feminist that she is — despite his best intentions otherwise! Susan's dedication is to her sisters in blood and in spirit, Liz Gingell and Ruth Gingell-Potts.

About the Authors

MARISA ANLIN ALPS was born in 1970 and is of Chinese and Dutch descent. She has a B.A. from Simon Fraser University and currently works in the publishing industry. Her poetry has been broadcast on the CBC radio, and also appears in *Breathing Fire: Canada's New Poets*.

D'BI.YOUNG.ANITAFRIKA is an award-winning afrikan-jamaican dubpoet, monodramatist, and educator who has performed, published, and lectured globally. She is the author of the critically acclaimed "biomyth monodrama bloodclaat" and the originator of the orplusi performance methodology. To date anitafrika has created six albums, published three books, produced six plays, written the sankofa trilogy, starred in "lord have mercy" — Canada's first multiethnic sitcom, featured in trey anthony's "da kink in my hair," founded "anitafrika dub theatre" (At: anitafrika.com), participated in seven artist residencies, and garnered numerous awards and grants, all while raising her two young sons, moon and phoenix. Visit her website at dbiyoung.net.

MARGARET ATWOOD is the author of more than thirty books of fiction, poetry, and critical essays. She is the recipient of many awards including the Booker Prize for *The Blind Assassin*, and the Giller Prize and the Premio Modello (Italy) for *Alias Grace*. Her most recent book, *Oryx and Crake*, was long-listed for Canada Reads, 2011.

LILLIAN ALLEN is a poet, lyricist, and vocalist and Canada's foremost dub poet. Born in Spanish Town, Jamaica and now living in Toronto, Lillian Allen teaches at the Ontario College of Art. She is the author of numerous books of poetry and winner of two Juno Awards in 1986 and again in 1988.

DORIS ANDERSON was a Canadian author, journalist and women's rights activist. Among many hallmarks, Doris was made an Officer of the Order of Canada in 1974, appointed chair of the Canadian Advisory Council on the Status of Women in 1979 and was president of the National Action Committee on the Status of Women. She was also the editor of *Chatelaine* magazine and a journalist for the *Toronto Star*, and is the author of *Rebel Daughter*, and *The Unfinished Revolution: Status of Women in Twelve Countries*.

CONSTANCE BACKHOUSE is Professor of Law at the University of Ottawa. She has published many award winning books on the history of gender and race in Canada, the most recent of which is *Carnal Crimes: Sexual Assault Law in Canada, 1900–1975* (2008). She is also a co-editor of the Feminist History Society (At: FeministHistories.ca.).

NATASHA BAKHT is Associate Professor of Law at the University of Ottawa. Her research focuses on the intersections of religious freedom and women's equality. She has written extensively on religious arbitration and the rights of *niqab*-wearing women.

ISABELLA BAKKER is a Professor of Political Science at York University. A leading authority in the fields of political economy, public finance, gender, and development, her work was recognized when she was named a Fulbright New Century Scholar in 2004. Her work integrates public policy, economics, international studies and gender-based analysis. She is editor of *The Strategic Silence: Gender and Economic Policy*; *Rethinking Restructuring: Gender and Change in Canada*; and most recently, author (with Rachel Silvey) of *Beyond States and Markets: The Challenges of Social Reproduction*.

DEBORAH BARNDT is a mother, popular educator, photographer, and professor in the Faculty of Environmental Studies at York University. Her extensive publications include *Women, Food and Globalization: Women Working the NAFTA Food Chain* (1999) and *Tangled Routes: Women Workers on the Tomato Trail, Second Edition* (2008).

C. LESLEY BIGGS is Associate Professor in the Department of History at the University of Saskatchewan. She co-taught with Susan Gingell the first women's and gender course at the University. Her main areas of interest lie in the history and sociology of the professions with a particular focus on complementary and alternative healers, and the sociology of the body. Lesley was a recipient of the Master Teacher Award in 2009.

JOAN BORSA is Associate Professor of Art and Art History, and Women's and Gender Studies at the University of Saskatchewan. She is an independent curator and art critic, and in 2008 was the recipient of the Lieutenant Governor's Lifetime Achievement Arts Award administered by the Saskatchewan Arts Board.

BETH BRANT is a Mohawk writer whose writing explores First Nations literature, racism, and homosexuality. Brant's poetry, essays, and stories have appeared in countless books, including her own anthology *Writing as Witness: Essay and Talk* (1994). Her edited work, *A Gathering of Spirit: A Collection by North American Indian Women* (1989), was the one of the first books to involve only female Native American contributors.

LINDA BRISKIN is Professor in the Faculty of Liberal Arts and Professional Studies at York University. In addition to numerous articles, she has authored *Equity Bargaining/Bargaining Equity* (2006); co-edited *Women's Organizing and Public Policy in Canada and Sweden* (1999); *Women Challenging Unions: Feminism, Democracy and Militancy* (1993); and *Union Sisters: Women in the Labour Movement* (1983); and co-authored *Feminist Organizing For Change: the Contemporary Women's Movement in Canada* (1988), and *The Day the Fairies Went on Strike* (for children) (1981).

JANINE BRODIE is Canada Research Chair in Political Economy and Social Governance at the University of Alberta. Her research critically engages with many of the core challenges in Canadian politics and public policy: gender equality, political representation, regionalism, citizenship, social policy, globalization, continental integration and transformations in governance. To date, she has written or co-written eight books and has edited or co-edited three other books. She also is the co-editor of *Critical Concepts: An Introduction to Politics*, now in its fourth edition. In 2002, she was elected a Fellow of the Royal Society of Canada which noted that "the breadth of her scholarship and the strength of her academic leadership provide an impressive model for the Canadian political science community."

KLYDE BROOX is a Jamaican-born, literary and award-winning dubpoet. He is the author of the bestselling, "delightfully humorous and insightful," *My Best Friend is White* (2005). Klyde's poems and performances have been described as "bubbling with mass appeal."

ELIZABETH CLARKE is a poet, essayist, and activist. Her poems and essays have appeared in a variety of periodicals and anthologies including *Sojourner*, *Sinister Wisdom*, *Lesbian Ethics*, *The Disability Rag*, *Hanging Loose*, and *The Arc of Love*. Clarke holds an MFA in Creative Writing from Goddard College.

DUNCAN CAMPBELL is a book designer and visual artist, originally from Newfoundland, who resides in Regina, Saskatchewan. His artwork ranges from sculptural and media-based installations that explore social justice, politics, and gay identity, to illustrative paintings (under the pseudonym Marilyn Cooper) of everyday gay life.

DAVID CARPENTER is a writer of fiction, essays, and poetry. He lives in Saskatoon with the artist, Honor Kever. His most recent work of short stories, *Welcome to Canada* (2010), won the *Fore Word Review* (Michigan) silver medal for short fiction and the Independent Publishers (New York) gold medal for Western Canadian Fiction. His most recent work of nonfiction is an examination of hunting, its history, and culture, entitled *A Hunter's Confession* (2010).

VIRGINIA CAPUTO is Associate Professor of Women's Studies at Carleton University. As an ethnomusicologist and social anthropologist, her work lies at the intersection of feminism, anthropology, and expressive cultures. Her publications address issues of gender and music, the politics of childhood and youth, women and technology, and third wave feminism.

VERA CHOUINARD is Professor of Geography at McMaster University. Her research interests include feminist geography, impacts of state restructuring on disabled people, disability experiences and struggles in the Global South, and women's experiences of economic restructuring in Canadian Northern communities. She is also a disabled woman.

SANDRA KA HON CHU is a senior policy analyst with the Canadian HIV/AIDS Legal Network, where she works to promote the human rights of people living with, and vulnerable to, HIV/AIDS, in Canada and elsewhere. In 2009, Sandra co-authored *The Men Who Killed Me*, which featured the testimonials of seventeen survivors of sexual violence during the 1994 Rwandan genocide.

ELAINE COBURN is Assistant Professor of sociology in the department of Global Communications, and a permanent research member of the Centre d'analyse et d'intervention sociologiques (CADIS), at the Ecole des Hautes Etudes en Sciences Sociales (EHESS). She is the co-editor of the peer-reviewed, interdisciplinary journal *Socialist Studies/Etudes Socialistes* and on the editorial board of *New Cultural Frontiers*.

ELIZABETH COMACK is Professor of Sociology and teaches courses in feminist criminology and the sociology of law at the University of Manitoba. She is author of *Women in Trouble*, co-author, with Gillian Balfour, of *The Power to Criminalize*, editor of *Locating Law*, and co-editor, of *Criminalizing Women*. Her latest book is entitled *Out There/In Here: Masculinity, Violence, and Prisoning* (2008).

GERRY COULTER is Professor and Chairperson, Department of Sociology, Bishop's University, Sherbrooke, Quebec. He is the founding editor of the *International Journal of Baudrillard Studies* (At: ubishops.ca/baudrillardstudies). His publications may be viewed at: ubishops.ca/ccc/div/soc/soc/publications/pub-coulter.html.

SELENA CROSSON is nearing completion of her doctorate in history at the University of Saskatchewan. Her research interests include nineteenth and twentieth-century Canadian women's history and Bahá'i women's history. She has worked as a sessional instructor teaching Canadian history, women's history and the history of sexuality.

LORNA CROZIER is a poet, author and Chair of Creative Writing at the University of Victoria. Lorna has published twelve books of poetry, the most recent being *Small Beneath the Sky* (2009). Her books have received the Governor-General's Award, the Canadian Authors' Association Award, two Pat Lowther Awards, the Dorothy Livesay Award, and the National Magazine Gold Medal and first prize in the National CBC Literary Competition.

R.W. (RAEWYNN) CONNELL is University Chair in the Faculty of Education and Social Work at the University of Sydney and was formerly at the University of California Santa Cruz, the University of Toronto and Macquarie University. Raewynn's research focuses on gender, masculinities, education, social class, intellectuals, and social theory. She is the author of *Gender* (2002), *The Men and the Boys* (2000), *Masculinities* (1995), and several other books.

AFUA COOPER is a scholar, author, and poet. She earned her Ph.D. in Canadian history and the African Diaspora with a focus on the Black communities of 19th century Ontario. She has done ground-breaking work in uncovering the hidden history of Black peoples in Canada. Her most recent history publication is *The Hanging of Angélique: The Untold Story of Canadian Slavery and the Burning of Old Montréal* (2006). She is currently the Ruth Wynn Woodward Endowed Chair in the Women's Studies Department at Simon Fraser University.

DEBORAH HOW COTTNAM was a poet and school "mistress," who was born in 1725 and raised in Nova Scotia. Cottnam privately circulated her poetry under the pseudonym "Portia." Because the family fell on hard times, Cottnam, along with her daughter "Grizelda," opened a "Female Academy," first in Salem, Massachusetts, and then in Halifax and Saint John during the 1780s and 1790s. According to all accounts, the Cottnam offered a superior education for girls who attended the school. She died in 1806.

SHAWNA DEMPSEY and Lori Millan collaborate to create performance, film, video, bookworks, and installation projects. Their work has shown extensively in venues ranging from the Istanbul Biennial, to the Museum of Modern Art, to women's centres in Sri Lanka.

PAMELA J. DOWNE is Department Head and Associate Professor of Archaeology and Anthropology at the University of Saskatchewan. As a medical anthropologist, her research focuses on the cultural dynamics surrounding HIV/AIDS, the medicalization of violence, maternal and family health, and addiction.

MARILYN DUMONT was born in 1955 in Northeastern Alberta. As a Métis, she often writes of the Canadian positioning of Native women. Dumont's first collection of poetry, *A Really Good Brown Girl* (1996) won the Gerald Lampert Award for best first book of Canadian poetry. Her second collection, *Green Girl Dreams Mountains*, won both the 2001 Alberta Book Award for Poetry and the 2002 Writer's Guild of Alberta Stephan G. Stephansson Award for Poetry. She has been Writer-in-Electronic Residence at Windsor University and has taught creative writing at Simon Fraser University and Kwantlen University College.

HONORABLE LILLIAN E. (QUAN) DYCK, was born in North Battleford, Saskatchewan in 1945. Prior to being summoned to the senate in 2005, she was a professor in the Department of Psychiatry and Associate Dean (Programs), College of Graduate Studies and Research, University of Saskatchewan. Recipient of many awards and honours, she is a member of the Gordon First Nation, and proud mother of Nathan David Dyck.

GEORGINA FELDBERG was Associate Professor of Social Science at York University, Toronto where she taught in health and society, women's studies, and history. Her book, *Disease and Class: Tuberculosis and the Shaping of Modern North American Society* (1995) was awarded the Hannah Medal from the Royal Society of Canada. She is co-editor of *Women, Health and Nation* (2003).

URSULA FRANKLIN is a Canadian metallurgist, physicist, and professor, of forty years, at the University of Toronto. Franklin has written extensively on issues of feminism and pacifism, as well as the relationship between social justice and peace. She is perhaps best known for her work on the social and political effects of technology, summarized in her book *The Real World of Technology* (1992).

TAMI FRIESEN is a former Advocate and current Policy Developer at the West Coast Domestic Workers' Association, a non-governmental organization in Vancouver, which has been providing outreach, education and legal assistance to live-in caregivers for over fifteen years.

BERNIE FROESE-GERMAIN has been a researcher with the Canadian Teachers' Federation in Ottawa since 1995. In addition to co-authoring a national report on commercial activity in Canadian schools, he has authored publications on standardized testing, charter schools, online education, and educational accountability, and has written articles on various topics published in the education press. He is also an avid cyclist.

STEPHEN GAETZ is committed to a research agenda that foregrounds social justice and attempts to make research on homelessness relevant to policy and program development. He led Canada's first national research conference on homelessness at York University in 2005. Stephen Gaetz is Director of the Canadian Homelessness Research Network and the Homeless Hub (homelesshub.ca), a clearing house for homelessness research, at York University.

NATALIE GERUM graduated with distinction in Geography and Sociology at Mount Allison University in 2009. She is the recipient of the Gold 'A' Award for a series of significant and sustaining contributions in environmental sustainability at the University, and played a key role in the development of the Mount Allison Carbon policy. In 2010, she taught a one week intensive course "Place, Consciousness and Learning" at the Mount, based on recommendations emerging from her Honours thesis.

SUSAN GINGELL is Professor of English at the University of Saskatchewan and co-taught with Lesley Biggs their University's first Women's and Gender Studies courses. She currently researches the writing of the oral, and, in addition to publishing many articles, has edited a special number (83) of *Essays on Canadian Writing, Textualizing Orature and Orality,* and, with Wendy Roy, *Listening Up, Writing Down, and Looking Beyond: Interfaces of the Oral, Written, and Visual* (forthcoming).

LOUISE HALFE grew up on the Saddle Lake First Nations Reserve. Her first book of poetry, *Bear Bones & Feathers* (1994) was shortlisted for a series of awards, including the Spirit of Saskatchewan Award and the League of Canadian Poets Gerald Lampert Memorial Award. Her second book, *Blue Marrow,* was also shortlisted for several awards, including the Governor General's Literary Award for poetry.

JOANNA HARRIS is an associate with the firm of Thomas Rogers, specializing in family and children's law, matrimonial litigation, civil litigation, and class actions (particularly residential school claims). She served as Judicial Clerk for the Superior Court of Justice (2006–2007), and received her Master of Laws from Osgoode Hall Law School at York University in 2010.

ANNA HUNTER is a member of the Ktunaxa Nation and resides in Saskatoon with her daughter Alexandra. She teaches in the Department of Political Studies and in the Indigenous Peoples Justice Initiative at the University of Saskatchewan. She is also Director of the Aboriginal Public Administration Program.

FRANCA IACOVETTA is Professor of History at University of Toronto and co-editor of *Studies in Gender and History.* A historian of women, immigrants, and transnational radicals, her most recent book *Gatekeepers: Reshaping Immigrant Lives in Cold War Canada* (2006) won the Canadian Historical Association's Sir John A. Macdonald prize for the best book in Canadian history in 2008.

KARLA JESSEN WILLIAMSON is a *kalaaleq,* an Inuk, born in Greenland, and an Assistant Professor of Educational Foundations at the University of Saskatchewan. Dr. Jessen Williams has published a number of articles on Inuit gender relations in post-colonial Greenland community; edited *The Journal of Indigenous Studies*; was the first female Executive Director of the Arctic Institute of North America at the University of Calgary; and Senior Researcher for Inuit Tapiriit Kanatami, a national organization for the Inuit in Canada. Dr. Jessen Williamson is married to Dr. Robert Williamson, and is blessed with two children and two grandchildren.

YASMIN JIWANI is Associate Professor in Communication Studies at Concordia University. Her work focuses on media representations of race, gender, and violence. She is the author of *Discourses of Denial* and co-editor of *Girlhood: Redefining the Limits.*

ALLAN G. JOHNSON is a nationally recognized author in the U.S. and speaker on issues of social inequality. His books include *The Gender Knot* (2005), *Privilege, Power, and Difference* (2005), and *The First Thing and the Last* (2010). Visit his website at: agjohnson.us.

MORNY JOY is Professor in the Department of Religious Studies at the University of Calgary. She has published in the area of philosophy and religion, women and religion, postcolonialism, and intercultural studies in South and South-East Asia. Her book, *Divine Love: Luce Irigaray, Women, Gender and Religion,* was published in 2006. Recently, she has co-edited, with Jeremy Carrette, two posthumous volumes on the work of Grace Jantzen. Her next book examines the influence of continental philosophy on philosophy of religion.

DARLENE M. JUSCHKA is Associate Professor in Women's and Gender Studies, and Religious Studies at the University of Regina. She teaches theory related to feminisms, gender, sexuality, race, and the study of religion, along with courses investigating popular culture, non-human animals, and ritual, myth and symbol. She is the author an anthology *Feminism in the Study of Religion: a Reader* (2001), and *Political Bodies, Body Politic: The Semiotics of Gender* (2009).

IVAN KALMAR is Associate Professor of Anthropology and Sociolinguistics at the University of Toronto. He is the author of several books on topics ranging from orientalism and the Jews to semiotic and linguistic anthropology, and the Inuktitut. His most recent book is *Orientalism and the Jews* (with Derek Penslar).

PAT KAUFERT is currently Professor in the Department of Community Health Sciences in the Faculty of Medicine at the University of Manitoba. Her research has been in the general area of women's health, focusing on menopause, mammography, and midwifery but with a more recent interest in women, health policy, genetics, and research ethics.

LOIS KEITH is a published writer of fiction and non-fiction and her work has been translated into many languages. Her anthology of writing by disabled women, *Mustn't Grumble* (1994) won the MIND book of the year award. Her most recent novel is *Out of Place* (2003), the story of a disabled child who escapes war torn Vienna in the 1930s. Her current work includes writing, teaching creative writing at Birkbeck College, University of London and managing the equality and Diversity work at The Conservatoire for Dance and Drama.

VALERIE J. KORINEK is Professor of History at the University of Saskatchewan where she teaches Canadian cultural, gender, and sexual histories. She is the author of numerous journal articles, book chapters, and a scholarly monograph entitled *Roughing it in the Suburbs: Reading Chatelaine Magazine in the Fifties and Sixties* (2000). Presently, she is finalizing a manuscript on prairie queer communities and their histories, entitled *Prairie Fairies: Western Canadian Lesbian and Gay Communities, 1945–1980.*

HEATHER KUTTAI is a respected leader, administrator, coach, athlete, writer, and mother, and has been spinal cord injured for over three decades. She is a three-time Paralympic medalist and an experienced provincial and national team coach. She is the author of *Maternity Rolls: Pregnancy, Childbirth, and Disability* (2010).

ALISON LEE is Director of the *Good For Her Feminist Porn Awards* and continues to further engage audiences in dialogue about pornography and art through screenings and panel discussions. Her essay "The New Face of Porn" originally appeared in *This Magazine*, and was also anthologized in *The Best Canadian Essays* 2009.

DENNIS LEE is a composer and the author of many books of poetry and criticism. Winner of the Governor General's Award (1972) for *Civil Elegies and Other Poems*, Dennis Lee has served up *Alligator Pie* to countless children, as well as composing the song lyrics for "Fraggle Rock," a popular television program. In 2001 he became Toronto's first Poet Laureate.

JO-ANNE LEE is Associate Professor in the Department of Women's Studies at the University of Victoria. A sociologist by training, her research focuses on anti-racist, decolonizing theory and practice.

She has an extensive background in community development and organizing with women and girls in urban settings.

SYLVIA LEGRIS has published three poetry collections, the most recent of which, *Nerve Squall*, won the 2006 Griffin Poetry Prize and the 2006 Pat Lowther Memorial Award for the best book of poetry published by a Canadian woman. Her other books are *iridium seeds* (1998) and *circuitry of veins* (1996).

STEPHEN LEWIS is a Canadian politician, broadcaster, and diplomat. He led the Ontario New Democratic Party during the 1970s and was appointed Canada's ambassador to the U.N. in 1984. Lewis has done extensive humanitarian work in Africa, heading the Stephen Lewis Foundation, which helps individuals affected by HIV/AIDS, and has received the Order of Canada for his efforts. He is also the author of *Race Against Time: Searching for Hope in AIDS-Ravaged Africa* (2005).

JEANETTE LYNES is the author of five collections of poetry, most recently *The New Blue Distance* (2009) and *It's Hard Being Queen: The Dusty Springfield Poems* (2008). Her first novel, *The Factory Voice* (2009) was long-listed for the Scotiabank Giller Prize; it was also a *Globe and Mail* "Top 100" book for 2009. Jeanette co-edits *The Antigonish Review* and is the Coordinator of the MFA in Creative Writing in the Interdisciplinary Centre For Culture and Creativity at the University of Saskatchewan.

ELIZABETH MACKENZIE is a Vancouver artist whose work explores the complexity of familial and other interpersonal relations, and their representation. Her drawings, installations, and videos have been presented in numerous exhibitions and screenings across Canada, the United States, and Europe. For more information, see Elizabeth MacKenzie: negotiating doubt (blog) at: blogs.eciad.ca/elizabethmackenzie.

PEGGY MCINTOSH is Associate Director of the Wellesley College Center for Research on Women. A world-renowned lecturer, she consults with higher education institutions throughout the world on creating multicultural and gender-fair curricula. She is best known for authoring the groundbreaking article "White Privilege and Male Privilege: A Personal Account of Coming to See Correspondences through Work in Women's Studies" (1988).

ANGUS MCLAREN is Professor Emeritus of History at the University of Victoria and the author of eleven books, including *The Trials of Masculinity: Policing Sexual Boundaries, 1870–1930* (1997), *Sexual Blackmail: A Modern History* (2002), and *Impotence: A Cultural History* (2007).

MARILOU MCPHEDRAN is a human rights lawyer now serving as Dean of the University of Winnipeg Global College. She founded the International Women's Rights Project (University of Victoria Centre for Global Studies), before being named to the Ariel Sallows Chair in Human Rights at the University of Saskatchewan College of Law, and then appointed in 2007 as Chief Commissioner of the Saskatchewan Human Rights Commission. Marilou is Member of the Order of Canada since 1985 in recognition of her contributions to strengthening equality rights in the Canadian Constitution. She is also a founding mother of LEAF — the Women's Legal Education and Action Fund — and provides strategic counsel on "evidence-based advocacy" and "lived rights" locally and internationally.

ALLYSON MITCHELL is Assistant Professor in the School of Women's Studies at York University. Her research and practice meld feminism and pop culture to trouble representations of women and contemporary ideas about sexuality and the body via writing and art production. Her work has exhibited in galleries and festivals across Canada, the U.S., Europe, and East Asia. She has also performed extensively with Pretty Porky and Pissed Off, a fat performance troupe, as well as publishing both writing and music.

SHANI MOOTOO is a writer born in Dublin and raised in Trinidad mostly by her grandmother. Her work explores issues of identity, belonging, sexuality, gender, and sexual abuse. Her novel, *Valmiki's*

Daughter (2008) was long-listed for the Scotiabank Giller Prize while her book *Cereus Blooms at Night* (1996) was a finalist for the Giller Prize in 1997. Shani Mootoo's art has been exhibited nationally and internationally, and in the United States, mainly at the New York Museum of Modern Art.

FIONA NELSON is Associate Professor in the Department of Sociology, Coordinator of the Women's Studies Program, and Director of the Institute for Gender Research, at the University of Calgary. She is the author of two books: *Lesbian Motherhood: An Exploration of Canadian Lesbian Families* (1996) and *In the Other Room: Entering the Culture of Motherhood* (2009).

SHERYL NESTEL is Lecturer in the Department of Sociology and Equity Studies at the Ontario Institute for Studies in Education. She worked as a childbirth educator from 1981–1992, and was the director of the Humber College/Women's College Hospital Childbirth Educators Training Program between 1992–1997. Her book, *Obstructed Labour: Race and Gender in the Re-emergence of Midwifery* won the 2008 Book of the Year Prize from the Canadian Women's Studies Association.

ROXANA NG has been researching and working with immigrant women since the mid-1970s. Her chapter is based on her investigation on changes in the garment industry and her collaboration with immigrant garment workers since 1990. She is a sociologist who teaches in the Adult Education & Community Development program at OISE, University of Toronto.

bpNICHOL was a Canadian poet whose hand-drawn "concrete" poems received international acclaim in the 1960s. His publications, *Still water*, *The true eventual story of Billy The Kid*, *Beach Head*, and *The cosmic chef* all received the Governor General's Award for poetry. Nichol's work forever changed the way Canadian poets deal with text and meaning itself.

MARY NYQUIST is Professor at the University of Toronto, where she is jointly appointed to the Department of English, the Women and Gender Studies Institute, and the Literary Studies Program. Her interests include early modern literature, literature of revolution, post-colonial literature and critical race theory, and politics and poetic form. She has written on Anglo-British women novelists, mass-produced romance, modern poetry, and John Milton, and has co-edited, with Margaret Ferguson, *Re-Membering Milton: New Essays on Texts and Traditions* and, with Feisal Mohamed Milton, *Historicity and Questions of Tradition: Past and Present Essays by Canadians*. Her book, *Arbitrary Power: Slavery, Tyranny and the Power of Life and Death* is forthcoming.

M. NOURBESE PHILIP is a poet, essayist, novelist, playwright, and short story writer who was born in Tobago and now lives in Canada. She practised law for seven years in Toronto, but in 1983 she gave up law to devote more time to writing. She is author of many books including *She Tries Her Tongue*, *Harriet's Daughter* (runner up in the 1989 Canadian Library Association Prize for children's literature), and Genealogy of Resistance and Other Essays. In 2001, NourbeSe Philip was recognized for her work as "a revolutionary poet, writer and thinker" by the Elizabeth Fry Society of Toronto which presented to her their "Rebels for a Cause" award. She has also received of the YWCA Woman of Distinction award in the Arts.

NICOLE GERARDA POWER is Assistant Professor of Sociology at Memorial University and Chair of Affinity Group on Women, Gender and Health with the Newfoundland and Labrador Centre for Applied Health Research. She works mainly in the areas of work, occupational health and safety, fisheries, gender, and youth.

MARY PRATT is one of Canada's most respected realist painters, known for her perceptive depiction of light and the themes of domestic life. Pratt's work, which can be found in public and private collections, has been widely acclaimed. She has received several honorary degrees from Canadian universities, was named Companion of the Order of Canada (1996), and was awarded the Molson Prize in the Arts for the Canada Council (1997).

SUSAN PRENTICE is Professor of Sociology at the University of Manitoba, an active participant in Canada's childcare advocacy community, and is committed to public sociology and university-community collaboration. She is co-author with Martha Friendly of *About Canada: Childcare* (2009).

GILLIAN RANSON is Associate Professor in Sociology at the University of Calgary with research interests in gender, family life, and paid work. Her most recent book, Against the Grain: Couples, Gender and the Reframing of Parenting (2010), examines families who share paid work and childcare in non-traditional ways. Her current projects include a study of men who take parental leave.

MAUREEN REED is Professor in the School of Environment and Sustainability, and the Department of Geography and Planning at the University of Saskatchewan. Her research seeks to explain social and equity dimensions of environmental and land use policies as they affect rural places in biosphere reserves, national parks, and forest communities. She is co-editor with D. Draper of *Our Environment: A Canadian Perspective* (2008) fourth edition.

FRANCES ROBSON is an artist who often uses portraiture to speak about women's lives, especially her own. Robson has exhibited her photography across Canada and beyond, and has taught photography at the University of Saskatchewan since 1987. A graduate of the MFA program at the School of the Art Institute of Chicago (1985), Robson is the recipient of grants from the Saskatchewan Arts Board and Canada Council.

MARTIN ROCHLIN was born to Russian immigrant parents in the Bronx, New York, in 1928. A piano prodigy, Rochlin collaborated with Judy Garland, Pearl Bailey, Eartha Kitt, Martha Raye, Billie Holiday and other Hollywood celebrities for twenty-five years. In 1966 Rochlin earned his doctorate in psychology from the University of Southern California becoming a pioneer in the field of gay-affirmative psychotherapy. Rochlin was a leader in the campaign that led to removing homosexuality from the list of mental disorders in the *Diagnostic and Statistical Manual of Mental Disorders*. In 1974 he was one of the founders of the Association of Gay Psychologists, as well as the Los Angeles Gay and Lesbian Community Center. His work and advocacy on behalf of the lesbian and gay community earned him the moniker "Patriarch of Gay-Affirmative Therapy "in Southern California. Rochlin died in 2003.

LISA RUNDLE is a producer with the CBC's radio program *Q* and a former editor of rabble.ca. She is a co-editor of *Turbo Chicks: Talking Young Feminisms* (2001).

LIBBY SCHEIER was a Canadian poet, short story writer, and human rights activist. Scheier was highly involved with the Writers' Union of Canada and the League of Canadian poets. She taught creative writing at York and was the poetry editor of the *Toronto Star*. Some of her works include *Second Nature* (1986) and *Language in Her Eye — Writing and Gender (Views by Canadian Women Writing in English)* (1990).

CAROL SCHICK is Associate Professor in the Faculty of Education at the University of Regina. She uses feminism, critical race theory, and whiteness studies to live and work through tensions of post-colonial education and workplace experience as found on the Canadian prairies. Her most recent book is a co-edited collection with James McNinch, *I Thought Pocahontas Was a Movie: Perspectives on Race/Culture Binaries in Education and Service Professions* (2009).

GREGORY SCOFIELD is one of Canada's leading Aboriginal writers whose five collections of poetry have earned him both a national and international audience. He is known for his unique and dynamic reading style that blends oral storytelling, song, spoken word, and the Cree language. Scofield's most recent collections include *kipocihkan: Poems New & Selected* (2009) and *Love Medicine and One Song* (2009).

DENISE L. SPITZER is the Canada Research Chair in Gender, Migration, and Health at the University of Ottawa where she is also an associate professor with the Institute of Women's Studies and a Principal Scientist in the Institute of Population Health. Denise Spitzer is interested in how global processes — intersecting with gender, ethnicity, migration status and other social identifiers — are implicated in health and well-being. She is author of *Negotiating Identities: The Voices of African Women in Alberta, Canada* (2007).

VERNA ST. DENIS is Associate Professor in the Department of Educational Foundations at the University of Saskatchewan. Her research focuses on the working lives of Aboriginal teachers, critical race theory, and anti-oppressive teacher education. In 2008, she won the R.W.B. Jackson Award for most outstanding English language journal article. Recently she has completed a national study of Aboriginal teachers' professional knowledge and experience in Canadian public schools which was prepared for the Canadian Teachers' Federation and Canadian Council on Learning.

MARIA TRUCHAN-TATARYN lives and works with her husband and daughter in Ontario. Her research explores the impact of human differences on Canadian culture while her personal passion involves building caring local communities.

ARITHA VAN HERK is a novelist, writer, teacher, and editor working within Canadian literature, *belles-letters*, and contemporary culture. Her award-winning novels and essays have been published and praised nationally and internationally, and her work is the subject of dozens of studies, theses, and papers. Her most recent book is *Audacious and Adamant: the Story of Maverick Alberta*.

GAIL VANSTONE is Associate Professor and Coordinator of the Culture and Expression program in the Department of Humanities at York University. She is the author of *D is for Daring*, a study of the NFB feminist film studio (1974–1996) and is currently compiling a digital archive of filmmakers and other key players associated with Studio D. Her current digital media project *What Did She Say?* is designed as an interactive art installation bringing women's voices today into conversation with feminists from the second wave.

PAM WAKEWICH is Associate Professor in the Departments of Sociology and Women's Studies at Lakehead University. Her research has focused on gender, body, and health over the life course, and rural and northern health issues. She is currently co-authoring (with Helen Smith) as book on history, memory, and women's wartime work and identities.

RUSS WESTHAVER is Associate Professor of Sociology at Saint Mary's University, where he teaches research methods. His research interests are oriented to understanding the connections between gay men's health, health promotion, health knowledge, the body, and the pleasurable practices associated with risk taking, sex, and drug use. Previously, he was involved in the Sex Now Atlantic Canada Project.

SHANNON E. WYSS is a radical genderqueer from Washington, DC. She holds a master's degree in Women's Studies, and her principle academic interests are lesbian/gay/bisexual/trans/intersex issues, with a particular focus on trans lives and experiences. Her writing has appeared in several journals and publications and she is highly involved with the National AIDS Fund.

Introduction to the Second Edition

C. Lesley Biggs with Susan Gingell

Early one morning I woke up thinking about *Gendered Intersections* (as often happens when you are in the throes of a big project); all of the authors had emerged from the pages of the open book, and they were talking with one another. Some were chatting with the authors in neighbouring chapters; others were calling across to chapters in other sections of the book. I heard snippets of their conversations like "Nice to meet you!"; "What a great idea!"; "I hadn't thought about that topic in that way before"; "It's been a while since we last conversed," and "I disagree with you on that point!"

Initially, when this visual and auditory metaphor for the book came to mind, I was thinking about the contributors to the book, but of course, this project also involves the imagined conversations that the contributors have had with the authors that they cited in their texts, the communities to whom they belong, and ultimately, you the reader. If we include the statistics in the *Hypatia Indexes*, although the numbers are faceless, they too represent the experiences of thousands of women, men, girls, and boys. The authors (broadly speaking) include voices from the distant past, those who have been engaged actively in thinking, writing, and representing gendered intersections for some time — decades in some cases — while others are relative new-comers bringing fresh ideas and methodologies. All of the contributors are activists in their own way as community organizers, writers, academics, visual artists, poets, and storytellers — some criss-crossing these modes of communication. All are concerned in some way with the lives of women and men, boys and girls, and the ways race/ethnicity, class, sexualities, cultures, able-bodiness, and age shape those lives — the degree of emphasis changes according to the aspect of women's and men's lives being discussed by an author.

The contributors and the authors that they cite do not necessarily agree with one another, as will become evident as you read the book. In fact, in some cases they have diametrically opposed interpretations of events and subject matter. So, it will be up to you, the reader, to critically examine the various arguments and points of view and reach your own conclusions. Not even we, the editors, agree with all of the positions articulated in the book, although, some of the arguments have certainly given us pause and prompted us to reconsider our own ideas. Regardless of our personal views, however, we have included topics, issues, and ways of thinking that will ignite debate and push our collective understanding of gendered intersections to new ways of imagining and being in the world. What unites the contributors and the authors in our minds is that they are involved in *engaged* and *passionate conversations* about gendered intersections, ways of thinking that we hope you will embrace. These conversations now have been extended with the addition of the *Gendered Intersections* website (fernwoodpublishing.ca/gi2). There you will find audio recordings of some of the poems performed by the authors, as well as videos, links to other sources of information and women's organizations, and a variety of other resources.

The number of contributors to the book, and the authors they cite, is a tribute to the "staying power" of feminist thinking. As Maryellen Symons (2010) observes,

> We feminists are not modern, nor passé, but permanent. Feminism is a method of social ordering; a way of thinking that is different from patriarchy. It is an ordering based on equality, fundamentally different from the rank ordering of patriarchy. Equality is utterly

central to our thinking. It doesn't mean having identical properties; it means deserving equal concern, equal respect and consideration.

Gendered Intersections and the Women's and/or Gender Studies courses of which the book is a part provides a specifically feminist gender lens for you, the reader, to re-search, re-think, and re-imagine the worlds in which you live. We hope that you will go on beyond the course and the classroom to work — *in whatever ways work best for you* — at changing inequitable structures. For as Symons argues, "To change patriarchal ordering, we have to put our energy and attention to change structure and outlook."

The general format of the book has remained relatively unchanged since the first edition. The book is divided into eight sections — each with its own introduction, Hypatia Index, and articles, poems, and visual essays. In response to feedback, as well as our own experience of teaching with *Gendered Intersections*, we have incorporated or highlighted issues such as violence against women, and law, governance, and politics and public policy. You will note that two sections (1 and 4) include three parts respectively. Each part could have been presented as a separate section, but they are interconnected in our minds. The theme that unites Section 1, which includes parts on Pedagogy, History, and Gender and Difference, is knowledge creation, interpretation, and translation/transmission. These themes are not unique to Section 1, of course, but they are highlighted here. Section 4 includes parts on Spirituality, Health, and Violence. Again, in our minds, these topics are intertwined; it is difficult to think about mind, body, and spirit/soul (broadly defined) since they intimately affect each other, and that relationship becomes even more poignant when we think about the devastating effects of violence.

The book also has been expanded to include a greater representation of poetry and storytelling (Susan's specialty) which greatly enhances the diversity of voices (mostly Canadian but not exclusively) of poets and writers; they enrich our understanding of the texture of individual women's and men's lives. (For those of you who have not had a singularly positive experience with literary expressions [like me — Lesley here] then you are in for a treat; you do not have to have knowledge of poetry and prose in order to interpret them; but we encourage you to read them aloud in order to appreciate the writers' play with language and their lyricism.)

Lastly, the Hypatia Indexes have been extended to provide a global picture of a variety of issues. A number of our contributors focus directly on the relationship between gendered intersections in Canada and globalization in its many forms, but not all do. Nor is it possible or even appropriate, given both the specificity and diversity of Canadian experiences, to situate every issue in the book within a global context. However, in this era of transnational feminisms, we recognize that we, as citizens/residents of Canada, shape the lives of others living elsewhere in myriad of ways: through our economic, immigration, and refugee policies; the donation of aid to developing countries; the export of goods and services; and in the promotion of our cultural products. In turn, our lives in Canada are shaped by what happens elsewhere. Indeed, many of us in Canada are often the beneficiaries of globalization since we enjoy a good life as a result of the structured economic inequalities between the so-called developed countries and the Global South. Even though the Hypatia Indexes are a compilation of faceless statistics, the comparison between Canadian women's and men's experiences and those of people living in other countries often is startling in the extreme, and those statistics often are a grim reminder of the difficult, and sometimes horrendous, conditions under which women and men in other countries/nations live, work, and raise families. At other times, the statistics belie the myth that Canada is a "progressive" country;

other nations, including much poorer ones, have made far more advances in promoting equity for women than we have in Canada. What the statistics tell us is that equality for Canadian women should not be at the expense of women living in other countries. As Rosemary Brown, the first black woman elected to the Canadian House of Parliament, reminded us: "Until all of us have made it, none of us have made it" (cited in Munroe 2009).

REFERENCES

Munroe, Dawn. 2009. "Women's Quotes: Equality." *Famous Women Canadian*. At: famouscanadian-women.com/quotes/quotes page.htm#equality.

Symons, Maryellen. 2007. "Feminism in the Here and Now: Notes from Dr. Ursula Franklin's Speech. *Voices* 14, 1 (September). Toronto: Ontario Bar Association, Feminist Legal Analysis Section.

Introduction to the First Edition

Pamela J. Downe and C. Lesley Biggs

"The personal is political" is a feminist catch phrase with which most people interested in women's studies and gender issues will be familiar. It reminds us that even the most routine aspects of our daily lives can reflect influential political relations in our societies. As with many expressions, however, overfamiliarity can relegate it as important only for a bygone era. "That was the way it was for my mom," we often hear in my women's and gender studies classes as we introduce the "personal is political" for discussion. "But, like, with me, you know, I think we're over all that political stuff." The problem with this response lies not in the young women expressing these sentiments, who are usually as self-aware of their positions in society and as committed to social advocacy as those who actively embraced this slogan some thirty years ago. Instead, perhaps, the problem lies in how we politicize the world around us and the ways in which we communicate it to others. Who has been marginalized or silenced when only some aspects of select personal lives have been politicized to the exclusion of others? What have we continued to take for granted, and why? To what extent have we incorporated our own behaviours into the critical readings of power relations that inform the intersecting categories of gender, race, culture, class, ability, sexuality, age and geographical location?

One of our objectives in bringing together the diverse works that constitute this text is to offer a representation of how various scholars, artists and activists today are politicizing their lives and the lives of others. The contributors to this volume take up a wide array of topics in a variety styles to offer political renderings of everyday lives that incorporate both the groundbreaking ideas of the past and perspectives uniquely relevant to the first few years of the twenty-first century. As editors, our aim is to join those who are retreating from universalized images of women, girls, men and boys and instead provide analytical and creative insights into — to take one example — experiences of youth who are marginalized by class, homelessness and immigration. Rather than limit discussions of mothering to the experiences of able-bodied and heterosexual women, we disrupt the taken-for-granted interpretations of "mother" to consider experiences of mothers with disabilities and lesbian mothers, the dilemmas of those requiring other-than-mother care and creative representations of what it means to care for the next generation. In considering sexuality, we include perspectives that not only politicize women's bodies but also require us to examine masculinity, commercialized sex and how those marginalized through homophobia cope with pregnancy loss.

The topics covered here are not meant to be comprehensive or exhaustive. Rather than compile a series of overview or review essays, our intent is to present short, discussion pieces that take up only one or two aspects of any given topic. In fact, we specifically asked contributors not to write summarizing synopses like those that can be found in other excellent readers in women's and gender studies. We requested contributors to lend critical commentary to what they feel are among the one or two most interesting, important or noteworthy issues within a broader subject area. Our objective in designing this collection in this way is to provide readers with the opportunity to piece together their own "big picture," and we hope that they do so by attending to the intersections among the contributions as well as the emergent gaps and silences. And there are definite gaps in this text: the voices of Francophone women, transgendered people and children are most notably absent. This is not by design but by circumstance; some invitations to contribute were declined, a few chapters were never completed, and some scholars and artists working in these areas were and are unknown to us. We hope that these lamentable silences will be filled with the discussion and debate of readers and students.

Within any institutionalized academic field of study, there is a huge emphasis on the written word and research-based insight. For those of us mired in scholastic environments, this is required and necessary. While we should not embrace research-based knowledge as providing an exclusive truth, we should not shy from it either. Careful and considered research offers incredible insight into issues of great importance to women, men and children everywhere. Among those presented here are the gendered implications of Aboriginal self-government initiatives; dynamics of First Nations communities; the challenges faced by those living in poverty; the struggles of waged workers, food producers, scientists and home care workers; celebrations of spirituality and violations of bodies; fashion; globalization; pedagogical strategies for student-based learning initiatives; and various forms of community activism. It is important to remember, however, that as undeniably valuable as empirical research-based inquiry can be, it represents only one way of uncovering and communicating the complexities of everyday life and social process. There are other ways, and each offers us the opportunity to ask different questions, even ones not readily answered.

As computers become increasingly central to more people's lives, we are developing new ways of communicating, disseminating ideas and sharing humour. In this book, we include a sample of the kind of gendered commentary that circulates electronically to be read with levity and poignancy by diverse Internet users. What sex is your computer? Have you heard of "Menopause Barbie" or the story of the Princess and the Frog? What kind of cyber-rhythms and social networks are created through these sorts of circulating narratives? How do these rhythms and networks create as many divisions as connections among us in our local and global communities?

Poetic and artistic renderings of life reveal a great deal about the political circumstances in which social actors live, eat, communicate and embody pain and pleasure. We hope the pieces included here will inspire readers to become aware, if they are not already, of the poetic rhythms and visual aesthetics in their own lives. Like poetry and visual arts, life-writing — and particularly that which interweaves flights of fancy with a deeply personal but always shared reflection — offers us invaluable opportunities to question and explore how one narrator's social position articulates with our own and that of others. And then there is music, the "sound of the soul," as jazz great Ella Fitzgerald often called it. While there is certainly a lyricism, cadence and mellifluence in any writing classified as "good" (a political statement in and of itself), musical representations are very particular social texts that are both reflective and transformative.

In drawing together such diverse commentaries on the lives of women, men and children, we never lost sight of the fact that numbers can also function as a language. In a statistics-hungry and headline-oriented society, numeration offers a powerful way to tell a story and set a stage. The "facts" — which are usually generated from creative processes no more "objective" than Ann Harbuz's rendering of community life — are often used to define both the problems of injustice and inequities as well as the potential solutions. Statistical representations of human life are influential because they seem scientific, predictable and truthful. While the stories they tell are not as immediately apparent or moving as recollections of childhood sexual abuse or the telling of a father's death, they are just as strategically constructed. There are silences, interruptions, overstatements and turns just as in any analytical, poetic, artistic, humorous or musical text.

The statistical stories that follow our brief introductions to each section in this book are aptly named "Hypatia Index." Hypatia is known as one of the first influential women in mathematics and science. Historians estimate that she lived between the years 355 and 415 CE (Common Era). Known only through her letters, Hypatia travelled throughout the Mediterranean, garnering great respect as a philosopher and teacher of astronomy, geometry and algebra. She taught at a school in Alexandria, Egypt, and letters sent to her there would be addressed simply to "the philosopher," for everyone knew her as a learned woman. Hypatia's methodical and calculated approach to education and science was branded by the early Christians as a form of paganism, and yet, ironically, several very prominent men responsible for the rise of Christianity were among her admiring students (including Synesius of Cyrene, who later became the Bishop of Ptolemais). Ultimately, however, Hypatia's supposedly pagan beliefs in mathematics and the science of the stars so enraged her Christian neighbours that they dragged her from her classroom to a public square where she was stripped, raped and murdered (Molinaro 1990).

As the mathematician who discovered the principles of the hyperbola, parabola and ellipses, Hypatia was preoccupied with the connection of shapes and forms. Conversely, she was also concerned with gaps, codifying what was known, what should be discovered and what needs to be discussed. It is in this spirit that the Hypatia Indices were compiled for this text. We hope that readers will interpret these stories as they would any other, with an eye to the gaps, the fractures as well as the connections, that create elliptical tales of how our past, present and future lives are marked by gender, race, culture, class, ability, sexuality, age and geographical location.

We offer our sincerest thanks to all the contributors to this volume, who responded to an endless deluge of e-mail messages, phone calls and letters. It has been a privilege to work with all of you. We also thank Wayne Antony of Fernwood Publishing for his patience and ongoing support. Our collective efforts will be gratifying if this volume inspires further work, debate and reflection. As Hypatia is quoted as saying, "Reserve your right to think, for even to think wrongly is better than not to think at all" (cited in Dzielska 1995).

REFERENCES

Dzielska, Maria. 1995. *Hypatia of Alexandria*. Cambridge: Harvard University Press.
Molinaro, Ursule. 1990. *A Full Moon of Women: 29 Portraits of Notable Women from Different Times and Places*. New York: Dutton.

Section I

SETTING THE STAGE:
WHAT DOES IT MEAN TO BE A WOMAN OR A MAN?

C. Lesley Biggs

> The true representation of power is not of a big man beating a smaller man or a woman. Power is the ability to take one's place in whatever discourse is essential to action and the right to have one's part matter. —Carolyn Heilbrun (1998: 18)

The Context: Situating Feminist Thought

What does it mean to be a woman or a man? This seemingly simple question has been a source of much contemplation and debate over many centuries, but whereas men as a group have had considerable power to define what being a man means in specific historical and social contexts, women have characteristically been more defined than self-defining. What distinguishes industrial from pre-industrial societies, however, is that significant numbers of women have sought to define for themselves what it means to be a woman.

To claim that relative to men, women have less power is not to say that women in the past had no power. To counter such an idea, one need only point to Sappho (born sometime between 630 and 612 BCE), who was one of the great ancient Greek lyric poets; to Egyptian pharaoh Hatshepsut (1508 BCE?–1458 BCE), who greatly expanded her people's wealth by re-establishing trade cut off in earlier times; to Wu Zetian (625 CE–705 CE), who after the death of her second husband, Emperor Gaozong, crowned herself Emperor of China, thus interrupting the Tang Dynasty and creating her own, the Zhou Dynasty; to Elena Lucrezia Cornaro Piscopia (1646–1684), the first woman ever to receive a PhD; to Phyllis Wheatley (1753–1784), the first published African-American poet, who was sold into slavery at seven, and was by age twelve reading Greek and Latin classics; to Louise Arbour (1947–), a justice of the Supreme Court of Canada and Chief Prosecutor of the International Criminal Tribunals for the former Yugoslavia and Rwanda; or to Kim Campbell (1947–), the first female prime minister of Canada.

Women of ruling classes in many cultural contexts have wielded considerable political influence by virtue of their class and family connections, and even non-ruling-class women were able to exert some forms of power because their labour was central to economic production in the household. Nor can we say that all women passively accepted patriarchal control. Over the centuries, some women have resisted attempts by a father or husband, religious authorities, or the state to impose restrictions on their lives. In the Western context, however, one difference between the pre-modern and modern periods is that the position of women is no longer seen as "biologically predetermined" or "preordained by God." Rather "the woman question," as the issue of women's self-determination was first known, has entered public discourse, permeating all spheres of social, economic, political, and cultural life.

The hard-won gains over the course of the past three hundred years would not have happened if there had not been feminist movements to champion women's issues and women's rights. Western feminism, as an organized political force, has its origins in the industrialization and urbanization experienced first in seventeenth-century England. These experiences can be seen as moments of awakening, where "the natural order" of things was disrupted. Women's needs, issues, and desires became visible — perhaps for the first time in history. Yet, feminists have not spoken with a single voice — not now, not historically.[1]

Steeped in the language of women's rights, liberal feminists of the early twentieth century — the so-called first wave of Western feminism[2] — argued in favour of (formal) equal rights under the law including, *inter alia*, the right to vote, own property, have custody over children, and enter into financial transactions. Recognizing that women do not necessarily compete with men on a level playing field, the discourse of women's rights was extended later in the twentieth century to include equal opportunities for women, contingent upon the state enacting social and economic reforms.

Marxist feminism draws on the work of traditional Marxist theory, particularly the *Origin of the Family, Private Property and the State* by Fredrick Engels (1972), in which he posits that women's oppression was based on the sexual division of labour. Engels argued that capitalism benefits from this division of labour because women performed tasks necessary to reproduce workers — most of whom were men — on a daily and generational basis, while men were "free" to enter the paid labour force, where they exchanged their labour power for a living wage. But traditional Marxism could not explain why women do "women's work," nor could it explain various forms of male dominance expressed through violence and sexual assault. This "unhappy marriage of Marxism and feminism" (Hartmann 1981) spurred socialist feminists to combine the insights of Marxism with those of radical feminism, a theoretical approach that emerged in the 1960s.

Beginning with the insight that women as a group have been subordinated to men in every time and place, radical feminists argued that inequalities between women and men are grounded in the prevailing organization of procreation. Because women bear children and are physically weaker than men (at least by conventional standards of strength measurement), certain social relationships have emerged in order to ensure the survival of the biological family. Unlike anti-feminist arguments that insist that these biological relationships provide a justification for male dominance, radical feminist arguments maintained either that women's ability to bear children is evidence of the superiority of women's bodies (Firestone 1970; Griffin 1980; Rich 1976); or that the inherently aggressive testosterone-driven male body is the source of male dominance (Daly 1978; Dworkin 1974). Other strands of radical feminism, which could be more accurately termed cultural feminism, examined the institutional structures and familial arrangements that socialize girls and boys to become feminine and masculine (e.g., Gilligan 1982). In some cases, cultural feminists incorporated the insights of psychoanalytic theory while rejecting Freud's view that "anatomy is destiny" (e.g., Chodorow 1978); others drew on existentialism and extended Simone de Beauvoir's adage, "one is not born, [but] rather becomes a woman" (de Beauvoir [1952] 1974).

The insights and strategies of second wave feminism — the liberal, Marxist/socialist, and radical feminists of the 1960s — produced significant improvements in the lives of many women in Western societies. For example, more women entered the universities, and within universities, women's and gender studies, as well as gay studies, native studies and black studies, among others, gained a foothold. Women won the right to earn equal pay for equal work, to work in an environment free from sexual harassment, and to enter into the professions (such as law, medicine, and engineering). Women were able to exercise more control over their bodies when they had access to birth control and abortion, could have drug-free births and/or have midwives attend births, if women so chose. Feminists also established rape crisis centers, shelters for abused women, and employment and mental health services aimed at the special needs of women. These accomplishments are impressive. But, as the effects of the last decade of fiscal and social conservatism demonstrate, these hard-won gains can be undermined or reversed.

Feminism was arguably one of the most successful political movements of the twentieth century. But not all women benefited equally from the efforts of what we now know to be the concerns of white, middle-class women. Many women — poor women, lesbians, women of colour, women with disabilities, native women — felt alienated from the mainstream feminist movement. By the mid-1980s, many of the ideas of second wave feminism came under attack. At the centre of the debate was the assumption by the early feminist theorists that their experiences represented the universal experience of womanhood (i.e., "every woman is just like me," regardless of race or class or age or ability or sexuality). Even the conceptualizing of feminism in waves would be criticized as Eurocentric since the timelines may not fit the historical experiences of different groups of women.

Women from marginalized groups began to explore their own experience, and these feminist theorists pointed to how race, class, able-bodiedness, and sexuality produce different configurations of oppression, forms of resistance, and strategies for change, as well as privilege, among women (Harding 1991; Hill Collins 1990; hooks 1989; Smith 1987). By theorizing "the personal is the political," a rallying crying of the women's liberation movement of the 1960s, these "standpoint" theorists were able to see the ways in which women could be members of both an oppressed and an oppressing group — sometimes simultaneously.

The period from the mid-1980s to the present has been widely characterized as the third wave of feminism. Arguing against essentialism, postmodern feminists eschew the notion of Woman as an essential, ahistorical, and authentic category (Butler 1990; Irigaray 1985; Kristeva 1982.) Rather than ask, "What is Woman?" which assumes that if we unpeel the layers of patriarchal practices, we will find the "true" and "authentic" Woman, postmodern feminists ask, "How did this category come to be constructed in the first place?" Using the tools of deconstruction, postmodern feminists seek to uncover the technologies of power that have been deployed to establish the "truth" about Woman. "The central project," as Judith Grant observed, "is to investigate the mechanisms of power that have forged the female identity in order to resist identity itself" (Grant 1993: 131).

Postmodern feminism's focus on the meaning of Woman has necessarily led to examinations of the ways in which gender is constituted through language. For example, the modern Enlightenment concept of male and female as "opposites" is repeated in numerous pairings such as nature/nurture, nature/art, culture/nature, sun/moon, rational/irrational, reason/emotion and head/heart (cited in Grant 1993). At a glance, we can see the ways in which gender is deeply encoded in the English language. The inequities of power between ideas associated with masculinity and those associated with femininity are reflected in and reproduced in the ordering of the words and their valuation. Male terms most frequently are given priority in grammatical constructions (e.g., he and she, boys and girls, Mr. and Mrs., King and Queen), and where female terms are generally given priority (e.g., bride and groom, ladies and gentlemen) confining factors of pre-eminent status operating for a limited time or restrictive expectations of feminine behaviours are in operation. Moreover, the status of female terms in originally parallel male-female word pairs such as *governor* and *governess* or *lord* and *lady* tends to deteriorate over time (Schulz 1975). Thus governors remain powerful figures in every context, but the word *governess* came most often to denote a low-status educator and childcare worker; and while the term "cleaning lady" is now commonplace, the idea of a garbage lord remains risible.

Concepts such as Woman and Man, and masculine and feminine, can be decoded to reveal that they are historical and social rather than "essential," "authentic," or "natural" categories. As a result, postmodern feminists have shifted the focus of analysis away from women to the study of gender, examining the relationships between women and men, femaleness and maleness, and femininity and masculinity, and intersections with other categories of social relations. Thus, it is now common to speak of masculinities and femininities, i.e., in the plural, rather than in the singular.

As well as deconstructing gender codes embedded in language, postmodern feminists also seek to uncover the silences in texts. This project was initially begun by modernist feminists who queried the absence of women from great bodies of artistic and intellectual work otherwise known as the canon in respective fields. Much of the early work of second wave feminism was centred on uncovering and recovering women's contributions to literature, the performing and visual arts, religion, and science. Later this analysis was extended to examine the very categories that have been used to evaluate women's (and men's) contributions to social, political, and economic life. For example, the concept of work was equated with paid labour, but when feminists examined the work that women do — much of it unpaid, domestic labour — they argued that this type of work has been undervalued and should be counted in measures such as the Gross Domestic Product (Waring 1999). Moreover, the re-evaluation of work has led writers to challenge the values underlying mainstream economics, arguing that economic well-being should not be only measure of "the wealth of nations" (Smith 1776), but should include measures of social well-being (e.g., the Human Development Index).

Postmodern feminisms are not without their critics. "Where do the lives of 'real' women, thinking, acting people who live in and construct the world of the everyday fit into the analysis of discourse?" ask materialist feminists (e.g., Harstock 1990). Women and men are living, embodied beings and not simply texts. What role do notions of agency and resistance play in the ephemeral, postmodern world of discourse? As well, since female liberation is understood as freedom from limiting discursive categories, what is the vision of a more just and equitable society for women? In response, many contemporary feminists adopted Donna Haraway's (1991) notion of "situated knowledges," a concept that attempts to link a notion of subjectivity (thinking, knowing actors) that refuses the transhistorical category of Woman while simultaneously insisting that feminist theories and practices engage with the "real" world that exists outside of us. Standpoint theorists like Haraway argue that knowledge is always partial, multivocal, and historically contingent, but like the postmodernists, Haraway acknowledges the importance of "semiotic technologies" for making meanings in our everyday lives.

Since the 1990s, the issue of differences has become a central one within feminist theorizing, but it poses a new set of "dilemmas," as McLaughlin (2003) has observed. On the one hand, recognizing difference can lead to a positive affirmation of individual and group identities. On the other hand, "recognition implies certain levels of fixedness in the needs and identities" (McLaughlin 2003: 12); that is, the recognition of differences may lead to new forms of essentialism based on a (negative) identity as victims of suffering and pain. As a result, "the very expression of identity becomes 'invested in its own subjection'" (Brown cited in McLaughlin 2003: 12), having no way of moving forward. In response, many scholars have begun to analyze the production of identities. Thus the question is no longer "what are the differences between women and men, or blacks and whites, or homosexuals and heterosexuals?" but "what are the social, economic, cultural, and political conditions through which differences are produced?"

This approach was taken up by postcolonial feminisms, and its more recent iteration, transnational feminisms. Writers from and about the Global South, such as Gayatri Spivak (1990), Jacqui M. Alexander and Chandra Talpade Mohanty (1997), and Trinh T. Minh-ha

(1989) have made important contributions to the understanding of differences by linking the production of difference to global economic pressures (e.g., migration and the transfer of capital on an international scale), colonization and decolonization, nationalism, and cultural movements. These processes and institutions shape women's and men's lives — although not necessarily in the same ways.

The return to materialist analyses has also informed theorizing about "the cultural turn" in feminist theory, and particularly the analysis of discourse. Adopting the analyses of Michel Foucault, feminists have understood discourse as the matrix of texts, the specialized languages, and the networks of power relations operating and defining a given field. Discourses can be identified by their systematic re-presentation of ideas, opinions, ways of thinking and behaviour, which in the case of dominant or hegemonic discourses, are considered "legitimate," "natural," and/or "normal." These analyses have shifted away from studying discourses as a thing or as an object, to examining discourses as sets of discursive practices; that is, investigations focus not only on the content of a text, important as it is, but also on who produces the text, the conditions under which it is produced, and its reception. Thus the distinction between context (often represented as the social, economic, and/or cultural background) and text (the content) has been blurred. Instead, the material conditions and cultural expressions are interwoven through the networks of power relations operating and defining a given field. As a result, not only are the material effects of discursive practices acknowledged but so too are the discursive effects of material practices (Alarcón et al. 1999 cited in McLaughlin 2003: 13). For example, most women have been involved in cleaning, cooking, and caring for children, but until the 1970s, these activities were not seen as work. Rather they were understood as part of women's natural role, and as a result, were either not acknowledged or undervalued. However, with the rise of the feminist movement in the late 1960s, these material activities were translated into the discourses of work (for example, domestic labour, household labour, or unpaid labour), and as result, cleaning, cooking, and caring for children were seen in part as "work," thereby acquiring an economic value. This redefining then enabled women to lobby for renumeration in the event of a divorce, to qualify for insurance benefits in the case of an accident, and have this work enumerated in the census and a measure of the Gross National Product.

We return, then, to the question, what does it mean to be a woman? The ways in which feminists have thought about "the woman question" demonstrates the complexity of this issue: a variety of approaches have been taken over the last three centuries, which reflect competing understandings of power, resistance, and agency. There are no easy resolutions to these debates, but rather than interpret these competing views as "problems" for feminist theory, we might embrace them as opportunities to think creatively and critically "outside of the box." We invite you to join the conversation!

What about Men?

"So what about men?" you might be asking yourself? Isn't the section entitled "What Does It Mean to Be a Woman or a *Man*?" If the "woman question" has been debated over the centuries, the corresponding question, "what is a man?" has not engendered the same kind of discussion. For a long time, thinkers drawing on biological and anthropological models, naturalized and failed to submit to critical inquiry men's position as the dominant group; their superior position vis-à-vis women was deemed the "natural order," as were inequalities between men based on class, race, able-bodiness, sexuality, and age.

From the Enlightenment period to the twentieth century in Western industrialized cultures, "Man" has stood for the rational, knowing subject who represents the universal (as evidenced in our language in concepts such as mankind, "you guys," or in occupational titles like *policeman* rather than *police officer*, or *chairman* rather than *chair*). Men have also represented the norm by which women are measured — whether we are talking about men's intellectual prowess, their political, economic, cultural, or social accomplishments, or their physical strength.

Even within feminist theory, until the late 1980s, men's experiences as gendered beings were not subjected to scrutiny and deconstructed in the same way as women's. Collectively and individually, men represented "Man" — the embodiment of patriarchal oppression of women — although there was some recognition, particularly in Marxist/Socialist feminist theorizing, that all men were not created equal. However, beginning in the 1970s and gathering momentum in the late 1980s, men's studies has become a distinct area of scholarship. Initially inspired by feminist writers and drawing on sex role theory (popular at the time), these studies drew attention to the gap between the normative elements of the male sex role and the lived experiences of men (Kimmel and Messner 2010: xv). Not surprisingly, most men could not attain the ideals prescribed by male sex roles. Moreover, once men's studies exposed its ideological underpinnings, which served to justify male dominance over women, the concept of sex role could no longer be defended as a scientific concept.

In the late 1980s, research on men and masculinity went into two distinct directions. The first was the mythopoetic men's movement prominently represented by Robert Bly's (1990) bestselling book *Iron John*. Drawing on mythology, shamanic rituals, and drumming, Bly was instrumental in the establishment of men's groups that sought to reclaim men's "authentic" masculine souls and get in touch with emotional experiences which otherwise had been buried under traditional (i.e., patriarchal) forms of masculinity. The intent of the mythopoetic men's movement was to critique patriarchal views of masculinity, but its essentialist and universalizing assumptions not only undermined this critique but were appropriated by organizations like the Million Man March and the Promise Keepers to re-establish patriarchal control within families.

These initiatives took place largely outside of the academy, but within scholarly research, men's studies has moved to the social constructionist frameworks also being adopted by many feminists at the same time. This new scholarship represented "[a] challenge to the hegemonic definition of masculinity, [and it] came from men whose masculinity was cast as deviant: men of colour, gay men, and ethnic men" (Kimmel and Messner 2010: xvii). This research studies the construction of men as gendered beings who, although they as a group have power relative to women, are also hierarchically organized based on class, race, ethnicity, sexuality, age, and ability. These scholars speak of "masculinities" rather than "masculinity," just like most contemporary feminists eschew the respective singular "femininity." Researchers in men and masculinities examine the meanings of masculinity, how masculinity is organized and institutionalized, as well as the ways in which men resist patriarchal forms of masculinity. Thus, Simone de Beauvoir's famous adage can be rewritten to include men: "Men are not born, [but] rather made." Like women, men "do," or perform, gender (Butler 1990) in ways that intersect with other social relations, producing complex experiences and understandings of what it means to be a man.

Part I A – Pedagogy

"Knowledge is power" is the theme that informs the chapters in Part I of Section I. Feminist pedagogy is important to the creation of new knowledge for and about women and gender relations. Knowledge not only gives us the tools to understand the worlds we inhabit, but also empowers women and men to think critically. In a 1977 speech to the Douglass College

Convocation, Adrienne Rich urged the female graduates to "claim their education" by "refusing to let others do your thinking, talking, and naming for you" (Rich 1979: 233). We strongly endorse this view, as does Lillian Allen, who, in "Feminism 101" rewrites Rebecca West's famous quip, "I myself have never been able to find out precisely what feminism is: I only know that people call me a feminist whenever I express sentiments that differentiate me from a doormat."

While feminism is often presented as a political movement with its roots in the late nineteenth century, some women, as shown earlier, have resisted patriarchal expectations for women. In her poem, "A Piece for a Sampler," Deborah How Cottnam, a New Brunswick teacher of girls in the late eighteenth century, subverts traditional expectations of femininity associated with the domestic arts and embroiders a new picture for women, urging them to "Expand [their] Genius in its prime" since "How transient Youth, & Beauty are." In "I Am Invited to Women's Studies Class," second wave feminist Jeanette Lynes bumps up against a new generation of female students who have grown up in a world in which feminist ideas have been part of the culture (even if uneasily so). Compared to these savvy young third wavers, Lynes's experiences at the same age conditioned her to "being bauble, accessory to patriarchy." Still her poem cautions women against turning on one another because of the imprinting they may have taken from patriarchy.

The power of knowledge to transform an individual's life in the face of, and in spite of the trauma of childhood sexual abuse is poignantly recounted in "Once Upon My Mind." The author demonstrates how a child subjected to repeated abuse will struggle to make sense of what is happening to her, and she reports that "Reading my books became my lifeline to society, my umbilical cord to the world outside my tattered body." Reading didn't stop the abuse, as the author observes, but reading helped heal her "damaged psyche." The new knowledge thus garnered also gave the author the courage to write about her horrendous experiences and can offer hope to other victims of childhood sexual abuse.

Education is highly correlated with income, and is an important pathway to empowerment for women and men. From 1999 to 2009, women in Canada have consistently earned more bachelor's degrees than men (14.6 percent of all women compared to 13.1 of all men in 2009). Although more men than women continue to earn degrees above the bachelor's (6.9 percent of all men compared to 5.7 percent of all women in 2009), women have made great strides over the past decade given that in 1999 just 3.7 percent of all women earned a degree above the bachelor's compared to 5.8 percent of all men (Statistics Canada 2010: 125). Moreover, since the 1970s, feminist research on educational attainment and gender barriers — over-representation of male figures in textbooks, males' and females' different learning styles, and a masculinist-oriented curriculum — has had a significant impact on educational practices. So much so that some critics now argue that "girls rule in school." In his chapter, Bernie Froese-Germain examines the explanations for the media panic about boys' underachievement and the "boy turn" in research and policy related to gender and education. He concludes that there is a need for a more nuanced understanding of the ways in which gender relations inform curriculum, pedagogy, structures, and research programs in order to "make schooling more inclusive and equitable for boys, girls, and *all* children."

"Why can't *they* fit in, and just be like *us*?" is a common question implied if rarely directly posed by dominant groups. The assumption underlying this thinking is that the "Other" needs to be "fixed" in some way. Carol Schick and Verna St. Denis end Part 1 by arguing that changing thought patterns and cultural climates require a critical focus not only on the actions of others but on ourselves as well. In a university-level course on anti-racism, students learn not only what barriers prevent Aboriginal students from reaching their full potential, but also how taken-for-granted aspects of whiteness perpetuate those barriers.

Part I B – History

Two of the main questions that inform Part I B are "Whose stories get told when recounting the histories of 'Canadian peoples' (or to put the matter another way, what has the national pedagogy, the teaching about the nation, been")? and "How does that pedagogy need revising? Not that long ago, virtually no history of women or gender relations, or of Aboriginal peoples and visible or sexual minorities from marginalized peoples' perspective existed. Since the 1970s, the writing of women's history, as Franca Iacovetta observes in her chapter, has shifted from reclaiming women's history by focusing on great women and their contributions to producing histories that "sheds much light on the ordinary people's lives and tribulations." These histories have not only expanded the number of subjects studied by historians, challenging what constitutes history, but as Iacovetta argues, they have "offered compelling critiques of the dominant liberal, elite, white, masculine, and nationalist meta-narratives of Canadian history." Examples of discrimination — of which there are many — can no longer be represented as rare deviations from an otherwise exemplary record of "peace, order and good government." The myth of Canada as the land of "the strong and free" is no longer defensible; rather the nation-state of Canada was built on structural inequality and the oppression of Aboriginal peoples and racialized minorities, as well as women, sexual minorities, working class people, and those with disabilities.

Since the late 1980s, women's and gender histories have been extended to include critical race analysis, as well as a sharper view of the intersections of nation building, colonialism, and empire in the building of what most now know as Canada (but is alternatively understood by some Indigenous peoples as part of Turtle Island). Of course, the impact of these processes has been uneven, with benefits accruing largely to white settlers with devastating consequences for Aboriginal peoples and other racialized groups. In her chapter, Iacovetta traces the historiography of women's history and gender history, as well as exploring the debates about the desirable focus of Canadian history and the backlash against feminist and other critical analyses.

Most Canadians prefer to distance themselves from the slavery that figures so prominently in U.S. history and the current collective consciousness. We are generally happy to celebrate the fact that many towns and cities in Canada were destination points for the Underground Railroad, but are shocked to find out that slavery was practised in Upper and Lower Canada until the early 1800s. In her poem "Confessions of a Woman Who Burnt Down a Town," Afua Cooper explores the suffering of Marie Joseph Angelique, a Black slave woman, and the ordeal of her trial and sentence to torture, mutilation, and burning alive (the latter two punishments were ultimately commuted to a June 1734 hanging alone) when she was charged for burning down much of Montreal two months earlier.

Canada was built not only on the backs of Black slaves, but also on the backs of many ordinary women and men, especially from racialized groups. Building a transcontinental railway was Sir John A. MacDonald's dream connected to his bid to unite Canada in the face of U.S. expansion in the west, but completion of the railway was also the condition for British Columbia entering into Confederation in 1871. The project was rife with controversy over competition for the lucrative contract and the generous terms ultimately awarded to the Canadian Pacific Railroad, as well as tension between prairie regional interests and the national government (Lavallée 2011). What wasn't of concern, at least to these national leaders, was the appalling conditions under which approximately 7,000 Chinese male migrants worked to build the railroad. Not only were the Chinese workers paid less than their white counterparts, but an estimated 600 to 2,000 Chinese workers died between 1880 and 1885 while working in what today would be considered criminally unsafe conditions on the railroads (Library and Archives Canada 2009). To add insult to injury, after the railroad was completed, and in order to discourage Chinese remaining or immigrating to Canada, such workers had from 1885 to 1947 to pay a head tax. One of the consequences was that wives and families of immigrant male workers were left behind in China.

On July 1, 1923 (Canada Day), the federal government passed the *Chinese Exclusion Act*, known as "humiliation day" among Chinese Canadians (Munroe 2011). As a result, according to the *Canada In The Making Project* "only fifteen Chinese immigrants were allowed into Canada between 1923 and 1947 when the law was revoked," and the Chinese population in Canada dropped from 46,500 in 1931 to about 32,500 in 1951 (Munroe 2011).

Not until 2006, when Prime Minister Harper, as Sandra Ka Hon Chu observes, offered "an official apology and symbolic redress payments of $20,000 to surviving head-tax payers and persons who had been in conjugal relationships with head-tax payers deceased by 2006," did Canada move to acknowledge the systemic racism of its erstwhile policy. But, even then, Chu argues in her chapter, the emotional suffering Chinese women endured as a result of long periods of separation was not compensated for, and their full Canadian citizenship rights denied. Chinese women's experiences were "largely conflated with those of Chinese men," Chu explains, while harm and discrimination were constructed around the financial disadvantages accrued rather than the emotional injury incurred.

Not everyone, of course, suffered in such ways in the building of Canada. Members of white settler society, particularly those of Anglo origins representing the Empire, typically enjoyed a privileged life. However, motivated by many concerns — women's rights, particularly the right to vote; high rates of infant and maternal mortality; fears of "race-suicide" and grinding poverty brought about by rapid industrialization and urbanization — many upper class women sought to improve the lives of women and girls. The National Council of Women of Canada (NCWC) was one organization formed with such an aim. Established at a public meeting of 1500 women on October 27, 1893, that elected Lady Aberdeen, wife of then-Governor-General of Canada (Lord John Campbell Gordon Aberdeen), its first president, the NCWC contributed to the passage of the *Act to Confer the Electoral Franchise Upon Women* at the federal level in 1918. It was also instrumental in the establishment of many Canadian institutions — some of which, including the NCWC itself, continue today. The photograph of the NCWC founders included in this section on history is a tribute to the organization's accomplishments, but the image simultaneously re-presents the embodiment of class, gender, and race power at that era. Look at the image carefully, and ask yourself who is present and who is not? Why are Lady and Lord Aberdeen at the centre of the image, and why is Lord Aberdeen even included in the photograph? Can you attach any meanings of Empire to the conservatory in the background? And what might the dog lying at a woman's feet, and another being held, symbolize?

Judge Emily Murphy, Henrietta Muir Edwards, Irene Parlby, Nellie McClung and Louise McKinney all had connections to the NCWC (Griffiths 1993); they also constitute "The Famous Five" who challenged existing laws that deemed women not to be persons. How did they find out women were not legally persons? Emily Murphy, a self-taught legal expert, became the first female magistrate in the Empire when she was appointed to the Alberta Bench (Jackel and Cavanaugh 2011). But on her first day of work, Eardley Jackson, a lawyer, challenged Murphy's right to be there since women were not deemed persons under the *British North America Act* (BNA). After a thirteen-year battle, the Famous Five appealed to the Judicial Committee of the Privy Council in London, England, "the true Supreme Court for Canada at that time," and the Privy Council found on October 18, 1929, that women were, in fact, "persons" under the BNA Act (Alberta Heritage 2004).

On October 18, 1999, a bronze statue of the Famous Five on Parliament Hill in Ottawa was unveiled to commemorate the seventieth anniversary of the Person's Case. The statue was intended to commemorate the Famous Five as nation-builders, but it was embroiled in controversy because Judge Emily Murphy was a strong supporter of eugenics, and lobbied for Alberta's *Sexual Sterilization Law* (1928). The legacy of that law was still being felt by its sterilized victims, including Leillani Muir, who successfully sued the Alberta government in 1996 for procedural negligence and damages. After the Muir decision, a class-action lawsuit on behalf of sterilized victims followed soon after. In light of the history of the Famous Five and this contemporary controversy, how do we "read" the statue?

The statue invites individuals to sit at the table with the Famous Five and imagine themselves as feminist nation-builders. Tracy Kulba (2002) asks, in her analysis of the statue and the statue controversy, "What kind of feminist, and what kind of nation-builders do we want to be?" Senator Lillian (Quan) Dyck, who is of "mixed Chinese and Cree Indian heritage, and [has] encountered racism all [her] life," finds the Famous Five statue a place of solace, comfort, and inspiration. The photographs of Senator Dyck dancing, sitting, and having tea with the Famous Five enables us to re-imagine Canada as a nation in which our differences enrich and enhance what it means to be a Canadian. In embracing the Famous Five, Senator Dyck signals both the continuities and discontinuities between first, second, and third wave feminisms.

Much has been made about the tensions between so-called second and third wave feminists, but as the interview between then 84-year-old Doris Anderson, "one of Canada's best-known feminists," and well-known third waver, Lisa Rundle reveals that many of the same issues — inequality in pay, need for a universal childcare program and better access to safe, legal abortion — beset both generations. After four decades of activism, Anderson declares that she "Still Ain't Satisfied!" In her interview with Rundle, Anderson reflects on her career as a former editor of *Chatelaine* at a time when women couldn't get a legal abortion or information about birth control, and child abuse was a dark secret. Anderson boldly went where few women went before, engaging Canadian women with issues that mattered deeply to them — while offering "10 Ways to Dress up Hamburger!" Anderson recalls the optimism engendered by the establishment of the Royal Commission on the Status of Women, but the former president of the National Committee on the Status of Women and of the (now defunct) Canadian Advisory Council on the Status of Women, laments the lack of progress in producing equality between women and men. In Anderson's view, gender equality will come more quickly if there is proportional representation of women and men in Parliament. What do you think?

After reading the chapters on women's and gender history in Canada, we hope that you are interested in learning more about the diverse contributions that women and men have made in the pursuit of equality relations. Take the test "So You Think That You Know Canadian Women's/Gender History?" as one measure of your knowledge! (Short answers to the history test appear in Chapter 13. More detailed answers and more questions can be found on the *Gendered Intersections* website: fernwoodpublishing.ca/gi2.

Part I C – Gender and Difference

In the so-called first and second waves of feminism, women organized around the assumption that they had a common identity based on similar gender experiences. But feminist critics of first and second wave feminisms have put that myth to rest. Women's and men's lives and identities are complex and intersections of class, gender, sexuality race, ethnicity, religion, ability, age, and nation produce multiple identities and allegiances. These complex aspects of identity sometimes complement, but more often than not, contradict one another, leading to tensions not only between different groups of people, but also within individuals. Part 1 C highlights some of the key issues that we believe have shaped and continue to inform debates within feminism.

One of the resounding criticisms directed at second wave feminism was its white, middle-class bias. Echoing the now (in)famous speech "Ain't I a Woman" delivered by Sojourner Truth (1797–1883), a former black slave, given to a women's rights convention in Akron, Ohio, in 1851, dub poet d'bi.young anitafrika challenges the history of feminism presented in "feminism 101" — not to be confused with Lillian Allen's version! "We a guh talk about gloria steinem/betty friedan/di liberation of di white middle-class oomaan/from oppreshun in society." The solution for many second wave feminists was for women to enter the work force in order to reduce (white) women's financial dependence upon men. But, as both Sojourner Truth and d'bi.young.anitafrika argue, black women — mammies, tanties, aunties, and nannies — have always worked, raising "black and white pickney." anitafrika refuses the linear history of white feminism, inviting readers instead to "step step step into [her] head."

If anitafrika challenges the white-washed history presented in Feminism 101, then Jo-Anne Lee's study of racialized girls provides insight into the experiences of young women who have to negotiate "being different" in Victoria, British Columbia, a city that has marketed itself as "*a little bit of olde England*," that is, Victoria intentionally capitalizes on its whiteness. Whether Canadian-born or children of immigrants, these teenagers experienced racism and isolation; they try to fit into mainstream white culture while at the same time meeting the often traditional expectations of their parents. A tall order for teenage girls! But Lee found that these young women "possessed a wealth of cultural knowledge," recognizing that "identity is a continuing creation."

Main Street often refers to a road that runs through the centre of a town or city, but it also evokes an imagined social and cultural space where people come together to shop, get a bite to eat, or have coffee. Main Street is where the mainstream "hangs out." In Shani Mootoo's short story being "Out On Main Street" is particularly problematic for the narrator and her partner Janet, self-described as "watered-down Indians." As Trinidadians of Indian descent, they do not fit into the culture of émigrés from India. Neither speaks any of a number of Indian languages; nor is the pair particularly religious; moreover they are lesbians. Stepping out on to Main Street then is fraught with risk as the couple deal with racism, sexism, and homophobia. And yet in the pursuit of sweet gustatory pleasures — burfi and gulub jamoon — they strut their stuff.

Gregory Scofield has spent a lot of time pondering the politics of identity as a Native man, as a gay man, as a man raised by women — often in fear of other straight and gay men, and as a writer. The concept of two-spiritedness, first mooted perhaps by gay American Indians in the 1980s, has been adopted as a badge of solidarity in response to discrimination both within and outside North American Indigenous communities. In his chapter, "You Can Always Count on an Anthropologist (To Set You Straight, Crooked or Somewhere In-Between)," Scofield queries the meaning of "two-spiritedness," asking if we are all in some way two-spirited because we have our good selves and our bad selves or because we carry the spirits of our ancestors with us. In his quest, Scofield found no clear equivalent for "two-spiritedness" in the Cree language, but closely related words led him to a reading of himself as one likely to hear strong words that would be difficult to hear but also one urged to diligent pursuit of understanding and acceptance of his "Creator-made self, [his] God-given power," and his sacredness, all "still steeping in [his] spirit" like the tea in the pot that people gathered round in the kitchens of his youth. Acknowledging difference, Scofield yet envisions our commonalities: "Turtle Island is a place of sacred and not so sacred people, all of us looking for a sense of belonging, a validation of our existence — maybe even a platform to stage our resistance, for whatever reason."

Questions of identity are often central issues among groups who are disadvantaged in some way, but until recently at least, the identities of dominant groups were rarely scrutinized — "whites are taught to think of their lives as morally neutral, normative, and average, and also ideal." Whites were/are the mainstream, the unhyphenated Canadians, the norm by which other groups were measured, either implicitly or explicitly. Peggy McIntosh was one of the first writers to interrogate that "invisible knapsack of white privilege" which allows people with white skins to navigate through their everyday world relatively freely. McIntosh drew up a list of twenty-six daily experiences that she took for granted that negatively racial-ized[3] colleagues could not. If you consider not only differences of race/ethnicity, but also of class, gender, sexuality, and ability, in what ways do you experience privilege, or more aptly, as McIntosh concludes, *unearned advantage* and *conferred dominance*?

Through the institutionalization of patriarchal norms, forms of social organization, and culture, "the law of the father" (the literal translation of *patriarchy* from Latin) has been embedded in most, if not all cultures. But, when asked whether or not women can be patri-archal, the answer is almost always a resounding "yes!" How can it be that women are victims of patriarchy yet also perpetrators of patriarchal oppression? In his chapter, Allan Johnson examines the nature of patriarchal power and urges us to move away from individual models of power (which focus on "bad" people — usually men) and in which blame is assigned to individuals' behaviour, personalities, motivations, and attitudes. At the same time, Johnson also advises us to reject models of power that blame "the system" for all of society's problems while holding nobody to account for social inequalities. In its place, he offers a process and relational model of patriarchal power in which individuals participate; we are shaped by and shape patriarchal relations, but Johnson insists "we are not it [patriarchy]!" Patriarchal relations are embedded into our culture, language, and social organization. "Above all," Johnson argues, "patriarchal culture is about the core values of control and domination in almost every area of human existence." And bitter medicine as Johnson's analysis is, his chapter urges recognition that, "We are involved; we are part of the problem; the question is whether we'll choose also to be part of the solution."

If men are sometimes perpetrators of oppression, can they also be victims of patriarchal power? Again, the answer is "yes!" Just as marginalized groups of women challenged white, middle-class, straight women's conceptions of *woman* and what the important women's is-sues were, marginalized men have also challenged the concept of *man* or men as having a homogeneous identity and universal experiences. In "Understanding Men," R.W. Connell provides an overview of the research on studies of masculinities. Moving from essentialist views of masculinity — characteristic of "the mythopoetic movement" noted above — Connell argues for an understanding of men which theorizes them as gendered beings and examines the social construction of masculinities. Connell draws our attention to multiple masculinities arranged in hierarchies of hegemonic and marginalized masculinities; to their active construction, their dynamic relations, and their internal complexities; and to the emergence of a transnational elite of men whose power is tied increasingly to globalization, and new patterns of colonization. Like women, men "do gender" which is situated and intersects with other social relations.

By the time that you have finished reading the chapters in Section 1, you'll probably want to read something that is a more light-hearted. On occasion, you receive an e-mail that makes you laugh out loud. "I Want to Be a Woman" is one of those wickedly funny e-mails that pokes fun at patriarchal images of women. See, feminists do have a sense of humour!

NOTES

1. It is not possible in such a short space to examine the nuances of the debates both within and between categories of feminist thought. For comprehensive analyses of the various strands of feminism, see Grant 1993; Jaggar 1983; Tong 1989. Nor are the examples of feminist writers cited in this section meant to be exhaustive; they are/were illustrative but influential thinkers.

2. University of Victoria Women's Studies professor Jo-Anne Lee called our attention to the too-ready assumption underlying wave theory that feminism, at least as an organized political movement, begins with white women in Europe.

3. The term "negatively racialized" was first proposed in Susan Gingell 2010: 4. The term was coined to recognize that using the term *racialized* to refer only to people who are disadvantaged by the process of racialization obscures how dominance is conferred upon whites by such a process. The problem is analogous to using the term *gender* to refer only to females, thus leaving unrecognized and undisturbed the unearned advantage that the process of gendering accords to males relative to females of their social groups.

REFERENCES

Alberta Heritage. 2004. "The Famous Five: Heroes for Today: Emily Murphy." At: abheritage.ca/ famous5/achievements/ emily_murphy.html.

Alexander, Jacqui M., and Chandra Talpade Mohanty (eds.). 1997. *Feminist Genealogies, Colonial Legacies, Democratic Futures.* New York: Routledge.

Bly, Robert. 1990. *Iron John.* New York: Perseus Books.

Butler, Judith. 1990. *Gender Trouble: Feminism and the Subversion of Identity.* New York: Routledge.

Canada. Royal Commission on the Status of Women. 1970. *Report.* Ottawa: Information Canada.

Canada in the Making. 2001–2005. "Asian Immigration." Canadiana.org. At: www2.canadiana.ca/ citm/specifique/ asian_e.html.

Chodorow, Nancy. 1978. *The Reproduction of Mothering: Psychoanalysis and the Sociology of Women.* Berkeley: University of California Press.

Daly, Mary. 1978. *Gyn/Ecology: The Metaethics of Radical Feminism.* Boston: Beacon Press.

de Beauvoir, Simone. [1952] 1974. *The Second Sex.* Translated by H.M. Parshley. New York: Bantam.

Dworkin, Andrea. 1974. *Woman Hating: A Radical Look at Sexuality.* New York: E.P. Dutton.

Engels, Frederick. 1972. *The Origin of the Family, Private Property and the State.* New York: International Publishers.

Firestone, Shulamith. 1970. *The Dialectic of Sex: The Case for Feminist Revolution.* New York: Morrow.

Gilligan, Carol. 1982. *In a Different Voice: Psychological Theory and Women's Development.* Cambridge: Harvard University Press.

Gingell, Susan. 2010. "Unearned Advantages of White Faculty." *University Affairs* 51.10 (December): 4.

Grant, Judith. 1993. *Fundamental Feminism: Contesting the Core Concepts of Feminist Theory.* New York and London: Routledge.

Griffin, Susan. 1980. *Woman and Nature: The Roaring Inside of Her.* New York: Harper Colophon.

Griffiths, N.E.S. 1993. *The Splendid Vision: Centennial History of the National Council of Women of Canada, 1893–1993.* Ottawa: Carleton University Press

Haraway, Donna. 1991. "Situated Knowledges." In Donna Haraway, *Simians, Cyborgs and Women: The Reinvention of Nature.* New York: Routledge.

Harding, Sandra, 1991. *Whose Science? Whose Knowledge? Thinking from Women's Lives.* Ithaca: Cornell University Press.

Harstock, Sandra. 1990. "Foucault on Power: A Theory of Women?" In Linda Nicholson (ed.), *Feminism/Postmodernism.* New York: Oxford University Press.

Hartmann, Heidi. 1981. "The Unhappy Marriage of Marxism and Feminism: Towards a More Progressive Union." In Lydia Sargeant (ed.), *Women and Revolution.* Boston: South End Press.

Heilbrun, Carolyn. 1998. *Writing a Woman's Life.* New York: Ballantine Books.

Hill Collins, Patricia. 1990. *Black Feminist Thought: Knowledge, Consciousness and The Politics of Empowerment*. New York and London: Routledge.

hooks, bell. 1989. *Talking Back: Thinking Feminist, Thinking Black*. Boston: South End Press.

Irigaray, Luce. 1985. *The Sex Which Is Not One*. Translated by Catherine Porter and Carolyn Burke. Ithaca: Cornell University.

Jackel, Susan. 2011. "Emily Murphy." Revised by Catherine Cavanaugh. Historical Dominion. At: thecanadianencyclopedia.comindex.cfm?PgNm=TCE&Params=A1ARTA0005529.

Jagger, Alison. 1983. *Feminist Politics and Human Nature*. Totova, NJ: Rowan and Allanheld.

Kim, Alison, Tingen, Candace, M. and Teresa K. Woodruff. 2010. "Sex Bias in Trials and Treatment Must End." *Nature* 465 (June 10).

Kimmel, Michael S., and Michael A. Messner. 2010. *Men's Lives* (eighth edition). Boston: Allyn & Bacon.

Kristeva, Julia. 1982. *Powers of Horror: An Essay on Abjection*. New York: Columbia University Press.

Kulba, Tracy. 2002. "Citizens, Consumers, Critique-al Subjects: Rethinking the 'Statue Controversy' and Emily Murphy's *The Black Candle* (1922)." *Tessera* 31 (Winter).

Lavallée, Omer. 2011. *The Canadian Encyclopedia*. Entry: The Canadian Pacific Railroad. Historical Dominion. At: thecanadianencyclopedia.com.index.cfm?PgNm= TCE&Params= A1ARTA0001322.

Library and Archives Canada. 2009. "The Early Chinese Canadians 1858–1947." At: collections-canada.gc.ca/chinese-canadians/ 021022-1200-e.html.

McLaughlin, Janice. 2003. *Feminist Social and Political Theory: Contemporary Debates and Dialogues*. Houndsmill, Basingstoke, Hampshire, and New York: Palgrave McMillan.

Minh-ha, Trinh T. 1989. *Woman, Native, Other: Writing Postcoloniality and Feminism*. Bloomington: Indiana University Press.

Munroe, Susan. 2011. "Chinese Head Tax and the Chinese Exclusion Act in Canada: Discrimination in Chinese Immigration to Canada 1885–1947." *About.Com*. At: canadaonline.about.com/od/ historyof immigration/a/chineseheadtax.htm.

Rich, Adrienne. 1979. "Claiming an Education." In Adrienne Rich, *On Lies, Secrets and Silence: Selected Prose, 1966–1978*. New York and London: W.W. Norton.

___. 1976. *Of Woman Born: Motherhood as Experience and Institution*. New York: Norton.

Schulz, Muriel. 1975. "The semantic derogation of woman." In Barrie Thorne and Nancy Henley (eds.), *Language and Sex: Difference and Dominance*. Rowley: Newbury House Publishers.

Smith, Adam. 2000 [1776]. *The Wealth of Nations*. Adam Smith reference archive. At: marxists.org/ reference/archive/smith-adam/works/wealth-of-nations/index.htm.

Smith, Dorothy. 1987. *The Everyday World as Problematic: A Feminist Sociology*. Boston: Northeastern University.

Spivak, Gayatri. 1990. *The Post-Colonial Critic: Interviews, Strategies, Dialogues*. London: Routledge.

Statistics Canada. 2010. *Canada Year Book*. At: statcan.gc.ca/ads-annonces/11-402-x/index-eng.htm.

Tong, Rosemary. 1989. *Feminist Thought: A Comprehensive Introduction*. Boulder and San Francisco: Westview.

Waring, Marilyn. 1999. *Counting for Nothing: What Men Value and What Women are Worth*. Toronto: University of Toronto Press.

Compiled by C. Lesley Biggs

- Canada's overall ranking among 182 countries, assigned by the United Nations in 2007, based on all measures of human development: 4[2]
- The overall ranking of the United States in 2007 based on all measures of human development: 13
- Canada's international ranking as assigned by the United Nations in 2007 based on a measure of gender empowerment: 12
- The international ranking of the United States in 2007 based on a measure of gender empowerment: 18
- Canada's international ranking as assigned by the United Nations in 2002 based on a measure of gender empowerment: 7[3]
- The international ranking of the United States in 2002 based on a measure of gender empowerment: 11
- The number of countries whose Human Development Index (HDI) and Gender-Related Development Index ratio in 2007 exceeds Canada's: 73/155
- The overall ranking of Canada in 2005 based on all measures of human development: 4
- The overall ranking of the United States in 2005 based on all measures of human development: 6
- Percentage of women in Canada's population in 2004: 50.4[4]
- Number of years a female infant born in Canada in 2001 can expect to live: 82
- Number of years a male infant born in Canada in 1997 can expect to live: 77
- Number of years an Aboriginal female infant born in Canada in 2001 can expect to live: 76.8
- Number of years an Aboriginal male infant born in Canada in 2001 can expect to live: 70.9
- Percentage of Aboriginal females in 2001 under 15 years of age: 32
- Percentage of non-Aboriginal females in 2001 under 15 years of age: 19
- Percentage of Canadian women in 2004 who were over age 65: 15
- Percentage of Canadian women in 2001 who identified themselves as visible minority: 14
- Percentage of Canadian women in 2001 who identified themselves as North American Indian, Métis, or Inuit: 3
- Percentage of women in Canada who report having a disability: 13.3
- Percentage of men in Canada who report having a disability: 11.5
- Percentage of women in 2001 who were born outside of Canada: 19
- Percentage of women in 1921 who were born outside of Canada: 20
- Percentage of women in Canada who have a university degree; or college certificate or diploma; or trade certificate; or some post-secondary education, in 2001: 15, 17, 8, 11.
- Percentage of men with a university degree in 2001: 17
- Percentage of women in Canada with a university degree in 1971: 3
- Percentage of men in Canada with a university degree in 1971: 7
- Percentage of doctorates awarded in 2001 earned by Canadian women: 27

- Percentage of all university students in Canada who are women in the 2008/2009 academic year: 57.6 [5]
- Proportion of the overall increase in Canadian university enrolment between 1997/98 and 2000/01 accounted for by women: 78 percent
- Percentage of women in Canada between the ages of 20–24 who had not gone beyond high school in 2001: 26
- Percentage of men in Canada between the ages of 20–24 who had not gone beyond high school in 2001: 36
- Percentage of Aboriginal women in 2001 not completing secondary education: 40
- Percentage of Aboriginal men not completing secondary education: 44
- Percentage of non-Aboriginal women in 2001 not completing secondary education: 29
- Percentage of Aboriginal women in 2001 over the age of 25 who have graduated with a university degree: 7
- Percentage of Aboriginal people in 2001 aged 25 and over with a university degree who were women: 62.
- Percentage of Aboriginal women in 2001 aged 25 to 44 who were attending school either full- or part-time: 17
- Percentage of non-Aboriginal women in 2001 aged 25 to 44 who were attending school either full- or part-time: 13
- Percentage of women and men in Canada in 2003 identified as having limited reading skills: 20
- Percentage of women in Canada in 2003 over age 66 identified as having limited reading skills: 53
- Percentage of men in Canada in 2003 over age 66 identified as having limited reading skills: 49
- Percentage of women in South Africa in 2008 who meet the illiteracy criteria as set by UNESCO: 11.9[6]
- Percentage of men in South Africa who meet the illiteracy criteria as set by UNESCO in 2008: 10.1
- Percentage of women in Chad who meet the illiteracy criteria as set by UNESCO in 2008: 78.1
- Percentage of men in Chad who meet the illiteracy criteria as set by UNESCO in 2008: 56.2
- Number of people, worldwide, who meet the criteria of illiteracy as set by UNESCO in 2008: 744 million
- Estimated percentage of those who meet the criteria of illiteracy as set by UNESCO who are women: 64
- Estimated number of people worldwide who do not have access to improved sanitation in 2010: 2.6 billion[7]
- Estimated number of people worldwide who do not have access to improved water in 2010: 884 million.[8]
- Percentage of rural households in Sub-Saharan Africa in which women are responsible for collecting water: 94[9]
- Increase in time needed by Nepalese women for water collection after they received improved water services: 4 to 5.[10]
- Maximum number of minutes (which is considered adequate access to a water supply) for a household in Tanzania to collect water and return: 30[11]

- Number of rural households in Tanzania in 2010 that meet the adequate access to a water supply. 29.6
- Percentage of rural households in Tanzania in 2009 that can access only unprotected water: 59.6
- Average weight (in kilograms) of water that women in Africa and Asia carry on their heads: 20[12]

NOTES

1. The original Hypatia Index was compiled by Pamela Downe, with the assistance of Ellen Whiteman. Except when otherwise indicated in the main text, the sources cited in this Index apply to the line where first referenced and then to all those that follow until another endnote appears.
2. United Nations, 2009, *Human Development Report 2009: Human Mobility and Migration*. At: hdrstats. undp.org/en/countries/country_fact_sheets/cty_fs_CAN.html. The HDI provides a composite measure of three dimensions of human development: living a long and healthy life (measured by life expectancy), being educated (measured by adult literacy and gross enrolment in education) and having a decent standard of living (measured by purchasing power parity [PPP], income). The gender-related development index (GDI), introduced in the Human Development Report 1995, measures achievements in the same dimensions using the same indicators as the HDI but captures inequalities in achievement between women and men.
3. United Nations, 2002, *Human Development Report 2002: Deepening Democracy in a Fragmented World*. At: hdrstats.undp.org/en.
4. Statistics Canada, 2006, *Women in Canada: A Gender-Based Statistical Report* fifth edition, Ottawa: Ministry of Industry. At: statcan.gc.ca/pub/89-503-x/89-503-x2005001-eng.pdf
5. Statistics Canada, 2010, "University Enrolment," *The Daily* July 14. At: statcan.gc.ca/daily-quotidien/100714/dq100714a-eng.htm.
6. UNESCO Institute for Statistics. At: stats.uis.unesco.org/unesco.
7. WHO/UNICEF Joint Monitoring Programme (JMP) for Water Supply and Sanitation. At: wssinfo. org/datamining/introduction.html. An improved sanitation facility is defined as one that hygienically separates human excreta from human contact.
8. An improved drinking-water source is defined as one that, by nature of its construction or through active intervention, is protected from outside contamination, in particular from contamination with fecal matter.
9. United Nations, 2000, *The World's Women 2000: Trends and Statistics*, New York: United Nations.
10. United Nations, Division for the Advancement of Women. Department of Economic and Social Affairs, 2005, *Women and Water*. This example demonstrates the need to incorporate a gendered perspective when providing new services. The report found that, "The tapstands and the tubewells [were] located along the roadside where the [women could not] freely bathe and comfortably wash their clothes used during menstruation, for shame of being seen by males" (p. 4). At: un.org/womenwatch/daw/public/Feb05.pdf.
11. United Republic of Tanzania, 2009, *Poverty and Human Development Report 2009*, MKUKUTA Secretariat, Poverty Eradication Division, Ministry of Planning, Economy and Empowerment. At: tz.undp.org/docs/Tanzania_PHDR_2009.pdf.
12. This weight is equivalent to the average U.K. airport luggage allowance. At: wateraid.org/uk/what_we_do/statistics.

1

Feminism 101

Lillian Allen

Instead of being the doormat
get up and be the door

NOTE

Lillian Allen, 1993, *Women Do This Every Day*, Toronto: Women's Press, p. 35. Reprinted with permission.

A Piece for a Sampler

Deborah How Cottnam

Observe in time, ye growing Fair!
How transient Youth, & Beauty are;
These gayest Charms! How quickly gone!
How often blighted in their dawn!
Attend then, to your better part,
Attain each useful, pleasing, Art;
Expand your Genius in its prime,
You mind inform, improve your time;
New pleasures, each, new days shall give,
And Virtue's bloom, shall time out-live.

NOTE

Deborah How Cottnam [c. 1793] 1994, "A Piece for a Sampler." In Carole Gerson and Gwendolyn Davies (eds.), *Canadian Poetry: From the Beginnings Through the First World War*, Toronto: McClelland & Stewart. See also Loyalist Women in New Brunswick. At: atlanticportal.hil.unb.ca/acva/ loyalistwomen/en/documents/cottnam.

I Am Invited to
Women's Studies Class

Jeanette Lynes

Not their politics that faze me, their peach-yogurt skin.
I might as well be Mrs. Robinson in a room of Elaines.

How did it feel, being bauble,
        accessory to patriarchy?

Might I have a glass
of water, please?

How could you sleep, demoted to air
        head, sex toy,
no more than
        an exotic dancer?

That came later, Winnipeg. Before that, my art was pure, all moves
connected—   flier to base
        scorpion to liberty,
        banana to basket toss.

Could you be deluded? Surely you can't deny being a contemporary
of Barbie?

My glass empty. Led out, an Elaine squeezes my hand, whispers:
I always wanted the camper. And Ken.

NOTE

Jeanette Lynes, 2003, *The Ageing Cheerleader's Alphabe,t,* Toronto: Mansfield. Reprinted with permission.

4

Once Upon My Mind

Anonymous

As the toxic by-product of marital rape, I began my tiny life on rather unsteady ground. Ironically, my personality and spirit have been greatly moulded by my own experiences of brutality and violation. My initial experiences with rape began at an enigmatic age, and were committed by a body, face, and hands that elude the tentacles of my memory. The only indicators of these first events are the perverse dreams that dominated my nights as a four year-old. In these dreams, I was always singled out from a line-up of young children; a gun was pointed at my genitals and I was forced to perform and witness acts that frighten me even in the daylight hours of my adult life.

[*Enter the elves, dwarves, flying carpet, fire-breathing dragon, a virginal princess, and Prince Charming. They mill about in the bedroom of a young girl, uncertain how to play out their stories for they are confronted with the experiences of a grown woman in the body of a child. The elves find her Dad's stash of pot and ask the dragon for a light. Meanwhile, the princess rummages about, trying to locate the phone number of the last stepfather, a real party animal. Gradually, the thick, green haze relaxes the guests and they begin to discuss how to help the tiny child. Decisively, they agree to grant the child the ability to read.*]

"But she's only five," argues the dragon. "She isn't scheduled for reading for at least another year."

"Well she wasn't scheduled for sex for another fifteen years," retorts the flying carpet viciously. "If we don't grab her now, she's going to miss her childhood."

[*Enter the Knight-in-Shining-Armour, Lester Literature…*]

When I first started reading, I wasn't exceptionally young. By the age of seven, however, I had completed all of the Bobbsey Twins, Nancy Drew, and Hardy Boys series, and was desperately searching for more books. I was the only child in grade one who was permitted to withdraw books from the high school shelves in the school library. The following summer, I pored over *The Tales of Narnia*, Tolkien's trilogy, and *Watership Down*. I was borrowing eight novels a week from the town library and, consequently, was accused by my parents of being abnormal and lazy. Toward the end of grade two, I began to cultivate an appreciation for Kurt Vonnegut; his black wit and satire resonated in my ears as I received my daily spankings, listened to the screaming of my parents, and packed my toys as we left to live with yet another man. My teacher called my parents after my class had completed its annual standardized intelligence test. "Are you aware that your daughter is reading beyond a grade twelve level?" she demanded breathlessly. "We are aware that she reads too much," was the reply, I am certain.

"You are such a little bitch!"

"Once upon a time, there was a beautiful princess…" the dwarves dreamily recite.

"If you ever tell anyone about this, I'll tell them what a bad girl you've been—who do you think they'll believe? Me or you?"

"*…who lived in a magical, far away land. The king and queen loved her very much and the three of them often spent their days together, flying kites beside the lake, rolling in buttercups, and riding gallant horses across their vast kingdom.*"

"But they beat her, right?" the girl asks suspiciously.

"Never!" exclaimed the dwarves. "Now listen to the story."

"But my mum is calling…" the child frets. "If I don't answer her…"

"Where the hell are you? I am so sick and tired of your bullshit, you little brat! I wish you had never been born!"

"Well, maybe I can stay just a little longer," she ventures. "What colour was the princess's horse?"

Reading became an escape from what was occurring around me—and what I knew was still to come. Curling up on the floor of our frosty-pink teacherage, the sun would flush over me through the south-facing picture window. Within seconds, I was worlds away from my home and my life. I couldn't hear the screaming or the insults and I didn't have to think about what a loathsome burden I was to my parents. I still felt the stinging slaps and my sleep was dominated by nightmares, but in the hours between dawn and dusk, I finally had some control over my life.

My second experience with rape began at the antiquated age of nine. My parents (Mum had decided to move back in with Dad, stepfather #2) made friends with a couple from the Netherlands, Peter and Ann, who had come to ranch in Alberta. Dad, who was also from the Netherlands, delighted in finding people with whom he could speak Dutch, and so we spent every weekend on their cattle and horse ranch. Every weekend, Dad regained more of his native tongue, while Peter meticulously and secretly instructed me on the complexities and necessities of "becoming a woman."

Initially, I felt only fear toward Peter. While in the company of other adults, he would play "wrestling games" with his three children and me. During the course of these games, he would grab me by the arms, stare into my wide eyes, and then squeeze until I yelped in pain. Then he would shove me aside, telling the other children that they shouldn't play with me because I would just cry like a baby. Leaving the room, my cheeks flushed with embarrassment and injury, I would hear my mother's voice telling Peter that I needed to be "toughened up."

For a year and a half, our relationship remained one between the feared and the fearful. Repeatedly, he would tear open my childish body and repeatedly, I would bind it back together with words from a page. It was when Peter began to defile my love for literature that I finally learned to feel rage and hatred. Afraid to close my eyes while staying in their home, I heard the hall boards creaking in the middle of the night. Frantically, I slammed my eyelids shut and attempted to make my breathing seem slow and deliberate, as though I were sleeping. First, he gently whispered my name, but I kept my eyes tightly shut. Then his voice became angry and he hissed, "You were reading by the hall light, weren't you?" Frozen, I swore, "No! I was sleeping!" Knowing then that I was awake, he slipped his hands beneath the covers and asked, "Why bother with all those books? That's all I ever see you do, is read. That's not normal, you know—you're just a girl. You need to develop other interests." As I curled my arms and legs about my body and all of my muscles tensed against his probing hand, he became angry. "Don't lie to me! I know that you were reading. You think you are smarter than me, don't you? We'll see who's smarter. What are your books going to do for you now?" Then, throwing my books from the nightstand, he climbed into the bed. "Just shut up and relax. Just relax… relax…."

The dragon weeps.

"Please tell me a story!" the girl shrieks. "Hurry! Tell me! Tell me the one about the princess and the pea, about Rapunzel — anything!!" Looking madly about, she sees the heads of her friends silently bowed.

"He's right," whispers a dwarf, "what good can we do you now, against him?"

"I need you!" she cries wildly, but the books lie lifeless on the floor.

Turning away to the window, the Knight in Shining Armour meekly assures, "We'll be here when he leaves."

Despite Peter's condemnations of a girl who read, I continued to pack books in my bag every weekend. I had nothing else. I could not talk to my parents and I could not escape the visits. In the summer, I would wander away from the ranch house to spend my afternoons reading in the fields. In the winters, I snuck off to the barn or a quiet room in the basement. Eventually, Peter always found me, but, before and after each contact, I drowned myself in the words of other places, times, and people. This dulled the pain, the shame, and the fear.

The books I chose to read while being raped were quite different from those I read throughout the week. Often, I would seek out tales of people whose lives were far worse than mine: tales of prostitution, murder, starvation, or homelessness. Always believing that the abuse would end, I thought that I would survive if I could convince myself that the situation was not as tragic as it appeared. The abuse didn't end, however — not until we moved to another province — when I began studying Dad's university texts.

"What's she reading now?" the princess whines. "What about one of our stories?"

"It's psy-cho-lo-gy," the girl pronounces slowly. "One in four girls under the age of eighteen has been sexually abused," she reads aloud. "Often, the perpetrator is well-known to the child, thereby causing feelings of distrust and betrayal. The victim may also experience feelings of rage, fear, shame, and exhibit symptoms such as withdrawal, nightmares, and inappropriate sexual behaviour."

"Why are you doing this to yourself?" pleads Prince Charming.

"I need to understand what's happening to me… maybe I will find out what I need to do to make it stop."

The text provided no strategy to make the abuse come to a halt, but it did help me to understand the emotions and behaviours that were transforming my personality. I came to understand that the abuse from my parents and Peter caused me to feel isolated from those around me. Reading my books became my lifeline to society, my umbilical cord to the world outside my tattered body….

* * *

I first wrote this story — part lifewriting, part fiction — for a university class in 1997. When I was asked to submit it for this collection, I reread it with a fiercely critical eye; stylistically, I have matured since I wrote "Once Upon My Mind," but I strongly resisted the urge to dismantle and recreate each sentence. The ending, however, I have deleted entirely. Five years ago, I could not imagine how the story should or would end, and so I created a scene in which the speaker eventually reaches a point of healing and bids farewell to her fairy-tale friends. The ending was trite, and the character was unfaithful to those who had brought her through the very toughest times of her life. More accurately, she (and I) have always kept books close to our hearts, and now I find myself completing a graduate degree in English literature and teaching undergraduate courses as an assistant. Like a burn victim, I grafted the pages of countless books to the raw flesh of my damaged psyche: those pages covered me, grew into my tissue, healed me, and became a part of my being. To quit reading would be equivalent to tearing open long since healed, but still aching, scars: to cast away literature would be to bury some of my dearest friends. No, rather than rewrite the ending, I hope I never find one.

5

Educating Boys
Tempering Rhetoric with Research

Bernie Froese-Germain

For a hot button education issue (and there are more than a few to choose from), look no further than the gender gap in schools. Every release of major test results, it seems, is accompanied by much hand-wringing over the fact that boys are falling further behind girls in achievement and other areas (Froese-Germain 2004).

To assist us in walking through this debate, Marcus Weaver-Hightower's thorough review of the literature on boys' education in a recent issue of the American Educational Research Association's *Review of Educational Research* is, in my opinion, very useful. He begins by dividing the research into four overlapping categories:

- popular-rhetorical literature: this literature "generally argues that boys are disadvantaged or harmed by schools and society and that schools are 'feminized'" (more on this later);
- theoretically oriented literature: this is "concerned with cataloguing types of masculinity and their origins and effects; [and] examines how schools and society produce and modify masculinities";
- practice-oriented literature: this, as the heading suggests, is "concerned with developing and evaluating school- and classroom-based interventions in boys' academic and social problems"; and
- feminist/pro-feminist responses: these are described as critiques of the "boy turn, moral panics over boys, notions of 'underachievement,' and popular-rhetorical backlashes." These critiques also tend to have a social justice focus and can usefully provide important checks and balances to the discussion — I'll also return to this issue later. (Weaver-Hightower, 2003: 474)

According to Weaver-Hightower, there are various reasons for the "boy turn" in gender and education research and policy, dating back to about the mid-1990s (see also the work of Bouchard et al. 2003). These explanations include the following aspects:

- media panic over boys' educational achievement and the emergence of popular and rhetorical books and articles (see, for example, Hoff Sommers 2000);
- earlier feminist examinations of gender roles and the use of narrow initial indicators of gender equity (e.g., test scores and enrollment data);
- economic and work force changes, and the "worldwide 'crisis of masculinity' that drives, and is driven by, the moral panic over the schooling and rearing of boys." (Weaver-Hightower 2003: 478);
- explicit feminist backlash politics; and
- pervasive New Right and neoliberal education reforms.

Making explicit the intersection between gender equity issues and the accountability and privatization agendas in education, Weaver-Hightower believes that the "structure of [the New Right's] educational reforms, particularly the interconnected processes of privatization and accountability, have accomplished more than its antifeminist rhetoric ever could" (Weaver-Hightower 2003: 476).

This restructuring of education is evident particularly in places like England with its system of public school choice and the creation of a competitive education market. The intense focus on high-stakes testing combined with the ranking and reporting of test scores in "league table" format — to facilitate consumer choice — has pressured administrators and teachers to "overvalue test performance lest they lose students and, consequently, their schools or their jobs" (Weaver-Hightower 2003: 477). This combination of factors has resulted in what Weaver-Hightower describes as "educational triage" with both gender and racial consequences. On the gender implications, he cautions that

> because boys outnumber girls in the lower test score ranks, funding will go disproportionately to them; moreover, advances in equalizing the curriculum, particularly in language arts, may be rolled back to better suit boy.... [E]ducational reforms championed by the New Right have created a "structural backlash"... that operates to challenge feminist victories without having to engage in explicit antifeminist rhetoric. (Weaver-Hightower 2003: 477)

In the current climate of market-driven and standardized education reform, educators harbour no illusions that advancing gender and other forms of equity in education poses significant challenges (see Larkin and Staton 2001).

The issues emerging from the research on boys are enormously complex and multifaceted. Weaver-Hightower's discussion of the formation of masculine identity and the notion of multiple masculinities competing with each other for dominance is of particular interest. In this struggle, visible minority, working class and gay males often lose out to the hegemonic male group. Moreover, Weaver-Hightower points out that one of the weaknesses in the research is a lack of awareness about the dualistic focus of this work (e.g., boy/girl, masculine/feminine, heterosexual/homosexual), effectively ignoring transgender, multiple sexuality, and other issues. As with the gay rights and other social and political movements, the struggles and concerns of transgendered people are showing signs of picking up momentum as a political force (Armstrong 2004).

Feminist critiques of the "boy turn" include highlighting the serious shortcomings of using large-scale standardized testing as a measure of student learning and, specifically, of gender equity. Alternative indicators of gender equity paint a more nuanced, accurate picture in which neither boys nor girls "rule in school" as it were (Sadker 2002: 240). Rather Sadker argues that "both girls and boys confront different school challenges, and they respond in different ways." Sadker highlights some of the progress made — and the challenges remaining — for both genders in a number of areas including grades and tests, academic enrolment, special programs (such as special education and gifted programs), health and athletics, and classroom and school interactions between teachers and students. For example, on the latter, Sadker reports that, "females have fewer academic contacts with instructors in class. They are less likely to be called on by name, are asked fewer complex and abstract questions, receive less praise or constructive feedback, and are given less direction on how to do things for themselves. In short, girls are more likely to be invisible members of classrooms" (238–39).

Other feminist critiques include looking more carefully at "which boys," rather than mistakenly assuming "all boys," are in trouble. In the same way that not all girls are excelling, not all boys are doing poorly. Disaggregating boys by race, social class, geography (urban vs. rural), and other factors reveals that differences in educational achievement among boys as a group exist.

With the "boy turn" there is also the danger that policy and research, as well as funding, could focus on boys at girls' expense. For example, on the assumption that the curriculum has become too "feminized" and that this shift is hurting boys, Weaver-Hightower counters that,

> as some argue… the "feminine" nature of the English curriculum is debatable at best, for many of the authors covered in contemporary schooling… are still from the "dead White men" camp, and many of the themes are masculine or sexist and the protagonists male. If we accept this argument, then *increasing* the "fit" of the curriculum to boys' concerns will only exacerbate existing inequality. (Weaver-Hightower 2003: 486–87, emphasis in original)

However, he does hasten to emphasize the need to

> avoid a kind of "zero-sum" thinking in this matter, for just as feminist scholars argue that girls have not benefited in education at the expense of boys… attending to boys' concerns does not *necessarily* mean taking from girls. In fact, some practice-oriented researchers have been careful to state their aims explicitly to avoid harming the achievement of girls. (Weaver-Hightower 2003: 487, emphasis in original)

Feminist analyses of the "boy turn" also address concerns associated with proposed solutions such as single-sex schooling, which appears to be growing in popularity. Weaver-Hightower notes that such proposals can "fall short because all-boys arrangements can be breeding grounds for virulent sexism… or can become dumping grounds for boys with discipline problems" (Weaver-Hightower 2003: 487). Riordan describes the issue of single-sex schooling as being "overpoliticized and underresearched" (as cited in Viadero 2002), with the few credible studies having mixed results. But the call for single-sex schooling is being heeded by some governments. For example, despite the lack of good evidence, the U.S. federal Department of Education is proposing legislative changes — to Title IX civil rights protections prohibiting sex discrimination in publicly funded schools — to encourage same-sex classes and schools.

The "feminization" of the teaching profession is all too often implicated in boys' lagging academic performance. The growing number of women among the ranks of elementary and secondary teachers, while not a new trend, has been accentuated by a steady decline in the number of men (who are either leaving classrooms or not choosing teaching as a profession, especially at the elementary level). At the same time, the "feminization" of the teaching profession is further complicated by an imbalance favouring men in educational leadership positions, as well as impending teacher shortages and the related issues of recruitment and retention.

Increasing the diversity of the teaching profession — including the proportion of males — to better reflect student and community diversity is undeniably an important equity goal. Robertson (2003) however dispels the notion that simply putting more men into classrooms will magically improve boys' learning, or that having fewer men is detrimental to the education of boys. As always there are complex issues and concerns embedded here, including the need to challenge restrictive, unhealthy notions of masculinity. Delany, for example, contends that expecting male teachers to come into schools as role models has a problem: what if they don't have the professional development, skills and training to engage boys in issues of gender, and reinforce undesirable notions of dominant masculinity? (cited in Davis 2003: 26)

The "underachievement" of boys has caught the attention of the men's movement, whose goal is to restore, in its view, lost masculine/masculinist rights and privilege. But Mclean argues that this outlook is wrong-headed:

> boys are... deeply affected by the collective pressures of masculine culture but left to themselves they are unlikely to identify it as the source of their problems.... Unfortunately, much of the current men's movement has responded to this situation by identifying women as the problem, rather than joining with women in challenging the gender system which impacts so negatively on both boys and girls in different ways. (cited in Davis 2003: 26–27)

While men can, and must, play a critically important role in boys' lives, Mclean emphasizes that

> This assertion is not based on some belief that "boys need men" in ways that women cannot fulfill. Rather, I believe it is unrealistic to expect boys to challenge the dominant culture of masculinity, if adult men are not challenging it themselves. This has nothing to do with "role modelling." (cited in Davis 2003: 27)

Other critics argue that good teaching has less to do with gender than with the quality, commitment, and ability of teachers. For example, Catherine Davis, Women's Officer with the Australian Education Union, quoting from its 1997 submission to the National Inquiry into the Status of Teachers, states:

> the profession should be attempting to attract the best and most suitable people into the profession, regardless of gender. If teachers mirror more accurately the society in which they operate — in terms of gender, class and ethnicity — so much the better. But teaching ability must remain the primary consideration. (cited in Davis 2003: 27)

Davis rejects the view that the "feminization" of the teaching profession is the main source of its problems as well as an explanation for the "underachievement" of boys. Rather, femininization is the result of a complex set of processes rather than the causes of the profession's problems:

> the profound problems facing the profession today — the failure to attract the next generation of teachers, the impending retirement of the majority of the teaching workforce, plus low salaries and heavier, more complex workloads — have little to do with the predominance of women. The solution to the critical issues facing school teaching is an industrial one. It is about significantly increasing teacher salaries, recognizing and remunerating valued classroom experience, and properly supporting teachers inside and outside the classroom, during and after initial training. (Davis 2003: 24)

Since teaching has been historically viewed as "women's work" and continues to be devalued in our society, the "feminization" label is convenient for those who want to pin the profession's problems on women (Davis 2003: 26). Moreover, the "feminization" label as applied to the teaching profession can be misleading. While women are over-represented in elementary teaching, women are underrepresented in senior management — which results in education systems continuing to be controlled largely by men.

Despite the complex issues underlying "the feminization" of the teaching profession, there is a push in some jurisdictions to hire more male teachers without necessarily incorporating a gender analysis. For example, based on research conducted by the Ontario College of Teachers and a province-wide campaign to encourage more men to enter the teaching profession, the (former) Ontario Minister of Education Gerard Kennedy publicly stated that boys' academic problems are linked to the growing shortage of male teachers (Leslie 2004). However, Jane Gaskell, Dean of the Ontario Institute for Studies in Education of the University of Toronto (OISE/UT) points out that the research on this point is unclear, and believes the "gender gap is more of a labour issue than an education problem," noting that "it's telling us that jobs are still gender differentiated" (cited in Sokoloff 2004).

This disconnect between policy and research parallels a similar distinction between the theory and practice traditions, a familiar yet valid refrain, within the education system. Teachers and teacher educators should and could make better use of the conceptual knowledge base, and educational researchers should be informing their work with classroom and school practice and experience. This theory-practice nexus speaks to the potential contribution of approaches such as participatory action research in marrying these traditions. The need to encourage greater use of teacher-researchers has been recognized by teachers' organizations, and they are actively supporting this approach in their work with classroom teachers.

With respect to boys' (and girls') education, Weaver-Hightower encourages educational researchers, policy makers, and others to conceive of gender in its "relational interdependencies" — that is, to formulate "curriculum, pedagogy, structures, and research programs that understand and explore gender (male, female, and 'other') in complexly interrelated ways and that avoid 'girls then, boys now'" (Weaver-Hightower 2003: 489–90).

Not only is this useful advice in moderating some of the strong rhetoric in this debate, it is entirely consistent with the long-standing mandate of public education to make schooling more inclusive and equitable for boys, girls, and all children.

NOTE

Bernie Froese-Germain, 2004, "Educating Boys: Tempering Rhetoric With Research," *Professional Development Perspectives* 4(4). Canadian Teachers' Federation/Fédération canadiennes des enseignantes et des enseignants. A longer version was published by Bernie Froese-Germain, 2006, "Educating Boys: Tempering Rhetoric With Research," *McGill Journal of Education* 41(2): 145–54. Adapted and reprinted with permission.

REFERENCES

Armstrong, J. 2004. "The Body Within: The Body Without." *Globe and Mail* June 12.
Bouchard, P., I. Boily, and M.-C. Proulx. 2003. *School Success by Gender: A Catalyst for the Masculinist Discourse.* Ottawa: Status of Women Canada.
Bourne, P., and C. Reynolds. 2004. "Girls, Boys and Schooling." *Orbit* 34,1.
Davis, C. 2003. "Gender Blind." *Australian Educator* 40, (Summer).
Froese-Germain, B. 2004. "Are Schools Really Shortchanging Boys? Reality Check on the New Gender Gap." *Orbit* 34,1.
Hoff Summers. C. 2000. *The War Against Boys: How Misguided Behaviour Is Harming Our Young Men.* New York: Simon and Shuster.
Larkin, J., and P. Staton. 2001. "Access, Inclusion, Climate, Empowerment (AICE): A Framework for Gender Equity in Market-Driven Education." *Canadian Journal of Education* 26,3.

Leslie, K. 2004. "Boys Need Male Teachers, Minister Says. Only 1 in 10 Teachers under 30 a Man." *Toronto Star* April 28.

Robertson, H.-J. 2003. "Une génération castrée?" *Phi Delta Kappan* 85,1 (Sept.).

Sadker, D. 2002. "An Educator's Primer on the Gender War." *Phi Delta Kappan* 84,3 (Nov.).

Sokoloff, H. 2004. "Gender Gap Moves to the Head of the Class." *National Post* April 28.

Viadero, D. 2002. "Evidence on Single-Sex Schooling Is Mixed." *Education Week on the Web.* Editorial Projects in Education, 21,40 (June 12).

Weaver-Hightower, M. 2003. "The 'Boy Turn' in Research on Gender And Education." *Review of Educational Research* 73,4 (Winter).

6

Critical Autobiography in Integrative Anti-Racist Pedagogy

Carol Schick and Verna St. Denis

This chapter draws on our experiences of teaching a required cross-cultural and First Nations course in a teacher education program. The question of how to teach feminist, anti-racist, cross-cultural courses in a teacher education program is an issue many people have addressed (see, for example, Cochran-Smith 2000; Hytten and Warren 2003). Those who teach such courses are likely familiar with the reluctance on the part of both students and teachers to hear the difficult things that need to be said and to unpack their own assumptions about inequality. In spite of our hopes that students would become aware of and active in producing anti-oppressive social relations, we have come to the realization that feminist and anti-racist education, including our own, can inadvertently reinforce relations of domination.

We are teachers in a pre-service teacher education program at two universities in western Canada. Verna is a Cree and Métis woman who has taught cross-cultural education and native studies in teacher education programs since the early 1980s. Carol is a white-identified woman whose experience of more than twenty years includes secondary and university teaching and research in the production of gendered and racialized identities. We are both committed to the production of equitable and just social relations within the context of teacher education. Our joint scholarship is evolving from a collaborative relationship that began in the late 1980s and continues to grow from mutual admiration and respect. This history forms the foundation of a trusting working relationship that requires ongoing care-taking and negotiation.

Our students are predominantly white-identified, mostly lower middle-class Canadian citizens, many from third generation, non-Anglo immigrant families. Students arrive with various understandings and assumptions about what they will encounter in such a course. Most think they are going to learn about the Other and be informed of strategies for how they will "deal with" the Other in the classroom. In this Canadian prairie context, it is Aboriginal peoples who form the greatest critical mass to challenge normative practices of a dominant white culture. The Other is typically understood to be Aboriginal peoples even though other visible minority groups also make the area their home.

Students come to our courses thinking that they are going to learn of the Other, to learn how they can be helpers, to discover how to incorporate practices of the dominant society. This is the assumption of superiority that whiteness permits: what we have and who we are is what the world needs whether it wants it or not. This sense of normative superiority is connected to what it means to be a respectable citizen and teacher (Fellows and Razack 1998). Students are very surprised to find that the curriculum is not about the Other, but about their own identity production as it is mediated by race, class, gender and other social positions.

We agree with Coco Fusco (in Goldberg 1993: 59), who warns that, "To ignore white ethnicity is to redouble its hegemony by naturalizing it. Without specifically addressing white ethnicity there can be no critical evaluation of the construction of the other." By not examining whiteness and keeping it "invisible," white students and teachers can conclude, "I don't have a culture. Therefore I can be a helper to Aboriginal people in their efforts to define theirs." Challenging students to look at their own identities disabuses them of the notion that they will be the "helpers" who can evaluate the "exotic other" (hooks 1992). We critique the practices of positioning of the Other as an exotic spectacle that the dominant culture may appreciate and consume. As students like to say: "I am fascinated by all the cultures. I love learning about them," a preoccupation in which students unselfconsciously participate as consumers whose only troubling moment is in the plethora of choice. The onus remains perpetually on Aboriginal teachers and students to explain themselves, to exhibit the markers by which they can be known as the Other (St. Denis, Bouvier and Battiste 1998). In most well intended multicultural information programs about Aboriginal people, the fundamental position of whiteness as dominant remains largely unexamined and is the standard of what passes for normal. By ignoring the production of racial identities, whiteness as a racial identity can be simultaneously invisible and a marker of difference.

Doing White Anti-Supremacist Pedagogy

Our course begins with readings that highlight the social and material practices involved in the production of knowledge, providing students with a basis from which they might be open to voices silenced by knowledge/power relations. We stress that Canadian history is not only a description of *what happened*; historical accounts also indicate *what has been produced* as a consequence of what stands as history. For example, the fact that very little attention was paid to the lives of Aboriginal women at the time of settlement on the prairies has contributed to the assumption that the women lack(ed) social and economic power. As a consequence of this, Aboriginal women's knowledge was (is) not considered worth recording. Instead, what have been produced as significant and worthy of record keeping are the lives of white, middle-class men and sometimes women. One can see the assumptions about whose history was considered worth writing as well as the consequences of that recording: the advancement of the interests of white settlers and the marginalization of the lives and rights of First Nations peoples.

The histories of Canadian settlement are produced through stories of triumphal whiteness and the silencing of other accounts. In exploring the histories of racially marginalized groups students begin to question the myth that Canada has always been a fair nation. We also examine how members of a contemporary white working class — holding similar class positions as many brown and black working-class people (Weis, Proweller and Centrie 1997) — struggle to maintain firm boundaries of racial distinction. Students become increasingly aware that they have a racial identity and that it is produced in a specific context of social, historical and material practices of nation building (e.g., Frankenberg 1996; Norquay 1993). The myth of meritocracy is kept intact through the assumption of equality and fairness, and the silencing of racialized minority history.

The second point of emphasis explores the impossibility of examining a particular form of oppression as if it were separate from other oppressions. Because identities are interlocking, and not singular, students explore the production of class, gender, sexuality, disability and race as intersecting identity formations. The readings (including Gregory 1996; Ng 1993; Wendell 1989) demonstrate how dominant identities rely on peripheral, marginalized, stigmatized identities for self-definition, for defining who "we" are because "we" are not "them." This is described as "dominance through difference" (Fellows and Razack 1998).

Critical Autobiography in Social and Political Analysis

In the autobiography, a major course assignment, students engage in reflective social and political self-analysis, including an examination of their experiences of gender, race and class.

Employing information from their own histories, they are expected to write an analytical essay (and not a chronological report) that incorporates a minimum of ten course readings. They are encouraged to comment on their social production, exploring how their own families achieved and are achieving what is commonly understood as "respectability and legitimacy."

As many feminist writers (e.g., Norquay 1993; Overall 1995, 1998) have indicated, we are mindful that the nature of personal experience can be highly problematic. The problem of including personal experience and reflecting on it critically is a necessary tension in the work we do. We stress that experience is valuable, but it does not, by itself, provide insight. The autobiography assignment is more than simply "telling one's story"; we ask students to "write in ways that trouble the already-familiar stories" (Kumashiro 2000). This implies going beyond normalized identity categories to examine experience through the social, economic and historic frames in which it is produced.

As students come to understand that identifications change with education, place of residence, language spoken and the anglicizing of immigrant names, they also see how they are produced as white and how identifications can shift and change. Students are encouraged to comment on what their gender, sexuality, ability, class and race afford or cost them, and how these identifications are dependent upon social practices and histories. Students describe how, in their own lives, privileges are both denied and assigned; they analyze the effects of privileging on the reproduction of inequality.

One of the challenges is how to support students to de-naturalize their own social production. The task of writing a critical autobiography that does not simply repeat familiar histories is akin to pulling the rug out from under oneself while standing on it. Understanding the implications of one's personal history and social identity — admittedly, a life-long activity — is at the heart of understanding the effects of inequality and also at the heart of doing feminist, anti-racist teaching. Discovering hidden and normalized construction of their raced and gendered identities is challenging as well as rewarding for students.

We invite students to consider what has been taken for granted in the telling of their histories. For example, if the students are white, how has their racial identity made the teaching profession seem like an obvious and "natural" career choice, more so if they are women? If they come from white families with working-class histories, how has their arrival at university been made to seem like solely a consequence of their own hard work and achievement? How is it that the same hard work of racial minority groups so often remains invisible and unrewarded?

Students move away from the concept of white teachers as unimplicated "helpers" in the "progress" of racial minorities as they begin to understand that dominant identities are co-produced through stigmatizing and marginalizing "others." This represents a significant shift in their learning. They invariably re-assess who they are through activities that require them to talk to each other and write about what they are learning. Through these processes, students work through their desire *not to know*. The fact that the course is mainly about their social production alternately centres and decentres students. We are not surprised if they offer some resistance to learning because, for most students in our courses, an analysis of power relations that are productive of social — including racial — identifications is unfamiliar in language and concept. Student resistance is, in some ways, useful to them as a defence against what they would rather not know or are not prepared to understand.

Student resistance to deconstructing their own social positioning is rarely overt; no one has ever refused outright to do the assignment. There are, however, several ways to avoid the topic of one's own white privilege, even while seeming to be talking about inequality and acts of discrimination. A student might, for example, claim, "I learned so many things about my white privilege in the course that when I see Aboriginal people, I now realize I was really wrong in my previous attitude toward them. My family is still really closed to the whole topic and I can't talk to them about it." This fictitious student references Aboriginal people and uninformed family members in ways that signal the student's comparatively "enlightened" thinking. While we certainly hope students learn many things about the effects of discrimination, this kind of talk still avoids looking at the effects of white privilege. The focus on her own "progress" moves the attention from critical anti-racism to a demonstration of her enriched cultural awareness, rather than a deconstruction of whiteness.

In another example, a fictitious male student demonstrates how he tries to "donate" (Norquay 1993) his racial privilege in a way that may be "well intended," but along with being impossible, it also fails to take into account the effects that one's social positioning can have in social situations: "I had an Aboriginal friend who wasn't asked to represent our school team in the geography challenge even though her marks were the tops. I made the team and her marks were higher than mine. The two of us agreed that this just wasn't fair; we were both really mad. I told her she should report it to the principal because it wasn't right. I really wanted her to do something about it. I even coached her on what to say. But she didn't go and the whole thing got dropped." In this example, the laudable desire of many students to speak out against inequality is made but this fictitious student fails to realize the effects of racial and gender privilege. The student recognizes the unequal treatment but does not see the disadvantage a minority person can face in lodging a protest with a person in power. He does not recognize that his expectation of a fair hearing — which has been afforded him by his lifelong experience of racial and gender privilege — is not something on which a racial minority woman can readily count. The presumption that one can even raise such a protest is also shaped by his white male positioning. A person with less social power may be more cautious in attempting to interrupt the status quo, even where the status quo is harmful.

As professors of anti-oppressive education, we learn continually to assess the teaching and curriculum we offer. We are always impressed by what students are willing to learn. When there is student resistance, we have learned to ask what it is that students are afraid to know and that we still need to teach. It is from student resistance and trauma that we see the extent of what is at stake for them (and us) in learning about the implications of being a white teacher and professor. In the autobiographical assignment written by each student, we have evidence that, indeed, something has been taught by us and by learning that students have taught themselves.

Conclusion

Teaching about the production of white identities is never unproblematic, especially with the potential that whiteness will be recentred in the process. What we mean by this is the potential for white people to imagine this "newly discovered" talk about race is all about them. We understand that white people, including one of the authors of this paper, who take up these issues, are free to see themselves as unimplicated helpers. There is also the possibility that they will see themselves as a little better at being white if whiteness is defined as liberal, accepting, tolerant and innocent of nation building that depends on the Other for an heroic image of self. An examination of the concept of "race" and the production of whiteness as integral to racism begins the process of making race privilege visible. Through an examination of current and historical social and political issues, and through writing their autobiographies, students come to understand that identities are not fixed. They also understand that through an investment in whiteness, however, schooling practices have every possibility of reinforcing relations of domination — even in multicultural and anti-racist courses.

Cochran-Smith, Marilyn. 2000. "Blind Vision: Unlearning Racism in Teacher Education." *Harvard Educational Review* 70,2.

Fellows, Mary Louise, and Sherene Razack. 1998. "The Race to Innocence: Confronting Hierarchical Relations among Women." *The Journal of Gender, Race and Justice* 1,2.

Frankenberg, Ruth. 1996. "'When We Are Capable of Stopping We Begin to See': Being White, Seeing Whiteness." In B. Thompson and S. Tyagi (eds.), *Names We Call Home: Autobiography on Racial Identity*. New York: Routledge.

Goldberg, David Theo. 1993. *Racist Culture: Philosophy and the Politics of Meaning*. Oxford: Blackwell Publishers.

Gregory, Susan. 1996. "The Disabled Self." In M. Wetherall (ed.), *Identities, Groups and Social Issues*. London: Sage Publications.

hooks, bell. 1992. *Black Looks: Race and Representation*. Toronto: Between the Lines.

Hytten, Kathy, and John Warren. 2003. "Engaging Whiteness: How Racial Power Gets Reified in Education." *Qualitative Studies in Education* 16,1.

Kumashiro, Kevin K. 2000. "Toward a Theory of Anti-Oppressive Education." *Review of Educational Research* 70,1.

Ng, Roxana. 1993. "Racism, Sexism, and Nation Building in Canada." In C. McCarthy and W. Crichlow (eds.), *Race, Identity and Representation in Education*. New York: Routledge.

Norquay, Naomi. 1993. "The Other Side of Difference: Memory-Work in the Mainstream." *Qualitative Studies in Education* 6,3.

Overall, Christine. 1998. *A Feminist I: Reflections from Academia*. Toronto: Broadview Press.

___. 1995. "Nowhere at Home: Toward a Phenomenology of Working-Class Consciousness." In C.L.B. Dews and C.L. Law (eds.), *This Place So Far from Home*. Philadelphia: Temple University Press.

St. Denis, Verna, Rita Bouvier and Marie Battiste. 1998. *Okiskinahamakewak — Aboriginal Teachers in Saskatchewan's Publicly Funded Schools: Responding to the Flux*. Regina, SK: Saskatchewan Education, Research Networking Project.

Thomas, Barb. 1994. "Learning from Discomfort: A Letter to my Daughters." In C. James and A. Shadd (eds.), *Talking About Difference: Encounters in Culture, Language and Identity*. Toronto: Between the Lines.

Weis, Lois, Amira Proweller and Craig Centrie. 1997. "Re-Examining 'A Moment in History': Loss of Privilege Inside White Working-Class Masculinity in the 1990s." In M. Fine, L. Weis, L.C. Powell and L.M. Wong (eds.), *Off White: Readings on Race, Power, and Society*. New York: Routledge.

Wendell, Susan. 1989. "Toward a Feminist Theory of Disability." *Hypatia* 4,2.

Gendering Trans/National Historiographies
Feminists Rewriting Canadian History
Franca Iacovetta

I address here the issue of gendering national historiographies in Canada by considering national narratives and counter narratives and the efforts to integrate more effectively gender, class, race and sex in Canadian history. I will accentuate the positive aspects, but then comment on difficulties. Over the last thirty-five years, Canadian feminist historians — whether they have identified primarily as women's or gender historians or some other type of historians — have been critical of the writing and teaching of far more inclusive, if uneven and contested, Canadian histories.

Women's and, more recently, gender history in Canada has enjoyed a degree of ongoing institutional support. There is an established and growing literature in Canadian women's history and a rapidly growing number of gendered histories — which include many studies that do not fit a homogenizing postmodern gender history label, but are grounded analyses of gender relations and power within different social arenas. Specific figures are not available but, qualitatively speaking, there are Canadian feminist historians in history departments, women and/or gender studies, and Canadian studies programs across the country. There is no specific journal in Canadian women's and gender history, but the established Canadian women's studies journals and history journals are receptive venues for publication. Faculty teach specific courses in these fields and integrate women and gender into their survey and other courses.

The Canadian Committee on Women's History (CCWH, founded in 1975) is the most successful of the societies affiliated with the Canadian Historical Association. Although the most prestigious awards and endowed chairs still go mostly to men, and men still outnumber women at the full professor rank, the greater influence of feminist historians within the wider profession is evident in their increased presence as journal and book series editors and as winners of many scholarly prizes, in the strong presence of women's and gender history on conference programs, and in the growing number of their students who are in full-time positions. However, although one can pursue a career in Canadian women's and gender history, most scholars simultaneously train in various fields.

Canada's history, historiography, and institutional structures have been influenced by many factors, including its historical relationship to Britain (and the British empire) and to its powerful neighbor, the United States; French-English relations; and, more recently, official multiculturalism.

Canadian historians, including feminists, were not in the vanguard of earliest efforts to internationalize national history, but early women's history in Canada, as elsewhere, was inspired by second wave feminism and a western feminist agenda. While not explicitly transnational or international in focus, many of the earlier studies — including those on suffragists and radicals — certainly took account of the broader international movements involved. (A project is now underway to more effectively internationalize Canadian first wave feminism.)

Since the 1970s, Canadian women's and, later, gender historians, along with a diverse group of social historians working with different approaches, have studied an increasingly wide array of once marginal or neglected groups and under-studied processes (capitalist state formation, industrialization, patriarchy, bourgeois hegemony, heterosexuality). In bringing more female subjects to Canadian history's table — including nuns, teachers, Aboriginal fur traders, telegraph operators, homesteaders, immigrant socialists, Black abolitionists, murderesses, asylum patients, battered wives, domestics and unwed mothers — women's and gender historians did more than simply enlarge the picture. Some also offered compelling critiques of the dominant liberal, elite, white, masculine, and nationalist meta-narratives of Canadian history. These narratives had long privileged powerful and public men who also often benefited, politically or financially, from the process of nation building and they ignored most women, the Aboriginal peoples displaced to accommodate white settlers, and such racialized laborers as the Chinese railway workers who helped link Canada "from sea unto sea."

There were key differences between the Marxist, feminist, and other approaches, but this still-growing body of work sheds much light on ordinary people's lives and tribulations, undermined the assumption that formal political events necessarily define historical turning points for women and others, redefined immigrant workers and women as nation builders and reclaimed the alternative or oppositional worlds of such groups as First Nations, rebels and revolutionaries, and sexual transgressors, including free-love red Finns, prostitutes, so-called delinquent girls and gays and lesbians. Studies of residential schools, Chinese head taxes, the Hindu woman question, Japanese-Canadian internment, rape and domestic violence, criminalization of homosexuality, and many others have challenged Canada's self-styled myths, many of them drawn in contrast to the United States. These include the myth of Canada as the peaceable kingdom that did not require violent revolution to become a nation, as a superior liberal country free of U.S.-style racism, and as an enlightened nation of immigrants — not just a big and assimilating one — that has long respected cultural diversity.

Moreover, some counternarratives and even oppositional historiographies emerged. In response to a whiggish historiography that recognized certain instances of state-sanctioned racism, but portrayed them as unfortunate blips in Canada's growth and maturity as a nation, progressive historians, including feminist legal, African Canadian and migration historians, have documented the persistent presence, rather than occasional flare-up, of racism and begun to scrutinize the processes of racialization. The work on early slavery, anti-Semitism, colour-coded courts and the guest worker systems established for not-white "Third World" workers after 1967 (when Canada supposedly adopted a non-racist immigration policy) has exposed racism as a defining element of Canada's history. Canadian self-image as a tolerant state and humanitarian nation, especially compared to the U.S. bully, sags under the weight of the many studies of state repression, police intimidation, Royal Canadian Mounted Police (RCMP) infiltration, and deportations. Similarly, new cold war histories have undermined the conventional view that Canada led a much less paranoid and repressive cold war than the United States, and also map the alternative and militant histories of reds, gays and others. Again, feminist historians have helped produce these oppositional literatures.

Building on this new scholarship, Canadian feminist historians, from the late 1980s and especially 1990s onward, began writing more synthetic national histories of women as well as producing course readers that, with each new edition, have become more explicitly informed by critical gender and race analyses. They have figured prominently among the Canadian historians writing more explicitly gendered and raced national and regional survey texts, and those acting as historical consultants for film and television series dealing with the histories of "the Canadian peoples," now a common phrase that indicates a recognition of a multiplicity of peoples, identities, and experiences. Beginning in the late 1980s, this important shift from a paradigm of global sisterhood to one of unequal sisters paralleled U.S. patterns; here, Black, working-class and immigration historians both critiqued the sister-hood model and produced histories of exploited but proud and defiant groups of women. The shift has been reinforced by current critical race studies that explore the links between gender, race and nation-building; citizenship processes of inclusion and exclusion; and the histories of South Asian, Caribbean and other racialized women workers from not-white countries of the southern hemisphere. As elsewhere, many — but by no means all, perhaps not even most — Canadian feminist historians have rejected the sharply polarized women's history/gender history dichotomy in favour of recognizing a symbiotic, but not tension-free, relationship between the two. This position reflects a converging interest among women's and gender historians in scrutinizing the differences of race, ethnicity, class, religion, sexual-ity, age and, more recently, (dis)ability, as they interact with women's multiple and shifting subjectivities. These historians also examine how gender shaped circumstances even when women were not present.

While not entirely new, Canadian contributions to the expanding literature on gender, race, nation and empire have returned attention to Canada's colonial history as a white settler society, while and sharpening analysis of its continuing neo-colonial state policies vis-à-vis Aboriginal peoples. Although much Canadian social history compared Canadian cities to U.S. ones and traced cross-border mobility and organizing, some historians explored Canada's complicity in the British imperial-colonial project. This resulted in an international orientation towards England and the "white" and "coloured" dominions of the former British empire, as well as more interest in scholarship produced outside of Canada. There is now renewed focus on the broader forces of imperialism as well as the intimate relations, both tender and violent, between colonizer and colonized, and the variety of relationships and mixed-race populations that these produced.

Having accentuated the positive, I will briefly note challenges and backlashes. First, it certainly can be argued that, despite all this activity, the dominant narratives have been only modestly revised. The power of the liberal nationalist framework[1] is well-known to activist historians who have fought for a more inclusive high school curriculum and heritage culture: the so-called new subjects are often incorporated in ways that reinforce, not disrupt, Canadian myths. The labour and multicultural programs that integrated women, immigrant workers and First Nations and Métis subjects often whitewashed or erased the history of state racism, class struggle and patriarchy at the core of these histories (a good example is the executed of resistance leader Louis Riel). I these once maligned or ignored subjects were transformed into members of the all-embracing liberal Canadian family. Second, many still view gender as belonging to women while men stand as the universal norm. Many male colleagues still consider it acceptable to tell feminist colleagues that "I don't do gender" and ask them to cover the field for them. Tokenism — as in the insertion of one paper on women (now often called gender) in a book or journal theme issue that otherwise shows little interest in gender — is still widespread.

There are still Canadian women historians who, despite plenty of evidence to the con-trary, say that more attention to gender will undermine a politically edged women's history. They also contend that attention to race will mean abandoning women, despite the fact that although so many of Canada's feminist gender historians, particularly those on the left, write both women's and gender history and with class- and race-critical eyes. But only a few have publicly mocked efforts to build bridges across theoretical and generational differences. I see these efforts as echoing earlier Marxist feminist efforts to work through a class/patriarchy divide, thus producing a rich literature demonstrating the symbiotic relationship between class and gender. At the recent CCWH meetings, some senior members worried (needlessly) that newcomers might lobby to add gender to the group's name; at the same time, younger women cannot fathom how their work in gender history can be seen as anything but feminist and political. Whenever the issue of attracting young women of colour to an overwhelmingly white organization is raised, so far only awkward silence has followed. More generally, critical race scholars note that many Canadian feminist historians still privilege gender oppression over race oppression as the main cause of women's subordination; they call for a more careful interrogation of these and other categories.

Canadian feminists historians have had to deal with backlash from the right, too — and, alas, from certain left historians. Leading the conservative backlash, political and military historian J. L. Granatstein charged that the "sssssssocial" (as in socialist with a sneer) historians had "killed" Canadian history by replacing the grand tales of political, diplomatic, and military progress with studies of the downtrodden, the trivial, and the inconsequential. His ill-conceived little book, *Who Killed Canadian History?* generated an enormous (too much) response from feminist, labour and gay historians, much of it in the form of declarations that women's history, or sexuality history, or labour history, *is* Canadian history. Such response unwittingly lent credence to Granatstein's national framework and at times echoed a liberal pluralist position. This situation speaks to the thorny question well-known to feminists and anti-racist activists: how do we make clear to others the important distinctions between feminist and anti-racist calls for inclusion or diversity (a position that calls for some fundamental restructuring of society and a distribution of resources and power towards the previously excluded), and simple-minded liberalism (that, for instance, confuse token nods towards inclusivity, such as government posters that present Canada as a collage of differently coloured faces, with real social change)? Significantly, the loudest calls to critique the categories of the nation have come from race-critical, postcolonial and migration historians, especially feminists of colour, many of whom write history from outside the discipline.

Granatstein's swipes at the feminists for helping to murder Canadian history were offensive. Equally offensive, however, to socialist feminists like myself, is the aggressive polemics of certain male labour historians, who, drawing increasingly narrow definitions "real" labour history, erroneously collapse all gendered perspectives into what they derisively call a "po-mo" camp. This characterization misrepresents the work of socialist feminists who developed gendered analyses of the working classes outside of post-modernist circles, or whose close attention to the social and analytical power of gender, race/ethnicity, sexuality or religion in labour history never involved a rejection of a class or materialist analysis. This is not to deny the value or importance of linguistic and discursive analyses, of course. Indeed, a number of socialist feminist historians (myself included), like other left historians, have moved beyond the highly dichotomized debates: we work at incorporating a variety of key insights from these and other theoretical paradigms into our analytical frameworks.

There are new and old challenges. Within Canada, the French/English divide grows wider, and the presence of parallel academic structures (journals, conferences) means that fewer Quebec historians practice in English Canada, while English Canadians increasingly cannot read French and feel little obligation to write national or comparative studies that include Quebec. (Hence, many titles read "in English Canada" rather than "in Canada.") Among women's and gender historians, as others, the call to diversify Canada's historical profession racially has so far failed to find meaningful ways of addressing the special situation of Francophone Quebeckers who quite rightly object to the assumption that they are part of the privileged Canadian white majority. At the same time, Anglo-Canadian historians who have responded to the race debate with the question, "What about Quebec?" sometimes speak as though Quebec itself has not become a multiracial Francophone world. With a few exceptions, such as new important work on international adoption and sex trade workers, few Canadian women and gender historians have yet experimented with a methodology that includes the whole of the Americas or with transnational methodologies, but these are early days for such methodologies. Still, given that, as with other national historiographies, most Canadian history is written with other Canadian historians in mind, will global or transnational histories of Canada enjoy a larger or smaller Canadian reading audience?

NOTES

Franca Iacovetta, 2007, "Gendering Trans/National Historiographies: Feminists Rewriting Canadian History," *Journal of Women's History* 19,1 (Spring): 206–13. Adapted and reprinted with permission. Given the space limitations, it is not possible to cite the many examples of the types of scholarship described in this chapter. Please see the original article cited above or the journal website. The content note below is purely explanatory.

1. I refer to efforts that interpret and promote the history of Canada as the linear progression towards an ever-improving nation with an ever-expanding commitment to protecting core liberal values like freedom and equality. Liberal interpretations have emphasized various themes, such as the progression from colony to nation and then to middle-power promoting justice in the world; the growing willingness of the two official founding groups, English and French, to tolerate, then accommodate and, finally, celebrate the cultures of "others"; a state that has largely respected civil liberties and provided increasingly expansive social welfare supports. What gets downplayed is the history of racism and the fact that liberal reforms of immigration or patriarchal laws or improved labour and welfare legislation are not simply the gifts of a benevolent state but usually a response to political mobilizations that threaten to embarrass or undermine the legitimacy of those in power, and that reforms (or hard-won rights) can be eroded or discarded.

REFERENCES

Granatstein, J.L. 1998. *Who Killed Canadian History?* Toronto: Harper Collins.

Iacovetta, F., 2007. "Gendering Trans/National Historiographies: Feminists Rewriting Canadian History." *Journal of Women's History* 19,1 (Spring).

Confessions of a Woman
Who Burnt Down a Town
(Inspired by the story of Marie Joseph Angelique)

Afua Cooper

Listen to Afua Cooper performing her poem at the Gendered Intersections website:
fernwoodpublishing/gi2

I buried the twins that evening
they died of smallpox
were only eight months old
Madame came too to the funeral
and said to me by way of consolation
"C'est la vie,
I too have lost my own."
I went back to work
went back to work in Madame's house
that same evening and at supper she yelled at me
and boxed me full in the face because
I overturned the gravy bowl in her lap

I remember my journey from my island to this island
Rhode Island to Montreal
Lived in Rhode Island all my life till
monsieur came from Montreal on one of his business trips
he bought me because he said I looked like a healthy wench.
Monsieur died soon after and madame never forgave me
But I had nothing to with it, he died of consumption

The twins died too.
After we buried them that evening
my heart changed position in my chest
and I was seized with one desire and one desire only
and that was to leave the prison of this island
But where could I go
because throughout the whole world
in all the continents people who look like me
were bound

But still, all I could see was
my feet running, no chains, no rope, no shackles
free

Madame talking to her best friend
and confessor Father Labadie
"I'm going to sell that negress, she's getting too much
for me, she's getting too uppity
And furthermore since François died I just can't seem to manage
    too well
Look a buyer for me father, perhaps the church is interested."
I bring in the food and pretend like ah neva hear
and I serve the food good and proper
was on my best behaviour
roll back mi lip and skin mi teeth
roll back my yai and show the white
den I went back to mi room in the cellar
and mek mi plan

Smoke, smoke, too much smoke
only intend fi one house fi burn
fire, fire, too much fire
but it done go so already
and I running
my feet unshackled, unbound,
free
running pass di city limits
while behind me the fire rage
and my raging heart change back into its rightful position

He was running too
an apprentice, from France
I gave him all my food to take me or show me
the way to New England but he tek the food
and leave me while I was sleeping
an the constables caught me

I don't utter a word as I sit in the jailhouse
Father Labadie come to confess me
but I refuse
their god is not my god
"Arson is one of the worst crime in New France, Marie,"
he say to me, "Confess now and save your soul."
I spit on the ground
outside, the mob want to rip me from limb to limb
but I not afraid, a strange calm fill my body
and I at peace, peace, perfect peace.

Guilty, the judge pronounce
and the sentence: to be tortured, my hands cut off
my body burned and the ashes scattered
to the four corners of the earth

I break down, my body crumple in a heap
and before my eyes I see the twins
and they look so alive as if they waiting
for me to come nurse them
The sentence is reduced
Now I am to be hanged only and my body burned
Father Labadie come back for di confession
And I confess
is I Marie who set the fire
I say yes
I start it in madame's house by the river
50 building destroy
the hospital, the cathedral
I confess

is I Marie who burn this city
so write that down Father Labadie
write down my story so it can be known in history
with my heart burning I take the sacrament
and accept the final rites
outside the guard is waiting
to take me to my hanging
outside the guard is waiting
to take me to my dying
outside the guard is waiting
to take me to my burning

Soon I will be free from the prison of this island
and I will fly and fly and fly

NOTE

In June 1734 Marie Joseph Angelique, a Black slave woman, was hanged in Montreal for burning down much of that town in April 1734. Poem from Afua Cooper, 2006, *Copper Woman And Other Poems*, Toronto: Natural Heritage Books. Reprinted with permission.

9

Complicating Narratives
Chinese Women and the Head Tax

Sandra Ka Hon Chu

Seeking to curtail Chinese immigration to Canada, in 1885 the Canadian government passed the *Chinese Immigration Act*, which mandated that all Chinese immigrants, with the exception of clergymen and merchants, pay a $50 head tax.[1] Realizing that $50 was an inadequate deterrent, the government increased the head tax to $100 in 1900 and again in 1903 to $500, an amount that was equivalent to approximately two years' wages for a Chinese labourer working in Canada at the time (Chan 1983: 67).

Over a century later, in December 2000, Shang Jack Mack, Quan Ying Lee, and Yew Lee filed a class action law suit with the Ontario Superior Court of Justice seeking the return of the amounts of the head tax paid by them, their spouses, or their direct descendants to the government of Canada.[2] Of the three plaintiffs, only Shang Jack Mack had personally paid the head tax. Quan Ying Lee was the widow of a head-tax payer, and Yew Lee was her third child, both of whom had immigrated to Canada in 1949.

Despite the focus of the legal arguments on compensation for the head tax, the plaintiffs stressed "the single most devastating consequence of the various forms of the *Act* was the separation of families and the resulting impediment to the growth of the Chinese Canadian community"[3] — a harm that would have been shared by Chinese men and women alike. Nevertheless, the plaintiffs framed the case primarily in terms of head tax compensation — a harm that most Chinese women could only claim as surviving spouses of head-tax payers. In 2001, the case was dismissed and appeals to the Ontario Court of Appeal and the Supreme Court of Canada were rejected. The redress campaign thus returned to the political arena where lobbying by head-tax claimants culminated in Prime Minister Stephen Harper's 2006 official apology and symbolic redress payments of $20,000 to surviving head-tax payers and persons who had been in conjugal relationships with head-tax payers deceased by 2006.

While Chinese immigrants during the era of the head tax did not conform to Canadian immigration law's model citizens who were "White, particularly British-origin, Protestants" (Abu-Laban and Gabriel 2002: 38), Chinese men have since found it easier to articulate their discrimination in terms of racial subordination. Since redress was largely predicated upon payment of the head tax, the claims of Chinese women, most of whom had not been directly financially harmed by discriminatory legislation, were contingent on the head tax paid by their spouses. Both Chinese women and men experienced emotional injury as a result of discriminatory immigration legislation, but such harms were characterized as subsidiary in relation to monetary loss in the head-tax payers' class action.

In the national dialogue about the head tax, the experiences of Chinese women have been largely conflated with those of Chinese men. In part, the state's inability to recognize the harms done to Chinese women can be attributed to the paucity of narrative tropes available to describe Chinese women's confrontation with discriminatory state policy and the corresponding strength of existing narratives describing Chinese women's rightful place at home in China (Chu 2006). The separation of Chinese women from their spouses in Canada was rendered "natural" by the Canadian state, and consequently Chinese women's absence from discourses of Canadian citizenship was only to be expected.

Historical Background

From its beginning in the late 1840s, immigration from China was overwhelmingly a male activity (Sugiman 1992, cited in Women's Book Committee, 17; Con et al. 1982: 17). Until the 1950s, the majority of Chinese women with spouses in Canada remained in China where they cared for children and, often, extended family (Das Gupta 2000: 146 and 159; Li 1998: 46). The few Chinese women who did come to Canada were often labelled as prostitutes (Sugiman 1992, cited in Women's Book Committee: 19). Nevertheless, the larger Canadian population initially welcomed them in limited numbers as an outlet for Chinese men's sexuality.[4] Although the politics of racial purity already made entering into familial relations with white women difficult for Chinese men, Chinese women were seen as lessening the threat of miscegenation that single Chinese men posed to the dominant white society (Das Gupta 2000: 153). At the same time, the concern for "racial purity," a cornerstone of British-Canadian nation-building and key to immigration policy, meant that reproduction by women from the perceived "lower races" was also seen as undesirable (Abu-Laban and Gabriel 2002: 38). As such, Chinese women experienced a paradoxical relationship with white settlers; while their presence mitigated the "vice" of Chinese male sexuality, that presence also enabled Chinese reproductive life.

Upon the completion of the Canadian Pacific Railway, the Canadian government passed successive iterations of the *Chinese Immigration Act* and imposed an increasingly higher head tax on Chinese immigrants. Married Chinese women's migration to Canada depended significantly on their husband's race, financial status, and occupational classification. Wealthy merchants, whose businesses were favoured by the Canadian government, were allowed to migrate to Canada with their wives and children; these merchants and their families were all exempt from the head tax, while poor labourers paid a heavy tax that unfairly deprived them of most of their families (Adilman 1984: 56).

According to Tamara Adilman (1984), the head tax was the most important constraint on Chinese women's entry into Canada (55). Effectively, the fee ensured that the majority of the Chinese-Canadian population would continue to be male: women were viewed as expensive economic liabilities and not productive workers who would be able to repay the head tax. Nevertheless, a major anxiety of the white population was that "if Chinese were allowed, without restriction, to bring their wives to Canada, they would reproduce at an alarming rate and [might] eventually outnumber whites" (Adilman 1984: 64). This fear culminated in the passage of a new *Chinese Immigration Act* in 1923. Referred to as the "Exclusion Act" by Chinese Canadians, the new act prohibited the immigration of virtually all Chinese, except for consular officials, children born in Canada, students and merchants.

The effects of the law were dramatic. According to David Lai (1988: 58), between 1923 and 1947, only twelve Chinese were admitted to Canada as immigrants. Peter Li (1998: 72) reports that in 1941, of the 29,033 Chinese men living in Canada, 20,141 had wives outside the country. While their spouses were abroad, women in China struggled to raise their children, often with the assistance of their extended families (Li 1998: 69; Yee 1996: 45; Sugiman 1992: 102, cited in Women's Book Committee). The *Exclusion Act* was not repealed until 1947.

One frequently proffered explanation for the apparent reluctance of Chinese women to emigrate with their husbands during the era of the head tax is the prevalence of Confucian values in Chinese culture, values which stress the importance of family (Sugiman 1992, cited in Women's Book Committee: 17; Yung 1986: 10). According to Sucheng Chan (1991: 95) "given the central importance of filial piety in traditional Chinese culture, the moral duty of wives to remain in China to wait on their parents-in-law was greater than their obligation to accompany their husbands abroad." Dutiful wives were thus left home to tend to the family while their husbands went overseas in search of fortune (Yung 1986: 11). Chinese women were stereotypically described by Chinese patriarchal discourse as *Nei-jen*, or "inside people," a notion that emanated from centuries of Confucian prescriptive literature defining women's place in the domestic sphere (Adilman 1984: 54).

The obedience of Chinese wives was summarized by Commissioner John Gray of the Royal Commission on Chinese Immigration (RCCI) when he maintained that "the married woman is subject to the will of her husband, and sometimes to the control of her husband's mother" (RCCI [1985] 1978: 269). In this version of the stereotype, Chinese women are represented as passive figures who exist to serve men. This paradigm suggests that Chinese women who did not migrate to Canada remained in China out of deference to their husbands and not because of the severely racist, sexist, and classist immigration legislation directed towards their community.

While there is no question that patriarchal cultural values, a sojourning mentality and differentials in the cost of living all worked in tandem to limit the number of Chinese female immigrants during the early decades of the Chinese influx, the assumption that cultural restraints were solely responsible for the skewed sex ratio of the Chinese immigrant community should be challenged (Zhao 2002:9). According to Li, "there is a profound difference between the ideals of traditional familism, as incorporated in the ethical precepts of neo-Confucianism, and the form of the Chinese family as an empirical reality... economic necessity compelled both the husband and the wife to participate actively and jointly in agricultural production" (1998: 62). Given the poor economic conditions at home, where most women, particularly among rural Chinese, needed to work to support the immediate and extended family, sufficient economic incentives existed, George Peffer (1999: 6) suggests, for tolerating, and even encouraging, female emigration from China rather than prohibiting it. In Li's view, a more important reason for the gross disproportion between males and females in Chinese immigrant communities was anti-Chinese sentiment among the white public (Li 1998: 61).[5] Coupled with the animosity directed towards Chinese women in particular, the severe marginalization of the Chinese in Canada had an equal, if not more profound, impact on discouraging the migration of women than "family-oriented" Confucian values, Li argues.

Although the influence of Confucianism appears to have been overstated, a conception of Chinese women as "inside people" was compatible with existing Canadian narratives describing women's place within the private sphere. The understanding that Chinese women were *Nei-jen* rendered their absence from Canada "natural." As a result, the impact of discriminatory immigration legislation on Chinese women has been left unexamined and the phenomenon of transnational households in the Chinese-Canadian community could be attributed to Orientalist notions of the solitary Chinese male and the domesticated Chinese female.[6] Given the ideological framework confining maternalized Chinese women to the home, it is hardly surprising that any harm arising from forced separation has yet to be considered by the Canadian state.

Conclusion

While Chinese women during the era of the head tax presumably experienced harms just as severe as those experienced by their male partners, reparation law has not, thus far, recognized the particularities of their experience. A narrative trope which seemingly robbed Chinese women of their agency diminished the harm of legislated separation from their spouses. Because Chinese women were characterized as passively subject to law, they were deemed unable to comprehend harm, much less "talk back" to dominant discourses confining them to one-dimensional narratives. Thus, not only have the head tax and twenty-four years of legislated exclusion subjected Chinese women to the emotional injury of forced separation, but they also have reinforced the message that Chinese women are limited to narratives characterized by subordination.

These narratives can be reconstructed. An awareness of their restrictive nature may enable Chinese Canadian women to transcend the arrested development entailed by such scripts. Recent works of literature documenting Chinese women's experiences during the period of the head tax already signal a shift in those narratives (see for example, Chong 1995; Lee 1990, 2007). Correspondingly, Chinese Canadian women's participation in a reparation movement may enable the reclamation of their rights through their own narratives which reject stereotypes of docility and portray Chinese women as more than passive objects of oppression. A reparation movement predicated upon the emotional injury associated with separation may also underscore the particular conditions of Chinese women's historical struggles and, in turn, affirm this experience of harm for the larger community. Then, the current notion of harm would be recoded, or at least destabilized. For Chinese Canadian women, complicating the traditional legal paradigm may be a critical way to prevent their being disappeared.

NOTES

Sandra Ka Hon Chu, 2006, "Reparation as Narrative Resistance: Displacing Orientalism and Recoding Harm for Chinese Women of the Exclusion Era," *Canadian Journal of Women and the Law* 18(2): 387–437. Adapted and reprinted with permission.

1. The term "Chinese" is used in this article to describe a socially constructed race of people, since discrimination against the Chinese was based on purely physical racial grounds. As such, naturalized Chinese Canadians were subjected to the same anti-Chinese legislative bills as alien Chinese.
2. Statement of Claim of Shang Jack Mack, Quan Ying Lee and Yew Lew at para. 1.
3. Memorandum of Argument of the Applicant for Leave to Appeal, *Shang Jack Mack et al.* v. *Attorney General of Canada*, Court of Appeal File No. C36799 at para. 7.
4. According to J. Brian Dawson, Alberta Supreme Court Justice Nicholas Beck stated in 1913 that if some Chinese led immoral lives in Canada, "the Dominion Parliament [was] to be held responsible [as it had imposed] the poll tax on Chinese women of $500" so that few Chinese could "afford to pay this sum for a prospective wife or go home to get married." *Calgary Albertan* November 27, 1913 (cited in Dawson 1991: 123).
5. In Canada, the hostile treatment of Chinese migrants is evidenced in the 1902 *Royal Commission Report on Chinese and Japanese Immigration* (1902: 263) in which a Chinese merchant from Vancouver testified that "a large proportion of [Chinese men in Canada] would bring their families here, were it not for the unfriendly reception they got here during recent years."
6. According to Said (2003: 3), "Orientalism" is the process by which Western states have, for at least the past five centuries, defined themselves in opposition to "Oriental" others. The construction of the Oriental male as perpetually isolated reinforces the assumption that the legislated separation of Chinese families was voluntary and natural to Oriental others.

Abu-Laban, Yasmeen, and Christina Gabriel. 2002. *Selling Diversity: Immigration, Multiculturalism, Employment Equity, and Globalization*. Peterborough: Broadview Press.

Adilman, Tamara. 1984. "A Preliminary Sketch of Chinese Women and Work in British Columbia 1858–1942." In B. Latham and R. Pazdro (eds.), *Not Just Pin Money: Selected Essays on the History of Women's Work in British Columbia*. Victoria: Camosun College Press.

Chan, Anthony. 1983. *Gold Mountain: The Chinese in the New World*. Vancouver: New Star Books.

Chan, Sucheng. 1991. "The Exclusion of Chinese Women, 1870–1943." In S. Chan (ed.), *Entry Denied: Exclusion and the Chinese Community in America, 1882–1943*. Philadelphia: Temple University Press.

Chong, Denise. 1995. *The Concubine's Children*. Toronto: Penguin Canada.

Chu, Sandra Ka Hon. 2006. "Reparation as Narrative Resistance: Displacing Orientalism and Recoding Harm for Chinese Women of the Exclusion Era." *Canadian Journal of Women and the Law* 18, 2.

Con, Harry, Ronald Con, Graham Johnson, Edgar Wickberg and William Willmott. 1982. *From China to Canada: A History of the Chinese Communities in Canada*. Toronto: McClelland and Stewart.

Das Gupta, Tania. 2000. "Families of Native People, Immigrants, and People of Colour." In N. Mandell and A. Duffy (eds.), *Canadian Families: Diversity, Conflict and Change*. Toronto: Harcourt Canada.

Dawson, J. Brian.1991. *Moon Cakes in Gold Mountain: From China to the Canadian Plains*. Calgary: Detselig Enterprises.

Lai, David Chuenyan. 1988. *Chinatowns: Towns Within Cities in Canada*. Vancouver: UBC Press.

Lee, Jen Sookfong. 2007. *The End of East*. Toronto: Knopf Canada.

Lee, Sky.1990. *Disappearing Moon Café*. Vancouver: Douglas and McIntyre.

Li, Peter. 1998. *The Chinese in Canada*, second edition. Toronto: Oxford University Press.

Peffer, George. 1999. *If They Don't Bring Their Women Here: Chinese Female Immigration Before Exclusion*. Urbana: University of Illinois Press.

Royal Commission on Chinese and Japanese Immigration. 1902. *Report*. Ottawa: King's Printer.

Royal Commission on Chinese Immigration [1885] 1978. *Report*. New York: Arno Press.

Said, Edward. 2003. *Orientalism*. London: Penguin.

Women's Book Committee. 1992. *Jin Guo: Voices of Chinese Canadian Women*. M. Sugiman (editor). Toronto: Chinese Canadian National Council and Women's Press.

Yee, Paul.1996. *Struggle and Hope: The Story of Chinese Canadians*. Toronto: Umbrella Press.

Yung, Judy. 1986. *Chinese Women of America: A Pictorial History*. Seattle: University of Washington Press.

Zhao, Xiaojian. 2002. *Remaking Chinese America: Immigration, Family, and Community, 1940–1965*. New Brunswick. NJ: Rutgers University Press.

10

The National Council of Women of Canada

Over a Century of Education and
Advocacy for Women and Children

National Council of Women of Canada

The National Council of Women of Canada[1] (NCWC), "one of Canada's oldest advocacy associations" (Strong-Boag and MacDonald 2011), was founded in 1893 and continues its work to improve the lives of women and children. The idea for the NCWC developed out of the World's Congress of Representative Women hosted by the International Council of Women (established in 1888) in May 1893. Attracting 1500 women, the NCWC held its inaugural meeting on October 27, 1893, in the Horticultural Building in Toronto. Lady Aberdeen, wife of Lord John Campbell Gordon Aberdeen, the Governor-General of Canada, became the NCWC's first president. The Council is an umbrella organization comprised of fifteen Local Councils, six provincial councils, one study group, and twenty nationally organized societies (federates).

NCWC's current mandate — "to empower all women to work together towards improving the quality of life for women, families, and society through a forum of member organizations and individuals" — has not changed much since its inception. In the early decades of the twentieth century, the NCWC became involved in improving the lives of women in prison: it had matrons appointed to institutions where women prisoners were housed; and in factories it instituted women inspectors where women, particularly immigrant women, worked. In 1907 and again in the 1940s, the NCWC recommended equal pay for work of equal value. The NCWC also worked tirelessly for child welfare: the Council pushed for free libraries and supervised playgrounds for children as well as teaching domestic science and manual training in schools. It supported the creation of many public health measures, including a pure water supply, the pasteurization of milk, and medical inspection in schools. Under Lady Aberdeen's leadership, the NCWC was instrumental in establishing the Victorian Order of Nurses in 1897.

The NCWC was active in the suffrage movement (although not all members agreed with the goal) and contributed to the passage of the *Act to Confer the Electoral Franchise Upon Women* at the federal level in 1918. NCWC also played a key role in the 1929 Persons Case, in which the Judicial Committee of the Privy Council declared women to be persons (Griffiths 1993). In the 1930s, the NCWC was involved with the study and prevention of the spread of venereal diseases. In the 1950s, the NCWC supported the development of the Women's Bureau of Labour Canada (1954), and recommended that pensions plans be adapted for women. In the 1960s, it recommended broadening the grounds for divorce (1961), advocated for the dissemination of birth control information, and supported the call for the Royal Commission on the Status of Women, resulting in the now disbanded Canadian Advisory Council on the Status of Women (Strong-Boag and MacDonald 2011). In the 1970s, the NCWC passed a resolution asking for the removal of abortion from the Criminal Code, recommended programs to protect prostitutes and to assist in their rehabilitation, as well as being involved in the formation of the Federal Bureau of Aging (1978).

In the 1990s, NCWC joined with twenty-three other national women's organizations in the "Fair Share Campaign" (1997), which recommended that the federal government increase the funding to the Women's Program to a minimum of $2 for every woman and girl child in Canada. (Unfortunately, the federal government did not heed this call; then, in the last decade, the Women's Program was severely cut.) In 1998 NCWC established a Task Force on World Trade Organization Treaties to study and monitor the impact of these agreements on

National Council of Women at Rideau Hall, October 1898. (Lady and Lord Aberdeen in centre; Lady Majorie Gordon at left.) Photo credit: Topley Studio/Library and Archives Canada/PA-028034.

political, social, cultural and environmental issues, with particular attention to the effect on women. From 1998 to 2007 NCWC has actively supported *Campaign 2000*, a cross-Canada public education movement to increase awareness of and support for the all-party House of Commons resolution to end child poverty in Canada by the year 2000. Clearly this goal was not reached, but *Campaign 2000*, along with *Make Poverty History*, continues to lobby for a federal action plan to reduce poverty in Canada.[2]

The NCWC has received many awards and honours for its work. It was incorporated by an act of Parliament in 1914. On May 13, 1993 His Excellency the Right Honourable Raymond John Hnatyshyn awarded the NCWC with a coat of arms and a crest (bearing Lady Aberdeen's motto, *Altior*, meaning "ever higher") in celebration of the NCWC's one hundredth Annual General Meeting. In 1997 NCWC was accredited by the Economic and Social Council (ECOSOC) of the United Nations and received Consultative Status (II). In August 2005, Parks Canada and the Historical Site and Monuments Board of Canada installed a National Historic Site commemorative plaque in the Allen Gardens where the first meeting of the NCWC took place — an important tribute to the work NCWC has done since its inception to improve the lives of Canadian women.

NOTES

1. For more information, please see the NCWC website at: ncwc.ca.
2. For more information and report cards on poverty, see *Campaign 2000* at: campaign2000.ca and at: makepovertyhistory.org/takeaction.

REFERENCES

Griffiths, N.E.S. 1993. *The Splendid Vision: Centennial History of the National Council of Women of Canada, 1893–1993*. Ottawa. Carleton University.

Strong-Boag, Veronica. 2011. "The National Council of Women of Canada." Revised by Diane MacDonald. *The Canadian Encyclopedia*. Historica-Dominion. At: thecanadianencyclopedia.com/index.cfm? PgNm=TCE&Params=A1ARTA0005614.

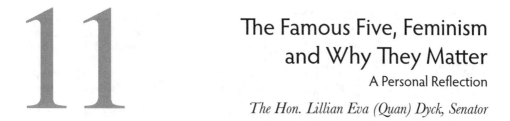

11

The Famous Five, Feminism and Why They Matter

A Personal Reflection

The Hon. Lillian Eva (Quan) Dyck, Senator

I have mixed Chinese and Cree Indian heritage, and have encountered racism all my life. My parents' lives were scarred by racial discrimination; my mother told me and my brother never to tell anyone that we were Indian. We had to pretend that we were just Chinese; it was the lesser of two evils. It wasn't until I earned a PhD that I had the courage to reveal my Cree Indian roots. How could anyone say or do anything derogatory to me when I had the highest earned academic degree? I naively thought that my academic status would protect me from racial discrimination.

While I could hide my Indianness, I could not hide my femaleness. As a female born in 1945, I was very aware of what girls and women could not do. The societal messages were clear: girls don't become professionals like doctors, scientists, or police officers. Likewise, non-white people weren't seen as suitable for many careers paths either. I was fortunate, however, and attended a very good high school with supportive teachers who set me on the path to university.

In my career as a professor and neuroscientist, I faced overt sexism. I was told many off-colour sexist jokes; the more I objected, the more it seemed to please my tormentor. I was told that I ought to resign because I had a husband. I was told that I was treated the same as my male colleagues, when I knew I was not. After a few years, I began to doubt my perception of reality. I was not alone. Other women, other scientists, had similar experiences and had come to the same conclusion — that they were being discriminated against. I joined the women's group on campus and began to speak and write about sexism in the academy.

In my wildest dreams I never imagined that one day I would be a senator. It is a position to which many politicians apparently aspire, and to which I was granted the privilege and honour in the spring of 2005. While I was an accomplished scholar, research scientist, and senior university administrator, I don't think that is why I was summoned to the senate; rather, my public contributions were the reason. I spent many years speaking to various audiences to encourage participation of women and Aboriginals in science. I gave many speeches about discrimination against women and Aboriginals in the educational system and in the workforce. Though I was told not to engage in these kind of activities, since they weren't seen as a legitimate thing for a scientist to do at that era, that's what got me into the senate — standing up for women, Aboriginals, and minorities. I was called a strident feminist, a troublemaker, a "women's libber." In May 2010, however, I

Lillian Dyck with Irene Parlby and Nellie McClung

Lillian Dyck with Henrietta Muir Edwards and Louise McKinney

Lillian Dyck with Emily Murphy

received an award from the Aboriginal Human Resources Council for being "A Champion of Change." One's actions often are judged by others and the verdict — well, it's all in the eye of the beholder!

One of my first invited speeches as a senator was entitled, "Women's Equality: Are We There Yet?" I was the keynote speaker at the Women's History Month Dinner (Person's Case Award) in Regina. I talked out about the Famous Five and their efforts resulting in women becoming "persons" in the eyes of the law, and thus eligible to be senators. I thank these ladies often. I pass by the Famous Five monument on Parliament Hill every time I go to the senate chamber, and I silently whisper my thanks to them for their courage and persistence. If I feel downhearted, discouraged, tired, or frustrated, I visit them and am revitalized by their calm, strong spirits. I sit on the chair by Emily Murphy and feel her comforting presence. I stand between Irene Parlby and Nellie McClung, and I am re-energized by their indomitable strength of spirit. I imagine myself having a cup of tea with Henrietta Muir Edwards and Louise McKinney, plotting our next strategy in a lady-like fashion. The Famous Five are cast bigger than life-size; how appropriate, they made women's lives bigger — more equal to those of men. In the summer months, I see many school children and tourists visiting the Famous Five monument. I am happy to know that these visitors are learning about women's rights and five of our famous feminist heroines.

NOTE

The Famous Five was the name given to the five Alberta women whose campaign to have women legally declared persons ended successfully in 1929.

12

Still Ain't Satisfied

Doris Anderson and Lisa Rundle

After welcoming me into her downtown Toronto apartment, Doris Anderson, former editor of *Chatelaine* and one of Canada's best-known feminists, had some questions for me. "Why don't young women vote?" she asked. I wish I knew the answer. "I vote," I said, and then ventured: "A sense that it won't make any difference?" By the end of the interview, I suspected young women may soon feel differently. Certainly, if Anderson has her way, all women will.

It might have something do with the fact that Anderson, eighty-four, has long been extremely proficient at talking to your average women. Flipping through copies of *Chatelaine* from 1957 to 1977, I found it jarring at first to see her editorials on abortion appearing alongside recipes. But the packaging of the forward-thinking with the traditional is so... logical. And it's a reminder that the two solitudes of regular women and feminists need not be so far apart as the keepers of the status quo would like us to believe.

Today, thirty-five years after the report of the Royal Commission on the Status of Women, a document that gave shape to the second wave women's movement and that Anderson helped bring about, I wanted to know more about the woman, the magazine she guided, and the times in which she did it.

Herizons/Lisa Rundle: What did it mean, in 1957, for you to become the editor of *Chatelaine*?

Doris Anderson: It was a job that I was thrilled to get. I'd been looking at *Chatelaine* since I was a kid—my mother always got it. And the editor for many years was a woman. But I had to fight for the job [I was already on staff]. They were going to give it to a man on staff and, without even thinking about it, I said "If you do that, I'll quit."

There were only two women editors of women's magazines in the whole of North America at one point when I was editor.

Lisa Rundle: *Chatelaine* decided not to serialize Betty Friedan's *The Feminine Mystique* because the editors looked at it and thought: "We've covered these issues." What did it feel like to be ahead of the text that's credited with sparking the second wave women's movement in North America?

Doris Anderson: I was a feminist long before the word had been invented. And I decided that the one thing we had going for us as a Canadian magazine (at a time when Canadian magazines were losing money and readers to richer U.S. magazines) was to tell Canadian women what was happening in Canada. And a lot of women used to say to me: "I never read women's magazines." These were very bright women at home with kids, and they were climbing the walls half the time in boredom. But they considered women's magazines beneath them. So I thought: "You're going to be reading *Chatelaine* when I'm through with it."

In almost every issue we had an article that really got women talking, and these were often about all the awful things women had to cope with: the fact that you couldn't get an abortion if your life was in danger or you were raped (I published the first of those articles in

1958); a social worker couldn't give out any information on birth control. I published one of the first articles in North America on the abuse of children and I got a raft of letters saying I was being sensational, this didn't happen. But soon that became a very serious concern. And of course, battered women — nobody talked about that.

Lisa Rundle: When did you get the conviction to talk about these things no one else was talking about?

Doris Anderson: What brought me into journalism was this idea that you could write about things and possibly change them. We tried to balance all this feminist stuff. We ran food and fashion like every other magazine. We ran a Mrs. Chatelaine contest every year. It was incredibly popular with readers, and it also brought the staff down to earth about who we were talking to. But we also tackled things that astound me now — we tackled lesbianism and sex. When Kinsey came out and reported that only one woman in four enjoyed sex, I thought, "That's awful." Then there were all these books to help women understand sex. It would have been better to educate the men.

What Betty Friedan did was pull all this together in her book. But my managing editor read it and said there's nothing in here we haven't covered, except how awful women's magazines are for not covering these issues. So we passed it up.

Lisa Rundle: I looked through several old *Chatelaines*, and it's shocking to read your editorials about contentious issues, to see them in there beside the recipes and the knitting patterns.

Doris Anderson: [laughs] "10 Ways to Dress up Hamburger!" We used to joke about it: "O.K., if we're going to do this serious story, we better have '16 Ways To Do Your Hair This Summer.'"

Lisa Rundle: You were writing about these vital issues, but you were also getting letters from readers saying, "You've turned my nice women's magazine into a feminist rag." So when did it start to feel that the issues had broader public appeal?

Doris: Anderson: The circulation kept going up, and that saved my skin. The guys upstairs didn't care for what I was doing. But they couldn't argue with the circulation. *Maclean's* had always been the big money-maker, but *Maclean's* began to lose money and *Chatelaine* continued to make money. I also got a lot of positive letters. And we were committed to involving the readers, running their letters. We paid women — readers — the going rate for stories about their own lives.

Lisa Rundle: It's thirty-five years since the report of the Royal Commission on the Status of Women and you, through *Chatelaine*, were instrumental in getting the commission called. You wrote an editorial in support of it. Can you evoke the time before the commission for readers — is there one particular injustice that stands out for you?

Doris Anderson: There were all sorts of things. For example, I didn't get married until I was thirty-six — I didn't think that marriage was a great deal for women — and I'd been supporting myself for years. I had money in the bank; I'd had a credit card for years. And yet when I got married, my husband had to sign it. And he owed the bank a lot of money! I couldn't get over it. And in parts of the country, a father had to give consent for a child who needed an operation. So here's a child in danger and they have to find the father; the mother can't give consent for the operation. It was ludicrous. In some places in Newfoundland, a woman had to get her husband to sign if she was going to get a library card. Can you imagine?

Lisa Rundle: It's dangerous for a woman to have a library card!

Doris Anderson: Yes! And the abortion law, of course. The very first editorial I wrote was about how we needed more women in Parliament. And as a matter of fact, I could run that editorial almost word-for-word today. It's changed, but not enough.

Lisa Rundle: At that time, how did you argue that it was important to have women in Parliament?

Doris Anderson: Well, [I argued] that women were 51 percent of the population, and they were well-educated, and here was a great resource. We've got one of the worst childcare systems — we only look good compared to the United States. European countries have had — for decades — far better childcare, and we're still only talking about it. So if you don't have women in Parliament, you don't get these things addressed. There are still women living in poverty — ingle mothers, older women — still too big a gap in pay between men and women. So it was these types of things that the Royal Commission set out to address, and did address.

Lisa Rundle: In 1970, you could buy a copy of the commission's report for $4.50. What did that report mean to women? Did your average woman care?

Doris Anderson: Let me backtrack a bit. The government didn't think we needed a Royal Commission. It was Laura Sabia threatening to have women march on Parliament that frightened them into doing it. But everybody — mainly men reporting on it — thought it was a joke when they first held their [the Commission's] hearings from coast to coast. Christina McCall wrote a wonderful article in *Chatelaine* called "What's So Funny about the Royal Commission?"

The reporters thought it was hilariously funny that there would be a royal commission about women at all. Why not have one about men? And then the stories started coming out about battered women, women in poverty, Native women, and it became more serious.

They [the government] only printed 25,000 copies of the report. It was a cheap commission. So it sold out within a week and became one of the big sellers of the time. The government totally misjudged how important this commission was.

Lisa Rundle: NAC, the National Action Committee on the Status of Women, was created to organize around getting the commission's recommendations implemented. The sense was that it would be a relatively short-term project, rather than that some of these recommendations, like a national child-care program, still would not have been achieved in 2005.

Doris Anderson: It was like everything else that's happened. We've had over thirty years of organizing, trying to persuade political parties to involve more women, and we haven't gotten anywhere. Well, we've gotten somewhere — now one in five MPs is a woman — but again, compared to most European countries we look pathetic. Compared to Rwanda, Mozambique... we're thirty-seventh in the world. It's terrible. Which is why I'm pushing for some form of proportional representation [as opposed to our current first-past-the-post system]. It's the only way we're going to change it.

Lisa Rundle: There's a sense now that the government throws a royal commission at an issue as a distraction — a way of muting protest. Was that the sense with this commission?

Doris Anderson: No. I think people took them much more seriously back then. And this was such an unusual one. We have royal commissions on fish, on the mining industry. And women felt once the recommendation came out, "Now that they know, surely something will be done." But very little was done. Gradually, we've learned through the years. And the equality provisions in the *Charter of Rights and Freedoms* were a great example. We were told the wording in the *Charter* would be fine. But the wording was lousy. We had to fight like tigers to get it changed. And we got a whole new clause [Section 28: "Notwithstanding anything in the *Charter*, the rights and freedoms referred to in it are guaranteed equally to male and female persons."] The American women are stunned we got it. They'd been trying for eighty years to get something similar and failed. But all of the cases won under the *Charter* had to be fought hard, right up to the Supreme Court.

Lisa Rundle: Looking back, is there anything strategically that could have been done differently?

Doris Anderson: I was so frustrated after being president of NAC and of the Canadian Advisory Council on the Status of Women — asking myself, "Why do we still have such lousy childcare and such a gap in pay?" — that I wrote a whole book [*The Unfinished Revolution*]. I went to twelve different countries and compared their progress. The only thing I can truly say that I think we could have done better is to change the electoral system; but of course that wasn't on the radar screen at all. But the countries that had proportional representation automatically got more women in Parliament. And more egalitarian policies followed.

Lisa Rundle: So, should women be calling for a royal commission on the status of women now? Would that be a helpful tool?

Doris Anderson: No. I met with a group of women in the Maritimes a couple of summers ago, and they were all gung-ho to call for another royal commission. But it takes two or three years to do it, and I think we've got all the information we need. Really, what we need to do is move. That's why I'm putting a lot of energy these days into changing the electoral system [through Equal Voice]. Five provinces are seriously engaged in looking at proportional representation, and also the federal government. I'm convinced we're not going to get anywhere without it.

NOTE

Lisa Rundle, 2006, "Still Ain't Satisfied," *Herizons* 19,3 (Winter). Adapted and reprinted with permission.

REFERENCES

Anderson, Doris. 1991. *The Unfinished Revolution: The Status of Women in Twelve Countries*. Toronto: Doubleday Canada.
Friedan, Betty. 1963. *The Feminine Mystique*. New York: W.W. Norton.

13

So You Think You Know Canadian Women's/Gender History?

C. Lesley Biggs, Susan Gingell and Selena Crosson

Detailed answers to these questions, plus more questions and answers, are at the Gendered Intersections website: fernwoodpublishing.ca/gi2

I   Aboriginal and Other Founding Nations, Invader-Settlers and Slavery: Pre-Twentieth Century History

1. Did Indigenous women generally enjoy greater equality to Indigenous men in the pre-contact era than they do today?
2. What was the name given to the Indigenous women who were life and economic partners to the European fur traders, who often later discarded the Indigenous women in favour of European women?
3. What Aboriginal woman was considered a key ally of the British during the American Revolution?
4. Which women are known as the founding mothers of New France?
5. Which eighteenth-century black woman resisted her slavery by setting fire to her mistress's house and in the process burned down a significant part of Montreal?

II   Legal Recognition of Women's, Indigenous and Gay Rights

A   Women's Rights
6. Can we accurately say that Canadian women were enfranchised first in 1918?
7. In 1966, which province enacted Canada's first maternity leave legislation?
8. When did Canadians gain the legal right to distribute birth control information?
    a) 1899   b) 1929   c) 1959   d) 1969   e) 1979
9. When were employment restrictions on married women in the federal public service removed?
    a) 1918   b) 1929   c) 1945   d) 1955
10. What name was given to the five Alberta women whose campaign to have women legally declared persons ended successfully in 1929?

B   Aboriginal Rights
11. When did "status" Indian women get the vote?
    a) 1940   b) 1950   c) 1960   d) 1970
12. Following agitation by women like Jeannette Corbière-Lavell (Anishinaabe), Yvonne Bédard (Iroqouis), Sandra Lovelace (Maliseet), and Mary Two Axe Earley (Mohawk), what bill returned "Indian status" to First Nations women who had lost it under the terms of the *Indian Act* by marrying a white man?
13. Who was the first woman to have her Indian status reinstated?
14. What woman began a distinguished career by supporting Inuit land claims in 1975;

was President of the Inuit Broadcasting Corporation from 1983 to 1988; served as Canadian vice-president for the Inuit Circumpolar Conference from 1986 to 1989; and went on to become President of the Inuit Tapirisat of Canada, the national political voice of Inuit in Canada, from 1991 to 1996?

C   Gay Rights

15. In 1965, what sentence was given to Everett George Klippert for admitting to police that he had sex with men?
a) 6 months   b) 2 years less a day   c) 10 years   d) life sentence, with a dangerous offender designation

16. What bookstore successfully challenged the Canadian censorship laws on the basis that gay publications, even those that were sexually explicit, were protected by the freedom of speech and expression clauses in the *Canadian Charter of Rights and Freedoms*?

17. When did gays win the right to be legally married in Canada?
a) 1985   b) 1995   c) 2000   d) 2005

18. Which Canadian church was the first to perform gay marriage?
a) Unitarian   b) United   c) Roman Catholic   d) Anglican

III   The Political System

19. Who was the first woman leader of a Canadian political party?

20. Who was the first woman Member of Parliament?

21. Who was the first black woman Member of Parliament and the first woman to run for the leadership of a Canadian federal party?

22. Who was the first woman appointed as Governor General of Canada?

23. Who was the first Member of Parliament to declare publicly that he was gay?

24. In 2010, the percentage of seats in the Canadian House of Commons held by women was?
a) 12.3%   b) 22.4%   c) 32.5%   d) 42.4%

IV   Women, Governance, the Legal System and the Judiciary

25. In the 1890s, when Clara Brett Martin, the first Canadian female lawyer, was seeking to enter law school, what reason did editorialists offer for opposing women becoming lawyers?

26. Who was the first female First Nations chief?

27. What Canadian feminist legal organization was incorporated on April 17, 1975, within two days of the enactment of the equality provision of the Canadian *Charter of Rights and Freedoms*, in order to ensure that women and girls would fully experience the equality rights legally guaranteed by the *Charter*?

28. Who was the first woman Justice of the Supreme Court of Canada?

29. Which Canadian female judge has achieved international recognition for her promotion of justice and human rights?

V   Organizing for Change

30. In 1946, nine years before Rosa Parks challenged Alabama's policy of segregat-

ing seating on public buses, for what act in New Glasgow, Nova Scotia, was Viola Desmond jailed and fined?

a) sitting in the whites-only section of a movie theatre
b) sitting in the whites-only section of a restaurant
c) drinking out of a whites-only fountain
d) attempting to enter a whites-only railway car

31. What profession shared by all three of Canada's female Governors General has led a number of other Canadian women into positions of prominence since the mid-1980s?

32. Building on the work of the Voice of Women for Peace (VOW), what was the largest Canadian umbrella organization of women's groups in the mid-1980s, lobbying for the equality of women, childcare, minority and gay rights, poverty reduction, and the elimination of violence against women?

33. What national Indigenous women's organization launched the Sisters in Spirit campaign to try to end the epidemic of disappearances and murders of Indigenous women in Canada?

34. Inspired by Marilyn Waring's (1988) book *If Women Counted*, what did Carol Lees, then a Saskatchewan homemaker, contribute in the 1990s to the fight for women's equality that will be lost now that the Harper government successfully ended the mandatory completion of the Census long form?

35. What national organization of women with disabilities began in 1985?

VI Artists

36. What was the name of the red-haired orphan character from Prince Edward Island created by Lucy Maude Montgomery in the early twentieth century and now famous around the world?

37. Which "scribbling" pioneer sisters were recreated in the work of two of Canada's most famous twentieth-century female writers?

38. What British Columbia artist's work has become emblematic of Canada's west coast?

39. What Cape Dorset graphic artist is known for her lively prints and drawings showing "the things we did long ago before there were many white men"?

40. What popular country music artist sparked outrage among ranchers because of her "Meat Stinks" campaign?

41. Pakistani-born, Canadian-raised, freelance writer, broadcaster, and filmmaker Zarqa Nawaz, took her experiences as a practicing Muslim as the inspiration for what popular CBC television comedy series now distributed internationally?

42. What Indo-Canadian director of the movie trilogy *Earth, Water* and *Fire* has won international acclaim for her controversial films set in India, films that challenge inequitable Hindu traditions as well as injustice, hypocrisy, intolerance and colonialism?

43. Which human rights activist for Japanese Canadian resettlement claims wrote the award-winning novel *Obasan* (1981), one of the *Literary Review of Canada's* selections for the list of the 100 Most Important Canadian Books?

44. What is the title of the autobiography of Métis author and community worker Maria Campbell, which not only told her life story but also informed readers of the physical, emotional, and spiritual violence the Métis of her generation experienced

from both white and First Nations neighbours?

45. Who was the classical ballerina who joined the National Ballet Company in 1969 and went on to become the company's Principal Dancer and Artistic Director, the Director of the Canada Council for the Arts (2004-2008), and a highly regarded advocate for the arts in general?

VII Sports

46. Who was the first person to swim successfully across Lake Ontario?
47. Who won the Overall World Cup Championships in 1967 and 1968 for downhill skiing, as well as the Olympic gold medal for giant slalom in 1968, and was named Canada's female athlete of the twentieth century?
48. What well-known sports figure and activist first came to prominence as a "boy" in 1959?
49. What male Canadian middle-distance runner of the early 1960s worked for gender and race equality in sport?
50. What Canadian female team took home the silver medal in 1998, after falling to the Americans in the game's inaugural year as an Olympic sport, but won gold in 2002, 2006, and 2010?
51. How many women are in 2010 among the 514 athletes and builders celebrated in the Canadian Sports Hall of Fame?
    a) 48   b) 74   c) 120   d) 144

VIII Health

52. Who is recognized (along with Paul de Chomedey de Maisonneuve), as founder of the Hôtel-Dieu hospital in Montreal, and the first lay nurse in North America?
53. Who was the first female medical doctor in Canada?
54. When did birth control first become legal in Canada?
    a) 1926   b) 1946   c) 1966   d) 1976
55. Who opened the Don Mills Birth Control Clinic, the first such clinic in a high school in North America, and later went on to become the host of the "Sunday Night Sex Show?"
56. What 1970 event has been billed as "the first feminist protest in Canada" and shut down the House of Commons for the first time in its history?
57. Which founding member and later President of the Aboriginal Nurses Association of Canada championed public health services for Aboriginal people in multiple roles, including special advisor to the Minister of National Health and Welfare, Monique Bégin?
58. Who was Canada's first female astronaut and the world's first neurologist in space?
59. Which province first legally recognized and regulated midwifery?
60. Is the excision for non-therapeutic reasons of the external female genitalia (commonly known as female genital mutilation) illegal in Canada?

IX Education and the Sciences

61. In 1882, at which Canadian university did anatomist Kenneth Fenwick and a group of male students threaten to transfer to the University of Toronto, where lectures

would not be "watered down" by the presence of three undergraduate female students?

62 Carrie Derick, the first woman hired as a professor in Canada, was a professor in which discipline?

a) Nursing   b) Genetics   c) English   d) Education

63 Which highly distinguished Quaker woman with a doctorate in experimental physics joined the University of Toronto's Department of Metallurgy and Materials Science in 1967, becoming the first woman named University Professor, the most prestigious position at the University of Toronto, in 1984; published more than seventy scholarly papers and major contributions to books on the structure and properties of metals and alloys, and on the history and social impact of technology; and won the United Nations Association in Canada's Pearson Peace Medal in January 2002; but, having been for many years paid lower wages than her male peers, had to join other prominent University of Toronto female faculty to sue the university for an equitable pension?

64. Who was the first Canadian female astronaut and an International Space Station (ISS) pioneer who participated in an ISS assembly and boarded the Space Station?

65. When were the first Women's Studies courses offered in Canada?

a) 1968   b) 1970   c) 1972   d) 1975

66. What list-serve is an electronic network of individuals and organizations interested in women-centred policy issues in Canada?

REFERENCES

Kogawa, Joy. 1981. *Obasan*. Toronto: Lester and Orphen Dennys.

Waring, Marilyn. 1988. *If Women Counted: A New Feminist Economics*. San Francisco: Harper and Row.

SHORT ANSWERS

1. Yes. Although there was a sexual division of labour in Aboriginal communities in the pre-contact period, Aboriginal women then had considerably more social and political authority than they do today.

2. Country wives

3. (Mary) Molly Brant, or Degonwadonti

4. Filles du roi

5. Marie-Josèphe Angélique

6. No. Women with property voted in Québec elections during the 1830s.

7. British Columbia

8. 1969

9. 1955

10. The "Famous Five"

11. 1960

12. *Bill C-31*

13. Mary Two-Axe Early

14. Rosemarie Kuptana

15. Life sentence, with a dangerous offender designation

16. Little Sister's Book and Art Emporium

17. 2005

18. Unitarians

19. Alexa McDonough

20. Agnes MacPhail

21. Rosemary (Wedderburn) Brown

22. Marie Jeanne Mathilde Sauvé

23. Svend Robinson

24. 22.4 percent

25. Editorials opposed women lawyers because it was believed that the physical attraction between them and all-male judges and juries would subvert justice.

26. Elsie (Taylor) Knott

27. Legal Education and Action Fund (LEAF)

28. Bertha Wilson

29. Louise Arbour

30. Sitting in the whites-only section of a movie theatre

31. Journalism

32. National Action Committee on the

Status of Women (NAC)

33. Native Women's Association of Canada
34. Carol Lees refused to fill out a 1991 Census Canada form which required anyone who had not worked for pay in the previous five years to check "Never worked in life."
35. DisAbled Women's Network (DAWN)
36. Anne of Green Gables
37. Margaret Atwood and Margaret Laurence
38. Emily Carr
39. Kenojuak
40. k.d. lang
41. *Little Mosque on the Prairie*
42. Deepa Mehta
43. Joy Kogawa
44. *Halfbreed*
45. Karen Kain
46. Marilyn Bell
47. Nancy Greene
48. Abby (Ab) Hoffman
49. Bruce Kidd
50. Canadian Women's Hockey Team
51. 74 women (17.3 percent) among the 422 athletes and builders
52. Jeanne Mance
53. Dr. Emily Stowe
54. 1966
55. Sue Johanson
56. The Abortion Caravan
57. Jean Goodwill Cuthand
58. Roberta Bondar
59. Newfoundland
60. Yes, female genital mutilation is considered aggravated assault under the Criminal Code.
61. Queen's University
62. Genetics
63. Ursula Franklin
64. Julie Payette
65. 1970
66. Policy, Action, Research List (PAR-L)

ain't I a oomaan

d'bi.young.anitafrika

Listen to d'bi.young.anitafrika perform her poem at the Gendered Intersections website:
fernwoodpublishing.ca/gi2

teachah seh: welcome class to feminism 101
we a guh talk about gloria steinem/betty friedan
di liberation of di white middle-class oomaan
from oprreshun in society
di solushun of which is to go out dere
into di work force and work

darkness/di absence of light skin
widout white skin
darkness/I have been force-working
since I was brought here

teachah seh: oomaan get di vote inna 1918
mi nuh really understand weh she mean
when you say oomaan/be more specific
if me remembah correct/1918 me nevah did a vote yet

georgy, you best go gets cleaning ups now
yuh hear, aunt jemima gonna make you some real nice pancakes

cum mek we look pon dis ya shituashun
dis feminism 101 where we elaborate pon betty friedan
gloria steinem
cannot have room for I
it forces di exclushun of di black oomaan
black black black bush oomaan

and ahdri zhina said step into my head
cum on and step step step into my head
black bush womban
step into my head where fear and loathing
stalk single strands of my kinky hair
beauty looks warp as you exotify me
a-sexualized/demonized

but we both agree
dat mammy raise black and white pickney
dat tanty raise black and white pickney
dat auntie raise black and white pickney
yuh nanny raise black and white pickney

mi lips a likkle ticker/mi nose a likkle broader
me ass a likkle rounder/mi skin a likkle darker
makes me an outsidah

and darkness is di embrace of di absence of light
darkness is black womb/weh we all come from
black oomaan
di beginning a feminism
ain't I a oomaan sojourner
truth come find me

NOTE

d'bi.young, 2006, *art on black*, Toronto: Women's Press. Reprinted with permission.

15 Talking about "Us" Racialized Girls, Cultural Citizenship and Growing Up under Whiteness

Jo-Anne Lee

It matters the way you look, all the time,

It matters what kind of hair

It matters like your head to toe

It includes body image

Clothes

Your personality, your attitude

How much make-up you wear
How big your boobs are

How big your ass is, how small, anything, or legs and stuff

What kind of shoes you wear

Or if you wear the same clothes or something

If you have any piercings

— Collective response to,

"So what matters in how you look?"

Introduction

"White" Victoria, the capital of British Columbia, situates its civic identity almost entirely in its historic role as a colonial outpost of the British Empire. There are constant and inescapable reminders of the colonial era in public architecture, art, statues, cultural activities, neighbourhoods, the ubiquitous tea shops, and in civic discourses and tourist literature that proclaim Victoria as "a little bit of olde England" that is "more English than the English." People of British backgrounds form the city's largest ethnic group.[1] They also feel a sense of belonging. Regimes of representation such as are found in capital cities are heavily coded with cultural symbolism, and these representations are constitutive and not just expressive of our identities. Our physical and cultural environment not only reflects how we think about ourselves but also how we shape our sense of who we are.

This chapter draws on young women's narratives and offers insights into ongoing processes of cultural citizenship formation — processes of making selves and being made as selves within a context of dominant whiteness. These processes are localized through different gendered and racialized regimes of representation and identity (Friedman 1998: 3; Grewal and Kaplan 1994: 1–36). This chapter foregrounds the complex, contradictory cultural knowledges that many racialized girls possess that enables them to survive, resist and make sense of living within and across multiple borders.

Talking About "Us"

My research team and I talked to racialized immigrant and Canadian-born teens and young women about their experiences growing up in Victoria.[2] Through focus groups organized around ethnic, national, religious, sexuality or "racial" identifications, we explored questions about identity and Canadianness. For the majority, this was the first time they had talked about living and growing up in Victoria. In living under whiteness, most had never experienced being in a group with others like themselves where they could discuss their differences within sameness.

Over time, racialized women and girls gradually become culturally white, in part through physical, social and cultural separation from others like themselves. Focus group participants laughed, cried, joked, shocked and confronted each other as they shared stories of growing up as "different." They also implicitly knew that the categories that assembled them were not stable, unified and unifying categories because each brought with them a slightly different experience.

Isolation and the Lack of Oppositional Solidarity

A consistent theme of isolation and separation from other girls like themselves emerged as the young women told us that they were often the only non-white girl in their class, group of friends or neighbourhood. Racial minority teens who grow up in white cities like Victoria don't see themselves reflected in public life, in the media or in their peer groups.

> Lari: I'm the only black person that I see. There's Africa Day and that's it.…

> Anii: [my community gets together] only in Vancouver 'cause, um, there's like parties in Vancouver. We have like people from my country and stuff.

There are few opportunities to meet others like themselves, share their experiences about where they come from, talk about what it is like being from a different culture or reflect on what it is like being a minority living under whiteness.

They say that teachers and school counsellors often don't understand what they and their families are going through or have gone through. There is little sympathy for the impact of migration, readjustment and settling in on their schoolwork. They have few people, inside or outside of the family, with whom they can process their feelings about a range of issues, such as the constant, but unspoken, presence of violence. In one focus group discussion, daughters of Chilean refugees told us they rarely had the opportunity to talk about their family's refugee experiences. As they talked together, they began to slowly piece together stories of their parents' experiences with violence and the death of family members:

> Stephanie: My father was exiled; he was tortured in Chile by Pinochet, for two years. He was in the stadium in Santiago… they don't want to talk about it… it's hard for them, my mother and father… it's a trauma.

Tania: Yeah, my dad came here because my dad was on the black list. I don't know much, anything about the torture....

Stephanie: There were people against Pinochet, the military, and everyone was involved. My mom wasn't, but my dad was, he went to talks and stuff.

Although adults do not talk to them about these issues and keep these stories from them, perhaps to save them from pain, silence does not prevent these girls from knowing and feeling. Queer women talked about the isolation that was mixed with racism:

Hazel: It wasn't like you could go to the counsellor, either. Like we knew in our group of friends, we knew that was the last place you went, that they would not understand where you're coming from, that they'd tell your parents, and that they'd develop this file on you. And we just knew we couldn't go to the counsellor.

Jo-Anne: Who could you talk to about this stuff?

Hazel: Just some friends. Not the white girls.

Rowen: Yeah, I just never [talked]. I just felt alone, like even with my close friends, like they're still my friends, but even to this day, I can't really talk to them about racism, because they'd bring it back to themselves about you know.... "I feel really guilty for being white, what can I do about it?" You know, I don't want that either.

The women, all in their early twenties, vividly recalled their pain of feeling Othered. In tear-choked words, they spoke passionately of their struggles around wanting to talk to white friends about experiences of racism and sexism, yet not wanting their white friends to feel guilty about their racism and not wanting to take that on as well. Racialized women face a triple burden in negotiating their identities: restricting their conversations with white friends, shouldering the burden of white guilt about racism and repressing and disavowing their own experiences with racism and sexism.

Responsibilities at Home and Isolation

Silence and repression around family expectations and responsibilities are another area of difficulty. Because many immigrant families struggle to make ends meet by working at two or more jobs or on double and triple shifts, older daughters have to take responsibility for their younger siblings and household chores. However, many parents and teachers do not realize the stresses and pressures that this places on immigrant teens. Respondents told us they had few people they could talk to about their conflicting family responsibilities and school expectations. They found it challenging to satisfy everyone's expectations: their parents', the ethnic community's and the schools'. School personnel, for the most part, seemed indifferent to their issues.

Living Difference through Whiteness

In high school culture where acceptance is monitored closely and continuously through style of dress, talk, behaviour and friends, being different is not easy. Racialized teens talked about the strain of trying to be socially accepted and successful at school, while also trying to meet the expectations of parents at home.

Canadian-born girls told us that the responses of teachers and counsellors are sometimes inappropriate and insulting. Many report that because of their physical features, they are assumed to be English as a Second Language (ESL) students even when they are able to speak English fluently and have lived here all their lives. Those immigrant girls and young women whose skin colour allows them to pass as white find their accented English marks them as different, and therefore inferior, which they find confusing.

Mixed-race girls reported continual questions about their identity. They often have to defend and justify their appearance which, for them, is a form of violation:

Ate: What are you?

Psycho: What are you? Neither this, nor the other. That is just the most annoying question because when a white person walks up to me, every time you meet a white person — they go, "what are you, what's your ethnic background?"

Ate: You're white, you're brown. I just think that is so stupid because my colour is different from you. You have no right to inquire what my family background is. I find that really annoying.

Canadian-born and immigrant teens who entered Canada as pre-schoolers, reported that as they matured, their taken-for-granted friendships became more awkward. Some young women remembered clearly that in elementary grades, they had already felt excluded and isolated, and with puberty, their "difference" seemed to become more complicated and subtle. With age, it became more difficult to identify what they were experiencing. Was it sexism, racism, ageism, classism, homophobia, religious and linguistic intolerance or all these "isms" working together? Others attempted to ignore their difference and tried their best to be "the same," by immunizing themselves against negative views of their "difference."

Racialized Sexism

For the most part, the younger women deal with all the usual challenges of growing up female in Canadian society, but they also face a host of other issues that they will continue to encounter as they mature. For example, although most teens experiment with their looks, emerging sexuality and bodily changes, racialized female teens also must contend with everyday racialized sexism:

- When you are dark skinned and called "ho" or "slut," it's more than about sex, it's also about racism.
- Stereotypes are part of how you live your life even if you know it's not true. Boys talk about different kinds of girls they want for sex. Asian girls are supposed to be small and boys say stuff about their tight pussy.
- South Asian girls are supposed to be hairy, but we aren't.
- We don't act like the girls in the rap videos, but that's the idea we have to live with.
- Girls in the videos wear bras and hot pants, and they expect black girls to dress like that. It makes them look slutty and dirty.

Several girls told stories about being in grades six or seven and having a crush on a boy but never having a chance because he only had eyes for the popular girls in school, and they were always white, blonde and blue-eyed. Eventually, these experiences of rejection result in some racialized girls internalizing the message that they are "second-class" and not attractive.

Despite over thirty years of official multiculturalism, being Canadian also still means being blonde, blue-eyed and fair-skinned to these girls. They know and see themselves standing outside of full citizenship and they live their exclusion from citizenship through their skin and bodies.

However, in a multicultural society, teens consume (and are consumed by) many discourses and one of the most influential is, ironically, teen popular culture. Drawing on teen culture, school peers appreciate girls' racialized "difference" as a type of specialness (Minh Ha 1989). Latina Canadian girls are appreciated for their ability to dance, and African Canadian girls for their association with black American culture of hip-hop, rap music and break dancing. But increasingly, even this specialness is being eroded as white girls and boys co-opt elements of American black and Latin pop culture, transforming them into hybridized, bleached versions that are more highly valued in their school culture. But although blonde braids, expensive hip hop clothes and dance lessons are easily accessible to white, middle-class teens, the physical fact of phenotypic blackness remains undesirable. For black girls, it is a no-win situation. Rap music videos often portray black women as highly sexualized objects of the male gaze, which only reinscribes negative images of black female sexuality. Thus, racialized girls not only have to contend with racism but also with a heterosexist popular culture that places their bodies under the male gaze. The epigram at the beginning of this chapter — the girls' response to the question, "So what counts in how you look?" — reflects the tyranny of heterosexist male objectification of female bodies.

Charting a Way Forward

Racialized teens in our study displayed a wealth of cultural knowledge about living across and between multiple cultures and deployed many strategies of coping and surviving under dominant whiteness. Despite having few opportunities to develop "oppositional solidarity" (Tatum 1999), they do play with their identities. They talked about making self-conscious decisions about where, when, how and with whom they could present different sides of themselves:

> Maxwell: I think we do that unconsciously. We do it without thinking. We're told, "you should act this way at home," but when we go out in the world, we have other environments, we act differently and we act maybe in our own skin. But, who knows what's normal for us?... When you're not at home, when you are at school, you act a lot differently.... I think I'm more the "Indian" girl when I'm at home. You know you're doing things girls are supposed to do in your culture and it's not a bad thing at all. But I don't think I would do it if I were within a white majority, I think I'd act within the majority.... I think identity is a continuing creation.

As Canada becomes more culturally, racially and ethnically diverse through globalization and migration, there will be a growing need to perform transnational, transcultural citizenship. The conscious transformational, transnational and transcultural tactics of positioning that are evident in these young women's narratives signal some of the shifts that are already being incorporated into crafting subjectivities. We glimpse in their self-narratives complex strategies that they use in their interactions with others. Yet unrecognized and invalidated, many racialized girls and young women thrive and flourish at school and in their communities by deploying knowledge about cultural citizenship.

1. Victoria has a proportionately lower percentage of immigrants than the national or provincial average, or Vancouver (15 percent in Victoria; 24 percent in B.C.; and 42 percent in Vancouver), and visible minorities (8 percent in Victoria; 17 percent in B.C.; and 43 percent in Vancouver). Only 15 percent of Victoria's total population was born outside of Canada, most come from the U.K. and Europe (58 percent), Asia (20 percent), the U.S. (12 percent), South and Central America (5 percent) and Africa (4 percent) (1996 Statistics Canada Census).

2. We spoke to about a hundred racial minority teens and young women aged twelve to twenty-eight years. About sixty-five girls and young women from ten different ethno-racial-cultural backgrounds participated in focus group discussions that met two or three times. An additional ten girls participated in individual interviews. Eight teens participated in popular theatre workshops and a girls advisory group to help plan a girls conference. Another thirty-five young racialized women participated as volunteers and mentors to these girls at the girls conference. (At: itsaboutus.com)

REFERENCES

Friedman, S.S. 1998. *Mappings: Feminism and the Cultural Geographies of Encounter.* Princeton: Princeton University Press.

Grewal, I., and C. Kaplan. 1994. *Scattered Hegemonies: Postmodernity and Transnational Feminist Practice.* Minneapolis: University of Minnesota Press.

Kelly, J. 1998. *Under that Gaze: Learning to Be Black in White Society.* Halifax, Fernwood Publishing.

Minh Ha, T.T. 1989. *Woman, Native, Other: Writing Postcoloniality and Feminism.* Bloomington: Indiana University Press.

Tatum, B.D. 1999. *Why Are All the Black Kids Sitting Together in the Cafeteria? And Other Conversations.* New York: Basic Books.

Twine, F.W. 1996. "Brown Skinned White Girls: Class, Culture, and the Construction of White Identity in Suburban Communities." *Gender, Place and Culture* 3.

16

Out on Main Street

Shani Mootoo

Janet and me? We does go Main Street to see pretty pretty sari and bangle, and to eat we belly full a burfi and gulub jamoon, but we doh go too often because, yuh see, is dem sweets self what does give people like we a presupposition for untameable hip and thigh.

Another reason we shy to frequent dere is dat we is watered-down Indians — we ain't good grade A Indians. We skin brown, is true, but we doh even think 'bout India, unless something happen over dere and it come on de news. Mih family remain Hindu ever since mih ancestors leave India behind, but nowadays dey doh believe in praying unless things real bad, because, as mih father always singing, like if is a mantra: "Do good and good will be bestowed unto you." So he is a veritable saint cause he always doing good by his women friends and dey children. I sure some a dem must be mih half sister and brother, oui!

Mostly, back home, we is kitchen Indians: some kind a Indian food every day, at least once a day, but we doh get cardamom and other fancy spice down dere so de food not spicy like Indian food I eat in restaurants up here. But it have one thing we doh make joke 'bout down dere: we like we meethai and sweetrice too much, and it remain overly authentic, like de day Naana and Naani step off de boat in Port of Spain harbour over a hundred and sixty years ago. Check out dese hips here nah, dey is pure sugar and condensed milk, pure sweetness!

But Janet family different. In de ole days when Canadian missionaries land in Trinidad dey used to make a bee-line straight for Indians from down South. And Janet great grand-parents is one a de first South families dat exchange over from Indian to Presbyterian. Dat was a long time ago.

When Janet born, she father, one Mr. John Mahase, insist on asking de Reverend MacDougal from Trace Settlement Church, a leftover from de Canadian Mission, to name de baby girl. De good Reverend choose de name Constance cause dat was his mother name. But de mother a de child, Mrs. Savitri Mahase, wanted to name de child sheself. Ever since Savitri was a lil girl she like de yellow hair, fair skin and pretty pretty clothes Janet and John used to wear in de primary school reader — since she lil she want to change she name from Savitri to Janet but she own father get vex and say how Savitri was his mother name and how she will insult his mother if she gone and change it. So Savitri get she own way once by marrying this fella name John, and she do a encore, by calling she daughter Janet, even doh husband John upset for days at she for insulting de good Reverend by throwing out de name a de Reverend mother.

So dat is how my girlfriend, a darkskin Indian girl with thick black hair (pretty fuh so!) get a name like Janet.

She come from a long line a Presbyterian school teacher, headmaster and headmistress. Savitri still teaching from de same Janet and John reader in primary school in San Fernando, and John, getting more and more obtuse in his ole age, is headmaster more dan twenty years now in Princes Town Boys' Presbyterian High School. Everybody back home know dat family good good. Dat is why Janet leave in two twos. Soon as A level finish she pack up and take off like a jet plane so she could live without people only shoo-shooing behind she back....

"But A A! Yuh ain't hear de goods 'bout John Mahase daughter, gyul? How yuh mean yuh ain't hear? Is a big thing! Everybody talking 'bout she. Hear dis, nah! Yuh ever see she wear a dress. Yes! Doh look at mih so. Yuh reading mih right!"

Is only recentish I realize Mahase is a Hindu last name. In de ole days every Mahase in de country turn Presbyterian and now de name doh have no association with Hindu or Indian whatsoever. I used to think of it as a Presbyterian Church name until some days ago when we meet a Hindu fella fresh from India name Yogdesh Mahase who never even hear of Presbyterian.

De other day I ask Janet what she know 'bout Divali. She say, "It's the Hindu festival of lights, isn't it?" like a line straight out a dictionary. Yuh think she know anything 'bout how lord Rama get himself exile in a forest for fourteen years, and how when it come time for him to go back home his followers light up a pathway to help him make his way out, and dat is what Divali lights is all about? All Janet know is 'bout going for drive in de country to see light, and she could remember looking forward, around Divali time, to the lil brown paper-bag packages full a burfi and parasad that she father Hindu students used to bring for him.

One time in a Indian restaurant she ask for parasad for dessert. Well! Since den I never go back in dat restaurant, I embarrass fuh so!

I used to think I was a Hindu *par excellence* until I come up here and see real flesh and blood Indian from India. Up here, I learning 'bout all kind of custom and food and music and clothes dat we never see or hear 'bout in good ole Trinidad. Is de next best thing to going to India, in truth, oui! But Indian store clerk on Main Street doh have no patience with us, specially when we talking English to dem. Yuh ask dem a question in English and dey insist on giving de answer in Hindi or Punjabi or Urdu or Gujarati. How I suppose to know de difference even! And den dey look at yuh disdainful disdainful — like yuh disloyal, like yuh is a traitor.

But yuh know, it have one other reason I real reluctant to go Main Street. Yuh see, Janet pretty fuh so! And I doh like de way men does look at she, as if because she wearing jeans and T-shirt and high-heel shoe and make-up and have long hair loose and flying about like she is a walking-talking shampoo ad, dat she easy. And de women always looking at she beady eye, like she loose and going to thief dey man. Dat kind a thing always make me want to put mih arm round she waist like, she is my woman, take yuh eyes off she! and shock de false teeth right out dey mouth. And den is a whole other story when dey see me with mih crew cut and mih blue jeans tuck inside mih jim-boots. Walking next to Janet, who so femme dat she redundant, tend to make me look like a gender dey forget to classify. Before going Main Street I does parade in front de mirror practicing a jiggly-wiggly kind a walk. But if I ain't walking like a strong-man monkey I doh exactly feel right and I always revert back to mih true colours. De men dem does look at me like if dey is exactly what I need a taste of to cure me good and proper. I could see dey eyes watching Janet and me, dey face growing dark as dey imagining all kind a situation and position. And de women dem embarrass fuh so to watch me in mih eye, like dey fraid I will jump up and try to kiss dem, or make a pass at dem. Yuh know, sometimes I wonder if I ain't mad enough to do it just for a little bacchanal, nah!

Going for a outing with mih Janet on Main Street ain't easy! If only it wasn't for burfi and gulub jamoon! If only I had a learned how to cook dem kind a thing before I leave home and come up here to live!

2.

In large deep-orange Sanskrit-style letters, de sign on de saffron-colour awning above de door read "Kush Valley Sweets." Underneath in smaller red letters it had "Desserts Fit For

The Gods." It was a corner building. The front and side was one big glass wall. Inside was big. Big like a gymnasium. Yuh could see in through de brown tint windows: dark brown plastic chair, and brown table, each one de length of a door, line up stiff and straight in row after row like if is a school room.

Before entering de restaurant I ask Janet to wait one minute outside with me while I rumfle up mih memory, pulling out all de sweet names I know from home, besides burfi and gulub jamoon: meethai, jilebi, sweetrice (but dey call dat kheer up here), and ladhoo. By now, of course, mih mouth watering fuh so! When I feel confident enough dat I wouldn't make a fool a mih Brown self by asking what dis one name? and what dat one name? we went in de restaurant. In two twos all de spice in de place take a flying leap in our direction and give us one big welcome hug up, tight fuh so! Since den dey take up permanent residence in de jacket I wear dat day!

Mostly it had women customers sitting at de tables, chatting and laughing, eating sweets and sipping masala tea. De only men in de place was de waiters, and all six waiters was men. I figure dat dey was brothers, not too hard to conclude, because all a dem had de same full round chin, round as if de chin stretch tight over a ping-pong ball, and dey had de same big roving eyes. I know better dan to think dey was mere waiters in de employ of a owner who chook up in a office in de back. I sure dat dat was dey own family business, dey stomach proudly preceeding dem and dey shoulders throw back in de confidence of dey ownership.

It ain't dat I paranoid, yuh understand, but from de moment we enter de fellas dem get over-animated, even armorously agitated. Janet again! All six pair a eyes land up on she, following she every move and body part. Dat in itself is something dat does madden me, oui! but also a kind a irrational envy have a tendency to manifest in me. It was like I didn't exist. Sometimes it could be a real problem going out with a good-looker, yes! While I ain't remotely interested in having a squeak of a flirtation with a man, it doh hurt a ego to have a man notice yuh once in a very long while. But with Janet at mih side, I doh have de chance of a penny shave-ice in de hot sun. I tuck mih elbows in as close to mih sides as I could so I wouldn't look like a strong man next to she, and over to de l-o-n-g glass case jam up with sweets I jiggle and wiggle in mih best imitation a some a dem gay fellas dat I see downtown Vancouver, de ones who more femme dan even Janet. I tell she not to pay de brothers no attention, because if any a dem flirt with she I could start a fight right dere and den. And I didn't feel to mess up mih crew cut in a fight.

De case had sweets in every nuance of colour in a rainbow. Sweets I never before see and doh know de names of. But dat was alright because I wasn't going to order dose ones anyway.

Since before we leave home Janet have she mind set on a nice thick syrupy curl a jilebi and a piece a plain burfi so I order dose for she and den I ask de waiter-fella, resplendent with thick thick bright-yellow gold chain and ID bracelet, for a stick a meethai for mihself. I stand up waiting by de glass case for it but de waiter/owner lean up on de back wall behind de counter watching me like he ain't hear me. So I say loud enough for him, and every body else in de room to hear, "I would like to have one piece a meethai please," and den he smile and lift up his hands, palms open-out motioning across de vast expanse a glass case, and he say, "Your choice! Whichever you want, Miss." But he still lean up against de back wall grinning. So I stick mih head out and up like a turtle and say louder, and slowly, "one piece a meethai — dis one!" and I point sharp to de stick a flour mix with ghee, deep fry and den roll up in sugar. He say, "That is koorma, Miss. One piece only?"

Mih voice drop low all by itself. "Oh ho! Yes, one piece. Where I come from we does call dat meethai." And den I add, but only loud enough for Janet to hear, "And mih name ain't 'Miss.'"

He open his palms out and indicate de entire panorama a sweets and he say, "These are all meethai, Miss. Meethai is Sweets. Where are you from?"

I ignore his question and to show him I undaunted, I point to a round pink ball and say, "I'll have one a dese sugarcakes too please." He start grinning broad broad like if he half-pitying, half-laughing at dis Indian-in-skin-colour-only, and den he tell me, "That is called chum-chum, Miss." I snap back at him, "Yeh, well back home we does call dat sugarcake, Mr. Chum-chum."

At de table, Janet say, "You know, Pud [Pud, short for Pudding; is dat she does call me when she feeling close to me, or sorry for me], it's true that we call that 'meethai' back home. Just like how we call 'siu mai' 'tim sam.' As if 'dim sum' is just one little piece of a food. What did he call that sweet again?"

"Cultural bastards, Janet, cultural bastards. Dat is what we is. Yuh know, one time a fella from India who living up here call me a bastardized Indian because I didn't know Hindi. And now look at dis, nah! De thing is: all a we in Trinidad is cultural bastards, Janet, all a we. *Toutes bagailles*! Chinese people, Black people, white people. Syrian. Lebanese. I looking forward to de day I find out dat place inside me where I am nothing else but Trinidadian, whatever dat could turn out to be."

I take a bite a de chum-chum, de texture was like grind-up coconut but it had no co-conut, not even a hint a coconut taste in it. De thing was juicy with sweet rose water oozing out a it. De rose water perfume enter mih nose and get trap in mih cranium. Ah drink two cup a masala tea and a lassi and still de rose water perfume was on mih tongue like if I had a overdosed on Butchart Gardens.

Suddenly de door a de restaurant spring open wide with a strong force and two big burly fellas stumble in, almost rolling over on to de ground. Dey get up, eyes red and slow and dey skin burning pink with booze. Dey straighten up so much to overcompensate for falling forward, dat dey find deyself leaning backward. Everybody stop talking and was watching dem. De guy in front put his hand up to his forehead and take a deep Walter Raleigh bow, bringing de hand down to his waist in a rolling circular movement. Out loud he greet everybody with "Alarm o salay koom." A part a me wanted to bust out laughing. Another part make mih jaw drop open in disbelief. De calm in de place get rumfle up. De two fellas dem, feeling chupid now because nobody reply to dey greeting, gone up to de counter to Chum-chum trying to make a little conversation with him. De same booze-pink alarm-o-salay-koom-fella say to Chum-chum, "Hey, howaryah?'

Chum-Chum give a lil nod and de fella carry right on, "Are you Sikh?"

Chum-chum brothers converge near de counter, busying deyselves in de vicinity. Chum-chum look at his brothers kind a quizzical, and he touch his cheek and feel his forehead with de back a his palm. He say, "No, I think I am fine, thank you. But I am sorry if I look sick, Sir."

De burly fella confuse now, so he try again.

"Where are you from?"

Chum-chum say, "Fiji, Sir."

"Oh! Fiji, eh! Lotsa palm trees and beautiful women, eh! It is true that you guys can have more than one wife?"

De exchange make mih blood rise up in a boiling froth. De restaurant suddenly get a gruff quietness 'bout it except for a woman I hear whispering angrily to another woman at de table behind us, "I hate this! I just hate it! I can't stand to see our men humiliated by them, right in front of us. He should refuse to serve them, he should throw them out. Who on earth do they think they are? The awful fools!" And de friend whisper back, "If he throws them out all of us will suffer in the long run."

I could discern de hair on de back a de neck a Chum-chum brothers standing up, annoyed, and at de same time de brothers look like dey was shrinking in stature. Chum-chum get serious, and he politely say, "What can I get for you?"

Pinko get de message and he point to a few items in de case and say, "One of each, to go please."

Holding de white take-out box in one hand he extend de other to Chum-chum and say, "How do you say 'Excuse me, I'm sorry' in Fiji?"

Chum-chum shake his head and say, "It's okay. Have a good day."

Pinko insist, "No, tell me please. I think I just behaved badly, and I want to apologize. How do you say 'I'm sorry' in Fiji'?"

Chum-chum say, "Your apology is accepted. Everything is okay." And he discreetly turn away to serve a person who had just entered de restaurant. De fellas take de hint dat was broad like daylight, and back out de restaurant like two little mouse.

Everybody was feeling sorry for Chum-chum and Brothers. One a dem come up to de table across from us to take a order from a woman with a giraffe-long neck who say, "Brother, we mustn't accept how these people think they can treat us. You men really put up with too many insults and abuse over here. I really felt for you."

Another woman gone up to de counter to converse with Chum-chum in she language. She reach out and touch his hand, sympathy-like. Chum-chum hold the one hand in his two and make a verbose speech to her as she nod she head in agreement generously. To italicize her support, she buy a take-out box a two burfi, or rather, dat's what I think dey was.

De door a de restaurant open again, and a bevy of Indian-looking women saunter in, dress up to weaken a person's decorum. De Miss Universe pageant traipse across de room to a table. Chum-chum and Brothers start smoothing dey hair back, and pushing de front a dey shirts neatly into dey pants. One brother take out a pack a Dentyne from his shirt pocket and pop one in his mouth. One take out a comb from his back pocket and smooth down his hair. All a dem den converge on dat single table to take orders. Dey begin to behave like young pups in mating season. Only, de women dem wasn't impress by all this tra-la-la at all and ignore dem except to make dey order, straight to de point. Well, it look like Brothers' egos were having a rough day and dey start roving 'bout de room, dey egos and de crotch a dey pants leading far in front dem. One brother gone over to Giraffebai to see if she want anything more. He call she "dear" and put his hand on she back. Giraffebai straighten she back in surprise and reply in a not-too-friendly way. When he gone to write up de bill she see me looking at she and she say to me, "Whoever does he think he is! Calling me dear and touching me like that! Why do these men always think that they have permission to touch whatever and wherever they want! And you can't make a fuss about it in public, because it is exactly what those people out there want to hear about so that they can say how sexist and uncivilized our culture is."

I shake mih head in understanding and say, "Yeah. I know. Yuh right!"

De atmosphere in de room take a hairpin turn, and it was man aggressing on woman, woman warding off a herd a man who just had dey pride publicly cut up a couple a times in just a few minutes.

One brother walk over to Janet and me and he stand up facing me with his hands clasp in front a his crotch, like if he protecting it. Stiff stiff, looking at me, he say, "Will that be all?"

Mih crew cut start to tingle, so I put on mih femmest smile and say, "Yes, that's it, thank you. Just the bill please." De smart-ass turn to face Janet and he remove his hands from in front a his crotch and slip his thumbs inside his pants like a cowboy 'bout to square dance. He smile, looking down at her attentive fuh so, and he say, "Can I do anything for you?"

I didn't give Janet time fuh his intent to even register before I bulldoze in mih most un-femmest manner, "She have everything she need, man, thank you. The bill please." Yuh think he hear me? It was like I was talking to thin air. He remain smiling at Janet, but she, looking at me, not at him, say, "You heard her. The bill please."

Before he could even leave de table proper, I start mih tirade. "But A A! Yuh see dat? Yuh could believe dat! De effing so-and-so! One minute yuh feel sorry fuh dem and next minute dey harassing de heck out a you. Janet, he crazy to mess with my woman, yes!" Janet get vex with me and say I overreacting, and is not fuh me to be vex, but fuh she to be vex. Is she he insult, and she could take good enough care a sheself.

I tell she I don't know why she don't cut off all dat long hair, and stop wearing lipstick and eyeliner. Well, who tell me to say dat! She get real vex and say dat nobody will tell she how to dress and how not to dress, not me and not any man. Well I could see de potential dat dis fight had coming, and when Janet get fighting vex, watch out! It hard to get a word in edgewise, yes! And she does bring up incidents from years back dat have no bearing on de current situation. So I draw back quick quick but she don't waste time; she was already off to a good start. It was best to leave right dere and den.

Just when I stand up to leave, de doors dem open up and in walk Sandy and Lise, com-ing for dey weekly hit a Indian sweets. Well, with Sandy and Lise is a dead giveaway dat dey not dressing fuh any man, it have no place in dey life fuh man-vibes, and dat in fact dey have a blatant penchant fuh women. Soon as dey enter de room yuh could see de brothers and de couple men customers dat had come in minutes before stare dem down from head to Birkenstocks, dey eyes bulging with disgust. And de women in de room start shoo-shooing, and putting dey hand in front dey mouth to stop dey surprise, and false teeth, too, from falling out. Sandy and Lise spot us instantly and dey call out to us, shameless, loud and affectionate. Dey leap over to us, eager to hug up and kiss like if dey hadn't seen us for years, but it was really only since two nights aback when we went out to dey favourite Indian restaurant for dinner. I figure dat de display was a genuine happiness to be seen wit us in dat place. While we stand up dere chatting, Sandy insist on rubbing she hand up and down Janet back — wit friendly intent, mind you, and same time Lise have she arm round Sandy waist. Well, all cover get blown. If it was even remotely possible dat I wasn't noticeable before, now Janet and I were over-exposed. We could a easily suffer from hypothermia, specially since it sud-denly get cold cold in dere. We say goodbye, not soon enough, and as we were leaving I turn to acknowledge Giraffebai, but instead a any recognition of our buddiness against de fresh brothers, I get a face dat look like it was in de presence of a very foul smell.

De good thing, doh, is dat Janet had become so incensed 'bout how we get scorned, dat she forgot I tell she to cut her hair and to ease up on de make-up, and so I get save from hearing 'bout how I too jealous, and how much I inhibit she, and how she would prefer if I would grow *my* hair, and wear lipstick and put on a dress sometimes. I so glad, oui! dat I didn't have to go through hearing how I too demanding a she, like de time, she say, I pre-vent she from seeing a ole boyfriend when he was in town for a couple hours *en route* to live in Australia with his new bride (because, she say, I was jealous dat ten years ago dey sleep together.) Well, look at mih crosses, nah! Like if I really so possessive and jealous!

So tell me, what yuh think 'bout dis nah, girl?

NOTE

Shani Mootoo, 1993, *Out on Main Street and Other Stories*, Vancouver: Press Gang. Reprinted with permission.

You Can Always Count On an Anthropologist

(To Set You Straight, Crooked or Somewhere In-Between)

Gregory Scofield

Yesterday I spent the better part of the afternoon thumbing through the *Alberta Elders' Cree Dictionary*, hoping to find a word or description for "two-spirited," a label remotely close to its English counterpart, like homosexual, queer, transsexual, transvestite…. But the closest I could come to such a word was *nîso achâhkowak*, which literally translates to "two spirits" and which, if used in a sentence, might read, "The house was haunted by two spirits."

Apparently the Cree elders were as mystified as I was about the whole two-spirited description. How do you translate such a concept, the idea of a third or fourth gender? After all, don't we carry the spirits of our mother and our father, our grandmothers and our grandfathers? Moreover, on a purely biological level, our gender appears to be determined by the X or Y chromosome. Then again, who really knows what sacred ceremony takes place inside the womb? The Cree dictionary doesn't appear to have a translation for the word *hermaphrodite*.

Nevertheless, the afternoon wasn't entirely wasted. I stood at the kitchen window watching the late October leaves fall in tufts of two or three, reciting the new words I'd learned: *ka nîsohkwakanehk*, two-faced; *nîswayak kohpakarnahikehk*, two-fisted; *nîswaw*, two-fold; *nîspîwâpiskos*, two pence; *nîswaw ka pimastek*, two-ply. But I found myself chanting the word *nîskwayak ka itapatahk* over and over. The image of my late aunty suddenly came to mind. I could see her watching the kitchen clock, her eyes dark and stormy. "*Wahk-wa*, Harry!" I could hear her say. "*Tapway ê-kimôcitan*! Dat sneaky doo-diming son of a bitch husband of mine!"

If Harry was a doo-dimer, I began to think, then was he also two-spirited? Did he possess a good husband spirit and a bad husband spirit? Did those spirits ever come into conflict, ever come to blows? And was Harry the bingo-playing version of Sybil, the famous schizophrenic whose multiple personalities stumped everyone from psychics to psychiatrists? *Nîskwayak ka itapatahk* — I wondered, are we all genetically built to be doo-dimers? And if so, does this mean we're all two-spirited?

But this wasn't the first or second time I had pondered the politics of identity. In fact, most of my writing career has been punctuated by labels such as "angry," "streetwise," "Métis," "gay," and "two-spirited." It seemed with each new book I was helped into yet another coat of identity, and although there was a certain truth to each one, I found the coats of academics or reviewers, even other Native people, ill-fitting or too restrictive. Yet I understand the wearing of coats and colours, badges and buttons. Perhaps even the "two-spirited" badge, the term itself, had been coined by gay American Indians. Having worked with gay, lesbian, and transgendered Native people, I fully understood the need for solidarity and a sense of uniqueness, a defined and supportive place among the dominant white gay male culture. Racism, class discrimination, and sexism can be even worse within our own community than they are in general society. Furthermore, the daily burdens of family and ostracism carried by many urban gay/lesbian/transgendered Native people only add to their sense of isolation and disconnection.

I hadn't heard the term "two-spirit" until the late '80s. On my own quest for sexual/

cultural understanding and acceptance, I searched out books on the topic. There were two particular books that I found insightful: *The Spirit and the Flesh: Sexual Diversity in American Indian Culture* by Walter L. Williams (Beacon Press, 1986, 1992) and *The Zuni Man-Woman* by Will Roscoe (University of New Mexico Press, 1991). Both books are anthropological in scope, espousing the idea of sacredness among those individuals born with both male and female spirits. Both authors elaborated on the cultural and spiritual significance of such individuals, citing the Zuni world view of multiple genders and the bestowing of holy powers. This embodiment of multiple genders greatly intrigued me, although I found it difficult to understand in relation to the Cree spiritual world and the teachings I'd been taught. One's sacredness or *pawatew*, the spirit helper who becomes part of one's identity, defines one's life-long responsibilities, and one's lifelong responsibilities define one's sacredness, one's *pawatew*.

Nonetheless, this confusing but politically fringed coat remains hanging in my closet. I grew up in a household of women where the teapot sat on the table, a piping hot goddess whose stories were steeped in Métis and *nehiyawewin*, Cree traditions. I grew up with lace that warmed winter windows and the smell of Pine-Sol, smoked moosehide and cinnamoned apples. I grew up learning to cook and sew. I grew up learning the finer qualities of intimacy and diplomacy. I learned to pee sitting down. And I learned to deaden myself against my stepfather's rages, to gather up my mother's bones after one of his beatings. And always the teapot, our goddess, was ready to speak of wars both won and lost. I grew up among warrior women, hearing their songs of sisterhood and survival. I grew up singing beside them, and I carry their songs to this day.

And yet my sense of masculinity, my own state of being male in the world, suffered a great deal. My fear of men was largely influenced by my mother and my aunties, an uneasy cohabitation of tyrant and loyalist, perpetrator and protector. It seemed appropriate to blame my vacant father, my abusive stepfather and uncle for all of our suffering. Men, or so I believed, were the epitome of everything wrong in the world. They could neither demonstrate love nor compassion, understanding nor acceptance. To complicate matters even more, my adolescent attraction towards men made me feel ashamed and disloyal. My body felt like a liability, my desires a muddled dichotomy of lust and loathing. The very thought of surrendering myself emotionally, mentally, spiritually, or physically to another man filled me with panic. I vowed not to repeat the mistakes my mother and aunties had made. Instead, I was able to detach my body from my mind. I learned to use sex as a self-indulgent weapon. Little did I know that the majority of the human race had learned the exact same. This revelation, however, was my first real insight into men. They, too, could be vulnerable and suspicious, scared and filled with self-doubt. They, too, were capable of feeling emotion, although I now realize society does not, for the most part, support this notion. Over time my own sense of masculinity was also shaped by these expectations. So perhaps, given my childhood, I was fortunate to be raised by women, to develop my own idea of masculinity and its meanings.

But still one's sacredness, one's *pawatew*, like sexual identity itself, is not easy to define. I've often wondered if the act of sex or the refusal of it between lovers can be considered two-headed, two-hearted, two-spirited? Or is the act of sex simply just that — an act? An acting out of love and hate, tenderness and brutality, joy and sorrow, freedom and captivity; an unconscious demonstration of our two-headed, two-hearted, two-spirited selves? Or does it simply come down to the mysterious site of our bones and our quest to uncover their ancient meanings, our own anthropological dig into self and spirit? Moreover, when we brush away the dirt of societal expectations, do we find our bones in a state of straightness or crookedness, or somewhere comfortably in between? And who among us, having experienced love and hatred, tenderness and brutality, joy and sorrow, freedom and captivity, can say that there is only one way to excavate our true sacredness, our *pawatew*?

These thoughts lead me back to the teapot from my childhood, the goddess whose stories were steeped in *nehiyaw*, Cree tradition, and whose stories flowed, piping hot, filling my imagination. My aunty Georgina's stories about the northern lights, love medicine or *Wihtikiw*, the Legendary Eater of Humans, were veiled in mystery, complicated like the brightly coloured beads she stitched into place on a pair of moccasins. These were nighttime stories — stories that she'd picked from the muskeg, stripped from the birch trees, lifted from beneath a rock and place upon the table, beside the tin of bannock and the teapot. These were stories not meant for TV or books. These were stories that could not be recorded, stories that had to be held and passed around like a newborn baby. These were stories meant to teach a small boy how to use his strength and senses, his awareness and instinct. These were lifetime stories, gifts of *maskihkîy*, medicine.

This type of "thought" medicine, I believe, can be brewed from the most seemingly insignificant root. My bookshelf, for example, has become a sacred lodge of poetic singers, young and old storykeepers, trickster-talkers, political warriors, and history weavers. Whereas once I only housed the books of Aboriginal authors, I've learned to open my lodge to anyone who thinks in terms of medicine and the passing of sacred knowledge — anyone who wishes to add his or her gift to the giveaway ceremony of communal stories.

One such story came to my attention many years ago. It was the collected work of a white anthropologist who'd spent years among the Plains Cree on the Little Pine reserve in Saskatchewan, documenting the traditions and customs of the people who lived there. At first I was not interested in yet another anthropological dig into the Native psyche. A few moments later, however, I was drawn back to the book. It was the work of a white anthropologist, I reasoned, and therefore I was entitled to edit his research for inaccuracy, for gross misinterpretation. I flipped through the index and was astonished by the pages of information. Everything I wanted to know about Cree kinship terms, male and female roles, the raising of children, storytelling and mythical beings, art and games, birth and death, housing and food preparation, social customs and vision quests, was at my fingertips.

I followed the long column of words beginning with the letter H until I found the word *homosexuality*. According to the anthropologist and his Cree informant, named Fine-Day, there was a gay precursor before me, the Cree version of the Lakota *winkte*; the Mohave *alyhas*; the Navajo *nadle*; the Zuni *Ihamana*; the Tewa Pueblos *quetho*; the Crow *bade*; the Cheyenne *he man eh*; the Omaha *mexoga*; the Zapotec *ira'muxe* and the Aleut *shopan*.

My Cree forerunner was called *ayekkwew*, "neither man nor woman" or "man and woman." It was reported that *Piciw-iskwew*, which was said to mean "he moves and makes his home/house among women," died from wearing a dress that had been worn by a menstruating woman. He had been killed by the power of the woman's menstrual blood just as the Cree believed a man would have been. Only if he had been born a woman would he not have been harmed.

I was alarmed by the story, and yet at the same time I was intrigued by the phenomenon, the spiritual significance of *Piciw-iskwew*'s death. This was, or so it appeared, brought about by his born gender and his male inability to nullify the spiritual/physical power of women. I couldn't help but wonder, would wearing a dress that he made himself have protected him? Furthermore, I recall thinking seriously about the idea of two-spiritedness. If the Creator had gifted *Piciw-iskwew* with two spirits, then why had his female power not protected him? Moreover, if *Piciw-iskwew* knew the consequence of wearing the menstruating woman's dress, then why had he done so?

Although the story was difficult to understand, I did come to a certain conclusion. *Piciw-iskwew*'s death was a direct result of him breaking Cree spiritual law. The female energy and his male physical being had in the end killed him. Did this mean, therefore, that the idea of two-spiritedness among the Cree was conceptual rather than spiritual?

As I mentioned earlier, I was raised exclusively by women. The homes/houses of my childhood were far removed, at least emotionally, from the homes/houses of men. Had you known my women, the indignity they suffered, you would not blame them. I have only recently, in my own home, learned to live among men comfortably. My *niwicewakan*, "the one I go around with," is loving and kind. He is the son of a farmer, smart in the ways of landscape and animals. His father has the sight to predict bad weather and strange happenings, although he does not believe in omens. He often teases me about my taste for wild meat but never complains about my cooking. He once told me that I was a hard worker, a good housekeeper. He thanked me for hemming his pants. I took the compliment, giving thanks to my *iskwewak*, my women.

So does this make me two-spirited in my father-in-law's eyes? I'm certain if I asked him, he would look at me strangely as if I had said, "Do I look like a farmer today?" Knowing him as I do, his response would go something like this: "Jesus Christ — you're a human being like everyone else!" A human being, yes. And like all human beings, I strive to understand my *pawatew*, my lifelong responsibilities. The lessons and teachings I've received from both men and women.

Based upon the anthropologist's interpretation and spelling of the word *ayekkwew*, I found nothing close to its meaning in the Cree dictionary. I did find, however, two similar words: *ayakwemaw* pl. *ayakwemawak* (VTA): *The words spoken give her/him a tough time*, i.e., it is a reprimand. I also found the word *ayahkweyihtamowin* pl. *ayahkweyihtamowina* (N1): *Being diligent; diligence.* My best (and not so fluent) interpretation of these words as they relate to two-spiritedness is: *It may constitute a tough time hearing strong words, but be diligent.*

My own diligence, both steady and wavering, to understand and accept my Creator-made self, my God-given power, my *pawatew*, is still steeping in my spirit. Until I fully understand the gifts I've been given, I am grateful for the sight of my two eyes, the ability to create with my two hands. So again, does this make me two-spirited? Perhaps. Perhaps not. I do know, however, that Turtle Island is a place of sacred and not so sacred people, all of us looking for a sense of belonging, a validation of our existence — maybe even a platform to stage our resistance, for whatever reason. One could conclude, I suppose, that these inherent needs are one and the same, an endless step towards self-definition. Then again, perhaps definition is really about interpretation.

Take the simple act of eating together. Many potatoes ago, I sat down for dinner with my adopted Cree brother and his family. Quite casually, I asked him, "*Peta een patakwa.*" He looked up from his plate disapprovingly, as if I'd asked him to pass the kitchen stove. "We don't say *een patakwa*," he corrected. "That's what half-breeds call them. The proper way to say it is *n-patakwa*." He slid the bowl of potatoes across the table, digging back into his proper spuds. A few moments pass uncomfortably. Being a half-breed myself, half devil/half angel, as my aunty used to say, I mentally slipped off to my own secretive coulee. The potato resistance of 1982 was about to begin.

"Hey, bro'," I said, "if I'm gonna eat my *n-patakwa*, I'll need you to pass me *mistemihkwan.*" My sister-in-law dropped her face, trying desperately to quell her laughter.

Even the half-breeds knew an *etimihkwan* was not dinner conversation. A spoon, which in Cree has a double (female) meaning for….

And to think I'd made inference to my bro' being not just any old spoon. But a big spoon. A huge, self-important spoon that could dish up more *een patakwa* than a forklift. At that, he left the table. Within seconds, the resistance was over. And Riel and Dumont both enjoyed a good smoke.

NOTE

Gregory Scofield, 2008, "You Can Always Count on an Anthropologist: (To Set You Straight, Crooked or Somewhere In-Between)," in Drew Hayden Taylor (ed.), *Me Sexy: An Exploration of Native Sex and Sexuality*, Vancouver, Toronto, Berkeley: Douglas & McIntrye. Adapted and reprinted with permission.

REFERENCE

LeClair, Nancy and George Cardinal. 1998. *Alberta Elders' Cree Dictionary/alperta ohci kehtehayak nehiyaw otwestamakewasinahikan*. Edmonton: University of Alberta Press.

18

White Privilege
Unpacking the Invisible Knapsack

Peggy McIntosh

Through work to bring materials from Women's Studies into the rest of the curriculum, I have often noticed men's unwillingness to grant that they are overprivileged, even though they may grant that women are disadvantaged. They may say they will work to improve women's status, in the society, the university, or the curriculum, but they can't or won't support the idea of lessening men's. Denials which amount to taboos surround the subject of advantages which men gain from women's disadvantages. These denials protect male privilege from being fully acknowledged, lessened or ended.

Thinking through unacknowledged male privilege as a phenomenon, I realized that since hierarchies in our society are interlocking, there was most likely a phenomenon of white privilege which was similarly denied and protected. As a white person, I realized I had been taught about racism as something which puts others at a disadvantage, but had been taught not to see one of its corollary aspects, white privilege, which puts me at an advantage.

I think whites are carefully taught not to recognize white privilege, as males are taught not to recognize male privilege. So I have begun in an untutored way to ask what it is like to have white privilege. I have come to see white privilege as an invisible package of unearned assets which I can count on cashing in each day, but about which I was "meant" to remain oblivious. White privilege is like an invisible weightless knapsack of special provisions, maps, passports, codebooks, visas, clothes, tools and blank checks.

Describing white privilege makes one newly accountable. As we in Women's Studies work to reveal male privilege and ask men to give up some of their power, so one who writes about having white privilege must ask, "Having described it, what will I do to lessen or end it?"

After I realized the extent to which men work from a base of unacknowledged privilege, I understood that much of their oppressiveness was unconscious. Then I remembered the frequent charges from women of color that white women whom they encounter are oppressive. I began to understand why we are justly seen as oppressive, even when we don't see ourselves that way. I began to count the ways in which I enjoy unearned skin privilege and have been conditioned into oblivion about its existence.

My schooling gave me no training in seeing myself as an oppressor, as an unfairly advantaged person, or as a participant in a damaged culture. I was taught to see myself as an individual whose moral state depended on her individual moral will. My schooling followed the pattern my colleague Elizabeth Minnich has pointed out: whites are taught to think of their lives as morally neutral, normative and average, and also ideal, so that when we work to benefit others, this is seen as work which will allow "them" to be more like "us."

I decided to try to work on myself at least by identifying some of the daily effects of white privilege in my life. I have chosen those conditions which I think in my case *attach somewhat more to skin-colour privilege* than to class, religion, ethnic status, or geographical location, though of course all these other factors are intricately intertwined. As far as I can see, my African American co-workers, friends and acquaintances, with whom I come into daily or frequent contact in this particular time, place, and line of work, cannot count on most of these conditions.

1. I can if I wish arrange to be in the company of people of my race most of the time.
2. If I should need to move, I can be pretty sure of renting or purchasing housing in an area which I can afford and in which I would want to live.
3. I can be pretty sure that my neighbors in such a location will be neutral or pleasant to me.
4. I can go shopping alone most of the time, pretty well assured that I will not be followed or harassed.
5. I can turn on the television or open to the front page of the paper and see people of my race widely represented.
6. When I am told about our national heritage or about "civilization," I am shown that people of my color made it what it is.
7. I can be sure that my children will be given curricular materials that testify to the existence of their race.
8. If I want to, I can be pretty sure of finding a publisher for this piece on white privilege.
9. I can go into a music shop and count on finding the music of my race represented, into a supermarket and find the staple foods which fit with my cultural traditions, into a hairdresser's shop and find someone who can cut my hair.
10. Whether I use cheques, credit cards, or cash, I can count on my skin color not to work against the appearance of financial reliability.
11. I can arrange to protect my children most of the time from people who might not like them.
12. I can swear, or dress in secondhand clothes, or not answer letters, without having people attribute these choices to bad morals, the poverty, or the illiteracy of my race.
13. I can speak in public to a powerful male group without putting my race on trial.
14. I can do well in a challenging situation without being called a credit to my race.
15. I am never asked to speak for all the people of my racial group.
16. I can remain oblivious of the language and customs of persons of colour who constitute the world's majority without feeling in my culture any penalty for such oblivion.
17. I can criticize our government and talk about how much I fear its policies and behaviour without being seen as a cultural outsider.
18. I can be pretty sure that if I ask to talk to "the person in charge," I will be facing a person of my race.
19. If a traffic cop pulls me over or if the IRS (Internal Revenue Service) audits my tax return, I can be sure I haven't been singled out because of my race.
20. I can easily buy posters, postcards, picture books, greeting cards, dolls, toys, and children's magazines featuring people of my race.
21. I can go home from most meetings of organizations I belong to feeling somewhat tied in, rather than isolated, out-of-place, outnumbered, unheard, held at a distance, or feared.
22. I can take a job with an affirmative action employer without having co-workers on the job suspect that I got it because of my race.
23. I can choose public accommodation without fearing that people of my race cannot get in or will be mistreated in the places I have chosen.
24. I can be sure that if I need legal or medical help, my race will not work against me.
25. If my day, week, or year is going badly, I need not ask of each negative episode or situation whether it has racial overtones.
26. I can choose blemish cover or bandages in "flesh" color and have them more or less match my skin.

I repeatedly forgot each of the realizations on this list until I wrote it down. For me white privilege has turned out to be an elusive and fugitive subject. The pressure to avoid it is great, for in facing it I must give up the myth of meritocracy. If these things are true, this is not such a free country; one's life is not what one makes it; many doors open for certain people through no virtues of their own.

In unpacking this invisible knapsack of white privilege, I have listed conditions of daily experience which I once took for granted. Nor did I think of any of these perquisites as bad for the holder. I now think that we need a more finely differentiated taxonomy of privilege, for some of these varieties are only what one would want for everyone in a just society, and others give license to be ignorant, oblivious, arrogant and destructive.

I see a pattern running through the matrix of white privilege, a pattern of assumptions which were passed on to me as a white person. There was one main piece of cultural turf; it was my own turf, and I was among those who could control the turf. *My skin color was an asset for any move I was educated to want to make.* I could think of myself as belonging in major ways, and of making social systems work for me. I could freely disparage, fear, neglect, or be oblivious to anything outside of the dominant cultural forms. Being of the main culture, I could also criticize it fairly freely.

In proportion as my racial group was being made confident, comfortable, and oblivious, other groups were likely being made unconfident, uncomfortable, and alienated. Whiteness protected me from many kinds of hostility, distress, and violence, which I was being subtly trained to visit in turn upon people of color.

For this reason, the word "privilege" now seems to me misleading. We usually think of privilege as being a favoured state, whether earned or conferred by birth or luck. Yet some of the conditions I have described here work to systematically over-empower certain groups. Such privilege simply *confers dominance* because of one's race or sex.

I want, then, to distinguish between earned strength and unearned power conferred systematically. Power from unearned privilege can look like strength when it is in fact permission to escape or to dominate. But not all of the privileges on my list are inevitably damaging. Some privileges, like the expectation that neighbors will be decent to you, or that your race will not count against you in court, should be the norm in a just society. Others, like the privilege to ignore less powerful people, distort the humanity of the holders as well as the ignored groups.

We might at least start by distinguishing between positive advantages which we can work to spread, and negative types of advantages which, unless rejected, will always reinforce our present hierarchies. For example, the feeling that one belongs within the human circle, as Native Americans say, should not be seen as privilege for a few. Ideally it is an *unearned entitlement*. At present, since only a few have it, it is an *unearned advantage* for them. This paper results from a process of coming to see that some of the power which I originally saw as attendant on being a human being in the U.S. consisted in *unearned advantage* and *conferred dominance*.

I have met very few men who are truly distressed about systemic, unearned male advantage and conferred dominance. And so one question for me and others like me is whether we will be like them, or whether we will get truly distressed, even outraged, about unearned race advantage and conferred dominance and, if so, what we will do to lessen them. In any case, we need to do more work in identifying how they actually affect our daily lives. Many, perhaps most, of our white students in the U.S. think that racism doesn't affect them because they are not people of colour; they do not see "whiteness" as a racial identity. In addition, since race and sex are not the only advantaging systems at work, we need similarly to examine the daily experience of having age advantage, or ethnic advantage, or physical ability, or advantage related to nationality, religion, or sexual orientation.

Difficulties and dangers surrounding the task of finding parallels are many. Since racism, sexism, and heterosexism are not the same, the advantaging associated with them should not be seen as the same. In addition, it is hard to disentangle aspects of unearned advantage which rest more on social class, economic class, race, religion, sex and ethnic identity than on other factors. Still, all of the oppressions are interlocking, as the Combahee River Collective Statement of 1977 continues to remind us eloquently.

One factor seems clear about all of the interlocking oppressions. They take *both active forms* which we can see *and embedded forms* which, as a member of the dominant group, one is taught not to see. In my class and place, I did not see myself as a racist because I was taught to recognize racism only in individual acts of meanness by members of my group, never in invisible systems conferring unsought racial dominance on my group from birth.

Disapproving of the systems won't be enough to change them. I was taught to think that racism could end if white individuals changed their attitudes. [But] a "white" skin in the United States opens many doors for whites whether or not we approve of the way dominance has been conferred on us. Individual acts can palliate, but cannot end, these problems.

To redesign social systems we need first to acknowledge their colossal unseen dimensions. The silences and denials surrounding privilege are the key political tool here. They keep the thinking about equality or equity incomplete, protecting unearned advantage and conferred dominance by making these taboo subjects. Most talk by whites about equal opportunity seems to me now to be about equal opportunity to try and get into a position of dominance while denying that *systems* of dominance exist.

It seems to me that obliviousness about white advantage, like obliviousness about male advantage, is kept strongly inculcated in the United States so as to maintain the myth of meritocracy, the myth that democratic choice is equally available to all. Keeping most people unaware that freedom of confident action is there for just a small number of people props up those in power, and serves to keep power in the hands of the same groups that have most of it already.

Though systemic change takes many decades, there are pressing questions for me and, I imagine, for some others like me if we raise our daily consciousness on the perquisites of being light-skinned. What will we do with such knowledge? As we know from watching men, it is an open question whether we will choose to use unearned advantage to weaken hidden systems of advantage, and whether we will use any of our arbitrarily awarded power to try to reconstruct power systems on a broader base.

NOTE

Peggy McIntosh, 1988, "White Privilege: Unpacking the Invisible Knapsack," excerpted from Peggy McIntosh, 1988, "White Privilege and Male Privilege: A Personal Account of Coming to See Correspondences through Work in Women's Studies," Working Paper 189, Wellesley College Center for Research on Women, Wellesley MA. Copyright fees are donated to National SEED Project on Inclusive Curriculum (Seeking Educational Equity and Diversity). Reprinted with permission.

REFERENCE

Combahee River Collective. 1977. "The Combahee River Collective Statement." At: circuitous.org/scraps/combahee.html.

19

Patriarchy, the System
An It, Not a He, a Them or an Us

Allan G. Johnson

"When you say patriarchy," a man complained from the rear of the audience, "I know what you *really* mean — me!" A lot of people hear "men" whenever someone says "patriarchy," so that criticism of gender oppression is taken to mean that all men — each and every one of them — are oppressive people. Not surprisingly, many men take it personally if someone mentions patriarchy or the oppression of women, bristling at what they often see as a way to make them feel guilty. And some women feel free to blame individual men for patriarchy simply because they're men. Some of the time, men feel defensive because they identify with patriarchy and its values and don't want to face the consequences these produce or the prospect of giving up male privilege. But defensiveness more often reflects a common confusion about the difference between patriarchy as a kind of society and the people who participate in it. If we're ever going to work toward real change, it's a confusion we'll have to clear up.

We have to realize that we're stuck in a model of social life that views everything as beginning and ending with individuals. Looking at things in this way, we tend to think that if evil exists in the world [it's] because there are evil people who have entered into an evil conspiracy. Racism exists, for example, simply because white people are racist bigots who hate members of racial and ethnic minorities and want to do them harm. There is gender oppression because men want and like to dominate women and act with hostility toward them. There is poverty and class oppression because people in the upper classes are greedy, heartless, and cruel. The flip side of this individualistic model of guilt and blame is that race, gender, and class oppression are actually not oppression at all, but merely the sum of individual failings on the part of blacks, women, and the poor, who lack the right stuff to compete successfully with whites, men, and others who know how to make something of themselves.

What this kind of thinking ignores is that we are all participating in something larger than ourselves or any collection of us. On some level, most people are familiar with the idea that social life involves us in something larger than ourselves, but few seem to know what to do with that idea. When Sam Keen[1] laments that "THE SYSTEM is running us all," he strikes a deep chord in many people. But he also touches on a basic misunderstanding of social life, because having blamed "the system" (presumably society) for our problems, he doesn't take the next step to understand what that might mean. What exactly *is* a system, for example, and how could it run us? Do *we* have anything to do with shaping *it*, and if so, how? How, for example, do we participate in patriarchy, and how does that link us to the consequences it produces? How is what we think [of] as "normal" life related to male dominance, women's oppression, and the hierarchical, control-obsessed world in which they and our lives are embedded? Without asking such questions we can't understand gender fully and we avoid taking responsibility either for ourselves or for patriarchy. Instead "the system" serves as a vague, unarticulated catch-all, a dumping ground for social problems, a scapegoat that can never be held to account and that, for all the power we think it has, can't talk back or actually *do* anything.

So, the system is invoked in contradictory ways. On the one hand, it's portrayed as a formidable source of all our woes, a great monster that "runs us all." On the other hand, it's ignored as a nebulous blob that we think we don't have to include in any solutions. But we can't have it both ways. If we see patriarchy as nothing more than men's and women's individual personalities, motivations, and behaviour, for example, then it probably won't even occur to us to ask about larger contexts — such as institutions like the family, religion, and the economy — and how people's lives are shaped in relation to them. From this kind of individualistic perspective, we might ask why a particular man raped, harassed, or beat a woman. We wouldn't ask, however, what kind of society would promote persistent *patterns* of such behaviour in everyday life, from wife-beating jokes to the routine inclusion of sexual coercion and violence in mainstream movies. We are quick to explain rape and battery as the acts of sick or angry men; but we rarely take seriously the question of what kind of society would produce so much male anger and pathology or direct it toward sexual violence rather than something else. We rarely ask how gender violence might serve other more "normalized" ends such as male control and domination. We might ask why a man would like pornography that objectifies, exploits, and promotes violence against women. But it's hard to stir up interest in asking what kind of society would give violent and degrading visions of women's bodies and human sexuality such a prominent and pervasive place in its culture to begin with.

What Is Patriarchy?

Patriarchy is more than a collection of individuals (such as "men"). It is a system, which means it can't be reduced to the people who participate in it. If you go to work in a corporation, or attend a university, for example, you know the minute you walk in the door that you've entered "something" that shapes your experience and behaviour, something that isn't just you and the other people you work with. You can feel yourself stepping into a set of relationships and shared understandings about who's who and what's supposed to happen and why, and all of this limits you in many ways. And when you leave at the end of the day you can feel yourself released from the constraints imposed by your participation in that system; your focus shifts to other systems such as a family or a neighbourhood bar that shape your experience in different ways.

Similarly, patriarchy is a kind of society organized around certain kinds of relationships and ideas. As individuals, we participate in it. Paradoxically, our participation both shapes our lives and gives us the opportunity to be part of changing or perpetuating it. But *we are not it*, which means that patriarchy can exist without men having "oppressive personalities" or actively conspiring with one another to defend male privilege. To demonstrate that gender oppression exists, we don't have to show that men are villains, that women are good-hearted victims, that women don't participate in their oppression, or that men never oppose it. If a society is oppressive, then people who grow up and live in it will tend to accept, identify with, and participate in it as "normal" and unremarkable life. That's the path of least resistance in any system. It's hard not to follow it, given how we depend on society and its rewards and punishments that hinge on going along with the status quo. When oppression is woven into the fabric of everyday life, we don't need to go out of our way to be overtly oppressive in order for an oppressive system to produce oppressive consequences. As the saying goes, what evil requires is simply that ordinary people do nothing.

Patriarchy's defining elements are its male-dominated, male-identified, and male-centred character, but this is just the beginning. At its core, patriarchy is a set of symbols and ideas that make up a culture embodied by everything from the content of everyday conversation to literature and film. Patriarchal culture includes ideas about the nature of things, including men, women, and humanity, with manhood and masculinity most closely associated with being human and womanhood and femininity relegated to the marginal position of the "other." It's about defining women and men as opposites, about the "naturalness" of male aggression, competition, and dominance and of female caring, cooperation, and subordination. It's about the valuing of masculinity and maleness and the devaluing of femininity and femaleness. It's about the primary importance of a husband's career and the secondary status of a wife's, about childcare as a priority in women's lives and its secondary importance in men's. It's about the social acceptability of anger, rage, and toughness in men but not in women, and of caring, tenderness, and vulnerability in women but not in men.

The symbols and ideas that make up patriarchal culture are important to understand because they have such powerful effects on the structure of social life. By "structure," I mean the ways gender privilege and oppression are organized through social relationships and unequal distribution of rewards, opportunities, and resources. This inequality appears in countless patterns of everyday life in family and work, religion and politics, community and education. It is found in family divisions of labour that exempt fathers from most domestic work even when both parents work outside the home, and in the concentration of women in lower-level, pink-collar jobs, and male predominance almost everywhere else. It is in the unequal distribution of income and all that goes with it, from access to health care to the availability of leisure time. It is in patterns of male violence and harassment that can turn a simple walk in the park or a typical day at work or lovers' quarrel into a life-threatening nightmare. More than anything, the structure of patriarchy is found in the unequal distribution of power that makes oppression possible, in patterns of male dominance in every facet of human life, from everyday conversations to global politics. By its nature, patriarchy puts issues of power, dominance, and control at the centre of human existence, not only in relationships between men and women, but among men as they compete and struggle to gain status, maintain control, and protect themselves from what other men might do to them.

Above all, patriarchal culture is about the core values of control and domination in almost every area of human existence. From the expression of emotion to economics to the natural environment, gaining and exercising control is a goal of great continuing importance. In this context, the concept of power takes on the narrow definition of "power over" — the ability to control others, events, resources, or oneself in spite of resistance — rather than alternatives such as the ability to cooperate with others, to give freely of oneself, or to feel and act in harmony with nature. To have power over and to be prepared to use it are defined culturally as good and desirable (and characteristically "masculine"), and to lack such power or to be reluctant to use it is seen as weak, if not contemptible, (and characteristically "feminine").

The System in Us in the System

One of the most difficult things to accept about patriarchy is that we're involved in it, which means we're also involved in its consequences. As I stated in the beginning, this acceptance is especially hard for men who refuse to believe that they benefit from women's oppression because they can't see how this could happen without being personally oppressive in their intentions, feelings, and behaviour. For many men, being told they're *involved* in oppression can only mean they *are* oppressive.

How then are men and women involved in patriarchy? One way to see how people connect with systems is to think of us as occupying social positions that locate us in relation to people in other positions. We connect to families, for example, through positions such as "mother," "daughter," and "cousin"; to economic systems through positions such as "vice -president," "secretary," or "unemployed"; to political systems such as "citizen," "registered voter," and "mayor"; to religious systems through positions such as "believer" and "clergy." How we perceived the people who occupy such positions and what we expect of them depend on cultural ideas — such as the belief that mothers are naturally better than fathers at childcare or the expectation that fathers will be the primary breadwinners. Such ideas are powerful because we use them to construct a sense of who we are and other people are. From this perspective, *who* we and other people think we are has a lot to do with *where* we are in relation to social systems and all positions that people occupy. We wouldn't exist as social beings if it weren't for our participation in one social system or another. It's hard to imagine just who we'd be and what our existence would consist of if we took away all of our connections to the symbols, ideas, and relationships that make up social systems. Moreover, we can think of a society as a network of interconnected systems within systems, each made up of social positions and their relations to one another.

Like all social systems, patriarchy exists only through people's lives. To some extent people experience patriarchy as external to them; but this doesn't mean that it's a distinct and separate thing, like a house in which we live. Instead, by participating in patriarchy we are *of* patriarchy and it *of* us. Both exist *through* the other and neither can exist without the other. In addition, patriarchy isn't static; it's an ongoing *process* that's continuously shaped and reshaped. Since the thing we're participating in is patriarchal, we tend to behave in ways that create a patriarchal world from one moment to the next. But we have some freedom to break the rules and construct everyday life in different ways, which means that the paths we choose to follow can do as much to change patriarchy as they can to perpetuate it.

We're involved in patriarchy and its consequences because we occupy social positions in it, which is all it takes. Since gender oppression is, by definition, a system of inequality organized around gender categories, we can no more avoid being involved in it than we can avoid being female or male. *All* men and *all* women are therefore involved in this oppressive system, and none of us can control *whether* we participate, only *how*.

Conclusion

Patriarchy is a system which includes cultural ideas about men and women, the web of relationships that structure social life, and the unequal distribution of rewards and resources that underlies oppression. We need to see new ways to participate by forging alternative paths of least resistance, for the system doesn't simply "run us" like hapless puppets. It may *be* larger than us, but it doesn't exist except *through* us. Without us, patriarchy doesn't *happen*. And it's where we have power to do something about it and about ourselves *in* it. We are involved; we are part of the problem; the question is whether we'll choose also to be part of the solution.

NOTES

Allan G. Johnson, 1977, "Patriarchy, the System: An It, Not a He, a Them, or an Us," *The Gender Knot: Unraveling Our Patriarchal Legacy*, Philadelphia: Temple University Press. Reprinted with permission.

1. Editors' note: Sam Keen is a well-known American author and philosopher. In 1991, he published *Fire in the Belly: On Being a Man* (Bantam Books), widely regarded as a rallying cry for the mythopoetic men's movement, a movement urging men to get in touch with their authentic (essential) masculinity by reimagining "the ideals of heroism, strength, and potency for a fuller life" in order to pursue "an alternative vision of virtue and virility."

20

Understanding Men
Gender Sociology and the New International Research on Masculinities

R. W. Connell

Debates about Men and Boys

In the last decade there has been an upsurge of concern with issues about men and boys. In the public realm there have been social movements focused on the reform or restoration of masculinity, such as the "mythopoetic" movement, the Million Man March and the Promise Keepers (Messner 1997). In education there has been much talk of boys' "failure" in school and the need for special programs for boys (Connell 1996; Gilbert and Gilbert 1998). In health there has been increasing debate about men's health and illness (Sabo and Gordon 1995; Schofield et al. 2000), and a popular therapeutic movement addresses men's problems in relationships, sexuality and identity.

In a way this is surprising, because men remain the principal holders of economic and political power. Men make up a large majority of corporate executives, top professionals and holders of public office. Worldwide, men held 93 percent of cabinet-level posts in 1996, and most top positions in international agencies (Gierycz 1999). Men continue to control most technology and most weaponry; with only limited exceptions it is men who staff and control the agencies of force such as armies, police and judicial systems.

This used to be thought "natural," either prescribed by God or a consequence of biology. Essentialist views of gender are still popular and are constantly reinforced in the media. However they are increasingly under challenge. The women's liberation movement, and the many feminisms that have followed on from it, have produced a massive disturbance in the gender system and in people's assumptions about gender. And what affects the social position of women and girls must also affect the social position of men and boys. Large numbers of men now acknowledge that their position is under *challenge*, that what they once took for granted must be re-thought. They may or may not like it, but they cannot ignore it.

The "Ethnographic Moment": Significant Conclusions

We now have a growing library of ethnographic studies from around the world, across a number of the social sciences, in which researchers have traced the construction of masculinity in a particular milieu or moment.

Though each study is different, there are many common themes. Some of the most important findings of this research may be summarized in six theses:

1. Multiple Masculinities

Historians and anthropologists have shown that there is no one pattern of masculinity that is found everywhere. Different cultures, and different periods of history, construct masculinity differently. Equally important, more than one kind of masculinity can be found within a given cultural setting. Within any workplace, neighbourhood or peer group, there are likely to be different understandings of masculinity and different ways of "doing" masculinity.

2. Hierarchy and Hegemony

Different masculinities do not sit side-by-side like dishes in a smorgasbord; there are definite relations between them. Typically, some masculinities are more honoured than others. Some may be actively dishonoured, for example homosexual masculinities in modern Western culture. Some are socially marginalized, for example the masculinities of disempowered ethnic minorities. Some are exemplary, taken as symbolizing admired traits, for example the masculinities of sporting heroes.

The form of masculinity that is culturally dominant in a given setting is called "hegemonic masculinity." "Hegemonic" signifies a position of cultural authority and leadership, not total dominance; other forms of masculinity persist alongside. The hegemonic form need not be the most common form of masculinity. Hegemonic masculinity is, however, highly visible. It is likely to be what casual commentators have noticed when they speak of "the male role."

Hegemonic masculinity is hegemonic not just in relation to other masculinities, but in relation to the gender order as a whole. It is an expression of the privilege men collectively have over women. The hierarchy of masculinities is an expression of the unequal shares in that privilege held by different groups of men.

3. Collective Masculinities

The gender structures of a society define particular patterns of conduct as "masculine" and others as "feminine." At one level, these patterns characterize individuals. Thus we say that a particular man (or woman) is masculine, or behaves in a masculine way. But these patterns also exist at the collective level. Masculinities are defined and sustained in institutions, such as corporations, armies, government, schools, workplaces, sports organizations and in informal groups, like street gangs. Masculinity also exists impersonally in culture. Video games, for instance, not only circulate stereotyped images of violent masculinity. They require the player to enact this masculinity (symbolically) in order to play the game at all.

4. Active Construction

Masculinities do not exist prior to social behavior, either as bodily states or fixed personalities. Rather, masculinities come into existence as people act. They are accomplished in everyday conduct or organizational life, as patterns of social practice; that is, we "do gender" in everyday life. However, masculinities are far from settled. From bodybuilders in the gym, to managers in the boardroom, to boys in the elementary school playground, a great deal of effort goes into the making of conventional, as well as non-conventional masculinities. Recent research on homosexual men shows that for these men too, identity and relationships involve a complex and sustained effort of construction.

5. Internal Complexity

One of the key reasons why masculinities are not settled, is that they are not simple, homogeneous patterns. Close-focus research on gender, both in psychoanalysis and ethnography, often reveals contradictory desires and logics. A man's active heterosexuality may exist as a thin emotional layer concealing a deeper homosexual desire. A boy's identification with men may co-exist or struggle with identifications with women. The public enactment of an exemplary masculinity may covertly require actions that undermine it. Masculinities may have multiple possibilities concealed within them.

Since different masculinities exist in different cultures and historical epochs, we can deduce that masculinities are able to change. That is, masculine identities are not fixed but are dynamic; particular masculinities are composed, de-composed, contested and replaced. Sometimes this process of contestation and change finds spectacular public expression, in large-scale rallies or demonstrations. More often it is local and limited. Sometimes it becomes conscious and deliberate; at other times it is non-conscious.

Critique and New Directions

In masculinity research, there are real difficulties in defining "masculinity" or "masculinities" (Hearn1996, 1998a; Clatterbaugh 1998). These terms are certainly used in inconsistent ways by different authors. They are often used in ways that imply a simplified and static notion of identity, or rest on a simplified and unrealistic notion of difference between men and women. Hearn and Clatterbaugh are both inclined to drop the concept of masculinities because they think the real object of concern is something else — "men." If, as Clatterbaugh (1998: 41) puts it, "talking about men seems to be what we want to do," why bother to introduce the muddy concept of "masculinities" at all?

But then, why would we talk about "men" in the first place? To talk at all about a group called "men" presupposes a distinction from and relation with another group, "women." That is to say, it presupposes an account of gender. And whichever conceptual language we use, we need some way of talking about men's and women's involvement in that domain of gender. We need some way of naming conduct that is oriented to or shaped by that domain, as distinct from conduct related to other patterns in social life. Hence the need for a concept of "masculinities."

In addition to problems of definition, research on the social construction of masculinities has placed a good deal of emphasis on the uncertainties, difficulties, and contradictions of the process (Messner 1992; Thorne 1993; Connell 1995). Whether the outcomes are stable or unstable, mostly fluid or mostly fixed, is an empirical question, not one to be settled in advance by theory. There are some cases, both in research and in practice (e.g., in work concerning domestic violence), where patterns of masculinity are quite tough and resistant to change (Ptacek 1988). There are other situations where masculinities are unstable, or where commitment to a gender position is negotiable.

Recognizing this possibility raises important questions about when, and why, people hold on to a certain subject position, adopt or reject the possibility of movement.

Finally, the development of global social structures has meant an interaction between the gender orders of colonizers and colonized, sometimes resulting in hybrid or novel gender patterns. Globalization has, further, created new institutions which operate on a world scale, and which provide new arenas for the construction of masculinities: transnational corporations, global markets, global media, intergovernmental institutions.

In these complex and large-scale social processes new patterns of masculinity may emerge. I call these "globalizing masculinities," appearing as they do on a global stage, oriented to a global gender order. Within the contemporary world gender order, the emerging hegemonic form seems to be a masculinity based in multinational corporations and international capital markets, which I call "transnational business masculinity" (Connell 1998).

Briefly, the most powerful group of men in the world are transnational businessmen and the politicians, bureaucrats and generals associated with them. The masculinities of these milieux are historically based on the bourgeois masculinities of the rich countries (Roper 1994; Donaldson 1998; Wajcman 1999). But some new patterns seem to be emerging: a shift towards mobile career structures with very conditional loyalties; a personalized rather than dynastic approach to marriage; the abandonment of commitments to social responsibility through the welfare state or corporate welfare.

While the embodiment of transnational business masculinity has yet to be studied in detail, two points leap to the eye. One is the immense augmentation of bodily powers by technology (air travel, computers, telecommunications), making this to a certain extent a "cyborg" masculinity. The other is the extent to which international businessmen's bodily pleasures escape the social controls of local gender orders, as their business operations tend to escape the control of the national state; along with globalization of business has gone the rapid growth of an international prostitution industry.

Uses of Social Research on Masculinities

Social research is useful at three levels: increasing understanding, solving practical problems, and guiding long-term change. A better understanding of masculinities and men's gender practices is worth having simply because gender is an important aspect of our lives. If we value living in knowledge rather than in ignorance, this subject is significant for education, research and reflection. If we are to think about it at all, we need to think about the whole of the gender equation and all the groups included in it.

There is also a hard practical purpose. Contemporary masculinities are implicated in a range of toxic effects including high levels of injury, such as those caused by road crashes; patterns of ill health and mortality resulting from poor diet, drug abuse, inadequate use of health services; high levels of victimization (men are the majority of victims of reported violence) and imprisonment (about 90 percent of prison inmates are men in countries like Australia and the U.S.). The toxic effects also impact the lives of others: rape and domestic violence against women, homophobic violence and racism (Hearn 1998; Tillner 1997). In dealing with these problems at a practical level, one is constantly led beyond the immediate situation; for instance, a campaign against men's violence against women is led towards issues of prevention as well as an immediate response.

Studies of men and masculinities may also help to identify men's interests in change. There have been two polar positions here: the idea that men share women's interest in changed gender relations, and the idea that men as the dominant group have no interest in change at all. The real position is more complex. Men as a group gain real and large advantages from the current system of gender relations. But some men pay a heavy price for living in the current system, as the observations just made on toxicity go to show. Particular men, or particular groups of men, share with certain women and interest in social safety, in prevention of discrimination, in more inclusive and less hierarchical economies. It is possible to define, for many issues, bases for coalitions for change. More generally, research on multiple forms of masculinity may help people to recognize the diversity of masculinities, and the open-ended possibilities in gender relations — and thus to see alternatives for their own lives.

In the growing gender disparities of the former communist countries, and the decline of the welfare state in the West, we see examples of decline not advance in gender equity. But history is not a one-way street. A more democratic gender order is possible, and some groups of men are working towards it (Segal 1997; Pease 1997). If we are to realize democracy in the gender order, many men must share the burden, and the joy, of creating it.

NOTE

R.W. Connell, 2002, "Understanding Men: Gender Sociology and the New International Research on Masculinities," *Social Thought and Research* 24. Adapted and reprinted by permission.

Clatterbaugh, Kenneth. 1998. "What is Problematic about Masculinities?" *Men and Masculinities* 1,1.

Connell, R.W. 1998. "Masculinities and Globalization." *Men and Masculinities* 1,1.

___. 1995. *Masculinities*. Cambridge: Polity Press.

___. 1996. "Teaching the Boys: New Research on Masculinity, and Gender Strategies for Schools." *Teachers College Record* 98, 2.

Donaldson, Mike. 1998. "The Masculinity of the Hegemonic: Growing Up Very Rich." *Journal of Interdisciplinary Gender Studies* 3,2.

Gierycz, Dorota. 1999. "Women in Decision-Making: Can We Change the Status Quo?" In Ingeborg Breines, Dorota Gierycz and Betty A. Reardon (eds.), *Towards a Women's Agenda for a Culture of Peace*. Paris: UNESCO.

Gilbert, Rob, and Pam Gilbert. 1998. *Masculinity Goes to School*. Sydney: Allen & Unwin.

Hearn, Jeff. 1998. "Theorizing Men and Men's Theorizing: Varieties of Discursive Practices in Men's Theorizing of Men." *Theory and Society* 27,6.

___. 1996. "Is Masculinity Dead? A Critique of the Concept of Masculinity/Masculinities." In M. Mac an Ghaill (ed.), *Understanding Masculinities*. Philadelphia: Open University Press.

McMahon, Anthony. 1999. *Taking Care of Men: Sexual Politics in the Public Mind*. Cambridge: Cambridge University Press.

Messner, Michael A. 1997. *The Politics of Masculinities: Men in Movements*. Thousand Oaks: Sage.

___. 1992. *Power at Play: Sports and the Problem of Masculinity*. Boston: Beacon Press.

Pease, Bob, 1997. *Men and Sexual Politics: Towards a Profeminist Practice*. Adelaide: Dulwich Centre Publications.

Ptacek, James. 1988. "Why Do Men Batter their Wives?" In Kersti Yllo and Michele Bograd (eds.), *Feminist Perspectives on Wife Abuse*. Newbury Park: Sage.

Roper, M. 1994. *Masculinity and the British Organization Man since 1945*. Oxford: Oxford University Press.

Sabo, Donald, and David Frederick Gordon (ed.). 1995. *Men's Health and Illness: Gender, Power, and the Body*. Thousand Oaks: Sage.

Segal, Lynne, 1997. *Slow Motion: Changing Masculinities, Changing Men* (second edition). London: Virago.

Thorne, Barrie. 1993. *Gender Play: Girls and Boys in School*. New Brunswick: Rutgers University Press.

Tillner, Georg. 1997. "Masculinity and Xenophobia." Paper to UNESCO meeting on Male Roles and Masculinities in the Perspective of a Culture of Peace. Oslo.

Walker, Linley, Dianne Butland and Robert W. Connell. 2000. "Boys on the Road: Masculinities, Car Culture, and Road Safety Education." *Journal of Men's Studies* 8,2.

Wajcman, Judy. 1999. *Managing Like a Man: Women and Men in Corporate Management*. Sydney: Allen & Unwin.

21

E-Mail
I Want to Be a Woman

Subject: [Fwd: Fwd: Fwd: I Want to be a Woman]
From: Pamela Downe <downep@duke.usask.ca>
Date: August 1, 2003
To: <undisclosed recipients>

Hi Everyone,
Some of these are really great!
>
>>
>>>I want to be a woman: Quotations about women by women
>>>
>>>1. The hardest years in life are those between ten and seventy.
—Helen Hayes (at seventy-three)
>>>
>>>2. I refuse to think of them as chin hairs. I think of them as stray eyebrows.
—Janette Barber
>>>
>>>3. Who ever thought up the word "Mammogram"? Every time I hear it, I think I'm
supposed to put my breast in an envelope and send it to someone.
—Jan King
>>>
>>> 4. A few weeks ago I went to play catch with my golden retriever. When I bent over
to pick up the ball, my prosthesis fell out. The dog snatched it, and I found myself chasing
him down the road yelling "Hey, come back here with my breast!"
—Linda Ellerbee
>>>
>>>5. Things are going to get a lot worse before they get worse.
—Lily Tomlin
>>>
>>>6. You know the hardest thing about having cerebral palsy and being a woman? It's
plucking your eyebrows. That's how I originally got pierced ears.
—Geri Jewell
>>>
>>>7. A male gynecologist is like an auto mechanic who never owned a car.
—Carrie Snow
>>>
>>>8. Laugh and the world laughs with you. Cry and you cry with your girlfriends.
—Laurie Kuslansky
>>>

>>>9. My second favorite household chore is ironing. My first being hitting my head on the top bunk bed until I faint.
—Erma Bombeck
>>>
>>>10. Old age ain't no place for sissies.
—Bette Davis
>>>
>>>11. The phrase "working mother" is redundant.
—Jane Sellman
>>>
>>>12. Every time I close the door on reality it comes in through the windows.
—Jennifer Unlimited
>>>
>>>13. Thirty-five is when you finally get your head together and your body starts falling apart. —Caryn Leschen
>>>
>>>14. I try to take one day at a time, but sometimes several days attack me at once.
—Jennifer Unlimited
>>>
>>>15. If you can't be a good example, then you'll just have to be a horrible warning.
—Catherine Aird
>>>
>>>16. Behind every successful woman... is a substantial amount of coffee.
—Stephanie Piro
>>>
>>>17. Behind every successful woman... is a basket of dirty laundry.
—Sally Forth

Forging Femininities and Masculinities through Media and Material Cultures

C. Lesley Biggs

> My father did not *invent* Tinkerbell or the bluebell fairy. Rather he used what were cultural fantasies to name something about his deep and complex feelings for his daughter. In return, I, his daughter, took those fantasies to my heart and my unconscious, making them my own. (Walkerdine 1997: 181)

Open the newspaper, turn on the television, listen to the radio, watch a film, drive to the supermarket, surf the Internet; what do you find? A bedazzling array of images — visual and sound — and messages that boggle the mind. From the peccadilloes of *Playboy* and *Playgirl* to the homemakers' advice offered by *Chatelaine* magazine; from the thunderous symphonies of Beethoven to the gender-bending performances of k.d. lang; from the apple pie images of family in *Leave It to Beaver* to the antics of *The Simpsons*; from the racist images of Aunt Jemima to the flattened images of racial diversity in Calvin Klein ads; from tampons soaked in blue ink to the dazzling whiteness of Mr. Clean; and everything in between, we cannot escape this image-saturated culture in which we live. Or can we?

Some of us love all that the consumer culture has to offer. We rush out to buy the newest CD by our favourite artist; can't wait for the release of the next major blockbuster film; read the next bestselling book; or "gotta have" this year's fashions, or the latest hairstyle. Others of us decry mass consumption. At best, we see that consumers are the victims of unrelenting advertising that exploits our fears and anxieties. At worst, we see consumers as cultural dupes who have been seduced by the glitter and glamour of celebrity capitalism. We lament the degradation of our land, water and air, and the tremendous waste of natural resources to produce and sell products. We point to extreme poverty amidst great wealth both within Canada and between Canada and developing countries; and we organize protests against companies that exploit child labour or whose employees work for a pittance in sweatshops. Some of us have a love/hate relationship to the media and consumer culture. We find pleasure in the perfectly muscled body of an athlete but criticize the slim, youthful body as *the* measure for judging an individual's worth; we appreciate the aesthetics of good films, television, and music but abhor the violence, sexism, classism and racism infused in much of media culture; and we value the range of choices that we have as consumers, but we also diligently recycle our bottles, cans, and waste paper and buy products that haven't been tested on animals. And some of us — women, that is — as Valerie Korinek in this section points out, experience "guilty pleasures." Although so many of us are aware that romance novels, women's magazines, popular music, soap operas and "chick flicks" are "politically incorrect," we "read, view, and listen guiltily, or in very extreme cases, secretly, to this material."

Since the beginning of the industrial revolution, women have often been identified with mass consumption, which as Sue Thornham (2000) observes, is negatively positioned in the production/consumption binary.[1] More specifically, women have been associated with conspicuous consumption; the unrelenting demand for more and more consumer goods to satisfy the needs of the domestic sphere and personal adornment. The modern equivalent is the grasping, mindless "'shopaholic'" who is coded female. If women are mindless consumers, then they represent the irrational as opposed to the rational, discerning (read male) consumer. While it may have been true that women in the not-too-distant past were the primary consumers, does this hold true for today? What of men's relationship to mass culture? To what extent are men now the targets of advertising?

Of course, women are not only consumers of media and consumer culture, they are also commodified objects and objects of desire. "Sex sells," as the saying goes, and there is no shortage of material to prove this point. Perhaps the more interesting question is how women (and men) are represented to sell what kinds of products? Under what conditions are relations of difference (race, able-bodiedness, class, age, sexuality) inscribed into the media and consumer culture? How have these images changed over time? How do we decode the meanings of these images? Is there one "correct" read of an image, or are they many? And if multiple interpretations are possible, what conditions structure those readings?

Perhaps the most important question of all is, "what is the impact of these images on 'real' women and men?" Early analyses of the sexist biases in "social texts" such as children's literature and television focused on their content (for example, the absence or presence of female characters and the ways in which these characters were portrayed). By identifying sexist stereotypes and presenting alternative visions of gender relations, the hope was that both male and female readers would develop a less distorted picture of reality and provide a broader range of images of women and men, and girls and boys. The assumption was that changing children's thinking about gender would lead to a change in behaviour. In itself, as Valerie Walkerdine (1990) observes, critiquing sexist images is a worthy goal, but she argues that it is limited and perhaps a tad naïve. In Walkerdine's view, there are two difficulties with this approach. First, there is no guarantee that the desired change in thought and action will actually occur, and second, "that unproblematic transformation will come about through the adoption of non-stereotyped activities. Such an approach assumes a passive learner or rather a rationalist one, who will change as a result of receiving the correct information about how things *really* are" (Walkerdine 1990: 89, emphasis in the original). Instead, Walkerdine argues that cultural products do not exist outside of the "real" world but are sites where we construct meaning, where we seek to create identities for ourselves and define who we are. Readers (in the broadest sense of the word) are actively engaged in complex ways with the media, consumer and popular cultures, accepting some elements while rejecting others.

The point is to understand how we insert ourselves into the dominant discourses of femininity and masculinity; that is, how do we learn to be feminine and masculine. "How can it be," asks Walkerdine, "that femininity [and de facto] is a fiction and yet lived as though it were real, felt deeply, as though it were a universal truth of the psyche?" (Walkerdine 1990: xiii). In answer to her question, she suggests that fantasies are the vehicles through which we insert ourselves into cultural scripts about femininity and masculinity. We are desiring subjects through which we seek to represent ourselves as actors in our own stories and as the fantasized objects of another's desire.

What are some of these fantasies? Many of them centre on a romantic, heterosexual narrative of the "some day my prince will come" variety; to be as beautiful and as sexy as our favourite pop star or movie idol; to have the ideal body; to have the ideal home (á la Martha Stewart); to be the perfect mom; to achieve respectability. Our fantasies are structured by the familial and social worlds in which we live and operate in a dynamic relationship with a variety of cultural products that not only reflect and reproduce practices of femininity and masculinity, but are constitutive of them. Fantasies are sites of pleasure, which is the source of their power, motivating us to engage with cultural products. We buy that magazine or listen to that CD over and over again as a way of creating meaning. But fantasies are also sources of anxiety because most of us cannot realize our dreams and desires, and therein lies their power — striving to fulfil our elusive wishes regulates to varying degrees our actions and limits our imaginative possibilities. Walkerdine argues that as readers of these cultural products, we enter into these cultural practices as ways of resolving, however imperfectly, these psychic and social struggles.

Not everyone, of course, and probably not even most of us at all times, accept willy-nilly the cultural scripts that are handed to us. Either as individuals or as part of subcultures, we resist the dominant definitions of femininity and masculinity (as well as other social relations which structure but do not determine our lives). This defiance was evident in the case for readers of *Chatelaine* magazine who opposed the "Mrs. Chatelaine Contest," an annual essay competition begun in 1961 that valorized homemaking and community service. Valerie Korinek, in her chapter, recounts the ways in which a group of women highjacked the contest by nominating themselves for the award of "Mrs. Slob," women who neither had the time, resources nor inclination to be the "perfect homemaker" envisioned by the editors of *Chatelaine*. Korinek shows that the female readership of *Chatelaine* was a diverse lot who used "key concepts of second wave feminism (that they, in part gleaned from feminist articles published in *Chatelaine*) to critique the more traditional magazine content." Korinek urges us to "critically explore women's cultural products because behind the stereotypical façade, they may well lurk non-traditional and/or subversive content, consumers and producers."

Mrs. Slob's critique of the narrowness of women's roles predated the political activism of second wave feminism. But by the 1970s, second wave feminism was in full swing, and women were asking questions. "Why have there been no great women in film, literature, the fine arts, or music?" "Frustrated by the lack of prominent (or any) positions for women film-makers and film crew members in the National Film Board," Kathleen Shannon "lobbied relentlessly for the establishment of Studio D, which in 1974 became 'the only state-funded feminist film studio of its kind in the world.'" In her chapter, Gail Vanstone explores the legacy of Studio D. As a "voice of, by and for women," Studio D produced over 100 films by the time that it was closed in 1996. But Studio D was not without its controversies as Shannon's second wave agenda clashed with newly emerging feminist culture critics. Accompanying Vanstone's chapter is a poster for the National Film Board's (NFB) award-winning 1992 film *Forbidden Love: The Unashamed Stories of Lesbian Lives*. The NFB's website describes the film as "compelling, often hilarious and always rebellious, nine women paint a portrait of lesbian sexuality against the backdrop of tabloid headlines, book covers and dramatizations from lesbian pulp novels" (NFB 2010). Check out the poster and ask yourself: In what ways are second wave ideas embedded in this image?

Women, as cultural producers, have participated in many artistic practices, but often their work has not been celebrated or considered part of the canon — "a body of works… considered to be established as the most important or significant in a particular field." (Not surprisingly, canon has its roots in ecclesiastical law, but one cannot help but think of the homnyn "cannon" — a mounted gun. In the struggle for meaning, the can(n)on obliterates ideas that don't fit prevailing views.) In the world of music, women have always participated as musicians and performers, but their contributions were rarely recognized as "artistic" or creative. In the early 1970s, feminist musicologists also asked the question, "Why are there no great women composers or musicians?" but this line of inquiry quickly led to the interrogation of the gendering of musical expression. "Feminist scholars," Virginia Caputo observes, "have argued forcefully that music derives multiple meanings from its broader context and that music has much to do with gender as it intersects with other social lines of difference including race, class and sexuality."

In her chapter, Caputo explores the ways in which principally Canadian female artists reinforce elements of patriarchal femininity through their musical practices (e.g., Shania Twain and Celine Dion), those who simultaneously reinforce and challenge these conventions (e.g., Sarah McLaclan and Alanis Morissette), and those who subvert normative expectations of femininity (e.g., k.d. lang). In addition, Caputo examines the concept of "girl power," a phenomenon most widely associated with the Spice Girls, which has generated complex and contradictory responses among audiences and feminist cultural critics alike. Does "girl power" represent a way for young girls to freely express their sexuality or is it yet another mechanism of patriarchal exploitation of girls' sexuality?

The media — whether or not we are talking about newspapers, television, radio, or increasingly the Internet — not only reports on the news, but also has a profound impact on perceptions of the world in which we live. What gets reported, who does the reporting, how the story is told — all influence our interpretation of events and the people who participate in them. In particular, the media's power to persuade has had a major effect on the reception by Canadians to immigrants. Yasmin Jiwani's analysis of the representation of immigrants in the media reveals — at best — a deep ambivalence toward newcomers, especially toward those whose skin colour is not white and/or whose first language is not English.

Unlike overt forms of racial discrimination of the past, the construction of immigrants as the "Other" relies on "inferential racism," and is "encoded in the language of culture and nature." Immigrants are "not like" us Canadians; "'They' are the ones with backward, traditional, barbaric and different customs. 'We' are the ones who are civilized, benevolent, law-abiding and accepting of difference." Moreover, these discourses are deeply gendered; immigrant women are portrayed simultaneously as victims of traditional patriarchal culture and customs, and the exoticized desirable "Other." In contrast, immigrant men are imbricated in criminologic discourses and represented as "gangstas" or otherwise involved in illegal activities. The irony here is that Canada has always been a land of immigrants—indeed Canada's economy is dependent in part on a steady flow of immigrant labour. Moreover, immigrants have enriched the cultural and social life of Canada with the infusion of different and diverse cultural beliefs, traditions, and practices.

What then are the effects of these images on immigrant girls and young women? Like Jo-Anne Lee in her chapter, Jiwani found that these girls and young women carry "'the burden of representation' wherein they feel they are judged by how the media portrays their particular community." As a result, "they are continually made to 'walk the hyphen' between membership in their own communities and finding a sense of inclusion in the larger society." Welcome to Canada!???

Despite the fact that the media is implicated, and in many cases complicit, in producing and perpetuating hierarchies of difference, the experiences of everyday life can offer a counter-narrative to dominant discourses. The dissonance between hegemonic views of the "Other" and self and community representations can make a space in which marginalized groups can create positive and affirming images. Dissatisfied "with creating dark, brooding, political art about gay rights and sexuality" Duncan Campbell began painting "colourful, whimsical paintings of muscle-bound men in love." But in Campbell's view these "pretty pictures" did not conform to his idea of "serious" art, so he adopted the *nom de plume* of Marilyn Cooper. But despite his best intentions to create "completely apolitical" work, Campbell/Cooper found that these depictions of "gay men living in a world without shame, struggle or politics, may be even more political than [his] other, more overt attempts to deal with gay issues."

For centuries, nursery rhymes and fairytales have enchanted and scared the wits out of children as they encounter dragons, monsters, and talking animals, Prince Charmings and beautiful Princesses, witches, wizards, and wicked stepmothers, ogres and fairies. Children, particularly girls, are entranced by these tales, but (to borrow from bpNichol — see Chapter 31) they are also entranced into a world in which images of women and girls vacillate between the innocent (yet desirable) victims of patriarchal cruelty (exercised both by men and women), the jealous and malevolent hag, and in the absence of a "real" mother, the kindly fairy godmother, governess, or nurse (Warner 1994). Female characters were rarely "heroes."

In the 1980s, writers and storytellers began rewriting patriarchal fairytale, but with a new twist. In this genre known as fractured fairytales, popularized by Robert Munsch's *The Paper Bag Princess*, the female character has become the sassy, brave, smart, and resourceful young woman who saves the day with her wit and cleverness. Denis Lee's poem "I Eat Kids Yum! Yum!" continues this tradition. The female persona encounters a monster, but "The child was not amused./She stood there and refused./Then with a skip and a little twirl/She sang the song of a hungry girl:/ 'I EAT MONSTERS BURP!'" Of course, you will have to read the rest of the poem to find out what happens!

Many of us grew up with the idea that "someday my prince will come," and that "we will live happily ever after." In the email "A fairy tale for the assertive woman of the 2000s,"the Princess considers the life (preparing meals, cleaning clothes, bearing children, and feeling forever grateful and happy to do) proposed by the Frog, who will be transformed back into Prince with one (teeny weeny) kiss. But the Princess has other ideas. WARNING! COARSE LANGUAGE.

NOTE

1. Mass culture is not only gendered but it is overlaid with class connotations. Mass consumption/production implies ready-made, or off-the-rack, as opposed to individual, tailor-made and unique products. Mass culture is almost synonymous with popular culture, which is juxtaposed against high culture, suggesting authenticity and refined taste as opposed to the coarse instincts of the *hoi polloi*.

REFERENCES

Bordo, Susan. 1993. *Unbearable Weight: Feminism, Western Culture, and the Body*. Berkeley: University of California Press.

Munsch, Robert. 1980. *The Paper Bag Princess*. Toronto and Vancouver. Annick Press.

NFB (National Film Board). 2010. *Forbidden Love: The Unashamed Stories of Lesbian Lives*. At: onf-nfb.gc.ca/eng/collection/film/?is=28593.

Thornham, Sue. 2000. *Feminist Theory and Cultural Studies*. London: Holden Headline Group.

Walkerdine, Valerie. 1997. *Daddy's Girl: Young Girls and Popular Culture*. Cambridge, MA: Harvard University Press.

___. 1990. *School Girl Fictions*. London and New York: Verso Books.

Warner, Marina. 1994. *From Beast to the Blonde: On Fairy Tales and Their Tellers*. London: Vantage.

Wilson, Elizabeth. 1985. *Adorned in Dreams: Fashion and Modernity*. London: Virago.

Compiled by C. Lesley Biggs

- Worldwide circulation of the feminist publication *Ms. Magazine* per month in 2010: 110,000 copies[2]
- Minimum number of copies that *Playboy* magazine guarantees to its advertisers (the rate base) in 2010: 1.5 million copies[3]
- Number of copies that Playboy magazine sold in 1971 — its peak year: 7.2 million
- Value of *Playboy Enterprises Inc.* in 2010: $230.9 million (U.S.)[4]
- Estimated circulation of *Chatelaine* magazine in 2008: 507,438[5]
- Estimated gross revenue of *Chatelaine* magazine in 2008: $56.5 million[6]
- Estimated advertising revenue of *Chatelaine* magazine in 2008: $50.4 million
- Number of copies per month for all titles of teen magazines sold in the United Kingdom in 1998: 2,441,163[7]
- Number of copies per month for six titles of teen magazines sold in the United Kingdom in 2008: 568,095[8]
- Age when girls express a desire for a thinner body ideal: 6 or 7[9]
- Percentage of Canadian women who are dissatisfied with their bodies: 90[10]
- Average number of Barbie dolls received each year by girls aged 3 to 11 years: 3[11]
- Number of Barbie dolls that are sold worldwide every second: 2
- Revenue of the American toy industry: $15 billion (U.S.)[12]
- Estimated height of Barbie: 6 feet[13]
- Estimated height of average American woman: 5 foot 4 inches
- Estimated weight of Barbie: 101 pounds
- Estimated weight of average American woman: 145 pounds
- Average waist on a woman's size 4 garment in 1997: 25.5 inches[14]
- Average waist on a woman's size 12 garment in 1942: 25 inches
- Ranking of the game Solitaire by female personal computer game players aged 25 to 54 in 2008: 1[15]
- Ranking of the game Solitaire by male personal computer game players aged 25 to 54 in 2008: 1
- Ranking of card games on personal computers in 2008: 1
- Number of personal computer users who played World of Warcraft in 2008: 1.8 million
- Number of men aged 25 to 54 who played World of Warcraft in 2008: 675,713
- Number of women aged 25 to 54 who played World of Warcraft in 2008: 428,621
- Percentage of the most popular videos depicting sexual imagery on Black Entertainment Television in 2001: 84[16]
- Ratio of women in these videos who were dressed in mildly provocative or provocative clothing or wore no clothing at all compared to male characters: 2:1
- Percentage of characters who were male the 101 top-grossing G-rated films from 1990 to 2004: 75
- Percentage of American teenage women who indicated that clothes were their number one item to buy: 48[17]
- Percentage of American teenage boys who indicated that clothes were their number

one item to buy: 24

- Price of Louis Vuitton Bowling Monogram Etoile handbag: $3,100 (U.S.)[18]
- Per capita Gross Domestic Product (GDP) of Afghanistan in 2009: $800 (U.S.)[19]
- Retail price of one pair of Jimmy Choo black leather biker boots: $1,050 (U.S.)[20]
- Percentage of Canadian residents living below after-tax low income cut-offs (below the poverty line) as defined by Statistics Canada: 9.2[21]
- Available income per day for four persons living at the after-tax low income cut-off ($33,946) as defined by Statistics Canada in 2007: $93.00
- Price of Estée Lauder Re-Nutriv Ultimate Lifting Eye Crème (0.5 oz.): $100 (U.S.)[22]
- Per capita GDP of Niger in 2009: $700 (U.S.)[23]
- Percentage of recorded music purchases in the United States in 2008 accounted for by female consumers: 51.5[24]
- Percentage of the female paid labour force working in professional occupations in art and culture as defined by Statistics Canada in 2006: 1.5[25]
- Percentage of the male paid labour force working in professional occupations in art and culture as defined by Statistics Canada in 2006: 1
- Percentage of men who read literature in the United States in 2008: 41.9[26]
- Percentage increase in men's reading rates between 2002 and 2008: +4.3
- Percentage of women who read literature in the United States in 2008: 58
- Percentage increase in women's reading rates between 2002 and 2008: +5
- Estimated number of Internet users worldwide in 2010: 1,966,514,816[27]
- Percentage of the world's population which has access to the Internet in 2010: 28.7
- Percentage of Canadians in the top quintile (more than $95,000) who used the Internet in 2007: 91[28]
- Percentage of Canadians in the lowest quintile (less than $24,000) who used the Internet in 2007: 47
- Percentage of Canadians living in small towns or rural areas who accessed the Internet in 2007: 65
- Percentage of Canadians living in urban areas who used the Internet in 2007: 76
- Percentage of women in Canada in 2009 who used the Internet: 79.7[29]
- Percentage of men in Canada in 2009 who used the Internet: 81
- Percentage of 4,374 Canadian students across 13 institutions in 2009 who own their computers: 93.4[30]
- Percentage of 4,372 Canadian students across 13 institutions in 2009 who use computers for word processing: 99.5
- Percentage of 4,372 Canadian students across 13 institutions in 2009 who use their computers for email and web browsing: 95
- Average number of hours that American children between 8 and 18 years of age in 2004 spent each day using entertainment media (television, commercial or self-recorded video, movies, video games, print, radio, recorded music, computers, and the Internet): 6.35[31]
- Average number of hours per day spent by American children between 0 and 6 years of age in 2004 using screen media (television, movies, computers): 2
- Percentage of children in the United States 8 years and older who had a television in their bedrooms in 2002: 68
- Percentage of children in the United States who had a television in their bedrooms in 1998: 50[32]
- Number of women who have received an Academy Award for Best Director: 1[33]

- Percentage of commercial broadcast American television stations owned by women in 2007: 6[34]
- Percentage of commercial broadcast American television stations owned by people of color in 2007: 3
- Decline in the total number of African-American owned stations between 1998 and 2007: 70
- Percentage of women who are top executives among communications companies in the Fortune 500 in 2007: 15
- Number of women who anchored the prime-time television news program for the "big three" networks — ABC, CBS, NBC — in 2006: 1[35]
- Percentage of reporters/writers and newsroom supervisors working in daily newspapers in the U.S. in 2006 who are white: 90
- Percentage of reporters/writers and newsroom supervisors working in daily newspapers in the U.S. in 2006 who were male: 66.6
- Percentage of American women who worked as directors, executive producers, producers, writers, cinematographers, and editors working on the top 250 domestic grossing films in 2007: 15
- Percentage of American films released in 2007 which employed no women in any of these roles: 21
- Number of American films released in 2007 in which no men played at least one of these roles: 0
- Rate at which male compared to female characters appeared on American television for kids in 2008: 2:1
- Rate at which female compared to male characters are likely to be presented on American television in 2008 in sexy attire: 4:1
- Percentage of speaking characters (both live and animated) appearing in a study of American G-rated films from 1990-2005 who were female: 28
- Percentage of narrators in a study of American G-rated films from 1990-2005 who were male: 4/5
- Percentage of characters appearing in a study of American G-rated films from 1990–2005 who were white: 85
- Percentage of global stories about politics and government in 2009 in which women were the only news subjects:[36] 19[37]
- Percentage of Canadian stories about politics and government in 2009 in which women were the only news subjects: 25
- Percentage of global news subjects in 2009 who were female: 24
- Percentage of Canadian news subjects in 2009 who were female: 30
- Percentage of expert opinion presented in the news globally in 2009 that was male: 80
- Percentage of Canadian expert opinion presented in the news in 2009 that was male: 71
- Percentage of news content globally in 2009 that focused specifically on women: 13
- Percentage of Canadian news content in 2009 that focused specifically on women: 20
- Percentage of television and radio presenters worldwide in 2009 who were women: 49
- Percentage of Canadian television and radio presenters in 2009 who were women: 40
- Percentage of stories worldwide in 2009 that highlighted gender equality or inequality: 6
- Percentage of stories in Canada in 2009 that highlighted gender equality or inequality: 12

- Percentage of actors in the 2007 American prime-time season who were women: 40[38]
- Number of Americans who watched *Desperate Housewives* on April 26, 2009: 13.5 million[39]
- Number of American households that watched the premiere of *The Biggest Loser: Couples* on January 5, 2009: 11 million[40]
- Number of visits to FIFA website during the 31 days of the FIFA World Cup (soccer) in 2010: ¼ billion[41]
- Worldwide audience for the FIFA World Cup (soccer) finals between Spain and the Netherlands held in South Africa in 2010: 700 million viewers[42]
- Estimated revenue accrued by FIFA for television rights to the FIFA World Cup (soccer) in 2010: 2.5 billion (U.S.)[43]
- Estimated number of NBC and CBC viewers for the Stanley Cup final playoff game between the Chicago Blackhawks and Philadelphia Flyers in 2010: 12.36 million[44]
- Estimated number of viewers who watched the Canadian Women's Hockey Team receive the Olympic gold medal after defeating Team U.S.A. on February 25, 2010: 11.3 million[45]
- Revenue generated by the global diet industry in 2010: $59.7 billion[46]
- Revenue generated annually by the global cosmetic surgery industry in 2008: $31.7 billion[47]
- Ranking of liposuction of all cosmetic surgery procedures performed worldwide in 2009: 1 (18.8%)[48]
- Percentage of liposuctions of all cosmetic surgery procedures performed in Canada in 2009: 20.3
- Ranking of breast augmentation of all cosmetic surgery procedures performed worldwide in 2009: 2 (17%)
- Percentage of breast augmentations of all cosmetic surgery procedures performed in Canada in 2009: 25.9
- Ranking of blepharoplasty (upper or lower eyelid lift) of all cosmetic procedures performed worldwide in 2009: 3 (13.5%)
- Percentage of blepharoplasty (upper or lower eyelid lift) of all cosmetic procedures performed in Canada in 2009: 15.8
- Estimated total number of cosmetic procedures performed on women worldwide in 2009: 84.7[49]
- Average salary of a player with the National Hockey League in the 2008 season: $1,906,793[50]
- The median salary of a player with the National Basketball Association in the 2008–2009 season: $3 million[51]
- The salary of a player in the Women's National Basketball Association after 3 years of service in the 2010 season: $51,000[52]

NOTES

1. The original Hypatia Index was compiled by Pamela Downe, with the assistance of Ellen Whiteman. Except when otherwise indicated in the main text, the sources cited in this Index apply to the line where first referenced and then to all those that follow until another endnote appears.
2. Jay Lefkowitz, 2008, "Truth in Advertising," *The Wall Street Journal* January 25. At: online.wsj.com/article/SB120121678290915051.html.
3. Susan Krashinsky, 2010, "Why Hef Wants to Take Playboy Private," *Globe and Mail* July 12. At:

theglobeandmail.com/globe-investor/why-hef-wants-to-take-playboy-private/article1636658.

4. At: topics.nytimes.com/top/news/business/companies/playboy-enterprises-inc/index. html?scp=1&sq=Playboy Enterprises Inc.&st=cse.

5. At: rogerspublishing.ca/portfolio/consumer/chatelaine_eng.

6. James Adams, 2010, "Can Ken Whyte Save *Chatelaine*," *Globe and Mail* May 21. At: theglobeandmail.com/news/arts/can-ken-whyte-save-chatelaine/article1577214.

7. The magazines include *Smash Hits, Just 17, Looks, Jackie, Mizz, Company, 19, Number One, Girl, Blue Jeans* and *My Guy*. At: magforum.com/glossies/teen.htm.

8. The magazines include *Sugar, Bliss, Top of the Pops, Shout, Mizz* and *Kiss*.

9. Hayley Dohnt and Marika Tiggemann, 2006, "Body Image Concerns in Young Girls: The Role of Peers and Media Prior to Adolescence," *Journal of Youth and Adolescence* 35, 2.

10. "FAQ Title," Canadian Women's Health Network. At: cwhn.ca.

11. Ana Enriquez, 2003, "Sounding Barbie's Alarm: A Toy Factory Worker's Story," *Maquila Network Update* (June). At: maquilasolidarity.org/campaign/toy/barbiefactorx.htm.

12. Claire Renzetti and Daniel J. Curran, 1995, *Women, Men and Society* (third edition), Boston: Allyn & Bacon.

13. ANRED, 2002. At: anred.com/stats.html.

14. Michael Kesterton, 1997, "Social Studies." *The Globe and Mail* March 28.

15. Neilsen Co., 2009, "The State of the Video Gamer: PC Game and Video Game Console Usage Fourth Quarter." At: blog.nielsen.com/nielsenwire/wp-content/uploads/2009/04/stateofvgamer_040609_fnl1.pdf.

16. American Psychological Association, 2007, *Report of the Task Force on the Sexualization of Girls*. At: apa.org/pi/women/programs/girls/report-full.pdf.

17. Magazine Publishers of America, 2004, *Teen Market Profile*. At: magazine.org/content/files/teenprofile04.pdf.

18. At: louisvuitton.com.

19. At: cia.gov/library/publications/the-world-factbook/geos/af.html.

20. At: saksfifthavenue.com.

21. Statistics Canada, 2009, *Income in Canada, 2007*, Ottawa: Ministry of Industry. At: dsp-psd.pwgsc.gc.ca/collection_2009/statcan/75-202-X/75-202-x2007000-eng.pdf.

22. At: saksfifthavenue.com.

23. At: cia.gov/library/publications/the-world-factbook/geos/ng.html.

24. Recording Industry of America, 2008, *2008 Consumer Profile*. At: riaa.com/keystatistics.

25. Statistics Canada, 2006, Census, *National Occupational Classification for Statistics (60) 2006 Class of Worker (6) and Sex (3) for the Labour Force 15 Years and Over of Canada, Provinces, Territories, Census Divisions and Census Subdivisions, 2006 Census — 20% Sample Data*. At: 12.statcan.gc.ca/census-recensement/2006.

26. U.S. National Endowment for the Arts, 2009, *Reading on the Rise: A New Chapter in American Literacy*. At: nea.gov/research/ReadingonRise.pdf.

27. Internet World Stats, 2010, June 30. At: internetworldstats.com/stats.htm.

28. Statistics Canada, 2008, *The Daily* July 12. At: statcan.gc.ca/daily-quotidien/080612/dq080612b-eng.htm.

29. Statistics Canada, 2010, "Characteristics of Individuals Using the Internet." At: 40.statcan.gc.ca/l01/cst01/comm35a-eng.htm.

30. Media Awareness Network, 2010, *Digital Literacy in Canada: From Inclusion to Transformation. A Submission to the Digital Economy Strategy Consultation*. At: media-awareness.ca/english/corporate/media_kit/digital_literacy_paper_pdf/digitalliteracypaper.pdf.

31. American Academy of Pediatrics, Council on Communications and Media, 2009, "Policy Statement on Media and Violence," revised from 2001. At: appolicy.aappublications.org/cgi/content/full/pediatrics;124/5/1495.

32. Public Agenda On-Line, 2003, "The Family: Major Proposals." At: publicagenda.org/issues/angeles_graph.cfm?issue_type=family.

33. Kathryn Bigelow won in 2009 for *The Hurt Locker*.

34. National Organization of Women, "Women in the Media Fact Sheet." At: now.org/issues/media/

women_in_media_facts.html.

35. CBS hired Katie Couric, who was the first female solo anchor of a weekday network evening news broadcast and the program's managing editor.

36. News subjects are defined as the people who are interviewed or whom the news is about.

37. Global Media Monitoring Project, 2010, "Report." At: whomakesthenews.org/images/stories/website/gmmp_reports/2005/gmmp-report-en-2005.pdf.

38. At: womensenews.org/story/commentary/070425/prime-time-tv-sweeps-women-all-time-lows.

39. Benjamin Toff, 2009, "Ratings: *Desperate Housewives* Draws Highest Audience on Sunday," *New York Times* April 27. At: mediadecoder.blogs.nytimes.com/2009/04/27/ratings-desperate-housewives-draws-highest-audience-on-Sunday.

40. Rick Porter, 2010, "TV ratings: '*NCIS*,' '*Biggest Loser*' sack Orange Bowl Tuesday," *Zap 2 It* January 6. At: blog.zap2it.com/frominsidethebox/2010/01/tv-ratings-ncis-biggest-loser-sack-orange-bowl-tuesday.html.

41. At: fifa.com/worldcup/organisation/media/newsid=1273696/index.html#fifa+attracts+over+quarter+billion+visits+world+engages+online+with+2010+cup.

42. Oneindia News, 2010, July 13. At: news.oneindia.in/2010/07/13/fifa-world-cup-2010-finals-spain-holland-tv-audien.html.

43. At: eufootball.biz/finance/7151-2010_world_cup_expected_revenue.html.

44. At: nhl.com/ice/news.htm?id=531630.

45. At: channelcanada.com/Article4139.html.

46. Jessica Rao, 2010, "It's the Year of the Value Diet," June 18. At: cnbc.com/id/37492840/It_s_The_Year_of_The_Value_Diet.

47. SoCal Cosmetic Network, 2009, "Cosmetic Surgery Industry to Exceed $40 billion by 2013," September 11. At: .socalcosmetics.com/cosmetic-surgery-industry-to-exceed-40-billion-in-revenues-by-2013.

48. Science 2.0, 2010, "Worldwide Plastic Surgery Statistics Are In: The U.S. Wins by a Nose," August 9. At: science20.com/news_articles/worldwide_plastic_surgery_statistics_are_and_us_wins_nose. See "Total Procedures for Top 25 Countries" for individual country statistics.

49. International Society of Aesthetic Plastic Surgery, 2009, "Biennial Global Survey." At: .isaps.org/uploads/news_pdf/Analysis_iSAPS_Survey2009.pdf.

50. At: tsn.ca/nhl/story/?id=240324.

51. *USA Today*, 2010, "Databases. Salaries." At: content.usatoday.com/sports/basketball/nba/salaries/mediansalaries.aspx?year=2008-09html.

52. "Women's Basketball Online." At: womensbasketballonline.com/wnba/rosters/salary.html.

"Mrs. Slob's" Manifesto
A Case Study in Critical Reading of *Chatelaine* Magazine

Valerie J. Korinek

Few students and scholars within the field of women's and gender studies are unfamiliar with the guilty pleasures of consuming women's cultural products. Whether your products of choice are romance novels, women's magazines, popular music, soap operas or the so-called "chick flicks," we are simultaneously aware of the elitist scorn of many feminist and anti-feminist critics alike who dismiss this material as brainless, escapist fare. So fans, particularly those university educated ones, read, view and listen guiltily, or in very extreme cases, secretly, to this material. Meanwhile, untroubled by these concerns, the entertainment conglomerates happily rake in the profits because of the immense popularity of these gendered genres. Within the past ten to twenty years, this blanket condescension has been unsettled by a number of feminist academics — working in fields as diverse as history, English, sociology, cultural studies and anthropology — who have begun to critically study the myths about these products.[1] While results of these studies vary, what the scholars have discovered is that the world of women's cultural products is significantly more complex and important than its critics acknowledge.

What follows is a case study drawn from the pages of Canada's premier adult women's magazine — *Chatelaine*. This chapter demonstrates the important role that readers' creativity and agency played in interpreting the magazine's material. In this situation a contest chosen to award Canadian homemakers was hijacked by a lively group of women who identified themselves as "slobs." Clearly, this was an unconventional ending for a traditional women's magazine contest — and yet the Mrs. Chatelaine Contest highlights a number of important factors. First, it demonstrates the ways in which a diverse readership interpreted the material. Second, it highlights the ways in which readers employed key concepts of second wave feminist ideals (that they, in part, gleaned from feminist articles published in *Chatelaine*) to critique the more traditional magazine content. In the pages of *Chatelaine* magazine in the fifties and sixties, Canadian women were exposed to a wide-ranging amount of material on topics we now consider representative of second wave feminist concerns — pay equity, divorce legislation, working outside the home, child welfare, sexuality and reproduction. Additionally, *Chatelaine* was one of the key media voices that implored the federal government to investigate women's status. Later they gave significant coverage to both the study and the final *Report of the Royal Commission on the Status of Women* (Canada 1970). Third, it confirms the importance of close readings of so-called "traditional" material. The fate of the Mrs. Chatelaine Contest illustrates the need to explore critically women's cultural products, because behind the stereotypical facade, there may well lurk non-traditional and/or subversive content, consumers and producers.

The "Mrs. Chatelaine Contest"

In 1961, *Chatelaine* created the Mrs. Chatelaine Contest, an annual essay competition open to all Canadian homemakers. The preferred entrant was a married woman with children. Women who entered were required to answer questions about their families, thoughts about marriage and mothering, favourite recipes, descriptions of their home's interior design.

According to E.H. Gittings, Assistant Advertising Sales Manager for *Chatelaine*, the contest's popularity had exceeded Maclean Hunter's expectations: "We received approximately 5,700 entries from our English edition and 400 entries from our French edition. Some of the entries were very elaborate indeed. They included such things as samples of pies, cookies, tape recordings of their voices and, in practically all cases, it was obvious that these readers had spent literally days preparing their entries. Mrs. Saxton who won the contest last year, confessed after she had been selected that she had spent over 150 hours preparing her entry."[2] By all accounts, both in number of entries received and in the amount of time contestants put into their entries, the contest was a success. Of course, the prizes were also very enticing. They included two first-class tickets to Paris, hotel accommodation, $1,000 cash and a new wardrobe.

J.L. Adams, *Chatelaine* Manager for Eastern Canada, described the first winner, Mrs. Joyce Saxton, of Plenty, Saskatchewan, as a "charming and delightful person."[3] A farm wife and mother of three children, Saxton was a hyper-energetic housewife who was active in nine community groups in addition to her farm wife duties: "[she] preserved 140 quarts of fruit preserves last summer, 60 jars of jellies, 260 packs of frozen fruit and vegetables; sews most of her children's clothes and some of her own."[4]

Not all readers were cut from the same cloth. For them, the Mrs. Chatelaine Contest highlighted actual or imagined inadequacies in their various roles as wives, mothers and often workers. One woman, Beatrice Maitland of Chatham, N.B., took matters into her own hands and decided to write to the magazine and nominate herself for the "Mrs. Slob 1961" contest (Maitland's invention). The following excerpt from her first letter to editor Doris Anderson provided her humourous critique of the standards required of "Mrs. Chatelaine" and is a wonderful example of readers creativity in fashioning "oppositional" readings of *Chatelaine* material:

Yesterday was the closing date for your Mrs. Chatelaine contest, but I didn't enter.... I wish someone, sometime, would have a competition for "Mrs. Nothing!!" A person who isn't a perfect housekeeper, a faultless mother, a charming hostess, a loving wife, or a servant of the community. Besides being glamourous as a model, talented as a Broadway star and virtuous as a Saint. I have studied your questionnaire carefully but my replies are hopelessly inadequate.... To start with my appearance is absolutely fatal.... I am overweight, pear-shaped and bow legged. Consequently, not having much to work on I don't bother and cover it up with comfortable, warm old slacks.... Now, housework. Failure there too as I am a lousy housekeeper.... Entertaining? Practically never.... A game of cards or just talk with a few beers. No fancy food, drinks or entertainment.... Meals?... We prefer plain meat and potato-vegetable meals with no frills. For birthdays our children choose the dinner. What's the menu? Usually hamburgers and chips. You can't win. Make a fancy meal from a magazine and they look like they are being poisoned.... The decor is middle English European junk shop, especially when the children start doing their homework. Community activities? I have always belonged to and worked with other organizations... but I have become so sick of and bored with meetings I quit.... My philosophy as a home-maker — I guess that is, be happy, don't worry. You do what you can with what you've got when you feel like it. Consequently I'm never sick and I've got no nerves or fears. That is poor me.... So if you want to run a contest for "Mrs. Slob 1961" I would be happy to apply and would probably win hands down. Thank you for your enjoyable magazine and my apologies for taking up your time.[5]

Maitland's self-deprecatory style of humour and her parody of the conventions of the contest made for a witty letter. However, there was a considerable edge to her "manifesto," since she challenged the preferred reading of the contest — that all Canadian women aspired to or could afford the easy affluence of suburbia. The "Mrs. Chatelaine" mantel was awarded on the basis of family life, community volunteer work, philosophy of marriage and child rearing, interior design and fashion sense. Many readers were quick to condemn articles which they felt were geared to "higher-income" earners and not average Canadians. The tensions between the magazine's middle-class presumptions and the large number of working-class and rural readers was a constant source of friction. As an RCAF (Royal Canadian Air Force) wife with three kids, Maitland was clearly not part of the "better-sort" of reader the magazine's advertisers and publisher sought.

Anderson's response praised Maitland's "wit" and "good humour" and acknowledged that the "Mrs. Chatelaine contest sets up pretty formidable rules but, in our defense, the woman who won it last year was a fairly average homemaker in western Canada who lived on a farm."[6] Neither Anderson nor Maitland anticipated the response that would follow the publication of her letter in the February 1962 issue. According to Maitland's own description, having her letter published in *Chatelaine* was akin to having a "best-seller." "When I wrote that letter to you, back in the fall, I never dreamed that such a furore would ensue," Maitland wrote. "My stars! It's as good as having a best-seller! Strangers have shook my hand and said, 'Welcome to the Club.' And it's buzzing all over our PMQ [Permanent Married Quarters]. I have also had a lot of letters all very much in agreement. Who would have thought there were so many slobs in the country?"[7]

Who would have guessed so many slobs read *Chatelaine*? Despite the magazine's attempts to encourage household perfection and reward the ideal Canadian homemaker, the Mrs. Slobs refused to re-create themselves in that mold. With Maitland's treatise as their rallying cry, they wrote to her and to the magazine professing support and encouragement to all the other Canadian slobs. Anderson's reply acknowledged that Maitland's letter and the ensuing letters in her support provided a wake-up call for the magazine: "You certainly did stir up a furore. I for one found it extremely interesting to realize what a great load of guilt most of the housewives of this country carry around on their shoulders. It makes me a little guilty that women's magazines probably contribute as much as any medium to this feeling. Thank you for reminding us."[8]

The letters professing solidarity with Maitland came from all regions of the country. This brief sampling captures the spirit of the letters (see Korinek 1996). Most continued Maitland's critique of the contest's middle-class bias and rather limiting role prescribed for Canadian wives and mothers. F. Miller of New Westminister, B.C., wrote: "I received my issue of *Chatelaine* about one half hour ago and turned immediately to 'The last word is yours.' I say Three Cheers for Mrs. Beatrice Maitland."[9] C. Cserick of Ottawa deduced that the magazine was to blame for its unattainable style of homemaking and its focus upon the suburban family. "To be brutally frank I love *Chatelaine*," Cserick wrote. "But dear old *Chatelaine*, you write very little about us — don't you — we don't have a home of our own — 2 bedrooms is all, but we do like to read, listen to good music, watch good TV shows, take in a really excellent movie, drink gallons of coffee at odd hours, love our husband and kids, care for them and do 100 menial jobs a day."[10] Finally, a letter from Mrs. Neil Ferguson of Dutch Brook, Nova Scotia, warrants attention for its explicit class analysis. "In the last two Mrs. Chatelaine contests it was quite well-to-do women that won. Do people from the middle-class income bracket ever enter these contests?" Ferguson wondered. "There are a lot of women that would certainly enter if they could fill out the entry forms but how can they say how well they entertain when they are racking their brains as to what to cook up for their family for a hearty good meal when maybe there is very little pay coming in to provide the proper ingredients for a proper meal...."[11] Clearly, readers' class identifications were elastic. Nevertheless, regardless of their incomes, they believed that the magazine's material should be accessible to all readers. Anderson's responded that the winners had both been in the $5,000 income bracket, "average" for Canadian families at that time and thus not beyond the realm of the majority of readers.

Throughout the decade, the debate over the "perfection" of Mrs. Chatelaine was re-visited yearly, after the publication of the winner and the regional runners-up. The oppositional and alternate readings, along with the large numbers of women who decoded the preferred meaning and honed their contest entries year after year, indicate the variety of ways Canadian women "read" the periodical. Intended as a celebration of homemaking, it often became a celebration of slobs, the working-class and regional difference. The editorial and advertising directives (which hoped that this feature would support the departmental features, and thus the advertisers' products) often fell on blind eyes because many Canadian women could not identify with its presumption of a middle-class, homemaking role for all women. Hence, they offered oppositional readings, or alternate and critical commentary, about what they considered an "unrepresentative" and hence unfair contest. They didn't meekly follow the prescription to become homemakers and they didn't cancel their subscriptions. Instead, they demanded that the magazine change. And *Chatelaine* did. By 1969, the contest was not afforded as prominent coverage in the periodical, and that year's winner was a working wife and mother who bluntly told readers that she had no time for volunteer groups.

In the seventies the contest was quietly abandoned. The concept was revamped into a new annual feature called *Chatelaine's* "Woman of the Year." The "Woman of the Year" was nominated by the editorial staff and once again, the emphasis was on celebration. Instead of home-making skills, this time the magazine applauded Canadian women's *forté* in the public realm, including, politics, the arts, academe, business or volunteering. In 1992, the magazine gained attention and some notoriety for nominating the pride of Consort, Alberta, singer/songwriter k.d. lang. By the convention of the Woman of the Year format, lang did double duty as both the subject of a lengthy profile article (which focused on her professional accomplishments) and as that issue's "cover girl." Although the singer believed that she and the magazine had an agreement regarding the re-touching of the cover photo, prior to publication lang's portrait was airbrushed to include makeup, and the resultant cover image received considerable commentary. At the time of the publication, lang's lesbianism had not been made official public knowledge. However as one of the most poorly kept "secrets" within the field of Canadian popular music, her sexual orientation would not have been unknown to the editors. Their selection of "the maverick" (their words) lang, then, can be attributed to two overt goals — to recognize her achievements and to attract a more diverse crowd of "younger" readers. Amongst themselves, it was also, no doubt, covertly, a bit of subversive fun for those readers who were in the know — a wink, wink, nudge, nudge towards the conventions of the women's magazine world. For the vast majority of unassuming readers, the article could be read "straight" as a tale of feisty, western-Canadian gal who'd made good in the North American music industry. In return for their unconventional choice, the feature was immortalized in one of lang's best-selling songs, "Miss Chatelaine," which gently pokes fun at her cover-girl debut.

What links the experiences of Mrs. Slob and "Miss Chatelaine," beyond their obvious value as compelling stories, is the way they demonstrate the magazine's variety and playfulness in addition to the reader's agency. Within the corporate entity that was *Chatelaine* magazine, editors and writers were often broadly political, even feminist, and occasionally delighted in planting subversive articles, images or letters. Equally, readers were not passive dupes — they were engaged in decoding the magazine based on their own interests and from their own regional, racial, class and gendered identities. Ultimately a close reading of Mrs. Slob's "manifesto" validates the importance of research on the so called "mundane" women's cultural product. We need more work on these topics if we are to accurately understand why countless readers and consumers find these products compelling fare.

NOTES

Valerie Korinek, 2000, *Roughing It in the Suburbs: Reading Chatelaine Magazine in the Fifties and Sixties*, Toronto: University of Toronto Press. Adapted and reprinted with permission of the publisher.

1. This is a burgeoning field of academic study. For further exploration of gender, popular culture and consumption see: Adams (1997); Ballaster et al. (1991); Currie (1999); Hermes (1995); Meyerowitz (1994); Radway (1991); and Schwichtenberg (1993).

2. Public Archives of Ontario [PAO] Maclean Hunter Record Series [MHRS] F-4-a-b Box 431, E.H. Gittings, Assistant Advertising Sales Manager for *Chatelaine* to Mr. F.D. Adams, 22 June 1961.

3. PAO MHRS F-4-1-b Box 431, J.L. Adams, Manager for Eastern Canada (*Chatelaine*) to L.M. Hodgkinson, 14 February 1961.

4. "Meet Mrs. Chatelaine," 1961, *Chatelaine*, April, 111.

5. PAO MHRS F-4-3-a Box 434, Mrs. Beatrice Maitland, Chatham, NB, to Doris Anderson, 1 November 1961.

6. PAO MHRS F-4-3-a Box 434, Doris Anderson to Mrs. Beatrice Maitland, 10 November 1961.

7. PAO MHRS F-4-3-a Box 434, Mrs. Beatrice Maitland to Doris Anderson, 2 February 1962.

8. PAO MHRS F-4-3-a Box 434, Doris Anderson to Beatrice Maitland, 12 February 1962.

9. PAO MHRS F-4-3-a Box 434, Mrs. F. Miller, New Westminister, BC, to Doris Anderson, 12 January 1962.

10. PAO MHRS F-4-3-a Box 434, Clara Cserick, "Slob par excellence," Ottawa to Doris Anderson, 27 January 27 1962.

11. PAO MHRS F-4-3-a Box 435, Mrs. Neil Ferguson, Dutch Brook, NS, to Doris Anderson, 25 September 1962.

REFERENCES

Adams, Mary Louise. 1997. *The Trouble with Normal*. Toronto: University of Toronto Press.

Ballaster, Ros, et al. 1991. *Women's Worlds: Ideology, Feminism and the Women's Magazine*. Toronto: MacMillan Educational.

Canada. 1970. *Report of the Royal Commission on the Status of Women*. Hull: Information Canada.

Currie, Dawn. 1999. *Adolescent Magazines and their Readers*. Toronto: University of Toronto Press.

Hermes, Joke. 1995. *Reading Women's Magazines: An Analysis of Everyday Media*. New York: Polity Press.

Korinek, Valerie J. 1996. "Mrs. Chatelaine versus the Slobs: Contestants, Correspondents and the Chatelaine Community in Action, 1961–1969." *Journal of the Canadian Historical Association* 7.

Meyerowitz, Joanne (ed.). 1994. *Not June Cleaver: Women and Gender in Postwar America: 1945–1960*. Philadelphia: Temple University Press.

Radway, Janice. 1991. *Reading the Romance: Women, Patriarchy and Popular Literature*. Chapel Hill: University of North Carolina Press.

Schwichtenberg, Cathy (ed.). 1993. *The Madonna Connection: Representational Politics, Subcultural Identities, and Cultural Theory*. Boulder, CO: Westview Press.

D is for Daring
The Women Behind the Films of Studio D

Gail Vanstone

Studio D of the National Film Board (NFB) was founded in 1974, the only state-funded feminist film studio of its kind in the world.[1] Studio D's collective imagination was directed towards placing women's issues at the centre of national interests.

Studio D was inspired by second wave feminism: frustrated by the lack of prominent (or any) positions for women filmmakers and film crew members in the NFB, Kathleen Shannon, a respected NFB editor and filmmaker in the *Challenge for Change* series, lobbied relentlessly for Studio D's inception. Shannon became the studio's backbone and its longest-serving executive producer.

Created on the heels of the release of recommendations contained in the *Royal Commission on the Status of Women* (1970), Studio D constituted a significant thread in the fabric of women's activism broadly drawn across Canada to create a more equitable situation for its female citizens. Styled as a "voice of, by and for women," Studio D claimed the role of cultural producer mediating between the state and its women as citizens/constituents. Its 1996 closure signalled an official retreat from women's issues and a new chapter in the struggle of Canadian women nationally to have their voices heard and their stories taken seriously.

Studio D leaves behind it a complex legacy, an archive of over a hundred films from its early "realist" documentaries such as Shannon's *Working Mothers* series to later more stylistically complex films like the Genie award-winning *Forbidden Love: The Unashamed Stories of Lesbian Lives* (1992).[2] (See the accompanying image of the poster for this film.) This collection of documentaries captures landmarks of, and tensions arising from, feminist activity in the 1970s, 1980s and 1990s: it provides a unique, though not uncontested, account of the Canadian women's movement from the mid-1970s to the late 1990s. How many of these films will survive the transition from film and video stock to digitized material is a pressing question for feminism and film.

Critics charged that Studio D was a haven for white middle-class filmmakers. This was essentially a veiled complaint against liberal feminism for operating within existing power structures. Radical and socialist feminists agitating for dramatic social change scorned liberal feminism for its problematic mainstreaming of gender, depending on government and organizational policies to ensure that women secure the same legal rights, and educational and work opportunities as men. Even though Shannon's own political philosophy was closely aligned with her more radical sisters, the very location and operation of Studio D in the embrace of the NFB, an instrument of the state, made it a lightning rod for such criticism. Studio D was an understandable target, if we weigh liberal (1970s) feminism against more sophisticated models, for instance the feminist anti-race and/or post-colonial developments of the 1980s and 1990s.

Further, Shannon was suspicious of emerging models of feminist film criticism derived from Marxist, semiotic, and psychoanalytic approaches rooted in dense theoretical language which Shannon regarded as elitist and inscrutable for the "ordinary woman." As a result, Studio D was at odds with some independent filmmakers exploring filmic narrative and structure from the perspective of these critical approaches. Vilifying the studio for excluding certain feminist filmmakers and producing naïve or politically dicey documentaries, its critics could be found variously in the ranks of government, the academy, and the religious and political right. Its champions, many drawn from the same spheres, far outnumbered its detractors. In retrospect, the studio's legacy is impressive. Many women working in film in Canada today were associated in one way or another with Studio D. Overall, Studio D stands as an intriguing study and a site of contradiction. Studio D was an official instrument of a second wave feminism that organised both the Studio's institutional structure and its documentary film production around the process of consciousness raising hitched to the concept "the personal is political." Studio D was also a cultural producer mediating between the state and its women as citizens/constituents.

Forbidden Love: The Unashamed Stories of Lesbian Lives, ©1992 National Film Board of Canada. All rights reserved; reprinted with permission.

NOTES

1. For a more detailed history, see Gail Vanstone, 2007, *D Is For Daring: The Women Behind the Films of Studio D*, Toronto: Sumach Press.
2. Employing a hybrid structure, the filmmakers explore ways of knowing in a "serious" yet "playful" narrative structured around two film styles: documentary and melodrama. Real-life interviews of ten lesbians and portions of 1950s archival footage are interspersed with melodramatic dramatizations from a fictitious pulp romance novel bearing the same title as the film.

REFERENCE

Canada. 1970. *Report of the Royal Commission on the Status of Women*. Hull: Information Canada.

Music and Gender

Virginia Caputo

> The distinction that needs to be drawn is between how people use music and how people perceive music…. I'm interested here in the social process, that begins with perception, but it centers in engagement, in meanings being made through listening experiences as they are woven into the fabric of daily life. (Feld 1990: 164–65)

> Music is a domain in our lives through which we can express desire, establish relationships, and actualize self. (Diamond 2000: 131)

Music is a dynamic cultural discourse that intertwines with people's lives in important ways. It is part of a broad network that people use to express, negotiate, share and contest meaningful aspects of their lives. Gender is one such aspect of social life. Performers, composers and consumers of music from various social and cultural locations engage in the process of negotiating gender meanings through music. Thus music provides an important site to explore diverse ways that people experience and understand gender, and to look at how they negotiate and play with ideals, beliefs and stereotypes of gender, even as they accommodate them in their everyday life experiences.

In this chapter, I explore some of the links between music and gender with a view to understanding how social categories such as male, female, masculinity, and femininity are embodied through music. For women's studies scholars, music as a social and cultural practice provides a window through which to view a variety of expressions of femininities and masculinities that may exist simultaneously within the same context. Understanding the impact of patriarchal constructions of femininity and masculinity, and finding ways to effect positive change in these constructs are also centrally relevant to women's studies. For these reasons, among others, music, and popular culture more generally, have become increasingly important sites for understanding the process of gendering through sounds, texts, images and representations (music, magazines, videos, television programs, films) and the ways they depict and encode relations of power in society.

The chapter begins with a very brief overview of some of the key questions in the scholarly study of music and gender from the viewpoint of both musicology and popular music studies. The next section highlights the work of a number of Canadian mainstream popular music artists. It illustrates how music can be used to make and remake understandings of gender at individual, interpersonal and institutional levels. The chapter ends with a discussion of the concept of "girl power."

Scholarly Studies of Music and Gender

In the late 1970s, feminist scholars began exploring the links between gender and musical practices. Early research efforts in musicology — the scholarly study of music — focused on the catalyst question: why have there been no great women musicians and composers? Subsequent research examined questions regarding institutional access, women's involvement in composition, systems of valuation of certain musical genres over others, the implications of canon formation for women musicians, women's roles in music historically, patronage in music, and so on. Two key assumptions underscore this work: (a) gender is a distinct social force in the ways music is practised and understood; and (b) music is tied to its socio-political context (McClary 1991: 79). By arguing that music derives multiple meanings from its broader context, feminist scholars working in this area have argued forcefully that music has much to do with gender as it intersects with other social lines of difference including race, class and sexuality. Moreover, scholars have argued that dichotomies such as high/popular music, mind/body and other dualisms need to be interrogated using a feminist lens. With regard to music and sexuality in particular, the rational/emotional binary has contributed historically to the perception that music is an emotional activity and, therefore, relegated to a feminine realm. Feminist music scholars in the 1990s debated this feminization of music and the way in which it gave rise to homophobia in music history and criticism (Brett, Wood and Thomas 1994; Cusick 1994). Using queer theories of gender, these scholars asserted the importance of exploring sexuality as another kind of difference and position from which to listen to and speak about music and musical experiences that work in tandem with gender.

Popular Music Studies

Popular music is an umbrella term for a number of different styles and repertoires of music, including pop, jazz, hip hop and rock, that lie outside of what is commonly understood as "classical" music. Popular music scholars examine the process by which people make meanings and ascribe values to the sounds of music (Wicke 1990). Some popular music scholars focus on exploring the ways in which music connects with gendered social experiences in the lives of women and girls. They explore listening and consumption practices, women's involvement in popular music as performers and producers of music, constructions of gendered and racialized identities in popular music performance, the rise of girl groups, portrayals of women in song texts and music videos, gender and genres (rock music, blues, hip hop, riot grrrl, teen pop music), the body in performance, issues of difference and diversity, sexualities and music performance and reception and music and gendered subjectivities, to name a few (Frith and McRobbie 1979; Rose 1994; Whiteley 1997; Dibben 1999; Bradby and Laing 2001; Fast 2001; Pegley 2008).

For feminist scholars of popular music, one of the key concerns has been to interrogate the process by which gendered subjectivities reflect, challenge and resist patriarchal constructions of femininity through music. For example, some scholars investigating the portrayal of women and the impact of this portrayal on those consuming the music have asked questions such as, what values and ideas about women are promoted through popular music and how are these ideas sustained? What roles are available for women in music in contemporary contexts and how can these roles be expanded? What is the impact of patriarchal images, words and sounds in the lives of women? How can music be used to effect change in the lives of women and girls? How do gender, race, sexuality and class intersect in popular music? These are a few of the questions that are part of understanding the process of gendering that works through music and musical practices. The next section explores this process in greater detail.

Music and the Process of "Gendering"

Music, like other cultural practices, encodes and is guided by ideologies of gender. In the nineteenth and early twentieth centuries, for example, certain kinds of music and musical activities were deemed appropriate for women (singing and playing the piano within the home, teaching piano to children) and for men (playing and conducting orchestras, teaching in academies of music). With regard to European art-based music, musicologists Susan Cook and Judy Tsou (1994) have argued that these ideas extend to questions of creativity and genius as well. In their view, gender influences all aspects of music.

These historical ideas about the gendering of music resonate in contemporary contexts where gender remains integral to the ways musical practices and activities are currently perceived and defined. One illustrative example is the centrality of singing and playing acoustic instruments as a way for contemporary female artists to participate in mainstream popular music. These activities reinforce elements of patriarchal definitions of femininity: i.e., an emphasis on body versus mind (sound produced through the body alone rather than by instruments); reproduction versus production (women assuming musical roles as performers rather than composers); and "nature" versus "culture" (acoustic rather than electronic instruments).

Mainstream popular music provides many examples of artists who participate in music primarily as vocalists. They include Beyoncé, Shakira, Britney Spears, Rihanna, Katy Perry, Ke$ha, Miley Cyrus, Mariah Carey and Lady Gaga. Celine Dion, Nelly Furtado and Shania Twain are three Canadian artists that can be added to this list, although Twain has sometimes been credited with co-writing material on her CDs, and Furtado is known as a songwriter and record producer. For the most part, marketing strategies and promotional materials for these artists emphasize their gender, singing voices, body image and feminized/sexualized styles. Other Canadian female musical artists participate in both reinforcing and challenging these conventions of femininity through their music and performance styles. Artists such as Sarah McLachlan, Alanis Morissette, and k.d. lang actively participate in the process of gendering through the genres in which they participate and by cultivating an image that resists and blurs gender boundaries.

Sarah McLachlan, for instance, adheres to certain gendered expectations as a singer and acoustic pianist. However, as a respected songwriter and the driving force behind Lilith Fair, one of the most financially successful North American concert tours of 1997, she also challenges gender conventions. Her Lilith Fair efforts were acknowledged by a 2000 Juno Award for international achievement. Despite the commercial success of the Lilith Fair tour, however, media reviews of the concerts tended to focus on the appearance of the performers rather than their abilities as instrumentalists, vocalists and songwriters, or the style and presentation of the performances. In 2010, Sarah McLachlan returned with a second Lilith Fair tour, featuring over ninety artists traveling to twenty-three cities in Canada and the U.S. Despite raising close to $500,000 for women's charities, the tour suffered low ticket sales and a lukewarm media response that forced the cancellation of a number of dates.

Similarly, Alanis Morissette both upholds and challenges gender normative expectations. She is known primarily as a vocalist who sings introspective songs about identity, love, romance and heartbreak. Yet Morissette disrupts patriarchal definitions of femininity by composing most of her own material, crafting a stage appearance that does not coincide with stereotypical femininity and cultivating an "angry" persona that includes being loud and using "off-colour" language in her songs.

k.d. lang also plays with gender boundaries, behaviours and images of femininity in her music and performance practice. In her early work, lang's writing focused on love and romance, yet she often parodied the stereotypical female singer ("Miss Chatelaine") to blur boundaries of gender and sexuality. Her career has been marked by controversy because of her militant veganism and the revelation in 1992 of her lesbianism. By this time, however, lang had become a successful songwriter and record producer.

Like performers, listeners and consumers of music and music videos participate in the process of gendering. Whether explicit or not, ideologies of gender not only inform people's choices regarding the types of music they listen to and the videos that they view, but these ideologies also are maintained and modified in this process. Music videos are particularly important as they hold a powerful place in a media-saturated and visually oriented society (Pegley 2008). They can both perpetuate stereotypical images of femininity and provide a way for some artists (such as electronic music and performance artist, Peaches) to challenge and transgress gender ideologies.

"Girl Power" and Popular Music

Power is central to understanding the process of gendering because it marks the connection between music and the social and cultural circumstances of its production, performance and reception. Feminist popular music scholars examine the power that music holds for people, especially young girls. For these audiences of listeners, music sustains particular social values and meanings. The re-emergence of the phenomenon of "girl power" in the late 1990s is one illustration of the connection between music, gender, and power.

The concept of girl power is commonly associated with the hugely successful all-female 1990s British pop group the Spice Girls. The group was originally comprised of five women vocalists; no instrumentalists appeared in their videos. Each of the women had a stage name — Posh, Ginger, Baby, Scary and Sporty Spice — that individualized and personalized each performer. Apart from the Spice Girls, several iterations of girl power existed in the music of Riot Grrrl bands in the United States in the early 1990s, including Bikini Kill, Bratmobile, Sleater-Kinney and Huggy Bear, as well as other artists performing at this time, including Hole, Elastica and Madonna before them (see Kearney and Leonard 1997). Since the 1990s, girl power has continued to be associated with a number of all-women bands, bands with strong female leads and solo artists from a variety of genres, such as alternative rock, hip hop, r & b and pop, including Veruca Salt, Alicia Keys, Pink, Destiny's Child and the Black Eyed Peas featuring Fergie, to name a few.

Girl power has generated considerable debate in popular music and feminist circles, and is an example of a value that is projected through musical texts and images that can be read in a variety of ways. Some scholars view popular cultural icons, such as Madonna, Riot Grrrls and the Spice Girls, as empowering for women and girls. These artists are lauded for the progressive ways they use the contradictions in stereotypical femininity to resist and re-appropriate identity constructions. Other scholars argue that these artists are negative role models because they reinforce the view that appearance is a key source of female power. From this viewpoint, girl power seduces women and young girls into adhering to patriarchal scripts of femininity, thereby subverting possibilities for active resistance to such forces. Critics also draw attention to the power relations embedded in the term "girl power," arguing that the qualifier "girl" infantilizes adult women by linking them with a category of younger, vulnerable people in non-adult status, positions so that the images can only be read as demeaning and disempowering.

In Canada, the debate over girl power and questions regarding how female artists resist and challenge patriarchal values continue to inform feminist criticism in popular music circles. Canadian female popular music artists and bands encompass a wide range of genres, styles and images (from Avril Lavigne to Susan Aglukark; Jann Arden to Loreena McKennitt; Tegan and Sara to Nelly Furtado; Sarah Harmer to Andrea Lindsay; Sarah Slean to Kathleen Edwards; Diana Krall to Jully Black; Terry Clarke to Deborah Cox; Metric to Dragonette; Ranee Lee to Molly Johnson; Joni Mitchell to Feist; and Rita MacNeil to Chantal Kreviazuk, to name a few). Taken together, they reach an audience comprised of millions of young women worldwide, numbers that alone underscore the significance of examining the connections between gender, power and popular music in an increasingly technologically oriented and media-saturated world.

REFERENCES

Bradby, Barbara, and Dave Laing. 2001. "Introduction to Gender and Sexuality, Special Issue." *Popular Music* 20,3.

Brett, Philip, Elizabeth Wood and Gary C. Thomas (eds.). 1994. *Queering the Pitch. The New Gay and Lesbian Musicology.* New York and London: Routledge.

Cook, Susan, and Judy Tsou (eds.). 1994. *Cecilia Reclaimed: Feminist Perspectives on Gender and Music.* Urbana: University of Illinois Press.

Cusick, Suzanne G. 1994. "Gender and the Cultural Work of a Classical Music Performance." *Repercussions* 3,1.

Diamond, Beverley. 2000. "The Interpretation of Gender Issues in Musical Life Stories of Prince Edward Islanders." In Beverley Diamond (ed.), *Gender and Music: Negotiating Shifting Worlds.* Urbana: University of Illinois Press.

Dibben, Nicola. 1999. "Representations of Femininity in Popular Music." *Popular Music* 18,3.

Fast, Susan. 2001. *In the Houses of the Holy: Led Zeppelin and the Power of Rock Music.* Oxford Press.

Feld, Steven. 1990. *Sound and Sentiment: Birds, Weeping, Poetics, and Song in Kaluli Expression.* Philadelphia: University of Pennsylvania Press.

Frith, Simon, and Angela McRobbie. 1978. "Rock and Sexuality." *Screen Education* 29.

Kearney, Matu Celests. 1997. "The Missing Links: Riot Grrrl — Feminism—Lesbian Culture." In Sheila Whitely (ed.), *Sexing the Groove: Popular Music and Gender.* New York: Routledge.

McClary, Susan. 1991. *Feminine Endings: Music, Gender and Sexuality.* Minnesota: University of Minnesota Press.

Pegley, Kip. 2008. *Coming to You Wherever You Are: MuchMusic, MTV and Youth Identities.* Wesleyan University Press.

Rose, Tricia.1994. *Black Noise: Rap Music and Black Culture in Contemporary America.* Hanover, NH: University of New England/Wesleyan University Press.

Whiteley, Sheila (ed.). 1997. *Sexing the Groove: Popular Music and Gender.* London and New York: Routledge.

Wicke, Peter. 1990. *Rock Music: Culture, Aesthetics and Sociology.* Cambridge: Cambridge University Press.

25

"Walking the Hyphen"

Discourses of Immigration and Gendered Racism

Yasmin Jiwani

Whether or not we read the daily papers or listen to the daily broadcast news, it is evident that the topic of immigration is a major and continuing preoccupation of the media. Headlines regularly report on the plight of refugees, the status of female immigrants, and the criminal activities of immigrant men and women. The media, however, not only communicate news and information about immigration but also structure our understandings of immigration through the portrayal (both verbally and pictorially) of immigrants and immigration. Through their ability to frame and define the phenomenon of immigration, the media exert enormous power in shaping perceptions of and responses to immigrants and the issue of immigration. In the first section of this chapter, I outline key features of the dominant economic, cultural and criminologic discourses on immigration and immigrant groups, which rely on a seemingly simple binary of "us" and "them." In the second section, I explore the impact of these images on young women of colour, and their sense of identity and belonging. Although many of these media images are oppressive, young women find creative ways of defining themselves in relation to members of their own community and members of their peer groups in the larger, dominant society.[1]

Media Discourses of Immigration

Both print and television news coverage representations of immigration are embedded in the wider discourses of racialized "difference" and "otherness." In most cases, the racialized nature of the discourse is not explicit and overt. Rather, it is encoded in the language of culture and nature (Essed 1990; Henry and Tator 2002; Thobani 2007), in what has been called "inferential racism" (Hall 1990). This kind of racism is reinforced with the continued reliance on a very problematic binary of "us" versus "them." "They" are the ones with backward, traditional, barbaric and different customs. "We" are the ones who are civilized, benevolent, law-abiding and accepting of difference (Abu Laban 1998; van Dijk 1993; Jiwani 2006).

As a racialized discourse, immigration is perceived to be synonymous with the problem of an invasion of others wherein these others are seen as economically, culturally, and racially different. As a gendered discourse, immigration is feminized and seen as consisting of an invasion of dependent others who are unable/unwilling to work and support themselves but who selfishly take advantage of the benevolence of the Canadian state and its peoples (Folson 2004).

There is a long-standing media-propagated myth that racialized immigrant groups are "stealing" jobs, taking unfair advantage of the welfare system, and/or draining the health-care system. This myth is set against the harsh reality that faces many immigrants who find themselves "deskilled." Their credentials are often unrecognized by Canadian employers and they are excluded from participating in the labour market because of their lacking "Canadian experience" (Henry et al. 1995; Galabuzi 2001). Deskilling often results in women being able to acquire jobs that are often menial and significantly lower paid with scarcely any benefits (Ng 1993; Thobani 2007). For men, deskilling often results in a lack of employment altogether.

A dominant feature of the discourse of immigration is the emphasis on culture. The language that is often used to define immigrants tends to utilize euphemisms such as "eth-nocultural" and "multicultural," thereby suggesting that only these groups possess "cultures" and therefore stand out against a universal, non-cultural background. This kind of inferential racism has the effect of portraying immigrants as threats to Canadian culture. Racialized immigrants are represented as "diluting" or "denigrating" Canadian culture by insisting on the retention of their own cultural traditions that are often characterized as being rude and an affront to the assumed polite rationality of white Euro-Canadian communities.

The cultural discourse of immigration is also deeply gendered. Often, the tendency is to portray immigrant groups as having cultures that are inferior and barbaric. One common and strategic way by which this is accomplished is to point to the presumably disadvantaged and inferior status of women within immigrant groups (Thobani 2007). Thus, these women are seen as being oppressed by their cultural traditions and at the mercy of men who are only interested in retaining their patriarchal power (Razack 1998; Yeğenoğlu 1998). In news stories concerning gender-based violence, the media and the courts often look to cultural traditions to explain why particular immigrant women have been killed by their spouses (Jiwani 2006; Narayan 1997). Young women from racialized immigrant communities are represented in the media as being "in conflict," caught between their supposedly backward cultures and the progressive and liberated culture of western society (Bannerji 1993; Jiwani 1992).

At the same time, the cultural discourse of immigration also exoticizes immigrant groups. The food, fashions and music of immigrant groups are often embraced because they are "different," even trendy, while there remains little public acceptance of the immigrants them-selves. In the popular media, the discourse of exoticization is gendered with the continued manufacturing of iconic images of women of colour as dragon ladies, martial arts experts and docile, submissive sexual objects[3] (Jiwani 2005; Said 1978; Shohat and Stam 1994). In contrast, men of colour appear as gangsters, deviants, bumbling super-heroes who are part of the dynamic interracial duo (Zackel 2000).

In the news media, immigrant groups are primarily represented as threats to the social order. They are often portrayed as being engaged in criminal acts (such as illegal immigra-tion, gang involvement, human trafficking and smuggling). Here too, the discourse is often gendered. Immigrant men are most often portrayed as perpetrators, actively engaged in criminal activities, whereas the women are represented as victims who have been trafficked and sold as chattel. Women are rarely seen as having active agency in attempting to define their own realities. Implicit in these images is the notion that the loyalty of immigrants can-not be assumed but has to be established over and over again through legislative, social and policing mechanisms.

Girls and Young Women

According to recent statistics, 22.6 percent of the visible minority population in 2006 was composed of children aged fourteen and younger (Statistics Canada 2006). According to Kobayashi et al. (1998), the 1996 Census revealed that one out of every ten immigrants is a female under the age of fifteen. Most of these young women and girls come into the country as dependents of their parents and sponsors. That dependency is compounded by age, class, legal status, gender and race (Jiwani et al. 2001). In a series of focus groups and interviews with young immigrant women of colour (fourteen to eighteen years of age), many reported being extremely aware of their racial differences and linked this to their sense of belongingness or lack thereof.[4] For many, identity is relational — it is contextual, based on how others define them (see also Kelly 1998). As one Persian young woman stated: "I think they see me as Iranian. Like the brown people, Moroccan, Iranian are like all one…. they don't see me as white like they call Canadian."

The experiences of dislocation and displacement resulting from migration accentuate the need to find a sense of belonging. For many young women and girls, the salient aspect of their life is the constant negotiation of trying to fit in the dominant society, and attempting to fit into their own communities. This process of negotiation is marked by the prevailing internal and external discourses of race and gender. Thus, normative prescriptions regarding how to behave as a young woman or girl may be different in the external, dominant society as compared to the standards operative within their own communities (see Handa 1997). Racism and sexism from the external society often results in young girls retreating into their own communities. Sexism from within their own communities often forces them out into the external society. This tension between two worlds not only takes its toll but it also forces young women to engage in creative ways of defining themselves in relation to members of their own community and members of their peer groups in the larger, dominant society (Ramachandran 2010).

What are some of the ways in which immigrant girls are made to feel as if they don't belong? The discourse of otherness communicates itself through a variety of mechanisms beginning with language, comportment, knowledge of the dominant system's norms and mores, and social experiences of exclusion, exoticization, marginalization and alienation. For many racialized girls, the sense of not fitting in is deeply rooted around the ways in which their appearance is exoticized, othered or rendered inferior and different. Witness this exchange from a focus group conducted with girls from Afro-Caribbean backgrounds:

Girl: They're always touching hair.
Girl: "Can you show me how to [jam]?"
Girl: And I'm telling them, "Don't touch my hair again. You're going to mess it up." And they still touch your hair.
Girl: Or the stupidest question, "What colour is your blood?" "What do you think? Purple."

This exchange not only reveals the way in which hair is a marker of difference but members of the dominant group do not hesitate to violate the bodily boundaries of the exoticized other, reinforcing relations of power between the dominant and subordinated.

Media-based stereotypes of exoticism also reinforce experiences of difference and exclusion. As this young South Asian Canadian woman reported:

[The media] shows it (India) as being very exotic, with Madonna and her mendhi [henna] and saris being turned into drapes and the masala and everything being exotic. When I went to India it was not like that: it seems very exotic but on the other hand, it's shown as a welfare culture, it's the kids on the UNICEF ad. So on one hand it's like this big rich silk industry which does henna on the side and on the other hand it's the nude baby with the over-swelled tummy on the UNICEF ad.

In this example, India is represented as the other, a land of "exotic" cultural practices and impoverishment.

Such representations make it difficult for young immigrant women of colour to counter the discourses of otherness and difference to which they are continually subjected. Instead, many end up carrying what Kobena Mercer (cited in Cottle 2000) has described as the "burden of representation" wherein they feel they are judged by how the media portrays their particular community. For example, a Persian young woman speaks about her reaction to watching the film *Not Without My Daughter* in the context of her English class:

> I start[ed] crying and I was so upset and I talked to my teacher and told her this is not how it is for me. Now I realize that all the people who are Chinese, Japanese, from all over the world, would think of Iran based on this.

Negotiating Identity

Confronted with exclusion and stigmatization wherein they are made to feel othered and where their difference is consistently devalued, racialized immigrant girls and young women have developed strategies by which to defend themselves against the corrosive impact of racism. Reliance on their family and friends is one such strategy. As this young South Asian woman noted: "Home is my safe place, not only from violence but from anything else." And an Iranian young woman said, "But Persians, if you're in that group, you feel safe because there's a lot of us and if something happens to one, there is a lot of people to help back the person up." Additionally, for many of the young women we spoke to, identity was conceptualized in relational terms. In other words, it was dependent on the context in which they found themselves. As this young South Asian woman put it:

> Like if someone was to ask me where I was from, I'm still from Pakistan. I'm always going to be from Pakistan and ultimately, somewhere deep down inside, that's my baseline foundation. But I have a Canadian flag on my backpack and if I were to backpack for year... I'd be Canadian. ("Jumpstart" workshop with girls of colour)

Conclusion

Media discourses about immigration and immigrant groups are deeply raced and gendered. The larger discourse on immigration tends to problematize immigrants as an invading force, threatening the fabric of Canadian society, its economic pillars and social sanctity. Immigrant groups are represented as racialized others who make excessive demands on the social and cultural benevolence of Canadian society. At the same time, racialized immigrant cultures are exoticized and women of colour are often sexualized, while men tend to be criminalized and/or denied of their masculinity.

The discourses of othering and difference which are part and parcel of the larger discourses concerning immigration and immigrant communities, structure and shape the lives of young immigrant women of colour. Pressured to "fit in," many of these young women are rejected and excluded from the dominant society. This impacts their sense of identity and belonging as they are continually made to "walk the hyphen" (Batth 1998) between membership in their own communities and finding a sense of inclusion in the larger society.

NOTES

1. This research was made possible by funding from SSHRC Strategic Theme Grant #829-1999-1002. The term "gendered racism" is derived from Philomena Essed's (1990) work on *Everyday Racism*. The phrase "walking the hyphen" comes from Indy Batth's (1998) illuminating thesis on South Asian girls and sports.
2. See, for instance, the information provided by the Media Action Network for Asian Americans (2000).
3. For a more detailed discussion of this study, see Jiwani et al. (2001).

Abu-Laban, Yasmeen. 1998. "Keeping 'Em Out: Gender, Race, and Class Biases in Canadian Immigration Policy." In V. Strong-Boag, S. Grace, A. Eisenberg and J. Anderson (eds.), *Painting the Maple: Essays on Race, Gender, and the Construction of Canada*. Vancouver, BC: University of British Columbia Press.

Bannerji, Himani. 1993. "Returning the Gaze: An Introduction." In H. Bannerji (ed.), *Returning the Gaze: Essays on Racism, Feminism and Politics*. Toronto: Sister Vision Press.

Batth, Indy. 1998. "Centering the Voices from the Margins: Indo-Canadian Girls' Sports and Physical Activity Experiences in Private and Public Schools." Master of Arts thesis, Department of Human Kinetics, University of British Columbia.

Berman, Helene, and Yasmin Jiwani (eds.). 2001. *In the Best Interests of the Girl Child, Phase II Report*. London: Centre for Research on Violence Against Women and Children, University of Western Ontario.

Cottle, Simon. 2000. "A Rock and A Hard Place: Making Ethnic Minority Television." In S. Cottle (ed.), *Ethnic Minorities and the Media*. Philadelphia: Open University Press.

Essed, Philomena. 2002. "Towards a Methodology to Identify Converging Forms of Everyday Discrimination." At: un.org/womenwatch/daw/csw/essed45.htm

___. 1990. *Everyday Racism: Reports from Women in Two Cultures*. Claremont, CA: Hunter House.

Folson, Rose Baaba. 2004. "Representation of the Immigrant." In Rose Baaba Folson (ed.), Calculated Kindness: Global Restructuring, Immigration and Settlement in Canada. Halifax: Fernwood Publishing.

Galabuzi, Grace-Edward. 2001. Canada's Creeping Economic Apartheid: The Economic Segregation and Social Marginalisation of Racialised Groups. Toronto: CSJ Foundation for Research and Education.

Hall, Stuart. 1990. "The Whites of Their Eyes." In M. Alvarado and J.O. Thompson (eds.), *The Media Reader*. London: British Film Institute.

Handa, Amita. 1997. "Caught Between Omissions: Exploring 'Culture Conflict' among Second Generation South Asian Women in Canada." Ph.D. thesis. Toronto, ON: University of Toronto, Graduate Department of Sociology and Education.

Henry, Frances, and Carol Tator. 2002. *Discourses of Domination, Racial Bias in the Canadian English Language Press*. Toronto: University of Toronto Press.

Henry, Frances, Carol Tator, Winston Mattis and Tim Rees. 1995. *The Colour of Democracy: Racism in Canadian Society*. Toronto: Harcourt Brace Canada.

Jiwani, Yasmin. 2006. Discourses of Denial: Mediations of Race, Gender and Violence. Vancouver: University of British Columbia Press.

___. 2005. "The Eurasian Female Hero(Ine): Sydney Fox as the Relic Hunter." Journal of Popular Film & Television 32,4.

___. 1992. "Canadian Media and Racism, to Be and Not to Be: South Asians as Victims and Oppressors in the Vancouver Sun." Sanvad 4,45 (August).

Jiwani, Yasmin, with Nancy Janovicek and Angela Cameron. 2001. *Erased Realities: The Violence of Racism in the Lives of Immigrant and Refugee Girls of Colour*. Vancouver: FREDA. Also at: harbour.sfu.ca/freda/reports/gc203.htm.

Kelly, Jennifer. 1998. *Under the Gaze, Learning to be Black in White Society*. Halifax: Fernwood Publishing.

Kobayashi, Audrey, Eric Moore and Mark Rosenberg. 1998. *Healthy Immigrant Children: A Demographic and Geographic Analysis*. Ottawa: Human Resources Development Canada.

Mahtani, Minelle. 2001. "Representing Minorities: Canadian Media and Minority Identities." Canadian Ethnic Studies 33,3.

Media Action Network for Asian Americans. 2000. *A Memo from MANAA to Hollywood: Asian Stereotypes, Restrictive Portrayals of Asians in the Media and How to Balance Them*. At: manaa.org/a_stereotypes.html.

Mirchandani, Kiran, and Evangelia Tastsoglou. 2000."Towards a Diversity Beyond Tolerance." Studies in Political Economy 61.

Narayan, Uma. 1997. *Dislocating Cultures/Identities, Traditions and Third World Feminism*. London and New York: Routledge.

Ng, Roxana. 1993. "Racism, Sexism, and Immigrant Women." In S. Burt, L. Code and L. Dorney (eds.), *Changing Patterns: Women in Canada*. Toronto: McClelland & Stewart.

Ramachandran, Tanisha. 2010. "No Woman Left Covered: Unveiling the Politics of Liberation in Multi/Interculturalism." Canadian Woman Studies 27,2/3.

Razack, Sherene. 1998. *Looking White People in the Eye: Gender, Race, and Culture in Courtrooms and Classrooms*. Toronto: University of Toronto Press.

Said, Edward. 1978. *Orientalism*. New York: Random House.

Shohat, Ella, and Robert Stam. 1994. *Unthinking Eurocentrism, Multiculturalism and the Media*. London and New York: Routledge.

Statistics Canada. 2006. "Canada's Ethnocultural Mosaic, 2006 Census: National Picture." At: 12.statcan.ca/census-recensement/2006/as-sa/97-562/p9-eng.cfm.

Thobani, Sunera. 2007. Exalted Subjects, Studies in the Making of Race and Nation in Canada. Toronto: University of Toronto Press.

Van Dijk, Teun A. 1993. *Elite Discourse and Racism*. London and New York: Routledge.

Yeğenoğlu, Meyda. 1998. *Colonial Fantasies, Towards a Feminist Reading of Orientalism*. Cambridge: Cambridge University Press

Zackel, Frederick. 2000. "Robinson Crusoe and the Ethnic Sidekick." *Bright Lights Film Journal* 30.

26

Coffee Boys

Duncan Campbell

Artist's Statement

In the nineties, unaware of my blossoming dissatisfaction with creating dark, brooding, political art about gay rights and sexuality, and much to my own surprise, I began outputting colourful, whimsical paintings of muscle-bound men in love. These interruptions to my "serious" art were so disconcerting, I immediately shirked all responsibility for them and created a *nom de plume*, "Marilyn Cooper,"

to take the blame. Little did I know that the work attributed to Marilyn Cooper would eventually become an equal, and valid component of my artistic output.

When I create a Marilyn Cooper painting my concerns are strictly formal: pretty colours, curvy lines and decorative edges are all hallmarks of the Marilyn style. The subject matter flows from my own life and observations of the gay community, and could be just as easily representative of straight life, had I been born that way. In spite of my best intentions to be completely apolitical with this work, I like the fact that pretty pictures of gay men living in a world without shame, struggle or politics, may be even more political than my other, more overt attempts to deal with gay issues. The work lives in a world beyond politics, and is, therefore, potentially more dangerous to the status quo.

Coffee Boys, mixed media on paper

NOTE

Reprinted with permission of Duncan Campbell.

I Eat Kids Yum Yum!

Denis Lee

A child went out one day.
She only went to play.
A mighty monster came along
And sang its mighty monster song:

I EAT KIDS YUM YUM!
I STUFF THEM DOWN MY TUM.
I ONLY LEAVE THE TEETH AND CLOTHES.
(I ESPECIALLY LIKE THE TOES.)

The child was not amused.
She stood there and refused.
Then with a skip and a little twirl
She sang the song of a hungry girl:

"I EAT MONSTERS BURP!
THEY MAKE ME SQUEAL AND SLURP.
IT'S TIME TO CHOMP AND TAKE A CHEW –
AND WHAT I'LL CHEW IS YOU!"

The monster ran like that!
It didn't stop to chat.
(The child went skipping home again
And ate her brother's model train.)

NOTE

In Margaret Atwood (ed.), 1987, *The CanLit Food Book: From Pen to Palate — A Collection of Tasty Literary Fare*, Toronto: Totem Books. Reprinted with permission.

E-Mail
The Princess and the Frog

Subject: [Fwd: Fairytale]
From: C. Lesley Biggs <lesley.biggs@usask.ca>
Date: June 12, 2003
To: <undisclosed recipients>

Hi!
I laughed out loud at this one!
LB

>A fairy tale for the assertive woman of the 2000s
>>
> Once upon a time, in a land far away, A beautiful,
> independent, self assured princess, happened upon a frog as
> she sat contemplating ecological issues on the shores of an
> unpolluted pond in a verdant meadow near her castle.
> >
> The frog hopped into the Princess' lap and said: Elegant
> Lady, I was once a handsome Prince, until an evil witch cast
> a spell upon me. One kiss from you, however, and I will turn
> back into the dapper, young Prince that I am and then, my
> sweet, we can marry and set up housekeeping in yon castle with
> my Mother, where you can prepare my meals, clean my clothes,
> bear my children, and forever feel grateful and happy doing
> so.
> >
> That night, on a repast of lightly sautéed frogs legs
> seasoned in a white wine and onion cream sauce, she chuckled
> to herself and thought: I don't fucking think so.
> >

Section III

SEXUALIZING WOMEN AND MEN

Pamela J. Downe, C. Lesley Biggs and Susan Gingell

Human sexuality, as contemporary Western societies predominantly understand it, is the creation of modernity, claims famed sociologist Anthony Giddens in *The Transformation of Intimacy* (1992). His point is that the meanings attached to sexuality vary across time, cultures, and other social groupings. People in late modern Western cultures most often conceive of sexuality as a site of reproduction, erotic pleasure, and romantic love while other cultures do not necessarily include the latter in their conception of sexuality. Perhaps the broadest definition we might safely venture is to say that sexuality is a person's "erotic desires, practices, and identities" (Jackson and Scott 1996: 2), and these are always subject to change.

Recognizing a spectrum of beliefs and sexual practices including homosexuality, bi-sexuality, queer sexuality, transgendered sexuality, and heterosexuality, scholars and many non-scholars today are much more inclined to speak of sexua*lities* than of sexua*lity*. Giddens' observation that divergent tendencies of modern life get played out on the hotly contested terrain of sexuality is substantiated by reactions to Canadian Lorna Crozier's poem, "The Sex Lives of Vegetables." In August of 1985 *Arts Manitoba* magazine published the sequence in which Crozier plays with the perception that the shape of many vegetables is sexually suggestive. For example, in "Peas" (1985: 99), she writes, "Your tongue finds them clitoral / as it slides up the pod. / Peas are not amused. / They have spent all their lives / keeping their knees together." In response, a member of the Manitoba provincial parliament rose in the legislature to demand public funding be withdrawn from a magazine that would publish such pornography (Crozier 1990: 91). Such outrage at the frank and funny sequence is at the same end of the response spectrum as someone's sending the poet a hateful, threatening letter whose envelope was bordered in black electrician's tape (Crozier 1990: 93). However, the audience at the 2007 *Words Aloud* Festival roared out loud when they heard Crozier read "Carrots" (Crozier 2007) with its image of the phallicly shaped vegetables "fucking / the earth. / A permanent erection/ they push deeper / into the damp and dark." Thus, we can see both how contentious a subject sexuality can be, and how various the responses to its publically circulated representation are.

Because of the power associated with reproduction and intimate emotion, many societies have attempted to regulate sexuality through governmental, religious, and social sanctions including the imposition of moral codes and state laws. But attempts at regulation are rarely successful. Section III of the book concerns itself with the varying expressions and experiences of sexuality, the everyday and taken-for-granted regulatory practices that shape sexual identities.

The authors in this section implicitly or explicitly support the notion that "what we do sexually, and what we think about what we do sexually, are as much a product of our interactions with each other and with our cultural assumptions about sexuality, as sexuality is about drives and biological imperatives to reproduce" (Kimmel and Plante 2004: xi). This section focuses, then, on the cultural aspects of sexuality rather than on the biological bases of reproduction and sexual identity which have dominated research for almost two hundred years. In part, the culturalist approach represents a response to the legacy of early twentieth-century beliefs (much influenced by Freud) that "biology is destiny," and that heterosexuality represents "mature" sexual identity in, individuals who have passed successfully through the psychosexual stages of development (oral, anal, phallic, and genital). Moreover, in the view of the Victorians, sexuality was tied to one's moral character; men could be randy (because it was in their "nature") while women were supposed to be chaste and pure; that is, women were not to be seen as overly keen in wanting sex; rather they should demurely accept the attentions of their male suitors, but save their virginity for the marriage bed. The stereotypes of forceful males and coy females are still prevalent today despite a mountain of experience showing far greater variation in the sexual behaviours of both sexes. Today, most scholars in Women's and/or Gender Studies and in Queer Studies eschew simplistic explanations of sexuality, keeping firmly in view the complex conditions under which sexual expressiveness occurs.

Sexuality is highly gendered. In fact, the word "sex" is derived from the Latin verb *secare*, meaning to section or divide (Selkirk 1988). Given this etymological origin, it is not surprising that popular and scientific attempts to understand and regulate sex and sexuality have been greatly concerned with distinguishing between male and female desire and activity. This insistence on dividing the world into two genders begins at birth when parents, family, friends, and health-care practitioners ask, "Is it a boy, or a girl?" (Note the sequencing of the genders in the question — boy child is positioned almost always first in the pairing, reinforcing the privileged position of the male over the female child.) But what happens if an individual refuses to be defined in these binary terms? In her chapter, Shannon Wyss identifies "hirself" as genderqueer, "which refers to people who are neither men nor women, neither masculine nor feminine, but are a gender for which we have no word in the English language." In response to an innocent question by her young friend "Shante," Wyss asked, "How did i see my own gender? How did i wish to be gendered? Did i really want to keep trying to fit into a tiny gender box? Could i do my gender another way?" Like gender and sexual radicals before "hir," Shannon became "the nightmare of the religious right," but also, "and, sadly," as s/he observes, "of many feminists, especially second wave middle-class American women who grew up in the 1960s and 1970s." Despite having struggled for women's rights and lesbian rights, this generation of feminists often was hostile to people who identified as genderqueer in part because their own identities were still tied to gender boxes that pigeonhole individuals as either male or female. Disappointed with this response, Wyss was able to find support within both gender radical and mainstream women's communities, but if the feminist revolution is to continue, Wyss argues that a respectful dialogue needs to take place across generations of feminists.

Christine Overall (2000) argues that heterosexuality, defined primarily through men's experiences of intimate pairing with women, has become an institution. She explains: "By the institution of heterosexuality… what I mean is the systematized set of social standards, customs, and expected practices which both regulate and restrict romantic and sexual relationships between persons of different sexes" (2000: 262). In other words, the institution of heterosexuality is one that pervades all other social institutions and creates a supposedly "normal," and in fact, normative expectation that everyone is heterosexual. As Mariana Valverde (2000: 256) describes it, "This institution [of heterosexuality] is not located in any downtown skyscraper or in any government department, but it is so pervasive in today's society that it resembles the proverbial water of which fish are unaware."

Through the institution of heterosexuality, men's desires and activities are privileged.

As a result, women's sexual pleasure has been defined for centuries as secondary and almost always seen in relation to men's; that is, the satisfaction of male sexual desire took centre stage in heterosexual sexual relations and focused on *his* orgasm. At the same time, fear of women's sexuality has been a pervasive theme in mythology, the arts, religious texts, political tracts, etc., and productive of images as perverse as the *vagina dentata*, the toothed vagina that would cannibalize the male organ. As a result, women's sexuality has been subjected to patriarchal control, and what better way to regulate women's sexuality than by controlling women's knowledge of their own bodies, particularly their genitalia.

Shawna Dempsey realized that women, including lesbians, rarely saw images of their vulva, except perhaps in porn. Dempsey and her artistic collaborator Lorri Milan set out to create a five-minute performance piece *We're Talking Vulva* (later produced as a video) to provide information about the vulva. But, in the construction of a larger-than-life giant foam costume, Dempsey "realized that the performance's real power is in celebrating a part of our bodies that has been demonized." Dancing and rapping through her day, this fun-loving Giant Vulva "publicly talks about all of the embarrassing, private things that each of our own vulva do." The performance was created in 1986; the question is do women (and men) still need this information? From our interactions with our students, we say "yes!" What do you think?

"I never had one," the poet bpNichol writes, as he begins his contemplation of the vagina. Working against the patriarchal "pen-is-penis" tradition named in Margaret Atwood's *The Handmaid's Tale*, Nichol admits to having vagina envy: "I always wanted one. I grew up wanting one. I thot cocks were okay but vaginas were really nifty." Being a sound poet who appreciates rhyme, Nichol says he "liked that name [vaginas] for [the female organ] because it began with 'v' and went 'g' in the middle." In the poem, Nichol traces his journey as he exits from his mother's vagina — "the mouth where real things are born" — and he acknowledges it as the source of his existence. He exits to his childhood and adolescence when misinformation and silence about vaginas were the norm; and finally to "When sex happened, [and he] realized it was all a matter of muscles… that was where all the power & the feelings sprang from — the muscles. Alive, alive, oh!"

What if Sigmund Freud had celebrated the vagina in his theory of psychosexual development instead of the concept of penis envy? But, "Freud never had one," Libby Scheier declares, stating the obvious to remind readers how self-centred our theorizing often is. Instead, Scheier argues that Freud's theory of penis envy was the result of his "compulsive obsession with penises," a preoccupation shared by our phallocentric culture. In her poem "Penises: 1" Scheier cuts penises down to size. (Ouch!) They are "kind of a pain," "vulnerable," "inconsistent," "fun, but they're never pretty." However, Scheier revises her views about the penis when she has a baby boy who likes to play with his penis and enjoys his erection; but he also likes playing with his trucks and cars, and his belly button, too. According to Scheier, her son's "got his penis in perspective. It's part of his body," and "not yet part of his brain." In the end, Scheier concludes that "As part of the male body/the penis is quite a nice part…. As container for the entire male body/including the brain/the penis in this case is a bore."

For at least three centuries, women in Western societies have been led by media representations, family pressure, or religious doctrine to believe that in order to be publicly recognized and valued, women "need" an intimate relationship with a man. Women's status is often subsumed by and dependent on the men with whom they pair. Women and, to a lesser but still significant extent, men who do not maintain public heterosexual relationships are often deemed abnormal because they are seen to be rejecting the pervasive institution of heterosexuality. Those who face the greatest stigma, though, are gay men, lesbian women, and transgendered people.

In the late nineteenth century, doctors and scientists (predominantly in Britain and Germany) became interested in classifying human sexuality not only by gender, as had been done before them, but also by "type." With heterosexuality as the unquestioned and institutionalized baseline, categories of supposedly "abnormal" sexuality were developed. Few sexual "abnormalities" received the popular or scientific attention of "the invert" also known as the homosexual. With the seal of medicine and science, same-sex relationships became increasingly stigmatized as illnesses and moral failings, although earlier in the nineteenth century, such relationships among women, were called "romantic friendships" and were neither stigmatized nor deemed threatening (Faderman 1981, 1991), perhaps because actual sexual activity in such relationships was largely unimaginable. As David Evans (2004: 94) concludes, "Homosexuality has been pathologized and criminalized, with all forms of punishments and discriminations condoned by Church and state, at a misguided attempt at deterrence." Even as late as the 1970s, "there were cases in Canada of women being committed to psychiatric hospitals and subjected to heavy drugs and electroshock because their parents or husbands convinced doctors that lesbianism was a sign of madness" (Valverde 2000: 257–58). However, not all cultures have had such prejudicial attitudes toward homosexuality as Euro-Canadian ones have predominantly been. One indicator of a non-stigmatizing attitude to gay women and men is the naming "two-spirited" among some North American Indigenous peoples that Gregory Scofield writes about in "You Can Always Trust an Anthropologist" in Part C of this book, "Gender and Difference." There the sense of gay sexuality is one of plenitude, a doubling rather than a deficit.

Over the past forty years, gay men and lesbians have lobbied successfully for greater public acceptance (not just tolerance), but the extent to which the sexuality of gay men and lesbian women is currently regulated varies from community to community. Nonetheless, people in same-sex unions continue to face greater obstacles than do heterosexual couples. For example, the status of same-sex marriages remains a highly contested issue in Canadian society despite the fact that civil unions for same-sex couples have been recognized legally in every jurisdiction. This dissonance between formal rights and social acceptance is testament to the pervasiveness of heteronormativity — the commonplace but incorrect assumption that "everyone is heterosexual" — or should be (Nagel 2003: 49–50).

Not everyone, of course, accepts these assumptions. Russ Westhaver's chapter offers an analysis of how gay men carve a social space for themselves to experience the sensuality of music, drugs, and sexual contact. The circuit party is a community of attendees where gay masculinity and sexuality is expressed without the harsh and heteronormative gaze of broader society. The circuit party, however, comes with its own strategies for self-surveillance, the predominant one being that certain male body types are preferred over others. Westhaver's analysis reminds us that regulatory practices in a heterosexist society are never complete, but neither is sexual expression ever completely unmonitored.

If the circuit party is a site that attempts to escape the heteronormative gaze, then the *Heterosexual Questionnaire* turns the heterosexual gaze back onto itself. Few of us would consider asking a heterosexual "why they choose to be heterosexual?" because being heterosexual is seen as "natural." But gay men and lesbians are often asked "why they would choose to be a homosexual?" or "what do they think caused their homosexuality?" or "why do they insist on flaunting their homosexuality?" But what if we simply substituted heterosexual for homosexual in these questions, as Martin Rochlin did when he developed the *Heterosexual Questionnaire* in 1972? The results are surprisingly funny, but reveal the heteronormative assumptions that permeate cultural ideas and practices. The *Questionnaire* exposes the absurdities of these questions, their invasiveness into the private lives of individuals, and the double standards regulating heterosexual and homosexual behaviour. The test, by the way, is only for "self-avowed heterosexuals."

The creation of the Internet has led to a virtual explosion in sexualized images that are widely available to millions of people every second of every day. Of all the websites located on the World Wide Web, approximately twelve percent (24,644,172) are categorized as explicitly pornographic. The proliferation of pornographic images is a source of concern for both conservatives and feminist alike, and sometimes for the same reasons. Both, for example, fear the exploitation of children by child molesters searching for victims in chat rooms, as well as the sexualization of children at an increasingly younger age. For conservatives, pornography represents the undermining of "family values"; and for some feminists, pornography represents the continued sexual objectification of women, and a form of violence against women (either semiotic — that is in the sign systems of a culture or actual, as, for example, the violence in "snuff" films). These views often were strongly held by second wave feminists who, in the late 1970s and 1980s, offered compelling cultural and scholarly critiques of pornography, picketed porn shops, and fought legal battles to ban pornography. (This legal issue now is probably moot since the Internet is generally an unregulated site.)

Many third wave feminists, however, do not share the views of the previous generation of feminists. "Younger feminists," as Alison Lee observes in her chapter, "were taking a broader view of sex and sexuality including a more open attitude toward porn." Lee loves porn; she sees it "as a positive extension of human sexual expression," and an educational tool that allows women to explore their own erotic fantasies. But Lee is critical of the porn industry, which often exploits its sex workers, as well as producing unimaginative and narrowly defined tropes of sexual behaviour. In the sex-positive imagery imagined by Lee, women are represented as "active participants in their own sexual fantasy," but in order for sex-positive pornography to exist, women need to have control over its production and distribution. There are feminist pornographers, but not everyone in the feminist community agrees that these filmmakers are feminist. What does it mean to be a feminist in the context of this debate over pornography? Is feminist pornography possible in a patriarchal world? What would feminist pornography look like? Is it possible to create sexually explicit images without objectifying the participants in the image-making process? Is maintaining a distinction between pornography and erotica useful? Lee's chapter raises many compelling questions about feminist struggles to create a sex-positive society for both women and men.

The institution of heterosexuality subjects itself to regulation as well. Among the many examples are laws against sexual assault, religious prescriptions against birth control, and policies against sexual harassment, but perhaps the most obvious example of sexual regulation is that relating to commercialized sex work. Those engaged in prostitution whether by choice, necessity, or coercion, experience a great deal of stigma and surveillance. Having done much research into women's experiences in prostitution, Pamela Downe, in her chapter, tries to capture the diversity in such experiences. For some, prostitution is a site of great violation, indignity, and coercion. For others, it is a site of liberation, allowing them to achieve a level of economic security and freedom that they have not experienced elsewhere. For everyone, it is a site of ongoing and gender- differentiated regulation, although girls and women have always been the primary focus of such regulation.

Historically, vagrancy laws, contagious disease control strategies, and international conventions such as the well known *International Convention for the Suppression of the Traffic in Women and Children* were gender-specific, applying almost exclusively to the girls and women who were engaged in the exchange of sexual activity for material profit (Busby 2003: 103). The majority of these policies rendered prostitution illegal. In Canada today, prostitution is criminalized but not illegal. That means that exchanging sex for money is not illegal *per se*, but all the activities surrounding it — communicating for the purposes of the exchange, living off the avails of prostitution, pimping, and public loitering — are illegal. This legal regime creates a criminalized context for those who work both voluntarily and involuntarily in prostitution. Although current laws in Canada are framed in gender-neutral language and some provinces have implemented programs targeting the male clients of sex workers, "most prostitution-related charges are against women" (Busby 2003: 103). Moreover, Busby writes, "gender bias also exists with respect to sentencing disparities: 39 percent of women but only 3 percent of men convicted under the communicating for prostitution provisions in the *Criminal Code* received jail sentences, and women are significantly more likely to be detained in custody after arrest than men."

Because more often than not the criminalizing of prostitution has detrimental effects on the women and girls involved in it, very persuasive arguments in favour of decriminalization have been made. Decriminalization is not the same as legalization, the latter of which would involve the development of new kinds of regulation governing working conditions and taxation procedures; rather, decriminalization would remove some laws against the activities surrounding prostitution while leaving others, such as laws against pimping or the sexual exploitation of children, intact. Scholars like Deborah Brock (1998) and Fran Shaver (1996) argue that a decriminalized context would enhance women's access to resources and their ability to exit the trade or to work in safer and less stigmatized environments. Other scholars (e.g., Barry 1995; Jeffreys 1996) argue that decriminalization will further sanction the exploitation of women and girls in prostitution, and they doubt the extent to which a change in law will effect a change in social attitude and stigmatization. While there is merit in both arguments, neither adequately captures the diversity of experiences within prostitution. Portraying every sexual sale as if it were the same as the next and developing policy based on this over-generalized portrayal ignores the fact that commercialized sexuality is a multiple and complex phenomenon. The women and girls involved in the trade reflect this diversity in the stories they tell about their lives and their sexuality; in so doing, they resist and reject attempts to stereotype their experiences.

Sex is often thought (by the young) to be the purview of the young, but many women and men remain sexually active throughout the life course. The nature of that experience may change, however, as a result of having children, shifting responsibilities, and, yes, in part, declining hormones. At least that's what the pharmaceutical industry would like us to think. In their chapters, both Patricia Kaufert and Angus McLaren examine the medicalization of women's and men's sexuality as they age, revealing the chameleon-like ways in which the drug companies draw on and constitute gendered constructions of that sexuality. Kaufert traces the changing faces of menopause from adult woman to older woman, a transition completed when the woman is permanently infertile. This phase of adult sexual life is, like the others, not one of jarring and abrupt change but gradual transformation unless brought on by major injury or surgery such as a hysterectomy.

Despite menopause being a physiological process (as opposed to an event), it is not experienced in a universal way. Drawing on Margaret Lock's concept of "local bodies," Kaufert demonstrates that "bodies [including menopausal bodies] are formed by place and culture, which determine such things as what women eat, how their bodies are shaped by physical work, the spacing of their children." But, as Kaufert observes, "The menopausal body... is a product not only of how women lived their lives, but also how becoming menopausal is defined and 'managed'." In the 1970s, pharmaceutical advertisements presented women as aging crones. By the 1990s, these images had been replaced by those of active women enjoying their older years, as well as "the flower woman" (a woman who is situated in pastoral settings amid flowers, birds, and plants), "the cyborg woman" (a woman who is made up of human and technological parts), and "the horsewoman" (a construction of animal rights activists who "[have protested] the use of pregnant mares to produce urine, the raw material of one of the most widely marketed forms of estrogen).

As men age, they too experience changes to their sexuality. In the not too distant past, impotency was almost always a source of shame and secrecy, and for centuries, men and their health-care providers have sought various remedies to cure this problem. But in 1998, impotency became a public issue almost overnight when Viagra, billed as a new wonder drug, was launched onto the market, becoming the fastest selling pharmaceutical in history. How was it possible for Pfizer to create a billion dollar industry related to a condition that was thought to affect about 10 percent of men, most of whom were middle-aged and older? In other words, how did Pfizer, the developers of Viagra, create new markets for its impotence drug? In part, Pfizer and other health professionals, most notably urologists, were able to transform an affliction (often associated with fatigue, stress, and aging) to a medical problem (general sexual dissatisfaction), renaming it "erectile dysfunction." No longer understood as "a simple plumbing problem" by doctors, erectile dysfunction became a clinical issue, that without treatment threatened the vitality of men's lives, their identities, and personal relationships — all of which were taken to be synonymous with men's sense of masculinity.

In part, then, Pfizer's marketing campaign was able to capitalize on the (perceived) "crisis of masculinity" as straight, gay, white, black, and Hispanic men, the overworked, and the underemployed were forced to negotiate the changing structures of patriarchal power. Pfizer's success can also be attributed to its marketing strategies. Since male impotency was a taboo subject not discussed in public or in polite company, Pfizer initially adopted a conservative campaign that promoted traditional "family values," and directed its advertising at the heterosexual, monogamous, and middle-aged man. But having saturated this market, Pfizer developed new ones by targeting different groups of men who were younger, racialized, and/or gay.

The power of these images is realized ultimately in huge profits for the pharmaceutical industry, but what do these images also tell us about the manufacture of femininities and masculinities and women's and men's experiences of embodiment? To what extent are our bodily experiences responses to physiological changes that happen over the life course, and to what extent are those experiences shaped by social and cultural practices (like pharmaceutical advertising) that not only structure cultural assumptions, but help to construct the meanings and interpretations of those bodily experiences?

The scholarly engagement with the topic of sexuality takes into account the political context in which personal experiences occur. We need to reflect on the questions that reveal how sexuality is both a site of pleasure and sensuality and a site of political regulation. What everyday practices do you see around you that privilege particular representations of sexuality over others? How are heteronormative practices reinforced in our daily routines? How are these practices resisted and rejected? To what extent is sexuality represented in media as a diverse and flexible human quality? To what extent is sexuality shown as a fixed and biological phenomenon? How are expressions of sexuality gendered? Racialized? Class-based? Taking up these and other questions will continue to drive our ongoing exploration of this important area of human social life.

Barry, Kathleen. 1995. *The Prostitution of Sexuality: The Global Exploitation of Women*. New York: Harrington Park Press.

Brock, Deborah. 1998. *Making Work, Making Trouble: Prostitution as a Social Problem*. Toronto: University of Toronto Press.

Busby, Karen. 2003. "The Protective Confinement of Girls Involved in Prostitution: Potential Problems in Current Regimes." In Jane Runner and Kelly Gorkoff (eds.), *Being Heard: The Experiences of Young Women in Prostitution*. Halifax: Fernwood Publishing.

Crozier, Lorna, 2007. "'Sex Lives of Vegetables.' Words Aloud 2007, Canada." At: youtube.com/watch?v=bus-osLNXy4.

___. 1990. "Speaking the Flesh." In Libby Sheier, Sarah Sheard and Eleanor Wachtel (eds.), *Language in Her Eye: Writing and Gender: Views by Canadian Women Writing in English*. Toronto: Coach House.

___. 1985. "The Sex Lives of Vegetables" *Arts Manitoba* 15.

Evans, David. 2004. "Homosexuality." In Jo Eadie (ed.), *Sexuality: The Essential Glossary*. London: Hodder Headline.

Faderman, Lilian. 1981. *Surpassing the Love of Men: Romantic Friendship and Love Between Women from the Renaissance to the Present*. London: Women's Press.

___. 1991. *Odd Girls and Twilight Lovers: A History of Lesbian Life in Twentieth Century America*. London: Penguin.

Giddens, Anthony, 1992. *The Transformation of Intimacy: Sex, Love, and Eroticism*. Palo Alto, CA: Stanford University Press.

Jackson, Stevi, and Sue Scott. 1996. "Sexual Skirmishes and Feminist Factions." In Stevi Jackson and Sue Scott (eds.), *Feminism and Sexuality*. New York: Columbia University Press.

Jeffreys, Sheila. 1996. *The Idea of Prostitution*. Melbourne: Spinifex.

Kimmel, Michael, and Rebecca Plante. 2004. "Introduction." In Michael Kimmel and Rebecca Plante (eds.), *Sexualities: Identities, Behaviors, and Society*. Oxford: Oxford University Press.

Malszecki, Greg, and Tomislava Cavar. 2004. "Men, Masculinities, War and Sport." In Nancy Mandell (ed.), *Feminist Issues: Race, Class and Sexuality*. Toronto: Prentice-Hall.

Nagel, Joane. 2003. *Race, Ethnicity and Sexuality: Intimate Intersections, Forbidden Frontiers*. Oxford: Oxford University Press.

Overall, Christine. 2000. "Heterosexuality and Feminist Theory." In Barbara Crow and Lise Gotell (eds.), *Open Boundaries: A Canadian Women's Studies Reader*. Toronto: Prentice Hall Allyn and Bacon Canada.

Selkirk, Errol. 1988. *Sex for Beginners*. New York: Writers and Readers Publishing.

Shaver, Fran. 1996. "The Regulation of Prostitution: Setting the Morality Trap." In B. Schissel and L. Mahood (eds.), *Social Control in Canada*. Toronto: Prentice Hall.

Valverde, Mariana. 2000. "Lesbianism: A Country that Has No Language." In Barbara Crow and Lise Gotell (eds.), *Open Boundaries: A Canadian Women's Studies Reader*. Toronto: Prentice Hall Allyn and Bacon Canada.

Compiled by C. Lesley Biggs

- Percentage of Canadian teenagers — both male and female — who had had sex before age 15 in 2005: 8[2]
- Percentage of teenagers aged 15 to 19 who reported in 2005 that they had had sexual intercourse at least once: 45
- Percentage of sexually active Canadian females aged 15 to 19 who reported in 2005 that they had used condoms: 70[3]
- Percentage of sexually active Canadian males aged 15 to 19 who reported in 2005 that they had used condoms: 80
- Total number of pregnancies for young women aged 13 to 14 in Canada in 2005: 414[4]
- Total number of pregnancies for young women aged 15 to 17 and 18 to 19 respectively in Canada in 2005: 9,899 and 20,635
- Percentage of pregnancies for young women aged 15 to 19 of the total number of pregnancies in Canada in 2005: 29.2
- Percentage change from 1996 to 2005 in the number of Canadian women aged 15 to 19 who have had intercourse at least once: -8
- Percentage change from 1996 to 2005 in the number of Canadian men aged 15 to 19 who have had heterosexual vaginal intercourse at least once: 0[5]
- Percentage of never married, American females aged 15 to 19 in 2005 who reported never having heterosexual vaginal intercourse: 58.4[6]
- Percentage of never married, American females aged 15 to 19 in 2005 who reported never having heterosexual vaginal intercourse due to religious convictions or morals: 45
- Percentage of never married, American males aged 15 to 19 in 2005 who reported never having heterosexual vaginal intercourse: 57.4
- Percentage of never married, American males aged 15 to 19 in 2005 who reported never having heterosexual vaginal intercourse due to religious convictions or morals 35
- The average (modal) age at first heterosexual vaginal intercourse for never married, American females and males aged 15 to 19 in 2005: 15 to 16 years
- Percentage change from 1988 to 2006–2008 in never married American females aged 15 to 19 who had heterosexual vaginal intercourse: -9
- Percentage change from 1988 to 2006–2008 of never married American males aged 15 to 19 who had heterosexual vaginal intercourse from 1988 to 2006–2008: -17.8
- Percentage of never married American women aged 15 to 19 who indicated that they really didn't want sex to happen the first time: 9.8
- Percentage of never married American women aged 14 and under who indicated that they really didn't want sex to happen the first time: 18.0
- Percentage of never married American men aged 15 to 19 who indicated that they really didn't want sex to happen the first time: 4.8
- Percentage of never married American men aged 14 and under who indicated that they really didn't want sex to happen the first time: 6.5
- Percentage of never married American women aged 15 to 19 who indicated that the first time they had heterosexual intercourse they had mixed feelings about having sex

— "part of me wanted it to happen at the time and part of me didn't": 47.1

- Percentage of never married American men aged 15 to 19 who indicated that the first time they had heterosexual intercourse they had mixed feelings about having sex — "part of me wanted it to happen at the time and part of me didn't": 33.5
- Percentage of never married American women aged 15 to 19 who indicated that they really wanted to have sex happen the time first time: 43.1
- Percentage of never married American men aged 15 to 19 who indicated that they really wanted to have sex happen the time first time: 61.7
- Percentage of non-voluntary first sex for American females 18 to 24 years of age at interview 2006–2008 whose first experience of sex was before age 20: 7
- Percentage of 3161 women in the American military who reported a history of sexual assault in the military between 1994 and 1995: 24[7]
- Median number of female sexual partners in lifetime for American men 25 to 44 years of age in 2002: 6.7[8]
- Median number of male sexual partners in lifetime for American women 25 to 44 years of age in 2002: 3.8
- Percentage of American men 25 to 44 years of age who have had 15 or more female sexual partners in 2002: 29.2
- Percentage of American women 25 to 44 years of age who have had 15 or more male sexual partners in, 2002: 11.4
- Number of combination of sexual behaviours documented by the (American) National Survey on Sexual Health and Behaviour in 2009: 41[9]
- Percentage of American men aged 70 and over who masturbated alone throughout their lifetime: 80.4
- Percentage of American women aged 70 and over who masturbated alone throughout their lifetime: 58.3
- Percentage of American men 16 to 17 years of age who performed oral sex with a female partner in the past year (2008–2009): 18.3
- Percentage of American women 16 to 17 years of age who performed oral sex with a male sex partner in the past year (2008–2009): 22.4
- Percentage of American men 25 to 29 years of age who performed oral sex with a female sexual partner in the past year (2008–2009): 40.4
- Percentage of American women 25 to 29 years of age who performed oral sex with a male sexual partner in the past year (2008–2009): 49.9
- Percentage of American men aged 70 and over who had vaginal intercourse throughout their lifetime: 88.1
- Percentage of American women aged 70 and over who had vaginal intercourse throughout their lifetime: 89.2
- Percentage of men who reported in 2009 that their partner had an orgasm at the most recent sexual event: 85
- Percentage of women who reported in 2009 having had an orgasm at their most recent sexual event: 64[10]
- Year in which scientists introduced the term "homosexuality" to refer to a specific social category: 1871[11]
- Year in which the term "heterosexuality" was introduced into the scientific literature: 1901
- Percentage of American women in 2009 who identified as gay, lesbian or bisexual: 7[12]
- Percentage of American men in 2009 who identified as gay or bisexual: 8

- Percentage of Canadians aged 18 to 59 who reported in the 2009 Canadian Community Health Survey that they consider themselves to be homosexual (gay or lesbian): 1.1[13]
- Percentage of Canadians aged 18 to 59 who reported in the 2009 Canadian Community Health Survey that they consider themselves to be bisexual: 0.9
- Percentage of Canadian heterosexual youth surveyed in 2004 who acknowledged same-sex sexual behavior: 7.5
- Percentage of Americans in 1983 who considered homosexuality an "acceptable life-style": 34[14]
- Percentage of Americans in 2008 who considered homosexuality an "acceptable life-style": 48
- Percentage of Americans in 2008 who believed that homosexuality should be legal: 55
- Percentage of Americans in 2008 who believed that sex between an unmarried man and woman was "morally acceptable": 61
- Percentage of Americans in 2008 who believed that married men and women having an affair was "morally acceptable": 7
- Percentage of the French public in 2008 who considered homosexuality an "acceptable lifestyle": 81[15]
- Percentage of the German public in 2008 who considered homosexuality an "accept-able lifestyle": 68
- Estimated collective buying power of the Gay, Bisexual, Lesbian, Transgendered demo-graphic per year according to the Canadian Gay & Lesbian Chamber of Commerce: $100 billion[16]
- Estimated attendance at Toronto's Gay Pride Festival in 2009: 411,450[17]
- Estimated economic benefit of Toronto's Gay Pride Festival in 2009: $136 million
- Ranking of Toronto's Gay Pride Festival compared to all Gay Pride Festivals in North America with respect to attendance: 1[18]
- Ranking of Toronto's Gay Pride Festival of compared to Gay Pride Festivals worldwide with respect to attendance: 3
- Number of United Nations member states as of 2010 which support the U.N.'s statement on human rights, sexual orientation and gender identity calling for the decriminalization of homosexuality: 66[19]
- Number of United Nations member states as of 2010 that outlaw homosexuality: 70
- Number of dollars spent on Internet pornography every second: $3,000[20]
- Percentage that "sex," the number one search term in the world, accounts for all Internet searches: 25 (or n = 68 million)
- Estimated percentage of websites that are explicitly pornographic: 12 (or n = 24,644,172)[21]
- Estimated number of searches daily for "child pornography:" 116,000
- Estimated revenue from the pornography industry in the United States: $2.84 billion
- Estimated percentage of American women who are viewers of pornography: 33
- Percentage of all Internet porn traffic that takes place during the 9-to-5 workday: 70[22]
- Percentage of United Kingdom public in 2008 who agreed that viewing pornography was "morally acceptable": 29
- Percentage of French public in 2008 who agreed that viewing pornography was "mor-ally acceptable": 52[23]
- Percentage of German public in 2008 who agreed that viewing pornography was "mor-ally acceptable": 60
- Number of prostitution offences reported in Canada in 1987: 10,457[24]

- Number of prostitution offences reported in Canada in 2007: 4,724
- Percentage of female offenders found guilty of prostitution who received a prison sentence: in 2003/2004: 32[25]
- Percentage of male offenders found guilty of prostitution who received a prison sentence in 2003/2004: 9

NOTES

1. The original Hypatia Index was compiled by Pamela Downe, with the assistance of Ellen Whiteman. Except when otherwise indicated in the main text, the sources cited in this Index apply to the line where first referenced and then to all those that follow until another endnote appears.

2. Statistics Canada, *Trends in Teenage Sexual Behaviour and Condom Use*. At: statcan.gc.ca/pub/82-003-x/2008003/article/10664-eng.html.

3. Statistics Canada, 2009, Chapter 5: "Children and Youth," *Canadian Year Book*, chapter 5. At: statcan.gc.ca/pub/11-402-x/2009000/pdf/children-enfants-eng.pdf.

4. Statistics Canada, 2005, "Pregnancy Outcomes by Age Group," *Healthy Today, Healthy Tomorrow? Findings from the National Population Health Survey*. At: 40.statcan.gc.ca/l01/cst01/HLTH65A-eng. htm.

5. The rate for young men aged 15 to 19 who had sexual intercourse has remained constant at 43 percent.

6. United States, Center for Disease Control and Prevention, 2010, *Teenagers in the United States: Sexual Activity, Contraceptive Use, and Childbearing, National Survey of Family Growth 2006–2008*, Vital and Health Statistics, Series 23, No. 30. At: cdc.gov/nchs/data/series/sr_23/sr23_030.pdf.

7. J.S. McCall-Hosenfeld, J.M. Liebschutz, A. Spiro and M.R. Seaver, 2009, "Sexual Assault in the Military and Its Impact on Sexual Satisfaction in Women Veterans: A Proposed Model," *Journal of Women's Health* 18,6.

8. Center for Disease Control and Prevention, *Key Statistics from the National Survey of Family Growth*. At: cdc.gov/nchs/nsfg/abc_list_n.htm. N.B.: Includes partners with whom respondent had any type of sexual contact (anal, oral or vaginal intercourse).

9. Debby Herbernick et al., 2010, "Sexual Behaviour in the United States: Results from a National Probability Sample of Men and Women Ages 19–94," *Journal of Sexual Medicine* 7(suppl).

10. This difference is too large to be accounted for by some of the men having had male partners at their most recent event.

11. Nancy Mandell, 2001, "Introduction," in Nancy Mandell (ed.), *Feminist Issues: Race, Class and Sexuality*, Toronto: Prentice-Hall.

12. Kinsey Institute for Research into Sex, Gender, and Reproduction, "Frequently Asked Questions to the Kinsey Institute." At: kinseyinstitute.org/resources/FAQ.html#homosexuality.

13. Statistics Canada, 2010, "Gay Prid… By the Numbers, 2010" (August 17). At: statcan.gc.ca/ smr08/2010/smr08_144_2010-eng.htm.

14. Gallup, 2008, "Americans Evenly Divided on Morality of Homosexuality" (June 18). At: gallup. com/poll/108115/americans-evenly divided-morality-homosexuality.aspx.

15. Magali Rheault and Dalia Mogahed, 2008, "Moral Issues Divide Westerners from Muslims in the West" (May 23). At: gallup.com/poll/107512/Moral-Issues-Divide-Westerners-From-Muslims-West.aspx.

16. Marina Straus and Tara Perkins, 2009, "Looking for Gold at the End of the Rainbow," *Globe and Mail* (June 26). At: theglobeandmail.com/life/looking-for-gold-at-the-end-of-the-rainbow/ article1198800.

17. Pride Toronto, 2009, "Economic Impact Study, 2009." At: pridetoronto.com/downloads/ Economic_Impact_Study_2009.pdf.

18. Pride Toronto, 2010, "Pride Toronto Focuses on Celebrating 30 Years in Parade" (March 10). At: pridetoronto.com/press/pride-toronto-focuses-on-celebrating-30-years-in-parade.

19. Washington Review and Commentary, Weekly News from the White House, The Associated Press, "U.S. Joins United Nations in Decriminalizing Homosexuality Around the World! Only Country to Not Sign Charter During Bush Years!" At: traceyricksfoster.wordpress.com/2009/03/21/

us-joins-united-nations-in-decriminalizing-homosexuality-around-the-world-only-country-to-not-sign-charter-during-bush-years.

20. Andrea Swalec, 2010, "Internet Bosses Set to Approve .xxx for porn sites," *Globe and Mail* (June 24). At: theglobeandmail.com/news/technology/internet-bosses-set-to-approve-xxx-for-porn-sites/article1616449.

21. Michael Kesterton, 2010, "Social Studies: Facts and Arguments. On-line Porn," *Globe and Mail* (June 3). At: theglobeandmail.com/life/facts-and-arguments/hot-young-mentors-cycling-in-cities-and-advertising-that-smells/article1591584. November 13, 2010. Original source: Online MBA, "The Stats on Internet Pornography." At: onlinemba.com/blog/stats-on-internet-pornography.

22. Lauren La Rose, 2010, "Surfing Still Popular At Work," *Globe and Mail* (May 26). At: theglobe-andmail.com/news/technology/surfing-porn-still-popular-at-work/article1581940.

23. Magali Rheault and Dalia Mogahed, 2008, "Moral Issues Divide Westerners from Muslims in the West" (May 23). At: gallup.com/poll/107512/Moral-Issues-Divide-Westerners-From-Muslims-West.aspx.

24. Statistics Canada, 2009, "Canada at a Glance: Justice: Table 10: Reported Crime Statistics," CANSIM, table 252-0013. At: 45.statcan.gc.ca/2009/cgco_2009_004-eng.htm.

25. Rebecca Kong and Kathy AuCoin, 2009, "Female Offenders in Canada," *Juristat* 28, (no. 1). Cat. 85-002-XIE. At: statcan.gc.ca/pub/85-002-x/2008001/article/10509-eng.htm.

Sometimes Boy, Sometimes Girl
Learning to be Genderqueer through a Child's Eyes

Shannon E. Wyss

"Would you be my pretend daddy?"

So asked the adorable little girl who was sitting on my lap and whom i'd known since she was a baby. I'll call her Shante here. She was four years old. I was in my mid-twenties. And i was stunned. Sure, she'd never really been able to tell what gender i was. Sometimes she referred to me as "she"; sometimes she talked about me as "he." Occasionally, the other adults at the organization where i volunteered would try to correct her and tell her what the "right" pronouns were. But she always returned to using "she" and "he" interchangeably for me.[1]

In response to her question, i wrapped my arms around her as tightly as i could. I ached inside that she felt so deeply, at her young age, the absence of a biological father in her life. I kissed her and told her that, yes, i would be her pretend daddy. As far as i could tell, Shante promptly forgot about it and, five minutes later, was treating me like she always had.

Her question, however, burned in my mind for days, weeks, months afterwards. Indeed, it still burns there today, six years later. It is one of the few moments in my life that i can recall with deep clarity and that i can name with absolute certainty as a crucial, instantaneous "turning point." What did it mean, i wonder(ed), for this child to ask me to be her "pretend daddy," when she is black and i am white? What kind of "daddy" could i be, as a gentle, affectionate, unconditionally loving, unmacho, nurturing human being? Could i give Shante another idea of what masculinity is and can be? Or had she already incorporated the ways in which i interacted with her into what her vision of a daddy was?

When this girl asked me to be her pretend daddy, i had been studying transgender issues and becoming an ally of the trans community in the U.S. for five years. But all my reading and analysis had never really been about me. Sure, dressed in jeans, a sweatshirt and tennis shoes, i cut a somewhat ambiguous figure. Add to that my shaved head, my four-foot-eleven-inch frame and my skinny body, small breasts, makeup-less face, and unabashedly hairy legs, and you have a person who gets stared at on those rare occasions when i wear a skirt. I'm too unfeminine-looking to be a woman, people's eyes seem to say. But if i was pre-pubescent boy, i wouldn't have all that hair on my legs. So i get the "Is it a boy or girl?" stare a lot.

Mostly i just ignore people. And before Shante, i had never really stopped to reconsider, to own, to take responsibility for my dyke identity. In that one instant, however, this child crystallized for me the issues that have been lurking in the back of my mind for a year or more: How did i see my own gender? How did i wish to be gendered? Did i really want to keep trying to fit into a tiny gender box? Could i do my gender another way? Weren't folks' reactions to me — including Shante's — evidence of the fact that i was already doing it another way?

When Shante asked me her question, my feminism mushroomed to encompass gender non-conformity in a way that it never had before: genderqueerness (which refers to people who are neither men nor women, neither masculine nor feminine, but are a gender for which we have no word in the English language) was now about *me*. I had, in short, become the nightmare of the religious right and, sadly, of many feminists, especially second wave middle-class American women who grew up in the 1960s and 1970s. It was and continues to be frustrating to me that baby-boomer feminists,[2] lesbian feminists of the 1970s, and many others can't see that the things that concern me also affect the lives of all women. It is even harder to know that these same feminists will unleash such vitriol against us radical Generation X and Generation Y queers.

Each of us stands on the shoulders of those who have come before us. If it wasn't for lesbian feminists' struggle to have lesbianism accepted as a legitimate sexual orientation, i wouldn't be able to fight for the recognition of genderqueerness. If it wasn't for other feminists' insistence that women control their bodies, i wouldn't be able to advocate for the rights of trans people and intersexed folks to make their own decisions about their bodies. Unfortunately, many feminists who are older than i am seem to see my worldview not as a building upon theirs, but as a turning away from what they have stood for and as a threat to their very identities and existence. And while i have deep respect for their beliefs, even if i don't always agree with them, it is hard to believe that many of them have an equal amount of respect and open-mindedness for my points of view.

For instance, i have heard feminists allege that trans men are traitors to the feminist cause or that they have abandoned butch lesbians. Others lay exclusive claim to the definition of womanhood, arguing that male-to-female transsexuals are not "true women" because they were born with penises and were raised as boys. Some feminists state that male-bodied people who do a feminine gender are mocking bio-women, not expressing their inner selves. And still others articulate a concern that genderqueer identities undermine their own woman-hood. I see such people refusing to consider how their lives and trans lives might be similar, how trans issues might overlap with feminist and bio-women's issues. I see them advocating hatred of gender radicals, wanting us out of "their" feminist community, wishing to silence our experiences and insights and to distance themselves from gender non-conformity. This sort of split is indicative of the generation gaps endemic in the U.S. and of adults' refusal to respect the culture and the contributions of youth to society. But it also signals a fear, a deep and abiding terror that opening our gender boxes, loosening the bonds around our bodies and minds will somehow unleash a force that will destroy feminism, feminist gains, and "the women's community."

To be fair, i can also gladly describe the tremendous amount of support that i have received from many of the feminists in my own life. My best friend, a couple of my co-workers, another radical queer, a straight friend, my girlfriend, all have been tremendously supportive…. They think that my genderqueerness is completely legitimate…. All of them know from their personal lives what it's like to be on the fringes of society. They are bisexual, polysexual, polyamorous, queer, working class or of colour; they have dated interracially or have gone out with members of the "same sex"; they have seen war and strife in the Peace Corps. They are all amazing Generation X feminists.

I have also received support from more mainstream women. Since 1995, i have be-longed to a local feminist choir, which is populated mostly by middle-age white women. Some of them identify as straight, some are lesbian, a few are bi. Most of them hold jobs that are not connected directly with social justice work. Few of them have studied feminist or trans theory. Several years ago, when i decided to come out to them as genderqueer, i was concerned. What would they think? Would they kick me out? I knew that that was possible since my choir had, for over twenty years, defined itself as a feminist *women's* singing group. I worried about the freak-out factor…. I worried that, by coming out as genderqueer, i was jeopardizing my membership in the choir and my relationship with most members. I was not at all sure what kind of response to expect from these strong feminist women.

Much to my surprise, they accepted me totally. More than a few expressed their disappointment that i was worried about their reactions and had, as a result, waited for over a year to come out to them as genderqueer. Since that time, the group as a whole decided, with no prodding from me, to redefine itself. We are now no longer a feminist women's choir but a feminist choir. We have continued to have a very constructive and respectful dialogue about how inclusive to become, and i'm pleased that i have not been the only choir member to speak out in favour of more openness. We are, at least in theory, open to members of any sex or gender. And while no man or trans person has yet tried to join, i feel confident that, when and if such a day comes, the answer to that query about membership will not be "no." Hir[3] presence will undoubtedly cause some discomfort and consternation, for it will force the group to move away from thinking of itself as a women's choir in a much more concrete way than my presence ever could. But i also feel confident that, at least as the group stands now, we will be willing to deal with those challenges and to face the changes that a man's, trans person's, genderqueer's or intersexed individual's presence in the group will bring — and also to embrace the gifts that those types of feminists could contribute.

I look at my choir and see the small revolution that i have unwittingly wrought. My actions have changed a small corner of my world and, along with other members' support and openness, have made my choir a more welcoming place for any gender nonconformers who come after me. I know from what other singers have told me that my coming out has also created a more welcoming environment for bisexual members and for those who might otherwise not fit the strict rules of 1970s lesbian feminist communities. I look at this accidental accomplishment and i am incredibly proud. I think: maybe if i can change my chorus, then i can help to change "gender-unfriendly" feminists as well... .

We all have something to gain from trans and genderqueer feminist insights and lives.... It appears that Shante already knew that. She never seemed fazed that i didn't fit into one of her preconceived gender boxes. At four years old, she didn't know that i had to be one or the other, that i could never change. So she accepted me as sometimes boy/sometimes girl. Shante — this girl with her confusion over which pronouns to use for me — was more right about my gender identity than any other children or adults with whom we played. She knew, albeit unconsciously and apolitically, that gender isn't innate and that it's not binary — something that many adults have a difficult time grasping. Yes, i realize that she'll learn a different gender order as she gets older, as more and more messages of gender conformity and gender binarism are heaped upon her head. As the truism goes, bigots are taught, not born. And it saddens me to think that someday, should we ever meet again, Shante will likely demand to know "what" i am. She will no longer be content to see me as sometimes boy/sometimes girl. But the fact that she did, at one point in her life, know that gender is messy and fun and flexible, that she could create me in a certain gendered image to fill a deep void in her heart, gives me hope that the rest of us can relearn that, too, for we all undoubtedly knew that truth when we were four years old.

Yes, breaking out of our boxes can seem scary. But it can also be a hell of a lot of fun. And it promises to offer all of us much more room to grow than if we stay trapped in those prisons labelled man and woman. Despite what many feminists might believe, my genderqueerness is not an attack on women, a tearing down of their pride in womanhood or a demand that they change how they see themselves; my identity is about me and about wanting to make more options for all of us. But those options are just that — options. Wouldn't you rather that those two genders be rooms that you could choose to enter if they feel comfortable for you instead of cells that we are forced to inhabit from birth? I know that i would. I think that Shante felt similarly. And i hope that you do, too.

Shannon Wyss, 2006, "Sometimes Boy/Sometimes Girl," in Krista Scott-Dixon (ed.), *Transforming Feminisms: Trans/Feminist Voices Speak Out*, Toronto: Sumach Press. Adapted and reprinted with permission.

1. When not at the beginning of a sentence, i leave my first person subject pronouns lowercase. The fact that, in English, we only capitalize the pronoun "I" seems indicative of the self-centredness of much of Western culture: I am more important that you, she, he, it, we or they. As such, my use of "i" signals a rejection of egocentric cultural norms and values.

3. Baby boomers make up the generation born between 1946 and 1964; Generation Xers were born between 1965 and 1980; and members of Generation Y were born after 1980.

4. "Hir" (pronounced "here") is a gender-neutral, third person object or possessive pronoun. Its subject equivalent, in my writing, is "ze," although other authors use different gender-neutral subject pronouns, such as s/he.

30

We're Talking Vulva!

Shawna Dempsey and Lorri Millan

Artists' Statement: Shawna Dempsey

I first wrote and performed *We're Talking Vulva* for an international conference on women's sexuality called *Coming Together*, which was held in Toronto in 1986. The five-minute performance piece was the result of my realization that many women never see female genitalia, except perhaps in its pornographic representation (beaver shots). Mainstream pornography is much more about men's projected desires than women's experience or even biology, so porn is far from a good source of health information. Other images of our sexual organs found in medical texts or feminist health books are still available to relatively few women. Hence, we know little about this part of our bodies.

These thoughts came to me through conversations with friends. Even lesbians with whom I spoke were largely unclear about the vulva's name, its individual components, and their functions. And most people, regardless of their political awareness or orientation, were embarrassed I had brought it up.

In creating *We're Talking Vulva*, I was motivated by a desire to disseminate anatomical information. However, it was not until I constructed the giant foam costume and performed the piece that I realized that the performance's real power is in celebrating a part of our bodies that has been demonized.

Historically, our society has reduced our function entirely to that of our sexual organs: as fulfillers of male fantasy and as makers of babies. The vulva has been thought of as something to be used for another's pleasure and as proof of our inferiority, or incompleteness. During the middle ages, its cleft was considered to be the mark of the devil. Even those of us born within the last fifty years, when exploring our vulva as children, heard words like "dirty" and "don't touch." Even in this new millennium, "cunt" is still considered to be the most vulgar insult. Our feelings of shame and disgust around our bodies are deep-rooted.

Both the film and the performance *We're Talking Vulva* present an alternative image. Larger than life, the Giant Vulva publicly talks about all of the embarrassing, private things that each of our own vulva do. But these basic human functions are presented with open good humour, even pride. The Giant Vulva is unselfconscious. She has fun. And she's anything but passive. She goes about her day (shopping, banking, working at a construction site) with the most basic part of her female identity exposed. Indeed, it is her whole self. She raps and dances her experience, and in the process exorcizes some of the negative socialization we share about female anatomy.

NOTE

Available as a film by Shawna Dempsey, Lorri Millan and Tracy Traeger, 1990. Based on a performance by Shawna Dempsey.

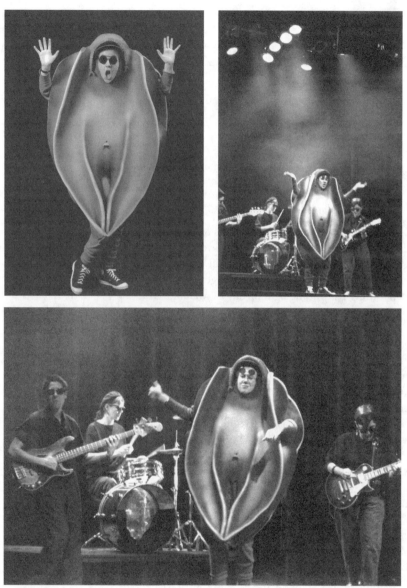

We're Talking Vulva, performance by Shawna Dempsey. Photos by Lorri Millan. Reprinted with permission of Shawna Dempsey.

31

The Vagina

bpNichol

1.

I never had one.

2.

I lived inside a woman for nine months & inside this male
shell all of my life. I floated around on that side of the wall
poking & kicking her not looking for exits till I needed them.
There came a time I needed you vagina to get thru into this
world. First thing I say at the light of day is "waaah," Ma.

3.

I thot they all were hairless even tho I bathed with my
mother I thot they all were like the little girl's who came
naked to the door I delivered the paper to when I was nine
even tho I read the typed porno stories my brother brought
back from the navy when I was ten I thot they all were
hairless like the nude women's in the sunbathing magazines in
the pool hall in Port Arthur even tho I had to know different
somewhere I thot they all were hairless & they weren't.

4.

I always wanted one. I grew up wanting one. I thot cocks
were okay but vaginas were really nifty. I liked that name for
them because it began with "v" and went "g" in the middle. I
never heard my mother or my sister mention them by name.
They were an unspoken mouth & that was the mouth where
real things were born. So I came out of that mouth with my
mouth flapping "waaah." Oh I said that. I said
"waaah" Ma again & again after I was born.

5.

When I was eleven this kid I knew took me to the drugstore
where he worked & showed me some sanitary napkins for
men. He said, "you wear these when you get your period." I
remember he pointed the box out to me & it was way up in the
back of this unlit top shelf. I figured I must have some kind of
vestigial vagina which was bound to open. I waited almost two
years. I never had one.

6.

When sex happened I realized it was all a matter of muscles.
I liked the way her muscles worked. She liked the way my
muscle worked. It wasn't the one thing or the other thing but
the way the two of them worked together. And that was
where all the power & the feelings sprang from — the muscles.
Alive alive oh.

7.

Doorway. Frame. Mouth. Opening. Passage. The trick is to
get from there to here thru her. Or the way Ellie misread that
sign on the highway for years: RIGHT LANE MUST EXIST. And of
course it's the old conundrum — the exit's the entrance. Exit
Ma & I exist. And when I feel in love with Ellie I was
entranced. Into a world. The world. This world. Our world.
Worlds.

NOTE

bpNichol, 1988, "The Vagina," in bp.Nichol, *Selected Organs: Parts of an Autobiography*, Toronto:
Black Moss Press. Reprinted with permission.

Penises

Libby Scheier

Freud never had one.

We're irritated with penises.
The psychiatrists
have shoved them down our throats for too long.
Penis envy and other silliness.
So there's backlash.

Penises are kind of a pain because
they are so vulnerable hanging out there like that
and men are so concerned about the way they hang
out there like that.
Penises are not consistent.
They make foolish demands
or lapse into abject defeatism.
They know no happy medium.
Penises are Jewish
When they fail they transfer the guilt,
when they succeed they take all the glory.

Penises are funny.
Sylvia said they look like chicken gizzards.
I said sausage and eggs
and old monkey skin
and hairs of an elephant's head.
Let's face it.
Penises are not goodlooking.
They can be fun, but they're never pretty.

Penises hang on grown men.
Children do not have penises.
Or so I thought.

But I had a baby boy.
He has a penis.
It's small and pretty like a little finger.
He does not yet have a piece of his brain
in the head of his penis.
Some days he wants to be a girl.

Some days he wants to be a boy.
It's no big deal for him.

He is intensely interested in trucks, trains, airplanes, boats,
crayons, paint, playdough, books, bikes, wagons, puppets, hats,
necklaces, blocks, dolls, doll carriages, rabbits, and nail polish —
which he insists on wearing ever since he saw it
on the fingernails of a friend of mine.
He doesn't confuse his interest in trucks with his penis.
He doesn't confuse his fondness for nail polish with his penis.
He pees with his penis.
He plays with it.
He likes playing with it.
He likes aiming his piss
and he likes his little erections.
But he's big on his feet and toes too.
And he greatly admires his belly button.
Let's face it.
He's got his penis in perspective.
It's part of his body.

Penis envy is a theory
that came from Freud's problem
which was a compulsive obsession
with penises
which was not surprising since he never had one.

As part of the male body,
the penis is quite a nice part.
Functional, humorous, unpredictable.
As container for the entire male body
including the brain
the penis in this case is a bore.

with apologies to bpNichol and
his wonderful poem, 'The Vagina'

NOTE

Libby Scheier, 1986, *Second Nature*, Toronto: The Coach House Press.

"The Best I Could Say Was That It Was like Bliss"

Thinking about the Circuit, Pleasure and the Subject

Russ Westhaver

How do ideas about sex, gender and desire intersect with living bodies? Like all important issues, this question is impossible to think about in the abstract. Notions like "sex," "gender" and "desire" are so broad as to be meaningless if not articulated in relation to lived sexed, gendered and desiring bodies. To raise a more productive question about ourselves as sexual subjects, I want to think about the relationship between "sexed" ideas and lived experience in the context of *circuit parties*.[1] Initially circuit parties can be understood as rave-like events — very large all-night dance parties. Well known DJs offer continuously mixed music to attendees who spend the bulk of their time dancing. These dance events run between six and upwards of twelve hours, and are understood as gay celebrations. Drug use and sexual activities are common components of the circuit.

Unlike raves, however, circuit party attendees are almost exclusively gay men and a cursory assessment of these events suggests the circuit is about an economy of pleasure, with particular notions of gender, body image, sex, drug use and community at the centre of its exchanges:

> I'm there for the same reason as others. I'm there for sex, drugs, music, meeting people, being in a gay space, forgetting the real world, being uninhibited for a night. (Peter)

Attendees uniformly dance shirtless while go-go dancers with perfectly chiselled gym toned bodies gyrate on pedestals above the crowd — a circuit party is, above all, a *very* sexy event. As a sexualised economy of pleasure, the circuit's currency is a particular brand of masculinity. The figures gracing circuit advertisements and promotional material are invariably muscular, with broad shoulders, well defined arms, a V-shaped back, washboard abdominal muscles, "bubble butts" and short cropped hair. The circuit is a man's world:

> I think it's a celebration of masculinity for sure. So you want to epitomize everything masculine about you. That's where the facial hair comes in; chest hair is coming back, the big muscles, the cock rings make your genitals protrude: everything that can epitomize male sexuality and being a man is epitomized on these dance floors. (Frank)

As a celebration of masculinity the circuit is a collective experience:

> At a circuit party you realise there are all kinds of other men there for exactly the same reason as you. And that's kind of an interesting experience. There's this whole world of like-minded people out there doing exactly the same thing you are and enjoying it for the same reasons you are. There's a common thread that goes through everybody. It's really an interesting way to bond with people. (Frank)

This notion of the circuit-as-community is widely shared by attendees. Community boundaries, however, require exclusion — a community depends on what it is not. Bill experiences this as he prepares for a circuit event:

> It seems like for me the only thing I don't feel decent about is my tummy. So when I know I'm gonna go to an event, where I'm gonna take my T-shirt off, my tummy has to be — not necessarily flat — but to a size that I don't mind having. (Bill)

While Bill might gloss this self-surveillance as a "choice", it emerges from an awareness of the value of the tight well-defined body:

> Personally, I wouldn't have as much pleasure going into an event like that if it were filled with fifty percent of fat men or overweight people. I wouldn't get off on that. (Bill, 36)

Not unexpectedly concerns about steroids, and their body sculpting magic, come into play:

> I hate that it's not natural, but on the other hand I'm one who loves to look at these beautiful guys — and if the steroids have got them to that place, then so be it. I don't really care because I'm not doing it personally. And you know what? Look at them. They're *beautiful*. It's a little bit unfair. I feel a bit of pressure to do them to equal up. I've been thinking about them a lot lately. (Peter)

At the same time, other drugs — MDMA (Ecstasy), ketamine (Special K), crystal methamphetamine (Crystal), Viagra, and gamma-hydroxybutyrate (GHB) are also well known to the bulk of circuit attendees.[2] It would be false, however, to suggest all attendees adhere to this hegemonic notion of masculinity or use drugs. A wide range of bodies find at least some transaction in the circuit's economy and not all attendees consume drugs.

Nevertheless, normative gender expectations privilege a particular aesthetic and a particular kind of masculinity is venerated. Buff men are at the top, dancing on podiums; the rest are ranked below. In this context, it is possible to raise questions about sexual categories and lived experience. How do gay men negotiate the gendered ideas of the circuit? I approach this question by spinning it in a slightly different direction: How have these experiences been "taken up" by intellectuals, community activists, circuit promoters, health proponents, writers, and others with an interest in the lives of gay men?

The best known critic of the circuit is Signorile (1997) who attacks the circuit's "cult of masculinity," arguing that anxieties about the buff body are hardly conducive to a positive sense of self and that the events' structures — loud music, an inability to clearly communicate, and an emphasis on appearance — lead to relationships premised on the pursuit of sex and devoid of real intimacy. Moreover, in light of the links between unsafe sex and drug use, the circuit is likely to be a place where gay men end up destroying friendship, community and love. Signorile calls for attendees to deprogram from the cult of masculinity and the pursuit of the buff body (see also Mansergh et al. 2001, Mattison et al. 2001, Lewis and Ross 1995).

An alternative view comes from proponents who see the dance floor as a place full of love and hope:

> Insight, breakthroughs, healing and a range of spiritual experiences are inherent in this form of ritual dance. In rediscovering our dancing body as the vehicle and container of joy and the experience of love and unlimited capacity to hold high levels of energy while remaining conscious, aware and present. (Maris 2000: 39)

Here, the circuit experience is a vehicle for personal development and the enrichment of interpersonal relationships.

While critics and proponents do offer more complex tales — both advocate safer sex and harm reduction strategies and demand real intimacy on the circuit — I use this typology to highlight the major terms of the circuit debate: the suggestion that the circuit is a site of danger versus the suggestion that by embracing the circuit, gay men might become more actualized subjects. Embedded in this debate are two assumptions. First, circuit party attendance has implications for gay men's social and political positioning. Things will get worse (drug addiction, self-esteem) or better (breakthroughs, insight) as gay men do the circuit. Second, the position that gay men have will improve via reflection on circuit experience — deprogramming, insights, or breakthroughs will emerge if attendees think about what the circuit offers. In making these claims, critics and proponents suggest there is a way of experiencing pleasure that is more productive than others.

Responding to the AIDS backlash in the 1980s, Leo Bersani (1988) raised some interesting questions about how we use the idea of sex — and, by association, pleasure — in sexual politics. The AIDS backlash involved clashes between two groups. Those on the right wished to silence the gay men, who were dying as the result of a poorly understood disease — an idea linked to the notion that gay men somehow deserved their fate insofar as they took sexual pleasure in un-Godly and unnatural ways. In contrast, gay activists argued for the right to have safer sex in whatever fashion. For these activists, models of sexual intimacy adopted by gay men challenged heterosexist notions of intimacy, sex, relationships and love. Across this spectrum of sexual politics is a peculiar commonality — what Bersani (1988) calls the *redemptive reinvention of sex*. "This enterprise cuts across usual lines of the battle field of sexual politics" and assumes a purity in sex might be recovered, as if sex could be "less disturbing, less socially abrasive, less violent, [and] more respectful of 'personhood'" than it currently is (Bersani 1988: 215). The Right assumed gay desire violated the divinely ordained purpose of sex. The challenge was to shepherd along those unable to see this — through force, if need be. Gay activists argued the sexual possibilities of the body were inherently *amoral* — what was *immoral* was the regulation the Right wished to exercise around what others did with their bodies. Implicit in both the violence toward gay men and sex-positive rethinking of same-sex desire is a redemptive project based on a "certain agreement about what sex should be" (Bersani 1988: 221).

Both arguments are "ways to defend our culture's lies about sexuality" (Bersani 1988: 222). The lie at the core of the redemptive reinvention of sex is that, with enough reflection, we might come to understand the true nature of sex. The lie is to think and act "as if the sexual… could somehow be conceived of apart from all relations of power; [as if sex] were, so to speak, belatedly contaminated by power from elsewhere" (Bersani 1988: 220). We are, he argues, fooling ourselves to think of sexual pleasure as something that might be "good," if only we were able to situate it in the "right" social relations. Bersani (1988) argues there is a constitutive link between sexual pleasure and the exercise or loss of power. Sexual pleasure always already involves a struggle with a "radical disintegration and humiliation of the self" or a "breakdown of the human itself in sexual intensities." It is not that sexuality exists *in* power relations. Rather sexual bodily pleasures emerge *from* relations of loss and control — and hence power.

In light of this idea, I consider an assumption guiding critics and proponents of the circuit alike. Both assume attendees have the capacity to mobilise the reflexive gaze necessary to negotiate through the dangers and potentials the circuit poses to the self and to one's community. This is a particularly modern view of the subject and social world, where an autonomous rational ego uses reflection to regulate the self and others as he or she calculates the potential benefits of the social field. The circuit, however, raises questions about the degree to which we can assume that subjects have the ability in the first place. Listening to attendees, one can hear language — and the cognitive, analytical, and reflexive possibilities that hinge on language — fail as it encounters the circuit's pleasures:

> You know what it was like? The best I could say was that it was like bliss. (Karl)

> I didn't know a body could sustain this much pleasure. My flesh threatened to come out of my skin. (Fieldnotes 1998)

> Your senses are completely heightened to a certain extent. Physically your touch and everything just seems more real I guess, or you… I'm short of descriptions for this. (Jaret)

Here, pleasurable experiences are inexplicable or ineffable. Unable to explain or represent their experiences, attendees argue, "you just have to be there to understand." As Jaret tells us, "I'm short on descriptions for this."

Reflection — deprogramming from the cult of masculinity or developing insight — depends on our ability to capture the experience through language. And yet, pleasurable experience — central to the circuit's structure — escapes language. This is not to suggest we cannot consider the dangers and possibilities associated with the pleasures of the circuit. It would be short-sighted to ignore the links between the circuit, sex, drug use, and the cult of masculinity. At the same time, to deny claims about community and bonding would be patronizing — these are real, lived experiences. Drug use, safer sex, and improved inter-personal relations of intimacy are real issues and I do not contest their significance. What I contest is that both critics and proponents do not take the pleasurable aspect of these pursuits seriously enough.

Critics' and proponents' call to re-evaluate the circuit assume the presence of a reflect-ing subject. In fact, however, upon the experience of his pleasures, the subject is *absent* from him- or herself. On the edge of pleasure, in a state *like bliss*, the self who might know and assess risks and opportunities through careful reflection, disintegrates. *My flesh threatened to come out of my skin.* Within pleasure there is no subject who understands, no self to be understood. Bodily pleasures are moments where the experiencing self is lost, where language — so central to critical and careful reassessments of risk and benefit — fails to capture the experiencing body. *I'm short of descriptions for this.* The body and its pleasures escape attempts to cordon it off, to capture, analyze it. One can, of course, always make reflexive gestures — but it remains important to recognize that, against pleasure, the self-reflecting gaze becomes inert.

If pleasure is closely linked to much — though certainly not all — of what destroys us (unsafe sex, drug use) *and* to what makes us better (the delight we take in self-expression and community), then the very definition of pleasure as It applies to the circuit needs to be rethought. Assuming that pleasure is something we can rationally know does not allow us to incorporate experiences into how we think about ourselves. In doing so, our analytical efforts fail because we deny what it means to have a body that has pleasure. Thus the question we might consider asking as we think about how gendered and sexed categories intersect with liv-ing bodies becomes: "How do we incorporate ineffable pleasurable experiences — so central to what destroys and fulfils our humanity — into current conceptualizations of the subject?"

1. The observations on which this discussion is based emerge from ethnographic participation in organizing and attending circuit events as well as in-depth interviews with gay men who have some investment and interest in the circuit experience.
2. GHB is a depressant, usually swallowed in liquid form, while MDMA and crystal methamphetamine are stimulants consumed through inhalation or orally. Ketamine is a dissociative anaesthetic that induces psychedelic episodes in humans and is usually inhaled.

REFERENCES

Bersani, L. 1988 "Is the Rectum a Grave?" In D. Crimp (ed.), *AIDS: Cultural Analysis, Cultural Activism.* Cambridge: MIT Press.

Lewis, L., and M. Ross. 1995. "The Gay Dance Party Culture in Sydney: A Qualitative Analysis." *Journal of Homosexuality* 29,1.

Mansergh, G., G. Colfax, M. Marks, M. Rader, R. Guzman and S. Buchbinder. 2001. "The Circuit Party Men's Health Survey: Findings and Implications for Gay and Bisexual Men." *American Journal of Public Health* 91,6.

Maris, P. 2000. "Soul Dance: Writhing in Ecstasy." *Circuit Noize* 24: 38–39.

Mattison, A., M. Ross, T. Wolfson, D. Franklin, and HNRC Group. 2001. "Circuit Party Attendance, Club Drug Use, and Unsafe Sex in Gay Men." *Journal of Substance Abuse* 13.

Signorile, M. 1997. *Life Outside: The Signorile Report on Gay Men: Sex, Drugs, Muscles and the Passages of Life.* New York: Harper Collins.

The Heterosexual Questionnaire

Martin Rochlin

This questionnaire is for self-avowed heterosexuals only. If you are not openly heterosexual, pass it on to a friend who is. Please try to answer the questions as candidly as possible. Your responses will be held in strict confidence and your anonymity fully protected.

1. What do you think caused your heterosexuality?
2. When and how did you first decide you were a heterosexual?
3. Is it possible your heterosexuality is just a phase you may grow out of?
4. Could it be that your heterosexuality stems from a neurotic fear of others of the same sex?
5. If you've never slept with a person of the same sex, how can you be sure you wouldn't prefer that?
6. To whom have you disclosed your heterosexual tendencies? How did they react?
7. Why do heterosexuals feel compelled to seduce others into their lifestyle?
8. Why do you insist on flaunting your heterosexuality? Can't you just be what you are and keep it quiet?
9. Would you want your children to be heterosexual, knowing the problems they'd face?
10. A disproportionate majority of child molesters are heterosexual men. Do you consider it safe to expose children to heterosexual male teachers, pediatricians, priests or scout-masters?
11. With all the societal support for marriage, the divorce rate is spiraling. Why are there so few stable relationships among heterosexuals?
12. Why do heterosexuals place so much emphasis on sex?
13. Considering the menace of overpopulation, how could the human race survive if everyone were heterosexual?
14. Could you trust a heterosexual therapist to be objective? Don't you fear s/he might be inclined to influence you in the direction of her/his own leanings?
15. Heterosexuals are notorious for assigning themselves and one another rigid, stereotyped sex roles. Why must you cling to such unhealthy role-playing?
16. With the sexually segregated living conditions of military life, isn't heterosexuality incompatible with military service?
17. How can you enjoy an emotionally fulfilling experience with a person of the other sex when there are such vast differences between you? How can a man know what pleases a woman sexually or vice-versa?
18. Shouldn't you ask your far-out straight cohorts, like skinheads and born-agains, to keep quiet? Wouldn't that improve your image?
19. Why are heterosexuals so promiscuous?
20. Why do you attribute heterosexuality to so many famous lesbian and gay people? Is it to justify your own heterosexuality?
21. How can you hope to actualize your God-given homosexual potential if you limit

yourself to exclusive, compulsive heterosexuality?

22. There seem to be very few happy heterosexuals. Techniques have been developed that might enable you to change if you really want to. After all, you never deliberately chose to be a heterosexual, did you? Have you considered aversion therapy or Heterosexuals Anonymous?

NOTE

Martin Rochlin (1928–2003) was the first openly gay clinical psychologist in Los Angeles. For his obituary, see Stephen F. Morin and Douglas Kimmel, 2004, "Martin Rochlin," *American Psychologist* 59, 9. The "Heterosexual Questionnaire," first published in 1972, is widely available on the Internet. See, for example, at: masculineheart.blogspot.com/2010/01/martin-rochlin-phd-heterosexual.html.

Why I Love Porn

Alison Lee

The first time I remember thinking critically about pornography, I was fifteen. It was the early 1990s, and my friend and I were going through a stack of discarded magazines, undertaking the well-loved teenage art of collage. Between the *Cosmos* and *National Geographics* was this out-of-place porno, just stuck in there. We made awkward jokes while flipping through it, and found a fake advertisement for "Gash Jeans," which depicted a naked woman bent over with her pants around her ankles. We added it to our collage, and next to it scrawled our own teenage thoughts about porn and sexism.

I'd seen porn before, having snooped through friends' parents' stashes or the collections kept by families for whom I babysat. But this was the first porn I remember laying eyes on after learning about feminism. Inspired by the punk-feminist Riot Grrrl movement of the early 1990s, I took books out of the library by feminist thinkers such as Andrea Dworkin, Catherine McKinnon and Robin Morgan, whose statement that "pornography is the theory, rape is the practice," summed up the attitude of many feminists of the previous generation.

Growing up on the bridge between second and third wave feminism was puzzling. I revered the anti-porn feminists who gave me my early education in women's studies — they knew, like I did, that women were being systematically harmed, and that it had to be stopped. At fifteen, I thought that watching porn made you hate women. By sixteen, I wasn't so sure. Younger feminists were taking a broader view of sex and sexuality including a more open attitude toward porn. Third wave feminists were more concerned with fighting for sex workers' rights than condemning pornography as a whole. While these schools of feminism weren't mutually exclusive, I had a hard time holding them both in my head without dealing with significant questions. Was I supposed to support the hard-working woman in front of the camera, or feel repulsed and sorry for her as an exploited sex object?

Since that collage-making session, I've looked at a lot of pornography in a lot of different contexts. I now see porn as a positive extension of human sexual expression, but I still have a lot of questions about big-picture issues around pornography and society. I've searched for answers in a lot of ways: as an undergrad studying sex and gender; as a sex store manager trying (unsuccessfully) to get porn in stock because my female customers demand it; and as a staff reviewer for a website that informed readers about where to get the best quality blowjob videos online. I've looked critically at sex, society, and porn for years now, and I still maintain that sex is an amazingly telling lens through which to view the world. This commitment to critical examination continues today with my work as manager of Good for Her,[1] a Toronto-based feminist sex store. At this store I also organize the Feminist Porn Awards, which honour the hard-working feminists who are revolutionizing the porn industry. If the very idea of someone who cut her teeth on anti-porn theory now handing out butt-plug-shaped trophies to pornographers doesn't make Andrea Dworkin spin in her grave, I don't what would.

After moving to Toronto in 2005, I'd been I out of work for almost five months when I found an intriguing help-wanted ad on Craigslist. The company was looking for writers to review adult websites. With a deep breath and undying love of ridiculous situations, I sent my résumé. The company owner explained the site's concept to me a few days later. My job was to give positive reviews of websites in order to direct online traffic to such enticing sites as "Black Dicks, White Chicks" and "Big Tits, Round Asses."

As someone who strongly identified as a feminist, I knew that taking this job did not reflect my politics. I still felt the sharp division between "good" porn and "bad" porn: this was definitely bad porn. I had no idea what to expect. The offices were nice, and the project was backed by a semi-retired millionaire who fed his love of toned Latino men by starting several small-time soft-core gay websites. I expected that the job would be strange and an experience unlike anything I'd ever done before, and it was. But I wasn't prepared for the overwhelming boredom that awaited me.

A year and a half into the gig, I was closing in on my 1000th review; it was becoming difficult to differentiate between websites. The names were nearly indistinguishable, the performers generally looked the same, and the content was often not just similar, but exactly the same, just sold under a different title in order to grab customers with an appetite for whatever niche the sites were selling. The work at this point was automatic. I could do it in my sleep: count the videos and photo sets, document the frequency of updates, and offer some kind of snappy line that made yet another mundane site sound sexily appealing.

Generally I didn't feel sorry for the women in these pictures, but, to tell the truth, I didn't really think of them all that much — the naked bodies blurred together. But then I came across photos of a woman I knew. Her face and naked body brought me back to reality: we'd had drinks together, talked feminist politics. I was shocked by the reminder that these were all real people with jobs that put them in the strangely public/private realm of porn. Viewing this content day-in and day-out, my desire to learn about porn as a cultural force and to think about it critically had been overrun by my blasé attitude. There was a difference between what I was viewing and the kind of porn that could be empowering and celebrated, and the difference was suddenly glaring.

My time writing about porn sites often left me feeling conflicted — how feminist was it really to be making money off the labour of (mostly) women? Could I still call myself a feminist if I was looking at naked women all day and not using my position to criticize the glaring sexism and racism that I was constantly viewing? I couldn't help but be disturbed by the sheer number of "reality" porn websites that had premises based on the idea of "tricking" unassuming women (who were obviously actresses following a script) into performing sex acts with promises of money or fame or sometimes just rides to their jobs, and then quickly yanking away these opportunities at the end of the scene. At the end of the day, I knew that what I was looking at was fantasy — a world built up of erotic shortcuts created to arouse (mostly) men. I took this job not so that I could call out the fucked-up parts of the industry, but so that I could pay my bills, and gain more knowledge about the wide world of porn.

What struck me most often when looking at these websites was how frequently I was left feeling sad that this was all that men were being offered. In my time working in sex stores, my own personal goal was to crack open the infinite world of sexuality for people, and especially for women, who are the primary clientele of the shops I've worked in. Seeing the world of Big Porn showed me that not only are women left out, but men are presented with an incredibly limited set of options to work from, with which to mould their own sexuality.

I left my porn review gig believing that the world of porn shouldn't be eradicated, but that it should instead live up to the boundless possibilities of the erotic, and that it should, and could, be able to reflect the diverse bodies, desires and dreams that make up human sexuality.

The Production of Feminist Porn

While there is a history of women writing stories and taking pictures and even making movies that have been intended or used to fuel erotic fantasies, it's only been recently that these films have been marketed as porn for women. Now women are claiming a stake in the means of production in what has traditionally been a male-dominated industry, and they are finding success both in and outside the larger industry. For example, Tristan Taormino, an acclaimed sex-columnist turned director, makes educational titles, such as *Tristan Taormino's Expert Guide to Anal Sex*, as well as racier projects. Her just released *Chemistry Volume 4: The Orgy Edition* takes six porn stars and puts them up in a house for thirty-six hours, Big Brother style, giving them the power to script their own scenes, and take part in the filming as well. The performers get a lot of say in how they want to be represented and exactly what kind of sex they want to engage in.

On the production side, more women are taking the reins with distribution, ensuring that they remain in control of how and where their work is displayed. With the success of porn on the web, performers running their own sites are increasingly able to reap a larger percentage of the profits and maintain creative control in ways that wouldn't be possible in the mainstream.

Feminist porn producers already depict women as active participants in their own sexual fantasy. The project going forward will be to continue to ensure safe, appropriate working conditions for those who appear in and produce porn, while continuing to work on traditional feminist goals, including eradicating the exploitation of women. Erika Lust's film company, for instance, donates five percent of its revenue to Equality Now and Womankind Worldwide, non-governmental organizations combating sexual exploitation.

The Debates Over Feminist Porn

In the spring of 2008, I organized the third annual Feminist Porn Awards, held in Toronto to recognize filmmakers who are doing it right, showing sex as positive and healthy. The Awards have categories such as Fiercest Female Orgasm, Deliriously Diverse Cast, and Most Tantalizing Trans Film. The films all depict consent and active desire, with women as agents of their libidos, rather than being shown as racialized or inferior objects. Leading up to the awards, which attracted an audience of upwards of 450 women (and even a few men), the bulk of my work hours were spent on trying to get the word out. I conducted many interviews with journalists who were confused by the very idea of feminists honouring porn flicks. A healthy part of my day became the Google search, looking for mentions in the media and on blogs. Most of the coverage I found was positive, and the negatives were hard to separate from online trolls looking to bait anyone with a different opinion. But the criticisms that I read most often, primarily on feminist blogs, focused on the impossibility of there ever being any such thing as feminist porn. The belief seems to be that recording a woman in a sex act was inherently degrading; the thought that any woman could choose to star in, or write and direct, her own porn is unfathomable to these critics. For all the problems that mainstream porn presents, I knew that women can — and do — choose to be involved in the industry, either within big productions or in their own indie affairs. I knew this because I'd been talking with many of these women for weeks, and asking them to be a part of these awards. I was talking directly with the vanguard of the new porn revolution.

One such woman is Erika Lust, a thirty-one-year-old mother of an incredibly cute tod-dler, and a pornographer. When Lust started making films, she wanted to provide something she couldn't find anywhere else — porn targeted at straight women. "I want to make movies for straight girls because we are a big group of people and we are supposed to go with the mainstream heterosexual porn, made by men for men," she says. "Lesbians, gays, trans… every group lately has their own porn, and I felt that nobody was thinking about the needs and desires of heterosexual women. We are supposed to be happy and satisfied with *Sex and the City*, *Desperate Housewives* or *Playgirl* movies, but we need more than that!" Lust's debut film, *Five Hot Stories for Her*, has won multiple awards (including a Feminist Porn Award for Movie of the Year in 2008).

This is not to say that everything is always perfect in feminist porn land; as has always been the case with feminism, there is never one solid vision of what "feminist" is, and what calling yourself a feminist pornographer really means. And there are disputes. Lust and another female director, Petra Joy from the U.K., were involved in a minor skirmish in the feminist porn blogosphere when Joy disputed the application of the feminist label for cer-tain sex acts caught on film: "If you want to show come on a woman's face that's fine, but don't call it feminist," she wrote on her website.[2] Lust took offense to this and shot back a passionate response in her blog, saying she was sad that "certain women devote their time and energy to pulling down the work of other women, instead of focusing on empowering our different approaches and points of view."

While Joy made sure to say she believed that any feminist could show whatever she liked in her films, the sentiment remained that there were, or should be, rules in place. Is showing semen on a woman's body inherently demeaning? If a performer is choosing to engage in these acts, and states either that it doesn't bother her or more, that she relishes it, can we condemn the result?

Conclusion

When I was a teenager making my first dives into feminism, I couldn't always wrap my head around the divides within pornography and notions of sex-positive expression in general. Even now, the call to support sex workers is too often predicated on getting them out of sex work, even if that is where they want to be. The idea that feminism was going to "save" women, either from performing in porn or from experiencing the presumed violent effects of porn, still smacks too much of paternalistic control. Women need to be supported in their decisions and choices around sex and sexuality, and that includes appearing on websites some find gross, or checking out porn on cable channels and finding new ideas and acts that turn them on even if it's porn free of politics.

Feminist porn may not be the answer to all of the critiques of pornography as a genre and an industry, but it is a start that looks to the infinite possibilities the future holds for porn. Access to porn is expanding every day. Consumers have the opportunity to demand better porn: we are doing just that on a larger scale than ever seen before. The new face of porn has an opportunity to disrupt stereotypes and address new viewers, all while creating a feminist view of sexuality. As Erika Lust says, "porn and feminism must be allies: they have to fight together against the conservative notion of considering [sex as something] that has to be only related with reproduction, and labelling [sexually] active women as whores. Both feminism and porn can help liberate women from what society expects from us: to be good, quiet, nice girls, not complaining, not arguing, not fighting, not enjoying sex, not be-ing powerful and provocative." Women can watch and make porn as a powerful statement against the status quo, one dirty DVD at a time.

Alison Lee, 2008, "Why I Love Porn," *This Magazine* 42,3 (Nov/Dec). Reprinted with permission.

1. At: goodforher.com.
2. At: petrojoy.com/weblog.

36

Tales of Selling Sex

Pamela J. Downe

What is prostitution? This seemingly simple question is actually far more complicated than it first appears. On one level, prostitution is, quite succinctly, the performance of sexual acts for the sole purpose of material gain. On another level, though, prostitution is surrounded by debates concerning its place in society, the degree of coercion that characterizes it and the extent to which it should be regulated through legislation. Commonly referred to as "the world's oldest profession," prostitution requires a considerable set of skills among those who are successfully involved in it. It takes great skill to survive in the often difficult and danger-ous circumstances associated with prostitution: to evade arrest, conviction and detainment in areas where selling sex is criminalized; to attract and handle clients; to negotiate with clients, managers and hostile bystanders; and to develop and maintain informal networks of peers often under necessary cloaks of secrecy. However, it is rare to find positive portrayals of those involved in prostitution. Instead, we are inundated with sensationalized and nega-tive images depicting red light districts where supposed "junkie whores" stroll the streets or racialized children from poor countries being forcibly trafficked as "sex slaves." Rarely do we hear from those with first hand knowledge of what it is like to be involved in prostitution.

For the past eleven years, I have conducted research across four countries and with ap-proximately two hundred young women who are involved in prostitution to varying degrees. Some are adult women working independently through escort services, hotels and bars. Some are much younger, living on the streets, and in need of the income that sex work provides. Some live and work in the eastern Caribbean, where they are forcibly relocated from one island to another to service the growing market of sex tourists. Some of these women are involved only occasionally in prostitution; others work more consistently. Most, but not all, abuse drugs and alcohol. Some of these women work with pimps; others do not. Some of the women have genuine affection for their pimps, calling them "boyfriends" and "husbands"; others do not. Some women work in prostitution because they have to, others because they want to. All have been exposed to violence, but to varying degrees. All of the women have admitted to wanting out of prostitution altogether, but coercive relationships with pimps and peers, necessity or convenience draw them back.

Working with these women has taught me a valuable lesson: "prostitution" is not one thing. Although it involves similar sexual acts, the meaning that those acts have are as diverse as the people who perform them. So what does prostitution mean to the young women with whom I have spoken and who are engaged in it?

Ashley-Mika

When I first met Ashley-Mika,[1] she was fifteen years old and had been working in prostitution for two years. After running away from an abusive home in a northern prairie community, she found herself on the streets of a mid-sized city. This urban environment exposed her, as a young Métis girl, to an intensification of racism and poverty. She found respite from the cold streets when she met Paul, a young man who offered her shelter, food and access to alcohol and drugs. He ultimately became her pimp, and required her to relocate from one city to another, across national borders and back. Ashley-Mika did not have control over the money she made, giving it all to Paul in exchange for shelter, food and crack-cocaine. Over the course of the nine interviews I conducted with Ashley-Mika, she described her involvement in prostitution in very telling ways:

> Like, what else was I gonna' do, you know? I was so young and I just hated it up there [home community], you know, I mean it got real bad, real bad. They was always yelling and hitting at me. I was nothing to them, nothing. Like, I just had to get out you know, so, like, I did. And [this city] seemed, like, so big, eh? But it was cold. It was cold like at home except I had no place to go. I didn't really know nobody, eh? I was the tough, loner kid, always being tough, you know? So then I met Paul and them and, like, they let me into their place when my feet was so cold they was blue. And it felt good, you know, just being inside and drinking and eating. So, I started letting them get on me so, you know, I could stay there, you know....
>
> Then one day, Paul goes, "I got a friend coming over and he likes you." So then he goes, "it's his birthday so you should go on him." So, like, I didn't want to get kicked out or nothing, eh? So, I go, "yeah, okay, whatever." And that just started it all, you know? At first I thought, you know, this is, like, easy money. Nothing to it. But after a bit, it starts to get to you. Paul got meaner, you know, and he started hitting at me when, like, when I was having my period or whatever, you know? I just would be feeling like shit, hung over, hurtin' from the drugs and then, like, the cramps and shit, eh? So, I'd be, like, "No, man, I don't want to do nothing today. I been working hard for you but today, like, no." And he'd freak out, started hitting and stuff. It was bad, bad as at home, you know? So, I'd be, like, what choice do I got? So I'd go work. But it was hard with my period. Like, it would be so much easier if I was a guy, you know? I could hit them all back, you know? I could tell 'em all to go to hell, you know? I could just relax maybe and, like, get some sleep, you know?
>
> ...The thing is, I'm Métis, eh? I don't really know what that means 'cept that I'm, like, I'm in the middle. I'm not white but I'm not Indian, you know? And that gets real hard 'cause I don't know how to act, like, who am I supposed to be? And I get these white guys, eh? They want me to, like, talk "Indian" to 'em, you know? What the hell does that mean? I'm just, like, this little Indian ho, you know? But I'm not. I mean, I don't feel Indian, but I know I look like it. So, I got these guys and they want squaw sex. That's what me and my friends call it, squaw sex. Indian guys want it too but not so much. I go more with the white guys, eh? They gots more money but they are meaner. I get beaten more by 'em. Like, what do they care? I'm just an Indian ho, you know? God, I want out sometimes.... But, like, what else what would I do? I can't go back to no foster home or nothing like that. But I'm getting really tired of it all, you know? I got cut up real bad by one of the other skanks out here, eh? I just don't know how much longer I got to live like this, you know? It's not about, like, being sexy, it's about getting sexed. It sucks. I don't know how much longer I got to live like this.

After our last meeting in late 2001, I never heard from Ashley-Mika again. I have tried desperately to contact her through her friends, trusted service providers and police officers, as well as child services, but to no avail. Whenever I hear a report that the police have found another body of a young street-involved girl, I freeze with fear because I think that it might be Ashley-Mika.

On Christmas Eve 1992, I found myself all alone, in the midst of my doctoral research, in San Jose, Costa Rica. Feeling quite lonely, I decided to treat myself to a dinner at a nice hotel. I was sitting in the bar when a woman who I would later know as Lisanna grabbed me and violently pushed me to the floor. Mistaking me for a North American sex worker encroaching on her potential clients, Lisanna — a twenty-four-year-old Costa Rican woman with two children — was protecting her "turf." After we were both thrown out of the bar, Lisanna recognized her mistake and fearing that I would go to the police, she offered to buy me a drink in a neighbouring restaurant. For some reason I agreed and over the next several weeks we gradually became friends. Lisanna was fascinated by my research into the health repercussions of violence and asked if she and her roommates (who were also involved in prostitution) could participate. Over the course of eighteen interviews, I learned how Lisanna became involved in prostitution and how it affects her:

> I started doing this because my brother needed to pay off the man who owned the land where we were living [in Nicaragua]. I was his payment. If you do not have the money, you can give the girl. That is how he thought. It worked for him, and his friends but it did not work for me. So, I left.… I came to Costa Rica and found my own way. I started working with Carlos [a well known local pimp] and I fell in love with him. All the girls do; he is beautiful. He is powerful and loving. He never raised a hand to me but the johns did and Carlos would do nothing. Nothing. I worried about AIDS and Carlos did nothing. I got pregnant and he did nothing. I loved him, but he did nothing. I came to know that if you do nothing, you are nothing. So I left him…
>
> I started to work for myself. I was a Nicaraguan in another country. I had no papers to say that I could be in Costa Rica. I have only three years of school and most people here are very well educated. What other job could I do? I had a son. He needed care. What was I to do but be a businesswoman and sell what I know will sell, sex. I am a good businesswoman. I have a group of clients who I trust. I try new ones and they beat me, rob me or refuse to pay. So never again for them. Some of the men really care for me.…
>
> I am a strong woman who has lived a lot. I think of my grandmother and, yes, she would be ashamed of me. But I do what I need to, for myself and my children. I live with my friends and we love each other and our children. In my next life, I will be a doctor, but in this life I am a businesswoman. And my business is sex.

Samantha

Samantha is a twenty-seven-year-old graduate student in physics who also works as a paid escort with a large and well-known agency. I met her in 2002 at a conference and she explained her involvement in sex work:

> Do clients want sex? Yeah. Do I give it to them? That depends. I actually have a lot of say in it. I got the guys back at the service who'll cover me if I need it. I got the other girls. I'm okay. When I agree to sex, I make money. I mean, I make a lot of money, tax free.… I made $77,000 last year, more than any guy I know. Tax free.… Do I do things that I don't like? That hurt? Yeah. But tell me, in your job, are there things you don't like? Things that hurt?

On what is known as the "carnival track" in the eastern Caribbean, Charlene is a sixteen-year-old girl who travels from island to island to sell sex to tourists. She works at the behest of three young men who threaten to abandon her, beat her and send her back to her home community in shame if she does not comply.

> I don't like what I do. It hurts. A lot. I been doing this for so long. I be moving and sexing. I be pretending to be a sexy girl for the tourists, I don't know who I is. I be tired and sick, that's who I know I be. But nobody be seeing that. They just see a piece of Caribbean ass, sexy ass. I don't want to be that. And I don't feel sexy. But I [have] no idea who I be. I be tired and sick.

Diverse Stories, Diverse Contexts

These stories of selling sex raise complex questions about gender, sexuality, cultural heritage and power. Different women, situated in diverse contexts, offer descriptions of their involvement in prostitution. Some, like Ashley-Mika and Charlene, see prostitution as damaging to themselves, their identities and their lives. They understand that their cultural heritage is sexualized in ways that they find demeaning. Other women, including Lisanna, see sex work as a business, a source of income when other alternatives are limited. Still others, like Samantha, find it empowering and liken it to any other job. All the women in my research projects have noted the gendered aspects of prostitution. Being a woman, a "sexy girl" as Charlene describes, is a burden for some and a benefit for others, but it is recognized as an integral part of prostitution by all. As the debates (that were described in the introduction to this section) rage on about decriminalizing, legalizing, controlling and eliminating prostitution, we must remember that prostitution is very complex and is experienced differently depending on social location. Although there is always something very magnetic about simple solutions — "all prostitution is exploitive and should be eliminated," or "all sex work represents free choice and should be condoned" — these solutions never fully address the complex experiences of the women with first-hand knowledge of the sex trades. Perhaps instead we should be concerned with understanding these complexities so that we may attend to them in nuanced, constructive and thoughtful ways.

NOTE

1.   All names used to describe research participants and their acquaintances are pseudonyms.

REFERENCES

Albert, Alexa. 2001. *Brothel: Mustang Ranch and Its Women.* New York: Ballantine Books.

Bell, Shannon. 1994. *Reading, Writing and Rewriting the Prostitute Body.* Bloomington: Indiana University Press.

Brock, Deborah. 1998. *Making Work, Making Trouble: Prostitution as a Social Problem.* Toronto: University of Toronto Press.

Delacoste, Frederique, and Priscilla Alexander (eds.). 1987. *Sex Work: Writings by Women in the Sex Industry.* San Francisco: Cleis Press.

Gorkoff, Kelly, and Jane Runner (eds.). 2003. *Being Heard: The Experiences of Young Women in Prostitution.* Halifax: Fernwood.

Hobson, Barbara. 1990. *Uneasy Virtue: The Politics of Prostitution and the American Reform Tradition.* Chicago: University of Chicago Press.

Hodgson, James F. 1997. *Games Pimps Play: Pimps, Players and Wives-In-Law.* Toronto: Canadian Scholars' Press.

Jeffreys, Sheila. 1997. *The Idea of Prostitution.* Melbourne: Spinifex.

Kempadoo, Kamala, and Jo Doezema (eds.). 1998. *Global Sex Workers: Rights, Resistance and Redefinition.*

New York: Routledge.

O'Neill, Maggie. 2001. *Prostitution and Feminism: Towards a Politics of Feeling*. Cambridge: Polity Press.

Roberts, Nicki. 1992. *Whores in History: Prostitution in Western Society*. London: Grafton.

Sanders, Teela. 2004. "Controllable Laughter: Managing Sex Work through Humour." *Sociology* 38,2.

Cyborgs, Flower Ladies and Horse Women

The Changing Face of Menopause

Pat Kaufert

This chapter is not about menopause *per se*, and I have no answers, either epidemiological or philosophical or spiritual, to questions on how the experience should be lived. My focus is rather on how menopause is imagined, thought about, manipulated, turned into a source of profit. As such, this chapter is part of an ongoing series of meditations on time, women, menopause and the perils of aging that have occupied me on and off for a number of years.

Meditation I: Time and the Menopause

Menopause is a marker in time, the body shifting from its fertile to its infertile state. It is also a passage through time; fertility is not suddenly lost, but declines slowly; hormone levels do not suddenly drop, but fluctuate. Menopause is repetitive time. The same passage is replicated in the body of every woman who ages beyond childbearing, with relatively minor variations from woman to woman. Or at least this is the assumption underlying most medical research on menopause. Medical anthropologists, such as Margaret Lock (1993), challenge this assumption and contend that bodies change and so also does menopause.

Margaret Lock uses the phrase "local biologies" as a reference to the ways in which bodies are formed by place and culture, which determine such things as what women eat, how their bodies are shaped by physical work, the spacing of their children. Jeanne Shea's (1998) study of menopausal woman in China suggests that we need to think also of bodies as a product of their historical period. She found that living through the cultural revolution as adolescents left such a deep imprint on some Chinese women that it remained the reference point for any change in well-being, even the ones associated with menopause. The cultural revolution is an extreme example, but the idea of a "historical biology" of the body has broader application. North American women turning fifty — the mean age of menopause — in 1980 will have been born in 1930 and will have been twenty in 1950. This means they were children of the Depression, who grew up during World War II, but not necessarily in the U.S. or Canada. For this is also the generation of the war brides and of the waves of migrants who flooded out of postwar Europe to Canada and the U.S. These women are the mothers of the baby boomers, the women written about by Betty Friedan (1963), remembered from countless old movies and TV shows. It is their daughters, born in the 1950s, who are now becoming menopausal. They were in their early twenties or late teens in 1970, becoming adults against a background of protest, whether against Vietnam or the *War Measures Act*; they cheered for Trudeau, marched for the ERA, joined the women's movement. Very few actually went to Woodstock, but all will have known the music. These are the baby boomers, endlessly analyzed and self-analyzing.

The bodies of this generation of women will not be quite the same as those of their mothers' generation. Women who were severely malnourished during the Depression or the war, for example, will not have laid down as strong a skeleton as their daughters. Their daughters' bodies will have been impacted by having ingested the contraceptive pill and smoked cigarettes and by having had fewer children, higher levels of employment, higher risks for breast cancer, heart disease and lung cancer, and a higher consumption of processed foods. None are the equivalent of living through war and revolution, but they carry enough physiological consequences to suggest that the body of the daughter at menopause will not be quite the same as the body of the mother.

The menopausal body, however, is a product not only of how women lived their lives, but also how becoming menopausal is defined and "managed." Women who turned fifty in 1970, for example, were promised that if they took high doses of estrogen, they would remain feminine forever. By 1980, the menopausal woman was advised to take estrogen for the management of menopausal symptoms, but for as short a time as possible and to watch out for endometrial cancer. Women turning fifty in 1990 were again told to take estrogen but with progestin, and this time they were promised that it would not only manage their symptoms but would protect their heart, their bones and their minds against cognitive decline but without significantly increasing their risk of breast cancer. Alongside these changes in medical advice went also a changing image of what it was to be a menopausal woman.

Meditation II: The Manufactory of Menopause

Menopause is a physiological process, but it is also a concept. How we think about, talk about, experience, treat or understand menopause has been in a fairly constant state of flux over the past thirty or so years. A "new" menopause has been repeatedly manufactured out of the reports of researchers, the pronouncements of clinicians, the images created by drug advertisements, and the chatter of the media. Money is lost and gained with each transformation, for menopause has evolved into a financial product, a multimillion dollar industry, a source of income for gynecologists and of funding for researchers, including the Women's Health Initiative (WHI), the most costly clinical trial in the history of research on women's health.

The promotion of a new menopause can be seen in the publicity materials of pharmaceutical companies in the 1990s relative to the 1970s. The images used in the mid to late 1990s show women admiring nature, exercising, playing with grandchildren, lunching with friends, talking to a daughter, swimming. They smile, glow with good health, display well maintained teeth, hair and skin. They are active rather than passive; while not youthful, they are very far from being crones. They are distinctly, but definitely sexual beings. The women shown in these images are in very marked contrast to an advertisement for estrogen therapy from the 1970s that showed a sad and depressed middle-aged woman, sitting in the office of a fatherly physician, complaining she was depressed, low in energy, having hot flushes.

Had medical science and clinical practice combined to transform the estrogen deprived woman of the 1970s into the fit and glowing woman of the 1990s? Or had the pharmaceutical companies decided that a beautiful, vital woman taking hormones was more likely to sell their product than the sad woman of the earlier advertisements, a burden to herself and others? Or do these images reflect a new way of thinking about menopause, aging and women's bodies?

Meditation III: Menopause and Cyborg Woman

One of the images in a pharmaceutical advertisement shows a very attractive woman in a white toweling bath robe. She is the very prototypes for the "new older woman": straight-backed, fit, of sound mind, strong heart, serene, presumably continent and definitely sexual. Is the message that without estrogen, her bones would crumble, the heart fail, her skin wither and her sexual organs atrophy. Is she reality, or a simulacrum; the cyborg lurking — as in all the best science fiction — below the shining surface?

Looking through the various brochures put out by the pharmaceutical companies in the late 1990s, I found some curious images: transparent women, aging skeletons, partial bodies and body parts, and cyborgs. One depiction of estrogen showed it as an abstract, but powerful force, wrapped protectively around the heart. In another representation, the menopausal woman is the perfect cyborg — her shining metal body maintained in a state of stasis, free of aging, without disease and without deterioration. In a third image, the body is indicated by a simple line and a scattering of body parts, the heart, the hip, the brain and the ovaries. (The "failure" of the latter organs being responsible for menopause.) It is almost as interesting to look at what was left out as what was put in — the things invisible or only partly visible. The colon, which was becoming interesting to researchers based on a few studies that suggested estrogen was protective against colon cancer, may have been difficult to represent, but why should the breast be missing? It is as if the complexity of the menopausal body were reduced only to those parts that responded positively to estrogen. The menopausal cyborg has neither lungs, nor liver, muscles or nerves, and hardly any arteries

Except that the colon, the endometrium and the breast are excluded, the choice of body parts reflects the concentration of research interest in the 1990s. Conferences were held to discuss hormones and the cardiovascular system; hormones and osteoporosis, hormones and Alzheimer's, hormones and ovarian failure. The WHI, the massive study of estrogen and menopause, was expected to provide an exact measure of the benefits of estrogen for each of these organs. Lung cancer, diabetes or the many autoimmune disorders that are part of women's experience as they age and became menopausal were largely ignored. The repeated message in the research and clinical literatures — presented in the form of tables, numbers, pie charts, histograms and graphs — is that once the supply of estrogen is cut off (as in the removal of a woman's ovaries) or gradually falls as in natural menopause — then these organs rapidly become pathological. The heart spasms; the spine compresses; the brain forgets words and goes into cognitive decline. The solution is to replace the lost estrogen, by creating a body that is part natural, part chemical — a cyborg.

Meditation IV: Horse Woman or Flower Woman

Flower Woman

Not all the images were cyborgs. At a conference of the North American Menopause Society in 1998, I found the same photographs of healthy smiling women but also an increasing number of flower, bird and plant images. The more pastoral approach flourished in the alternative health literature promoting "natural" products, but was also visible in the brochures of the pharmaceutical companies. This was woman and nature, but also woman as nature, a flower woman. The most charming flower woman appeared on the cover of a pamphlet distributed by the Canadian Society of Obstetricians and Gynecologists, which showed a woman growing out of the bush, dressed in pale yellow; slightly fey, her gentle romanticism in marked contrast to the brassy cyborg. It is an image of magic realism rather than clinical trials.

The choice of cover goes along with a relatively extensive discussion of alternative medicines for menopause, although preference is given to estrogen and progestin. The small body of feminist literature on menopause has long favoured alternative therapies for menopause ranging from meditation and acupuncture through to evening primrose oil and eating more soy products. Yet there is something slightly disconcerting in the promotion of "natural" products by pharmaceutical companies. Feminists may well be wondering whether they have won, or whether their most cherished therapies are being co-opted, their belief in menopause as a spiritual and natural passage transformed into an image which blurs the boundaries between woman and flower.

I was in New York when a group of animal rights activists picketed a conference on menopause and attracted the attention of the media by parading a woman in a blonde wig, wearing a body stocking and riding a white horse. They were protesting the use of pregnant mares to produce horse urine, the raw material of one the most widely marketed forms of estrogen. While not hidden, neither is this use of urine widely publicized; it falls within the category of facts that are well known but very little discussed. It was then that I registered the total absence of images of horses. There is the occasional dog or cat and lots of flowers and tress, but although I searched carefully, I never found any foals or nursing mares or pregnant ponies on the publicity literature for estrogen. Possibly the image of the galloping horse, a sign of freedom ingrained in the Anglo-American psyche, is not easily reconcilable with the vision of a pregnant mare hooked up to machines that siphon off her urine. There is rich material here for thinking about the boundaries between women and nature, or which animal products are culturally sanctioned for consumption and which are not.

Conclusion

Over the past thirty years as women aged and passed their menopause, they were told that their bodies were a source of danger to themselves, but also to the body politic, which was likely to collapse under the burden of their demands. Beneath the formal layers of the epidemiological risk and health promotion literature, the menopausal woman was presented with a subtext — a kaleidoscope of images from myths and fairy tales — in which the uncared-for female body aged and sickened, destroying its own beauty. But she was also shown a light side to becoming older, in which the caring/cared for female body remains fit, lean, disease free, serene in mind. It is made clear that the choice between light and dark is her responsibility; if she does not take her hormones and allows her body to deteriorate, then she becomes unworthy, undeserving of support.

The irony is that in the last two years, this story and these images have proved false. Sections of the WHI study were cancelled in July 2002 after it was discovered that women randomized to taking both an estrogen and a progestin were at higher risk for breast cancer, heart disease and stroke (Rossouw et al. 2002). The following year, data from the same project showed that women taking the same therapy were at increased risk for dementia (Shumaker et al. 2003). The combined therapy also increases the risk of ischaemic and haemorrhagic stroke (Wasserthell-Smoller et al. 2003). A second trial was cancelled by the British Medical Research Council in November 2002 (White 2002). Those images of fit and healthy women, with estrogen wrapped like a protective shield about the body were false. Rather than its risk decreasing, the menopausal body was at increasing danger the longer therapy endured.

REFERENCES

Friedan, Betty. 1963. *The Feminine Mystique*. New York: W.W. Norton.
Lock, Margaret. 1993. *Encounters with Aging: Mythologies of Menopause in Japan and North America*. Berkeley: University of California Press.
Rossouw, David, and the Writing Group for the Women's Health Initiative. 2002. "Risks and Benefits of Estrogen Plus Progestin in Healthy Postmenopausal Women: Principal Results from the Women's Health Initiative Study." *Journal of the American Medical Association* 288.
Shea, Jeanne. 1998. "Women in Middle Age: An Ethnographic Study of Menopause and Midlife Aging in Beijing." Unpublished PhD dissertation, Harvard University, Cambridge.
Shumaker, Sally, Claudine Legault, Stephen Rapp, Robert Wallace, et al. 2003. "Estrogen Plus Progestin and the Incidence of Dementia and Mild Cognitive Impairment in Postmenopausal Women: The Women's Health Initiative Study." *Journal of the American Medical Association* 289.
Wassertheil-Smoller, Sylvia, Susan Hendrix, Marian Limacher, Gerardo Heiss et al. 2003. "Effect of

Estrogen Plus Progestin on Stroke in Postmenopausal Women: The Women's Health Initiative Study." *Journal of the American Medical Association* 289.

White, Caroline. 2002. "Second Long Term HRT Trial Stopped Early." *British Medical Journal* 325.

Viagra
"Hard Science" Or "Hard Sell"?
Angus McLaren

On March 27, 1998, Viagra became the first oral medication to be approved by the United States Food and Drug Administration to treat erectile dysfunction. An unabated flood of books and articles has subsequently been devoted to analyzing the pill's impact. Among the more insightful is Meika Loe's *The Rise of Viagra: How the Little Blue Pill Changed Sex in America* (2004); but what does it mean to say sex is changed? Is Viagra a wonder drug? A magic bullet? The rejuvenating potion which doctors had sought for centuries? Many have suggested that Viagra's revolutionary impact in the first decade of the twenty-first century equals that which the contraceptive pill had on relaxing sexual mores in the 1960s.

The historian has to be skeptical of such extravagant claims. Each age, including the present one, has reconfigured the notion of male sexual failure. The arrival of the little blue pill certainly did not end male sexual anxieties. Indeed, much evidence exists that it actually heightened them. Specific social and cultural conditions were responsible for the appearance and profitability of a new generation of sexual pharmaceuticals in the 1990s.

The Medicalization of Men's Sexuality

For centuries men turned to doctors for pills and potions to restore their potency. But, in the post-World War Two era, medical doctors admitted they could do little for men suffering from impotence, and most accepted the common belief that ninety to ninety-five percent of cases could be attributed to psychological disturbances. The 1980s saw the emergence of a new paradigm, a swing towards the medicalization of male sexuality. Doctors were experimenting with new remedies including implants, vaso-dilating injections, and bypass surgery of the penile arteries. Urologists were one of the main beneficiaries of this heightened medical interest in male sexual dysfunctions: a new market in patients opened up, and pharmaceutical corporations with a financial interest in propagating such views increasingly employed doctors and scientists as consultants (Tiefer 1986).

Doctors had for years linked sexual dysfunctions to such diseases as diabetes and warned of the dangers of excessive drinking, smoking and bicycle riding. Now they associated impotence with the rise in the number of prostate operations, the increased use of certain prescription drugs and particularly the role of vascular obstructions. The message that impotence was a mechanical problem, and thus fixable, was what many men wanted to hear. However, the argument that urologists were better qualified than anyone else to treat impotence did not go uncontested. Thomas Szasz (1980) attacked the notion that "impotence" and "premature ejaculation" should be viewed as medical diseases. Leonore Tiefer (1995), a defender of sex therapy and a shrewd critic of the medicalization of sexuality agreed that sex was like dancing; to improve one had to practice, not ask a doctor for help. Her point was that sex therapy aimed at changing unhappy relationships; urology did not.

With the medical profession, the pharmaceutical corporations and health insurance companies in favour of a medical approach to male sexual dysfunctions, it is not surprising that it won out in the end. But the popular media's uncritical adoption of the medical model also contributed significantly to promoting impotence as a simple plumbing problem. Long before Viagra hit the market, the popular press, including, interestingly, women's magazines such as *Ms.*, popularized the view that doctors were in the process of triumphing over an age-old problem (McCarthy 1998). By the end of the 1980s, the media largely parroted the doctors' line that, in 90 percent of cases, the causes of impotence were physiological rather than psychological.

From Impotence to Erectile Dysfunction: The Invention of Viagra by Pfizer Corporation

The huge potential profits in life-style drugs naturally led companies to focus research efforts on products that made the most money. Perversely enough, the result was supplying expensive drugs such as Viagra and Prozac to healthy people in America and Europe rather than producing cures for the hundreds of millions of desperately ill and poor in developing nations.

Without the political swing to the right, the success of drugs like Viagra would have been attenuated. The economic downturn in the 1980s and the conservative governments' establishment of neoliberal economic policies provided an economic climate which helped pharmaceutical companies to maximize their profits through, among other things, the deregulation of the pharmaceutical industry, a government-university nexus in the development of research and marketing strategies, and the relaxing of advertising rules that allowed drug companies to engage in direct-to-consumer advertising. Thus patients were encouraged to demand drugs seen on television and in magazines, and drugs were increasingly easy to access on the Internet.

The Pfizer corporation asserted that, although it was not looking for a sex drug, events compelled it to discover one. The official story was that Pfizer scientists had hopes that a drug called sildenafil citrate would, by increasing blood flow to the heart, remedy angina. The drug failed as heart medication, but in 1991 an unexpected side effect was noted. Test subjects reported erections, and patients purportedly refused to give back their pills or even tried to steal more. In other words, happy male patients pushed Pfizer into carrying out further research on sildenafil as a possible remedy for impotence.

Now that Pfizer had a product, the next step was to sell it. The Pfizer advertising department thought that the name "Viagra," would work well as a marketing tool, as it conjured up ideas of "vigor" and "Niagara." Pfizer also astutely recognized the need to replace the word "impotence" with the term "erectile dysfunction." The new nomenclature made the corporation appear soberly scientific and quite distinct from shady sellers of love potions and aphrodisiacs. Eliminating "impotence" from its discourse undercut stigma, while the term "dysfunction" represented an acknowledgement that the "problem" was not a disease in the usual sense of presenting symptoms that would require a diagnosis and a prescribed treatment. The only way the doctor could tell if a patient "needed" Viagra was if the patient later reported improved or enhanced sexual performance.

The term "dysfunction" also provided an opportunity to expand the category of men to whom the drug might be marketed. Previous surveys suggested that, when strictly defined as the inability to get an erection, impotence sometimes afflicted perhaps ten percent of men. With drug companies playing such a central role in research, often loose definitions of erectile dysfunctions included self-reported unsatisfactory sexual experiences or the ambiguous category "mild erectile dysfunctions." Conflating all categories that hindered "satisfactory sexual performance" inflated overnight the number of American men with reputed potency problems from ten million to thirty million (Laumann et al. 1999). While skeptics observed that being sexually dysfunctional was perfectly normal if tired, stressed, or poor, the pharmaceutical corporations presented a common problem as a worrying illness.

Clearly Pfizer's strategy worked. Viagra immediately became the fastest selling pharmaceutical in history. Pfizer's stock went up 150 percent in 1998. Its sale of Viagra topped one billion dollars in 1999, when it enjoyed a profit margin of 90 percent. Was Pfizer's success due, as it claimed, to reaching a large, pre-existing "untapped market," or to its creation of a new market?

Putting the "Fun" Back in "Dysfunctional": The Marketing of Viagra

One can only speculate about how many men were impatiently awaiting the arrival of such a drug. What we do know is that Pfizer launched a sophisticated, if not complicated, campaign to convince millions that they needed its product. In part, Pfizer's message had to navigate the divide between "natural sexuality" and a serious "medical condition." In order to benefit from Viagra, a man had to plan carefully to take an (otherwise expensive) pill at least an hour before intercourse, which Pfizer asserted would now enable him to act "naturally." The drug manufacturers assured their customer that he should feel no shame inasmuch as he was only dealing with what was portrayed as a simple plumbing problem; but they also implied that a pill could magically transform a man's life, identity and relationships. The advertisements for Viagra and its competitors always showed happy couples slow dancing, holding hands, and laughing. Curiously enough, though the product supposedly only affected blood flow, the story line was always about romance.

Negotiating Masculinities

Although masculinity had been declared in crisis in almost every decade of the twentieth century, men faced new challenges in the 1980s and 1990s when, according to many observers, there was a backlash against the liberalism of the 1960s. They point to the rise of the Christian Right and its championing of "family values." Yet, in the same years, the general public's views were becoming more liberal. For example, levels of support for abortion and a tolerance of homosexuality generally rose. A more sexually pluralistic age was emerging in which the classic man and woman in the street found themselves discussing, if not approving, everything from test tube babies, transsexuals and "safe sex" to "date rape," pornography and "lipstick lesbians" (Faludi 1991). The growing popularity of common-law relationships, in which partners sought to be open about such issues as the domestic division of labour and sexual reciprocity, suggested that some men were seeking more equitable relationships. The media particularly attributed the appearance of the "New Man" — sensitive, anti-sexist, confused, cosmopolitan — to the influence of gays and feminists.

Physical performance was, at the start of the third millennium, still central to notions of masculinity. Publicity materials for Viagra and other erectile pharmaceuticals shored up an existing model of masculinity in which heterosexual male desire was taken as a given. Narrowing the definition of male arousal, drug companies implied that sex necessarily meant penetration. It followed that the harder the penis the better the sex, and doctors set about measuring the "quality" of the erection. Moreover, discussions of Viagra suggest that many men felt under increased pressure to prove themselves. The tensions apparently were mainly due to men attempting to sustain outdated ideals of masculinity that stressed power and control when the social world in which they lived had dramatically changed. Men saw Viagra, claim some researchers, as a "masculinity pill" which would fix the broken male machine (Loe 2004: 78).

Holding public discussions of the previously taboo topics of male sexuality and impotence was risky business. Initially, Pfizer targeted the respectable middle-aged and elderly married, and men who had survived prostate cancer. The needs of this group were "obvious," since most men (and their doctors) assumed that a loss of sexual vigour was a "natural" aspect of getting old. The pharmaceutical companies, in contrast, played up the notion that erectile dysfunctions were not "natural"; they were problems that could be cured by a pill. Furthermore, the companies promoted the idea that Viagra could prop up the traditional heterosexual marriage, in which the husband took the sexual initiative, and improve communication among monogamous, married middle-aged couples.

With sales plateauing by 2000, Pfizer shifted the focus of its advertisements from older men to baby boomers, who would, by 2030, represent one in four Americans over the age of sixty-five. To target a larger customer base, the corporation's advertisements increasingly portrayed younger, macho men. "We're talking about guys in their late 30s to 40s at the peak of their professional careers," observed an admiring marketing strategist. "They're burning themselves out with long hours at work. Their sexual lives are suffering" (Langreth 2000: 56). Almost as soon as Viagra arrived, young men were taking it. Partiers used it as "date insurance," bodybuilders to ward off the effects of steroids and ravers to add to their drug cocktails. By 2005 Pfizer was also edging away from the stress on respectability, running ads depicting a trim, forty-something man with a devil's horns leering at lingerie displays.

Pharmaceutical corporations recognized that the pressure for men to "perform" sexually was not restricted only to whites. From the start, some of advertisements for Viagra were directed at African-American consumers. In the 1970s, doctors were surprised that some non-Caucasians sought medical help for erectile dysfunctions: these doctors unconsciously accepted the racialization of masculine sexuality through clichés of black men's greater sexual potency and larger penis size. Impotence was understood culturally as a white man's problem. By the 1990s such crude stereotyping was to a degree attenuated, but this evolution in turn posed challenges. How did Blacks and Latinos, whom the culture had for centuries over-sexualized, deal with the possibility of being "under-sexualized?" Dr. Terry Mason, an African American urologist, argued that they had good reasons for being even more preoccupied than whites with restoring their potency: "To the extent that the Black man is so decimated in every other area of society, it's devastating for him to come home and not be able to sexually satisfy his mate" (Mason, cited in Leavy 1998: 157).

Gay men's experiences of using Viagra encapsulates many of the pill's contradictory influences. Gay men were never portrayed in Pfizer's advertising, but conservatives nevertheless expressed their alarm that Pfizer in its printed material always referred to the man and his "partner" (rather than his wife) benefiting from Viagra. Accessing a larger market presumably motivated the continued use of the gender-neutral term because the word "partner" was vague enough to cover both girlfriends and boyfriends. Thus straights and gays, the married and single, the monogamous and philanderers were all implicitly targeted.

Gay men's use of Viagra demonstrated that they too felt the pressure to conform to a specific standard of masculinity (Adams 2003). Perhaps even more than their straight counterparts, gay men bought into the idealization of youthful, virile male bodies They also had their own specific reasons for using an erectile drug. Men who indulged in anal sex needed a firmer penis. Some young men experimenting for the first time in a same-sex relationship wanted a drug which would help bolster their self-confidence. Those who attended circuit parties often used recreational drugs like ecstasy and cocaine, which could cause impotence: thus these men needed a pick-me-up.

Viagra did not end male sexual insecurities, but to claim as some of its critics have done that it created an era of performance anxiety is wide of the mark. Such male worries can be traced far back in time. However, in targeting the sexually insecure, companies have declared many erstwhile normal conditions to be medical problems, and for good or ill, Viagra's arrival made the once-taboo topic of impotence a subject of water-cooler and dinner-table conversation. Thanks to the modern media, then, more men than ever before may be prey to the idea that they are suffering a sexual dysfunction. The irony is that the new drugs, in focusing more attention on the erection, have put it more at risk.

NOTE

Angus McLaren, 2007, *Impotence: A Cultural History*, Chicago and London: University of Chicago Press. Adapted and reprinted with permission.

REFERENCES

Adams, Bob. 2003. "Keeping it Up." *Advocate* 38 (Nov. 11).

Faludi, Susan. 1991. *Backlash: The Undeclared War Against American Women*. New York: Crown.

Langreth, Robert. 2000. "Hard Sell." *Forbes* 166 (Oct. 16).

Laumann, Edward O., Anthony Paik and Raymond C. Rosen, 1999. "Sexual Dysfunction in the United States: Prevalence and Predictors." *Journal of the American Medical Association* 281.

Leavy, Mason. 1998. "Brothers (and Sisters) and the New Sex Pill." *Ebony* 53 (July).

Loe, Meika. 2004. *The Rise of Viagra: How the Little Blue Pill Changed Sex in America*. New York: New York University Press.

McCarthy, Sheryl. 1998. "The Hard Facts." *Ms.* 8.

Szasz, Thomas. 1980. *Sex by Prescription*. New York: Anchor/Doubleday

Tiefer, Leonore. 1995. *Sex Is Not a Natural Act and Other Essays*. Boulder, CO: Westview Press.

Tiefer, Leonore, 1986. "In Pursuit of the Perfect Penis: The Medicalization of Male Sexuality." *American Behavioral Scientist* 29.

Section IV

BODY AND SOUL:
SPIRITUALITY, HEALTH AND VIOLENCE

C. Lesley Biggs and Pamela J. Downe

How do we think about the relationship between the body and spirit/soul? In an excellent summary of ways of thinking about body and spirit/soul, Anthony Synnott (1993) identifies myriad ways in which various thinkers have thought about the body (and we might add that a much larger group of people practise these ideas in their daily lives without necessarily connecting them to a philosophical tradition). In some bodies of thought, body and spirit/soul are conceptualized as indivisible, i.e., in monist terms; in other cases, this relationship is understood in dualist terms, i.e., spirit/soul are seen as somehow separate and distinct. In some views, the body is described in idealist terms; that is, the beautiful body is a reflection of divine perfection; in other cases, the body is understood in materialist terms; i.e., the body is simply matter. In some belief systems, the spirit/soul is seen as superior to the body; in other cases, the reverse is true. Some hold body-negative views while others have body-positive ones.

These ideas, of course, do not exist separately but are either structured in a web of competing strands of thought, all of which can be found in one culture simultaneously, or interwoven into a coherent set of ideas that form a culture's belief system. Moreover, these views of the body and spirit/soul often are coded in relations of gender, race, ability, and sexuality — with women, negatively racialized people, persons with disability, and lesbians, gay men, bisexuals, and transgendered people relegated to subordinate positions in pairings of body and spirit/soul. In this chapter, we examine the interplay between these relationships and the ways that they are expressed in religious/spiritual practices, in conceptions and experiences of health, illness, and violence.

Meditations on the triunity of mind/reason, body, and soul/spirit have a long history in the Western tradition, dating back at least to the ancient Greeks. Hippocrates, known as the philosopher father of "modern medicine," and for whom the Hippocratic Oath of Care is named, wrote definitively in 400 BCE that spiritual beliefs in magic or gods should not be applied to the study and treatment of the human body. Only "charlatans" and "magi" (religious leaders) engage in this sort of irrational thinking, Hippocrates argued, and he called on his students to challenge such irrationality by medically treating only that which is observable to the trained practitioner. Although this argument set the groundwork for the mind/body divide that characterizes our present-day studies of religion and health, Margaret Lock and Nancy Scheper-Hughes (1996: 47) argue that it was the sixteenth-century writings of mathematician-philosopher René Descartes that most clearly formulated the ideas that are the immediate precursors of contemporary Western beliefs about the duality of mind and body. Descartes, a devout Catholic, argued that the human mind/soul was an immaterial substance which was unknowable because it came within the purview of God, while the body was a material substance, and therefore knowable. This distinction paved the way for the rigorous and objective examination of nature, including the human body. Many religious and medical theories today are still very much caught up in this idea, but they are increasingly met with strong opposition. Gender, race, class, ability and sexual orientation all figure prominently in arguments for and against maintaining a mind/body dichotomy. Regardless of whether we consider ourselves "religious," religious/spiritual practices, ideas, mythologies, and institutions have a major impact on all societies and many individuals. They are one way of making sense of the world around us, our relationships with one another, and our understandings of the divine. But women in most religions have been largely excluded from discussions concerning questions of epistemology, ontology, and existence; rather women's roles have been restricted to being the guardians of morality for their own children, as well as for the nation. In her chapter, Darlene Juschka provides an overview of feminist critiques of a variety of religious practices, but particularly the monotheistic systems in the East and West. Utilizing different strategies — rereading, reconceiving, and reconstructing — feminist critiques have challenged canonical writings, which defined some texts as orthodox and authoritative while others were designated as heterodox and non-authoritative, as well as their androcentric biases. In some cases, religiously oriented feminists sought to be more included in the well-established religious institutions in ways that were female-positive. In other cases, religiously oriented feminists rejected these institutions and sought to revitalize or create female-dominated religious systems that were centred in women's experience of family, relationships, and reproduction.

All religions have a creation, or cosmogonic, myth, i.e., one that explains the origins and organization of the cosmos. Creation myths, according to the *Encyclopedia Britannica*, situate human beings in relation to other human beings, nature, and the non-animal world. As a result, these myths set "the stylistic tone that tends to determine all other gestures, actions, and structures in the culture." The act of creating the world can be conceptualized in a number of ways: it can be attributed to a supreme being; the gradual emergence of fully formed beings below earth, out of formless chaos, or in the underworld; primordial parents; the breaking of a cosmic egg; and earth divers, which can refer to life emerging out of the water, or an animal diving into water retrieving mud to form land.

According to the book of *Genesis* in the *Bible*, God created the world in six days by divine fiat, a process that indicates God's omnipotence. The world the Judeo-Christian God created was paradise, an idyllic place of abundance and beauty, most powerfully elaborated as the Garden of Eden. Here human beings fell from grace when Eve bit into the fruit of the Tree of the Knowledge of Good and Evil and persuaded Adam to do likewise. Morny Joy's chapter "It All Began with Eve" traces the history of Christian doctrine which, over the millennia, has portrayed women's bodies as sources of spiritual contamination, evil, weakness, irrationality, and, in Eve's case, temptation. These views have, across the ages, often led to restrictions on women's freedom and sexual autonomy, and justified violence and sexual abuse of girls and women.

Although many in Western societies do not embrace such misogynist views, the legacy of these views nonetheless lives on as patriarchal institutions, and thus some women and men still conceive of women through the whore/Madonna dichotomy. As feminist cartoonist Liza Donnelly (2010) observes, her choices in growing up in the 1950s were to be a good girl or a slut! More recently, however, the persistence of virgin/whore dichotomy became evident in the controversy over comments made by a Toronto Police officer who told women at a 2011 York University safety forum that to keep themselves safe "women should avoid dressing like sluts" (slutwalktoronto). In response, Toronto women organized the first ever "SlutWalk," a march that protested the blaming of women for rape and other forms of sexual assault. The phenomena, with the aid of the Internet, went viral, and "SlutWalks" were held all over the world. The decision to name the protest "SlutWalk" moves to reclaim the word "slut" from its history as a shaming word, but not all women support either the attempted reclamation of the word or the tactics of some scantily clad women marching theatrically through the streets during SlutWalks. Do you think this new form of organizing around sexual assault against females actually plays to the patriarchal male gaze, or is it a great way to draw public attention to the prevalence of sexual violence against girls and women, particularly since Take Back the Night marches are losing their impact and had been criticized for fostering the myth that rape is mainly perpetrated by strangers to the victims? Do you think the attempt to de-stigmatize the word "slut" is an effort worth making, or is the term irredeemably tied to the virgin/whore dichotomy?

Feminist theologians and philosophers of religion, like Morny Joy in her chapter, have sought to reclaim Eve by looking to other cultures' non-misogynist interpretations of women's reproductive bodies; through imaginative retellings of Eve's story; by rethinking the concept of God in gender-neutral or non-anthropomorphic terms; and by embracing goddess worship or pantheism. Whatever the strategy, a central theme that unites these feminist theologians and philosophers is that "embodiment is a form of divinity," and therefore women have the right to be free from bodily coercion. But the rising backlash against feminists, particularly by fundamentalist religious groups, means that women's bodyright is not necessarily guaranteed.

The book of *Genesis* tells two creation stories: God is first said to have created man, both male and female, in his image (Genesis 1:27); in the second story, God is said to have formed man from the dust of the ground (Genesis 2:7) and woman from Adam's rib (Genesis 2:21–22). Lorna Crozier's poem "On the Seventh Day" is an excellent example of a feminist re-conceptualizing or retelling of the patriarchal story of the first *Genesis* creation myth — while also providing an account of the making of Crozier's beloved Canadian prairies. In this story, God is presented as "a dreamy sort" who daily forgets that he has created light, and therefore, continues to do so again and again. Reminded constantly (some would say "nagged") by his wife, God manages to complete creation by the end of the sixth day. But, according to God's wife, rather than thanking her, God spends the seventh day, the alleged day of rest, (re)writing history, "changing all the facts, of course, even creating Woman / from a Man's rib, imagine that! / But why be upset? [God's wife] thought. / Who's going to believe it?" Crozier's account thus challenges the distortions of all patriarchal histories that efface the crucial roles of women in creative and other activities.

The male bias of the Genesis stories is also challenged in a retelling of the Mohawk earth diver creation myth penned by Beth Brant, a Bay of Quinte Mohawk from the Tyendinaga Reserve. Brant tells the story of the creation of Turtle Island, (otherwise known as North America) and of humankind. She represents Sky Woman, who is central to the Mohawk creation story, as a queer woman in every sense of the word. In her thirst for knowledge, Sky Woman leaves the Sky People, and aided by Eagle and Muskrat, the earth diver who brings earth from the bottom of the waters to create an Eden-like paradise on Turtle's back, founds the human species. Brant invokes a matrilineal narrative in which Sky Woman, through immaculate conceptions, gives birth to First Woman. In a parallel to the death and resurrection of Jesus, when Sky Woman dies, new life, including the Three Sisters — beans, corn, and squash — and the moon and stars, springs from her body. First Woman learns from Moon that she is carrying twin sons. "One of these," Moon states, "is good and will honour us and our Mother. One of these is not good and will bring things that we have no names for. Teach these beings what we have learned together. Teach them that if the sons do not honour the women who made them, that will be the end of this earth." Which son do you think reigns today?

These creation myths represent not only stories about the origin of the world, but they also represent particular worldviews that are embedded in specific cultural practices. What happens then when one people with one set of narratives meets another with a quite different set? Initially, the history of Aboriginal-newcomer relations in Canada was marked by symbiotic relations each benefitting the other. But an imbalance in power between Aboriginal peoples and the newcomers grew with the arrival of Anglo-Europeans who were carriers of infectious diseases such as smallpox and tuberculosis that decimated Aboriginal populations, the decline of the fur trade, European appropriation and settlement of the land, processes that were assisted by their "superior" technologies. Later generations of the settlers would attempt to assimilate Aboriginal peoples into the dominant culture — with devastating results for Aboriginal people.

The Protestant and Roman Catholic churches played a prominent role in the colonization of Canada. Louise Halfe's poem "In Da Name of Da Fadder" demonstrates the insidious ways in which these religious institutions helped establish patriarchal hierarchies among Aboriginal people and racial hierarchies between Aboriginal and Anglo-European communities. During the ritual of Catholic confession, an unnamed Aboriginal woman delineates her "sins," which, influenced by the priest's teachings, she reports to include responsibility for her husband's violence to her, desiring the love and affection of another man in the absence of these comforts from her husband, and begrudging the disparities between her life and that of the *mōniyōs* (white man). Complementing this ironized litany of "sins," Halfe "poops" on the authority of the Pope and the Catholic Church, demonstrating that scatological humour is not just for kids!

Like Halfe, Jamaican-born Canadian poet Klyde Broox links the power and authority of the church with patriarchal values and relations. In a reggae-derived oral poetry known as dub, Broox says of patriarchy, "Don't pin it to the Trinity / It has no affinity with divinity." Having unmasked the patriarchal God, Broox then catalogues "Malesupremacist myths from coast to coast," myths which he represents as manifesting "Pay-triarchal ph-ill-osophy," in other words, "Guydeology, liedeology, [and] sexistology." In his list of "comic icons of perfection," Broox's targets include the many forms of "mas(k)ulinity" in popular culture, for example, "men of steel [who] don't feel." In Broox's view, "iron-man, caveman, brute strength [are] incongruent with a digitized environment," and homophobia is anathema: "I won't call a man Bman, seaman,[1] or demon / I cast no aspersion on any one orientation." Moreover, Broox warns "everyman," "Don't batter woman, you are the son of one," before concluding that "justice insists. / It's time to strip off mas(k)ulinity / To remake the image of God maskfree."

Although Canada has since European settlement been a predominantly Christian country, religious minorities have from the time of original settlement been part of the nation's populace because different immigrant populations brought their values and belief systems with them.[2] While these groups were often fleeing economic hardships or religious persecution, and contributed to the building of Canada, they often faced discrimination and/or racism based on language, culture, or creed as a result of white, Anglo- and Francophone xenophobia. The history of Jewish Canadians is a case in point. The first Jewish settlement was established in New France in 1760 (Sloame 2011), and Jews have had a presence in many communities across Canada ever since. Despite their history of persecution in Eastern Europe, the former Soviet Union, under the Nazi Regime, and more recently in North Africa, Canadian Jewish communities have faced virulent anti-Semitism in Canada throughout much of the twentieth century.

Ivan Kalmar questions the way he, as a Jewish man in a predominantly Christian country, is set apart and defined as different. In his chapter, Kalmar explores the implications of statements like "I didn't know you were Jewish!"; he contests stereotypes about "Jewish American Princesses (JAPs) and Jewish mothers; and he presents his views on God, Jesus, the Palestinians and Israel, and Christmas and Hanukkah. Encounters of peoples with different religious or spiritual beliefs and practices take place in what Mary Louise Pratt calls contact zones (Pratt 1991), social spaces where cultures meet, clash, and grapple with each other. In this particular case, differences in religious belief are established by the statement "I didn't know you were Jewish!" a remark that reveals that Christianity is the unquestioned norm. But just as Christianity is a way of life that extends beyond worship, being Jewish is more than Judaism. For Kalmar, being Jewish is "a culture, an ethnic identity, a shared history," but, as he also points out, Jews are diverse in their religious beliefs and their political views. In his tongue-in-cheek interrogation of non-Jewish assumptions about Jews and of anti-Semitic humour, Kalmer demonstrates the ways in which religious, racial, and gender differences intersect to construct Jews as "other" in everyday life while simultaneously revealing the complexity of Jewish identities and communities. So if you make the statement, "I didn't know that you were Jewish, or Muslim, or a believer of another faith different from your own, ask yourself as Kalmar does, "What would you have done if you had known?" More important still, "what are you going to do now that you do know?"

In Canada and many other countries around the world, the debate over Muslim women's attire (headscarves, the *hijab*, *chadri*, *jilbāb*, *khimar*, *niqab*, or *burqua*) emerges from contact zones in which Muslim communities and non-Muslim communities clash over women's rights, religious and political freedoms, and expressions of nationalism. Muslim women's attire has become a multivocal sign, a form of representation for the wearer, which is interpreted differently by both individuals and communities inside and outside Muslim worlds. Natasha Bakht documents several legal and quasi-legal attempts in Canada to ban the wearing of Muslim women's head attire. In debunking arguments that supported barring Muslim women's participation in certain sports and their voting in elections, Bakht argues that, "The justifications for banning Muslim women from participating in various activities reveal a tension between the need to protect Muslim women and the need to be protected from them." However, the need articulated by feminists and non-feminists alike to protect Muslim women from the patriarchal control of their families is increasingly less sustainable as many Canadian Muslim women choose to wear some form of head covering as a sign of empowered cultural identity. But the legacy of the traumatic events of 9/11 and the United States' war on terror, Canada's participation in the war in Afghanistan, and fears of homegrown terrorism and radicalism, as well as "unhelpful Muslim responses" that conflate religious practice with cultural tradition, have fuelled the Canadian racist imaginary, in which the tropes of "the imperiled woman," "the dangerous Muslim man" and "the civilized European" continue to circulate. How else can we explain the anti-Muslim furor and hysteria — much of which centers on the attire of Muslim women, who represent, as of the 2001 Census (CCW 2004), 1.8 percent of all Canadian women?

In many religious practices, purity of the body is equated with purity of the soul, and believers are encouraged to achieve a healthy body through dietary practices and exercise, as well as ritual forms of purification. This sentiment is captured, for example, in the Christian tradition by the idiom "Cleanliness is next to godliness," and during Ramadan, Muslims fast between sunrise and sunset so that they learn and maintain humility and patience. Before engaging in sacred rituals, many Turtle Island/North American Aboriginal cultures smudge themselves so that they enter into the sacred realm with open minds and hearts. In many traditional and/or religious communities, the mind, body, and soul are interconnected. But in our increasingly secular society, this triunity has been weakened, if not severed over the past century with the institutionalization of the biomedical model. In this view, the body is reduced to its mechanical components whose problems or flaws can be "fixed" *inter alia* by health-care practitioners, and through exercise, diet, and cosmetic surgery. For many, the "perfect" body has become a revered object, and the pursuit of the fit and/or healthy body has become a moral virtue in its own right. At the same time, other models of health offer counter narratives to the biomedical views. For example, the World Health Organization's definition of health as "a state of complete physical, mental and social well-being and not merely the absence of disease or infirmity," has gained considerable currency in recent decades (WHO 2011a) Similarly, the rise of complementary and alternative health-care (CAM) practices suggests that individuals are looking for more holistic approaches in attaining health. In many cases, CAM represents a reconfiguration of mind/body/spirit practices, some of which are explicitly tied to concepts of godliness, chi, forms of spiritual energy, etc.

Although biomedicine is dominant in Western industrialized countries, its privileged position has not gone uncontested. In the late 1960s, feminist health movements challenged the sexism within biomedicine in terms of the underrepresentation of women as doctors, as well as in the assumptions of the biomedical model itself. Feminist health activists pointed to gender biases in the diagnosis and treatment of women's health issues, particularly in the area of reproduction. Indeed, as Gina Feldberg notes in her chapter, the field of "women's health" has historically been characterized by a focus on "navel to knees." Women's biology was, and still is, seen primarily in relation to reproduction while non-reproductive aspects of their physiology are mistakenly described as being no different from men's. In the nineteenth century, when women were described by European and American scientists and medical practitioners as being innately sickly and weak, the focus was on the reproductive organs and functions: "Puberty was seen as a 'crisis'.… Menstruation — or the lack of it — was regarded as pathological throughout a woman's life.… A pregnant woman was indisposed and doctors campaigned against the practice of midwifery on the grounds that pregnancy was a disease — Menopause was the final, incurable ill, the death of the woman in the woman" (Ehrenreich and English 1973: 20–21). Women's experiences of tuberculosis, cancer, influenza, and pneumonia were all related directly to their reproductive capacities because women were primarily seen as "walking wombs" (Angier 1999). Have you ever wondered how female reproductive capacities would be viewed if men had them? Gloria Steinem did in relation to menstruation, and you can find her humorous take "If Men Could Menstruate" at: mum.org/ifmencou.htm.

Feldberg not only questions the ways in which women were reduced to reproductive capabilities in androcentric medical systems, she also challenges feminist scholars who adopt ableist assumptions about women's reproductive capabilities. Drawing on her own experience with infertility and reproductive technologies, Feldberg writes that "Hard personal struggle opened my eyes to the ways in which a kind of reproductive 'ableism' — or an assumption about the natural fertility of women and the ways in which the experience of birth unites us — has shaped and even distorted women's health scholarship and activism." She goes onto say that "The problem here, as I discovered, is that all our wombs were not alike, and they did not unite us." Some women are childless by chance not by choice; some women who are minoritized, or who are disabled have been sterilized against their will, or have been refused the technologies to become biological mothers. Most lesbians have no need for birth control, but they may wish to get pregnant by having access to appropriate reproductive technologies. These experiences point to the varied ways in which women experience fertility; the key issue that unites them is not having a womb, but having control over reproduction (i.e., when, where, with whom, and with what kind of technological assistance).

In demonstrating the varied experiences of reproduction, Feldberg's analysis highlights the importance of more "body stories," which situate bodily experiences within time, place, and culture. (Also see Chapter 37 for more detail). This approach is taken up explicitly in Pam Wakewich's chapter, which examines "body stories" in order to understand the ways in which "health, embodiment, and the body, are shaped and re-shaped through the life course, as well as how identities of gender, class, culture, and region (in this case 'northern-ness') are constituted within and through discourses on health and the body." Drawing on oral interviews conducted in Thunder Bay, Ontario, Wakewich found that women's ideas about their bodies and health change over the life course while men's are seemingly more stable. Women, when they were younger, focused on appearance practices and held to "a more conventional biomedical notion of the absence of disease"; but, as they aged, they assessed well-being in more environmental or holistic terms, as they balanced work, family, and leisure time. In contrast, men, who had a more difficult time recounting a body his-tory, defined health in terms of what would be considered 'typical' masculinist projects "of strength, or endurance in sporting activities, or the ability to do physical labour [especially for working-class men] or in relation to illness episodes." Both women and men were con-scious of different health capacities (both positive and negative), appearance standards, and bodily norms between the "north" (Northern Ontario) and the "south" (here she is referring to the Niagara triangle). This finding demonstrates the importance of "the region" or "the local" in shaping the experiences of health, embodiment, and the body. Now, think about where you live, or compare where you live now to somewhere you lived before. How does your sense of place shape your "presentation of self" and your experience of being healthy?

Including a sense of place in understanding health practices, behaviours, and systems in the analysis of dominant groups within Western societies is a relatively new conceptual tool for many social scientists. By contrast, in understanding local biologies, the intersection between place and culture has been central to anthropological inquiries into Indigenous cultures. In the past, the differences between Western and Indigenous cultures were perceived to be "obvious," and these asymmetrical analyses tended to reproduce the dominant group as "universal" and Indigenous (and other minoritized) groups as the "Other," and often as "backwards" and "uncivilized." However, as Indigenous peoples and scholars of indigeneity have had to grapple with the effects of colonization and decolonization, respect for Indigenous ways of knowing has been growing rapidly, both as sources of practical knowledge and as ways of healing the scars of colonization.

In her chapter, Karla Jessen Williamson wonders whether the silence around menstrua-tion in Greenland's Inuit culture is a product of colonial, patriarchal values or a vestige of pre-colonial ideas. This silence is particularly puzzling since Williams argues that positive and healthy attitudes about sexuality (through touching and discussion) is conveyed to children until *isuma*, Inuit conscience, has been formed, after which time Inuit believe that it is up to pre-adolescent children to develop their own sexuality. To answer her question, Williamson draws on the genderless language of Inuit culture and the concepts of *Timikkut* (through the physical), *tarnikkut* (through individual, personal soul) and *anersaakkut* (the life force whose energy remains autonomous from creation). Williamson concluded that during pre-Christian times, "Inuit women related their menstruating times to supernatural powers, and the practice of seclusion during female times demonstrates that Inuit women had a time on their own to internalize the alignment of *timikkut, tarnikkut, anersaakkut*." After contact and with the imposition/adoption of Christianity, *kalaallit* women "[gave] up the practices of seclusion during menstruation and birthing… [leaving] a vacuum so great in negation that no word has been found for it."

The onset of menstruation marks the beginning of female fertility, and in many cultures, this period in the life course marks the transition from girl- to womanhood, which is sometimes celebrated (as in earlier Inuit and Cree (nêhiyaw) cultures), but more often than not ignored. At the other end of the female lifecycle menopause marks the cessation of menses (a process which takes place over a number of years; see Chapter 37) and the ability to conceive. In some cultures, older women are revered for their wisdom, but in many modern societies, older women frequently become invisible and/or are otherwise marginalized. Images of the old hag, crone, or witch often disempower older women since these terms are reminders the woman is no longer young, beautiful, and sexual, the qualities often seen as the source of women's power. But, for these same reasons, many older women often feel freed from patriarchal scripts for women and thus more empowered than when they were younger. For example, in reference to menopausal changes in women's body heat, a feminist statement that circulated widely on the Internet declared that "They're not hot flashes; they're energy surges." Similarly, "Menopause Barbie" represents an ironic reimagining of a Barbie doll to which older women can relate. Gone is the ridiculous figure (which if scaled to real life proportions, would have Barbie measuring 36-18!-33) and eternal youth. Instead, Menopause Barbie wears bifocals, has bunions, facial hair, and flabby arms, and is now divorced. Now there's a role model!

Women's health research is no longer restricted to the analysis of reproduction, as the case of investigations into female cardiovascular disease shows; nor is it restricted to the concerns of white, able-bodied women. In particular, women with disabilities have become a powerful force in their own right, challenging assumptions of able-bodiedness within feminist and other health-care research, just as they have critiqued their exclusion or marginalization in other discourses and practices. Women and men who live with disabilities have argued that they can have rich and full lives; they want to be respected and treated with dignity rather than being seen as less valuable, less human than able-bodied individuals. According to the World Health Organization (2011b), "disability is a complex phenomenon, reflecting an interaction between features of a person's body and features of the society in which he or she lives." The World Health Organization (2011b) argues, "Disabilities is an umbrella term, covering impairments, activity limitations, and participation restrictions. An impairment is a problem in body function or structure; an activity limitation is a difficulty encountered by an individual in executing a task or action; while a participation restriction is a problem experienced by an individual in involvement in life situations." For many people with disabilities, the barriers they face have less to do with the disabilities themselves and more to do with social attitudes and practices that marginalize and disadvantage.

Just as able-bodied people's experience is gendered, so too is the experience of disability. Disabling attitudes and practices are captured in a poignant never-to-be-sent letter from Maria Truchan-Tataryn to her daughter, "Sophia," a young woman who has disabilities. In trying to explain "why at twenty [her daughter] seems to be imprisoned in [her] home, spending most of [her] time with [her] mother," Truchan-Tataryn expresses outrage at the ways in which society treats women like her daughter, who are vulnerable to sexual exploitation, are deemed "abnormal," and are subject to violence in a "multitude of mundane and ubiquitous ways... [that erode her] personal dignity." Looks and stares at the grocery store are just one example Truchan-Tataryn offers. In her view, attitudes towards persons with disabilities have not changed that much in the twenty or so years of disability activism, in part because these ideas are embedded in the fabric of societal institutions through the legacy of the eugenics movement, in which early twentieth-century feminists played a central role. Truchan-Tataryn argues that the status of persons with disabilities status is uncertain even though their rights are protected under *The Charter of Rights and Freedoms*. Comparing the *Latimer* and *Parvez* cases in which two young women were killed by their fathers — the first because Tracy Latimer's father believed that his daughter was suffering too much from the effects of cerebral palsy and endless surgeries, and the second because Aqsa Parvez refused to wear the *hijab*. Truchan-Tataryn asks why in the first case was public sympathy for Tracy's father poured out while in the second case, the public was hostile to Aqsa's father. Does someone having a disability mean that her/his life is worth less than that of someone who doesn't have a disability? Who gets to decide?

Disabilities can be expressed bodily in many ways, and in Western industrialized societies, young girl's and women's concerns about their body image has led to a host of physical and emotional/psychological problems that can manifest themselves in eating disorders, depression, and low self-esteem. In the beginning of her poem "hungergraphs," Sylvia Legris describes a woman struggling with an eating disorder as someone "so thin she could balance / an O.E.D. [an *Oxford English Dictionary*] on the points of her pelvic bones / and still leave room to fit a substantial paperback:/ *the alexandria quartet* or the *joy / of cooking*. Legris illustrates the devastating toll of an eating disorder on a woman's triune mind body-spirit as she is involuntarily hospitalized and force-fed when she refuses to eat, contemplates self-mutilation, and generally feels nothing. Ironically, the persona works in a bakery and is complimented on "her toothpick arms shoulder-blades jutting out of / her shirt / legs thin / as baguettes." But somehow through her despair, the persona learns to eat again, remembering every detail of that first meal, and her first cup of coffee with real cream and sugar, which, she says, "nourishes / my memory / long starved."

Legris' story of one woman's struggle with an eating disorder can be recounted thousands of times over. In Canada, based on 2002 statistics, an estimated 0.8 percent of all women and 0.2 percent of men reported an eating disorder. The rate increases to 1.5 percent of women between the ages of 15 and 24 (Government of Canada 2006), and represents the third most chronic health problem in this age group after asthma and obesity. While the incidence of reported eating disorders is relatively low, the evidence suggests that both girls and boys are preoccupied with their body image at an increasingly young age. As early as Grade 6, 23.2 percent of girls and 20.1 percent of boys reported being too fat, and by Grade 10 the rate had increased to a dramatic 43.8 percent of girls believing that they were too fat while the rate for boys remained stable at 19.9 percent (WHO survey cited in Government of Canada 2006: 100). By comparison, boys across all grades were more likely than girls to indicate that they were too thin rather than too fat. While the percentage of boys (10 percent) who reported dieting remained stable from Grade 6 to 10, the percentage of girls rose from 10.5 percent to 28.9 percent in the same period. As can be seen from the statistics, eating disorders are not just an individual problem, but also a social and cultural phenomenon — one that began in the 1980s, and does not appear to be abating. How do we explain this obsession with weight, and its disproportional effect on adolescent girls?

Women bear a paradoxical relationship to food. They nurture their families through breastfeeding young infants, and when they plant and harvest crops, shop, prepare, and serve food; much of this work, paid or unpaid, is taken for granted and occurs in a gendered division of labour in kitchens, restaurants, and supermarkets. As exemplified in the case of eating disorders, but more generally, women are more likely than men to restrict their consumption of food in order to adhere to dominant gender expectations. Hegemonic femininity exalts modesty, daintiness, and restraint, for example. Women also fear public ridicule if they consume large amounts of food in one sitting since doing so would signal a voracious appetite, an attribute which has multiple layers of meaning since it can denote being out of control, or eating like a man, or being sexually demanding (Finkelstein 1989). While women are exhorted to restrict their food consumption, girls and women are metaphorically consumed as is illustrated by such terms of endearment for girls as sweetie, cutie-pie, peach, honey and cookie while those for boys include tiger, buddy, and little man. Unlike boys, girls are described as edible items, implying that girls are to be eaten. Food itself is often gender coded: salads and chicken, for example, are seen as "lighter" and therefore more appropriately feminine whereas beef and potatoes are "heavier" foods, necessary to build or maintain men's strength and vigour (Counihan 1999: 124). In many cultures, men are offered the choicest pieces of meat first with the less desirable cuts going to women and children.

These contradictory messages of women's relationship to food are captured in Mary Pratt's painting "Bread Rising." In particular, Pratt draws a connection between the making of bread, a food that sustains and nourishes people in many places in the world, and breast cancer, one of women's greatest health challenges. Traditionally, homemade bread has been baked by women while men have produced bread for local and mass markets. Moreover, homemade bread is often associated with motherhood, domesticity, and femininity, evident for example, in images of women presenting steaming bread fresh out-of-the-oven to their families. Ironically, the term "breadwinner," a role associated with men being the primary income earners for their families, gained currency while women's traditional bread-making roles declined in the 1950s with the development of new bread-making techniques and the marketing of sliced bread. Pratt's choice then to depict bread dough as a "breast-like mound" formed by overactive yeast cells is, as she states, "quite ominous," and runs counter to popular images of women's bread-making role. Unlike women (and some men) with anorexia who strive to control their bodies by restricting the intake of food, women with breast cancer struggle with a body in which malignant cells are out of control. Given the social, cultural, religious importance of bread, as evidenced in the English language (with bread being referred to as "the staff of life," and used as a euphemism for money, a metaphor for invention, i.e., "the greatest thing since sliced bread," and a synecdoche for being a provider "putting bread on the table"), what associations do you think that Pratt is making between feelings of being "out-of-control," femininity, and breast cancer?

Legris' poem details the private, internal struggle of coming to terms with an eating disorder. At the same time, the act of writing the poem about eating disorders transforms a private matter into a public issue, allowing other women (and some men) in a similar situation to understand that they are not alone. Similarly, graphic representations of women's relationship to food and breast cancer raise awareness about these issues. Writing and artistic renderings represent different forms of self-expression and activism while challenging institutions to get them to accommodate people with disabilities (a duty that is required under provincial labour standards legislation) is another way of getting redress for inequitable treatment. In her chapter, Vera Chouinard documents her twelve-year battle with her university to make accommodations since she had rheumatoid arthritis, an autoimmune disease that causes painful inflammation of the joints and surrounding tissues. Not surprisingly, Chouinard's "[struggle] for inclusion and accommodation in academia [has] been a life-altering experience." In her work as a disabled woman scholar, Chouinard concluded that issues of gender and disability should not be added to the ever-expanding compendium of "special interests" in health research and intervention. Instead, she sees the lives of women with disabilities as being "inextricably linked" with those of able-bodied women. In order to prove that they indeed are "able," both able-bodied women and women with disabilities juggle jobs, domestic responsibilities, and the care of children and/or elderly parents. "Ironically," as Chouinard observes, "the more hyper-able [women] feel compelled out of fear to be, the more likely we are to become ill and impaired women." Very few of us will live disability-free lives (as a result of congenital problems, accidents, stress, or aging). Thus, as Chouinard observes, "by claiming disabled women's issues as our own, we take the first crucial step toward imagining and creating a society more enabling for every woman."

Chouinard's motivation to challenge her university was based on both a need to make her life more bearable and a gross sense of injustice. She was angry, and that emotion propelled her to action. Similarly, a group of third wave, feminist, fat activists based in Toronto was "pissed off" by the "tyranny of slenderness" (Chernin 1981). In response to fat phobia, Pretty Porky and Pissed Off (PPPO) engaged in performance art and utilized a variety of media to raise awareness about body size and its connection to health, happiness, and consumerism. Designed to generate a "belly laugh," images of these performances, stickers, and zines illustrate the chapter by Allyson Mitchell, a co-founder of PPPO. The goal of this fun-loving, "in your face" group is "to inspire others to keep fighting for representation of all bodies. We thought it crucial for fat people to see themselves reflected in art — to see our struggles and our beauty." With their BIG attitude, PPPO's work gives new meaning to the phrase "Super Size Me!"

The power of the "thin as ideal" imagery is that it is internalized by many women and girls (as well as by men and boys), so that the desire to be thin is seen as an individual "choice" rather than the result of a tyrant who exhorts girls and women to be thin. In the parlance of Michel Foucault, power is everywhere (the thin ideal is pervasive), and nowhere (no one person exerts power over others) simultaneously (Foucault 2004; Bartky 1990; Bordo 1993). Nonetheless, patriarchal control is exercised over female bodies as women and girls strive to achieve this ideal. (Think about what a woman or girl could do if she wasn't preoccupied with her weight or body image.) For many, this form of power doesn't seem like power in the traditional sense; that is, power is usually understood as the capacity to affect the actions of others, either positively (e.g., the power to inspire) or negatively (e.g., exerting authority or control over others). We all experience both forms of power, but the extent to which we experience these different power relations depends very much on class, gender, race, ablebodiness, sexuality, and age.

You might ask, "What is the relationship between power and violence?", and the answer would be that any misuse of power (physical, sexual, verbal, mental, emotional, or psychological) represents violence since it causes suffering and anguish for those subjected to such abuse. Of course, we are most familiar with physical violence, an issue that feminism has addressed since its early formulations. But despite four decades of activism and raising awareness about the pervasiveness of violence against women, this issue remains a major feminist and societal issue. Constance Backhouse, in her chapter, provides a selected history of the changes in sexual assault legislation over the past century. As Backhouse observes, "What will strike you, as the reader, are the changes in language, the definitions of rape/ sexual assault, the type of punishments, and the length of prison terms. These changes represent alterations in attitudes toward women, shifting patriarchal values, and women's rights in Canadian society." Many of these changes represent a significant improvement in women's treatment in the justice system after they have been sexually assaulted. But then Backhouse asks "'Are these changes enough?' and if not, "What will it take so that women, children, and men can live freely without the fear of sexual assault?" What do you think? Are these changes to the legislation enough?

The language of legislation is abstract and devoid of emotion, even when addressing issues like sexual assault. In contrast, Margaret Atwood in "A Women's Issue" viscerally depicts all too common acts of violence (either historical or contemporary). Setting the poem in what could initially be seen either as a museum or a law court, Atwood puts violence against women both on display and on trial. What these exhibits "have in common," Atwood concludes "is between the legs." Like Backhouse, Atwood laments the lack of progress on this "woman's issue," a too often publicly unnamed problem therefore suffered by women in silence. But this exhibition "is not a museum," where obsolete artifacts of the past are preserved and displayed; this is contemporary reality for many women. How would you answer Atwood's question "Who invented the word *love*?"

Fourteen women were murdered and another thirteen wounded in what has become known as the "Montreal Massacre," which took place at École Polytechnique on December 6, 1989. The deaths and injuries of these women, who were singled out by Marc Lépine because he believed that they "were just a bunch of feminists," was a chilling reminder of the pervasiveness of violence against women in Canadian society. In her chapter, pacifist, feminist, anti-nuclear activist, and physicist Ursula Franklin reflects on the meaning of the Montreal Massacre. Was this event an isolated act of a mad man, as many claimed? In answer to this question, Franklin agrees, but then goes onto say that "[this act] is not unrelated to what is going on around us. *That* people get mad may happen in any society, any place, every place. But *how* people get mad, *how* that escalation from prejudice to hate and violence occurs, what and who is hated, and how it is expressed, is not unrelated to the world around us." Violence against women is embedded in the cultural and institutional fabric of Canadian society.

Franklin herself is no stranger to violence. During World War II, she was sent to a Nazi work camp in Germany because her mother was Jewish. As a result, Franklin understands the importance of speaking out against violence even in the face of violence itself. For this reason, Franklin challenged the solidarity discourse that initially emerged in response to the Montreal Massacre (i.e., we are all brothers and sisters). What does solidarity mean, Franklin asks, when "In our memory and reflection [on the Montreal Massacre], we have to include the fact that these women were abandoned by their fellow students. We have to face it." At what point, Franklin asks us, do we speak up? When faced with a gun? A verbal threat? When we witness harassment? Writing in 1991, Franklin's challenge to us remains equally important today, but her (and other feminists') interpretation of that fateful day is being disputed twenty years on. Margaret Wente (2009), writing in the *Globe and Mail*, argued that "it's time [for Canadian society] to get a grip, and move on." The women who were killed or injured during the Montreal Massacre were not "victims of deep-rooted cultural misogyny" and to claim that "the rage of Marc Lépine reflected the rage of ordinary men embittered by seeing women get ahead… is a misandrist slur." The writing of history is often contested ground. How do you interpret what happened on December 6, 1989, and do you think that the Montreal Massacre should be commemorated still?

Even if (and that's a big "IF") we accepted Wente's assertion that the Montreal Massacre was a one-time act of a madman, Wente's individualist analysis would have a much more difficult time explaining the fact that Aboriginal women have the highest rates of violence for all persons who are victims of spousal abuse, spousal homicide, homicide by an intimate, and sexual assault. (Wente is correct, however, that Aboriginal men have higher rates of violence, but she fails to take into account that violence against Aboriginal men is highest in the categories of assault and homicide by acquaintances and strangers, indicating the situational nature of violence, and its intersections with gender, race, and class.) Aboriginal women have long been victims of violence, as Marilyn Dumont documents in her epistolary poem to Helen Betty Osborne, a seventeen-year-old Cree woman living in The Pas, Manitoba. In 1971, she was brutally raped and stabbed over 50 times with a screwdriver. In a summary of this spine-chilling case, Amnesty International reports that "Twenty years later, the Manitoba Justice Inquiry (MJI) concluded that the murder of Helen Betty Osborne had been fuelled by racism and sexism" (Amnesty International 2007). According to the MJI,

> Women in our society live under a constant threat of violence. The death of Helen Betty Osborne was a brutal expression of that violence. She fell victim to vicious stereotypes born of ignorance and aggression when she was picked up by four drunken men looking for sex. (Cited in Amnesty International 2007)

Osborne's four white killers were not brought to justice until 1986; one man was sentenced to life imprisonment for the murder of Osborne; one man was acquitted; and two men who were present for the abduction and murder were never charged.

The experience of Osborne was not, however, an isolated incident in the Pas. According to the MJI,

> We know that cruising for sex was a common practice in The Pas in 1971. We know too that young Aboriginal women, often underage, were the usual objects of the practice. And we know that the RCMP did not feel that the practice necessitated any particular vigilance on its part. (Cited in Amnesty International 2007)

Racism, sexism, the intergenerational effects of colonization — all too often expressed in physical, sexual, and psychological abuse — have been pervasive feature in the lives of Aboriginal women's lives both past and present. Writing a poem to Helen Betty Osborne, then, is an act of memorializing this tragic and preventable death, but by breaking the silence around this issue, and by bearing witness to Osborne's suffering, the poem also remembers or reconnects families and communities to the many Aboriginal women who were victims of abuse. As Métis writer Dumont points out, Aboriginal women were/are often targets: "Betty, if I set out to write this poem about you / it might turn out instead / to be about me /or any one of / my female relatives"; or it could be about Anna Mae Aquash, Donald Marshall, or Richard Cardinal, or "our grandmothers,/ beasts of burden in the fur trade." In other words, the poem "could be about hunting season instead, / about 'open season' on native women" (and some Aboriginal men).

Although the plight of missing and murdered women is, of course, well-known among Aboriginal people, this issue had failed to garner the attention of the police, governments, policy makers, and the general public until the release of Amnesty International's ground-breaking report *Stolen Sisters: A Human Rights Response To Discrimination And Violence Against Indigenous Women* in 2004. The report, which documents nine cases of murdered or missing Aboriginal women, "contributed to the shift in political climate and inspired Status of Women Canada and Indian and Northern Affairs Canada departments to prioritize this issue" (Sisters in Spirit website). The report is very clear about where the blame for the fate of these women lies:

> The social and economic marginalisation of Indigenous women, along with a history of government policies that have torn apart Indigenous families and have pushed a disproportionate number of Indigenous women into dangerous situations that include extreme poverty, homelessness and prostitution. (Amnesty International 2004: 2)

The report goes onto say that "These acts of violence may be motivated by racism, or may be carried out in the expectation that societal indifference to the welfare and safety of Indigenous women will allow the perpetrators to escape justice" (Amnesty International 2004: 2). Not all of the missing and murdered Aboriginal women were prostitutes; but the lives of those who were were no less valuable than those of other women; they were all somebody's daughter and a member of a community, and in many cases, they were a sister, partner/spouse, or mother. In Chapter 60, we provide a brief overview of the work *Sisters In Spirit*, as well as *Finding Dawn*, a film directed by Christine Welsh, that examines missing and murdered Aboriginal women in Canada through the lives of Dawn Crey, Ramona Wilson, and Daleen Kay Bosse, their families and communities, as well as Aboriginal activists seeking to end violence against Aboriginal women. A link to the film can be found on the *Gendered Intersections* website (fernwoodpublishing.ca/gi2) and it can be viewed at the National Film Board website (nfb.ca/playlists/films-influential-women/viewing/finding_dawn/).

When you hear the term "youth," what images immediately come to mind? Now if you change the term to "street youth," and then to "homeless youth," what images come to mind? "In popular culture," Stephen Gaetz observes, "adolescence is both celebrated as a time of adventure and freedom, but at the same time is seen as a period of confusion and stress with the potential for deviance." As we shift from "youth" to "street youth," a narrower set of meanings is conveyed from "kids" who are "dissatisfied and rebellious…who leave home for frivolous reasons (they don't like 'doing the dishes') or who are attracted by the excitement of downtown living" to young people who usually are escaping "a difficult home life." The main goal of homeless youth each day is to get enough to eat, find a place to sleep, and remain safe. This picture of the homeless youth is far less glamorous than the "fast-talking," "rebel-rousing," "hanging out at the local corner store" image of "street youth." Rather these youth may become "delinquents" or "deviants" in order to survive and get money. Because homeless youth often are forced to engage in risky illegal or quasi-legal behaviours, they are more vulnerable to becoming victims of violent crime than likely to be the perpetrators, as popular media representations would lead us to believe.

Living on the streets is very different for young men and women. Gaetz argues that "the streets are "a gendered space…they are a place where notions of masculinity, femininity, and sexuality are actively produced and reproduced, and opportunities structured." Drawing on the experience of Sandra, a seventeen-year-old "teenage girl," who grew up in a middle-class suburb of Toronto, who left home at the age of fifteen because her father beat her, Stephen Gaetz demonstrates in his chapter the ways in which street life is structured by class, race, gender, and sexuality. Like other homeless youth, Sandra is barely surviving by panhandling for money, but her middle-class background and education provide her resources that will more likely help her to get off the streets. As a female, Sandra is at great risk for gender-based aggression while her friends, who are racialized and/or gay or transsexual, are also subject to racially based and homophobic violence. So when you pass a young person on the street who is panhandling for money, how will you now think about "street youth or homeless youth?"

"Sticks and stones will break my bones, but names will never hurt me!" This aphorism often is used in response to schoolyard taunts, but is it true? For most of us, being called names is hurtful; sometimes we can shrug it off, but in other cases, we feel wounded. Now imagine that you are telling a new lover about your life and the experiences that have shaped you? What would you say if you had a history of sustained verbal abuse? This is the situation that Elizabeth Clarke recounts in her poem "How to Talk to a New Lover about Cerebral Palsy," in which she seeks the loving touch of her lover as she describes the pain and shame of "the words [that] sank into [her] body": spastic, retard, cripple, defect, gimp, crip. Over the centuries, people with disabilities in Europe (and many other places) have died due to exposure and drowning, or were banished. In more recent times, people with disabilities have been subjected to other indignities. In Clarke's experience, "Complete strangers / have patted my head, kissed / my cheek, called me courageous," while other people with disabilities have been the poster child for telethons, or relegated to nursing homes and the welfare lines. How does justice feel?

History is complicated. Nations are complicated. The political is complicated. Suffering is not (*Lessons of The Blood*, directed by James T. Hong and Yin Ju Chen).

NOTES

1. Bman is short for "battyman," a Jamaican pejorative for male homosexual. Seaman is a reference to the Marvel Comics — sometimes hot-headed anti-hero and sometimes hero — Namor the Sub-Mariner, whose mother was not mortal. Namor is thus linked to the other superheroes mentioned in the poem, but also to Columbus by marine operations that made Namor a hostile invader of the Americas. In Namor's case, he sought revenge for the nuclear destruction of his undersea home, Atlantis.

2. The website *Multicultural Canada* provides an excellent resource on the history of many different immigrant communities, their religious beliefs, economic and community life. At: multicultural-canada.ca/Encyclopedia.

REFERENCES

Alexander, Linda, Judith LaRosa and Helaine Bader. 2001. *New Dimensions in Women's Health*. Boston: Jones and Bartlett.

Amnesty International. 2007. "Stolen Sisters: Helen Betty Osborne." October 7. At: amnesty.ca/campaigns/sisters_helen_betty_osborne.php.

____. 2004. *Stolen Sisters: A Human Rights Response To Discrimination And Violence Against Indigenous Women*. At: amnesty.ca/campaigns/resources/ amr2000304.pdf.

Angier, Natalie. 1999. *Woman: An Intimate Geography*. Boston: Houghton Mifflin Company.

Bartky, Sandra. 1990. *Femininity and Domination: Studies in the Phenomenology of Oppression*. New York and London. Routledge.

Bordo, Susan. 1993. *Unbearable Weight: Feminism, Western Culture and the Body*. California: University of California Press.

Caron, Charlotte. 1993. *To Make and Make Again: Feminist Ritual Theology*. New York: Crossroad Press.

CCW (Canadian Council of Women). 2004. "Muslim Women in Canada: Fact Sheets." At: ccmw.com/press/press_room_factsheet.html.

Centres of Excellence for Women's Health. 2004. "Canada's Health System Failing Women in Rural and Remote Regions." *The Canadian Women's Health Network* 7,2/3.

Chernin, Kim. 1981. *Obsession: Reflections on the Tyranny of Slenderness*. New York: Harper Collins.

Condon, Marian. 2001. "Women, Society, Health and Health Care: Historical Roots and Contemporary Perspectives." In Marian Condon (ed.), *Women's Health: An Integrated Approach to Wellness and Illness*. Upper Saddle River, NJ: Prentice Hall.

Counihan, Carole M. 1999. *The Anthropology of Food and Body: Gender, Meaning and Power*. New York: Routledge.

Donnelly, Liza. 2011. "Drawing Upon Humor For Change." *TedTalks*. At: ted.com/talks/liza_donnelly_drawing_upon_humor_for_change.html.

Ehrenreich, Barbara, and Deirdre English. 1973. *Complaints and Disorders: The Sexual Politics of Sickness*. New York: The Feminist Press.

Encylopaedica Britannica. "creation myth." At: britannica.com/ EBchecked/ topic/ 142144/ creation-myth.

Finkelstein, Joanne. 1989. *Dining Out: A Sociology of Modern Manners*. New York: New York University Press.

Foucault, Michel. 1984. "Docile Bodies." In Paul Rabinow (ed.), *The Foucault Reader*. New York: Pantheon Books.

Government of Canada. 2006. "The Human Face of Mental Health and Mental Illness in Canada." Ottawa: Minister of Public Works and Government Services Canada. At: phac-aspc.gc.ca/

publicat/human-humain06/pdf/human_face_e.pdf.

Health Canada. 2002. "Women's Health Strategy." At: hcsc.gc.ca/english/ women/womenstrat/htm.

Hong, James T., and Yin Ju Chen (directors). 2010. *Lessons of The Blood*. Zukunftsmusik.

Lock, Margaret, and Nancy Scheper-Hughes. 1996. "A Critical-Interpretive Approach in Medical Anthropology: Rituals and Routines of Discipline and Dissent." In Carolyn Sargent and Thomas Johnson (eds.), *Medical Anthropology: Contemporary Theory and Method*. London: Praeger.

Mosca, L., J.E. Manson, S.E. Sutherland, R.D. Langdon, T. Manolio and E. Barrett-Connor. 2000. "Awareness, Perception, and Knowledge of Heart Disease Risk and Prevention among Women in the United States." *Archives of Family Medicine* 9.

National Aboriginal Women's Association. "Sisters In Spirit History." At: nwac.ca/programs/sis-history.

Pratt, Mary Louise. 1991. "Arts of the Contact Zone." *Profession* 91. New York: MLA.

Riley-Giomariso, Oma. 2001. "Cardiovascular Wellness and Illness." In Marian Condon (ed.), *Women's Health: An Integrated Approach to Wellness and Illness*. Upper Saddle River, NJ: Prentice Hall.

Sloame Joanna. 2011. "The Jewish Virtual Library." At: jewishvirtuallibrary.org/jsource/vjw/canada.html.

Stuckey, Johanna H. 2005. "Women and Religion: Female Spirituality, Feminist Theology, and Feminist God Worship." In Nancy Mandell (ed.), *Feminist Issues: Race, Class and Sexuality*. Toronto: Pearson Prentice-Hall.

Sunnybrook and Women's College Health Sciences Centre. 2003. "Canadian Women Less Healthy than Men." *Women's Health Matter News*. At: womenshealthmatters.ca/phprint.php.

Synnott, Anthony. 1993. *The Body Social: Symbolism, Self and Society*. London and New York: Routledge.

Wente, Margaret, 2009. "Montreal Massacre Death Cult." *Globe and Mail*. December 7. At: theglobe-andmail.com/news/opinions/montreal-massacre-death-cult/ article1392013.

World Health Organization (WHO). 2011a. "Frequently Asked Questions." At: who.int/suggestions/faq/en/index.html.

___. 2011b. "Health Topics: Disabilities." At: who.int/topics/disabilities/en/

- Estimated percentage of women affected by the 2010 French law banning the wearing of the *niqab* (full face veil): 0.0003 (n=2,000)[2]
- Percentage of Turkish women in 2007 who say they wore a headscarf in public: 45[3]
- Percentage of Turkish women wearing a headscarf in 2007 who said they wore one because it is a religious obligation: 49
- Percentage of Turkish women wearing a headscarf in 2007 who said they wore one because it is a symbol of Muslim identity: 35
- Percentage of Turkish women wearing a headscarf in 2007 who said they wore one in order to obey a male relative (father/brother/son): < 5
- Percentage of Britons in 2010 who would ban the *burqa*[4] (full body cover) in public places: 72[5]
- Percentage of Britons in 2010 who would ban the *niqab* in public places: 66
- Percentage of Britons in 2010 who would not ban wearing the *hijab* in public places: 75
- Percentage of Britons in 2010 who would forbid wearing the *niqab* at schools and universities: 75
- Percentage of Britons in 2010 who would forbid wearing the *niqab* in airports: 85
- Percentage of Britons in 2010 who believe that garments that conceal a woman's face are an affront to British values: 67
- Percentage of Britons in 2010 who claim the government should not be allowed to tell individuals what they can and cannot wear: 58
- Percentage of Canadians in 2010 who supported Quebec's legislation to ban wearing the *niqab* in public: 80[6]
- Percentage of Americans in 2010 who would approve banning the veil "that covers the whole face" in public places: 28[7]
- Percentage of Canadians in 2010 who believe that Canada is a tolerant society toward Muslims: 52[8]
- Percentage of Canadians in 2010 who believe that Canada is a tolerant society toward Aboriginals: 64
- Percentage of Canadians in 2010 who believe that Canada is a tolerant society toward gays and lesbians: 72
- Percentage of Canadian women in 2010 who believe that Canada should be a melting pot — immigrants should assimilate and blend into Canadian society: 49
- Percentage of Canadian men in 2010 who believe that Canada should be a melting pot — immigrants should assimilate and blend into Canadian society: 59
- Life expectancy for Canadian males born between 2005 and 2007: 78[9]
- Life expectancy for Canadian females born between 2005 and 2007: 83
- Life expectancy for women in Afghanistan in 2006: 43.3[10]
- The probability of female infants in Afghanistan in 2006 dying before the age of 5: 254/1000
- The probability of male infants in Afghanistan in 2006 dying before the age of 5: 260/1000
- Percentage of Afghan girls in 2006 who are married before the age of 16: 57

- Percentage of married women in Afghanistan in 2006 who used contraception: 15
- Frequency with which one Afghan woman died in childbirth in 2006: every 29 minutes[11]
- Percentage of births in Afghanistan in 2003 that were attended by skilled health personnel: 14
- Estimated maternal mortality rate[12] for Afghan women, the highest rate in the world, in 2008: 140/1000
- Estimated maternal mortality rate for Canadian women in 2008: 1.2/1000
- Estimated maternal mortality rate for Swedish women, the lowest rate in the world, in 2008: 0.5/1000
- Percentage of global maternal deaths in 2008 that took place in sub-Saharan Africa and South Asia: 87
- The average female-to-male sex ratio in India as of the 2001 census: 933:1000[13]
- The average male-to-female sex ratio for the infant-to-four-year-old age group in China as of January 2010: 123.26:100[14]
- The average male-to-female sex ratio in 2005 for second or more Chinese children in cities: 138:100; towns: 137:100; and rural areas: 146:100
- The average male-to-female sex ratio in 2005 among third children living in Beijing: 300:100
- Cost of an ultrasound in China to identify the gender of an unborn fetus: $12.00
- The average male-to-female sex ratio in all societies that record births: 103–106:100
- The percentage of males living in Canada in 2007: 49.5[15]
- Rate of induced abortions per 1000 females in Canada in 1996: 16[16]
- Rate of induced abortions per 1000 females in Canada in 2005: 13.7
- Percentage of Canadians in 2007 who believed that the law should protect human life from conception on: 30[17]
- Percentage of female Canadians in 2007 who believed that the law should protect human life from conception on: 34
- Percentage of Canadians in 2007 who believed that the law should protect human life after conception: 30; after three months of pregnancy: 21; after six months of pregnancy: 11
- Percentage of Canadians in 2007 who believed that human life should receive legal protection only from the point of birth: 33
- Percentage of female Canadians in 2007 who believed that human life should receive legal protection only from the point of birth: 30
- Percentage of Canadians in 2007 who believed that abortions should always be paid using the tax-funded health-care system: 32
- Percentage of Canadians in 2007 who believed that abortions should be financed using tax dollars but only in medical emergencies, such as a threat to the mother's life or in cases of rape or incest: 47
- Percentage of Canadians in 2007 who believed that paying for abortions should be a private responsibility, either out-of-pocket or using private health-care plans: 17
- Percentage of Americans in 2009 who identified themselves as "pro-choice:" 46[18]
- Percentage of Americans in 2009 who identified themselves as "pro-life:" 47
- Percentage of Canadian men who died from cancer, the leading cause of death among men in 2007: 30.8[19]
- Percentage of Canadian men who died from heart disease, the second leading cause of death among men in 2007: 22.2
- Percentage of Canadian women who died from cancer, the leading cause of death among women in 2007: 28.3

- Percentage of Canadian women who died from heart disease, the second leading cause of death among women in 2007: 20.7
- Percentage of new cases of prostate cancer, the leading diagnosis of all cases of cancer for men, of all primary sites of cancer in 2007: 27.1[20]
- Percentage of new cases of breast cancer, the leading diagnosis of all cases of cancer for women, of all primary sites of cancer in 2007: 26.9
- Relative risk between 1994/1995 and 2008/2009 of an Aboriginal or South/Southeast Asian woman being diagnosed with Type 2 diabetes compared to a white woman: 3.1:1[21]
- Relative risk between 1994/1995 and 2008/2009 of a low-income woman being diagnosed with Type 2 diabetes compared to a woman in the highest income bracket: 1.7:1[22]
- Estimated number of people worldwide living with HIV in 2009: 33.3 million[23]
- Percentage change in the incidence of HIV between 2001 and 2009 in 33 countries (including 22 sub-Saharan countries): -25
- Percentage of all people living with HIV globally in 2009 who are women: 50
- Percentage of all people living with HIV worldwide in 2009 who live in sub-Saharan Africa: 68
- Percentage of all women in the world living with HIV in 2009 who live in sub-Saharan Africa: 76
- Number of people living with HIV (including AIDS) in Canada in 2009: 65,000[24]
- Percentage increase of number people living with HIV (including AIDS) in Canada from 2005 to 2009: 14
- Percentage of all new HIV infections in 2009 diagnosed in Canadian gay, bisexual, and other men who have sex with men (MSM): 44
- Percentage of all new HIV infections in 2009 diagnosed in Canadian persons who inject drugs (IDU): 21
- Percentage of new HIV infections acquired from non-endemic countries among Canadian male and female heterosexuals in 2009: 25
- The percentage of new HIV infections acquired from endemic countries among Canadian male and female heterosexuals in 2009: 5.5
- Percentage of all new HIV infections acquired by Canadian women in 2009: 26
- Percentage of Canadian men who smoked in 2009: 22.6[25]
- Percentage of Canadian women who smoked in 2009: 17.7
- Percentage of Canadians in 2006 who reported having an activity limitation: 14.3[26]
- Percentage of Canadians in 2001 who reported having an activity limitation: 12.4.
- Percentage of Canadian men over the age of 75 in 2006 who reported having an activity limitation: 54
- Percentage of Canadian women over the age of in 2006 who reported having an activity limitation: 57.8
- Number of countries that have anti-discrimination and other disability-specific laws: 45
- Estimated percentage of women with disabilities of all women globally: 10
- Estimated percentage of women with disabilities of all disabled people living in low and middle-income countries: 75
- Estimated percentage of women with disabilities globally who are literate: 1[27]
- Percentage of Canadians in 1978/79 over the age of 18 who were either overweight or obese: 49.2[28]
- Percentage of Canadians in 2004 over the age of 18 who were either overweight or obese: 59.1
- Percentage of Canadian women in 2004 over the age of 18 who were either overweight

or obese: 53.4

- Percentage of Canadian men in 2004 over the age of 18 who were either overweight or obese: 65
- Percentage of Canadian men in the top 20% of household income in 2004 who were either overweight or obese: 26
- Percentage of Canadian women in the top 20% of household income in 2004 who were either overweight or obese: 20
- Estimated number of people worldwide who did not have enough to eat in 2009: 1.02 billion[29]
- Estimated percentage in 2006 of world's hungry who were women: 60
- Number of countries in which 65% of the world's hungry lived in 2009: 7[30]
- Number of people assisted by a food bank in Canada in March 2010: 867,948[31]
- Date on which the General Assembly of the United Nations passed the Declaration on the Elimination of Violence against Women (resolution 48/104): 1993
- Estimated percentage (based on data collected between 2004 and 2007) of women worldwide who will experience physical or sexual violence from men in their lifetime – the majority by husbands, intimate partners or someone they know: 70[32]
- Estimated number of people worldwide in 2006 who were trafficked: 800,000
- Percentage of persons trafficked worldwide in 2006 who were women and girls and who were trafficked for sexual exploitation: 79
- Proportion of murdered women in the United States in 2006 who were killed by intimate partners: 1/3
- Estimated number of women and girls worldwide in 2010 who are currently living with the consequences of female genital mutilation (FGM): 100 to 140 million[33]
- Estimated number of girls in Africa in 2010 from 10 years of age and above who have undergone FGM: 92 million
- Number of women who have been murdered in Cuidad Guarez, Mexico since 1993: 450[34]
- Estimated number of women who were raped during the war in Bosnia in the early 1990s 20,000 to 50,000[35]
- Estimated number of women who were raped during the Rwandan genocide during 100 days of conflict in 1994: 500,000
- Percentage of convictions for sexual violence of the 10,000 genocide-related trials heard by Rwandan courts: 3
- Number of rapes reported in South Kivu, Democratic Republic of Congo from March to May, 2008: 463[36]
- Date on which the U.N. Security Council unanimously adopted Resolution 1820 recognizing sexual violence as a tactic of war: 2008
- Number of incidents of spousal violence in Canada (i.e., violence against legally married, common-law, separated and divorced partners) that were reported to police in 2007: 40,200[37]
- Percentage of all police-reported violent crime in Canada in 2007 that were spousal assaults: 12
- Percentage of victims of spousal assault in Canada in 2007 who were female: 83[38]
- Percentage change between 1998 and 2007 in police-reported spousal violence: -15
- Percentage of all spousal assaults in Canada in 2007 in which police laid charges: 75
- Ratio of spousal violence in Canada in 2007 between current partners (legally married or common-law) and ex-partners: 2:1

- Number of children and youth in Canada who were the victims of a police-reported assault in 2007: 53,400
- Percentage of children and youth under the age of 18 in Canada in 2007 who were physically or sexually assaulted by someone they knew: 85
- Ratio of physical and sexual assault in Canada 2007 by a family member for girls compared to boys: 4:1
- Percentage of family-related sexual assaults in Canada in 2007 in which male family members were identified as the accused: 96
- Percentage of family-related physical assaults in Canada in 2007 in which male family members were identified as the accused: 71
- Number of incidents of family violence against seniors in Canada in 2007: 1,938
- Rate of violent victimization for senior men in Canada in 2007 compared to the male population: 163/100,000
- Rate of violent victimization for senior women in Canada in 2007 compared to the female population: 114/100,000
- Rate of violent victimization by a family member for senior men in Canada in 2007 compared to the male population: 43/100,000
- Rate of violent victimization by a family member for senior women in Canada in 2007 compared to the female population: 52/100,000
- Rate at which women in Canada in 2007 continue to be more likely than men to be victims of spousal homicide: 4:1[39]
- Number of shelters across Canada in 2008 providing residential services to women and children escaping abusive situations: 569
- Percentage of visible minority women in Canada in 2004 who reported being victims of spousal violence: 4
- Percentage of Aboriginal people in Canada in 2004 who reported being victims of spousal violence: 21[40]
- Percentage of non-Aboriginal people in Canada in 2004 who reported being victims of spousal violence: 7
- Rate at which Aboriginal women in Canada in 2004 were more likely to be victims of spousal assault than non-Aboriginal women or men: 3:1
- Percentage of Aboriginal women in Canada in 2004 who reported the most severe and potentially life-threatening forms of violence: 53
- Percentage of non-Aboriginal women in Canada in 2004 who reported the most severe and potentially life-threatening forms of violence:[41] 37
- Percentage of female Aboriginal victims who were killed by a family member: 45
- Percentage of female non-Aboriginal victims in Canada in 2004 who were killed by a family member: 68
- Rate of stalking in Canada in 2004 between Aboriginal and non-Aboriginal women: 2:1

NOTES

1. The original Hypatia Index was compiled by Pamela Downe, with the assistance of Ellen Whiteman. Except when otherwise indicated in the main text, the sources cited in this Index apply to the line where first referenced and then to all those that follow until another endnote appears.
2. Guardian.co.uk, 2010, "French Niqab Ban: Beneath the Veil" (July 15). At: *The Guardian,*guardian. co.uk/commentisfree/2010/jul/15/france-niqab-veil-ban-law.
3. Magali Reault, 2008, "Headscarves and Secularism: Voices of Turkish Women," *Gallup: Muslim West Facts Project* (February 8). At: muslimwestfacts.com/mwf/104362/Headscarves-Secularism-Voices-From-Turkish-Women.aspx.

4.	The burqa is an outer garment worn by some Muslim women that is meant to conceal the entire body. In addition to a full veil, the burqa usually features a net that covers the eyes.

5.	Visioncritical, 2010, "Public Opinions: Most Britons Would Ban Burqa in Public Places, Airports and Schools" (January 26). At: visioncritical.com/wp-content/uploads/2010/01/2010.01.26_Burqa_BRI.pdf.

6.	Angus Reid Public Opinion, 2010, "Most Canadians Support Quebec's Veil Ban" (March 29). At: angus-reid.com/polls/38670/most_canadians_support_quebecaas_veil_ban/.

7.	Pew Research Center, 2010, Pew Global Attitudes Project, "Most Americans Disapprove: Widespread Support for Banning Full Islamic Veil in Western Europe" (July 8). At: pewglobal.org/ 2010/07/08/widespread-support-for-banning-full-islamic-veil-in-western-europe.

8.	Angus Reid Public Opinion, 2010, "Canadians Endorse Multiculturalism, But Pick Melting Pot over Mosaic" (November 8). At: angus-reid.com/wp-content/uploads/2010/11/2010.11.08_Melting_CAN.pdf.

9.	Statistics Canada, 2010, "Life Expectancy at Birth, by Sex, by Province," CANSIM, table 102-0512 and Catalogue no. 84-537-XIE. At: statcan.ca/l01/cst01/health26-eng.htm.

10.	United Nations Development Fund, Ministry of Women's Affairs, 2008, "Women and Men in Afghanistan: Baseline Statistics." At: emro.who.int/ghd/PDF/afg_gender_statistics.pdf.

11.	This figure represents the highest maternal mortality rate in the world, followed by Chad and Somalia (120 deaths per 1000). World Health Organization, 2010, "Trends in Maternal Mortality: Estimates Developed by WHO, UNICEF, UNFPA, World Bank." At childinfo.org/files/ Trends in MaternalMortality, 1990 to 2008.pdf.

12.	Maternal mortality rates (MMR) is expressed as deaths per 1000 births.

13.	Government of India, Ministry of Home Affairs, "Census Data, 2001: India at a Glance: Sex Ratio." At: censusindia.gov.in/Census_Data_2001/India_at_glance/fsex.aspx.

14.	"All Girls Allowed: End Gendercide." At: allgirlsallowed.org/category/topics/gender-imbalance-china#_edn8. Although there are few statistics, the main explanation for the imbalance in the gender ratio is believed to the result of selective abortion of female foetuses or gendercide. See Wei Xing Zhu and Theresa Hesketh, 2009, "China's Excess Males, Sex Selective Abortion, and One Child Policy: Analysis of Data from 2005 National Intercensus Survey," *British Medical Journal* 338.

15.	Statistics Canada, 2010, "Population by Marital Status and Sex, 2003–2007." At: statcan.gc.ca/l01/cst01/famil01-eng.htm.

16.	Statistics Canada, 2005, "Induced Abortion Statistics: Table 3-1 Selected Induced Abortions Statistics, by Age Group and Area of Residence of Patient — Canada." At: statcan.gc.ca/pub/82-223-x/2008000/5202012-eng.htm.

17.	Environics Research Group, 2007, "Canadians' Attitudes Toward Abortion: Commissioned Research for LifeCanada" (October). At: lifecanada.org/html/resources/polling/2007PollReport.pdf. NB: The data does not necessarily add up to 100%. Some respondents answered "didn't know" or offered no opinion.

18.	Gallup, 2009, "U.S. Abortion Attitudes Closely Divided" (August 4). At: gallup.com/poll/122033/u.s.-abortion-attitudes-closely-divided.aspx.

19.	Statistics Canada, 2010, "Leading Causes of Death by Sex," CANSIM table 102-0561 and Catalogue no. 84-215-X.

20.	Statistics Canada, 2010, "Canadian Cancer Registry Database," (July 2010 file), CANSIM table 103-0550 and Catalogue no. 82-231-X.

21.	This data is based on a proportional hazards ratio, a term which refers to the proportional effect of an explanatory variable on the hazard or risk of an event. Nancy Ross, Heather Gilmour, and Kaberi Dasgupta, 2010, "14-Year Diabetes Incidence: The Role of Socioeconomic Status," *Healthy Today, Health Tomorrow: Findings from the National Health Survey*, Statistics Canada, Cat: 82-618-MWE2010008 (August 18). At: statcan.gc.ca/pub/82-618-m/82-618-m2010008-eng.htm.

22.	These findings about income and the onset of Type 2 diabetes among women remained significant when controlling for overweight, obesity, and ethno-cultural origin. No relationship between household income and the onset of diabetes was found among men when other factors were controlled for. Instead, Ross, Gilmour and Dasgupta report that "the onset of diabetes among men was related to being overweight or obese and to the number of secondary behavioural factors they reported, such as heavy drinking, smoking and physical inactivity."

23. UNAIDS, 2010, "Report on the Global AIDs Epidemic." At: unaids.org/globalreport / Global_report.htm.

24. AIDS Committee of Toronto (ACT), 2010, HIV/AIDS Statistics Canada. At: actoronto.org/home.nsf/pages/hivaidsstatscan.

25. Statistics Canada, 2010, "Smokers, by Age Group and Sex," *Health in Canada*, CANSIM, table 105-0501 and Catalogue no. 82-221-X. At: statcan.ca/l01/cst01/health73b-eng.htm.

26. Disability refers to limitations in individual's everyday activities due to a physical or psychological condition, or to a health condition. "Disability Statistics Canada." Disabled World. At: disabled-world.com/disability/statistics/disability-statistics-canada.php#ixzz17UlJuFva.

27. World Bank, "Women with Disability" (Article 3 & 6). At: web.worldbank.org/wbsite/external/topics/extsocialprotection/extdisability/0,,contentMDK:20193528~menuPK:418895~pagePK:148956~piPK:216618~theSitePK:282699,00.html.

28. Overweight and obesity are based on body mass index (BMI), which is a measure of an individual's weight in relation to his or her height. Overweight individuals have BMI of 25.9 to 29.9; obese individuals have BMI > 30, and are divided into three classes ranging from high to extremely high. Michael Tjepkema, 2005, "Adult Obesity in Canada: Measured Height and Weight," Statistics Canada. At: statcan.gc.ca/pub/82-620-m/2005001/article/adults-adultes/8060-eng.htm.

29. This number represents more than the combined populations of the U.S., Canada, and the European Union. At: wfp.org/hunger/stats.

30. The countries are India, China, the Democratic Republic of Congo, Bangladesh, Indonesia, Pakistan, and Ethiopia.

31. This figure for food bank attendance is the highest level on record. Food Banks Canada, 2010, "Hunger Facts 2010." At: cafb-acba.ca/main2.cfm?id=10718648-B6A7-8AA0-6A3C6F-3CAC0124E.

32. Say No to Violence — UNITE. End Violence Against Women, "Violence against Women: Facts and Figures." At: saynotoviolence.org/sites/default/files/Say_NO_VAW_Factsheet.pdf.

33 The World Health organization defines female genital mutilation (FGM) as "all procedures that involve partial or total removal of the external female genitalia, or other injury to the female genital organs for non-medical reasons."World Health Organization, 2010, "Female Genital Mutilation," Fact sheet N°241 (February). At: who.int/mediacentre/factsheets/fs241/en.

34. Amnesty International, 2009, "Amnesty International Public Statement: The Inter American Court of Human Rights Hears Important Case of Violence Against Women in Mexico," AI index: AMR 41/023/2009 (April 28). At: amnesty.org/en/library/asset/AMR41/023/2009/en/43217b05-ac2f-4d1d-bb08-ad51200596d1/amr410232009en.pdf.

35. United Nations, 2008, "Background document: Session II. Sexual Violence Against Women and Children in Armed Conflict," Parliamentary Hearing at the United Nations. New York, (20–21 November). At: ipu.org/splz-e/unga08/s2.pdf.

36. Integrated Regional Information Networks (IRIN), 2009, "DRC: Rape Cases Soar in South Kivu" (June 3). At: unhcr.org/refworld/docid/4a2e1016c.html.

37. Statistics Canada, 2009, "Family Violence in Canada: A Statistical Profile, 2009," Cat. No. 85-224-X. At: statcan.gc.ca/pub/85-224-x/2009000/aftertoc-aprestdm2-eng.htm

38. All subsequent entries pertaining to gendered violence in Canada refer to police reported data.

39. Spousal homicides are relatively rare in Canada, representing less than 1 percent of all homicides. Moreover, Statistics Canada reports that the "rates of spousal homicide for both male and female victims have been declining over the past three decades. This trend continued in 2007, with a rate of four spousal homicides per million spouses — this rate was the lowest over the 30-year period from 1978 to 2007" (p. 48).

40. Statistics Canada, 2006, *Measuring Violence Against Women: Statistical Trends, 2006*, Ottawa: Ministry of Industry. At: statcan.gc.ca/pub/85-570-x/85-570-x2006001-eng.pdf.

41. The most severe and potentially life-threatening forms of violence include being beaten or choked, having had a gun or knife used against them, or being sexually assaulted.

39

Feminists Pathways in the Study of (Religious) Beliefs and Practices

Darlene M. Juschka

Religious beliefs are world-making (Paden 2000): they have an incalculable effect on cultural and individual worldviews. As world-making, it is imperative that feminists examine and challenge prevalent systems of belief and practice — religion. However, religion itself is a slippery concept. Is religion a cultural phenomenon that invents and determines how we conceptualize our reality? Is it a political and/or epistemological concept that goes far in legitimating social control? Many scholars argue that religion is *sui generis*; that is, an essential and unique impulse found in human beings. However, human beings are meaning-making in that they seek to explain theirs and the world's existence, and mythic narratives, ritual scripts, and symbols have often functioned in this way. Such explanatory efforts, however, do not mean that religion is fundamentally or biologically inherent to human beings. Rather, systems of belief and practice have been, and continue to be, one of the narratives human beings have authored in order to define, explain, and shape existence.

Early Stages of Redefining Women's Religious Roles

In Euro-western societies, women and men who committed to systems of belief and practice like Christianities realized that women had much to offer society; but these contributions were anticipated to be moral rather than, for example, political, economic or epistemological ones. These latter masculinized social domains remained secured and protected from contamination by the feminine, which was seen as properly emotional but always gullible.

In the early to mid-twentieth century, Canada, like other Euro-western societies, was organized by a gender/sex ideology of separate spheres: the public arena was marked as male and masculine, and the private arena as female and feminine. For example, the Women's Christian Temperance Union (WCTU), founded in Canada in 1873 and active today, struggled to uplift society morally through the prohibition of alcohol, but the WCTU also supported women's suffrage, the abolition of slavery in the United States and the reformation of labour laws, with children and women in mind. However, the WCTU's endorsement and support of the eugenics movement and its effort to ensure social "purity" were egregious. Combining the desire for a genetically pure society with a belief in providence, or a belief that the deity had a divine plan for "man," the WCTU backed efforts to sterilize socially demarcated groups of women (and some men) who it deemed unfit as reproducers. Often defined by race, class, indigeneity or immigrant status, the unfit were classified as "degenerates," and were seen as a potential threat to the human genetic pool, taking humanity off the proper evolutionary path and, ultimately, away from deity.

The Second Wave and the Study of Systems of Belief and Practice

Women working and practising in the area of systems of belief and practice began to ask why some writings and authors (primarily men) were considered canonical, and others not, and why some interpretations of these texts were accepted while others were summarily rejected. In monotheistic systems, for example, feminists began to challenge the idea of designating some historical texts as orthodox and authoritative, and while others were deemed heterodox and non-authoritative. These feminists demonstrated that elite men had over the millennia determined what constitutes legitimate religious texts and their interpretations. Religiously oriented feminists, such as Rosemary Radford Ruether (Catholic), Rita Gross (Buddhist), Judith Plaskow (Jewish), Delores Williams (Afra-American Protestant Christian) and Leila Ahmed (Sunni Muslim), to name but a few, proposed new theological readings and interpretations of religious text, history, symbol, myth and ritual, and aspired to institute women's visibility within, and enable their enhanced contributions to, systems of belief and practice. Other feminists in the study of religion, such as Susan Starr Sered (1994, 1999) and Mieke Bal (1987, 1988), have examined the interplay between systems of belief and practice and gender/sex, women, sexuality and colonialism, and how specifically gender/sex and sexuality are central to conceptualizing being (ontology) and the world (existence).

Gendering Bodies and Texts:
Feminist Engagements with Systems of Belief and Practice

Many feminists, including those who study systems of belief and practice, observe that women's and men's different life experiences lead to differing perspectives, ethics and expectations. Moreover, in the last decades of the twentieth century, feminists have extended their analyses to include age, class, sexuality, race and geopolitical location. These categories that signify difference are central to shaping multiple aspects of systems of belief and practice such as the conceptualization of deity as either exclusively male or female (e.g., Buddha or Isis).

According to Sered (1994: 6), women in both male- and female-dominated systems of belief and practice express concerns that emerge from women's day-to-day existence, particularly those related to relationships, family, children, health, lactation, birth, oppression, education, death, food restrictions, and so forth. The centring of women's beliefs and practices in their life experiences is often interpreted as evidence for the innate effects of women's biology in their lives. However, such centring reflects more the social realities of women whose lives are dominated by male systems of belief and practice. We can see this centring in elaborate symbol systems such as the orthodox Jewish *Mikveh* bath, wherein women, following menstruation and childbirth (women in this state are referred to as *niddah*), fully immerse themselves in a pool of water in order to be ritually purified.[1] Blu Greenberg, an orthodox Jewish feminist, has argued against understanding this rite as deity's judgement on women's innate impurity, maintaining instead that the *Mikveh* rite should be understood as removing the *niddah* from a temporary state of impurity (with an emphasis on temporary since a state of impurity is a condition all Jews can enter for a number of reasons related to illness, blood, death, etc.[2]), as a renewal of her relationship with deity and as time set apart for her own personal space and self-care.

Sered argues that the centrality of family, relationships and reproduction in the daily lives of women is often reflected in the ways in which they express their religiosity, as the *Mikveh* rite suggests. Food, the inclusion of children, the informality of everyday space and the relatively free sharing of knowledge are often found in female-dominated systems of belief and practice. For example, organizations in which women, who tend not to be young, are in positions of leadership are more likely to make a conscious effort to create non-hierarchical structures and to repudiate privileged roles or kinds of contributions. In systems of belief and practice founded upon feminist consciousness, such as Reclaiming, co-founded by Starhawk, non-hierarchical structures are even more pronounced (Salomonsen 2002).

Due to women's acute sense of restriction within many systems of belief and practice such as Catholicism, Theravada Buddhism, Hasidic Judaism or Sunni and Shia Islam, feminists have worked largely to challenge women's exclusion from positions of recognized and legal authority. Feminists working in the study of religions have developed strategies by which to expose androcentrism, challenge the oppressive tendencies of institutionalized religions and reintroduce women as subjects into systems of belief and practice. These strategies include the processes of rereading, reconceiving and reconstructing systems of belief and practice (Juschka 2001, O'Connor 1989).

Rereading

The task of rereading means that all textual material is read to reveal androcentric tendencies, which assume only the male as subject, as the doer of action, even as the maleness of this subject is obscured by the pseudo-generic term, "man." This act of rereading is what Elisabeth Schüssler Fiorenza (1991) calls a "feminist hermeneutics of suspicion" or a reading against the grain of the text particularly with regard to the position of women and gender relations. In such a reading we see that women have been objects of study but rarely subjects. In positioning women as objects canonical texts have often been prescriptive, intending to define women as the Female — eternal, singular, sexual and problematic.

Rereading a historical, theological, or mythological text from a feminist perspective requires placing women at the centre of the discourse and framing questions with women in mind. Are women represented in the text? If so, how are they represented? If women are absent, why? And, what is the intention of the text when it comes to its descriptions of women? Mary Daly (1973), once a Christian theologian, began her odyssey out of Catholicism by rereading Catholic religious texts and pointing to their inherent androcentrism and misogynistic tendencies. Similarly, Phyllis Trible (1978) noted that Christianity, in both Catholic and Protestant versions, theologically privileged the second creation myth over the first. In the first creation myth, the deity is said to have created humankind and then designated them as simply male and female (Gen. 1: 27). In the second, more familiar story, after her discussion with the serpent, Eve convinces Adam to eat the fruit of the tree of knowledge, and, as a result, they are forced to leave the Garden of Eden (Gen. 2: 21–23). The implied equality between male and female in the Genesis 1: 27 creation myth has been, and continues to be, ignored by most mainstream and fundamentalist Christian groups, or the story is understood to express a lost human condition, lost, that is, through Eve's (read the Female's) transgression. Privileging one creation myth over the other means having a stake in the privileged version, and in the case of masculine-hegemonic Christianities, the gain is the legitimation of female/feminine subjugation to the male/masculine.

Reconceiving

Reconceiving canonical texts like the *Bible*, the *Qu'ran*, the *Tanakh* (Hebrew bible) or Buddhist sutras entails looking at non-canonical sources, searching beyond what was considered authoritative, such as orthodox literary texts, in order to reconceive the tradition. Reconceiving means bringing in different materials that are often considered heterodox (outside official canonical material) such as funerary inscriptions, or understood to be questionable historical documents (women's journals, letters and diaries). In reconceiving Hellenistic ritual practices, for example, feminists such as Joan Breton Connelly (2007) argued that not all temple priests were male: indeed, the temple to Artemis in Ephesus (modern-day Turkey) was completely overseen by women who managed the stone carvings, finances, festivals, votive offerings, sacrifices, and so forth. Documentation of such facts and other kinds of often fragmentary and far-flung evidence tells us that in ancient Greece through to the period of the Roman Empire, women were ritual specialists and shared this role with men.

Reconstructing consists not only of understanding the historical and theological aspects of the religion from a position inclusive of women, but also requires that one uses different methods by which to reconstruct a system of belief and practice. Also requisite is the retrieval of women's voices from the past, as well as attending to contemporary ones. In understanding Christian responses to medieval European witches, for example, the study of the *Malleus Maleficarum* (*The Hammer of Witches*, first published in 1484) is central. Composed by two Dominican monks, Henricus Institoris and Jacobus Sprenger, the work presents a particularly prejudiced and misogynistic view of women. For example, the monks inquire "why a larger number of sorcerers is found among the delicate female sex than among men?" and then offer the explanation that the female is weak, curious and naturally deceitful (Institoris and Sprenger [1484] 2006: 111–25). Such a view demonstrates an idealized notion of women as the Female/Feminine, who, whether angel or devil, is not to be trusted. (For example, Joan of Arc, a fifteenth-century French peasant girl who successfully guided the French army against the British, was figured as either a witch or a saint, and burned at the stake by the English when she was nineteen years old.) Writings such as the *Malleus* do not inform readers about women's lives, practices, or involvement in systems of belief and practice; instead readers encounter a masculinist conceptualization of the female/feminine (and male/masculine) within the system of belief and practice and in the social body at large. For example, in my own analysis of possession and witchcraft in early modern France, it became eminently clear that the discourse itself was gender-coded. Men who were diagnosed as possessed or accused of witchcraft were feminized in order that they fit the conceptualization of possession: witchcraft was understood as properly belonging to the female/feminine (Juschka 2009).

Feminist rereadings of canonical theological texts have also been done of the *Qu'ran*. Fatima Mernissi (1988, 1993) and Leila Ahmed (1992) challenge masculinist interpretations wherein women are devalued relative to men and placed normatively under masculine rule. In reconceiving Islam, Mernissi and Ahmed do not suggest that Islamic women abandon the religion; rather they argue for a critical approach to its history:

> even as Islam instituted, in the initiatory society, a hierarchical structure as the basis of relations between men and women, it also preached, in its ethical voice, the moral and spiritual equality of all human beings. Arguably, therefore, even as it instituted a sexual hierarchy, it laid the ground, in its ethical voice, for the subversion of the hierarchy. (Ahmed, 1992: 238)

In the process of restructuring their system of belief and practice, Merinissi and Ahmed challenge distorted views of women, especially of female sexuality, and pay attention to significant women in Islam such as Aisha, Muhammad's youngest wife, an intelligent and vocal advocate for Islam. Although many Euro-western feminists have wondered at the possibility of women's equal status within Islam, feminists like Mernissi and Ahmed have challenged them for their Eurocentric and colonialist perspective, a perspective that perceives and judges Islamic systems from the position of the "civilizing" colonizer.

Conclusion

Women have, in large part, been written out of the history of religions, their presence either ignored or subsumed under the pseudo-generic "man." In order to make visible those made invisible, feminist religion scholars have painstakingly chiseled away at the years of accumulated patriarchal sediment to present a more complex narrative of human history. Such a story fully acknowledges women as central to human meaning-making from the outset and as having influence on every past and present system of belief and practice. Despite the always important, if not central, place of the female and feminine in every religion, the study of women's true place in religious knowledge was given short shrift until feminists entered the scene and began to uncover a wealth of knowledge and insight through the examination of texts and artefacts by and about women.

NOTES

1. According to the book of Leviticus (15:19), found in the *Tanakh* and *Bible*, "When a woman has discharge, her discharge being blood from her body, she shall remain in her impurity for seven days; whoever touches her shall be unclean until evening." Also Leviticus 20:18 states: "If a man lies with a woman in her infirmity and uncovers her nakedness, he has laid bare her flow and she has exposed her blood flow; both of them shall be cut off from all the people." This rule, believed to be divinely inspired, set up the state of *niddah* for women, while the rite of the *Mikveh* bath provides a way for women to exit this state (and all others who enter a state of impurity, such as those who have been in close proximity to a corpse or have experienced skin diseases). This passage is developed and elaborated in other significant religious texts such as the *Mishnah* and *Talmud*.

2. Judaism in general focuses centrally on issues related to purity and impurity, particularly in relation to bodies (what goes into and leaves the body) and deity.

REFERENCES

Ahmed, Leila. 1992. *Women and Gender in Islam: Roots of a Modern Debate*. New Haven: Yale University Press.

Bal, Mieke, 1988. *Death and Dissymmetry: The Politics of Coherence in the Book of Judges*. Chicago: University of Chicago Press.

____. 1987. *Lethal Love: Feminist Literary Readings of Biblical Love Stories*. Bloomington: Indiana University Press.

Connelly, Joan Breton. 2007. *Portrait of a Priestess: Women and Ritual in Ancient Greece*. Princeton, MJ: Princeton University Press.

Daly, Mary. 1973. *Beyond God the Father: Toward a Philosophy of Women's Liberation*. Boston: Beacon Press.

Greenberg, Blu. 1998 [1981]. *On Women and Judaism: A View from Tradition*. Philadelphia: Jewish Publication Society of America.

Institoris, H., and J. Sprenger. [1484] 2006. *Malleus Maleficarum: The English Translation* 2. C.S. Mackay (ed. and trans.). Cambridge: Cambridge University Press.

Juschka, Darlene. 2009. *Political Bodies/Body Politic: The Semiotics of Gender*. London; New York: Equinox.

Juschka, Darlene (ed.). 2001. *Feminism in the Study of Religion: A Reader*. London; New York: Continuum.

Lesko, Barbara. 1989. *Women's Earliest Records from Ancient Egypt and Western Asia*. Atlanta, Georgia: Scholars Press.

Mernissi, Fatima. 1993. *The Forgotten Queens of Islam*. Mary Jo Lakeland (trans.). Cambridge: Polity Press.

O'Connor, June. 1989. "Rereading, Reconceiving and Reconstructing Traditions: Feminist Research in Religion." *Women's Studies* 17: 112.

Paden, W. 2000. "World." In W. Braun and R.T. McCutcheon (eds.), *Guide to the Study of Religion*. London; New York: Continuum.

Salomonsen, Jone. 2002. *Enchanted Feminism: Ritual, Gender and Divinity among the Reclaiming Witches of San Francisco*. London; New York: Routledge.

Schüssler Fiorenza, Elisabeth. 1991. *In Memory of Her: A Feminist Theological Reconstruction of Christian Origins*. New York: Crossroads.

Sered, Susan Starr. 1999. *Women of the Sacred Groves: Divine Priestesses of Okinawa*. New York: Oxford University Press.

____. 1994. *Priestess, Mother, Sacred Sister: Religions Dominated by Women*. New York; Oxford: Oxford University Press.

Trible, Phyllis. 1978. *God and the Rhetoric of Sexuality*. Philadelphia: Fortress Press.

It All Began with Eve

Morny Joy

It all began with Eve — a familiar but superficial phrase. For Eve, after all, is only a character in a story, a story that has been interpreted in many ways over the centuries. This basic story has come to link not only Eve but all women with evil, with weakness of will (because she was the one first tempted), as well as with irrational emotionality. Such a development seems odd, considering that the original sin was one of disobedience to God, who commanded that an apple in the garden of Eden not be eaten. Various later interpretations have also regarded Eve's body (after the banishment from Eden) as itself seductive and shameful and sexual relations as a necessary evil (for reproduction only). Women's sexuality (often associated with Satan) is regarded as defiling. While many women today, especially in the time of Madonna, "the material girl," feel that they have escaped these derogatory sexual stereotypes, such attitudes are still pervasive in western cultural traditions. Thus there remain many taboos connected with the way in which women experience and talk about their bodies. At the same time, crimes of hate and sexual violence against women continue.

Part of my research has been to try and understand the reasons for this misogyny and for women's internalized hatred of their own bodies (manifested today in extreme symptoms such as anorexia and self-mutilation). There can be no simplistic answers to the complex interconnection of causes — be they of a social, historical, psychological or religious nature — that have contributed to this situation. Perhaps a description of my own journey could help a new generation of women scholars to understand the vast changes in knowledge on this topic that have taken place in the past thirty years in religious scholarship.

I am now in my fifties, and I grew up in a conservative Catholic milieu in Australia, where the sinfulness of sex and shame of the body prevailed. Female talk about sexuality and menstruation were not discussed — even between friends and sisters. This was an extremely protected and repressed society. The first major challenge to these values came when I read Germaine Greer's *The Female Eunuch* (1970). Here, among other (then) amazing revelations, Greer discussed her "thrill of shock" when a friend described tasting her own menstrual blood (Greer 1970: 259).[1] I can remember initially being repulsed but then I began to investigate why this offended me. It was the start of a long journey which led me to the study of the origins of western philosophy and theology.

During the seventies and early eighties, while I was studying in Montreal for a PhD, there were a number of other events that jolted me into awareness. One was a television show where, to my astonishment, in broad daylight, in front of the cameras, women were being taught to use a speculum, so they could get to know and love their vaginas. Then, at the Montreal Museum of Fine Arts, I saw Judy Chicago's exhibit, *The Dinner Party*. This consisted of a triangular table, with place sittings for thirty-nine women (Chicago 1977). At each place, there was a vibrantly coloured plate, honouring outstanding women of myth and history, such as Sophia, Queen Elizabeth I, Pocahontas and Georgia O'Keefe. On closer inspection, it became obvious that all the dinner plates were spectacular depictions of each woman's genitalia. While I didn't care for some of the designs, I felt, after my original squeamishness, a surge of pride. My inhibitions began to fade that day. Perhaps today it is the *Vagina Monologues* (Ensler 1998) that arouses similar emotions and reactions in women — as again, what had previously been a taboo topic is brought to a graphic awareness.[2]

It was my explorations on the academic front that helped me achieve greater awareness of the history of hatred towards the body, and women's bodies in particular. The only problem was that at that time there were not many books available to help me in my search. Today, I still own the original copies of certain books that provided my initial insights. One is *Beyond God the Father* (1973), by Mary Daly, who demonstrates that because God was identified with men, women were not considered to be in God's image. In another work, Rosemary Ruether surveys the writings of the early Church fathers from the second to fifth centuries and demonstrates how St. Augustine (CE 354–430), influenced by Plato, posited the mind/spirit [associated with men] as superior to the body [associated with women]. "[The] definition of femaleness as body decrees a natural subordination of female to male, *as flesh must be subject to spirit in the right ordering of nature.* It also makes her peculiarly the symbol of the Fall and sin" (Ruether 1974: 157). In the same volume, Eleanor Commo McLaughlin discusses the work of Thomas Aquinas (CE 1224–74) and illustrates how Aquinas had been influenced by the flawed biology of Aristotle (BCE 384–322) who, lacking the contemporary knowledge of the X and Y chromosomes, regarded woman as a defective or "misbegotten" male.

McLaughlin is especially concerned by Aquinas's attitude to sexuality: "[P]hysical sex was always suspect and could never be the vehicle of love" (McLaughlin 1974: 229). She continues by observing that this attitude contributed to common beliefs that "[N]o Christian should receive the Eucharist the morning after he or she had sexual relations, or that a menstruating woman should not receive communion, or even enter a church. Menstrual blood was thought to be attractive to devils and unclean spirits" (229). To combat these attitudes, which remained dominant in conservative Christian theology, especially Catholicism, since the Middle Ages, McLaughlin believes that the first task is "to make explicit the assumptions received from this tradition about male/female difference and hierarchy, and to expose with the help of historical understanding the now patently invalid intellectual foundations of these typologies" (257).

During my years as a university teacher I have observed an immense amount of further research by women scholars that undertakes McLaughlin's recommendations. For example, cross-cultural research has revealed that many cultures, such as those of the indigenous peoples of North America and Australia, have women-centred celebrations for first menstruation (Gross 2001). But prejudices remain, such as the one I witnessed on television recently when a woman writer commented that there should be first menstruation celebrations in our society. The interviewer recoiled with distaste, if not horror. Menstrual taboos in particular die hard (O'Grady 2003). Another development has been the reinterpretation of the Eve story. Kim Chernin's imaginative retelling (1987) presents Eve as a curious woman, seeking new knowledge, rather than the first sexual sinner.

Many contemporary women scholars in religious studies, both theologians and philosophers of religion, believe that the traditional ideas of God have been bad for women. For some, the solution is to stop depicting God as a monolithic male figure. Others believe that the split between the (good) spirit or soul and the (bad) body should be eliminated. Certain women have decided to abandon the male image of God completely and replace him with the Goddess figure, who appears in a number of guises: as a Great Mother, worshipped since primordial times in both European and Asian cultures; as a remnant of a pagan or pre-Christian religion, surviving in the tradition of *wicca* (witchcraft); or as a symbolic representation of a psychological movement of self-empowerment (Christ 1979). According to Carol Christ:

> The symbol of Goddess has much to offer women who are struggling to be rid of the… devaluation of female power, [and]denigration of the female body…. As struggle to create a new culture… it seems natural that the Goddess would reemerge as a symbol of the newfound beauty, strength, and power of women. (1979: 286)

In this approach, God is no longer viewed as a transcendent, authoritarian male, but as a female or feminine presence that partakes in the natural world. While such a position may be very self-affirming for many women, there are critics who are concerned that such goddess projections, while imaginative, can become restrictive. They claim that women can become preoccupied with personal issues and reaffirm, rather than change, the cultural conventions that support the existing male and female divisions. In *Pure Lust,* Mary Daly worried that "fixation upon the 'Great Mother'" could prevent women from exploring other alternative modes of representing the divine (1984: 405). Daly herself, as she recounts in *Beyond God the Father*, is supportive of exploring non-anthropomorphic ways of appreciating God, for she views all gods/goddesses as potential idols. Instead of understanding "God" as a noun, Daly proposes seeing the word as a verb — so as to avoid any sexual stereotypes. In her iconoclastic approach, Daly then understands God as a source of energy — as a "form-destroying, form creating, transforming power that makes all things new" (1973: 43).[3] Women, identifying with this power, can free themselves from patriarchal impositions and transform the world.

While Daly imagines a psychological and physical liberation, Rosemary Ruether is influenced by a contemporary form of liberation theology that is more concerned with the living Christ than with a transcendent God. In liberation theology, Christ is recognized as a figure who came to bring justice to this world. Thus, Ruether supports social and structural change that addresses not just the injustice suffered by women, but that of all minorities. For Ruether, any human images of God are simply human projections and must be recognized as such. Ruether's own solution is to introduce the term "God/ess," which she understands as a gender-neutral, inclusive term, which should never be used to endorse "the existing hierarchical social order" (1974: 69). Instead,

> Images of God/ess must include female roles and experience. Images of God/ess must be drawn from the activities of peasants and working people, people at the bottom of society…. God/ess-language cannot validate roles of men or women in stereotypic ways that justify male dominance and female subordination. (Ruether 1974: 69)

For Ruether, along with other feminist religious thinkers, such as Elizabeth Schüssler Fiorenza (1993), women should never just work towards their own liberation but in solidarity with all human beings who suffer forms of oppression.

Another reinterpretation of God that moves away from an other-worldly ideal is pantheism. It appreciates the divine as the dynamic force inherent in the continuous process of a positive creation that rejects all forms of hierarchy. Grace Jantzen proposes that pantheism helps to challenge existing religious structures by illuminating the mutually reinforcing ways that oppression functions in a society. In describing her anti-hierarchal position, Jantzen notes the work of Patricia Collins, an African-American scholar (who is not herself a pantheist). Jantzen finds that:

Her [Collins's] approach is fruitful for encouraging thought about how forms of oppression dominate and reinforce one another: how, for example, heterosexism is embedded in the sexual control of all women, how concepts of race and class modify one another, and how religion has been used to legitimate and perpetuate an interlocking symbolic of domination. (Jantzen 1999: 124–25)

Advocating a total revision of traditional ideas of God and sexual ethics, Jantzen sees pantheism as encouraging different understandings of the divine, including the idea that the body itself, as part of creation, is divine. In this view, women's bodies and sexuality can no longer be vilified or treated with disrespect. "If we took for granted that divinity — that which is most to be respected and valued — *means* mutuality, bodiliness, diversity — the implications for our thought and lives would be incalculable" (Jantzen 1999: 269).

Although most peoples in western societies today accept the idea of personal autonomy and the right to control one's body, many abuses continue to take place, as documented by Christine Gudorf (1994). Gudorf claims that acts of violence against women can be described as sexual sins. She combines the need for justice, which is central to Ruether, with the idea of God as embodied in creation, promoted by Jantzen, and introduces the term "bodyright." This right refers to a women's right to be free from all forms of physical coercion. Gudorf does not confine her indictment to individual acts but refers to institutions, such as the Christians churches, which have even, at times, protected the perpetrators. "Until we enlarge our treatment of sexual sin from individual overt acts to include a critique of social models and institutions which give rise to them, our understanding of sexual sin will remain deficient" (1994: 18).

From the above examples, it seems that feminist writers in religion have broken through many of the barriers that allowed women's bodies to be degraded. I wish that such knowledge had been available to me in my youth. It is difficult to describe the deep pride and admiration I feel whenever I receive a new work of scholarship that stretches the boundaries of knowing by insisting on the interaction of both mind and body. The mind or spirit is no longer regarded as the sole source of knowledge and disconnected from the body. Yet the continuing saga of rapes, abductions and family violence breaks my heart. From my own perspective as an activist scholar, my hope is that my teaching and writing will inspire students to continue to work toward the establishment of the notion of bodyright. This would help to construct a society where violence against women — until recently something that was ignored, if not condoned, by both church and state — will be understood as a violation not just of the integrity of a woman's body but of her basic human rights.

NOTES

1. Greer's statement was even more of a shock, as the blood that the woman tasted was on her lover's penis.
2. In 1998, Ensler created V-day, an organization focused on combating violence against women. On St. Valentine's Day (V-Day) in 2002, over a thousand performances of the *Vagina Monologues* were performed throughout the world.
3. Daly enlarges on this: "As marginal beings who have no stake in a sexist world, women — if we have the courage to keep our eyes open — have access to the knowledge that neither the Father, nor the Son, nor the Mother *is* God, the Verb who transcends anthropomorphic symbolization" (1973: 97).

REFERENCES

Chernin, Kim. 1987. *Reinventing Eve*. New York: Harper and Row.
Chicago, Judy. 1977. *Through the Flower: My Struggle as a Woman Artist*. New York: Doubleday.

Christ, Carol. 1979. "Why Women Need the Goddess." In Carol Christ and Judith Plaskow (eds.), *Womanspirit Rising: A Feminist Reader in Religion*. San Francisco: Harper and Row.

Daly, Mary. 1973. *Beyond God the Father*. Boston: Beacon Press.

Ensler, Eve. 1998. *Vagina Monologues*. New York: Villard Books.

Fiorenza, Elisabeth Schüssler. 1993. *Discipleship of Equals*. New York: Crossroad.

Greer, Germaine. 1970. *The Female Eunuch*. London: Paladin.

Gross, Rita. 2001. "Menstruation and Childbirth as Ritual and Religious Experience among Native Australians." In Nancy Auer Falk and Rita M. Gross (eds.), *Unspoken Worlds: Women's Religious Lives*. Belmont, CA: Wadsworth Press.

Gudorf, Christine.1994. *Body, Sex and Pleasure: Reconstructing Sexual Ethics*. Cleveland: The Pilgrim Press.

Jantzen, Grace. 1999. *Becoming Divine*. Bloomington: Indiana University Press.

Joy, Morny. 1998. "Feminist Scholarship: The Challenge to Ethics." In Dawne McCance, (ed.), *Life Ethics in World Religions*. Atlanta: Scholars Press.

___. 1996. "No Longer Docile Daughters or Handmaidens of the Lord." *Women's Studies International Forum* 19, 6.

McLaughlin, Eleanor Commo. 1974. "Equality of Souls, Inequality of Sexes: Women in Medieval Theology." In Rosemary Ruether (ed.), *Religion and Sexism*. New York: Simon and Schuster.

O'Grady, Kathleen. 2003. "The Semantics of 'Taboo': Menstrual Prohibitions in the Hebrew Bible." In Kristin De Troyer, Judith A. Herbert, Judith A. Johnson and Anne Marie Korte (eds.), *Blood, Purity and Impurity: A Feminist Critique*. Bern, Switzerland: Peter Lang.

Ruether, Rosemary. 1983. *Sexism and God-Talk: Towards a Feminist Theology*. Boston: Beacon.

___. 1974. "Misogynism and Virginal Fathers of the Church." In Rosemary Ruether (ed.), *Religion and Sexism*. New York: Simon and Schuster.

On the Seventh Day

Lorna Crozier

On the first day God said,
Let there be light.
And there was light.
On the second day
God said, *Let there be light,*
and there was more light.

What are you doing? asked God's wife,
knowing he was the dreamy sort.
You created light yesterday.

I forgot, God said. *What can I do
about it now?*

Nothing, said his wife.
But pay attention!
And in a huff she left
to do the many chores
a wife must do in the vast
though dustless rooms of heaven.

On the third day God said,
Let there be light. And
on the fourth and fifth
(his wife off visiting his mother).

When she returned there was only
the sixth day left. The light
was so blinding, so dazzling
God had to stretch and stretch the sky to hold it
and the sky took up all the room –
it was bigger than anything
even God could imagine.
Quick, his wife said,
make something to stand on!
and a thin line of soil
nudged against the sky like a run-over snake
bearing all the blue in the world on its back.

On the seventh day God rested
as he always did. Well, *rest*
wasn't exactly the right word,
his wife had to admit.
On the seventh day God
went into his study
and wrote in his journal
in huge curlicues and loops
and large crosses on the *t*'s,
changing all the facts, of course,
even creating Woman
from a Man's rib, imagine that!
But why be upset? she thought.
Who's going to believe it?

Anyway, she had her work to do.
Everything he'd forgotten
she had to create
with only a day left to do it.
Leaf by leaf,
paw by paw, two by two,
and now nothing
could be immortal
as in the original plan.

Go out and multiply, yes,
she'd have to say it,
but there was too little room
for life without end,
forever and ever,
on that thin spit of earth
under that huge prairie sky.

NOTE

In Lorna Crozier, 1992, "On the Seventh Day," *Inventing the Hawk*, Toronto: McClelland and
Stewart. Reprinted with permission.

42

This Is History

Beth Brant

Long before there was an earth and long before there were people called human, there was a Sky World.

On Sky World there were Sky People who were like us and not like us. And of the Sky People there was Sky Woman. Sky Woman had a peculiar trait: she had curiosity. She bothered the others with her questions, with wanting to know what lay beneath the clouds that supported her world. Sometimes she pushed the clouds aside and looked down through her world to the large expanse of blue that shimmered below. The others were tired of her peculiar trait and called her an aberration, a queer woman who asked questions, a woman who wasn't satisfied with what she had.

Sky Woman spent much of her time dreaming — dreaming about the blue expanse underneath the clouds, dreaming about floating through the clouds, dreaming about the blue colour and how it would feel to her touch. One day she pushed the clouds away from her and leaned out of the opening. She fell. The others tried to catch her hands and pull her back, but she struggled free and began to float downward. The Sky People watched her descent and agreed that they were glad to see her go. She was a nuisance with her questions, an aberration, a queer woman who was not like them — content to walk the clouds undisturbed.

Sky Woman floated. The currents of wind played through her hair. She put out her arms and felt the sensations of air between her fingers. She kicked her legs, did somersaults, and was curious about the free, delightful feelings of flying. Faster, faster, she floated toward the blue shimmer that beckoned her.

She heard a noise and turned to see a beautiful creature with black wings and a white head flying close to her. The creature spoke. "I am Eagle. I have been sent to carry you to your new home." Sky Woman laughed and held out her hands for Eagle to brush his wings against. He swooped under her, and she settled on his back. They flew. They circled, they glided, they flew, Sky Woman clutching the feathers of the great creature.

Sky Woman looked down at the blue colour. Rising from the expanse was a turtle. Turtle looked up at the flying pair and nodded her head. She dove into the waters and came up again with a muskrat clinging to her back. In Muskrat's paw was a clump of dark brown dirt scooped from the bottom of the sea. She laid it on Turtle's back and jumped back into the water. Sky Woman watched the creature swim away, her long tail skimming the top of the waves, her whiskers shining. Sky Woman watched as the dark brown dirt began to spread. All across Turtle's back the dirt was spreading, spreading, and in this dirt green things were growing. Small green things, tall green things, and in the middle of Turtle's back, the tallest thing grew. It grew branches and needles, more and more branches, until it reached where Eagle and Sky Woman were hovering.

Turtle raised her head and beckoned to the pair. Eagle flew down to Turtle's back and gently lay Sky Woman on the soft dirt. Then he flew to the very top of the White Pine tree and said, "I will be here, watching over everything that is to be. You will look to me as the harbinger of what is to happen. You will be kind to me and my people. In return, I will keep this place safe." Eagle folded his wings and looked away.

Sky Woman felt the soft dirt with her fingers. She brought the dirt to her mouth and tasted the colour of it. She looked around at the green things. Some were flowering with fantastic shapes. She stood on her feet and felt the solid back of Turtle beneath her. She marveled at this wonderful place and wondered what she would do here.

Turtle swivelled her head and looked at Sky Woman with ancient eyes. "You will live here and make this a new place. You will be kind, and you will call me Mother. I will make all manner of creatures and growing things to guide you on this new place. You will watch them carefully, and from them you will learn how to live. You will take care to be respectful and honourable to me. I am your Mother." Sky Woman touched Turtle's back and promised to honour and respect her. She lay down on Turtle's back and fell asleep.

As she slept, Turtle grew. Her back became wider and longer. She slapped her tail and cracks appeared in her back. From these cracks came mountains, canyons were formed, rivers and lakes were made from the spit of Turtle's mouth. She shook her body and prairies sprang up, deserts settled, marshes and wetlands pushed their way through the cracks of Turtle's shell. Turtle opened her mouth and called. Creatures came crawling out of her back. Some had wings, some had four legs, six legs, or eight. Some had no legs but slithered on the ground, some had no legs and swam with fins. These creatures crawled out of Turtle's back and some were covered with fur, some with feathers, some with scales, some with skins of beautiful colours. Turtle called again, and the creatures found their voices. Some sang, some barked, some growled and roared, some had no voice but a hiss, some had no voice and rubbed their legs together to speak. Turtle called again. The creatures began to make homes. Some gathered twigs and leaves, others spun webs, some found caves, others dug holes in the ground. Some made the waters their home, and some of these came up for air to breathe. Turtle shuddered, and the new place was made a continent, a world.

Turtle gave a last look at the sleeping Sky Woman. "Inside you is growing a being who is like you and not like you. This being will be your companion. Together you will give names to the creatures and growing things. You will be kind to these things. This companion growing inside you will be called First Woman, for she will be the first of these beings on this earth. Together you will respect me and call me Mother. Listen to the voices of the creatures and communicate with them. This will be called prayer, for prayer is the language of all my creations. Remember me." Turtle rested from her long labour.

Sky Woman woke and touched herself. Inside her body she felt the stirrings of another. She stood on her feet and walked the earth. She climbed mountains, she walked in the desert, she slept in trees, she listened to the voices of the creatures and living things, she swam in the waters, she smelled the growing things that came from the earth. As she wandered and discovered, her body grew from the being inside her. She ate leaves, she picked fruit. An animal showed her how to bring fire, then threw himself in the flames that she might eat of him. She prayed her thanks, remembering Turtle's words. Sky Woman watched the creatures, learning how they lived in community with each other, learning how they hunted, how they stored food, how they prayed. Her body grew larger, and she felt her companion move inside her, waiting to be born. She watched the living things, seeing how they fed their young, how they taught their young, how they protected their young. She watched and learned and saw how things should be. She waited for the day when First Woman would come and together they would be companions, lovers of the earth, namers of all things, planters and harvesters, creators.

On a day when Sky Woman was listening to the animals, she felt a sharp pain inside of her. First Woman wanted to be born. Sky Woman walked the earth, looking for soft things to lay her companion on when she was born. She gathered all day, finding feathers of winged-creatures, skins of the fur-bearers. She gathered these things and made a deep nest. She gathered other special things for medicine and magic. She ate leaves from a plant that eased her pain. She clutched her magic things in her hands to give her help. She prayed to the creatures to strengthen her. She squatted over the deep nest and began to push. She pushed and held tight to the magic medicine. She pushed, and First Woman slipped out of her and onto the soft nest. First Woman gave a cry. Sky Woman touched her companion, then gave another great push as her placenta fell from her. She cut the long cord with her teeth as she had learned from the animals. She ate the placenta as she had learned from the animals. She brought First Woman to her breast as she had learned, and First Woman began to suckle, drawing nourishment and medicine from Sky Woman.

Sky Woman prayed, thanking the creatures for teaching her how to give birth. She touched the earth, thanking Mother for giving her this gift of a companion. Turtle shuddered, acknowledging the prayer. That day, Sky Woman began a new thing. She opened her mouth and sounds came forth. Sounds of song. She sang and began a new thing — singing prayers. She fashioned a thing out of animal skin and wood. She touched the thing and it resonated. She touched it again and called it drum. She sang with the rhythm of her touching. First Woman suckled as her companion sang the prayers.

First Woman began to grow. In the beginning she lay in her nest dreaming, then crying out as she wanted to suckle. Then she opened her eyes and saw her companion and smiled. Then she sat up and made sounds. Then she crawled and was curious about everything. She wanted to touch and feel and taste all that was around her. Sky Woman carried her on her back when she walked the earth, listening to the living things and talking with them. First Woman saw all the things that Sky Woman pointed out to her. She listened to Sky Woman touch the drum and make singing prayers. First Woman stood on her feet and felt the solid shell of Turtle against her feet. The two companions began walking together. First Woman made a drum for herself, and together the companions made magic by touching their drums and singing their prayers. First Woman grew, and as she grew Sky Woman showed her the green things, the animal things, the living things, and told her they needed to name them. Together they began the naming: heron, bear, snake, dolphin, spider, maple, oak, thistle, cricket, wolf, hawk, trout, goldenrod, firefly. They named together and, in naming, the women became closer and truer companions. The living things that now had names moved closer to the women and taught them how to dance. Together, they all danced as the women touched their drums and made their singing prayers. Together they danced. Together. All together.

In time the women observed the changes that took place around them. They observed that sometimes the trees would shed their leaves and at other times would grow new ones. They observed that some creatures buried themselves in caves and burrows and slept for long times, reappearing when the trees began their new birth. They observed that some creatures flew away for long times, reappearing when the animals crawled from their caves and dens. Together, the companions decided they would sing special songs and different prayers when the earth was changing and the creatures were changing. They named these times seasons and made different drums, sewn with feathers and stones. The companions wore stones around their necks, feathers in their hair, and shells on their feet, and, when they danced, the music was new and extraordinary. They prepared feasts at this time, asking the animals to accept their death. Some walked into their arrows, some ran away. The animals that gave their lives were thanked and their bones were buried in Turtle's back to feed her — the Mother of all things.

The women fashioned combs from animal teeth and claws. They spent long times combing and caressing each other's hair. They crushed berries and flowers and painted signs on their bodies to honour Mother and the living things who lived with them. They painted on rocks and stones to honour the creatures who taught them. They fixed food together, feeding each other herbs and roots and plants. They lit fires together and cooked the foods that gave them strength and medicine. They laughed together and made language between them. They touched each other and in the touching made a new word: love. They touched each other and made a language of touching: passion. They made medicine together. They made magic together.

And on a day when First Woman woke from her sleep, she bled from her body. Sky Woman marvelled at this thing her companion could do because she was born on Turtle's back. Sky Woman built a special place for her companion to retreat at this time, for it was wondrous what her body could do. First Woman went to her bleeding-place and dreamed about her body and the magic it made. And at the end of this time, she emerged laughing and holding out her arms to Sky Woman.

Time went by, long times went by. Sky Woman felt her body changing. Her skin was wrinkling, her hands were not as strong. She could not hunt as she used to. Her eyes were becoming dim, her sight unclear. She walked the earth in this changed body and took longer to climb mountains and swim in the waters. She still enjoyed the touch of First Woman, the laughter and language they shared between them, the dancing, the singing prayers. But her body was changed. Sky Woman whispered to Mother, asking her what these changes meant. Mother whispered back that Sky Woman was aged and soon her body would stop living. Before this event happened, Sky Woman must give her companion instruction. Mother and Sky Woman whispered together as First Woman slept. They whispered together the long night through.

When First Woman woke from her sleep, Sky Woman told her of the event that was to happen. "You must cut the heart from this body and bury it in the field by your bleeding-place. Then you must cut this body in small pieces and fling them into the sky. You will do this for me."

And the day came that Sky Woman's body stopped living. First Woman touched her companion's face and promised to carry out her request. She carved the heart from Sky Woman's body and buried it in the open field near her bleeding-place. She put her ear to the ground and heard Sky Woman's voice, "From this place will grow three plants. As long as they grow, you will never want for food or magic. Name these plants corn, beans, and squash. Call them the Three Sisters, for, like us, they will never grow apart."

First Woman watched as the green plant burst from the ground, growing stalks that bore ears of beautifully coloured kernels. From beneath the corn rose another plant with small leaves, and it twined around the stalks carrying pods of green. Inside each pod were small, white beans. From under the beans came a sprawling vine with large leaves that tumbled and grew and shaded the beans' delicate roots. On this vine were large, green squash that grew and turned orange and yellow. Three Sisters, First Woman named them.

First Woman cut her companion's body in small pieces and flung them at the sky. The sky turned dark, and there, glittering and shining, were bright-coloured stars and a round moon. The moon spoke. "I will come to you every day when the sun is sleeping. You will make songs and prayers for me. Inside you are growing two beings. They are not like us. They are called Twin Sons. One of these is good and will honour us and our Mother. One of these is not good and will bring things that we have no names for. Teach these beings what we have learned together. Teach them that if the sons do not honour the women who made them, that will be the end of this earth. Keep well, my beloved First Woman. Eagle is watching out for you. Honour the living things. Be kind to them. Be strong. I am always with you. Remember our Mother. Be kind to her."

First Woman touched her body, feeling the movements inside. She touched the back of Mother and waited for the beings who would change her world.

NOTE

Beth Brant, 1991, *Food & Spirits*, Vancouver: Press Gang Publishers. Adapted and reprinted with permission.

In Da Name of Da Fadder

Louise Halfe

In da name of da fadder, poop
on my knees I pray to geezuz
cuz I got mad at my husband for
humpin' and makin too many babies
I 'pologize cuz I mad and cried I
didn't have no bannock and lard
to feed dem cuz my husband
drank all da *sōniyās* for wine.

In da name of da fadder, poop
my husband slap, fist and kick me
I hit him back. I 'pologize poop
da priest said I must of done someding
wrong and I deserve it cuz woman is
'uppose to listen to man. I not a good
wife cuz my hands somedimes
want to kill him.

In da name of da fadder, poop
I lookit other man he is so
handsome my eyes hurt, he kind, gentle,
soft laugh and my body wants to
feel his hot face. I no geezuz
would be mad he said I must not
be durty in my doughts but
poop I want smile and warm arms.

In da name of da fadder, poop
Inside the sweatlodge I shame cuz
Indian *iskwew* don't know anydin'
In church priest said all us pagans
will go to hell. I don't know what da means,
all I no is I big sinner
and maybe I won't see geezuz when I die.

In da name of da fadder, poop
I dought da geezuz kind but
I is no good. I can't read hen write.
I don't understand how come *mōniyās* has

clean howse and lottsa feed and he don't
share it with me and my children.
I don't understand why geezuz say I be
poor, stay on welfare cuz *mōniyās* say
I good for nuddin' cuz I don't have
wisdom. Forgive me poop I is
big sinner.

NOTE

In Louise Halfe, 1994, *Bear Bones & Feathers*, Regina: Coteau Books. Reprinted with permission.

44

Mas(k)culinity

Klyde Broox

Listen to Klyde Broox perform his poem at the Gendered Intersections website:
fernwoodpublishing.ca/gi2.

Father, Son and Holy Ghost
Spill some blood and drink a toast
God's a man can back his boast
Omnipotent man, the Lord of Hosts
That's what men have preached the most
Malesupremacist myths from coast to coast
Mas(k)ulinity, mas(k)ulinity

Don't pin it on the Trinity
It has no affinity to divinity

Mas(k)ulinity, mas(k)ulinity
Don't spin it as divinity
Pay-triarchal ph-ill-osophy
"God made woman from man's anatomy
Men were meant to make more money"
Guydeology, liedeology, sexistology
Misogyny, on tv, in movies
Art-ificial personalities
Man-u-fractured sex-u-alities
Pseudo-manhood does no good
Hollywood male, oh so pale
That old tall tale, tickets on sale!

Men of steel cannot feel
Mission Impossible ideal
Onreel man-ipulated male-ego
Yo, bro; got to go with the flow
Got to be macho, you know
Fast cars, fights in bars, foreign wars
Mucho machismo por el muchacho
John Wayne, James Bond, Rambo
Shaft, Superfly, Dirty Harry
Makebelieve men who never marry
Guys without any family
Guns, guts, gory glory; cock and bull story

Superman, Batman, Spiderman
And so on; comic icons of perfection
I have no faith in those supposed superheroes
Johnny Ordinary means much more to me
Plain, simple, solid, stable, reliable role model
Vulnerable inside the tasks behind his mask
Many masks for men
Too many men in masks; who is the man?
Is not a question real men ask

Mask(u)linity mass-cue-linity

Don't pin it to the Trinity
It has no affinity with divinity

Mas(k)ulinity, mas(k)ulinity

Iron-man, caveman, brute strength
Incongruent in digitized environment
Strong-arm argument incoherent
Incoherent men often violent
Need some anger man-age-men-t
I won't call a man Bman, seaman, or demon[1]
I cast no aspersion on any one orientation
He-man, she-man, not me man
I-man just want to be free man
Want to warn everyman
Don't batter woman, you are the son of one
Black, White, Brown, Red, Yellow
Uptight or mellow, shortguy, longfellow
We all hailed, wailed, from the
Womb of Ma-ma, Ma-ma, Mamaaah!

Mas(k)ulinity, mas(k)ulinity

Don't pin it to the Trinity
It has no affinity with divinity

Mas(k)ulinity, mas(k)ulinity
Mirrors of mythology
Boys being boys find joys in toys
Still for all, as far as I can see
He who needs widescreen TV and SUV
To feel manly will probably also need therapy
Captive humanity trapped within our vanity
Mas(k)ulinity, mas(k)ulinity

Don't pin it on the Trinity; don't spin it as divinity
Sacred womanity is kindred to holymanity
From Genesis to a time like this; justice insists
It's time to strip off mas(k)ulinity
To remake the image of God maskfree

NOTES

This poem was re-versioned for this book, and Klyde wishes to acknowledge Susan Gingell's valuable feedback in the re-versioning and providing notes to the poem. The original poem is from Klyde Broox, 2005, "Mas(k)ulinity," *My Best Friend Is White*, Toronto: McGilligan Books.

1. Bman is short for battyman, a Jamaican pejorative for male homosexual. Seaman is a reference to the Marvel Comics — sometimes hot-headed anti-hero and sometimes hero — Namor the Sub-Mariner, whose mother was not mortal. Namor is thus linked to the other superheroes mentioned in the poem, but also to Columbus by marine operations that made Namor a hostile invader of the Americas. In Namor's case, he sought revenge for the nuclear destruction of his undersea home, Atlantis.

45

"I Didn't Know You Were Jewish"

… And Other Things Not to Say When You Find Out

Ivan Kalmar

Imagine that you and I have been acquainted with each other for some time. And now you learn that I have written this article. You are surprised and you say: "I didn't know you were Jewish!" Really? How touching. What would you have done if you had known? More important still, what are you going to do now that you do know?

Perhaps you mean to compliment me. I am not loud and aggressive. I am not interested in "jewing" people I have financial dealings with. If you are politically conservative, you might mean that I am not a subversive pinko radical. If you are on the Left, you might mean that I am not a Zionist Imperialist. In either case you mean, ultimately, that I am "Jewish but nice." But I don't need your compliment. To me, "Jewish" and "nice" are not opposites.

Notice: you did not simply ask me, "Are you Jewish?" I could take that; it is an ordinary question of personal information. You said, "I didn't know that…" and you said it because you don't speak to Jews the same way you speak to non-Jews. Let us go through some other things you might have said instead.

I don't care if a person is Jewish; to me all people are the same.

Maybe you think if you had said this, I would have been happier. Sorry. Yes, there are many Jews who would enthusiastically accept being "just human beings" rather than "Jews." I call such people EJI (pronounce it "edgy," an acronym for Embarrassed Jewish Individuals). I am not an EJI. No, I don't want you to treat me as a Jew rather than a human being because that implies that a Jew is not fully human. But I also don't want you to treat me as if I were not a Jew. I want to be treated as a Jew *and* a human being.

What's the JAP's Idea of an Ideal Home?

"Six thousand square feet with no kitchen or bedroom." Very funny. So you find out I am Jewish and you tell a "Jewish" joke. Why not, you think, the Jews are so funny. You want to please a Jew, you think, with a Jewish joke. And you choose a JAP joke. A JAP is, of course, a "Jewish American Princess." There is not a more vicious anti-female stereotype around. It is no compliment to Jewish men to have invented these vicious insults to Jewish women, who are portrayed as lazy, frigid, spoiled, and stupid. Indeed, a JAP is everything a woman means to a frustrated macho misogynist. I suspect the Jewish men who make up JAP jokes are unconsciously using a subtle and rather effective argument: "Look, our women are just as despicable as your women and in the same way; and we put them down just as much as you; therefore you goyish macho chauvinists, and us Jewish macho chauvinists have much in common."

When you, a non-Jew tell it, a JAP joke becomes both anti-female and clearly anti-Jewish. For you are not laughing about your own women (which would certainly be bad enough) but about ours. You laugh not only at women, but also at Jews.

My Mom's Such a Jewish Mother

For decades American Jewish comic performers have won great fame putting down their mothers. Telling their inanities in the first person, they have convinced the public, Jewish and

Gentile, to think that Jewish mothers are nagging, guilt-inducing monsters. I cannot really blame you for picking up a stereotype that is aggressively marketed by Jewish entertainers. By telling me that your mother is a Jewish mother, you wanted to say that we have much in common. But I hate the "Jewish mother" stereotype, another misogynous insult dressed in Jewish garb.

That mothering can be smothering is well known from all cultures. The "Jewish mother" is the anchor for all anti-mother resentment, felt just as much by Jews as by Gentiles. Indeed, "Jewish mother" has become a normal English expression for a passive-aggressive, guilt-inducing female progenitor. My mother is not a "Jewish mother," and I'd like you to leave her out of this.

What about the Palestinians?

Now I feel you are not even trying to be nice. Your expectation is that your question might irritate me. It does, but not for the reason you think: not because I hate Arabs or oppose the Palestinians' legitimate rights.

Of course, I have views on the Arab-Israeli conflict. And, of course, as a Jew I am ultimately on the side of Israel, the Jewish state. I am emotionally bound to Israel, a realization of a dream that my ancestors held for centuries. Moreover, Israel seems proof to me, like to most Jews, that another Holocaust would not be possible. If, God forbid, we have to go again, we will not go without a fight and we will not go without taking our enemy with us.

I also happen to believe in the rights of the Palestinian people: rights to self-determination, including a right to a state of their own, as long as the aim is not to take our state away from us. I deeply regret and am ashamed of the human rights abuses committed by the Israelis.

But I do not want to talk about this with you because your question, coming on the heels of my revelation that I am a Jew, makes me fear that to you "Jew" recalls "abusive Israeli occupier" (that is, Zionist Imperialist). If so, chances are you know little of the complexities of the Middle East; little of the large and widespread opposition, not only among world Jewry but also among Israeli Jews, to the Israeli army's practices; and little of the abuse committed by Palestinian terrorists, not only against Jews but also against fellow-Palestinians.

We All Believe in One God

Okay. This time you truly mean well. You want to show me that you and I are both God's children. True, those of us who are religious, Jews, Christians, and Muslims, believe in one God. Yet I don't think it is true that we believe in the *same* God. Our God does not have three persons like the Christian God: the Father, the Son, and the Holy Ghost. He did not become incarnate in Jesus. He has no human form at all; indeed, nowadays it bothers many of us that we refer to Him with the masculine pronoun, as if He were a man.

I respect your religion and I expect you to respect mine. But to equate all religions is not to respect them. A religion for all people would have to be a new religion that replaces all previous ones, and it is implied that this new religion would be more perfect than the old, "particularist" ones. Of necessity, religious universalists believe that their view of religion is better than that of the "particularists" and therefore create their own brand of religious one-upmanship.

What, however, distinguishes our Jewish religion and has distinguished it since the Middle Ages is that we are proudly particularist. We do not think that our religion is better for everybody, just that it is better for us. We are more tolerant of other ways of thinking about religion than the "universalists." We wish to keep our religion and let everyone else keep theirs.

When you invite me for dinner and ask me if I eat ham, you mean to show your understanding of the fact that traditional Jews do not eat pork. You want to make something I will eat; I understand and appreciate your concern. You mean to be considerate.

But remember this. If it is true that those of us who are religious have a concept of God that is not the same as that held by non-Jews (although there is great variation among us in terms of religious belief, just as there is among you), it is also true that many, perhaps most of us, have no concept of God at all. Those who are observant of the ancient behavioural code known as the *halakha* are a rather small minority. Even many of those who are affiliated with Orthodox synagogues don't really keep it. The Conservative, Reform, and Reconstructionist congregations, which comprise the majority of synagogue members in North America, have all modified or at least reinterpreted the *halakha*.

However, the great majority of us are not Orthodox. Jewishness is a matter of much more than religion: a culture, an ethnic identity, a shared history, family memories. It is perceived by us as a sort of magical identity, which we do not understand ourselves. Jewish identity consists of much more than Judaism. For many of us, Judaism is not even an important part of it.

If you don't see outward markers of Orthodoxy, chances are you are dealing with someone who is not strictly traditional. You are probably dealing with a Jew who is quite comfortable eating what you serve him or her. I certainly would be.

What Do You Think of Jesus?

And while we're dealing with religion, what about Jesus? Here and there I meet a religious Christian who longs to find out how it is possible for me, a member of Jesus' people, to "reject Him." So I am asked what I think about Him. The simple answer is that I don't think about Jesus.

I happen to be a devoted lover of Christian art and music. And I often find images of Christ deeply moving, a genuine symbolic depiction of the divine spirit. I am similarly touched when I see some images of the Buddha or of Hindu gods. But Jesus is no more an issue for me than Shiva is for you. I am not for or against Jesus and I have not rejected him. I have read the New Testament, and I find some of it quite interesting, and other parts quite stirring. But I am a Jew and happy to be one. I am not asking you to be a Jew; please do not ask me to be a Christian.

The problem is that if you are a Christian then Judaism *is* an issue for you. After all, Christianity started as a Jewish sect that opposed mainstream Judaism. (The early Christians' opposition centred mainly around Jesus: the Christians believed he was the Messiah, and the rest of us did not.) Judaism did not start in opposition to Christianity. But medieval myths libelled us as desecrating the Host, for the primitive Christian's image of the Jew is that of a Christ-killer, whose religion is devoted to opposing the concept of Jesus as the Messiah.

We respect Christianity, like we respect all other religions. But Jesus is to us simply a foreign religious personage. Next time you want to ask me what I think about Jesus, ask yourself what you think of Krishna.

Merry Christmas and Happy Hanukkah

Now here is one that most other Jews not only appreciate, they are positively thrilled by it. When you say Merry Christmas and Happy Hanukkah, you are recognizing that not everyone is Christian, you are noticing me as a Jew, and you wish me to share in the cheers of the holiday season. So why should I object?

I do not consider your greeting offensive, but I would like you to spend some time thinking about what it really means. Let us start with the issue of Christmas. In public, many Jews love to praise Christmas to the hilt, to make absolutely sure that they do not appear "different." Only in private, among other Jews, do some of them admit that their enthusiasm may have been a bit of a show.

But I hate Christmas. I hate Christmas because during the Christmas season I am put upon, time after time again, by well-meaning non-Jews to declare my difference from them. When I am wished a Merry Christmas, what am I to do? If I return the greeting, my Jewish conscience accuses me of not having the *chutzpah* to say "I do not celebrate it." If I do say this, however, I get into an unwanted discussion, often with someone I do not really wish to chat with; or I might spoil the holiday mood for someone I do care for. I am also not a little upset by the arrogance of people who think it a matter of course that *everyone* celebrates Christmas. To hear them talk about it, Christmas is as naturally part of December as snow in Minnesota.

I certainly do not hate Christmas for what it means to Christians. I like togetherness; I like peace on earth; and I like presents (so do the Jewish merchants in the shopping malls). I just wish it wasn't rubbed in my face when I am not part of it. So what do we do? We've come up with a Jewish version of Christmas: Hanukkah. Hanukkah is probably traditionally the least significant of Jewish festivals. Unlike major holidays, for example, on Hanukkah it is permitted to work. Yet the majority of non-observant Jews, the EJI, who do not even know the dates of such major festivals as Sukkoth or Shavuoth, do not fail to observe Hanukkah. This is profoundly ironic. The events that Hanukkah celebrates are not even in the Hebrew Bible, but in the Greek-language Book of the Macabees. The "zealots" of Israel, armed Pharisee fundamentalists, rose against the Graeco-Syrian rulers of the land, who were amply assisted by "assimilated Jews." Hanukkah or Rededication commemorates the zealots' victory. This resulted in their recapture of the Temple, where they relit the "eternal flame." (The little consecrated oil they had for the purpose miraculously lasted eight days — hence the eight days of the festival.)

How much Hanukkah has become a Jewish Christmas is demonstrated by office workers who put up "Happy Hanukkah" signs next to "Merry Christmas." When you say "Merry Christmas and Happy Hanukkah," you *do* help me avoid the tensions of Christmas; you made sure that I did not have to identify myself as "different" from you. But I would rather be uncomfortable than phony. As far as I am concerned, "Merry Christmas" posters will do just fine at the office without Happy Hanukkah. It would be nice, though, if next fall, when we really celebrate a major holiday, someone put up a sign saying, "Happy Rosh Hashanah."

By now you might feel overwhelmed. "Is there nothing I can say to a Jew without being considered insensitive?" you might ask. Relax. If you take what I have just said into consideration, chances are you will not say things that offend me. But if you slip up, don't worry. I know you mean well. Remember, I am not only a Jew. I am also a human being, like you.

NOTE

Ivan Kalmar, 2001, "I Didn't Know You Were Jewish… And Other Things Not to Say When You Find Out," in Carl James and Adriene Shadd (eds.), *Talking About Identity*, Toronto: Between the Lines. Adapted and reprinted with permission.

Victim or Aggressor?
Typecasting Muslim Women for their Attire
Natasha Bakht

Debates about the attire of Muslim women have been flooding the editorial pages of newspapers the world over. Whether it is the banning of headscarves in French schools, the dismissal of a Swiss schoolteacher for wearing a *hijab*[1] (*Dahlab v. Switzerland* 2001), the expulsion of a *hijab*-wearing Turkish student from medical school (*Şahin v. Turkey* 2005), or the dismissal of an American woman's small claims dispute for refusing to remove her full-face veil (*Muhammad v. Enterprise Rent-a-Car* 2006), people apparently cannot get enough of scrutinizing and penalizing Muslim women for what they wear. Many people have an opinion about how Muslim women ought to dress, including some Muslims who offer allegedly definitive answers to contentious questions by attempting to rely on "authentic religious requirements." Although Muslim and non-Muslim women have been concealing parts of their bodies for centuries, global publics seem far from reaching their saturation point on this topic. Several incidents suggest that the situation is no different in Canada. The justifications for banning Muslim women from participating in various activities reveal a tension between the need to protect Muslim women and the need to be protected from them.

Protecting Muslim Women from the *Hijab*

Perhaps the most commonly heard opposition to the veil is that women cover their faces or heads at the command of domineering men so that the veil is seen as a sign of Muslim women's oppression, as well as a general indicator of the supposed backwardness of Islamic culture. Sherene Razack (2008) has argued that three stereotypical figures, "the 'imperiled' Muslim woman, the 'dangerous' Muslim man and the 'civilized' European,'" repeatedly appear in the Western imaginary to justify the expulsion of Muslims from the political community. The idea that Muslim women who wear the *hijab* must be rescued from the confines of their community is pervasive indeed. For example, the tragic death of Mississauga teenager Aqsa Pervez was widely reported as resulting from her fundamentalist father's reaction to her refusal to wear the *hijab*.

As more Muslim women are vocal about their choice to don the *hijab*, and because these women are pursuing higher education, teaching in schools, and advocating in courts of law, fitting them into the stereotypical box of the "imperiled" Muslim woman is no longer logically possible. More recently, a novel version of the need to "protect" veiled women has emerged in Canada. Rather than protecting them from "dangerous Muslim men" or the symbolic assault that the *hijab* represents on women's equality, we must now step in to protect Muslim women from the dangers of the physical headscarf itself! For example, an eleven-year-old Ottawa girl was ejected from a soccer game in Quebec after she refused to remove her headscarf during the game. The referee claimed that removing the *hijab* was a necessary safety precaution. The Quebec Soccer Association's spokesperson noted "that the ban on *hijabs* is to protect children from being accidentally strangled" (reported by the CBC News 2007). Although five young teams walked out of the tournament as a result of the ban, the Fédération Internationale de Football Association (FIFA) upheld the referee's decision and refused to change the regulations—or explain them.

The FIFA rules do not explicitly ban the *hijab*; they simply give discretion to a referee to determine whether a headscarf is safe to wear. The effect of the FIFA ruling, however, undermines attempts to build bridges between Muslim minorities and the wider society, and sends the demeaning message to Muslim women/girls that soccer is not for them. Joe Guest, the Canadian Soccer Association's chief referee, pointed to the incongruity of the FIFA ruling with current practices. The ruling seems to indicate that "players can't wear prescription eye-glasses. But they do," he stated.

In the same vein, five girls were barred from taking part in a taekwondo tournament in Longueuil, Quebec, because they wore the *hijab*. Despite Muslim youth participating in provincial and international tournaments for more than five years, tournament organizers in Quebec said the sport's rules prevent women from competing in *hijab*. The World Taekwondo Federation (WTF) sanctioned this decision, and because the WTF is recognized by the International Olympic Committee, this ruling will have an impact on *hijab*-wearing women's ability to compete in the Olympics.

The decisions to exclude Muslim women from sport, often taken by federations comprised of all male and non-Muslim people, strike at the heart of religious freedom. Muslim women now apparently have to make a choice between their faith and sport. Rulings that preserve the discretionary powers of referees to exclude headscarves perpetuate the uncertainty with which Muslim women/girls must cope, never knowing until the last minute whether they will be ejected from a tournament despite months of training. Real safety issues can and should be dealt with legitimately. But sports officials have never pointed to a single incident where the *hijab* has endangered any player. The creation of "sport *hijabs*" which can come off easily because of a Velcro strap that is tied at the back of the neck have already been created and worn as a compromise to assuage safety concerns.

The perceived need to rescue Muslim women from the dangers of a scarf is indicative of racism. The idea that these feeble, ignorant creatures would not know what is good for them or how to save themselves from harm is grounded in the desire to "civilize" a group of people. The harm caused to such women is not the remote threat of being strangled by a headscarf but the steadfast commitment to exclude them from public life.

Protecting Canadians from Muslim Women

Westerners have barely dealt with the fact that some Muslim women want to wear the *hijab*. Now anti-Muslim hysteria is focusing on women who wear the *niqab*. In October 2006, comments made by British leader of the House of Commons, Jack Straw, sparked massive controversy about Muslim women who wear the full-face veil where only the eyes are visible. Mr. Straw asked Muslim women meeting with him to remove the *niqab*, stressing *his* discomfort in interacting with them and arguing that it acted as "a visible statement of separation and difference" (Cowell 2006, emphasis in the original).

Canada has not been immune to the growing agitation that has been expressed about Muslim women who cover their faces. In 2007, the Conservative government introduced Bill C-6, *An Act to Amend the Canada Elections Act (visual identification of voters)*.[2] The bill requires that voters who present identification in order to vote must have their faces uncovered to enable election officials to identify them visually. The bill is apparently an attempt to prevent voter fraud although little evidence of such a problem exists in Canada (House of Commons *Debates* 2007).[3] Interestingly, the Chief Electoral Officer of Canada indicated that he would not require women who wear *niqabs* to remove their veils in order to vote. He said that because voters are offered two alternatives to voting without photo identification (i.e., providing two pieces of non-photo ID or taking an oath), an uncovered face could not be a requirement under the *Canada Elections Act* since there could be no means of visually comparing the voter's face with a photograph. He also noted that the Act provides for other means of voting, such as by mail, that do not require the visual comparison of a voter with her photograph.

Despite these inconsistencies, politicians have insisted that showing one's face in order to vote is necessary for identification purposes. Thus, a *niqab*-wearing woman could, under Bill C-6, be forced to remove her veil at a polling station despite elections officials being potentially unable to compare her to her photograph on identity documents. This illogical situation strongly suggests that the only reason for the amendment is to target an already besieged and vulnerable minority group. "This is not about safety, not about security, not about fraud, it's about targeting a community that is seen as dangerous… [and] criminal" (*The Hill Times* 2007). As one Globe and Mail editorial pointed out, showing one's face would only prove that the voter "has a face" (*Globe and Mail* 2007).

Why have such a small group of women, already marginalized from mainstream society, provoked such a rash response from the highest levels of our political community? If people can vote in Canada without having to be visually identified, the only reason to insist on visually identifying some Muslim women for voting purposes is mistrust. Clearly, the government's relentless emphasis on the unsubstantiated danger of fraud and consequently requiring identification is a smokescreen.

Unhelpful Muslim Responses

Many Muslim women who do not cover their faces use religious arguments to oppose the wearing of the *niqab*. Raheel Raza stated: "Contrary to some peoples view [sic], covering the face is not a religious requirement" (Raza 2006). Responding to a Muslim woman losing her job because she wore the *niqab*, Farzana Hassan asserted, "There is nothing specified in the Qur'an that says you need to cover your face…. The veil is a tradition, a tool of oppression created by men" (*Canadian Press* 2006).

While no Quranic requirement to wear the veil exists, these Muslim critics show little willingness to accept that religiosity is differentially perceived by individual Muslims for a variety of reasons including race, national origin and cultural and personal beliefs. Diversities are so pronounced in this amorphous, divergent and shifting composition of individuals and groups that coming across Muslims who are in conflict with one another is not uncommon — just as coming across Christians at odds about what their religion requires of them is hardly rare.

Discerning the significance of religious requirements is not easy. Courts, which are typically in the business of assessing evidence, have recognized the futility in evaluating such requirements. The Supreme Court of Canada devised a test of religious belief in which an individual's sincere conviction is given predominance over the normative religious code professed by religious authorities or the religious community in question (*Syndicat Northcrest v. Amselem* 2004). Such a limited legal test both protects the convictions of individuals who may dissent from the mainstream views of their religious community, and sustains the idea that faith, even within a single belief system, will have multiple and mutable interpretations.

Many Muslims would be outraged by the contention that one is not a Muslim if one does not pray five times a day. They would rightly argue that what it means to be a Muslim depends on a variety of personal, cultural and religious factors. Just as the state cannot be in the business of determining religious requirements, it is unhelpful for Muslims to declare what is and is not requisite in the hopes of curtailing behaviour that has no negative impact on the rights of others.

These debates are interesting for their projection of contradictory views of Muslim women and girls. The first stereotype is based on the wide-spread belief that Muslim women are victims either of "dangerous Muslim men" or the garb these men prescribe. In either case, the women are believed to need protection and "civilized Europeans" must rescue these passive individuals who cannot help themselves. Under the guise of guarding Muslim women's safety, these "protectors" prevent the women from taking their rightful place as active participants in society. The second stereotype is that of the aggressor — a typecasting that has become particularly popular in a post-9/11 era and has justified the global surveillance and control of Muslim communities. The aggressive Muslim woman covers her face to disguise herself in order to defraud the electoral system. Society must be protected from these dangerous destabilizers who threaten to undermine the proper workings of the political system. Although other Canadians need not show their faces in order to vote, these particular Canadians cannot be trusted. These two stereotypes — equally and readily accessible in Canadian popular culture — are deployed in relation to the same group of women with no recognition of the contradiction between the two.

Decisions to limit head and face coverings must be subject to rigorous rationalization. Otherwise, the pronouncements of sports officials and politicians will serve to further marginalize Muslim women. Creating solutions to those situations when legitimate safety or identification issues are at stake is usually quite simple. However, they do not involve making declarations about the "correct" religious interpretation of modes of attire. One must respect women's agency regarding choice of dress and accommodate their needs generously. When opposition to Muslim women's attire is irrational, like the knee-jerk responses to difference illustrated above, one must ask what is really going on. Sadly, honest dialogue has been absent from these debates, and decisions have been rendered and buttressed without any appreciation for the actual lives of Muslim women.

NOTES

Natasha Bakht, 2008, "Victim or Aggressor: Typecasting Muslim Women for Their Attire," in Natasha Bakht (ed.), *Belonging and Banishment: Being Muslim in Canada*, Toronto: TSAR Publications. Adapted and reprinted with permission.

1. The *hijab* means both "modesty" and the "veil" in Arabic. Veils range from the headscarf (the *hijab*) through the face veil (the *niqab*) to the *burqa*, which covers the entire face and body.
2. Another not-so-subtle means of disciplining Muslim women is evident from the introduction of Bill 94 in Quebec, which essentially prevents *niqab*-wearing women from accessing any government services.
3. MP Brian Murphy noted: "There are no complaints… to cause us to be sitting here as a priority debating Bill C-6," House of Commons, 2007, *Debates*, No. 016 (14 November) at 867.

REFERENCES

CAIR-CAN. 2007. "Quebec Muslim Girls Banned from Tae Kwon Do Tournament." (April 15). At: <caircan.ca/itn_more.php?id=P2901_0_2_0_C>.

Canadian Press. 2006. "Canadian Muslim Leader Alleges Her Veil Views Sparked Vandalism." (October 31). At: <sisyphe.org/article.php3?id_article=2451>.

CBC News. "Muslim Girl Ejected from Tournament for Wearing *Hijab*." 2007. *CBC News* (February 25). At: <cbc.ca/canada/story/2007/02/25/hijab-soccer.html>.

Cowell, Alan. 2006. "Blair Criticizes Full Islamic Veil as 'Mark of Separation.'" *New York Times.* (October 18). At: <nytimes.com/2006/10/18/world/europe/18britain.html?_r=1&oref=slogin>.

Edmonton Journal. 2007. "FIFA Hijab Ruling Deserves Red Card" (March 6). At: <canada.com/edmontonjournal/news/opinion/story.html?id=59f06a4e-5043-4c33-b82a-acd43195b3e4>.

Globe and Mail. 2007. "A Bad Bill on Veils." (October 30).

Hill Times. 2007. "Visual Identification of Voters Bill C-6 Unfairly Targeting Muslim Women, Says Professor Bakht; Voter Fraud Shouldn't Be Addressed in Context of Religion." (November 5).

House of Commons. 2007. *Debates*. No. 016 (November 14) at 873, 875 (Mr. Paul Dewar).

Raza, Raheel. 2006. "Let's Pull the Veil off Our Minds." (October 14). At: <raheelraza.com/veils.htm>.

Razack, Sherene. 2008. *Casting Out: The Eviction of Muslims from Western Law & Politics*. Toronto: University of Toronto Press.

LEGAL DECISIONS

Muhammad v. Enterprise Rent-a-Car, No. 06-41896-GC (Mich. 31ˢᵗ Dist. Ct. Oct. 11, 2006).

Dahlab v. Switzerland, no. 42393/98 (15 February 2001).

Şahin v. Turkey [G.C.], no. 44774/98, (2005) 41 E.H.R.R. 8.

Syndicat Northcrest v. Amselem, [2004] 2 S.C.R. 551 at paras. 46–47.

Of Woman Born?
Reproductive Ableism and Women's Health Research
Georgina Feldberg

In 1993, after I lost my second pregnancy, I faced a fundamental feminist dilemma. I wanted a child very much, and in order to carry a child to term, I probably needed medical, or more specifically technological, assistance. However, as a feminist scholar of women's health, I was deeply committed to critiques of our increased reliance on medical technologies that violated and controlled women's bodies. My miscarriages occurred as Canada's Royal Commission on Reproductive Technology probed the status of reproductive health services. Barely two years earlier, when I first taught an undergraduate seminar in women's health, I had used the Royal Commission as a fulcrum around which to pivot what I believed were the central questions in women's health. By simulating the inquiries of the commission, I hoped that my students would learn about the rise of medical dominance and the ways in which it controlled women's reproduction; about the growth of technology and the ways in which it rendered women subservient; about health activism and its empowerment of women; and about the state's role in preserving and protecting women's health (Overall 1989).

The lessons I taught my students came back to haunt me as I became a participant in, rather than just a scholar of, infertility treatments. I grew less confident of the history of women's health that I had learned. Friends and colleagues offered their opinions about the perils of reproductive technology. Hoping to help steer my decision-making, they cited the findings of the Royal Commission and the central critiques of reproductive technology. Their advice was well-intentioned but not useful. Soon, I found that the theory I had taught, and which my colleagues and friends invoked, failed to speak to my personal experience. Their questions — Could I trust technology? Did I really understand the risks? Did I really need a child? — reflected the history of women's health activism but did not help my personal decision-making. I became part of a community of women that relied on reproductive technologies and, for varying reasons, found women's health scholarship limited. More than fifteen years, six miscarriages and one child later, I find that my personal experience tempered and reshaped my own health research, and lent new perspectives and directions to the history of our inquiries.

Feminist health researchers have attached particular significance and importance to personal experience. Anger at truly horrible encounters with physical and mental health systems inspired women to tell powerful stories, write plays, and paint pictures (Bialosky et al. 1998). I'm a scholar, not a poet or painter, so, until I grappled with my own repeated pregnancy losses, I recognized but did not feel the difference between arguments that worked in theory but not practice. When feminists tell us that "the personal is political," they exhort us not to be duped by positivist appeals to objectivity. They encourage us to be subjective in our research, admit our personal biases, and let our most heartfelt concerns guide our scholarship and our activism. Hard personal experience taught me that, despite our desire to validate and acknowledge the realities of women's lives, women's health scholarship can sometimes disregard, even disrespect, the range of women's experiences and needs. Hard personal struggle opened my eyes to the ways in which a kind of reproductive "ableism" — or an assumption about the natural fertility of women and the ways in which the experience of birth unites us — has shaped and even distorted women's health scholarship and activism.

My own experiences intersected with those of other women and with the history of women's health scholarship. Reproduction has defined and dominated North American interest in women's health for almost a century. A review of articles on women's health, published in women's health journals, demonstrates that, even at the turn of the twenty-first century, most women's health research continues to focus "navel to knees" — that is, on our reproductive systems (Clark et al. 2002). This focus reflects a 100-year tradition. Until the 1900s, childbirth was a leading cause of women's deaths. High rates of maternal mortality inspired suffragists and reformers to lobby for improved obstetrical care, birth control, child allowances and maternity benefits. During the early decades of the twentieth century, women and the state mobilized jointly around issues of maternal and child welfare (Comacchio 1993; Leavitt 1986).

As the study of women's health history grew popular, through the 1970s, reproduction and reproductive concerns dominated our inquiries (Feldberg et al. 2003). Activists and academics explored the origins and history of campaigns to ensure that women wanted to be pregnant, and that their pregnancies were safe. We underscored the importance of women's birthing experience and we probed the complex social, cultural, economic and political factors that had allowed male physicians to usurp female midwifery and steal a unique and universalizing female experience. The publication of *Witches, Midwives and Nurses* in 1973 set the stage for scholarship and activism that would reclaim woman's healing role and re-capture the contributions large numbers of non-professional and informally trained women made. In historical, sociological, and popular writings, we chronicled the ways in which women had lost control of the birthing process (Ehrenreich 1973, 1977; Biggs 1983). We explored the ways in which physicians' gynecologic and obstetrical interventions ex-ploited, even abused, women patients (Mitchinson 1979, 1982, 1984, 1991). We critiqued the introduction of physician-dominated hospital births, the development of birth control measures, and the medical interventions that embodied a male technological impulse to control female sexuality and suppress female rituals of healing (Corea 1985; Oakley 1976; Rothman 1982). We constructed a history of women's health in which pregnancy was *always* a natural condition, care provided by women was *always* better, and technological interven-tions were male-inspired assaults on women's physical and emotional well-being.

This history of women's health became a scholarly and political force in our struggle to reclaim pregnancy and birthing. As Canadian women's health collectives like the Montreal Women's Health Press and Healthsharing concentrated energy and attention on reclaim-ing reproduction, academics and activists invoked history to underscore traditional female methods of healing and expose the ways in which the changing power and prestige of sci-ence displaced and delegitimated women's practices (Biggs 1983). The focus on reproduc-tion was politically important, Lesley Biggs (2003) later suggested, because all women have reproductive systems and, despite the differences among us, our wombs and ovaries created the biological vulnerability that left us dependent on men. Second wave women's health activists believed that the struggle to control our bodies would unite us.

The problem here, as I discovered, is that all our wombs were not alike, and they did not unite us. The histories we wrote emphasised one, universal, experience of birth. We used that history to create unity. It inspired and prompted us to demand better and more sensi-tive health care. Our call to reproductive arms, however, obscured differences among varied groups of women. Even as recent women's health scholarship has broadened to appreciate difference and contend with the ways in which race, class, gender, sexual orientation, and other particularities of experience intersect, little or no attention has been paid to women's different reproductive abilities. Yet, these differences shape and create marginality within the health system and within the women's health movement. We remain ignorant of, and often insensitive to, the needs of women who are childless, by chance rather than choice.

Our history and scholarship are constrained by what I call reproductive ableism — the assumption that women will "naturally" conceive, carry and deliver children with ease. It can be found, for example, in editions of the Boston Women's Health Book Collective's classic *Our Bodies, Ourselves*, which presume that all women are fertile and concerned about conception. These books minimize the reproductive concerns of minority women and disabled women, who were sometimes sterilized against their will; they ignore infertility entirely. Reproductive ableism shaped our research into health-care delivery, our understanding of the social determinants of women's health and our activism. It shapes our sense of women's bodies and of the interconnections between physical and social well-being. It produces, often inadvertently, insensitivity to women's diverse reproductive needs and the influences of reproduction on women's lives. It guides our critiques of technology.

For example, after years of activism, we have successfully educated physicians to respect women's desire to control fertility. But physicians' eagerness to accommodate this desire for reproductive control can translate into a presumed universalism of experience that disregards the needs of some communities of women. Lesbian women continually battle a health-care system that assumes all young women need advice about birth control. Lesbians recount, with humour and frustration, encounters with physicians who have become trapped in their assumptions about what women want and/or need: "Are you sexually active?" "Yes." Are you using birth control?" "No." "You are sexually active but not using birth control? Are you trying to become pregnant?" Conversely, lesbian women battle the presumption that they neither want to nor will become pregnant. Significant numbers of lesbians view reproductive technology as a tool they can safely use to build their families. However conservative prejudices against "non-traditional families" limit their access to assisted reproductive technologies (ARTs). So does more critical women's health research, which seeks to limit and constrain the use of ART, which it assumes to be the domain of middle-class women who have delayed childbearing.

Reproductive ableism shapes and constrains our critiques of technology. As we fought to demedicalize childbirth, we also demanded access to safe abortions (Gordon 1976; Reagan 1997; McLaren 1986). But in our zeal to decriminalize the technologies and interventions that ensured women the right to safely terminate unwanted pregnancies, we overlooked the forced abortion and sterilization of women of colour or of women deemed mentally ill or "feeble-minded." We created one standard for the medical technologies and pharmaceuticals that allowed women to limit their pregnancies and another for those that women used to promote pregnancies.

In the most recent Canadian debates about regulation of reproductive technology, we almost missed the intersections between these technologies and allowed ourselves to fall into troubling debates. For example, when in 2001 a Standing Committee on Health revisited the Royal Commission's recommendations, the Committee argued that "reproductive materials and embryos [contain] the potential to mature into full personhood" and that "there must be a measure of respect and protection for the embryo that is based on its potential for personhood" (House of Commons, Standing Committee on Health 2001: 3). Our eagerness to regulate what were then new reproductive technologies (NRTs) almost blinded us to the ways in which this language violated the Supreme Court of Canada's ruling that the fetus has no legal status.

Similarly, years of women's health activism have ensured Canadian women rights to paid maternity leave and inspired workplace policies that safeguard women's reproductive health. We frame these accomplishments as victories in our ability to recognize women's productive and reproductive work. Yet our policies do not extend to attempts to conceive. As a mother, it is easy for me to leave a meeting because I need to get home to my child, or because the daycare is closing. Aspiring mothers — women who are undergoing fertility interventions — cannot easily say that they need to leave a meeting because they have to go home to take their shots. They hide the hours spent in clinics. Survey after survey asks women about the physical and psychological stresses of balancing work and family. Few questionnaires probe the stresses women encounter while trying to balance work and their silent or invisible struggles to have a child.

I ultimately abandoned the technologic solutions to childlessness. I did so because of fatigue more than anything else. With the assistance of international adoption, I became the mother of a beautiful and beloved daughter. My experiences left me with empathy for those who chose other paths, and it has, possibly forever, changed my outlook on women's health research. We enter the second decade of the twenty-first century facing many of the challenges that have faced us for centuries. Women, health scholars and activists alike, continue to struggle for reproductive autonomy and control. So do women who want a child. Over several decades, we have refined our agenda, and we have broadened our understanding of the communities of women. Despite our increased sensitivity to diversity and ability, we remain socially and politically resistant to differences in reproductive ability. Just as I was asked whether I really understood the risks of reproductive technology, I've been asked whether "I *really* want to talk" about reproductive ableism and the women it affects. Broadening our understanding of the experiences of Canadian women and debunking the myth of women's natural fertility can enrich not only our scholarship, but also our activism and policy (Reverby 2003).

REFERENCES

Bialosky, Jill, and Helen Schulman. 1998. *Wanting A Child: Twenty-Two Writers on Their Difficult but Mostly Successful Quests for Parenthood in a High-Tech Age.* New York: Farrar, Strauss and Giroux.

Biggs, C. Lesley. 2003. "Rethinking Midwifery in Canada." In Ivy Lynn Bourgeault, Cecilia Benoit and Robbie Davis-Floyd (eds.), *Reconceiving Midwifery: The New Canadian Model of Care.* Montreal: McGill-Queen's University Press.

___. 1983. "The Case of the Missing Midwives: A History of Midwifery in Ontario from 1795–1900." *Ontario History* 75.

Boston Women's Health Collective and Judy Norsigian. 2005. *Our Bodies, Ourselves* eighth ed. New York: Touchstone.

Clark, Jocalyn P., Georgina Feldberg and Paula Rochon. 2002. "The Representation of Women's Health in General Medical Versus Women's Specialty Journals: A Content Analysis." *BMC Women's Health* 2 (June).

Comacchio, Cynthia. 1993. *Nations Are Built of Babies: Saving Ontario's Mothers and Children, 1900–1940.* Montreal: McGill-Queen's University Press.

Corea, Gena. 1985. *The Hidden Malpractice: How American Medicine Mistreats Women.* New York: Harper.

Ehrenreich, Barbara, and Dierdre English. 1979. *For Her Own Good: 150 Years of the Experts' Advice to Women.* New York: Anchor Press.

___. 1973. *Witches, Midwives and Nurses: A History of Women Healers.* Old Westbury, NY: Feminist Press.

Feldberg, Georgina, Molly Ladd-Taylor, Alison Li and Kathryn McPherson. 2003. "Comparative Perspectives on Canadian and Women's Health Care." In Georgina Feldberg et al. (eds.), *Women, Health, and Nation: Canada and the United States Since 1945.* Montreal: McGill-Queen's University Press.

Franklin, Sarah, and Helena Ragoné (eds.). 1998. *Reproducing Reproduction: Kinship, Power, and Technological Innovation.* Philadelphia: University of Pennsylvania Press.

Gordon, Linda. 1976. *Woman's Body, Woman's Right: A Social History of Birth Control in America*. New York: Penguin.

House of Commons, Standing Committee on Health. 2001. "Assisted Human Reproduction: Building Families" (December). At: http://www2.parl.gc.ca/HousePublications/Publication.aspx?DocId =1032041&Language=E&Mode=1&Parl=37&Ses=1

Leavitt, Judith W. 1986. *Brought to Bed: Childbearing in America, 1750–1950*. New York: Oxford University Press.

Lock, Margaret, and Patricia A. Kaufert (eds.). 1998. *Pragmatic Women and Body Politics*. New York: Cambridge University Press.

McLaren, Angus, and Arlene Tiger McLaren. 1986. *The Bedroom and the State: The Changing Practices and Politics of Contraception and Abortion in Canada, 1880–1980* first ed. Toronto: McClelland and Stewart.

Mitchinson, Wendy. 1991. *The Nature of Their Bodies: Women and their Doctors in Victorian Canada*. Toronto: University of Toronto Press.

___. 1984. "A Medical Debate in English Canada: Ovariotamies." *Social History* 17,33.

___. 1982. "Gynaecological Operations on Insane Women: London, Ontario 1895–1901. *Journal of Social History* 15,3.

___. 1979. "Historical Attitudes toward Women and Childbirth." *Atlantis* 4.

Oakley, Ann. 1976. "Wisewoman and Medicine Man: Changes in the Management of Childbirth." In Juliet Mitchell and Ann Oakley (eds.), *The Rights and Wrongs of Women*. London: Penguin.

Overall, Christine. 1989. *The Future of Human Reproduction*. Toronto: Women's Press.

Reagan, Leslie J. 1997. *When Abortion Was a Crime: Women, Medicine, and Law in the United States, 1867–1973*. Berkeley: University of California Press.

Reverby, Susan. 2003. "Thinking through the Body and the Body Politic: Feminism, History, and Health Care Policy in the United States." In Gina Feldberg et al. (eds.), *Women, Health, and Nation: Canada and the United States Since 1945*. Montreal: McGill-Queen's University Press.

Rothman, Barbara Katz. 1982. *In Labor: Women and Power in the Birthplace*. New York: Norton.

Changing Perceptions of Health and Body Image Over the Life Course

Pamela Wakewich

Written on the body is a secret code only visible in certain lights; the accumulations of a lifetime gather there. In places the palimpsest is so heavily worked that the letters feel like braille. I keep my body rolled up away from prying eyes. Never unfold too much, tell the whole story. (Winterson 1993)

While efforts to incorporate the body into social theory have become prolific in the past two decades, it is only recently that social scientists have begun to explore the ways in which people actively constitute and experience the body in everyday life (see for example Shilling 2003; Malacrida and Low 2007). Analysts have tended to focus upon representations of the female body in the professional discourses of medicine and science, or the popular discourses of media and advertising, and to presume a direct link between these representations and women's experiences of the body (Bordo 2004). Even where authors seek to present alternative frameworks their analyses generally remain framed by the scientific and bio-medical categories and language that they wish to challenge (Price and Shildrick 1999). Body and identity are presented as static notions with the presumption that they remain fixed and homogenous through time, place and the life course.

These concerns are the points of departure for an oral history research project that I conducted in northwestern Ontario from 1994–97. Comparing the experiences of working-class and middle-class women and men, I explored how ideas about health, embodiment, and the body are shaped and re-shaped through the life course, as well as how identities of gender, class, culture, and region (in this case "northern-ness") are constituted within and through discourses on health and the body. This research uses techniques of feminist oral history to elicit what Barbara Duden calls "bio-logies" or body stories (Duden 1991) in order to bring into view the everyday processes and social relations through which the body is constituted and experienced.

Oral history is particularly suited to feminist research as it enables us to focus on people's perceptions and interpretations of the world around them, and provides a means to supplement and challenge dominant representations. Etter-Lewis (1991) argues that the technique is particularly suited to revealing the multilayered textures of people's lives. It allows us to hear how people articulate the complex intersections of culture, gender, and other key dimensions of their lives (see also Armitage, Hart and Weathermon 2002).

Oral history is not merely the representation of a life, but rather an active process of re-collection — a re-collecting or gathering together of aspects of our history in which we make and re-make sense of who and what we are (Freeman 1993). In this sense, the memories recounted are not seen as discrete *things*, but rather as *acts* and *imaginings* "the products of a conscious being bringing to mind what is not present" (Freeman 1993: 89). And while oral history interviews are always somewhat idiosyncratic (they begin with individual experience) as Anderson and Jack point out "a person's self reflection is not just a private, subjective act. The categories and concepts we use for reflecting upon and evaluating ourselves come from a cultural context" (1991: 18). Thus oral histories provide an entree to both the individual and the social body and how they are constituted in relation to one another.

The site of this research is the city of Thunder Bay in Northwestern Ontario, a community whose own identity is in many ways negotiated and liminal. It is at once "Northern" (officially considered part of the provincial north), and yet not northern (being located only fifty kilometres from the American border). It is urban (having a population of some 120,000) and yet rural, being physically isolated from other large centres by at least a full day's drive in either direction. It is an important regional business and service centre, and yet residents feel largely ignored and insignificant in provincial terms. Its population is culturally diverse, comprising a mix of various northern and eastern European roots, a significant First Nations population as well as recent migrants from Latin America and S.E. Asia, and yet conformity of style, speech and even behaviour is valued and remarked upon in public settings. And although the primary resource industries (such as the paper mills and grain elevators) are no longer as significant to the local economy as they once were, and women make up an increasingly large share of the city's labour force, the city maintains an image in the eyes of both residents and outsiders of being a "lunch bucket" or "working man's town" (Dunk 2003; Southcott 2006).

The oral history interviews were conducted with a purposive sample of forty middle and working-class women and men between the ages of thirty and sixty. All of the participants have lived in the area for most of their lives, although many have spent extended periods of time in other locations for work or education. Respondents' occupations are typical of those in the region and include college-trained nurses, teachers, forestry and mill workers, homemakers, self-employed small business people, tradespeople, semi-skilled health and social service workers and professionals.

Women's Images of Their Bodies

For most of the women, ideas about health and body image are intimately interlinked and have changed over the life course. For many, ideas about health and healthiness have evolved from a more conventional biomedical notion of the absence of disease which was adhered to at an earlier age, to the assessment of well being in more environmental or holistic terms. Respondents' notions of health discuss levels of physical energy, comfort in carrying out and balancing multiple roles, satisfaction with quality of work and family relations, and concerns about time for self and leisure as the following comment by Jennifer, a forty-one-year-old middle-class woman, suggests:

Q. Do you think your idea of what it is to be healthy has always been the same?

A. No. I'd say now, getting older that… there is no doubt that my sense of health is becoming much less separate from how I look, and much more to do with how I feel.

Behaviours associated with staying healthy had also changed over the life course. Many indicated that they did little consciously to stay healthy when they were younger but now were much more conscientious about eating well, getting regular exercise and rest. For women, time was the most important constraint to achieving optimal health. Most cited the difficulties of finding time for themselves (for leisure or exercise) while juggling multiple work and family roles.

In addition several of the women indicated that they didn't have a sense of entitlement to "time off." Women with younger children generally built their own leisure pursuits around activities which could include their children. One woman professional who had been very athletic in her youth expressed frustration at trying to get a "workout" for herself while doing activities with her children. Having recognized that the desires to spend time with her children and to exercise for herself were working at cross-purposes, she temporarily "resolved" the issue by putting her own needs on hold until the children were older.

In general the women were much more attentive to and aware of body image issues through the life course, yet the importance attributed to this had changed significantly for most of them. Many had previously dieted and monitored their weight carefully as adolescents and in their early twenties, yet most had abandoned the habit either due to a sense of frustration with its lack of success, or explicitly as a form of resistance to what they perceived as inappropriate medicalization and monitoring of their bodies by doctors, partners and others.

Some gender differences were readily apparent. Many of the men found it much harder to reflect on "body" history and required much more prompting to make connections between a sense of embodiment and specific activities or instances of their youth. Most often, men talked about embodiment in terms of a perceived sense of strength, or endurance in sporting activities, or the ability to do physical labour [especially for working-class men] or in relation to illness episodes. In comparison, women were more likely to evaluate their health in terms of coping with multiple roles and the quality of family relations. Women were also more likely to remark on their physical appearance or a sense of being "overweight" while few men made reference to presentation of self or appearance norms.

Most of the women talked about having multiple body images. They emphasized the fluidity and contextualness of their own perceptions. Body image was different at home and in public spaces, in the company of friends and with strangers, at times of healthiness and during illness experiences, and often between work and leisure. For many of the women, different body images were also related to the quality of relationships with their partners, or peer group. One woman who had divorced and remarried described a very different sense of body image with her new partner who she described as "comfortable with me as I am." Another woman indicated that comfort with her body shifts in relationship to contact with a group of women friends who are extremely physically active and concerned about appearance. Yet another, who had described herself as "borderline" anorexic in adolescence, but had overcome this during her early twenties found the weigh-in and fundal measurement during routine pregnancy check-ups very anxiety provoking. It created for her a very negative shift in body image that took many years to resolve.

The perception or definition of body image for many of the women was also fluid and changed over the life course. Often defined as body shape or physical appearance in adolescence, for some the notion expanded to a larger sense of "presentation of self" (Goffman 1959). For professional and business women this incorporated not only appearance and styles of dress, or "dressing for success" as many described it, but also a sense of self confidence, a feeling of accomplishment or skill in their field of work, and an improved sense of healthiness. For some of the working-class women, to be successfully relied upon by others, and to be seen to be coping were important aspects of the assessment of body image. Some narratives expressed a kind of idealization of a "northern" (almost akin to pioneer) woman for whom strength and endurance were key dimensions of a positive body image.

Consciousness of the body was also described as situational and again varied along class and gender lines. Most of the respondents indicated that they were not conscious of their bodies on an ongoing basis although a few women who were particularly concerned about weight described their bodies as constraints that they had difficulty ever transcending. However, most others indicated that body consciousness was situational, brought on by a particularly serious or sudden illness episode, by concerns about what to wear to a particular social event (i.e., a class reunion or family gathering), in the context of travel to a large urban centre such as Toronto where consciousness and monitoring of appearance seems more evident, or in the context of clothing shopping — especially the painful annual new bathing suit ritual. Body consciousness and anxiety for many of the women was also heightened by medical encounters (even routine check-ups) which frequently raised concerns about unhealthy weight independent of a woman's own assessment of her state of healthiness.

Both male and female respondents recognized different body and appearance norms between residents of the "north" [northern Ontario] and the "south" [a euphemism for the Niagara triangle]. The north was variously described as: more relaxed; less style conscious and preoccupied; more healthy due to access to the outdoors, better water and less pollution; less stressful because of its slower pace of life; and by contrast, less healthy because of the limited availability of fresh fruit and vegetables; less healthy because it is easier to hide an "overweight" body in all of the clothes worn for our cooler weather; and more stressful because of a lack of tolerance for diversity or heterogeneity among northern residents.

Body and body image were seldom discussed in individual terms, but rather almost always constituted in relational terms. Constructing the self was done in relation to a constructed "other." Thus, themes of northern-ness were discussed in terms of an imagined or real "south," norms or expectations of femininity were contrasted with norms of masculinity (and vice versa), middle class concerns about presentation of self and success were presented as apposite to stereotypes of working-class lack of care, or lack of discipline and working-class concerns about the lack of time and money to pursue idealized health and body images were construed in relation to the presumption of generic middle-class investment in, and resources to achieve those ideals. The homogeneity of northern styles and ideals presented largely ignored or "othered" the obvious ethnic and cultural diversity of the city and region.

Contemporary senses of health and body image for the respondents, particularly for the women, were referential to past notions and ideals and often made efforts to present an integrated or coherent history of embodiment. In some instances, where particularly troubling experiences of violence (such as sexual abuse) or social stigma were part of the respondent's past, the efforts at integration were contradictory or incomplete. The strong resonances of past experiences showed through the narrative surface giving a texture much like the "palimpsest" which Winterson so eloquently describes.

Body Image: Fluid and Contextual

These observations suggest that women's ideas about body and body image are fluid and contextual. They are shaped and re-shaped over time and the life course in relation to other aspects of identity and subjectivity. Ideas about the body are interlinked with notions of health and well-being, and evolve in relation to both individual and collective experience. Science, medicine and the media may play an important role in shaping and normalizing ideals and behaviours, particularly in our younger years, but they are often ignored or actively resisted when the images they present us with fail to match our own evolving sense of health or well-being. Thus, the analysis and incorporation of body and embodiment in social theory and feminist research must attend to the fluidity and contextualness of lay perceptions and ideals and explore their constitution and reconstitution in specific times and places and with particular attention to the quality and nature of the social relations in which they are shaped.

NOTE

For an extended version of this chapter, see Pamela Wakewich, 2000, "Contours of Everyday Life: Women's Reflections on Embodiment and Health Over Time," in Baukje Miedema, Janet M. Stoppard and Vivienne Anderson (eds.), *Women's Bodies, Women's Lives: Health, Well-Being and Body Image*, Toronto: Sumach Press.

REFERENCES

Armitage, Susan H., Patricia Hart and Karen Weathermon (eds.). 2002. *Women's Oral History: The Frontiers Reader*. Lincoln, NE: University of Nebraska.

Bordo, Susan. 2004. *Unbearable Weight: Feminism, Western Culture and the Body* second ed. Berkeley: University of California Press.

Duden, Barbara. 1991. *The Woman Beneath the Skin. A Doctor's Patients in Eighteenth-Century Germany*. London: Harvard University Press.

Dunk, Thomas. 2003. *It's a Working Man's Town: Male Working-Class Culture in Northwestern Ontario* second ed. Montreal: McGill-Queen's University Press.

Etter-Lewis, Gwendolyn. 1991. "Black Women's Life Stories: Reclaiming Self in Narrative Texts." In S. Gluck and D. Patai (eds.), *Women's Words: The Feminist Practice of Oral History*. London: Routledge.

Freeman, Mark. 1993. *Rewriting the Self: History, Memory, Narrative*. London: Routledge.

Goffman, Erving. 1959. *The Presentation of Self in Everyday Life*. Garden City, NY: Doubleday.

Malacrida, Claudia, and Jacqueline Low. 2007. *Sociology of the Body: A Reader.* Oxford: Oxford University Press.

Price, Janet, and Margrit Shildrik. 1999. *Feminist Theory and the Body: A Reader.* New York: Routledge.

Shilling, Chris. 2003. *The Body & Social Theory* second ed. London: Sage Publications.

Southcott, Chris. 2006. *The North in Numbers: A Demographic Analysis of Social and Economic Change in Northern Ontario*. Thunder Bay: Centre for Northern Studies.

Winterson, Jeanette. 1993. *Written on the Body*. London: Paladin.

Silencing Menstruation
among the Inuit

Karla Jessen Williamson

> When I was being brought up, questions surrounding sexuality were practically a taboo. If anything surrounding sexuality was explained, it certainly was done in a limited way. (Mariia, *Maniitsormioq*)[1]

As a *kalaallit*[2] anthropologist I have been interested in researching gender relations. The *kalaallit* live a very modern life, where one would assume that anyone should be able to talk freely about women's sexuality, but, as the excerpt above from an interview with another *kalaallit* woman suggests, contemporary *kalaallit* have not necessarily felt free to openly discuss issues surrounding menstruation. Why does such discussion remain so rare? Mariia wondered if this practice comes from our own Inuit cultural heritage or whether it was introduced with the processes involved in missionizing. I must admit that at the time Mariia asked her question, I did not see the relevance of the silence surrounding menstruation to our effort to understand the equal status of Inuit men and women. I was profoundly mistaken.

Transparency and Inuit Life

When I address issues of gender equality in my academic life, I do so with the knowledge that as an Inuk woman I enjoy status equal to that of Inuit men. I'm also aware that this status is significantly different than the status that I experience as a Danish or Canadian citizen. I am deeply appreciative of Inuit socio-cultural values, but I have also learned the lifestyle of a modern, middle-class individual in a Western setting. As I think about gender equality, then, I wonder how best to articulate Inuit women's status and explain it in ways that Westerners could understand and learn from.

Based on discussions of a focus group consisting of the six *kalaallit* women from my own Inuit community in Maniitsoq, in west Greenland, who became my research partners, I developed questions from which to explore *kalaallit* gender relations. While there are many profound questions related to this subject, I have chosen to focus here on what *kalaallit* women had to say about menstruation (Jessen Williamson 2006) and, most particularly, the silence around menstruation. One of the adult female interviewees of Maniitsoq admitted to having received virtually no information during adolescence about their emerging sexuality.

This lack of knowledge is unusual in light of the pre-contact child-rearing practices of the Inuit. Inuit adults in the Arctic, with whom I conversed regarding children and sexuality, expressed a positive attitude toward sexuality. Healthy engagement with one's genitalia is recognized as an important aspect of personal identity and self-value, traits that are the foundations for learning responsibilities later on. Inuit parents, grandparents and older siblings instill in their growing children a healthy familiarity with their own genitalia through playfully touching, squeezing, kissing and smelling, as well as making many remarks about the genitalia of their growing children. This behaviour continues until *isuma*, which Briggs (1970) identified as Inuit conscience, develops in the growing child. Once *isuma* has been formed, Inuit feel that pre-adolescent children have the impetus to carry on with the development of this positive, healthy and open attitude toward their sexuality (Jessen Williamson 1992). Given this openness to sexuality in children, the secrecy surrounding adolescent sexuality in general and menstruation in particular seems contradictory.

Secrecy and silencing among Inuit would not have been well-tolerated during pre-Christian times when Inuit depended on their transparent actions and thoughts to entice animals to give themselves to the people. This situation could only be achieved by living truthfully and openly so that the souls of the animals would recognize each Inuk as a person with good intentions (Fienup-Riordan 1990). Anyone who withheld feelings and thoughts surely would cause agony for the community. So why the secrecy surrounding adult female sexuality and menstruation?

Uncovering Pre-Colonial Knowledge

Mariia wondered to what extent this secrecy surrounding adult female sexuality and menstruation might be an extension of pre-Christian Inuit heritage or of the adoption of post-Christian ideas through colonization. This implies the existence in contemporary Inuit culture of different knowledge systems; but seeking knowledge from communities such as the Inuit, who are trapped in colonial systems to a considerable extent, requires particular research methods (Freire 1970). How was I to uncover the pre-colonial knowledge system among my people?

First, drawing on Ghosh's (1996) recommendation to create tools of reconstruction, I examined key elements of Inuit culture and found that, even though a gendered division of labour exists, gender was thought about very differently in Inuit culture than in Euro-western cultures. The Inuit understanding of human relations and humans' relationship with their surroundings, I argue, is based on a notion of genderlessness, a notion I explained at length in *Postcolonial Inuit Gender Relations in Greenland* (Jessen Williamson 2006). I offer three examples to show how the Inuit operationalized this notion. The first is manifest in the Inuit concept of intellect, which is understood as a life force, the nature of which cannot be divided by sex; nor is it solely a human quality. The second example is Inuit names, which, before the introduction of Christianity, were not gender specific. The same name could be held by male or female — what mattered was the essence of the name, not the sex. The third example concerns Inuktitut, the language of the Inuit, in which gender is not a feature of the grammar. Inuktitut makes no distinction between "he" or "she," as English, German, French or Danish languages do. Notions of genderlessness are therefore a better platform to explore Inuit gender relations than explicitly gender-based Western thought, which assumes and operates on inequity across gender.

Timikkut, Tarnikkut and *Anersaakkullu:* The Basis of Inuit Understanding

In talking about gender relations to the women in Maniitsoq, it became obvious to me that the notion of genderlessness alone was inadequate to fully explore the meaning of the data. While any Inuit could illustrate the concept with examples of the genderless qualities of individuals in their society, this notion is better understood if a key Inuit manner of understanding the self and the world is taken into account.

A widow's autobiographical narrative given to me in a lengthy interview revealed her troubled life through a dream world of nightmares and visions, déjà vu and premonitions — what Inuit call *timikkut, tarnikkut, anersaakkullu*. The only way I could make meaning of her tales in relation to her everyday life was to use the threesome to analyze her narrative. *Timikkut* denotes the physical because *timi* means "the body" and *-kkut* denotes "going through," "by way of," or "by means of." *Tarnikkut* means "through individual, personal soul." *Anersaakkut* recognizes the life force whose energy remains autonomous from creation (-*ullu* just means "and."). These physical and spiritual qualities are closely associated with the Inuit notion of genderlessness, but they go beyond equality between men and women. This triadic structure is applied to all of life and is the very basis for Inuit knowledge.

When children in Greenland experience life-altering events, they are told the three-part learning structure phrase: *timikkut, tarnikkut, anersaakkullu*. As children, we were encouraged to use these principles in an independent and confident manner, in order to acquire valuable knowledge, physical and spiritual, real and intangible. Given the interconnectedness and valuable qualities of all of creation, all aspects of life were important. After considering how ingrained the threesome had been in us, I hypothesized that these concepts had an equal impact on the widow's narrative. Her rendition of her life story finally made sense for me as I explored these terms. Just as *timikkut, tarnikkut, anersaakkullu* are equally important, so, in the accumulation of her knowledge of life, were all aspects of her own life, whether physical or spiritual, including dreams, imaginations and premonitions. Thus it is necessary to use the tripartite concept of *timikkut, tarnikkut, anersaakkullu* to understand the notion of genderlessness among the Inuit.

Menstruation in Other Cultures

To help my understanding of menstruation in Inuit culture, I turned to writing about the meaning of menstruation-related behaviours of peoples in cultures similar to that of *kalaallit* women. I discovered that Cruikshank et al. (1990: 11) found that Athapaskan and Tlingit women in the Yukon were admired when they were menstruating since they "acquired ritual and practical knowledge unavailable to men." This suggested to me that the meaning assigned to the seclusion of Athapaskan and Tlingit women while they were menstruating may be quite different from that of Europeans; that is, the latter sees seclusion in a negative light while the former interpreted this period as a time of reflection, meditation and integration to the surrounding environment and universe.

Finally, I also examined academic accounts of Inuit women's reproduction-related practices in Canada to see if I could find echoes of pre-Christian Inuit culture that had been reinterpreted within a Euro-western framework. One such story is offered by Kleivan and Sonne (1985: 13) who described the experience of a "Canadian Eastern Eskimo" woman during the birthing process and in the immediate post-partum period:

> Among the Eastern Eskimos in Canada, who exploited resources of both the sea and the land in a bipartite cycle, birth was regarded as so serious, and "infectious" that the mother had to be isolated. On the first sign of an approaching delivery the woman moved to a small igloo, in the summer, to a small tent. As a rule the seclusion continued for a few days after her delivery. And upon the mother's return to her family's dwelling with the new-born baby, she was to crawl in under the back end of the tent cover or through a fresh hole in the rear of the igloo… [as] she was [considered] too "infectious" to be permitted to pass through the customary entrance used by everyone else.… [A] few days after her delivery… [and the] two entire months [of seclusion] the mother was immediately reintegrated into her community, since she was considered non-infectious, as soon as her period of seclusion was terminated… Reintegration into the community was ritualized by the mother appearing in every single hut or tent in the settlement to announce the end of her seclusion and receiving pieces of meat as a token of her renewed community membership.

Reading this account, I was struck by the term "infectious," as I had not come across such a word in modern *kalaallisut* (the language of the *kalaalit*, a dialect of Inuktitut) in relation to menstruation. When women menstruate we simply say *aaqartoq*, literally meaning "has blood." The term for infection is *tunillaaneq*, but this term has not been used in the context of menstruation — at least not in my time. In further analyzing the term as a present-day reader, I also discern that the term "infectious" suggests the endangerment of others close to menstruating Inuit women. Could menstruating and birthing Inuit women pose a threat to others? If so, how? Could it be that Europeans view menstruation and birthing as unclean, thus labelling the women as infectious, in need of being isolated, whereas Inuit see the need for menstruating and birthing women to be kept apart from others because they were in the midst of the awesomely powerful processes of giving life to another? Could the separation result from the perception others need to be protected from women's extraordinary power at these times, power that would threaten to unbalance gender and other social relations?

Menstruation and Colonialism

The concept of *timikkut, tarnikkut, anersaakkullu*, provides a mental map of the activities of the pre-Christian Inuit, one that would include females willingly removing themselves from others during the particular times of menstruation and birthing. The mental mapping allows us to see why these activities were observed. The physical aspect of an activity — menstruation and birthing in this case — is always obvious, but it is just one aspect (*timikkut*). In this exercise, the physicality is menstruation and birthing. But the physicality is also a reflection of other dimensions, namely *tarnikkut anersaakkullu*. So while *timikkut* speaks to physical activity, *tarnikkut anersaakkullu* are mental abstractions speaking to the Inuit understanding of souls and creation and how to connect them to the physical. They are equally important to the Inuit and deal specifically with the understanding of how one integrates the land, the animals, and the souls. It is the understanding of the interconnectedness that grants an Inuk the ability to materialize her or his own potential.

The time of birthing and the menstruation period can be understood, then, to depict or illustrate the spiritual, cosmological alignment with the physical aspect of Inuit women, and thus brings together the three aspects of *timikkut, tarnikkut, anersaakkullu*. It is probable that these periods of separation were periods of "sanctity." Inuit women likely had time to meditate during these times of seclusion, to contextualize their roles in terms of family and society, and align them to form spiritual and cosmological relations. This process meant balancing the three dimensions: physical, spiritual and cosmological.

I argue that Inuit women related their menstruating times to supernatural powers, and the practice of seclusion during female times demonstrates that Inuit women had a time on their own to internalize the alignment of *timikkut, tarnikkut, anersaakkullu*, and, likely, to become empowered individually in relation to their surroundings. Much of that time would have been spent thinking, evaluating and imagining: finding ways of materializing *tarnikkut anersaakkullu*. Much female knowledge would have been solidified during such times, and would parallel the knowledge that men acquired while they were out alone hunting.

To answer Mariia's question about why modern *kalaallit* women continue to see issues surrounding menstruation as taboo, I argue that *kalaallit* women lost their power, through Christianity, by giving up the practices of seclusion during menstruation and birthing. This left a vacuum so great in negation that no word has been found for it. Once individuals have been shamed, they avoid talking about what shames them. Inuit women gave up their ability to integrate the spiritual, cosmological realities with the physical: this denial of their integrated power must have been as great as their silence today about menstruation. In working on this reconstruction, I regretted that my own periods of menstruation as a modern westernized Inuk were passed so dismally and have been nothing but manifestations of vulnerability, harassment, embarrassment and irritation. I can only imagine the power of valuing these periods from a significantly different perspective. I know that all women and girls around the world deserve to appreciate their physical selves and their sexual potential during such "sanctified activities." Can we ever regain our female potential?

Genderlessness in Inuit Culture

The notion of genderlessness and the concepts of *timikkut, tarnikkut, anersaakkullu* are not necessarily expressed explicitly in everyday Inuit life. Individuals do not make a point of behaving in a "genderless" manner: in fact, Inuit do practise a deep-seated gendered division in their activities. However, this separation does not detract from the opposite sex, but complements it (Bodenhorn 1990). And, while individuals may not always evaluate their daily life experiences according to the tripartite construct, many people in Greenland do rely on the model to convey their experiences, especially in situations that require serious decision making within family settings. Balancing *timikkut, tarnikkut, anersaakkullu*, while remaining respectful of genderless qualities, is a difficult task. Very few individuals achieve a state of balance, even in their elder years. Nonetheless, both abstractions have given me an opportunity to illustrate the complexities Inuit undergo in their attempt to maintain equal status for men and women.

Finding an answer for Mariia proved difficult and took considerable time and thought. At the end of our research project, she was profoundly affected by the information I gave her: "You know, I am not a stupid person and I know how to operate in my *kalaallit* and Danish contexts. But this blows me away," she said.

Anersaartorta, anersaartorta	Let us breathe and breathe
Tarnigissaarta, tarnigissaarta	enticing the spirit
Nukik qamannga pisoq ujartorlugu	to unleash the strength from within.
	Saskatoon, spring 2009.

1. A *Maniitsormioq* is a person from Maniitsoq.
2. In this chapter, I use the term Inuit to refer to pan-Inuit values and *kalaallit* when I am referring to people in Greenland of Inuit descent, since that is what they call themselves.

REFERENCES

Bodenhorn, Barbara. 1990. "'I'm Not the Great Hunter, My Wife Is': Inupiat and Anthropological Models of Gender." *Études/Inuit/Studies* 14, 1–2.

Briggs, Jean L. 1970. *Never in Anger: Portrait of an Eskimo Family*. Cambridge, MA: Harvard University Press.

Croll, Elisabeth, and David Parkin (eds.). 1992. *Bush Base, Forest Farm: Culture, Environment and Development*. New York: Routledge.

Cruikshank, Julie, Angela Sidney, Kitty Smith and Annie Ned. 1990. *Life Lived Like a Story: Life Stories of Three Yukon Native Elders*. Lincoln: University of Nebraska Press.

Fienup-Riordan, Ann. 1990. *Eskimo Essays*. New Brunswick, NJ: Rutgers University Press.

Freire, P. 1970. *Pedagogy of the Oppressed*. New York: Continuum.

Frideres, James S. 1992. *A World of Communities: Participatory Research Perspectives*. Toronto: Captus University Publications.

Frink, Lisa, Rita S. Shepard and Gregory A. Reinhardt (eds.). 2002. *Many Faces of Gender: Roles and Relations through Time in Indigenous Northern Communities*. Calgary: University of Calgary Press.

Ghosh, Ratna. 1996. *Redefining Multicultural Education*. Canada: Harcourt Brace.

Guemple, Lee. 1995. "Gender in Inuit Society." In Laura F. Klein and Lillian A. Ackerman (eds.), *Women and Power in Native North America*. Norman: University of Oklahoma Press.

Jessen Williamson, Karla. 2006. "Postcolonial Inuit Gender Relations in Greenland." Ph.D. dissertation. Department of Anthropology. University of Aberdeen.

___ . 2004. "Gender Issues." In Niels Einarsson, Joan Nymand Larsen, Annika Nilsson and Oran R. Young (eds.), *Arctic Human Development Report*. Reykjavik: Stefansson Arctic Institute.

___ . 2000. "Celestial and Social Families of the Inuit." In Ron F. Laliberte, Priscilla Settee, James B. Waldram, Rob Innes, Brenda Macdougall, Lesley McBain and F. Laurie Barron (eds.), *Expressions in Canadian Native Studies*. Saskatoon: University of Saskatchewan Extension Press.

___ . 1992. "The Cultural Ecological Perspectives of Canadian Inuit: Implications for Child Rearing and Education." Master's thesis, Indian and Northern Education Program, University of Saskatchewan.

Jessen Williamson, Karla, and Laurence J. Kirmayer. 2010. "Inuit Ways of Knowing: Cosmocentrism and the Role of Teasing in Child Development." In C. Worthman, P. Plotsky, D. S. Schechter and C. Cummings (eds.), *Formative Experiences: The Interaction of Caregiving, Culture, and Developmental Psychology*. New York: Cambridge University Press.

Kleivan, Inge, and B. Sonne. 1985. *Eskimos, Greenland and Canada*. Leiden: E.J. Brill.

Subject: Menopause Barbie
Date: July 31, 2003
From: C. Lesley Biggs <lesley.biggs@usask.ca>
To: <undisclosed recipients>

Hi Everyone,

No comment!

Lesley
—

>>>Finally a Barbie I can relate to! At long last, here are some NEW Barbie dolls to
>>>coincide with OUR aging gracefully. These are a bit more realistic…

>>>1. Bifocals Barbie. Comes with her own set of blended-lens fashion frames
>>>in six wild colors (half-frames too!), neck chain and large-print editions
>>>of *Vogue* and *Martha Stewart Living*.
>>
>>> 2. Hot Flash Barbie. Press Barbie's bellybutton and watch her face turn
>>>beet red while tiny drops of perspiration appear on her forehead.
>>> Comes with hand-held fan and tiny tissues.
>>
>>>3. Facial Hair Barbie. As Barbie's hormone levels shift, see her
>>>whiskers grow. Available with teensy tweezers and magnifying mirror.
>>
>>>4. Flabby Arms Barbie. Hide Barbie's droopy triceps with these new,
>>>roomier-sleeved gowns. Good news on the tummy front, too —
>>> muumuus with tummy-support panels are included.
>>
>>>5. Bunion Barbie. Years of disco dancing in stiletto heels have definitely
>>>taken their toll on Barbie's dainty arched feet. Soothe her sores with the pumice
>>>stone and plasters, then slip on soft terry mules.
>>
>>>6. No-More-Wrinkles Barbie. Erase those pesky crow's-feet and lip lines
>>>with a tube of Skin Sparkle-Spackle, from Barbie's own line of exclusive
>>>age-blasting cosmetics.
>>

>>>7. Soccer Mom Barbie. All that experience as a cheer-leader is really paying
>>> off as Barbie dusts off her old high school megaphone to root for Babs and
>>>Ken, Jr. Comes with minivan in robin-egg blue or white, and cooler filled with
>>>doughnut holes and fruit punch.
>>
>>>8. Mid-life Crisis Barbie. It's time to ditch Ken. Barbie needs a change, and Alonzo
>>> (her personal trainer) is just what the doctor ordered, along with
>>>Prozac. They're hopping in her new red Miata and heading for the Napa
>>>Valley to open a B&B. Includes a real tape of "Breaking Up Is Hard to Do."
>>
>>>9. Divorced Barbie. Sells for $199.99. Comes with Ken's house, Ken's
>>>car, and Ken's boat.
>>
>>>10. Recovery Barbie. Too many parties have finally caught up with the ultimate
>>> party girl. Now she does Twelve Steps instead of dance steps. Clean and
>>>sober, she's going to meetings religiously. Comes with a little copy of *The
>>>Big Book* and a six-pack of Diet Coke.
>>
>>>11. Post-Menopausal Barbie. This Barbie wets her pants when she
>>>sneezes, forgets where she puts things, and cries a lot. She is sick and tired of Ken
>>>sitting on the couch watching the tube, clicking through the channels.
>>>Comes with Depends and Kleenex. As a bonus this year, the book *Getting
>>>In Touch with Your Inner Self* is included.
>>
>
>

Dearest Sophia

Maria Truchan-Tataryn

Dear Sophia,

I'm writing this letter in gratitude because as we've grown together, mother and daughter, you've given me a different perspective on the world, helping me see how our culture disables people because of difference. I'm writing this letter to you, even though I don't want you ever to read it. The facts are too ugly and hurtful. But I need to explain why at twenty you seem to be imprisoned in your home, spending most of your time with your mother. I need to explain, at least to myself, and to all "those" people (our society) who automatically leave you out when they say "all people" or "women." "Those" people so wrongly believe that disability itself excludes us from the mainstream, makes us into the Other. I need to tell them and you the truth.

Society devalues disabled people regardless of gender, but you, my love, are in potentially deadly danger because you are female, despite not following the script for female gender performance. As a woman with a disability, your identity in society is so uncertain that it shifts your status as a woman. Sexist practices target not only your gender but also your divergence from sexist constructions of your gender. Because these attitudes blame you for being both female and disabled, we can't hope to have an equitable society unless the social ramifications of your identity as a woman with a disability are acknowledged.

I know that your body gives you lots of trouble, but if others acknowledged you as a human being, as you are (with the drooling, not despite it), they'd see a strong, loving woman. As it is, culturally programmed stereotypes of disability that pass as knowledge prevent most people from seeing you as an equal human being. Because your body doesn't conform to what society decrees to be "normal" for a woman, you're branded as somehow non-sexual and marked as deviant. In effect, society treats you as not fully human.

But what constitutes normalcy, and who decides? Normal is hardly natural; the concept of normalcy flourishes on a fear of difference. Normal typically causes anxiety and constant vigilance. For example, I wonder how many women are content with their appearance. The idea of normal, that tyrannizes all women, has to exclude disabled women in order to regulate effectively all other women and the sexual economy in which they are positioned. Just as women in the West have, from the time of Aristotle, been subjugated for being abnormal men, people with disabilities are devalued as abnormal people. We must dismantle the notion of normal as naturally preordained, in order to dismantle social oppression.

You, who aren't paying the club fees to sculpt your body to "perfection," can help us see women's issues more critically. The "women's" health and beauty industry denies the sexuality of women with disabilities and ultimately represses all women's humanity. If we embraced disability as diversity, as a typical occurrence for people — after all, we will all experience disability in our lives — we would more easily see through the manipulative mechanisms around us enforcing homogeneity and suppressing any promise of creativity that difference might carry. Imagine… you cannot use your hands or speak, but you threaten the system! You show me what René Girard meant by saying in *The Scapegoat* that difference outside of the social norm threatens and incites terror "because it reveals the truth about the system, its relativity, its fragility, and its mortality." By constructing women with disabilities as asexual, society attenuates your humanness and your power.

Asexuality is perhaps the most pernicious myth imposed on women with disabilities. Rosemarie Garland Thomson writes that "cultural stereotypes imagine disabled women as asexual, unfit to reproduce, overly dependent, unattractive — as generally removed from the sphere of true womanhood and feminine beauty." You, Sophia, might say "So what? I don't care if I don't fit in." Lots of women don't fit in. But the horrible truth is that you are a target for violence and abuse simply because you are female and disabled — it's nothing personal.

Remember when you began to menstruate at thirteen? Our pediatrician suggested birth control drugs for you, but not for your older sisters. She admitted that even at school you were more at risk of rape. Her approach was to protect you from pregnancy since she couldn't protect you from predators that prey on vulnerability. Just being female increases your risk of being abused but, if your characteristics are atypical, Nora Groce tells us your risk of being hurt by others increases threefold. Even these statistics are probably under-reported, because abuse can masquerade as caregiving, friendship and service provision. Victims may have no way to communicate except through their abuser, so their chances of being heard or taken seriously are often non-existent. Worse still, women who report abuse are further degraded by official disbelief and accusations of attention seeking.

According to Dick Sobsey, not only is mistreatment normalized as caregiving, but often, unbelievably, it's perpetrated by the very people who receive awards for their involvement in the disability service industry. Group home workers, for instance, enjoy social status as exceptionally caring people. They're trusted with intimate care of residents, often with little accountability. Your father was invited to sit on the board of directors of a group home where a personal support worker raped a resident: but that worker kept his unionized job, and the resident had to choose between continuing to face her abuser or leaving her home and community. Yet, according to Sobsey, your disability is not the cause of your vulnerability to abuse; rather the "complex interactions between disability, society, culture, and violence" produce this vulnerability, leaving you, my love, at great risk.

When we think about violence, we often conceptualize it as physical violence. But, living with you, I've seen the multitude of mundane and ubiquitous ways in which your personal dignity is eroded. This too is violence. You are assaulted by the way people stare at you — at the grocery store, at the park. As a disabled woman, your self-esteem and your dignity are assaulted regularly in the most ordinary interchanges: people assert how awful it must be to care for you; they talk as if you weren't there, or as if you couldn't hear or understand; you are rejected from regular school classes and community programs; people refer to you as *lame*, a *spaz* or *retard*; you receive substandard medical attention. Hospitals want me to sign "Do Not Resuscitate" forms whenever you need emergency attention. There seems to be no end to the multitudinous ways our society will devalue you. As a disabled woman, your reality is so saturated with ableist values, practices and preconceptions that, without conscious effort, people can't even recognize you outside of stereotypes.

As you know, Sophia, I'm a feminist, and feminists have made significant advances in women's rights. Over the past 150 years, they've sought equality with men in politics, law, education, health care and within the home. In Canada, the Famous Five, who won the *Persons* case in 1929, had to appeal first to the Supreme Court of Canada, and then to the British Privy Council, before Canadian women were officially granted person status. But, here's the cruel irony. These early twentieth-century women's rights activists promoted their views of true womanhood by targeting other women as subnormal and distinct from themselves. Although these women were white, middle-class British-Canadians who rightly imagined themselves as equal to the men who excluded them from institutions of power, they still asserted their competitive equality as nation-builders by embracing the putative science of eugenics with its promise of social improvement. Leaders such as Emily Murphy and Nellie McClung, who were centrally involved in the *Persons* case, deliberately worked to shift cultural images of incompetence and weakness from females to people whom they identified as disabled. Indeed, these activists emphasized their superiority to the inferior personhood of disabled males.

Eugenicists believed that "defectives" must be identified, segregated, and controlled. Ultimately, as Angus McLaren tells us, asylums contained and routinely sterilized disproportionately high percentages of women, especially Aboriginal and Eastern European women. We have to confront this history if we hope to ever live in harmony with diversity. So much of the force of our social prejudice against disability can be seen as arising from the short, but formative, reign of eugenics in Canada.[1] Although no longer referred to as eugenics, eugenic practices such as sterilization of disabled women continue, Daniela Stehlik argues, under the guise of health care (2001). For me, the ease with which society condones surgical sterilization for young girls with disabilities symbolizes the violence of disabled women's dehumanization.

Many think that people with disabilities are protected under the *Charter of Rights and Freedoms*, but, currently, if you are a woman with disabilities, you cannot be sure of your status as a person. Because societal prejudices against people with disabilities are so entrenched, through no fault of your own, you are thrown back to the absurd space of non-person, not legally, but socially and attitudinally. The disability rights movement has pointed out for years that society's biased attitudes and inaccessible structures disable people far more than most bodily conditions; but, let's face it, in the past twenty years, reactions to us haven't changed much. We can still expect compulsive stares filled with fascination, pity, fear and something like horror. Ironically, the most oppressive aspect of the bias against disability is that ableism is so pervasive that when a devaluing double standard is used for a disabled person, most of us don't notice because we think that it's normal.

Can we really believe that vulnerable citizens are "taken care of" and protected? Just consider that, in 1993, when twelve-year-old Tracy Latimer was murdered by her father in Saskatchewan, the entire country buzzed with indignation at his sentencing. The national media and popular opinion overwhelmingly supported the murderer's self-righteousness, as Ruth Enns so forcefully wrote about in *A Voice Unheard*. Because Tracy had cerebral palsy, her father still, years later, maintains he was right to kill her. Most chillingly, popular support for this premeditated, unrepentant killing was reflected in the significantly reduced sentence given by the ostensibly "unbiased" law. But remember when in Ontario, in 2007, sixteen-year-old Aqsa Parvez was murdered by her father for refusing to wear the hijab? The country recoiled with concern. Cultural sensitivity watchers hit red alert for a short time, and then the entire disturbing affair was dropped by the media. There were no defences of the father's right to kill his daughter, no lobby demanding clemency for the father for acting out of love and concern for his offspring. So why would national opinion defend filicide in the Latimer case? Tracy was no more terminally ill than Aqsa. We cannot know if Tracy suffered more. Surely both daughters suffered from their father's interpretation of responsible parenting. Would either be dead if they were not female? These questions haunt me.

OK, this is where I come in. Here I am with no career, no income, financially dependent on my husband — some feminist! I've developed a permanent cringe at the example of womanhood that I offer to you and the world. Moreover, I'm not letting you, at twenty, live away from home; so we two live as extensions of each other. But I'm in my situation for the same reasons that you're in yours. Oddly enough, to a great extent it's because of others — ordinary people who don't even know us — that we are trapped. Like you, I'm a statistic, exploited and forgotten by society — without income, social status or sleep. Because I will not "put" you into a group home and pretend that you are living independently like your peers, we're both punished for not complying with the social directives of community institutionalization. Services meant to assist us are woefully inadequate, and "friends" must be paid. Lobbying for more home services perpetuates damaging notions of you as a burden to society while reinforcing the image of me as martyred by your insatiable neediness. We can't win; either we pretend we're happily marginalized, or we pretend to agree with the terms of a system that devalues our humanity. Our world, Sophia, simply does not want you. But since you do exist, others will be more likely to exploit you, hurt you, even kill you, with impunity.[2]

You will not read this letter I've written to you, but I'm determined that our position is seen not as privately ours but as a social issue: an issue of gender, violence, and systemic oppression of human diversity. I refuse to let our social conditions destroy my gratitude for having you as my daughter. Perhaps we'll live long enough for me to read you this letter, because, instead of explaining painful reality, it will describe a past chapter of history. Perhaps in our lifetime others will see you as a woman with dignity, and embrace you as you are. Then we as women and as a society will recognize new ways of resisting enforced homogeneity, enabling us to accept our own uniqueness and flourish in our interdependence.

Much love,
Mum

NOTES

1. Eugenics was the term coined by Charles Darwin's cousin Francis Galton, in 1883, for the belief in human perfectability through the selective breeding of superior human stock and the extermination of inferior human genes. The eugenic ideology that scapegoated perceived "difference" as depraved and damaging to social welfare and progress was discredited soon enough by science. Eugenic social enthusiasts also lost much of their public fervour after the world learned of the Nazi implementation of eugenic theory in the extermination camps. See Devereux 2006 and McLaren 1990.
2. Asch argues that, "Until it is legitimate, respectable, and acceptable to be a person with a disability in the world, until the nondisabled majority recognizes how ubiquitous impairment is and how likely it is that everyone will experience it themselves or in someone they love, and until the nondisabled majority perceives that the millions of people with impairments are fully human and can contribute in meaningful ways to the economy and the family, that world will fight against every legal or moral claim made upon it to change institutions, cultural practices, and institutional and physical structures to become readily inclusive" (Asch 2004: 15).

REFERENCES

Asch, Adrienne. 2004. "Critical Race Theory, Feminism, and Disability." In Bonnie Smith and Beth Hutchison (eds.), *Gendering Disability*. Piscataway: Rutgers University Press.
Devereux, Cecily. 2006. *Growing a Race: Nellie McClung and the Fiction of Eugenic Feminism*. Montreal: McGill-Queen's University Press.
Enns, Ruth. 1999. *A Voice Unheard: The Latimer Case and People with Disabilities*. Halifax: Fernwood Publishing.
Girard, Rene. 1986. *The Scapegoat*. Baltimore: Johns Hopkins University Press.
Groce, Nora E. 2005. "HIV/AIDS and Individuals with Disability." *Health and Human Rights* 8: 2.
McLaren, Angus. 1990. *Our Own Master Race: Eugenics in Canada, 1885–1945*. Toronto: McClelland and Stewart.

Sobsey, Dick. 1994. *Violence and Abuse in the Lives of People with Disabilities: The End of Silent Acceptance?* Baltimore: Brookes.

Stehlik, Daniela. 2001. "A Brave New World: Neo-Eugenics and Its Challenge to Difference." *Violence against Women* 7: 4.

Thomson, Rosemarie Garland. 2004. "Integrating Disability, Transforming Feminist Theory." In Bonnie Smith and Beth Hutchison (eds.), *Gendering Disability.* Piscataway: Rutgers University Press.

52

hungergraphs

Sylvia Legris

1

i heard once of a woman so thin she could balance
an *O.E.D.* on the points of her pelvic bones
and still leave room to fit a substantial paperback:
the alexandria quartet or the *joy
of cooking.*

2

                                   she *refuses* to eat

can't eat

21 years old
5 feet 5 inches tall
weigh 72 pounds

                         the problem with this subject
                              one of control

never felt so
out of control

when i came to the ward
they inserted a tube
through a hole in my left arm
monitored my every movement

                             behaviour modification
                             is always administered in a caring
canvas restraints   therapeutic manner
at my shoulders and feet

                             still
                           she remains uncooperative

treat me
like i don't exist
only see
what i won't eat

5

sometimes i dream i'm a whittler, a girl lost
in a forest, branches sticks twigs everywhere.
piled like bones.
i dream of carving:
watermelon into perfect pink balls. kitchen linoleum
into geometric patterns — X X X X X. my arms,
skinny birch limbs, into blunt potato cuts: happy faces
with fat grins, full bellies, can't you just see it,
the pictures i can make? can't you imagine
crimson print on linen curtains, drizzles and
dribbles of cadmium red on white carpet?
action painting.

     hmmm…

       action.

       look around. just

       look around.

i'm standing in the middle of my apartment, blinds down,
every light but one burnt out. i have a big fluorescent calendar
on the wall above the tv, numbers three inches high,
but still i can't keep track of the date half the time.

my father says i do this for attention.

like i enjoy throwing up after every fucking meal like i
enjoy feeling like some sort of freak like i enjoy feeling

       nothing.

i can't describe the numbness. everything tingles with
insects, live wires, my gums are peeling from my teeth.
my esophagus is raw. but most of the time i feel

       nothing.

and then
i have these dreams
of sharp objects, narrow edges, near misses.
colours so vivid. everything red and white red
against white. red against white.

---

contrast
so stark.

not that i intend to hurt myself i just
never feel real want to feel so badly
feel

                anything.

but this skin,
it's so thin it doesn't take long
to hit bone.

how deep do i have to dig?

how little a dead person bleeds.

11
what people won't see:

       a young woman works behind a bakery counter
       serving poppyseed creamcheese apple danish
       cherry blueberry rhubarb-strawberry lemon meringue pie
       12 varieties of cookies:
       shortbread crispsugar
       chocolatechip pinwheel oatmealraisin walnut spice
       hamentashen brownies fruitbars maplecream
       chocolatemacaroons and   ginger
                                 snaps

       all day customers comment
       on her weight
               how lucky

       toothpick arms shoulder-blades jutting out of
       her shirt

       legs thin
       as baguettes

13

the first time you eat
after not eating for years
you remember every detail:

breakfast   august 16

shell of the soft-boiled egg brown
pinkish-brown and rough
like wallpaper we'd pick off
in layers from our attic walls
each successive layer revealing
another pattern
an old personality

                my sister neatly cuts away the top of the egg
          exposing white jello-y flesh

i delve into the yolk
creamy yellow   colour
of pollen
trim rectangular strips
of toast   sagging
real salted butter
stings when it touches
my cracked mouth

                my sister fills a glossy cup
          with fresh steaming liquid

for years black and acid
beating against walls
coffee
colour of caramel
luscious and smooth
whitened and sweetened
realness of cream and sugar
beige earthenware mug
warm and soothing   cradled
against me
aroma hot   intoxicating
nourishes
my memory
long starved:[1]

NOTES

In Sylvia Legris, 1996, *Circuitry Of Veins*, Winnipeg: Turnstone Press. Adapted and reprinted with permission.

1.   "hungergraphs" ends with this colon.

Bread Rising

Mary Pratt

Using two packages of super-active yeast, I made bread dough and placed in a clear glass bowl.

As the breast-like mound began to rise, its cells, like cancer cells, started to multiply at an ever-increasing rate. Suddenly, it was out of control. No matter how many times I punched it down, the dough — the cancer — kept growing. The photographs I took were quite ominous, and I think I captured that in my painting.

Bread Rising, 1995. Reprinted by permission of Woodland Arts Foundation.

NOTE

Mary Pratt, "Bread Rising," in Barbra Amesbury, 1995, *Survivors in Search of a Voice*, Toronto: Woodlawn Arts Foundation. The original exhibition was toured by the Royal Ontario Museum.

Connecting Our Lives with Yours

Why Disability Is Every Woman's Issue

Vera Chouinard

Welcome to "My" World

This chapter begins with the "personal," that is, my life as a disabled woman working in academia, because it is from our experiences of oppression that we often find the strength, wisdom and resolve to begin imagining and working toward a better world for women. No matter how one approaches disability, however, it remains an issue that makes many feminists, students and activists, uneasy and unsure: why it is that so many women, worldwide, who have impaired bodies and/or minds, end up being dis-abled, and what we can do to change this? By dis-abled I refer not only to the marginalization and exclusion that results from physical barriers, such as a lack of curb cuts on sidewalks, but also to the wide range of less tangible yet pervasive and powerful social barriers that work to keep disabled people in disadvantaged places in society and space. These barriers are (re)created through social practices which construct women, children and men whose bodies and/or minds differ from prevailing norms of ableness as other: as less valuable members of society.

On Being a Disabled Woman Scholar in Canada

I became seriously ill with rheumatoid arthritis early in my academic career — just three years after starting work as an assistant professor. I recall saying to my partner, when the illness was diagnosed, that I didn't want to deal with *this* (i.e., serious complication in my life). Unfortunately, as I quickly discovered, I really had no choice. Severe, unremitting forms of this illness are a physical ordeal, with constant pain and fatigue and, in my case, inflammation in all the joints of my body. Although it was difficult to endure the symptoms, adjusting to the illness itself was less of an ordeal than struggling with the physical and especially social barriers to inclusion. The latter consisted of pervasive social attitudes and practices that, intentionally or not, communicated to me that I was no longer wanted in places of normal adult life such as the university.

My first struggle against physical barriers to doing my job turned out to be a harrowing and infuriating eight-month battle for an accessible parking spot close to the building where I worked. Although intensifying joint pain was making it increasingly difficult for me to walk even short distances, and despite medical documentation, the Head of Parking Services decided I wasn't ill enough to be granted such a spot. I remember being shocked and appalled that such a simple request was being denied, particularly since I had assumed, naively, that in an enlightened place such as a university, logic and reason would dictate that people would try to make an ill professor's job easier rather than harder to do.

Other struggles to remove physical barriers to my inclusion at the university followed, but the most daunting barriers were social in nature. I was horrified to discover, when first talking to administrators about possible ways of adjusting my workload and working conditions to accommodate my illness, that their view was that faculty and staff who became ill or impaired should simply "go away" (i.e., go on long-term disability benefits). After one such encounter, in tears at the thought of losing a job I loved, I met with a lawyer from the

Canadian Association of University Teachers. She looked at me and said, "They can't do that to you." She then explained how, under Canadian human rights law, employers have a duty to accommodate disabled employees to the point of undue hardship (usually defined in terms of economic costs). Her words gave me hope and a renewed determination not to be forced out of my job.

My struggle for accommodation was long and involved, and there were many days when I felt like giving up. It took four years just to get the university to agree that it would try to meet my needs. It took twelve years and a legal battle to force the university to deal with serious violations of my human rights, such as the fact that my salary had been frozen for over a decade despite the fact that I was promoted to associate and then full professor. And it took the intervention of the Canadian Association of University Teachers to force the university to honour the out-of-court settlement it had signed with me, so that finally, fourteen years after becoming ill, there is a more comprehensive and just accommodation agreement in place between the university and me.

My struggles for inclusion in academia have been a life-altering experience. They have taught me that gender and other differences matter when one is disabled. The fact that I was an outspoken woman in an all-male department and a radical scholar had negatively marked me as a "troublemaker" even before I became ill. Becoming physically impaired and vocal about accommodation issues added yet another layer to the processes of negative differencing to which I was subjected. Perhaps most importantly, my struggles for human rights and inclusion have helped me to realize that being dis-abled is not something that follows inevitably from having an impaired body or mind. Rather, it is an outcome of social attitudes, relations and practices which devalue the lives and contributions of those of us who differ from what prevailing norms and practices of ableness demand.

Disabled Women's Places in Society

As disturbing as my personal story may be, what makes it even more troubling is that, as I have discovered as a researcher concerned with laws and policies affecting disabled women's lives, a great many women with bodily impairments world-wide live in far more oppressed, desperate circumstances than I. In these days of increasingly precarious paid work, at least I have a job and one that is, gendered inequities in academic salaries notwithstanding, comparatively well-paid.

As a group, it is much more common for disabled women in Canada to be among those extremely vulnerable workers who are "last hired and first fired" (Fawcett 2000). Disabled women who are employed are paid much less than disabled men, earning a median income of $8,360 compared to $19,250; it is even more common for disabled women to be unemployed, with an estimated 74 percent without a job (DAWNOntario 2001). How do such high rates of exclusion from the labour force come about? Women who become seriously ill and impaired lose their jobs and have to depend for income either on private insurance (which they can't always get, since they must be able to prove themselves too ill to work to claim benefits) or on the below-poverty-line welfare rates of income support provided by neoliberal governments such as Ontario's. Women who seek employment when already impaired have especially few chances of finding and keeping a job, due to widespread discrimination in hiring (see Chouinard 2001; Lynk 2000).

As recent studies have shown, being a disabled women on the political-economic and cultural margins of life in Canada and other countries involves dealing with the ongoing devaluation of disabled women's lives as "not worth living" (Marris 1996). This is a physically, psychologically and emotionally draining and painful process. Being poor, unemployed, unwanted when applying for jobs and abandoned by governments that prioritize corporate profits and "deficit reduction" over social programs for persons in need are some of the class-related ways in which women with physical and mental impairments are being forced to struggle to survive in the most marginalized of places in society and space. But women with bodily impairments face the additional gendered burdens of being exploited and devalued as female members of Canadian society: such as concentration in poorly paid, non-unionized and unpaid places of "women's work," experiencing especially severe poverty and being regarded as "ugly" or unattractive according to male-defined norms of the female "body beautiful" as able, agile, slender, youthful and so on.

Connecting Our Lives and Struggles

What, then, do disabled women's lives have to do with the lives of women who are presently able-bodied? What does my life have to do with those of you who are able women? By making extremely negative economic, political and cultural examples of disabled women who struggle to survive and assert their human rights, the state, employers, service providers and other privileged members of our ableist society send a clear and harsh message that being and becoming a disabled woman is a fate worse than death. All women are therefore more likely to be terrified at the prospect of losing our jobs as a result of becoming chronically ill and disabled. As a result, we struggle to prove, over and over again, that we are exceptionally able by submitting to longer hours of work, ignoring personal needs and failing to spend time with those we love. We also shoulder unpaid domestic work, caring for disabled children and/or elderly parents whose health and well-being are increasingly jeopardized by neoliberal forms of governance, because, again, this shows ourselves and others that we remain fully "able" women. Ironically, of course, the more hyper-able we feel compelled to be, the more likely we are to become ill and impaired through stress-related impacts on our health or through the sheer exhaustion that results in calamities such as car accidents.

Ultimately, then, we live our lives in ways that mean we become more rather than less likely to become the "other" disabled women, whose identities and lives we've been taught to fear so intensely. And the more psychologically and emotionally invested we become in being the able women the elites in our neoliberal global order demand, the less able we become to challenge processes of oppression, such as those based on ability, gender and class, which empower and enable a few at the expense of so many others. Further, as enticing as being the women the elite demand may be, we should also make no mistake about how conditional the immediate rewards of being such women are. If, in our attempts to prove ourselves able, healthy, young, productive, fit or attractive, we should fail, as we surely will in societies in which intolerance toward differences in female bodies and minds is actively promoted, then we too can expect to be disciplined and punished for falling short of how women and their bodies are "supposed" to be.

Toward a More Enabling Future

I have argued that the forces leading to the oppression and marginalization of women with physical and mental impairments play out, although in different ways, in the lives of able-bodied women. We can no more understand disability without attending to the norms, relations and practices of ableness, and the gendered differences they make in our lives, than we can understand racism without whiteness, or sexism without male privilege. If disability is, in these senses, "every woman's issue," then perhaps it is time to find solidarity in our diversity and work together toward a more enabling society for all.

For too long, issues facing disabled women have been seen in the women's movement as having nothing to do with able women's lives. This has not only left disabled women marginalized and silenced in feminist organizing, it has also meant that there has been little or no opportunity to explore the many reasons why women need to act together on disability issues. These include: the fact that disabled women, as one of the most vulnerable and marginalized groups in our societies world-wide, cannot do it alone; the fact that when governments cut back help and support to disabled women, children and men, it is usually women who struggle to fill the breach through unpaid caring work that taxes their own health and well-being; and the fact that women are especially vulnerable to stress-related chronic illnesses, such as rheumatoid arthritis, which are extremely disabling. By claiming disabled women's issues as our own, we take the first crucial step toward imagining and creating a society more enabling for every woman.

REFERENCES

Chouinard, Vera. 2002. "Learning from the Margins of Citizenship: Ableness, State Restructuring and the War on DisAbled Women in Canada." Paper presented to the International Geographical Union (IGU) Commission on Gender Workshop on Gender and Policy, held in conjunction with Canadian Association of Geographers Annual Meeting, May 26–June 2, Toronto.

___. 2001. "Legal Peripheries: Struggles over DisAbled Canadian's Places in Law, Society and Space." *The Canadian Geographer* 45,1.

___. 1999a. "Body Politics: Disabled Women's Activism in Canada and Beyond." In R. Butler and H. Parr (eds.), *Mind and Body Spaces: Geographies of Illness, Impairment and Disability*. London: Routledge.

___. 1999b. "Being Out of Place: Disabled Women's Explorations of Ableist Spaces." In E. Teather (ed.), *Embodied Geographies: Spaces, Bodies and Rites of Passage*. London: Routledge.

___. 1996. "Like Alice through the Looking Glass." *Resources for Feminist Research* 24, 3 & 4.

Chouinard, Vera, and Ali Grant. 1995. "On Being Not Even Anywhere Near 'the Project': Ways of Putting Ourselves in the Picture." *Antipode* 27, 2.

DAWNOntario. 2001. "Economics of Disability." At <http://dawn.thot.net/economics_of_disability.html>.

Fawcett, Gail. 2000. *Bringing Down the Barriers: The Labour Market and Women with Disabilities in Ontario*. Ottawa: Canadian Council on Social Development.

Lynk, Michael. 2000. "Accommodating Disabilities in the Canadian Workplace." Paper presented to the Labour Studies Program, McMaster University. Available from author, Faculty of Law, University of Western Ontario, London, Ontario.

Marris, Veronica. 1996. *Lives Worth Living: Women's Experiences of Chronic Illness*. London: HarperCollins.

55

Pretty Porky and Pissed Off

Allyson Mitchell

The women of Pretty Porky and Pissed Off (PPPO), based in Toronto, worked together to fight fat phobia from 1996 to 2004. The group began with Allyson Mitchell, Ruby Rowan, and Mariko Tamaki and grew to a group of eight, including Mitchell, Tamaki, Lisa Ayuso, Gillian Bell, Joanne Huffa, A[b]i Slone, Tracy Tidgwell, and Zoe Whittall.

Pretty Porky and Pissed Off worked to raise awareness about body issues and fat phobia through sticker production, dance, and educational workshops, engaging in group consciousness-raising and protest. We produced zines, held fat girl clothing swaps, hosted free bake "sales," performed street theatre, and developed a cabaret performance style that included performance strategies such as monologue, dance, storytelling, singing and fat drag.

PPPO's philosophy advised: "our brand of activism is about everyBODY. Peoples come in all different sizes…. From XXL to Super Size, we want to spread the word that every body is a good body" (excerpt from PPPO's zine 1999, no longer published). PPPO attempted to work through the complications of fatness by making connections between fat and health, food and happiness, capitalism and size.

PPPO hoped to inspire others to keep fighting for representation of all bodies. We thought it crucial for fat people to see themselves reflected in art — to see our struggles and our beauty. Dancing together, appearing in public, making speeches, reaching out and sharing experiences with others creates culture and builds communities. When we stop simply consuming culture and start making it, we craft and change our realities. We can imagine alternative ways of living and being. We find the commonalities and differences in our experiences to build stronger voices capable of making positive social change.

Like all underground activist groups, we are part of a community with a history as cultural workers. We learned from our active fattie foremoms and dads. Encouraged by relentless fat activists like Charlotte Cooper, Nomy Lamm, Sondra Solovay and Max Airborne, we made sure that our voices and opinions were public: we joined others to fight against the isolation that we felt as large women. We plead with anyone whose body is "different" to tell their stories. Make more fat friends. Trust yourself when things don't sit right in your belly. Make some big opinions. Break some small attitudes. Do it with flair. Share it with us. We need you to take a stand. We can all make art that reflects our bodies and makes our culture see us, not as fat and shy, but as pretty, porky, and pissed-off.

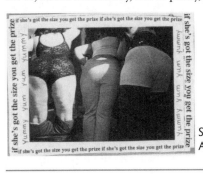

it's a Queen Size Revolt

Sticker produced by Pretty Porky and Pissed Off, 1999. Artwork by Allyson Mitchell.

Sticker produced by Pretty Porky and Pissed Off, 1999. Artwork by Allyson Mitchell.

Double Trouble/Baby Got Back Programme, MIX Festival, Anthology Film Archives, New York, November 23, 2002. Present, back left to right: Lisa Ayuso, Tracy Tidgwell, Mariko Tamaki; front left to right: Allyson Mitchell, Joanne Huffa, Zoe Whittall. Photo by Lex Vaughn.

Big Judy/Girl Friday Crashes Glass Ceiling, Mayworks Cabaret, Buddies in Bad Times Theatre, Toronto, May 7, 2004. Present: Tracy Tidgwell and Joanne Huffa. Photo by Lex Vaughn.

A Selected History of Sexual Assault Legislation in Canada, 1892–1983

Compiled by Constance Backhouse

In 1983, the Criminal Code was amended to replace rape and indecent assault with three types of sexual assault (levels one to three) in order to encourage victims to report sexual assaults to the police. In this new legislation, as a way of destigmatizing the crime, sexual assault was reconceptualized as a violent offence, so that the degree of physical violence, rather than its sexual nature, was taken into account. In addition, the legislation specified that victims of sexual assault could be both male and female, and that a spouse could be charged with sexual assault. During the first decade of the legislation, rates of reporting for level 1 sexual assault (the least level of violence) almost doubled, but from 1993 to 2007, they steadily declined; the rates for levels 2 and 3 sexual assault remained steady (Brennan and Butts 2008).

Getting a handle on statistics about sexual assault is notoriously difficult since most victims regard sexual assault as "a private matter" (Brennan and Butts 2008: 7). The *General Social Survey on Victimization* (2004) (GSS) shows that only one in ten victims report a sexual assault to the police, usually for levels 2 and 3. Based on 2004 GSS data, there were 1,977 incidents of sexual assault per 100,000; the vast majority of victims over the age of fifteen were women (3,248/100,000 as compared to 664/100,000 for men (Brennan and Butts 2008: 6). Despite widespread public awareness and almost four decades of activism by women's groups, sexual assault is still a major issue for women, children, and some men.

Most of us don't know anything about the law governing sexual assault, until we unfortunately need to know. In connection with my book, *Carnal Crimes: Sexual Assault Law in Canada, 1900–1975* (2008), I have compiled selected statutes to help summarize the laws for the past century and subsequent amendments. What will strike you, as the reader, are the changes in language, the definitions of rape/sexual assault, the type of punishments and the length of prison terms. These changes represent alterations in attitudes toward women, patriarchal values and an understanding of women's rights in Canadian society. The questions that you have to ask yourself are "Is it enough?" and, if not, "What will it take so that women, children and men can live freely without the fear of sexual assault?"

A Selected History of Sexual Assault Legislation in Canada, 1892–1983

The Criminal Code, 1892, **S.C. 1892, c. 29, s. 266.** [Note the bolding in this section is how the text appears in the legislation.]

[Rape defined.]
266. Rape is the act of a man having carnal knowledge of a woman who is not his wife without her consent, or with consent which has been extorted by threats or fear of bodily harm, or obtained by personating the woman's husband, or by false and fraudulent representations as to the nature and quality of the act.
  2. **No one under the age of fourteen years can commit this offence.**
  3 **Carnal knowledge is complete upon penetration to any, even the slightest degree, and even without the emission of seed. R.S.C., c. 174, s. 226.**

[Punishment for rape.]
267. Every one who commits rape is guilty of an indictable offence and liable to suffer death, or imprisonment for life. R.S.C., c. 162, s. 37.

[Attempt to commit rape.]
268. Every one is guilty of an indictable offence and liable to seven years' imprisonment who attempts to commit rape.

An Act to amend the Criminal Code, S.C. 1919–1920, c. 43, s. 7.

[Penalty of whipping added.]
300. Every one is guilty of an indictable offence, and liable to seven years' imprisonment and to be whipped, who attempts to commit rape.

An Act to amend the Criminal Code, S.C. 1921, c. 25, s. 4.

[Punishment for rape.]
299. Every one who commits rape is guilty of an indictable offence and liable to suffer death or to imprisonment for life and to be whipped. 55-56 V., c. 29, s. 267.

Criminal Code, S.C. 1953–54, c. 51, s. 135.

[Rape.]
135. A male person commits rape when he has sexual intercourse with a female person who is not his wife,
    (a) without her consent, or
    (b) with her consent if the consent
        (i) is extorted by threats or fear of bodily harm
        (ii) is obtained by personating her husband, or
        (iii) is obtained by false and fraudulent representations as to the nature and quality of the act.

[Punishment for rape.]
136. Every one who commits rape is guilty of an indictable offence and is liable to imprisonment for life and to be whipped.

[Attempt to commit rape.]
137. Every one who attempts to commit rape is guilty of an indictable offence and is liable to imprisonment for ten years and to be whipped.

An Act to amend the Criminal Code in relation to sexual offences and other offences against the person and to amend certain other Acts in relation thereto or in consequence thereof, S.C. 1980-81-82-83, c. 125, s. 19.

[Assault]
244.(1) A person commits an assault when
    (a) without the consent of another person, he applies force intentionally to that other person, directly or indirectly;
    (b) he attempts or threatens, by an act or gesture, to apply force to another person, if he has, or causes that other person to believe upon reasonable grounds that he has, present ability to effect his purpose; or
    (c) while openly wearing or carrying a weapon or an imitation thereof, he accosts or impedes another person or begs.

[Application]
(2) This section applies to all forms of assault, including sexual assault, sexual assault

with a weapon, threats to a third party or causing bodily harm and aggravated sexual assault.

[Consent]

(3) For the purposes of this section, no consent is obtained where the complainant submits or does not resist by reason of

(a) the application of force to the complainant or to a person other than the complainant;

(b) threats or fear of the application of force to the complainant or to a person other than the complainant;

(c) fraud; or

(d) the exercise of authority.

[Accused's belief as to consent]

(4) Where an accused alleges that he believed that the complainant consented to the conduct that is the subject-matter of the charge, a judge, if satisfied that there is sufficient evidence and that, if believed by the jury, the evidence would constitute a defence, shall instruct the jury, when reviewing all the evidence relating to the determination of the honesty of the accused's belief, to consider the presence or absence of reasonable grounds for that belief.

[Sexual assault]

246.1 (1) Every one who commits a sexual assault is guilty of

(a) an indictable offence and is liable to imprisonment for ten years; or

(b) an offence punishable on summary conviction.

[No defence]

(2) Where an accused is charged with an offence under subsection (1) or section 246.2 or 246.3 in respect of a person under the age of fourteen years, it is not a defence that the complainant consented to the activity that forms the subject-matter of the charge unless the accused is less than three years older than the complainant.

[Sexual assault with a weapon, threats to a third party or causing bodily harm]

246.2 Every one who, in committing a sexual assault,

(a) carries, uses or threatens to use a weapon or an imitation thereof,

(b) threatens to cause bodily harm to a person other than the complainant,

(c) causes bodily harm to the complainant, or

(d) is a party to the offence with any other person,

is guilty of an indictable offence and is liable to imprisonment for fourteen years.

[Aggravated sexual assault]

246.3 (1) Every one commits an aggravated sexual assault who, in committing a sexual assault, wounds, maims, disfigures or endangers the life of the complainant.

[Punishment]

(2) Every one who commits an aggravated sexual assault is guilty of an indictable offence and is liable to imprisonment for life.

NOTE

This compilation represents a selection of legislation governing rape and sexual assault. A complete history and more detail is at: constancebackhouse.ca/fileadmin/website/index.htm.

REFERENCES

Backhouse, Constance. 2008. *Carnal Crimes: Sexual Assault Law in Canada, 1900–1975*. Toronto: Irwin Law.

Brennan, Shannon and Taylor-Butts. 2008. *Sexual Assault in Canada: 2004 and 2007*. Ottawa: Canadian Centre for Justice Statistics, Statistics Canada. Ministry of Industry (Catalogue no. 85F0033M — No. 19).

57

A Women's Issue

Margaret Atwood

The woman in the spiked device
that locks around the waist and between
the legs, with holes in it like a tea strainer
is Exhibit A.

The woman in black with a net window
to see through and a four-inch
wooden peg jammed up
between her legs so she can't be raped
is Exhibit B.

Exhibit C is the young girl
dragged into the bush by the midwives
and made to sing while they scrape the flesh
between the legs, and then tie her thighs
till she scabs over and is called healed.

Now she can be married.
For each childbirth they'll cut her
open, then sew her up.
Men like tight women.
The ones that die are carefully buried.
The next exhibit lies flat on her back
while eighty men a night
move through her, ten an hour.
She looks at the ceiling, listens
to the door open and close.
A bell keeps ringing.
Nobody knows how she got here.

You'll notice that what they have in common
is between the legs. Is this
why wars are fought?
Enemy territory, no man's
land, to be entered furtively,
fenced, owned but never surely,
scene of these desperate forays
at midnight, captures
and sticky murders, doctors' rubber gloves

greasy with blood, flesh made inert, the surge
of your uneasy power.

This is no museum.
Who invented the word *love*?

NOTE

In Margaret Atwood, 1986 *Selected Poems 11: Poems Selected & New, 1976–1986*, Toronto: Oxford
University Press. Reprinted with permission.

Commemoration for the Montreal Massacre Victims

Ursula Franklin

The events in Montreal certainly and surely upset all of us deeply. As somebody who has taught for the last two decades in the Faculty of Applied Science and Engineering and who has tried to encourage young women to enter our profession, and as somebody who is a pacifist and a feminist, the events in Montreal deeply trouble me. They trouble me because any one of these young women could have been one of my students; could have been someone I encouraged by saying: "Look, you can do it. It's tough turf alright, but there are others. Nothing will change if we aren't there."

But these fourteen women are not here anymore. And many say what happened to them was an act of a madman, something more or less like a random printing error that had nothing to do with anything except the state of Marc Lépine's mind. I'm one of those who say, yes, it was the act of a madman, but it is not unrelated to what is going on around us. *That* people get mad may happen in any society, any place, every place. But *how* people get mad, *how* that escalation from prejudice, to hate, to violence occurs, what and who is hated, and how it is expressed, is not unrelated to the world around us. When a madman uses easily available weapons and easily available prejudices, it is not totally his problem, which will go away when he does. At another time, it could have been Jews who were lined up, it could have been black people, but in Montreal it was women — women in an engineering faculty — killed by somebody who wanted to be an engineer.

In remembrance, what is it that we are called upon to reflect? We remember the fourteen students in Montreal. But we also remember that they were abandoned. Our memory should not block out the fact that Marc Lépine, at one of the killing stations, went into a classroom in which there were men and women. He asked them to separate into two groups, and, when this didn't happen, he fired a shot to the ceiling. Then it did happen. The men left. Fourteen women were killed, and Marc Lépine could leave this classroom. It is not as much a question of how he got in, but it is a question of how he got *out*. In our memory and reflection, we have to include the fact that these women were abandoned by their fellow students. We have to face it.

We men and women have to ask: What does it take to make solidarity real? Is one shot to the ceiling or its verbal equivalent enough to abandon the victims? You may wish to think on what you would have done, maybe even what you are doing in less lethal situations. Is a joke enough to condone harassment? There's a lot to reflect upon. Many of the comments after the massacre were comments on what was called a "senseless killing." Are there people who can be abandoned? If reflection shows that all killing is senseless, we may ask why then do we have tools of killing around — if we agree that all killing is senseless. We may wish for a second to reflect how we, as a community, would have felt if the identical massacre had taken place in a bank, in a post office. Maybe, heaven forbid, in a hotel where the young women were prostitutes. How would we react?

We speak on occasion with fair ease about all of us being brothers and sisters. And maybe finally I could urge you, in memory of these our young colleagues, to reflect on what it means that someone is your sister, someone is a member of that human family. That doesn't mean that you have to like or love her, but it does mean you have to respect her presence as the right to be there on her own terms, not by gracious permission of the dominant culture, not only as long as she keeps her mouth shut and goes through the prescribed hoops: but because we are members of one family and each of us has an inalienable right to be, and to fulfill our potential. And if the grief we feel, the remembrance we must continue, and the reflections we have to share, bring us into a world in which it is not empty rhetoric when we speak of each other as brothers and sisters, then, I think, the memory of the students in Montreal will serve us well.

NOTE

Ursula Franklin, 1991, "Violence Against Women," *Canadian Woman's Studies/les cahiers de la femme*, 11, 4 (Summer). Reprinted with permission. The author gave this address at a commemorative service for the fourteen women murdered at École polytechnique, Montreal. Her address, given on January 19, 1990, was also read to the Senate by Roy Firth on February 21, 1990 as part of the request for a Senate Committee inquiry into violence against women.

59

Helen Betty Osborne

Marilyn Dumont

Betty, if I set out to write this poem about you
it might turn out instead
to be about me
or any one of
my female relatives
it might turn out to be
about this young native girl
growing up in rural Alberta
in a town with fewer Indians
than ideas about Indians.
in a town just south of the 'Aryan Nations'

it might turn out to be
about Anna Mae Aquash, Donald Marshall or Richard Cardinal,
it might even turn out to be
about our grandmothers,
beasts of burden in the fur trade
skinning, scraping, pounding, packing
left behind for 'British Standards of Womanhood,'
left for white-melting-skinned women,
not bits-of-brown women
left here in this wilderness, this colony.

Betty, if I start to write a poem about you
it might turn out to be
about hunting season instead,
about 'open season' on native women
it might turn out to be
about your face   young and hopeful
staring back at me   hollow now
from a black and white page
it might be about the 'townsfolk'   (gentle word)
townsfolk who 'believed native girls were easy'
and 'less likely to complain if a sexual proposition led to violence.'

Betty, if I write this poem.

NOTE

Marilyn Dumont, 2001, "Helen Betty Osborne," in Jeannette Armstrong and Lally Grauer (eds.), *Native Poetry in Canada: A Contemporary Anthology*, Peterborough: Broadview Press. Reprinted with permission.

"Canada's Shame"
582 Missing and/or Murdered Aboriginal Women

C. Lesley Biggs

Aboriginal communities in Canada have long been aware that many Aboriginal women have gone missing or have been murdered, especially in the western provinces, where the concentrations of Aboriginal people is highest.[1] For example, concerns about women missing from the streets of Eastside Vancouver and that a serial killer may be responsible were expressed as early as 1978 (Jiwani and Young 2006)! Yet only the grisly sensational discovery of the remains of twenty-six women on Robert Pickton's pig farm in 2002 finally brought the issue of missing and murdered Aboriginal women onto the national stage seemingly overnight. In addition, Amnesty International Canada published its report "Stolen Sisters: Discrimination and Violence against Indigenous Women in Canada" in October 2004, reinforcing the view that indeed the problem was of seismic proportions. Sisters in Spirit, the 2005 initiative of the Native Women's Association of Canada (NWAC) in response to the epidemic of violence against Aboriginal women, credits the "Stolen Sisters" report with having "contributed to the shift in political climate and inspired Status of Women Canada and Indian and Northern Affairs Canada departments to prioritize this issue" (NWAC n.d.).

The *Sisters in Spirit* (SIS) project, which "has been a catalyst for awareness and change from the community-based grass-roots to federal policy and program levels" (NWAC n.d.), began its work by creating a national database, the first of its kind in Canada. By July 2011, NWAC has documented 582 cases of missing or murdered Aboriginal women. *Sisters in Spirit* has used vigils, national workshops, and speaking engagements to raise public awareness about the targeting of Aboriginal women. In addition, *Sisters in Spirit* provides both support to the families of missing or murdered women as they navigate their way through the justice system and knowledge and resources to front-line workers.

NWAC has played a pivotal role in raising awareness about missing and murdered Aboriginal women, particularly in the face of political, media, and police apathy, yet their effectiveness has been undermined by the federal government. On October 29, 2010, Status of Women Minister Rona Ambrose announced $10 million for a national strategy to deal with missing and murdered Aboriginal women: $4 million was earmarked for the RCMP's Canadian Police Centre for Missing and Exploited Children while another $6 million was going to be directed to unspecified programming (APTN 2010). *Sisters in Spirit* received no funding. The announcement was mired in controversy (see APTN 2010 and Barrera 2010), but redirecting resources to the RCMP for general investigations of missing persons and unidentified remains means effectively that the over-representation of Aboriginal women as victims of this specific form of violence, in which the intersection of race, gender, and class configure prominently, was downgraded on the public policy agenda. More recently, the British Columbian government denied coverage of the legal costs of Aboriginal women's groups which wished

Grandmother Moon

Native Women's Association of Canada, Sisters in Spirit Campaign, reprinted with permission

to be represented in the Missing Women Commission of Inquiry into the police's handling of the Pickton case (Hall 2011).

The overwhelming number of crimes committed against Aboriginal women is revealed in the statistics, but numbers do not capture the human face of this tragedy. In her film *Finding Dawn*, Christine Welsh addresses this issue by focusing on the lives of three Aboriginal women— Dawn Crey, Ramona Wilson, and Daleen Kay Bosse — who had gone missing and then were found murdered. These women were loved by their families and communities, and they are missed by them.

Travelling to Vancouver's skid row, where Robert Pickton preyed on Aboriginal women, to the "Highway of Tears," in northern British Columbia where Aboriginal women disappear from Highway 16 at an alarming rate, to Saskatoon where both a serial killer and individual murderers have operated, Welsh "takes us on a journey into the dark heart of Native women's experience" (Blaney 2009). Challenging the stereotypes of Aboriginal women, *Finding Dawn* reveals the extent of the violence against Aboriginal women. Not only were the lives of young women cut short by racially motivated misogyny, but they left behind parents/children/sisters/friends/communities who loved and cared for them. Welsh doesn't go on this journey alone. "Along the road, Welsh discovers incredible strength and courage in individuals such as Native rights activists Professor Janice Acoose and Fay Blaney, who are bringing their communities together to stem the tide of violence against Native women" (Blaney 2009). In their individual and collective grief, Aboriginal communities have created ceremonies that "help the grief-stricken to heal, allow community members to rally round them, promote understanding and bring closure" (Blaney 2009). *Finding Dawn* is available for viewing through a link at the *Gendered Intersections* website (At: fernwoodpublishing.ca/gi2/) and through the NFB (At: nfb.ca/playlists/films-influential-women/viewing/finding_dawn/).

Pain, loss, and grief are all too familiar emotions for many Aboriginal women, their families and communities. But, at the same time, Aboriginal women and men have been working together to bring about positive and lasting change within themselves and their communities. In the video *From Stilettos to Moccasins*, Violet Naytowhow and the Canadian Institutes of Health Research Project Research Team recounts the ways in which the persona "survived through the pain," and through "honesty, strength, friends, and devotion," the persona is "no longer a prisoner in this world." By resolving her pain, she is able to "find [her] way home again," find peace, reclaim her spirit, and "honour in thy name." You can watch *From Stilettos to Moccasins* at the *Gendered Intersections* website (At: fernwoodpublishing.ca/gi2/).

NOTES

The title is taken from a placard displayed during a rally held in Ottawa, February 14, 2011, to protest federal government cuts to Sisters in Spirit (APTN 2011).

2. For example, almost 30 percent of Aboriginal people live in Saskatchewan and Manitoba, and seven of the nine Canadian cities with the highest percentage of Aboriginal residents are in western Canada (Silver 2006: 12–15).

REFERENCES

Amnesty International. 2004. *Stolen Sisters: A Human Rights Response to Discrimination and Violence Against Indigenous Women*. At: amnesty.ca/campaigns/resources/ amr2000304.pdf. June 7, 2011.

APTN (Aboriginal People's Television Network). 2011. "National News: This Is Sabotage by a Fascist Government." *Aboriginal People's Television Network*. (February 14). At: aptn.ca/pages/news/2011/02/14/this-is-sabotage-by-a-fascist-government/.

___. 2010. "National News: Native Women's Association Felt 'Betrayed' by Conservative Government." *Aboriginal People's Television Network*. (November 8). At: aptn.ca/pages/news/2010/11/08/native-womens-association-betrayed-by-conservative-government.

Barrera, Jorge. 2010. "'Internal Politics' Behind NWAC's Sisters in Spirit Shift: Brazeau." (November 15). *Aboriginal People's Television Network*. At: aptn.ca/pages/news/ 2010/11/15/ internal-politics-behind-nwacs-sisters-in-spirit-shift-brazeau.

Blaney, Fay. 2009. *Finding Dawn: A Guide for Teaching and Action*. Ottawa: National Film Board of Canada. At: onf-nfb.gc.ca/sg/100567.pdf.

Hall, Neal. 2011. "Missing Women Inquiry to Discuss AG's Denial of Funding for Participants." (June 7). *Vancouver Sun*. At: vancouversun.com/news/Missing+Women +inquiry+discuss+denial+funding+participants/4907639/story.html.

Jiwani, Yasmin, and Mary Lynn Young. 2006. "Missing and Murdered Women: Reproducing Marginality in News Discourse." *Canadian Journal of Communication* 31.

NWAC (Native Women's Association of Canada). n.d. "Sisters in Spirit History." At: nwac.ca/programs/sis-history.

Silver, Jim. 2006. *In Their Own Voices: Building Urban Aboriginal Communities*. Winnipeg and Black Point, NS: Fernwood Publishing.

Another Girl
An Atypical Story about a Typical Adolescent

Stephen Gaetz

Sandra is seventeen. When you first meet her, she seems like many other teenage girls. She likes music — in fact she prefers hip hop — and enjoys spending time with her friends whenever she can. She grew up in a middle class home in a Toronto suburb and is the oldest of three children. She doesn't really get along with her parents.

Youth as a Group?

What does this short profile tell us about Sandra? Not very much. Yet, it likely resonates to some degree with ideas and images we all share about teenagers. In fact, this depiction of Sandra relies on stereotypical notions regarding adolescents, their tastes and relationships with friends and family. When we talk about "youth," we often make the mistake of assuming that we are all talking about the same thing.

It is not hard to imagine why. In a country like Canada, we are constantly bombarded by standardized depictions of youth that emphasize shared and assumed innate qualities of lived experience. In popular culture, adolescence is celebrated both as a time of adventure and freedom and, at the same time, as a period of confusion and stress with the potential for deviance. Periodically in newspapers and magazines, the results of surveys on the attitudes of Canadian youth are presented as a means of assessing the state of adolescence today. Don't all young people like music, like spending time with friends and have conflicts with parents?

The discourses surrounding popular notions of "adolescent," "teenager" and "youth" are problematic when differences are played down or ignored altogether. Can we really be sure young people living in Inuvik or Montreal, male or female, gay or straight, from a privileged urban background or an impoverished rural one, all share commonalities by virtue of having been born in the same decade? If we ignore such differences, what remains of our concept of youth? We are left with an over-generalized conceptualization.

My experience working with street youth in Toronto challenges this problematic tendency to generalize. As a white male who grew up in a middle-class neighbourhood and whose conflicts with my own parents were fairly superfluous, it might have been easy for me to make wildly inaccurate assumptions about young people who are homeless. Popular depictions of street youth often focus on their so-called "deviance" and "delinquency," their personality and motivational deficits, their inability to "get along" with their parents or their inherently rebellious nature. All of these ideas about street youth — which carry a strong currency in Canada — are produced and reproduced through discourses that focus narrowly on the developmental issues of adolescents.

There is no doubt that the transition from childhood to adulthood brings significant changes in status and responsibility, and in physical and mental development. Yet, there are significant differences. Features of individual identity — gender, sexual orientation, ethnic and racial difference and class — intersect with personal histories in unique ways to produce both shared and distinct life worlds, which at the same time reflect the degree to which social power and opportunity are distributed unequally. A person's identity position will have a profound effect on how she or he experiences adolescence and the developmental shifts that are inherent in it.

Healing — Sandra's Story

Let's go back to Sandra's story, which highlights how structural factors — such as systemic sexism, institutionalized indifference to poverty, stigmatization of homelessness, age-based discrimination — intersect to shape the experience of adolescence.

At some point after you meet Sandra, it will dawn on you that she is homeless. You may not be able to tell right away by looking at her; she has short dark hair, and her clothes, though not clean, are neat. On most days she and her friends can be found sitting on the ground in front of a store on Queen Street. When she sees you, if she can catch your eye, she will ask you if you have any money or food because she is hungry.

On any given day, there are about 1,700 to 2,000 homeless youth living on the streets of Toronto. Some stay overnight in street youth shelters, others live in squats (abandoned buildings), public places (doorways, alley ways, parks and under bridges) or temporarily with friends ("couch surfing"). The reality is that in a given year, most street youth will experience all of these living situations. Life on the streets is inherently unstable. Much of their energy is devoted to meeting immediate needs, such as shelter, safety and food. Thinking about getting a job, going to school, planning for vacation — these are luxuries that few street youth can afford to ponder.

When people pass Sandra on the streets, they do not know that she grew up in a middle-class neighbourhood with a banker for a father and a teacher for a mother. They also do not know that her household was very violent when she was a child. When her mother died when she was thirteen, things just got worse. Her father became more and more depressed and was unable to care for her. She finally left home when she was fifteen, after her father hit her "for the last time." She still isn't sure who wanted her to leave home more: herself or her father.

Like many street youth, the circumstances that led to Sandra's homelessness are complicated. They do not easily correspond with popular representations of street youth as dissatisfied and rebellious young people who leave home for frivolous reasons (they don't like "doing the dishes") or as kids who are attracted by the excitement of downtown living. While these factors account for some of the street youth population, the reality is that young people who leave home for these reasons generally don't stay away from home for long.

What we do know is that most young people who wind up living on the streets are escaping a difficult home life. For a large percentage of street youth, physical, sexual and/or emotional abuse as well as ineffective parenting, family breakdown and substance abuse issues lead to their homelessness (Read et al. 1993; Gaetz and O'Grady 2002).

While it is true that youth from poor families are over-represented in the street youth population because they have fewer resources with which to deal with family and individual problems, one must remember that the main causes of homelessness (such as abuse) do cut across class boundaries. The fact that Sandra grew up in a nice suburban neighbourhood does not make her unique as a street youth. Her middle-class background, however, influences how she responds to her homelessness and the resources that she is able to access in order to leave the streets.

Sandra never imagined that she would be living on the streets in downtown Toronto. She and her friends would sometimes come downtown to see a movie or go shopping, but it was not a place she liked to hang around. Even now she finds it a bit unnerving. She feels that it is harder for girls to live on the streets, and that she can never be alone. She had to quickly learn how to take care of herself.

Within the population of homeless youth, males typically outnumber females by a two to one margin (Hagan and McCarthy 1997; Gaetz and O'Grady 2002). This certainly suggests that gender has an impact both on becoming homeless and on the experiences of homelessness. Because the streets are a "gendered space," becoming homeless presents different challenges for girls. The streets are a place where notions of masculinity, femininity and sexuality are actively produced and reproduced, and opportunities structured. For instance, it is not unusual for young men to colonize the streets in order to exercise independence, develop friendships and attachments, and explore cultural options and economic opportunities. Girls, then, may have to think about and negotiate their safety, the activities they engage in, how they present themselves and who they are attached to in ways that are different than boys.

Homelessness and Security

Sandra was clear that life on the streets is different for young men and young women. How would her life become even more complicated if she were black or lesbian?

Sandra's best friend is Michelle. They hang around together all the time. Michelle is two years older and has been on the streets for four years. Michelle, whose parents immigrated from India, also came from a middle-class home, but did not experience physical abuse as Sandra did. In fact, Michelle got on pretty well with her parents, until the day she told them that she thought she might be lesbian.

For most young people who are lesbian, gay or transgendered, the process of coming out is challenging. Tolerance for heterosexist and homophobic attitudes in communities, schools and at home renders sexual minorities invisible and makes it difficult for lesbian and gay youth to develop identities as many heterosexual teenagers do. As a result, many lesbian, gay and transgendered youth report higher incidences of depression and stress, lower self esteem, more suicide attempts and higher rates of alcohol and drug abuse (Taylor 2000).

Lesbian, gay and transgendered youth are also more likely than heterosexual youth to become homeless. Coming out often produces ruptures with family, friends, neighbourhood or ethno-racial community, making staying at home a difficult and, in some cases, a non-viable option. Many lesbian and gay youth are kicked out of their homes or leave on their own accord because their safety is no longer guaranteed at home or school. However, the streets do not necessarily offer a panacea. Being lesbian or gay adds one more risk factor for a youth who is homeless.

Michelle was the victim of gay-bashing last night. Because she doesn't have a health card, she did not seek medical help for the cut that will surely scar her forehead. Sandra tries to comfort her, knowing that the continual threat of violence is part of life on the streets. Since becoming homeless, Sandra herself has been attacked more than once. To feel safe, she recently got a dog. Even though she doesn't have enough money to feed herself many days, she does get food for her dog. At least she feels safe for now.

When street youth are discussed in the media, it is often with reference to crime. Public debates often focus on how street youth and their implied criminality scare shoppers and tourists away from downtown Toronto. What gets ignored in many of these debates is the fact that street youth are more likely than almost any other group to be victims of crime. While in any given year about 25 percent of Canadians report being victims of a crime, over 80 percent of street youth do (Gaetz 2002).

Being without secure shelter and a safe door to seek refuge behind makes street youth much more vulnerable to violent attacks, sexual assault and/or having their few possessions stolen. The fact that street youth are often compelled to engage in risky behaviours in order to make money also increases their chances of being assaulted or robbed.

> Sandra likes panhandling because she can sit with her friends. What she doesn't like about it is how people who pass by treat her. People shout "Get a job" and call her names. She suspects these people rarely talk to anyone else the way they talk to her. Sometimes creepy men come up to her and proposition her for sex. She worries that she might run into them again, in less public places. But the main thing she worries about, the thing that will really embarrass her, is meeting someone she knows from her past — an old friend, a teacher, a neighbour, her boss from the donut shop. She wonders, "what will they think of me now?"

Like many street youth, Sandra is compelled to employ a variety of strategies to earn money, some of which are illegal or quasi-legal. Holding down a regular job is difficult when you lack safe, affordable shelter. Without a home, street youth are at a disadvantage in the job market because they are unable to adequately prepare for a job search (they lack an address to put on an application and have no phone number for job callbacks). Even when they find work, it is difficult to get the proper sleep and nutrition necessary to work day in and day out. As a result, street youth do what they can to make money, including panhandling, squeegeeing (cleaning car windows), petty theft and prostitution. When you are cold, tired and hungry, you make different decisions. The subsistence activities of street youth allow them the opportunity to earn cash-in-hand on a daily basis, but these activities also carry great risks and affect self-esteem in ways that regular jobs generally do not.

> When Sandra was younger, she thought she might like to be a journalist when she grew up. She loves writing, and has always been interested in politics. To this day she still keeps a journal. Because she had to drop out when she became homeless, the prospect of going to university seems more and more remote. Still, she hopes that one day she will be able to make it as a journalist. But first, she has to get off the streets, which it turns out is a lot tougher than she ever imagined.

What happens to street youth? Do they spend their lives on the streets? Do they get off the streets and enter the so-called "mainstream"? Unfortunately, there is little research that satisfactorily answers these questions. Anecdotally, it is known that there are many different outcomes for street youth like Sandra. While some do overcome adversity and move on with their lives, others end up becoming part of the adult homeless population, or worse, dying before their time.

Sandra's dreams, desires and imagined future are perhaps not that dissimilar from other young people her age. However, her identity cannot be framed neatly by popular representations of youth. Sandra's life has been profoundly affected by her youthful experience of homelessness and by the factors that led to her life on the streets. Moreover, her understanding of adolescence is also shaped by important structural factors; the fact she is a girl means that she faces different challenges than homeless boys do. Her best friend Michelle has exposed Sandra to the costs of homophobia, and as a young woman, Sandra's concerns for her own safety on the streets are profound. As a very poor, homeless teenage girl, Sandra will see the world differently and she will experience growing up in ways quite distinct from other youth. She will also make decisions based on circumstances that other teenagers do not have to confront. Although we all are affected by our past, the factors that shape our past may be profoundly different, based on whether we are male or female, rich or poor, black or white, gay or straight, housed or homeless. The best strategies to adopt when working with young people in any capacity (as teachers, social workers or policymakers) are rooted in an appreciation of the significance of differences within the youth population.

REFERENCES

Gaetz, Stephen. 2002. *Street Justice II: The Legal and Justice Issues of Homeless Youth in Toronto.* Toronto: Justice for Children and Youth.

Gaetz, Stephen, and B. O'Grady. 2002. "Making Money — Exploring the Economy of Homeless Workers." *Work, Employment and Society* 16,3.

Hagan, J., and B. McCarthy. 1997. *Mean Streets: Youth Crime and Homelessness.* Cambridge: Cambridge University Press

Read, S., D. DeMatteo, B. Bock, B. Coates et al. 1993. *HIV Prevalence in Toronto Street Youths.* Toronto: The Hospital for Sick Children.

Taylor, H. 2000. "Meeting the Needs of Lesbian and Gay Young Adolescents." *The Clearing House* 73,4 (March/April).

How to Talk to a New Lover about Cerebral Palsy

Elizabeth Clarke

Tell her: *Complete strangers*
have patted my head, kissed
my cheek, called me courageous.

Tell this story more than once, ask
her to hold you, rock you
against her body, breast to back.

her arms curving round, only
you flinch unchosen, right arm trembles
Don't use the word *spastic,*

> In Europe after centuries
> of death by exposure
> and drowning,
> they banished us
> to the streets.

Let her feel the tension burn down your arms
tremors jump. Take it slow: when she asks
about the difference between CP and MS,

refrain from handing her an encyclopedia.
If you leave, know that you will ache.
Resist the urge to ignore your body. Tell her:

They *taunted me* retard, cripple.
defect. *The words sank into my body.*
The rocks and fists left bruises.

> Gimps and crips, caps
> in hand, we still
> wander the streets but now
> the options abound: telethons,
> nursing homes, and welfare lines.

Try not to be ashamed as you flinch and tremble
under her warm hands. Think of the stories you haven't
told yet. Tension locks behind your shoulder blades.

Ask her what she thinks as your hands shake
along her body, sleep curled against her,
and remember to listen: she might surprise you.

NOTE

Elizabeth Clarke, 1997, "How to Talk to a New Lover about Cerebral Palsy," in Kenny Fries
(ed.), *Staring Back: The Disability Experience from the Inside Out*, New York: Plume. Reprinted with
permission.

Section V

CARING FOR THE GENERATIONS: A LABOUR OF LOVE

C. Lesley Biggs and Pamela Downe

"The trouble with young people today," my [Pam here] father used to declare, "is that they don't know how to work hard." At the same time, my daughter would complain, "Old people just don't get it; we have more pressure on us than any other generation ever has." And, I confess, I have frequently bemoaned the trials of being among the "sandwich generation," where caring for both my children and my aging parents takes a greater toll than I would like. In these instances, my father, daughter, and I are characterizing and mischaracterizing the generations of people who make up our families and communities. We are not alone in doing so. People commonly speak about what life is like for a particular generation, so much so that "Baby Boomers," the "Me Generation," and "Gen-X" have become well recognized descriptors of those born in the post-World-War-II era, the late 1960s and the 1980s. Popular media and artistic productions celebrate and condemn the music, fashions, worldviews, and policies of entire cohorts, leading many to conclude that the "generation gap," a sociological and psychological term that was coined in the 1920s, still prevails.

The *Oxford English Dictionary* defines a "generation" as a single step in descent or pedigree. One generation of people born at the same time moves through life together occupying different generational positions in society; in Western ideology these positions are usually represented as chronological stages beginning with infants and children, followed by youth, young adults, middle-aged adults, and seniors. When speaking of generational distinctiveness, we must remember that no generation ever expresses itself uniformly, nor do all members of a generational cohort share identical experiences or worldviews.

This section of the book concerns itself with how generational positions are culturally configured and artistically represented. Together the chapters address an important set of questions: What are some of the rites of passage — ceremonies and rituals marking a transition from one social position to another — associated with different generational positions? How are these rites of passage represented in artistic works and popular media? What does it mean to be "a mother" or "to mother," or to be "a father" or "to father"? How do we care for vulnerable populations — children, the elderly, and those with disabilities? These issues cross the generations, and they are deeply embedded in relations of gender, sexuality, race, and ability.

While all rites of passage typically assemble families and communities, weddings and funerals are key markers of the transition from one stage of life to another. (Indeed, families often joke that they see each other only at weddings and funerals.) Weddings are usually joyous events because two people have formed an emotional bond and decided to spend their lives together, and because weddings are commonly taken to mark the formation of new families and the establishment of affinal kin (in-laws). In most societies, even those with varying definitions of marital unions, weddings are the most common marker of adult status and sanction sexual activity and reproduction.

Funerals, of course, are usually sombre occasions, as the living both celebrate the life of the deceased and mourn the passing of a loved one or friend. When the deceased has lived to a ripe-old age, a funeral is often understood to represent the passing of a generation. But when people die young, families and communities also mourn lost potential and the rites of passage that will go unmarked. A funeral is a time of remembrance and a time of remembering as families and communities knit themselves together in new ways in the absence of the deceased.

Ten weddings and a funeral are the subjects of two paintings by Ann Harbuz (1908–1989), *Ten Weddings* and *July, 2010*. Together they offer, as curator Joan Borsa observes, a commentary on "the social landscape from the perspective of someone who not only understood what it meant to live, work, and survive within the land [she] represented, but who also longed to articulate the economic, climatic, and psychological extremes which had frequently tested their [her subjects'] limits." Condensing space and time, *Ten Weddings* documents the history of one family as its generations move from being Ukrainian settlers in Canadian prairie and small town environments to city-dwellers. *Ten Weddings*, however, is not the expression of a sentimental or nostalgic longing for the past. As Borsa argues, Harbuz offers a "highly analytical response to the interplays between private and public realms and to the enforcement of 'acceptable' behaviour through the institutions of marriage, family, and heterosexuality." Playing with psychological interiors and public representations of family, as well as the gendered constructions of domestic and public space, Harbuz complicates might what otherwise would be construed as joyful occasions. In a scene that would be easy to miss, the "happiness" of the wedding is, as Borsa notes, pierced with gendered violence as a father whips his adolescent daughter for her illegitimate pregnancy.

In *July 25, 1920*, we see a family experiencing the distressful rite of passage brought on by the death of the wife and mother. The father's presence is commanding: "his riveting gaze, his hands clasped in prayer and the noticeable absence of an adult female figure in a home with six young children, speak to the solemn and psychologically charged occasion of a mother's death." The painting not only reveals the psychological isolation of grief, but the stark interiors of the home also mirror the geographic and economic isolation felt by families living in the 1920s on the Canadian prairies.

Although Harbuz was a painter, her work does not in terms of technique, the surfaces on which she painted, the materials that she used to frame her work, and some aspects of her subject matter, accord with widely held standards of what is considered "fine art." As a result, Harbuz's work raised broader questions for Borsa as she contemplated the body of the painter as a woman and the gendered conditions under which Harbuz practised her art. As a self-taught painter, Harbuz did not conform to the conventions of landscape paintings, those "formal compositions of scenic, but unpeopled land," and "picturesque vistas" which suggest that "[the painter's] ultimate goal was to offer aesthetic respite and transcend everyday existence." Nor did her paintings exhibit the technically proficient, modernist styles to which [Borsa] had been introduced. In the world of the fine art, Harbuz's style would have been regarded as "naive," "folk," "primitive," or "undisciplined"; however, Borsa rejects this dichotomy between "folk" and "fine" art. Instead she situates Harbuz in her cultural, geographic, and social context (her gender, her Ukrainian background, age, marital status, and place of residence), and demonstrates that Harbuz was a keen and critical observer of the individuals, families, and communities of which she was a part. Together painter Harbuz and art historian Borsa make visible the everyday lives of "those whose labour and practices are all too easily misunderstood or forgotten."

Once we get over what is for many of us the angst-ridden time of adolescence, a time when most teenagers are exploring their identities separate from their families, many come to appreciate our parents for their love and support. In her poem "Chinese 5 Spice," Marisa

Anlin Alps tenderly recalls her parents' affection through their hands and their labours of love manually performed. Alps testifies that for her mother, that work involves growing and preparing the food that her family eats: "My mother's hands smell of ginger / traces of sesame oil, Chinese 5 spice / the colour of miso, her long fingers / sift through the black mushrooms and / vegetables piled on the kitchen counter." In contrast, Alps' father works on a boat — "The other woman" in his life according to her mother: "My father's hands are wide and / lined with rough work... / They smell of the sea, / salt ropes and diesel engines, of the / sails stored in the forepeak." Although a clear division of labour exists between father and mother, this marriage is based on mutuality and respect as expressed in Alps' father's appreciation for his wife's food. In other ways, however, it is not a traditional marriage (particularly in the generation in which this union was formed) since Alps' mother is Chinese and her father is white. Just as the foods of both parents' cultures are savoured in this household, so too are Alps and her brother, "a blend of their [parents'] own particular recipes."

Since the publication of Adrienne Rich's book *Of Woman Born: Motherhood as Experience and Institution*, mothering has become a central focus of feminist analysis. In 1976, little was known about "the nature and meaning of motherhood" because, as Rich points out, "women have not been the makers and sayers of patriarchal culture" (Rich [1976] 1995: 11). Since then feminists have sought to understand the experience of mothering — its joys and frustrations, the passionate love and resentments, its pleasures and pain — because mothering is central to women's lives (either as mothers or daughters) and to the lives of their children, families, and communities. But feminist excavations of mothering are not simply a matter of personal concern; rather examining motherhood is a political act designed to expose the ill-conceived patriarchal structures and values that have restricted women's capabilities and potentialities. Of central importance here is the issue of imagining mothering in a feminist or non-patriarchal world.

Most feminist analysts either implicitly or explicitly begin with Rich's "distinction between two meanings of motherhood, one superimposed on the other: the *potential relationship* of any woman to her powers of reproduction and to children; and the *institution*, which aims at ensuring that potential — and all women — shall remain under male control" (Rich [1976], 1995: 13, emphasis in the original). For Rich, a woman's powers of reproduction centre on "the biological capacity to bear children and her ability to nurture human life, and the magical power invested in women by men, whether in the form of Goddess-worship or the fear of being controlled and overwhelmed by women" (ibid.). In contrast, the institution of motherhood refers to the patriarchal structures that have "ghettoized and degraded female potentialities" (ibid.), and includes a plethora of advice books on how to mother; the "scientific" pronouncements of a long line of mostly male psychologists, psychiatrists, social workers and other experts; the proselytizing on the virtues of motherhood by clergy of all religious denominations; the staid reports of governments; and the saccharine-sweet images of mothers portrayed in the media.

Adopting Rich's methodology, the authors in the remainder of this section begin with the experiences of mothering and its intersections with the dominant discourses of motherhood as a way of understanding "the nature and meaning of motherhood." But, it will become quickly apparently, no singular definition of motherhood is offered here. Rather, what is revealed are rich, diverse, and complex accounts of mothering. Rather than arguing, as Rich does, that woman's power, her ability to nurture all human life, will be strengthened if released from the shackles of the patriarchal institution of motherhood, these authors demonstrate that practices of mothering emerge within particular social and historical contexts.

In a study of lesbian women becoming mothers, Fiona Nelson pursues the question of what it means to be a mother. Moving beyond a biological definition, Nelson contends that the title "'Mother' is conferred by individuals such as extended family, the created family, other mothers and institutions such as the state, religious/spiritual bodies, the health industry and society at large." Given "this matrix of socio-cultural bodies," the journey into the culture of motherhood is relatively unproblematic for married, heterosexual, white women, but for lesbian women — both gestational and non-gestational mothers — it is fraught with difficulties. Nelson demonstrates that becoming a mother is a social process and not simply a biological occurrence.

Another major issue for feminists is the relationship between a pregnant woman and her fetus: are they separate individuals or are they one? Such questions haunted Elizabeth MacKenzie while she was pregnant and continue to inform her art as she negotiates being a mother and an artist. While most contemporary popular imagery of pregnancy presents mother and fetus as autonomous subjects, MacKenzie found that pregnancy was "a marginal state of existence that is fraught with ambiguity, since it calls into question the boundaries of self." In *Her/s*, MacKenzie asks where does a woman's body begin and end in relation to her fetus? Does the woman's body belong to her or is it overtaken/invaded by an alien fetus? While these are issues of personal experience, they are also deeply connected to the larger questions of women's reproductive rights and bodily autonomy. What are the implications of the self/other distinction for the abortion debate or *in utero* surgery, or the incarceration of women who are addicted to substances? Who owns women's bodies?

The subject of myth and fantasy, fact and fiction, motherhood has simultaneously been venerated, for example, in the figure of the Christian Virgin Mary — the self-sacrificing and nurturing "good mother" — and feared, as represented in the Greek myths of Medea and Clytemnestra — "bad mothers," who unleashed their fury and destroyed their children and the men around them. Although classical myths no longer hold the same sway over Western culture they once did, the dichotomy of the good/bad mother persists in contemporary Western conceptions of mothering. Mother's Day, observed on the second Sunday of May, is the one day of the year (Is it enough???) on which we celebrate our mothers by sending a card, preparing a meal for her or taking her out to dinner, giving a gift, or telephoning. The idea of Mother's Day is a relatively new one, but celebrating mothers has a long history dating back to antiquity. According to the website "Mother's Day Central," "past rites typically had strong symbolic and spiritual overtones; societies tended to celebrate Goddesses and symbols rather than actual Mothers." In Europe, the early Christians used the fourth Sunday of Lent to honour their "Mother" Church, the church in which they were baptized. In the 1600s, Lenten Sunday was declared "Mothering Day" by a clerical decree in England. This holiday, according to "Mother Day's Central" was a compassionate gesture to the working classes in England since it not only "provided a one-day reprieve from the fasting and penance of Lent," but "Mothering Day" allowed workers to return to their families so that they could enjoy a family feast—with Mother as the guest of honour.

When the Puritans arrived in America, they discontinued the tradition of Mothering Day, as well as Christmas, since these holidays had become increasingly secularized. In 1870, however, Mothering Day was reinvented in the U.S. with the Mother's Day Proclamation of 1870, a protest against the carnage of the nation's Civil War. The proclamation, which was reproduced and circulated in an email, and we have included in this section, is a good example of (first wave) maternal feminism subverting Victorian notions of women's "proper sphere" and "the cult of domesticity." Feminists of the day were able to translate the values of women as nurturers into arguments for political and social rights for women.

Mother's Day has been used by many groups as a day of protest, and is part of a longer tradition in which women, drawing on their role as mothers and nurturers, have been active in peace movements. For example, in 1915, Nobel Prize winner Jane Addams became the first president of the Women's Peace Party, which was formed in the United States to protest the outbreak of the First World War (National Women's History Museum). Russian women, who initially celebrated International *Women's* Day on the last Sunday of February, used that day in 1917 to protest the deaths of two million Russian soldiers who died in the First World War and to strike for "bread and peace" (International Women's Day).

More contemporary examples include Las Madres de Plaza de Mayo, mothers and grandmothers who protested the disappearance of their children during the "Dirty War" (1976–1983) in Argentina, led by military dictator Jorge Rafael Videla Redondo (Asociación Madres de Plaza de Mayo). In addition, the Abuelas de Plaza de Mayo, the grandmothers, seek the return of their children and grandchildren, who were kidnapped along with their parents, or born in detention and then "adopted" by families supportive of the regime. "Our demand is concrete," write the Abuelas, "that the children who were kidnapped as a method of political repression be restored to their legitimate families" (Abuelas de Plaza de Mayo). Similarly, mothers of "the disappeared" in other countries such as Chile, Uruguay, Paraguay, and Bolivia have used their status as mothers to protest brutal juntas. In Ireland, Nobel Peace Prize winners Mairead Corrigan and Betty Williams founded the Peace People in 1976 after the three children of Anne McGuire, Corrigan's sister, died in a tragic accident, the result of a fatally wounded Irish Republican Army gunman being chased by a British army patrol. McGuire was severely injured and committed suicide a few years later (BBC News 2006). In England, the women's peace camps at Greenham Common (1981–2000) protested the U.S. nuclear missile base in England (Greenham Common Women's Peace Camp). In 1997, the Four Mothers Movement was founded by Rachel Ben-Dor, Miri Sela, Ronit Nachmias, and Zahara Antavi, Israeli women who had sons serving in Lebanon, to protest Israel's "silent war" in Lebanon (Mujeres Mediterráneas).

These are a few examples of women protesting based on their status as mothers. Can you think of others? Invoking mothers' or women's special status as nurturers raises interesting questions about the strengths and pitfalls of this political strategy. What are the political and social consequences of the view that all women/mothers are inherently nurturing? When men participate in peace movements, do they invoke their status as fathers, or do they appeal to other gendered narratives? If Mother's Day began as anti-war protest, how did it transform into a sentimental occasion devoid of political content?

While women continue to be the primary caregivers of children, the majority of children under the age of twelve are cared for by women other than their mothers, including nannies and caregivers in licensed child-care centres and unlicensed homes. As a result of a hodge-podge of policies and practices, high quality and affordable childcare remains elusive for many families. What is needed, Susan Prentice contends, is a universal childcare system. Taking into account the needs of children's and workers' rights, Prentice argues that such a system would provide excellent quality of care to children, and good, rewarding jobs to adults. Why Canada has failed to develop an effective national childcare program is complex, but the experience of progressive European governments indicates that "where there is a political will there is a way." Despite Prentice's commitment to a universal child-care system, she admits that it poses vexing questions for feminists. She asks: Is the call for a universal childcare system a "cop-out"? Would a Canadian system of universal, high quality, affordable care be a sign that our country didn't respect "caring," and was retreating from valuing women's traditional roles? Is it anti-feminist to want to redistribute the work of caring for children?

For those who can afford a live-in caregiver (often referred to as a nanny), having one is a solution for the care of children, elderly parents, and people with disabilities. The benefits for families of a live-in caregiver are often enormous since she provides continuous support, stability, and piece-of-mind because her employers know that their loved ones are well-looked after. For the live-in caregivers, the situation is much more precarious and dependent upon the respectfulness and goodwill of their employers. Canada has a long history of recruiting domestics to fill labour shortages, and in some cases, with the secondary agenda of supplying future wives. In the late nineteenth century, 90,000 women were recruited from the British Isles to serve as childcare workers, cooks, housekeepers, launderers, maids, servants, and cleaning women (Cohen 1994). Between 1917 and 1930, another 80,000 were recruited under the Servant-Turn-Mistress Program (ibid.).

After World War II, recruitment strategies shifted from white women of Anglo descent and Northern European women to women from Central Europe (Germany, Italy, and Greece), Asia, and the West Indies. Rina Cohen (1994: 84) argues that "Canada's foreign domestics policy was explicitly racist, restricting the number of black immigrants to Canada." However, under the Caribbean Domestic Scheme of 1910–11, one hundred women from Guadalupe were brought to Quebec as a source of cheap labour (Calliste 1994). In 1955, in response to a shortage of white, British and Northern European domestic workers, Canada opened its doors to black female workers under the West Indies Domestic Scheme, which required domestic labourers to remain in service for a year. This program remained in place until 1967 when a new *Immigration Act* was passed, granting entrance into Canada based on a points system for educational and occupational status. Most domestic servants were unable to meet these requirements. But, in 1973, again in response to the demand for domestic labour by white, middle-class families, the federal government established the Employment Authorization Program, which granted only temporary visas to domestic workers.

In response to organizations like the International Coalition to End Domestic Exploitation (INTERCEDE), the Legal Education and Action Fund (LEAF), the YWCA, and church and women's groups, many of the most egregious discriminatory criteria and practices have been rescinded, but the current policy still places domestic workers in vulnerable positions (Cohen 1994). In 1992, in response once again to a contemporary shortage of Canadians willing to perform this form of domestic work, the federal government established the Live-in Caregiver Program (LCP), a specialized program of Citizenship and Immigration Canada. In return for three years of services, live-in caregivers, many of whom are negatively racialized, are eligible to apply for permanent residence. These women were, of course, subject to conditions, as Tami Friesen documents in her chapter: participants must live in their employers' homes and are only allowed to work for the one employer named on their work permit. If a live-in caregiver wants to change employers, she must go through a lengthy bureaucratic process to get a new permit. But, as we write, one case of domestic slavery in Canada has come to light, demonstrating the ways in which the LCP can easily be abused (see Hall and Duggan 2011). Based on their gender, race, and class, and their temporary status, live-in caregivers are a vulnerable to physical, sexual, economic, and psychological abuse. According to Friesen, "Women under the LCP are often underpaid, work excessive hours, experience violations of privacy, and receive inadequate food and accommodation. Caregivers may also experience social isolation, family separation, and lack of awareness of their employment rights." Living in fear of deportation, as well as losing their income and homes, live-in caregivers often are reluctant to file a complaint against employers who exploit them. In response to community groups concerns about the well-being of live-in caregivers, the federal government has taken only a few ameliorative steps (e.g., establishing a contract between live-in caregivers and their employers)—despite calls from the United Nations Committee on the Elimination of Discrimination against Women to ensure the rights and dignity of live-in caregivers under the LCP.

The good mother is a synecdoche for other norms which reproduce the ideal mother as white, heterosexual, and able-bodied, and this image of the mother is inextricably tied to the preservation of the nuclear family as an ideal form. Mothers who do not fit these norms, or who fail to live up to the ideal image of the good mother, risk public vilification, being made the subject of gossip, and in the worst cases face the loss of their children (or the threat thereof) through custody disputes or apprehension by social services, and endure incarceration. Not every woman, however, is capable of caring for her child(ren); mental illness, problems with addictions, or extreme poverty can stand in the way. How do we, as feminists, support women with pressing social and psychological problems while "protecting the interests of the child"? Is motherhood a right justified by the biological capacity to bear children, or is it a responsibility negotiated in relation to contemporary, and often conflicting, values around mothering, and to a lesser extent, fathering?

Motherhood is not only an institution or an experience, it is also a practice, for which there is no shortage of advice about how best to mother — while considerably less advice exists about how best to father. For example, beginning with *The Common Sense Book of Baby and Childcare* (1946), Dr. Benjamin Spock's books on mothering, and baby and childcare guided childrearing practices in North America for several generations, and are prime exemplars of advice books to mothers. Ironically, Spock presented this book as a "handbook for parents," and encouraged fathers to be actively involved in raising their children, but Spock speaks directly to young mothers. Translated into 39 languages and selling 50 million copies, Spock's books offered a "revolutionary" view of childrearing while speaking to a need for information. In a world where many women no longer have daily contact with their mothers or grandmothers due to time, geographic distance, and the fact that many grandmothers are working in the paid labour force, many of these advice books can be very helpful to women (and men) as they navigate parenthood.

However, these books often not only provide advice but are normative in nature. For example, such books did much to develop the now conventional wisdom that children should not sleep with their parents. But, until 150 years ago, most children slept with their parents as a matter of course, and in many parts of the world, children still sleep with their parents. In part or in whole, the reasons were practical; households, particularly among the poor, did not have separate bedrooms. As incomes increased and ideas of individual privacy took hold, children and parents began to sleep separately. However, some parents began to question this practice, leading to the phenomena of "The Family Bed" (an idea that emerged along with the importance of breastfeeding, which was promoted by the La Leche League) that extolled the benefits of parents and children co-sleeping.[1]

As a supporter of the family bed, artist Frances Robson wanted to illustrate the love and intimacy that her family experiences while sleeping together. The opportunity arose when Robson was asked, "what would you want to do with your art if you were going to die in six months?" Robson replied, "I wanted to make lots of photographs of my family and I together, showing me with them in a way that would remind them of our closest moments and that I loved them very much." The result was *The Family Bed*. For Robson, her husband and children, the family bed is a space where family bonds are strengthened. But for others the close physical intimacy of the family bed raises questions about children's and adults' sexuality, and the relationship between the two. In addition, concepts such as the family bed are controversial within feminist circles. Seen as a package, some argue that the family bed, along with extended breastfeeding and homeschooling, is consistent with patriarchal values that simultaneously exalt and devalue motherhood by perpetuating the view that "biology is destiny" and that women's main role in life is to mother. Other feminists, often drawing on essentialist arguments, argue that alternative parenting styles (such as that involving the family bed) represent a way of resisting patriarchal views of motherhood by placing "women and children first." The line, as you can see, between patriarchal and non-patriarchal constructions of motherhood is a fine one, as these ideas can be subverted to fit particular worldviews.

There are no simple cultural scripts for women with disabilities. In her moving account, Heather Kuttai recalls the pain of growing up female in a society that defines women with disabilities as asexual. Not only did Kuttai insist that her sexuality be given expression, she defied convention by also becoming a mother. Working against the script that reads "a mother is an adult, an adult is a sexually capable person, a sexually capable person is physically capable," Kuttai lovingly narrates the joy and pain of being a mother to her son, Patrick, in a society that judges self-worth by physical and sexual attributes. Through this journey, "despite the absence of scripts, [Kuttai], like other women with disabilities, [has] become a capable author by necessity."

The examples in this section reveal the range of mothering but are by no means exhaustive. What does mothering and motherhood mean to women who mother in blended families, women otherwise known as stepmothers (and what's in that name?); or wish to mother but can't (the childless); or choose not to mother (the childfree) or to have an abortion; or conceive through the use of reproductive technologies. What do mothering and motherhood mean to grandmothers?

Perhaps the greatest lacuna in feminist writing is an analysis of the nature and meaning of fatherhood, particularly if we compare the voluminous feminist writings on motherhood to the relative paucity of feminist writing about fatherhood. However, drawing on Rich's distinction between motherhood as an experience and institution, the same analysis could apply to fatherhood — with all of its attendant complexities and contradictions. These tensions are evident in David Carpenter's reflections on his relationship with his father, "the hero of [his and his brother's] boyhood, the naysayer of their manhood." Carpenter wrote "My Father's Dying" late one night, after having just disabled his elderly father's car, "sever[ing] his last connection to freedom, shot his horse as it were." With wit and humour, the poem explores the many sides of his father — the athlete, the storyteller, the control freak, the petty tyrant, the loving father, the devoted husband, the gregarious dad and the repressive one, the hard taskmaster, and his sons' greatest fan. For Carpenter, writing this poem was a way of healing old wounds, grieving his loss, and expressing his love for his father; it also reveals that negotiating masculinity is fraught with joys and pitfalls for both father and son.

The concept of fatherhood has been tangled up with patriarchal values and beliefs — remember that patriarchy means law of the father — but this interlocking of ideas doesn't represent the only configuration possible for fatherhood. We end this section with a beautiful image of a male dancer elegantly balanced on one foot while he holds an infant outstretched out on his arm and hand. The image conveys tenderness and strength, grace and trust, joy and love. Both dancer and babe are smiling. We hope that when you see the photograph, you will too!

NOTE

1.   The concept of the family bed was popularized by Tine Thevenin, a La Leche League leader, who wrote *The Family Bed*, which was originally self-published in 1981, and sold 30,000 copies. For more information, see Katie Allison Granju, n.d., "The Family Bed: An Evolutionary Approach To Family Sleep." At: breastfeeding.com/ reading_room/family_bed.html

Abuelas de Plaza de Mayo. "History of Abuelas de Plaza de Mayo: Children Who Disappeared or Who Were Born in Captivity." At: abuelas.org.ar/english/history.htm.

Asociación Madres de Plaza de Mayo. At: madres.org/navegar/nav.php.

BBC News. 2006. "Legacy of NI Peace Movement (August 11). At: news.bbc.co.uk/2/hi/uk_news/ northern_ireland/4781091.stm.

Calliste, Agnes. 1994. "Race, Gender, and Canadian Immigration Policy: Blacks from the Caribbean, 1910–1932." *Journal of Canadian Studies* 28,4.

Cohen, Rina. 1994. "A Brief History of Racism in Immigration Policies for Recruiting Domestics." *Canadian Woman's Studies* 14,2.

Four Mothers. n.d. "Four Mothers: Leaving Lebanon in Peace." At: 4mothers.org.il/peilut/ about.htm.

Greenham Common Women's Peace Camp. At: greenhamwpc.org.uk.

Hall, Neal, and Evan Duggan. 2011. "East Vancouver Couple Accused of Domestic Slavery: Woman's Passport Had Allegedly Been Confiscated after She Entered Canada." *Vancouver Sun* (June 9). At: vancouversun.com/news/East+Vancouver+couple+accused+domestic+slavery/4913604/story. html#ixzz1OtbFRPu9.

International Women's Day. n.d. "International Women's Day: Factsheet." At: internationalwomensday. com/iwd_factsheet.pdf.

Mother's Day Central. n.d. "Mother's Day History." At: mothersdaycentral.com/about-mothersday/ history.

Mujeres Mediterráneas. 2004. "The Four Mothers Movement: Leaving Lebanon in Peace." November 28. At: mediterraneas.org/article.php3?id_article=50.

National Women's Peace Museum. "Reforming Their World: Women in the Progressive Era." At: nwhm.org/online-exhibits/progressiveera/peace.html.

Spock, Dr. Benjamin. 1946. *The Common Sense Book of Baby and Childcare*. New York: Duel, Sloane and Pearce.

Caring for the Generations: A Labour of Love
Hypatia Index[1]

Compiled by C. Lesley Biggs

- Estimated number of people worldwide in 2010: 6,887,829,448[2]
- Estimated number of people worldwide in 2010 over the age of 60 years: 2.4 billion (35%)
- Male-to-female sex ratio of children worldwide in 2010 ages 1 to 4: 101.5:100
- Male-to-female sex ratio of adults worldwide in 2010 between the ages of 45 to 49: 1:1
- Male-to-female sex ratio of adults worldwide in 2010 over the age of 100: 23.8:100
- World population growth rate[3] in 1963 — the highest in the twentieth century: +2.19 percent
- World population growth rate in 2009: +1.133 percent
- Canadian population growth rate in 2010: +0.804 percent
- Niger population growth rate — the fastest in the world in 2010: +3.66 percent
- Annual global growth rate as of 2009 for the population of older persons (60 years and over): +2.6 percent[4]
- Annual global growth rate as of 2009 for the population of the oldest old (80 years and over): +3.8 percent
- Ratio of persons worldwide in 2009 aged 80 years or over (the oldest old) to the number of older persons (60 years and over): 1:7
- Ratio of persons worldwide by 2050 aged 80 years or over (the oldest old) to the number of older persons (60 years and over): 1:5
- Year in which the number of older persons (60 and over) worldwide is expected for the first time to exceed the number of children (ages 15 and under): 2045
- The potential support ratio (number of potential workers to support an older person) worldwide in 1950: 12
- The potential support ratio worldwide in 2009: 9
- The projected support ratio worldwide in 2050: 4
- Percentage of women of persons worldwide in 2009 who were 80 years of age and over: 63
- Percentage of women of persons worldwide in 2009 who were 100 years of age and over: 81
- Total population of Canada in 2009: 33.7 million[5]
- Canada's total fertility rate, or the average number of children per woman, in 2007: 1.66
- Nunavut's total fertility rate, highest fertility in the country, in 2009: 2.97
- Newfoundland and Labrador's total fertility rate, the lowest in the country: 1.46
- Alberta's population growth in 2008–2009: 2.5
- Ontario's population growth in 2008–2009: 1.0
- Percentage of Canadians in 2009 living in metropolitan areas: 68
- Year in which the number of older persons (60 and over) in Canada is expected for the first time to exceed the number of children (ages 15 and under): 2017
- Percentage of Canadians in 1960 who were over 65 years of age: 8
- Percentage of Canadians in 2009 who were over 65 years of age: 14
- Projected percentage of Canadians who will be over 65 years on age in 2036: 23 to 25

- Percentage of Canadians in 2009 aged 65 years and older who are women: 55.8
- Percentage of Canadians in 2009 who are under 14 years of age: 16.6
- Total Aboriginal identity[6] population in 2006: 1,172,785
- Percentage of total Canadian female population in 2006 who were Aboriginal identified: 3.8
- Percentage of total Canadian male population in 2006 who were Aboriginal identified: 3.7
- Percentage of Aboriginal identity population in 2006 who were aged 14 years and under: 29.7
- Percentage of the total Canadian population in 2006 who were aged 14 years and under: 16.6
- Percentage of Canadian parents from very low-income[7] homes in 2006/2007 who expected their children to attend university: 50
- Percentage of Canadian parents from higher income[8] homes in 2006/2007 who expected their children to attend university: 67
- Percentage change in population of Canada from 2001 to 2006: 5.4
- Percentage change in population count for Aboriginal identified persons from 2001 to 2006: 20.6
- Percentage of all children (aged 14 and under) in the provinces of Saskatchewan and Manitoba in 2006 who were Aboriginal identified: 28[9]
- Percentage of Aboriginal identified children aged six and under in Canada in 2006 who live in a three generational (parents, children, grandparents) home: 9
- Percentage of Aboriginal identified children aged six and under in Canada in 2006 for whom at least one grandparent was involved in raising the child: 43
- Percentage of Aboriginal identified children aged six and under in Canada in 2006 who spoke an Aboriginal language: 18[10]
- Percentage of Aboriginal identified children aged six and under in Canada who spoke an Aboriginal language in 2006 who spoke Cree: 53
- Percentage of Aboriginal children aged six and under in Canada in 2006 for whom they were expected by parent/guardian to become fluent in an Aboriginal language: 29
- Percentage of Aboriginal identified children aged six and under in Canada in 2006 for whom health care was unavailable: 21
- Percentage of Canadians in 2006 who were first generation immigrants: 19.8[11]
- Percentage of Canadians in 2006 who were second generation immigrants: 12.1
- Percentage change from 2001 to 2006 in the number of foreign-born people in Canada: 13.6
- Percentage of all first generation immigrants who emigrated from Europe in Canada in 2006: 16.1
- Percentage of all first generation immigrants who emigrated from Europe in Canada in 1971: 61.6
- Percentage of all first generation immigrants who emigrated from Asia, including the Middle East, in Canada in 2006: 58.3
- Percentage of all first generation immigrants who emigrated from Asia, including the Middle East, in 1971: 12.1
- Percentage of the foreign-born population in Canada 2006 reported a mother tongue[12] other than English or French: 70.2
- Percentage of the foreign-born population in Canada in 2006 whose mother tongue was a Chinese language (the largest language group among the foreign-born population): 18.6

- Percentage of children aged 15 and under of the world's population in 2007: 28 (1.9 billion)[13]
- Percentage of children aged 15 and under in more developed countries in 2007: 17
- Percentage of children aged 15 and under in least developed countries in 2007: 41
- Number of deaths worldwide of children under the age of five in 1990: 12.5 million (or 90/1000 live births)[14]
- Number of deaths worldwide of children under the age of five in 2008: 9 million (or 64/1000 live births).
- Number of children worldwide aged 5 and under who died every day in 2008: 25,000
- Percentage decline between 2000 and 2007 in child deaths globally from measles: 74
- Percentage decline between 2000 and 2007 in child deaths in Africa from measles: 89
- Percentage of primary-age children worldwide who attended primary school in 2007: 80
- Percentage of children worldwide who completed the final grade (grade 5) of primary school in 2008: 90
- Number of school-age children worldwide who were not in school in 2007: 101 million
- Percentage of out-of-school children worldwide who were girls in 2007: 52.7
- Number of countries that have ratified the United Nations Convention on the Rights of the Child: 191/193[15]
- Percentage of fathers in Canada in 2001 who took a leave after the arrival of a child (either through birth or adoption): 37.9[16]
- Percentage of fathers in Canada in 2006 who took a leave after the arrival of a child (either through birth or adoption): 55.2
- Percentage of mothers in Canada from 2001 to 2006 who took a leave after the arrival of a child (either through birth or adoption): 90
- Percentage of parents in Canada in 2006 who could not take a leave for financial and employment reasons: 79.8
- Percentage of parents in Canada in 2006 who did not take a leave because they preferred not to compromise their career: 24.5.
- Percentage of marriages in Canada in 2006 that ended up in divorce: 50.4
- Percentage of cohabiting couples in Canada in 2006 that dissolved: 49.6
- Percentage of cohabiting couples in Quebec in 2006 that dissolved (the highest rate for all provinces): 67.6
- Percentage of married and cohabiting couples in Canada in 2006 that dissolved and who had dependent children: 41.1
- Number of families in private households in Canada in 2006: 8,896,840[17]
- Percentage of all families in Canada in 2006 who were married couples (with and without children): 68.6
- Percentage of all families in Canada in 2006 who were common-law couples (with and without children): 15.5
- Number of lone parent families in private households in Canada in 2006: 1,414,060
- Percentage of lone parent families in private households in 2006 who were female: 80.1
- Percentage of households in Canada in 2006 who owned their own home: 68.4[18]
- Percentage of households in Canada in 2006 who spent 30% or more of their income on shelter: 24.9
- Percentage of homeowners in Canada in 2006 who spent 30% or more of their income on their mortgages: 25.7
- Percentage increase between 2001 and 2006 in median annual shelter costs for renter

households in Canada: 12.8
- Percentage increase between 2001 and 2006 in the consumer price index in Canada: 11.3
- Percentage increase between 2001 and 2006 in median annual shelter costs for owner households in Canada: 21.6
- Percentage of women in Canada in 2006 living alone who owned their own home: 48.7
- Percentage of men in Canada in 2006 living alone who owned their own home: 46.7
- Percentage of women in Canada in 2006 living alone who were 65 years of age or older: 50
- Number of shelter beds available on a regular basis in Canada in 2010: 16,758[19]
- Ratio of one person sleeping in a shelter in Canada to people living with housing vulnerability: 1:23
- Percentage of homeless or vulnerably housed people surveyed in 2009 who had a mental illness: 52
- Percentage of homeless or vulnerably housed people surveyed in 2009 who had a traumatic brain injury at some point in their lives: 61
- Percentage of homeless or vulnerably housed people surveyed in 2009 who had been beaten up or attacked in the past year: 38
- Percentage of homeless or vulnerably housed people surveyed in 2009 who had trouble getting enough to eat: 33
- Average lifespan of homeless or vulnerably housed people compared to the Canadian population: -7 to 10 years
- Number of individuals who reported living on the street in Metropolitan Vancouver during a 24 hour point-in-time count in 2008: 2,660[20]
- Number of accompanied and unaccompanied children (under the age of 19) who reported living on the street in Metropolitan Vancouver during a 24 hour point-in-time count in 2008: 94 & 59.
- Percentage of street/service homeless population who tried to stay in a shelter on the night of the count, but was turned away either because the shelter was either full or the person was inappropriate for the shelter: 19
- Percentage of the homeless in Metropolitan Vancouver who were men: 72
- Percentage of homeless people during a 24 hour point-in-time count in 2008 who were Aboriginal: 32
- Percentage of homeless women during a 24 hour point-in-time count in 2008 who were Aboriginal: 45
- Percentage of American men in 2007 who stated a preference for a boy child: 45[21]
- Percentage of American women in 2007 who stated a preference for a boy child: 31
- Percentage of American men in 2007 who stated a preference for a girl child: 21
- Percentage of American women in 2007 who stated a preference for a girl child: 35
- Percentage of American adults in 2007 who said that they would prefer a boy child because men can relate to males better/have more in common: 23
- Percentage of American adults in 2007 who said that they would prefer a boy child because a boy can carry on the family name: 20
- Percentage of American adults in 2007 who said that they would prefer a boy child because boys are easier to raise: 17

1. The original Hypatia Index was compiled by Pamela Downe, with the assistance of Ellen Whiteman. Except when otherwise indicated in the main text, the sources cited in this Index apply to the line where first referenced and then to all those that follow until another endnote appears.

2. U.S. Census, 2010, "World Mid-year Population by Age and Sex" (June), International Data Base World Population. At: census.gov/ipc/www/idb/worldpopinfo.php.

3. Population growth is defined as "the average annual percent change in the population, resulting from a surplus (or deficit) of births over deaths and the balance of migrants entering and leaving a country." C.I.A., *The World Fact Book*. At: cia.gov/library/publications/the-world-factbook.

4. United Nations, Department of Economic and Social Affairs: Population Division, 2010, *World Population Ageing: 2009.* At: un.org/esa/population/publications/WPA2009/WPA2009-report. pdf.

5. Statistics Canada, 2010, *Canada Year Book*, Ottawa: Ministry of Industry. At: statcan.gc.ca/pub/11-402-x/2010000.

6. The Aboriginal identity population comprises the Aboriginal groups (North American Indian, Métis and Inuit), multiple Aboriginal responses and Aboriginal responses not included elsewhere. Statistics Canada, 2010, *Canada Year Book*, Ottawa: Ministry of Industry. At: statcan.gc.ca/pub/11-402-x/2010000/pdf/aboriginal-autochtones-eng.pdf.

7. Very low income refers to household income below the low-income cut-off. *Low income cut-offs (LICOs)* -— more commonly known as Canada's "unofficial" poverty lines — are established by Statistics Canada using data from the Family Expenditure Survey (now known as the Survey of Household Spending). LICOs indicate the level of income at which a family may be in "straitened circumstances" because it spends a greater proportion of its income — 20 percentage points more — on necessities of food, shelter and clothing than does the average family of a similar size. Canadian Council on Social Development, "A Profile of Economic Security in Canada, Economic Security Fact Sheet #2: Poverty." At: ccsd.ca/factsheets/economic_security/poverty/index.htm.

8. Higher income level refers to household income above the low-income cut-off. Note that a two-level measure for income is a crude measure. The fact that these differences were statistically significant at .001 level indicates a strong correlation between household income and parental expectations.

9. Statistics Canada, 2008, "Aboriginal Identity Population by Age Groups, Median Age and Sex, 2006 Counts for Both Sexes, for Canada, Provinces and Territories," 2006 Census. At: statcan.ca/census-recensement/2006/dp-pd/hlt/97 558/pages/page.cfm?Lang=E&Geo=PR&Code=01&Table=1&Data=Count&Sex= 1&Age=2&StartRec=1&Sort=2&Display=Page.

10. Statistics Canada, 2008, "Profile of Aboriginal Children, Youth, and Adults," 2006 Census. At: statcan.ca/ census-recensement/2006/dp-pd/89-635/P4.cfm?Lang=eng&age=1&ident_id=1 &B1=0&geocode1=001&geocode2=000.

11. Statistics Canada, 2007, *The Daily*, 2006 Census, Immigration, Citizenship, Language, Mobility, and Migration (December 4). At: statcan.gc.ca/daily-quotidien/071204/dq071204a-eng.htm.

12. Mother tongue is defined as the first language learned at home in childhood and still understood by the individual at the time of the census.

13. Population Reference Bureau, 2008, "2008 World Population Data Sheet." At: prb.org/pdf08 /08WPDS_Eng.pdf.

14. UNICEF, 2009, *The State of the World's Children*, Special Edition. At: unicef.org/sowc09/report/report.php.

15. The United States and Somalia are the only two countries that have not ratified the Convention on the Rights of the Child. Fewer countries have ratified 11.b Optional Protocol to the Convention on the Rights of the Child on the Involvement of Children in armed conflict, and 11.c Optional Protocol to the Convention on the Rights of the Child on the Sale of Children, Child Prostitution and Child Pornography. New York, May 25, 2000.

16. Pascale Beaupré and Elisabeth Cloutier, 2007, *Navigating Family Transitions: Evidence from the General Social Survey 2006*, Statistics Canada, Ministry of Industry, Catalogue no. 89-625-XIE — No.002.

At: statcan.gc.ca/pub/89-625-x/89-625-x2007002-eng.pdf.

17. Statistics Canada, 2007, (2006), "Census Families in Private Households by Family Structure and Presence of Children, by Province and Territory." At: statcan.gc.ca/l01/cst01/famil54a-eng.htm.

18. Statistics Canada, 2008, *The Daily*, "2006 Census: Changing Patterns in Canadian Homeownership and Shelter Costs" (June 4). At: statcan.gc.ca/daily-quotidien/080604/dq080604a-eng.htm.

19. "Homelessness is defined as living in a shelter, or on the street, or in other places not intended for habitation" including those who were couch surfing (staying with families or friends temporarily). "A person is considered vulnerably housed, if a person has a place to live, but at some point in the year had been either homeless or who had moved at least twice." The results of REACH[3] study showed that these are not distinct groups, but people move between these two groups. Research Alliance for Canadian Homelessness, Housing, and Health, 2010, *Housing Vulnerability* and "Health: Canada's Hidden Emergency: A Report on the REACH Health and Housing in Transition Study" (November). At: homelesshub.ca/ ResourceFiles/HousingVulnerabilityHealth-REACH3-Nov2010.pdf.

20. Social Planning and Research Council of B.C. (SPARC BC), Eberle Planning and Research, Jim Woodward & Associates Inc., Judy Graves, Kari Huhtala, Kevin Campbell, In Focus Consulting and Michael Goldberg, 2008, *Still on Our Streets: Results of the 2008 Metro Vancouver Homeless Count* (December), commissioned by Greater Vancouver Regional Steering Committee on Homelessness. At: metrovancouver.org/planning/homelessness/ResourcesPage/HomelessCountReport2008Feb12.pdf.

21. The question asked by the Gallup poll was "Suppose you could only have one child. Would you prefer that it be a boy or a girl?" Frank Newport, 2007, "Americans Continue to Express Slight Preference for Boys: Little Changed Since 1994," Gallup (July 5). At: gallup.com/poll/28045/Americans-Continue-Express-Slight-Preference-Boys.aspx.

63

Ann Harbuz
Playing with Convention

Joan Borsa

I was introduced to Ann Harbuz's work through my family. My mother and Ann Harbuz were raised in the same community and are of the same generation. After curating several smaller exhibitions of Ann Harbuz's artwork and struggling with the ways self-trained artists such as Harbuz have been represented, I decided a few years of research and a much larger exhibition were in order. The resulting exhibition, *Ann Harbuz: Inside Community, Outside Convention,*[1] was sponsored by the Dunlop Art Gallery, Regina, and travelled to six Canadian museums and public art galleries from 1995–1998.

Born in 1908 in Winnipeg, Manitoba, to parents who had emigrated from Ukraine, Ann Harbuz (nee Napastiuk) spent most of her life in the district of North Battleford, Saskatchewan. After a life of caring for others (siblings, husbands, and children); working as a housewife and mother; running a small store in Ponoka, Alberta; and doing odd jobs to supplement her income, at the age of fifty-three, Ann Harbuz began her first series of paintings. By the time of her death in 1989, she had produced well over one thousand paintings and painted objects, most of which she sold or gave away as gifts. The documentation on this work (including its whereabouts) is sketchy, and the range of styles and quality of execution uneven. As more people passed through Ann's studio-home, she received increasing numbers of requests for commissioned paintings based on both personal photographs and commercial reproductions. Making money was a novel experience and Ann was not adverse to these commissions. All of these works are now in the public domain, which certainly complicates how we perceive her practice, illustrating how important the editing process has been in establishing an artist's professional reputation.

Since my first visits to Ann Harbuz's studio (in the late 1970s), I have been intrigued by her unorthodox approach to painting and by her eclectic mixing of media, methods, and materials. Having studied painting at the University of Saskatchewan, I thought I was somewhat versed on Saskatchewan art, but work like Ann Harbuz's had not been part of my formal studies, and it was difficult to know how to deal with her obvious difference. The school of landscape painting to which I had been exposed emphasized formal compositions of scenic, but unpeopled land, as if the ultimate goal was to offer aesthetic respite and transcend everyday existence. Harbuz's paintings did not adhere to this version of picturesque vistas, nor to the technically proficient, modernist styles to which I had been introduced. Yet, I felt more kinship with her methods and her point of view, with her inclusion of cultural activities and historical references set in specific geographical locations. In Ann Harbuz's paintings the landscape was not only inhabited but abundant with settlement and social exchange. As if simultaneously assessing and representing the inner and outer workings of a world she shared with others, Harbuz's interpretations of nature and people's lives were up close, not always beautiful, and laboriously in-process. Clearly these were "social landscapes"[2] from the perspective of someone who not only understood what it meant to live, work, and survive within the land they represented, but who also longed to articulate the economic, climatic, and psychological extremes which had frequently tested their limits.

Harbuz's work is both eccentric and innovative; she painted on objects and surfaces that ranged from old vinyl records, kitchen cupboards, dust pans, birch bark logs, metal cream cans, and fences as well as properly gessoed and stretched canvases. Her frames were home-made or purchased at Zellers; the shapes of her canvases were slightly crooked; her technical skills were not refined (in an art school way); and her subject matter led into narratives about classed, labouring bodies which seldom experienced leisure, let alone the sublime. Her production was steeped in marginalized stereotypes — she was an older, rural, ethnic, self-trained female artist. She made work about agrarian experience, Ukrainian-Canadian culture, prairie settlement, physical labour, rural communities, motherhood, local history, and women's lives. I understood that in many professional contexts this would be considered "small town" art, marked by class dynamics and the conditions of its own dis-empowerment. It was not destined for *Documenta*, the National Gallery of Canada, *Flash Art*, or the *Venice Biennale*. In short, in an art world infested with hierarchies, economics, sex appeal, exoticism, and the race for the new, Ann Harbuz, her world, and her work would not ignite enough sparks. Why, I asked myself, in the midst of my intense interest in contemporary art and cultural theory, was I drawn to work that was mostly about the past and connected to an ethnic and cultural enclave I thought I was leaving behind? These questions prompted me to pay greater attention to the classification systems, documentation, exhibitions, and commentary which surrounded Harbuz's work. It quickly became apparent that neither the complexity of Harbuz's art practice nor the politics of the labels "folk," "naïve," and "primitive" which encircle the self-trained artist had received due critical attention. My goal was to open up a critical space for a form of production which had been both marginalized and misrepresented. I began to research parallels in other disciplines and other artistic practices, searching for forms of analysis that would productively lead me astray.

It did not take long before I was immersed in Carol Shields' writing, in particular her book *Swann* (1993), which addressed the blind spots within our critical responses to unorthodox or marginal forms of cultural expression. Like Ann Harbuz, the central character in Shields' book, Mary Swann, lived in relative isolation in a rural community. She is portrayed as an obscure and closeted writer whose challenging prose and poetry fall outside conventional genres and modes of literary expression. Shields' book offered valuable insights into the many reactionary and dismissive comments I had heard within the communities with which Ann Harbuz had been closely associated. It was not uncommon to hear that Ann was considered somewhat of an oddity, that she was not a "real" artist. Her involvement in art was frequently seen to be a role outside her class, education and life experience. It *was* unusual for a woman of her generation and social position to paint. However, it is not Ann, but her conviction and prolific output that seem peculiar, given the conventions and restrictions of her day. As I read Jeanette Winterson's book *Art Objects: Essays on Ecstasy and Effrontery*, I was reminded, once again, that all art is much more than its subject matter or medium, and much more than its point of origin: "It is not necessary to be shut up in one self, to grind through life like an ox at a mill, always treading the same ground. Human beings are capable of powered flight: we can travel across ourselves and find that self multiple and vast. The artist knows this" (Winterson 1995: 116).

In much of Harbuz's work, it is apparent that she moves away from reductive readings of art as merely a reflection of an artist's life or the sum total of its subject matter, technical execution, or narrative structure. In re-staging and re-interpreting past events, Harbuz challenges us to look closely, to see the details and interconnected parts, to comprehend the "inside" of a situation; yet simultaneously, she manages to set in motion a picture even big-

July 25/1920, acrylic, ink on masonite, 32.2 x 42.3 cm, 1978, Saskatchewan Arts Board permanent collection, photo Saskatchewan Arts Board. Reprinted by permission of Joan Borsa.

ger than what is portrayed. Playing with the boundaries of space and memory, she offers us glimpses into how she experienced, assessed, and understood a particular social world and her position in it.

Within the spatial ordering of Harbuz's two-dimensional works, we frequently see an interior/exterior divide, as well as a suspended or traversing perspective. In her painting *July 25, 1920*, an interior space of domestic grief functions like a cut-out, inserted into a larger prairie topography. The stark appearance of the central male figure, his riveting gaze, his hands clasped in prayer and the noticeable absence of an adult female figure in a home with six young children, speak to the solemn and psychologically charged occasion of a mother's death. Outside the home the physical environment is equally turbulent — colours jar and set the nerves on edge. A scratchy surface-quality reminiscent of pelting rain projects an unsettling reverberation. One cannot help but notice the horse-drawn wagon containing a coffin — the only other sign of activity within the sparsely populated landscape. But it is not only the news of a mother's death that impacts. The evidence of geographical isolation in combination with the minimal furnishings of the one-room home exaggerates the scene within. As if signalling more repressed or complicated speech, specific social contexts and subtexts are frequently buried in the overall composition. As Chilean art critic Nellie Richard (1986) has suggested, artists are not always overt in their use of social and political commentary. Images can be layered and may carry subtle cultural codes as a way of obscuring difficult personal circumstances or traumatic events.

In *Ten Weddings*, one of Harbuz's most animated and ambitious paintings,[3] a series of

Ten Weddings, acrylic and pen on masonite, 60.0 x 90.4 cm, 1978, Collection of the Regina Public Library, PC2001.4, photo: Grant Kernan/AK Photos. Reprinted by permission of Joan Borsa.

events particular to one family history is condensed into concentrated units of space/time, interior/exterior interplays. Bringing together a time frame of approximately forty years and a radius of about one hundred miles, Harbuz humorously reassembles the weddings of ten siblings into one compact landscape. But next to the diagonal line of traditional wedding receptions is a smaller more private scene that one could easily miss. Near one of the houses, quite centrally located, a man holds a horsewhip, his arm raised and directed at a young woman within his immediate reach; supposedly, a father responding to the news of his unwed teenage daughter's pregnancy. This seemingly innocuous insert and its proximity to the sanctioned space of family convention complicates the conceptual underpinnings of this work. Here and in other paintings, multiple views of a common theme are frequently juxtaposed, as if establishing elements of a larger debate or acknowledging the complexities of factors affecting individuals and their everyday lives. It would be simplistic to describe *Ten Weddings* as a documentation of Ukrainian customs and prairie communities, a record of one particular family and their ten children, or a prairie landscape. Of equal importance is Harbuz's highly analytical response to the interplays between private and public realms and to the enforcement of "acceptable" behaviour through the institutions of marriage, family, and heterosexuality.

In *Ten Weddings*, as in many of Harbuz's paintings, the obvious starting point is a specific cultural ritual associated with traditional Ukrainian-Canadian rural communities. But the scanning of social geography and the mapping of specific life events quickly move beyond the more immediate cultural innuendoes and geographical sites. In *Ten Weddings* the children not only grow up, marry and start lives of their own, they leave parents and grandparents, small towns, and rural communities behind. The procession of newlyweds, all bound for the skyscrapers looming in the distance also comments on the process (and price) of widespread urbanization and cultural assimilation, a situation which Ann Harbuz's generation would have experienced firsthand.

In these and other works, it is her own world upon which Harbuz casts a critical gaze — not to judge, nor as a distancing manoeuvre, but to make visible people, places, events, histories, and interactions whose marginal social status all too easily casts them aside.

Over and over again Harbuz's images offer astute observations of culturally coded conventions, pointing both to what it means to inhabit specific bodies and to the ways life experience is socially ordered. As art historian Griselda Pollock (1992: 140) has written, while both men and women artists have "the right to enjoy *being the body* of the painter" at work in their studio, not all bodies are equally positioned or enjoy situations which allow the time and energy to actualize active artistic practices. Ann Harbuz was never able to completely leave her domestic responsibilities behind, nor did she live under conditions in which making art was highly valued. Nonetheless in her sixties, as she turned more fully to her art practice, she found ways of integrating her art into the rest of her life. Easels of half-finished paintings were in easy reach of the dining room table, the television set, or a pot of soup simmering on the stove. Clearly this dynamic home environment was multipurpose — but the sheer volume of paintings, hung salon style, everywhere visible and always changing, announced that art was finally taking precedence.

In many of Harbuz's images and painted objects, we witness a preoccupation with the material conditions of everyday life. Within a contemporary visual arts context, a younger and more theoretically motivated generation of artists have also explored how social relations, economic realities, and material conditions impact on people's lives. For example, Canadian artist Germaine Koh (about sixty years Harbuz's junior) has been knitting a blanket started in 1992 that she plans to knit for the rest of her life. About this project (*Knitwork*) Koh says, "I was thinking about how people labour for their whole lives and don't see the result of it" (Barnard 1996: 83). In *Knitwork*, a blanket with a beginning but no end, Koh utilizes the process of knitting as a tangible record of daily time. As a part of the gallery installation, Koh sits in the gallery space with her evolving blanket, actively engaged in the knitting process; her presence (or performance) connects the convention of knitting, the women who knitted, and the time and labour devoted to knitting, to a space of display — a space which both commemorates and legitimizes cultural value.

Ann Harbuz referred to her representations of endless acts of labour as her "busy pictures." Germaine Koh suggests her repetitive knitting actions are a "recuperation not only of traces of human lives and customs, but also and above all the recuperation of time" (Couëlle 1994: 42–43). Whereas Ann Harbuz moved at an accelerated pace so that she would have something of value to leave behind, Koh connects the process of knitting with an attempt to slow time down. In the medium of painting (significantly a "fine art" tradition), Harbuz found a form that could validate her "undisciplined," "self-trained," and "unorthodox" style. In the medium of knitting, Koh found a form and an activity that is regarded to be outside the fine art tradition, in fact reminding us of individuals like Harbuz whose labour and practices are all too easily misunderstood or forgotten. For both artists contact with the gallery system was an important step in establishing a context of cultural value. Through her appropriation of a fine art convention as well as through subsequent exhibitions, Harbuz found a forum where her ideas, her unique vision, and her particular form of articulation gained recognition and intellectual currency.

1. The exhibition catalogue is available at many public and university libraries as well as through the Dunlop Art Gallery, P.O. Box 2311, 2311 12th Ave., Regina, SK S4P 3Z5.

2. I have started to use the term social landscape in my attempt to extend descriptions and interpretations of art that has largely been categorized as "folk art" or "self-taught." In many works by Saskatchewan-based artists such as William McCargar, Molly Lenhardt, Dmytro Stryjek and Ann Harbuz, landscape takes on complicated social meanings, a space touched by intimate exchanges, daily experience, history and local knowledge.

3. Harbuz produced five paintings titled *Ten Weddings*. Each painting is unique, but all five versions contain the same compositional structure highlighting a diagonal row of ten outdoor wedding receptions.

REFERENCES

Barnard, Elissa. 1996. "The 250-Pound Blanket." *Halifax Chronicle Herald* (February 9).

Couëlle, Jennifer. 1994. "Il était une fois, le temps qui fuit." *Etc Montréal* (February 15–May 15).

Pollock, Griselda. 1992. "Painting, Feminism. History." In M. Narratt and A. Phillips (eds.), *Destabilizing Theory*. Cambridge: Polity Press.

Shields, Carol. 1993. *Swann*. Toronto: Stoddart.

Winterson, Jeanette. 1995. *Art Objects: Essays on Ecstasy and Effrontery*. Toronto: Alfred A. Knopf.

64

Chinese 5 Spice

Marisa Anlin Alps

My mother's hands smell of ginger
traces of sesame oil, Chinese 5 spice
the colour of miso, her long fingers
sift through the black mushrooms and
vegetables piled on the kitchen counter.
Shaping our meals with necessity,
garden soil and clay caught beneath
her nails, she washes her artist's hands
before she digs out the rice pot and
pours herself a glass of wine, sips
it as she stirs and simmers,
scented steam rising to greet the light.

My father's hands are wide and
lined with rough work, his fingers
blunt, stained with nicotine, the
coarse red hairs burnt short
near the nails. They smell of the sea,
salt ropes and diesel engines, of the
sails stored in the forepeak.
The other woman, my mother
says of *Carlota*, her sleek lines
hug the ocean like a lover,
moving with the wind in rhythm.

My father's best dish is eggs and toast,
but he relishes my mother's meals
like a gourmet, serving up lavish compliments,
recreating them in air — their flavours,
spices, aromas — they are closest to his
heart and heaven. He touches her hand and
murmurs *Mei Mei* before his half-finished
plate calls him back to earth.

This is how I see them together, here at the table.
Hands joined, the dark and the pale,
my mother's black hair, my father's red
my brother and I a blend of their own
particular recipes: a trace of her epicanthic fold,

a dash of his freckles, a hint of her oval face,
a seasoning of his wide shoulders,
a shade of her brown skin.

NOTE

Marisa Anlin Alps, 1999, "Chinese 5 Spice," in Andy Quan and Jim Wong-Chu, (eds.), *Swallowing Clouds: An Anthology of Chinese-Canadian Poetry*, Vancouver: Arsenal Pulp. Reprinted with permission.

Becoming a Lesbian Mother

Fiona Nelson

Since 1988 I have been talking with women in Alberta about their experiences of becoming mothers for the first time; here I focus primarily on lesbian mothers. There are several means by which a woman can become a lesbian mother. She might conceive through heterosexual intercourse as the result of a primary heterosexual relationship or in the context of a more "casual" heterosexual encounter. Alternatively, she might use donor insemination, purchase semen through a sperm bank and be inseminated by a medical professional; she might have an intermediary who would transport fresh semen from an anonymous donor and then self-inseminate or be inseminated by her partner. Finally, she might use the sperm of a man known to her, who might or might not be involved later in the child's life.

These are the main ways a lesbian woman could become a *biological* mother. Until recently, intercourse has been the most common. A sizable proportion of lesbian mothers conceived their children in prior heterosexual relationships, often marriages. After becoming mothers they came out as lesbian and, in many instances, moved on to lesbian relationships (very often taking their children with them). These women, in general, became lesbian mothers by being mothers first and then establishing a lesbian identity. In the past twenty years, however, based on my own observations (there is no scientifically compiled data), a virtual baby boom in the Canadian lesbian community has occurred, with growing numbers of couples and single lesbian women opting for donor insemination. These women become lesbian mothers by establishing a lesbian identity first and then pursuing motherhood.

There are also numerous non-biological means by which lesbian women might become mothers. A single lesbian woman, or a lesbian couple, might adopt a baby/child through public, private or international adoption. Adoption laws are complex, varying by country and province. There has, thus, not been consistent access to adoption by lesbian women across Canada, although recent years have seen a liberalization of adoption laws. A lesbian woman might also become a mother because she has entered into a relationship with a woman who had children in a prior heterosexual or lesbian relationship. An increasingly common route to motherhood is to be the non-biological mother in a relationship where the partner conceives by donor insemination. In these latter instances, where one of the mothers is a biological mother, the non-biological mother might legally adopt the child(ren), or pursue other avenues of legal protection of her relationship with the child(ren). The laws surrounding this sort of adoption have been debated province-by-province with access to adoption increasing across the country.

Simply considering the many ways in which lesbian (and, of course, non-lesbian) women can become mothers raises the question of what motherhood actually is. How does one become a mother and is it merely a legal status or something more? Whose recognition counts when it comes to being recognized as a mother?

Being a mother is not simply a biological condition; nor does it rest solely on the roles played or tasks completed; rather "mother" is an extremely complex and highly contested status. Sociologists speak of motherhood as an "achieved status," denoting that it is achieved through some effort that places women in a new social category. For a status to be achieved, however, there must be some recognition and acknowledgement, individual and/or institutional, that the status *has* been achieved. The individuals and institutions empowered to recognize and acknowledge some people as mothers exist in a myriad of social contexts. Each individual and institution carries a different weight of authority, and they may certainly, at times, disagree with each other. We can conceptualize these individuals and institutions as a web within which mothers (and non-mothers) exist and struggle to identify themselves and to achieve recognition and acknowledgement from others.

There are seven distinct, though broadly defined, "bodies" that are empowered to recognize and validate the status of "mother." The first of these is the state, which legislates who may and may not consider themselves "mother," "father" or "family." Canadian law has traditionally and formally recognized a birth mother but the status of her lesbian partner has been less clear, respected or protected, although this situation is gradually changing. The law is an important (albeit slow) instrument of change. Since 2005, same-sex marriage has been legal across Canada. Adoption laws vary by province and territory, but these laws are changing in the direction of greater access, regardless of sexual identity.

Second are religious/spiritual bodies (such as churches, synagogues, and temples), which can play a vital role for many people in identifying what is an appropriate family form. Conservative faith-based groups have been vocal in Canada, and elsewhere, in arguing that gay and lesbian people should not be recognized as families and should not be assisted or supported in the raising of children. On the other hand, many faith-based groups have offered support and blessings for lesbian and gay couples and families.

Third is the health-care industry, which plays a role in deciding who is most deserving of motherhood (e.g., in fertility clinics) and who can call or consider herself a "mother" (e.g., a birth mother's lesbian partner sometimes cannot. Lesbian women seeking medically assisted insemination have struggled occasionally with sperm banks, fertility clinics and/or doctors over getting assistance, as well as recognition of non-biological lesbian mothers as "mothers" and one of the parents who can be at the birth.

Fourth is that nebulous entity, society at large. For most people, "society at large" is experienced most saliently in the form of friends, acquaintances, neighbours, and co-workers. In a society where a woman can lose her job or home and be ostracized, harassed, assaulted, or even killed upon revealing her lesbianism, it can be difficult or dangerous for her to demand recognition as a lesbian mother. This situation can be particularly the case for non-biological lesbian mothers.

Fifth is the extended family, including family of origin and in-laws. Often the biological mother in a lesbian relationship is recognized by her parents, siblings, and other relatives as a mother, even if some family members are not comfortable with lesbianism. The partner of a woman who conceives by donor insemination can have a more difficult time convincing her family members to acknowledge that she is also the mother of the child. A woman who conceived while in a prior heterosexual relationship will almost definitely be recognized as a mother although her family might resist identifying her as a *lesbian* mother. This woman's lesbian partner may have a harder time being recognized by anyone as a mother to her partner's children.

The sixth body regulating "mother" status is the created family including such members as spouse/partner, other birth children, and step-children. To establish or maintain an identity of "mother" if one's immediate family members do not support it can be very difficult. When lesbian couples conceive by donor insemination, both women are likely to acknowledge each other as equally "mother" and to be equally primary to the children, even if, as sometimes happens, only one of them is called "mom." We might expect that this equality or symmetry of motherhood would also be the case for couples who enter motherhood together through adoption. In families in which children were conceived in a prior relationship, resistance on the part of the biological mothers and especially the children in recognizing the lesbian partner as "mother" can occur. In families in which children were conceived in heterosexual relationships and their biological mothers later came out as lesbian, an inability to imagine or understand what possible role a second mother might play often exists. Conceptualizing dual-motherhood seems to be much easier for couples who embark on motherhood together.

The seventh group is other mothers. I set this group apart from "society at large" because other mothers, as a group and as individuals, have particular kinds of power to informally regulate who can call herself "mother" and what it means to do so. The ability to enter, as a mother, into maternal discourse with other mothers is a key component in claiming the identity of mother. A mother is not merely a woman who takes care of her children; she is a woman who is acknowledged and treated *as a mother* by other mothers. I would argue, in fact, that there exists a "culture of motherhood," a social space shared by women who have been recognized by others as mothers. Biological lesbian mothers are generally accepted into this "club" but can feel marginalized because of the homophobia that they sometimes encounter from other mothers. Non-biological mothers can feel rejected because of their lesbianism and the perceived tenuousness of their claim to be mothers.

Being a Lesbian Mother

All women who journey into and through motherhood are embedded in this matrix of socio-cultural bodies with which they engage on a daily basis. We can begin to see how "becoming a mother" can be a much more straightforward process for some women (generally, married, heterosexual, white women who conceived through intercourse with their husbands) than for others. We cannot consider all the complexities here, but we can briefly explore a very small part of the journey into the culture of motherhood as it is experienced by partnered lesbian women who conceived by donor insemination.

Once lesbian women are visibly pregnant, other pregnant women and mothers interact with them in fairly predictable ways. General and often very public questions — Is this your first? When are you due? Do you want a boy or a girl? — serve as an initiation into the culture of motherhood. A pregnant lesbian woman can pursue these conversations although there is often a limit to how far the conversation can progress before she would have to either lie about her relationship/sexual identity or come out to the questioning stranger. Her partner really has no "in" to these conversations at all. As one of the non-biological lesbian mothers in my recent research pointed out, in order to engage in the pregnant-mommy talk, you really have to be pregnant; to be "expecting" in more abstract ways does not generally suffice.

A non-gestational lesbian mother, however, is in fact an expectant mother for the same length of time as is her partner. She has likely been involved in the pregnancy since the decision-making stage and may have been the person who inseminated her partner. Without the visible pregnancy, however, she tends not to be accepted into pregnancy chats with other mothers and pregnant women. Often, it is the gestational mother's responsibility to keep her partner feeling connected to the journey into motherhood, connected to the baby and connected, as a mother, to the family unit. In my research, lesbian couples who had sperm donors actively involved with the pregnancy and child-care found that making people understand that there were two mothers and a father was even more difficult than when only lesbian partners were involved. Health-care practitioners, for example, were likely to acknowledge only the birth-mother and the father. Non-gestational mothers in these families reported that they also felt very threatened and marginalized during the pregnancy by the presence of the donor/father, but these feelings subsided once the baby was born and both women became the custodial parents and primary care-givers.

Commonly, new mothers, even if they are strangers to each other, exchange birth stories. Gestational lesbian mothers can certainly enter into these conversations although they may feel the need to reveal or hide their lesbianism. The non-gestational mother, who is also the child's mother, is at a severe disadvantage here. Heterosexual adoptive mothers can, with reasonable impunity, admit that they adopted. A non-gestational lesbian mother is in a much more awkward situation. This mother must deal not only with the possibility of homophobia but also with the difficulty that other mothers might have even in recognizing her as a mother and including her in maternal conversations. Thus, she can, for the sake of casual conversations in parks and stores, face great effort and risk. One lesbian mother describes her experiences as follows:

> Mothers are funny like at… playgrounds or whatever they'll say things like "oh yeah how was the… birth?"… I'll answer as best I can and sometimes I find I'm irritated. Ah, but I'm irritated not at them asking me questions, I'm irritated that it's such a process to, to have to tell people, and be outed, and educate and you know sometimes you don't want to do it. I just want to go to the park and play with my kids.

Although a significant part of establishing oneself in the culture of motherhood in the beginning, the exchange of birth stories does die down, and the non-gestational status of the mother can then become much less significant. Heterosexual adoptive mothers can, to a large extent, simply blend in, but doing so is much more difficult for lesbian mothers. Often, they still have to explain each woman's relationship to the child and to each other.

There are many different ways to become a mother, and all mothers, regardless of sexual orientation, must negotiate maternal identity and status through interactions with other people and social institutions. Variations in personal and cultural beliefs about family, about gender roles and about sexual orientations, can make these negotiations particularly complex for lesbian mothers. These complexities are not intrinsic to lesbianism or lesbian families; they arise from the social context within which lesbian families exist.

REFERENCES

Aizley, Harlyn (ed.). 2006. *Confessions of the Other Mother: Nonbiological Lesbian Moms Tell All*. Boston: Beacon Press.

Arnup, Katherine. 1995. *Lesbian Parenting: Living with Pride and Prejudice*. PEI: Gynergy Books.

Clunis, M., and G.D. Green. 1995. *Lesbian Parenting Book: A Guide to Creating Families and Raising Children*. New York: Avalon.

Howey, N., and E. Samuels (eds.). 2000. *Out of the Ordinary: Essays on Growing Up with Gay, Lesbian, and Transgender Parents*. New York: St. Martin's Press.

Johnson, S.M., and E. O'Connor. 2001. *For Lesbian Parents*. New York: Guilford Publications.

Lehmann, J.M. (ed.). 2001. *The Gay and Lesbian Marriage and Family Reader: Analyses of Problems and Prospects for the 21st Century*. New York: Gordian Knot Books.

Nelson, Fiona. 2009. *In the Other Room: Entering the Culture of Motherhood*. Halifax and Winnipeg: Fernwood

Publishing.

___. 2007. "Lesbian Motherhood: Love and Challenge." In Vangie Bergum and Jeanne VanderZalm (eds.), *Motherlife*. Edmonton: Pedagon Press.

___. 1996. *Lesbian Motherhood: An Exploration of Canadian Lesbian Families*. Toronto: University of Toronto Press.

Sullivan, Maureen. 2004. *Family of Woman: Lesbian Mothers, Their Children, and the Undoing of Gender*. California: University of California Press.

Sullivan, T.R. (ed.). 1999. *Queer Families, Common Agendas: Gay People, Lesbians, and Family Values*. New York: Haworth Press.

Tasker, F., and J.J. Bigner (eds.). 2007. *Gay and Lesbian Parenting: New Directions*. New York: Haworth Press.

Tasker, Fiona L., and Susan Golombok. 1997. *Growing Up in a Lesbian Family: Effects on Child Development*. New York: Guilford Press.

Thompson, J.M. 2002. *Mommy Queerest: Contemporary Rhetorics of Lesbian Maternal Identity*. Amherst, MA: University of Massachusetts Press.

66

Her/s

Elizabeth MacKenzie

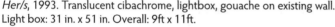

Her/s, 1993. Translucent cibachrome, lightbox, gouache on existing wall.
Light box: 31 in. x 51 in. Overall: 9ft x 11ft.

My first child was born in 1988 and in the years that followed, during which I gave birth to two other children, it became increasingly important for me, both as an artist and as a mother, to find a way to interrogate popular media's representations of pregnancy and maternity.

Pregnancy can be described as a marginal state of existence that is fraught with ambiguity since it continually calls into question the boundaries of self. Most current representations endeavour to simplify and clarify the process of pregnancy and therefore subdue anxiety. These representations promote the notion that pregnancy involves two separate individuals — the fetus and the pregnant woman.

Her/s, which consists of a photo light box and text painted directly on the gallery wall, was first exhibited in 1993. It came out of my desire to address some of the ambiguities surrounding representations of pregnancy, maternity and the female body as a site of reproductive function.

The word "Her/s" can be understood to mean possession or the (ungrammatical) plural of "her." Meanwhile the woman in the photograph shakes her head in a gesture of negation, which renders her identity anonymous, while the features of the startlingly visible and oversize embryo remain clear. Her/s represents the confusion of identity and personhood that occurs within pregnancy, making it difficult to make clear distinctions between oneself and another.

This movement between identification and estrangement, longing and aversion continues to represent my practice as a mother and an artist.

Subject: Mother's Day: This Is A Lovely Thing
Date: Tue, 23 May 2000 08:31:44 -0600
From: C. Lesley Biggs <lesley.biggs@usask.ca>
To: <undisclosed recipients>

Hi Everyone,

I have read a number of versions about the origins of Mother's Day. This is an interesting one!

Cheers,

Lesley

Happy Mother's Day To All:

> >Mothers' Day Proclamation: Julia Ward Howe, Boston, 1870
> >
> >Mother's Day was originally started after the U.S. Civil War, as a
> >protest to the carnage of that war, by women who had lost their
> >sons. Here is the original Mother's Day Proclamation from 1870:
> > ....
> >
> >Arise, then, women of this day! Arise all women who have hearts!
> >
> >Say firmly: "We will not have great questions decided by
> >irrelevant agencies. Our husbands shall not come to us, reeking
> >with carnage, for caresses and applause. Our sons shall not be
> >taken from us to unlearn all that we have been able to teach
> >them of charity, mercy and patience.
> >
> >We women of one country will be too tender of those of another
> >country to allow our sons to be trained to injure theirs. From
> >the bosom of the devastated earth a voice goes up with our own.
> >It says "Disarm, Disarm! The sword of murder is not the balance
> >of justice."
> >
> >Blood does not wipe our dishonor nor violence indicate possession.
> >As men have often forsaken the plow and the anvil at the summons
> >of war, let women now leave all that may be left of home for a

> >great and earnest day of counsel. Let them meet first, as women,
> > >to bewail and commemorate the dead.
> >
> > >Let them then solemnly take counsel with each other as to the
> > >means whereby the great human family can live in peace, each
> > >bearing after their own time the sacred impress, not of Caesar,
> > >but of TRUTH.
> >
> > >In the name of womanhood and of humanity, I earnestly ask that a
> > >general congress of women without limit of nationality may be
> > >appointed and held at some place deemed most convenient and at
> > >the earliest period consistent with its objects, to promote the
> > >alliance of the different nationalities, the amicable settlement
> > >of international questions, the great and general interests of
> > >peace.
> >
> > >Julia Ward Howe
> > >Boston
> > >1870

Childcare and
Mothers' Dilemmas

Susan Prentice

As a feminist sociologist, I research and write about family policy and social movements. My specialty is childcare policy in Canada, past and present. I am also active as a childcare advocate trying to develop a universal childcare system for all children who need or want it. Being a feminist "expert" on childcare at the same time as being a mother who uses childcare means I live with some striking contradictions every day. First, even on two good salaries, the expense of childcare is a squeeze. Our fees have dropped a bit since our children are no longer toddlers, but they're still around $9,000 a year — more than our Winnipeg mortgage. I also know, acutely painfully, that my ability to work and use childcare is at the expense of the childcare staff who are grossly underpaid for the important work they do. Finally, I live with the troubled knowledge that our children have the privilege of enriching, high quality care, but most children — some of whom need it more — don't have that privilege.

Childcare Crisis

The fastest way to understand why daycare is a political issue in Canada is to count: according to the 2006 census, Canada has about 2 million preschool children (birth to six) and 2.7 million school-aged children (seven to twelve). Among these nearly five million children, over three million have mothers in the paid labour force (Friendly et al. 2007). Dual-earner families are the norm, yet few policies and supports are in place to enable parents to combine employment and caregiving. Childcare is also needed when one or both parents are studying or in a training program. Salaried parents, in all their variety, are the parents we typically imagine when we think about childcare, but children and parents need early childhood care and education services for other reasons, too. Childcare is required if parents are to become involved in their communities, as volunteers or participants. Full-time homemakers may need or want childcare as respite from a job that is twenty-four hours per day, seven days a week. Some vulnerable children need childcare to promote appropriate development, or to provide social experiences. Childcare programs can welcome and help integrate newcomer children, as well as provide language exposure to children whose first language isn't English or French.

North Americans imagine that childcare is needed because a mother (or, less commonly, father) works for pay. For Canadians to argue that children should use early childhood care because it is good for them is highly unusual. In many European countries, by contrast, the common-sense assumption is that children need childcare because it provides many benefits to them and their families (Borchorst 1990; Jenson and Sineau 2001). Although this perception is relatively rare in Canada, it is supported by research. High quality childcare promotes healthy physical, social and linguistic development, and helps prepare children for the education system. Childcare contributes to the life-long good health of children, mitigates poverty, creates jobs, facilitates economic self-reliance and helps build healthy, safer and often more inclusive communities. When children play together in inclusive early childhood programs, they grow to appreciate diversity, and this in turn promotes equity among classes, levels of ability, racial and ethnic groups, and generations. For children, parents and communities, good childcare is a way to strengthen social solidarity.

Childcare and Women's Equality

Feminists have thought long and hard about childcare. Feminist theorizing and advocacy have been oriented to the dual goals of providing high quality childcare for children and their families, and doing so in ways that respect caregivers — whether those caregivers are mothers at home or paid staff. For feminists, the question has been: how can we organize care in an egalitarian way, respecting the diversity of children and parents and adequately compensating caregivers?

Using these criteria, traditional ways of caring for children fail the equality test. Caring for children — what some have called "mother-work" — is definitely labour. Male partners rarely share the workload equally with full-time mothers, meaning the work of childcare in families falls more heavily on women. The current ideal of "intensive mothering" means that women are always on-duty as mothers twenty-four hours a day, seven days a week, whether they are in or out of paid employment (Hays 1996). Yet, when women take time away from the labour force, they lose ground economically — jeopardizing career advancement and missing out on pension time and contributions. Evidence also shows that women who don't contribute to household finances typically have less decision-making power and authority within the family (England and Kilbourne 1990; Folbre 2001). When relationships end, formerly stay-at-home mothers all too often find themselves paying a very heavy price, as women's standard of living tends to fall after divorce and single mothers disproportionately raise children in poverty.

Some families turn to nanny-care as their alternative to full-time mother-care. Surprisingly little is known about nannies in Canada. Most frequently, families with nannies are affluent; nannies are expensive. A family seeking a nanny generally relies on immigrant women hired through the Live-In Caregiver Program (LCP). Many immigrant nannies are mothers who have left their own children behind to seek work in Canada. For these women, being a nanny is often exploitative. Under the LCP program, they risk deportation if they don't live with their employers for a minimum of two years. Employers deduct room and board from wages; working hours are almost always more than eight hours a day; and over-time pay is rare. Moreover, stories of violence and sexual exploitation are all too common. Compound these troubles with the reality many nannies confront as visible minorities in a racist society, and the "nanny" solution loses much of its gloss (Bakan and Stasiulus 1997).

Most families use the "gray market" of unlicensed care, a sort of underground (although not illegal) work. Typically, informal care providers can care for up to four or more children at a time before they are required to be licensed, but being unregulated creates problems for all involved. Parents and children lack safety and quality assurances. Informal providers rarely have early childhood education training, and few are able to offer a developmentally appropriate program to children. Informal providers often receive poor wages; many do not report their incomes. As a result, they often do not give parents receipts for childcare fees; parents in turn are unable to claim a portion of their childcare costs at income tax time. Informal care providers are also not covered by occupational legislation; if they are injured on the job (for example, with the steady stooping and lifting of children), they aren't covered for workplace injuries. Nor do they contribute to Employment Insurance or Canada Pension Plans, leaving them without resources if they become unemployed, and pensionless when they retire.

In contrast to full-time mothering, nannies, or unlicensed care, high-quality childcare centres, with well-paid and well-trained staff, can provide both excellent quality care to children and rewarding jobs to adults. Unfortunately, however, regulated childcare in Canada usually falls short of this ideal. The biggest reason is cost. Parents who need childcare must pay for it themselves. Across the country, preschool fees are commonly $7,000 or more a year per child. In most provinces, very low-income parents qualify for some fee subsidy. But the number of parents who need subsidies vastly outstrips the supply. As a result, in most childcare centres, parents are cleaved by class; they are typically either high-income earners who can afford full fees, or are extremely low-income families who have qualified for scarce subsidies. The great numbers of middle-income Canadians are "too rich" to qualify for subsidies, but find they can't afford to pay the fees.

The exception to this grim scenario is Quebec (Jenson 2001). Since 1997, Quebec has been building a universal childcare program. The province today has a childcare place for more than 34 percent of children aged birth to twelve. Quebec parents, whether they are employed, in school, or out of the labour market, pay the lowest fees in North America for early learning and childcare services, at just $7 per day per child. As in most European countries, the provincial government directly funds most of the costs of the system, meaning parent fees can be very low. The Quebec system is expensive, costing the province over $1 billion annually, but it is enormously popular with parents. Economists are supportive too because they've calculated that the generous childcare system has enabled more mothers to join the paid labour force. The increase in government revenues from taxes paid by newly employed parents is sufficient to cover 40 percent of the public cost of childcare each year (Baker, Gruber and Milligan 2006). Longer term, many economists calculate that childcare services more than pay for themselves.

Outside Quebec, the small supply of expensive childcare is nevertheless a lifeline for some parents. Yet childcare workers, 98 percent of whom are women, find themselves in jobs that are far from ideal (Doherty et al. 2000). The work of caring for children is physically and emotionally demanding, yet salaries and benefits don't begin to compensate. Although most childcare workers have specialized training and post-secondary education, they earned an average of just $21,519 in 2001, about sixty-two percent of the average full-time income for women, and home-based childcare providers earned even less. The saddest fact might be that most childcare workers discover, when they become parents, that they earn too little to afford childcare for their own children. Across the country, many trained staff are choosing to leave the childcare field for better paying jobs — a choice that can scarcely be faulted. The scenario for Quebec early childhood educators is significantly better: their pay and social status have risen considerably since the new childcare system began developing over a decade ago.

The Future of Childcare in Canada

Answers to why childcare is so under-developed in most of Canada vary widely. Some analysts attribute under-development to sexist ideology and the belief that families (read: "mothers") should be the primary caregivers. Others point out that prejudices against group care and ignorance about the importance of the early years explains why governments haven't acted. The federal government hasn't seen childcare as an essential public service — though several plans have been batted around over recent years. Unlike health care or education, each of which is seen as an entitlement of Canadian citizens, childcare is virtually absent from the political radar screen. In contrast, progressive European governments believe that work-family integration is a problem that they must help to solve (Knijn and Kremer 1997).

Some critics have deplored the women's movement's call for a universal childcare system.

These critics include conservatives who want to restore a nostalgic by-gone era of full-time mothers and breadwinning fathers, as well as a handful of more progressive critics who argue that the real problem is the low social value associated with caregiving and children. The solution, according to groups like Mothers Are Women, is to find ways to ensure full-time mothering is remunerated, not to build a national childcare system.

Such criticisms must make feminists pause. Would a Canadian system of universal high-quality, affordable care be a sign that our country didn't respect "caring," and was retreating from valuing women's traditional roles? Is it anti-feminist to want to redistribute the work of caring for children? As feminists we certainly want to affirm the importance of care and nurturance. It would be a perverse twist if feminism were seen to be saying that caring for children is so awful we want to hire workers so that we don't have to do it ourselves. But it seems equally untenable to insist that it is only parents — indeed only mothers — who must privately provide care to children at the expense of their own ability to participate in the world of paid work and community.

Many changes are needed to support children and their parents. Among them are shifts in how we organize and regulate the world of paid work. More employers need to develop (and pay for) policies that contribute to what used to be called work-family balance (now known as work-life reconciliation). Employers should provide their employees with maternity, parental and adoption leaves, as well as flexible policies to reconcile work and family. Creating work-family balance must include, at a minimum, family-friendly provincial legislation as well as more generous federal payment programs to support provincial childcare delivery. Solutions will be inadequate without greater involvement by men in the rewarding and demanding world of small children and domestic life — meaning our deepest ideas about gender must be radically shifted. Yet supporting children and their parents will also require a universal, publicly funded, high-quality system of childcare, even with all these other changes in place.

Childcare advocates have developed a set of principles for quality childcare in Canada (Friendly and Prentice 2009) arguing that, with these principles enacted, childcare would do the double job of providing quality care to children and respecting caregivers. The principles are as follows:

- regulated, licensed services;
- universal provision (including all children, regardless of income, class, ability or disability, region and parents' work status);
- high quality (reflecting best practices and a participatory approach to quality improvement and assurance);
- comprehensiveness (a systematic and integrated approach to policy development and implementation, including a range of service choices for all children and families);
- responsiveness (reflecting community values and diversity, as well as including community and parental input);
- accountability (services are responsible to the communities served and good governance is present);
- non-profit auspice (ensuring all dollars are directed to program and staff, making the most effective use of funds and providing highest quality care).

In combination with other public- and private-sector policies and far-reaching changes in gender norms, childcare can offer some resolution to the old but still contemporary problem that Carol Pateman calls "Wollstonecraft's Dilemma" (Pateman 1992). Like Mary Wollstonecraft so long ago, today's feminists are torn between wanting to validate and support women's caring work and wanting to liberate women from such work. A system of universal childcare can answer Wollstonecraft's dilemma: it could affirm, redistribute and adequately remunerate care-giving, and it would enable mothers (indeed all parents) to get jobs or education, participate in civil society and/or have leisure time. Childcare can support women (and children) in *both* the "public" *and* the "private" sphere. This is why feminists are working toward a universal childcare system for all Canadian children and their families.

REFERENCES

Bakan, A., and D. Stasiulus. 1997. *Not One of the Family: Foreign Domestic Workers in Canada*. Toronto: University of Toronto.

Baker, M., J. Gruber and K. Milligan. 2006. *What Can We Learn from Quebec's Universal Childcare Program?* Toronto: C.D. Howe Institute.

Borchorst, A. 1990. "Political Motherhood and Child Care Policies: A Comparative Approach to Britain and Scandinavia." In C. Ungerson (ed.), *Gender and Caring: Work and Welfare in Britain and Scandinavia*. Hertfordshire: Harvester Press.

Doherty, G., D.S. Lero, H. Goelman and J. Tougas. 2000. *You Bet I Care: A Canada-wide Study on Wages, Working Conditions and Practices in Child Care Centres*. Guelph: Centre for Families, Work and Well-being, University of Guelph.

England, P., and B. Kilbourne. 1990. "Markets, Marriages, and Other Mates: The Problem of Power." In R. Friedland and A.F. Robertson (eds.), *Beyond the Marketplace*. Hawthorne, NY: Aldine de Gruyter.

Folbre, N. 2001. *The Invisible Heart: Economics and Family Values*. New York: New Press.

Friendly, M., J. Beach, C. Ferns and M. Turiano. 2007. *Early Childhood Education and Care in Canada 2006* seventh ed. Toronto: Childcare Resource and Research Unit.

Friendly, M., and S. Prentice. 2009. *About Canada: Childcare*. Halifax and Winnipeg: Fernwood Publishing.

Hays, S. 1996. *The Cultural Contradictions of Motherhood*. New Haven: Yale University Press.

Jenson, J. 2001. "Family Policy, Child Care and Social Solidarity: The Case of Quebec." In S. Prentice (ed.), *Changing Childcare: Five Decades of Childcare Policy and Advocacy in Canada*. Halifax: Fernwood Publishing.

Jenson, J., and M. Sineau (eds.). 2001. *Who Cares? Women's Work, Childcare and Welfare State Redesign*. Toronto: University of Toronto Press.

Knijn, T., and M. Kremer. 1997. "Gender and the Caring Dimension of Welfare States: Toward Inclusive Citizenship." *Social Politics* 4,3.

Pateman, C. 1992. "Equality, Difference, Subordination: The Politics of Motherhood and Women's Citizenship." In G. Brock and S. James (eds.), *Beyond Equality and Difference*. New York: Routledge.

The Live-In Caregiver Program
Inequality Under Canada's Immigration System

Tami Friesen

The Live-in Caregiver Program (LCP) is a specialized program of Citizenship and Immigration Canada, which admits participants to Canada as temporary workers for up to three years. In exchange for completing twenty-four months of caregiving work for children, the elderly or the disabled in a private household, within three years of arriving in Canada, LCP participants are eligible to apply for permanent residence. Pursuant to the *Immigration and Refugee Protection Act Regulations*, participants must live in their employers' homes and are only allowed to work for the one employer named on their work permit. Working for another employer or living outside of their employer's home can result in a participant's removal from Canada. Participants can change employers, but only after receiving a new work permit through a lengthy bureaucratic process, which can take several months. (Details on the LCP are at: cic. gc.ca/english/pub/caregiver/index.html.)

While participants benefit from the opportunity to obtain permanent residence, the LCP fails to safeguard live-in caregivers from unfair and discriminatory treatment. A large majority of participants are women of colour. The onerous conditions of the LCP — temporary status, mandatory live-in requirement, employer-specific work permit, and twenty-four-month requirement — violate the fundamental rights of women and create vulnerability to economic, physical, sexual and psychological abuse. In fear of deportation, not being able to qualify for permanent residence, and of losing their home and income, caregivers are reluctant to change employers or lodge a complaint and often endure unbearable working and living conditions. Women under the LCP are often underpaid, work excessive hours, experience violations of privacy and receive inadequate food and accommodation. Caregivers may also experience social isolation, family separation and lack of awareness of their employment rights.

The unfair treatment and inequality inherent in the LCP is based on gender, race, and class. The federal government's rationale for the LCP is that there is a shortage of Canadians or permanent residents to fill the need for live-in care work. Arguably, the poor working conditions, low pay and stigma attached to domestic work helps to perpetuate this labour shortage. In addition, Canada's immigration selection criteria (the "point system" for independent immigrants) emphasize higher education and labour market participation in male-dominated occupations, and fail to recognize the economic disadvantage of women and the value of domestic work. Further, caregivers historically entered Canada with permanent resident status. When one examines the various caregiver immigration schemes over the past century, it becomes apparent that caregivers' legal status and rights in Canada began to deteriorate as caregivers' place of origin changed from Britain and other European countries to the Caribbean and the Philippines.

In an effort to ameliorate the unfair treatment of caregivers, the *Immigration and Refugee Protection Act Regulations* introduced the requirement of an employment contract for caregivers and their employers. The government's intent was to provide the fairest working arrangement for both parties and to create a clear understanding of expectations. However, an employment contract alone is insufficient to prevent exploitation of caregivers or to ensure clear avenues of assistance for caregivers. A contract's effectiveness requires an ability to negotiate contractual terms and strong enforcement mechanisms, both of which are lacking for live-in caregivers. There is a large power imbalance in the employer-employee relationship due to the restrictive conditions of the LCP, making fair negotiation a practical impossibility. Further, the federal government, despite having introduced the contract requirement, takes no responsibility for intervention or enforcement because the regulation of working conditions falls within the purview of provincial governments. Most provinces provide a complaint-driven enforcement model which, coupled with cutbacks to provincial employment standards, makes it especially difficult for live-in caregivers to access justice.

Community groups have long called for changes to the LCP to lessen these inequities, including granting caregivers permanent residence on arrival, abolishing the live-in requirement, providing caregivers with occupation-specific and not employer-specific work permits, decreasing the work requirement to one year, and a pro-active monitoring system of employers and employment conditions.

The United Nations Committee on the Elimination of Discrimination against Women recently heard these calls. In its draft report following its review of Canada's fifth report on compliance with the Convention on the Elimination of All Forms of Discrimination against Women (United Nations 2003) the Committee singled out the LCP, expressing its concern with caregivers' temporary status and the live-in requirement, stating:

> The Committee urges the State party to take further measures to improve the current live-in caregiver programme by reconsidering the live-in requirement, ensuring adequate social security protection and accelerating the process by which such domestic workers may receive permanent residency. (paragraph 42)

It is clear that the LCP, in its current form, is flawed and inequitable. Canada's immigration evaluation system requires modification to recognize the value of domestic work, the significant and unique contributions LCP participants make to Canadian society, and the human dignity of women.

NOTE

Tami Friesen, 2003, "The Live-In Caregiver Program: Inequality Under Canada's Immigration System," *Jurisfemme* 22,2 (Summer). At: nawl.ca/en/newlibrarypage/jurisfemme/68-jfvolume-22summer2003/303. Adapted and reprinted with permission.

REFERENCE

United Nations. 2003. "Convention on the Elimination of All Forms of Discrimination Against Women: The Fifth Periodic Report of Canada." Division for the Advancement of Women, Department of Economic and Social Affairs. At: un.org/womenwatch/daw/cedaw/ 28sess.htm.

Family Bed

Frances Robson

To my mother, whose warmth I will always remember.

The physical connection to my mother was very strong. With my own children and my husband, it is when I am touching them, snuggled cozily in bed at night that I feel the closest to them. This project evolved out of wanting to preserve, express and make visible those feelings of tenderness, intimacy and love. My desire to create this project was catalyzed when planning art goals with a photography class I was teaching in Kindersley, Saskatchewan. In addition to lifetime- and five-year goals, one of the questions asked, "What would you want to do with your art if you were going to die in six months?" I wanted to make lots of photographs of my family and me together, showing me with them in a way that would remind them of our closest moments and that I loved them very much. I also wanted the images to reveal for them who I was in my family as a person, mother and wife.

Thus, within my "Family Bed" work, I express my own experience of closeness and evolving identity in the growth of a family relationship. I visually capture candid glimpses of my personal space within my family, showing particularly the sometimes comforting, sometimes consuming feeling of being sandwiched in by flesh and of having a body that is very needed and is nurturing for others. The imagery centres on the body with the figures of myself, my husband, my daughter and our baby son engaged in the close physical connections of breastfeeding and sleeping in the family bed. Our body language, the shifting positions, tender embraces, pushing and crowding weave subtle images of dreams, hopes and fears from our inner lives. With sculptural grace, the resulting images are narrative, mythic and hauntingly dreamlike.

Process-wise, I made photos, from overhead, of my family sleeping in our bed. I used a camera on a boom with electronic flash. I programmed the camera to take a picture, for example, every fifteen minutes throughout the night or every two minutes at bed-time nursing. Over several months, more than twenty-five nights were photographed to draw upon in creating the "Family Bed" exhibition. The photographs are presented as very large contact sheets of thirty-five, thirty, or twenty shots and as shorter sequences of five and eleven images selected from a given night. To emphasize the sense of dreaminess, I used computer retouching techniques (Adobe Photoshop) to extend the bedsheets to the edge of the frame so it seems that the figures are lying/floating in a vast unending space.

This work is important in that it reveals a fresh particular example of one individual's experience of nurturing and closeness. This work is also political in that it expresses an experience of much physical intimacy — the warmth and tenderness of breastfeeding a toddler and sleeping with the whole family in one bed that is not practiced generally and is somewhat controversial in Western society with its stress on independence.

When we were expecting our first child, our midwives had encouraged family bed sleeping and we talked to other happy co-sleeping families whom we met through the Friends of the Midwives. We decided it would work for us. Since then, I have read *The Family Bed*

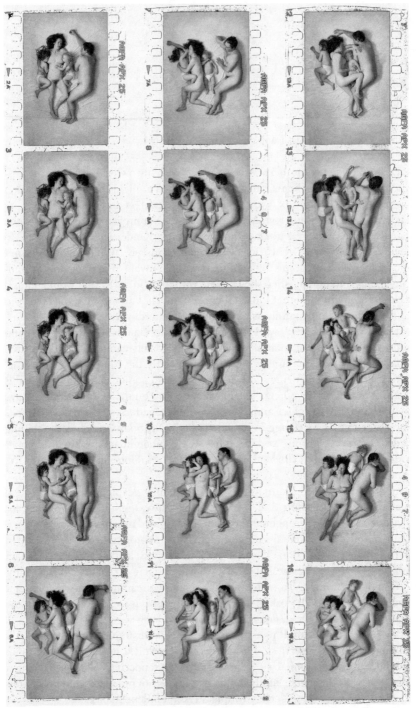

"Photographs made one night in January 1998 at 15-minute intervals." Medium: inkjet prints. Size: 48" X 57." Date: 2000. Reprinted with permission of Frances Robson.

"Photographs made one night in January 1998 at fifteen-minute intervals." Reprinted with permission of Frances Robson.

by Tine Thevenin (1987) and perused several internet sites[1] discussing the family bed, extended breastfeeding, and birth and bonding issues which seem to be all brought together in a widely followed approach called "Attachment Parenting." I became aware that family co-sleeping has always been common in many other cultures and parts of the world. Within my own family of origin, we all had separate beds, but my mother would come and warm up my bed and tell stories before I went to sleep. When she was a girl, as with many other pioneering families of the West, she slept in a bed with three of her siblings — two with their heads one way and two with their heads the other way — to make space in a family home with ten children.

This work will, I believe, promote discussion and consideration of the family bed and extended breastfeeding. While it presents a positive experience, it also explores some of the conflicts. It is sometimes difficult having to find other times or locations for parents' sexuality. Waiting for the children to get up and watch movies on weekend mornings is one solution to this creative challenge. A mate may feel left out sometimes. There are interruptions of sleep and frequent needs for milk and cuddling. After a lifetime of being alone in bed or with one mate, it is sometimes overwhelming to be a centre of attention and nurturing for a crowd. However, the rewards of closeness and of fostering my children's sense of security are more important.

I think the series also works as a symbol of the meaningful time and energy put into being a caregiver, being a partner and looking after oneself within a family. This work acknowledges the importance and complexity of family relationships and balance.

The work appeals to audiences on a more general level as well. Everyone sleeps and has curiosity about what goes on with his or her body during the night. What secret unconscious desires and relationships are expressed by their postures during sleep? Here we see the people move and squirm around, wiggle to the top or bottom of the bed, embrace and move apart, in a tender, sometimes humorous, dance-like choreography.

The archetypal family — youth and maturity in two generations — is suspended in time, resting, growing, dreaming, in a floaty infinite space. Within them flow the spirit, hope and meaning of the cycles of life and myths of creation.

NOTES

I would like to gratefully acknowledge the support of the Saskatchewan Arts Board, CARFAC Sask., The Photographers Gallery, my husband and children, and numerous very helpful friends and colleagues.

1. See, for example, bygpub.com/natural/family-bed.htm; breastfeeding.com; geocities.com/Heartland/8148/bed.htm.

REFERENCE

Thevenin, Tine. 1987. *The Family Bed*. New York: Perigree Books (Penguin/Putnam).

Dancing with Disability and Mothering

Examining Identity and Expectations

Heather Kuttai

When you were born, they looked at you and said, what a good girl, what a smart girl, what a pretty girl. (Page 1992)

Every so often, I look at a picture of myself from when I was six years old. A shiny cap of blond hair, a pair of big brown eyes, a smile that created a dimple in my left cheek, I admit it, I was cute. Gazing further down that picture reveals a dark green vinyl-upholstered, hospital-issued wheelchair — not so cute. No doubt about it, the combined image of that face and that wheelchair would be right at home on a charity poster and could have increased the number of pledges at a telethon. Looking at it, parents everywhere would be ever so much more grateful for their able-bodied children. Me, the ultimate poster child. Posters don't change, though, but I did. I grew up. Breasts, dating, sex, university, marriage, profession, childbirth are several of the veritable hallmarks of becoming a woman, a female person. Simple guides, prescriptions and scripts permeate the fabric of our society. But there are no simple scripts for a six-year-old with a spinal cord injury. That story, my story, is neither simple nor a fairy tale. Like many children, teens and adult women with a physical disability, I had to be my own author, simultaneously writing, revising and living an experience for which preparedness comes only in hindsight.

People see me/I'm a challenge to your balance/I'm over your heads/how I confound you and astound you/to know I must be one of the wonders of god's own creation. (Merchant 1995)

When my spinal cord was damaged in a motor vehicle accident at the age of six, my body changed forever. I didn't need the doctors to tell me that I had changed physically. What no one told me and which I had to learn by myself was that there were markedly different expectations for non-disabled girls my age. It seemed as though other people, like neighbours and teachers, for example, did not expect that I would do, never mind excel, at anything that was considered "normal." The adults in my life had no idea what life was going to be like for me or what they could expect for me. I was the only child with a disability in my school and one of few people who used a wheelchair in our community. Many times, the lack of expectations was best demonstrated by what was not said. I did not have the same predictions for the future as other girls my age seemed to. Rather, it was okay that I did not "get" math or if I did not complete the science labs because I could not reach the inaccessible microscope. While my scholastic success was not encouraged, similarly, thoughts concerning my physical attributes were not voiced. My girlfriend's fathers did not reciprocate the familiar ego-boosting banter that proud fathers shared amongst themselves. There was no mention of how "Heather will be a heartbreaker," for example. It was as though my disability interfered, or perhaps precluded and overshadowed, my attractiveness. My social currency had been altered. The pats on my head and the infantilized asexual reflection of me in their self-satisfied smiles reinforced, in my mind, that my lack of physical competency changed my present and future worth.

My adolescent years were some of the most confusing. Being able to demonstrate gender and sexuality roles were the heart of being seen as a capable actor in an adult female role. This was difficult for me to do considering the societal assumption that in order to be sexual one also needs to be physically able. Although my body was maturing with the height and curves similar to that of most young women, I still felt the need to prove that I was a "real" young woman, rather than an asexual kid in a wheelchair. For example, although I was probably not expected to attend my junior high school prom at age fourteen, and despite my anxiety over this social event, I needed to be there, to see myself reflected in the eyes of others as a young woman on the verge of being an actual woman. I needed to be beautiful, with my hair done, dress dazzling and skin exposed. It seemed extremely important to reshape the clay of my existence to fit into the mold of woman. To be what was denied, to be capable, sexual, and by consequence, valued was what I desperately wanted more than anything.

> I am 32 flavors and then some. I am beyond your peripheral vision so you might want to turn your head. (DiFranco 1995)

In university, I read and heard women complaining about being seen as sex objects. "For the ideal of beauty is administered as a form of self-oppression. Women are taught to see their bodies in parts, and to evaluate each part separately.... Nothing less than perfection will do" (Sontag 1990). I never had that experience. Instead, my experience was that, although I was seen as my body parts, it was because these parts were disabled. In addition, my body and my wheelchair were extremely visible and invisible simultaneously. It seemed that the wheelchair took up too much space and that my main, possibly only, definable characteristic was "disabled." Being seen as a "girl" or "woman" was a distant second, if it was considered an identifier at all, whereas my wheelchair and disabled body were the things that marked me.

> Lying deep in the dream of darkness/the soul of every child/has waited to be born a stranger/underneath the drum of his mother's heart. (Nielson-Chapman 1993)

Poster girl I may have been, poster woman — not likely; poster mother — not at all. In our culture a mother is syllogistically typified in the following way: a mother is an adult, an adult is a sexually capable person, a sexually capable person is physically capable. With three strikes against me, I again defied the rules dictated by convention and became not the studied "other" but an atypical mother. "Motherhood, the institution and experience that perhaps dominated all cultural conceptions of women — eclipsing even expectations of beauty, softness, or ever-present sexuality — often has been *proscribed* for a woman with a disability" (Fine and Asch 1988: 21, emphasis in the original). Informed by television, print, assorted other media instruments of cultural bombardment and the advice of similarly saturated friends, I understood the decision to have a baby is, more or less, the result of traditional expectations, childhood dreams, cheesy romance novels and peer pressure. Further, there is an assumption that having a baby is a natural progression in the life of a woman, pregnancy is "something they always wanted" or something they "always imagined themselves doing." Naturally there were for me, in total, zero expectations and therefore no childhood dreams, no novels, cheesy or otherwise, and no made-for-prime-time movies about pregnant women who used wheelchairs. So when I decided I wanted to "try" to become pregnant, it was not with exemplars of the "difficult but beautiful" struggle into motherhood, nor was it because it "felt" like the right time and place to "start a family." Rather, I knew I was capable of experiencing love beyond myself, beyond my physical limitations, beyond sex, beyond typical adult scripts.

In my internal assessment of capacity I felt reasonably confident that I could mother. On the pro side I had a healthy self-awareness, a solid education in sociology, women's studies, disability culture, history and rights, and a marriage with a loving partner. The cons, of course, began with the cultural claptrap and prescriptive role assumptions of a mother being physical, sexual and able. Concerns that I hadn't counted on stemmed from socialized, and yes, internalized assumptions that the physical-sexual-able triumvirate typifies the role of mother. Despite the fact that I lacked and/or was denied the norm-empowered freedom to identify and express myself as a sexual being, I became pregnant. On that life-changing night in the hospital, I sweated, I pushed, I bled, I tore, and yes, I, the poster child, gave birth; I became a mother.

Late nights, lost sleep, post-partum depression and five years of experience later, I have taken on a role that no one, not even I, can deny. I am Patrick's mother. When Patrick was an infant, I, like most young mothers, was overwhelmed and not at all confident in my abilities. Since there was no script for wheelchair using women to take on the role of mother, I was ill equipped to deal with this new part of my identity. I remember one time at 3 a.m. as I sat breast-feeding him, I thought about all the things I would never do with him. I mourned not being able to teach him how to ride a bike or go tobogganing with him. I especially grieved not being able to have a slow dance with him, which I believed to be a special mother-son bonding or rite-of-passage experience. In my mind, he should be tall and handsome and graduating from school or perhaps getting married, and I should be a proud mom wearing a dress with a made-for-dancing skirt and a big carnation pinned just below my left shoulder. He would glide me around the floor and everyone watching would acknowledge by their nods, smiles and approving looks that we were mother and son. The more I thought about this image, the sadder I became. I believed the image was not possible. That night I descended into a depression I had not known before. Struggling with my despair, I did the only thing that seemed natural, something that I had done frequently to comfort my young self in my bedroom or hospital bed whether by playing a soft stereo or through a pair of earphones or picking up my guitar. I simply sang to him. The singing calmed us both and helped him to sleep. Since then, I sing him to sleep each night that we are together. Singing, in my "mother's voice" not only works but has transformed a coping skill into a bonding experience.

Between his second and third years, my son's appreciation for music grew beyond the need to hear the soothing and sleep-instilling sound of his mother's voice. Like myself at his age, he constantly pressed me to play music on the stereo. One evening, a lullaby that I regularly sang to him, and one of the few children's songs I knew, began to play on the stereo. Patrick froze. He stopped his dancing and listened. "Visit the Moon" had begun playing. He walked over to me, stepped up on the footrest of my wheelchair, looked me in the eye and said, "Mommy, this is our song. Will you dance with me?" With tears in my eyes, I told him I'd love to. He put his arms around my waist and lay his head against my chest and we slowly danced to the entire song. It wasn't a special event that had brought us here. It was an ordinary day. While short and in desperate need of a haircut, he was undeniably handsome. We were not dressed in formal attire; we wore jeans and t-shirts. And there was no one watching. There was just the two of us, the music and the golden light of a prairie sunset pouring in through the windows, warming the room as we danced. I hope that if I am granted one memory to carry over in the moment before I die, it is that one.

> everything I do is judged/mostly I get it wrong, oh well/the bathroom mirror has not budged/the woman who lives there can tell/the truth from the stuff that they say/she looks me in the eye/would you prefer the easy way?/well okay, then don't cry... I do it for the joy it brings/because I'm a joyful girl/because the world owes me/nothing we owe each other the world... (DiFranco 1996)

How do I measure up as a mother? A woman pushing a wheelchair in a crowded shopping mall with a child crying at the top of his lungs and thrashing his body about in a tantrum generally attracts attention. Even in tranquil moments I know we are noticed. I also believe that if I am not being judged, I am, at the least, being evaluated. As a mother, how am I reflected in the eyes of others? At the best of times I feel that my biggest obstacle is the constant struggle to prove my motherly worth. "Parents, [with disabilities] especially mothers, feel judged harshly by other parents for common and slight mistakes. Many parents feel that their child must be cleaner and better behaved than others or they will be seen as inadequate parents unable to attend to their children's daily needs" (Olkin 1999: 130). Because I was not expected to be one, I feel pressure to be an exceedingly good, if not perfect, mother and I feel a lot of guilt when I struggle or make a mistake.

I know my self worth is not determined by my physical ability, my sexuality, or my capacity to be seen as an adult, but rather by the choices I make and the perspective I take. Despite the absence of scripts, I, like other women with disabilities, have become a capable author by necessity (Kuttai 2010). The fact that society values certain physical and sexual attributes or the rituals that contribute to our personal formation is not likely to change. At the same time a woman's sexual voice, a mother's voice, and her expectations are not easily captured in an all-encompassing image. Twenty-seven years later, as I gaze at a different image, this time in a family portrait (the brown eyes are the same, the blond hair has turned brown with a few stands of grey and the ugly hospital-issued wheelchair has now disappeared, replaced by a red, streamlined and dare I say it, sexy, model), how do I reflect on my efficacy as a mother? I am not sure but one thing is certain: the absence of prescribed scripts does not prevent me from writing, editing, evaluating and ultimately, choosing my own.

REFERENCES

DiFranco, Ani. 1996. "Joyful Girl." *Dilate*. Righteous Babe Records.
____. 1995. "32 Flavours." *Not a Pretty Girl*. Righteous Babe Records.
Fine, Michelle, and Adrienne Asch (eds.). 1988. *Women With Disabilities: Essays in Psychology, Culture, and Politics*. Philadelphia: Temple University Press.
Kuttai, Heather. 2010. *Maternity Rolls: Pregnancy, Childbirth and Disability*. Winnipeg and Black Point, NS: Fernwood Publishing.
Merchant, Natalie. 1995. "Wonder." *Tigerlily*. Elektra.
Moss, Jeff. 1978. "I Don't Want to Live on the Moon." *Elmopalooza*. Sony Music.
Nielsen-Chapman, Beth. 1993. "Dancer to the Drum." *You Hold the Key*. Artemis Records.
Olkin, Rhoda. 1999. *What Psychotherapists Should Know about Disability*. New York: Guilford Press.
Page, Steven. 1992. "Good Boy." *Gordon*. Reprise.
Sontag, Susan. 1990. "A Woman's Beauty: Put-Down or Power Source?" In Pat C. Hoy, Esther H. Schor and Robert DiYanni (eds.), *Women's Voices: Visions and Perspectives*. Toronto: McGraw-Hill.

Breaking Bounds

Lois Greenfield

Daniel Ezralow and Adee. Photo by Lois Greenfield, 1984, Image 843_BW_05_03. Reprinted with permission of Lois Greenfield. Other Breaking Bounds images are at: loisgreenfield.com/contact/index.html.

My Father's Dying

David Carpenter

Listen to David Carpenter perform his poem at the Gendered Intersections website:
fernwoodpublishing.ca/gi2

Blocked arteries from a massive heart attack
Alzheimer's aphasia dementia three kinds of cancer
Death is confused
Death wants a second opinion

Dad the father Dad the son Dad the
family tyrant with a short fuse a ready laugh
ready laugh and a short fuse
awakens every morning with clenched fists
like a man in a brawl
around him don't let your guard down
above all never admit to a weakness
If it hurts don't let it show

they'll skin you alive
they'll cut you in two
they were the government
the rival team rival companies
cars on a busy road your boss senior colleagues
the banks all other loaning agencies society
never let your guard down

on the subject of various girls
don't get involved
politics
don't get involved
idealistic causes
don't get involved
learning to play an instrument
don't get involved
learning to save money
now yer talking

a big kid known as Shags
used to swagger down into the ravine
and beat the crap out of us
I told him once if he tried that again

my dad would come to his home
and kick him in the nuts
for some reason the kid never tried it again
which made me wonder about the magic of words
and the omnipotence of my father

he could have died World War II
but they sent him packing
tuberculosis   they said   blood in the urine
thirty-five years old and a kid in the cradle
they sent him back to Edmonton
one in the cradle another on the way
the writer of these lines
his scornful son

the coronary came at sixty-three
Mum phoned me from the hospital
I spotted her standing outside the ward
as soon as he saw me she shook her head
no   her gesture said
he's not going to make it
thirty-one years ago

when your father is over ninety
senile and dying
however slowly
you tend to seek advice
doctors   lawyers social workers
counselors health professionals
they all say the same thing
take his car away

he should have died in World War II
but they sent him packing
lungs a-hacking
the rest won't rhyme

my father gets smaller and smaller by the year
smaller by the month
cancer in the lymphatic system
cancer in the prostate
cancers all over his head
seep and bleed and fester anew
like a bombed-out town
like World War 11
the rest won't rhyme
I play on my harp from time to time
the rest won't rhyme

good to see you   Dad
how'd you get out here
took the plane   how are you feeling
Your mother's ready to go dancing
good for her
how'd you get out here
I took the plane
you take the car this time

he used to drive downtown and get lost
try to go home to the old house
with the new owners
his license has been suspended
his insurance invalid
I took the bull by the horns
oh yes   I took the bull by the horns
I put a hammerlock on the steering wheel
and a forged note from the City of Victoria
license suspended
did it in the dead of night
didn't sleep a wink
I watched TV all night long
wondering when my father would discover it
my little conspiracy
behold   my own son seeks my car
all night long I watched the Olympics from Nagano
I watched Elvis skate with a pulled groin muscle
win a silver in a wrenching howl of pain
my dad had gotten through to Elvis
if it hurts don't let it show
all his life behind the wheel my dad
had been free as a rustler
I had just shot his horse
you want to sleep at night   guys
don't shoot your father's horse

a few years ago
he told me his secret
after the heart attack I said
I just want to make it to seventy
I hit seventy and I said well seventy-five
when I made it to seventy-five
and your mother and I moved out here
all my arteries were shot
but the little ones the
capillaries
yeah   the capillaries
they took up the job

so I said wouldn't it be great
if I made it all the way to eighty
and I made it to eighty
well   I'll never make it to ninety
any fool knows I'll never make it to ninety
so why not shoot for eighty-five   eh

my father will be ninety-four this summer
because the capillaries took up the job
the century will expire before my father does
this country will expire before my father does

on the subject of death
don't get involved

how did you get out here
I drove
how
I said I drove
in that car of yours

he wanders at night
sometimes into the wrong apartment
the people who run the building want to kick him out
send Mum and Dad to a nursing home
lie around with a bunch of old duffers
no thanks he says
no thanks my mother says
they'll have to drag us out in a box he says
can we change the subject my mother says
how did you get out here

I flew out one time to say goodbye
he had gone outside to check on his car
gone out in the dark in his nightshirt
lost his balance and grabbed for the rail
the rail turned out to be a vine and he crashed
into a pile of cinder blocks
broke five ribs and collapsed a lung
crawled inside   gasping
Mum phoned the ambulance
(never let your guard down)
 I arrived at the ICU
as soon as Mum saw me she shook her head
the gesture meant no
he's not going to make it
the oxygen they pumped into him and gone astray
instead of the usual scrawny carcass
I beheld my father puffed up like the Pillsbury doughboy

subcutaneous emphysema
he recognized me
had a dream   makes me feel like a fool
some guy was after me   in an alley
couldn't see him very well   looked like a thug
he knew I was hurt   couldn't move or fight back
so I played possum   pulled in my leg
when he came up on me   shoot me or something
stab me   I kicked out with my leg
woke up   I'd knocked over the beside table
the bedpan   felt like a fool
that was Death   I said
and he wheezed with laughter
the next day he complained about cold soup
the day after that he tyrannized the nurses
the day after that he declared war on the ICU
tore a strip off his loving wife
tore another strip off me
my dad was on the mend

the millennium will expire
before my father dies
cancer   heart   stroke   dementia   aphasia
alzheimer's   collapsed lungs
Death stalking him down a dark alley

never let your guard down   Death
or my dad will kick you in the nuts

this was meant to be a song
the song of David for Saul
really   it should be a song
Dave to Saul
rhymes and all

in the meantime he has
his food brought to him
regular transfusions of rye
his disabled car
his wife and sons
their worried looks
their wary love

1999

NOTE

In David Carpenter, 2003, "My Father's Dying," *Troutstream Creed*, Regina: Couteau Books. Reprinted with permission.

March 26, 2002

Dear Lesley,

Thanks for your invitation to include my poem in your anthology. I understand that you want me to write a short piece based on my work. Well, here goes.

In the last year of my father's life, I found myself traveling more and more to British Columbia to take care of my parents. As many people my age will understand, it was a tough time for my parents and a tough time for Honor (my wife) and me. Honor's mother died the same year my father did. We simply had to put our careers on hold and do what had to be done.

I brought a lot of emotional baggage to the task of caring for my dad. We had always been more or less embattled from the time of my early teens. He had learned most of what he knew about life from growing to manhood in the shadow of the Great Depression. He was a vigorous man, an athlete, a good storyteller, very sociable, but also quite shy. Although he loved us all, he was a control freak, a petty tyrant whose two sons were supposed to grow up as visible symbols of the things he stood for: respectability, stoicism in the face of difficulties, honest hard work, emotional and fiscal restraint, and love of the out-of-doors. He was a devout family man, always interested in the daily lives of his two sons, never unfaithful to his calling as husband and father, but he simmered with anger when his boys chose paths that seemed to stray from his limited outlook on life. Every April Fool's Day we went all-out to play pranks on him: parking the car around the corner so that he would think it had been stolen, or phoning him in disguised voices announcing various calamities at his office. The tyrant and the loving father. The gregarious dad and the repressive one. The hero of our boyhood, the naysayer of our manhood. Our hard taskmaster and our greatest fan.

I wrote "My Father's Dying" one night while staying in the guest room of his apartment building. I couldn't sleep. Acting on legal advice, I had just disabled Dad's car and forged a note from the City of Victoria reminding him that his license had been suspended. All night long I lounged in front of a TV set in a state of darkest gloom. I had disabled my father's car, severed his last connection to freedom, shot his horse as it were. As the Nagano Olympics rolled on through the night, I wrote the poem. When at last I stopped writing, it was six a.m. Some poems you write because you want to: others you write because you have to. Of all the rituals I observed during my father's dying and after his death, writing this poem was the most healing. I've read it in quite a few cities, and on good nights, when ghosts are at rest, I suspect my dad is glad to hear the laughter of the crowds, secretly pleased to be my show and tell.

There it is, Lesley. Hope you can use it. Call me if you need anything else.

— David

GENDERED ECONOMIES AND WAGED WORK

C. Lesley Biggs

"What do you do for a living?" This is one of the most frequently asked questions when we first meet someone. It is testament to the centrality of work in our lives, both as a source of economic security and as a measure of self-worth. Implicit in this question, however, is a particular definition of work — one that is inextricably linked to a moral framework in which paid labour is valued while unpaid labour is not only undervalued but invisible. Even though the majority of women, regardless of marital status, now participate in the paid labour force for a significant portion of their lives, gendered definitions of work persist because women perform the bulk of unpaid labour — childcare, elder care, homemaking/housework, and formal and informal volunteer activities.

One of the greatest achievements of first and second wave feminists is to have made women's participation in the labour force and the relationship between paid and unpaid labour part of public debates. At the turn of the twentieth century, suffragists initially lobbied for women's right to vote, but their campaign soon broadened to include educational, labour, health, and welfare reforms. Eventually, the suffragists won the vote and made other significant gains in protecting women and children, but equality remained elusive. By the beginning of the Great Depression in 1929, much of the momentum of first wave feminists had been lost. With the advent of World War II, women's participation rates in the labour force skyrocketed; they were needed in the factories while the men were away at war. But when the veterans returned, married women at least were forced to return to the home. However, working for a living — even for a short time — became a fact of life for many young women. In the 1960s women's employment expanded in the service and public sectors, converging with unprecedented numbers of married women entering the labour force and the rise of second wave feminism. Once again, issues around women's work were back on the public agenda and given their fullest expression in the report of the Royal Commission on the Status of Women (1970). Liberal feminists focused their attention on discrimination in wages, hiring and promotion policies, better childcare, and improving women's educational opportunities.

The focus of the Royal Commission was creating equal opportunities for women in education and in the workplace; that is, the playing field between women and men was leveled so that they could compete on equal terms. This liberal framework on which the Royal Commission was based does not guarantee equality of outcome; nor does it challenge the organization of women's and men's work and its relationship to domestic labour. While socialist feminists agreed with the many problems identified by the Royal Commission, they pointed to the structural barriers to women's participation in the labour force, specifically the industrial and occupational segregation of the labour force by gender. Overall since the 1970, work in goods-producing industries[1] has declined, but in 2009, only relatively few women worked in the goods-producing industries (Ferraro 2010). Women represented 30.1 percent of the manufacturing labour force; 19.5 percent worked in primary resource industries, and 6.4 percent in transportation, trades, and construction (Ferraro 2010). However, when the downturn in the economy hit in 2008, its impact was felt most strongly in the good-producing industries, leading to higher rates of unemployment for men compared to women (Ferraro 2010). Even in the new millennium, women remain concentrated in occupations in which women traditionally have worked. In 2009, 67 percent of all employed women as compared to 31 percent of men were working in one of teaching, nursing and related health occupations, clerical or other administrative positions, or sales and service occupations[2] (Ferraro 2010). However, the proportion of women employed in traditionally female-dominated occupations has been declining slowly since 1987 when 71.8 percent of employed women worked in these jobs. Most of this decline can be accounted for by the decrease in clerical and administrative jobs, while women's representation in management, business and finance, and in non-traditional health-care occupations has increased significantly (Ferraro 2010; also see Hypatia Index VI for more details). Men tend to be distributed more evenly across occupational categories. But not all men — not even the majority of men — work in high-powered, high-paying jobs; in 2009, 20.1 percent of all men worked in sales and service; 26.3 percent in trades, transport, and construction, and 6.3 percent in processing, manufacturing, and utilities (Ferraro 2010). Not surprisingly, these employment patterns have significant effects on earnings.[3] In 1967, women made, on average, 58.4 percent of what men made; in 2009, women made 83 percent of what men made (Williams 2010). These statistics obscure as much as they reveal. As the data in Hypatia Index indicate, women's income and hence quality of life greatly depends upon their family status (whether they are lone parents or in two-parent families, single or attached); the age and number of children (which affects women's decision whether to work in the paid labour force, and whether they will work full- or part-time); education (which is positively correlated to income); race, ethnicity, immigration status, able-bodiedness, and sexual orientation. The intersections of these relationships produce complex patterns of employment and wage differentials.

Beginning in the 1970s, socialist feminists examined housework and childcare as activities that are necessary for the well-being of families and individuals, as well as intrinsic to the functioning of capitalism. More recently, feminists have examined unpaid labour as "caring work," affirming women's activities rather than reinforcing the negative connotations associated with this kind of labour. What actually constitutes caring work and why it remains "women's work" is hotly debated within feminist circles (see Benoit 2000). Nonetheless, women continue to perform the bulk of unpaid household work including primary childcare and shopping, averaging 4.3 hours per day of unpaid work, but down from 4.8 hours per day in 1986 (Lindsay 2008). More men, particularly younger men, are engaged in domestic labour; in 2005, men aged 25 to 54 averaged 2.5 hours per day doing unpaid household work, up from 2.1 hours per day in 1986. Upon hearing a statistic that men had increased their participation in household tasks by six minutes in 1982, cartoonist Nicole Hollander's character "Sylvia" declared, "Mercy… It's a revolution, and I'm still in my bathrobe!" I think that we are still waiting — and waiting — for the real revolution. So, one of the vexing questions is how do we encourage men to take on more of the responsibilities of caring work?

As more and more women participate in the paid labour force (in 2009, for example, 64.4 percent of women with a child under the age of three worked fulltime), the stresses and strains of the "double day" are no longer private issues (Ferraro 2010: 7). Calls for a balance between the job and family, however, are coming at a time of significant economic restructuring. Since the late 1980s, with the shift to the "knowledge economy" and to capitalist globalization, new patterns of work are emerging: more women are engaged in non-standard work (in 2007, 40 percent of women, as compared to 30 percent of men were engaged in part-time, self-employed, or temporary work) (Bowlby 2008); for some, the closure of factories, the demise of the fisheries, layoffs in the public and private sectors, and fluctuating commodity prices for agricultural products make economic instability a fact of life; moreover, the new information technologies have led to the polarization of the labour market into "good" jobs, which require a small group of highly skilled knowledge workers who are able to garner high wages, and "bad" jobs, which require a much larger group of less skilled workers who work for considerably lower rates of pay.

The effects of restructuring have been, and probably will continue to be, uneven on women and men. Many of these changes have had tremendously negative consequences for women and their families, as they struggle to make ends meet and balance family life and waged work. But it is not clear that all of the effects are negative. For example, does the shift toward non-standard work for women represent a way of balancing job and family responsibilities, giving them greater flexibility and less stress; or does it represent another way in which women's work is being ghettoized in low-paying jobs with little or no security?

So far, most governments and employers have been slow to respond to these job/family conflicts. Unions have demanded more flexible work arrangements (e.g., flex time, job sharing, and telecommuting), improved maternity and paternity leaves, on-site childcare, and provisions for elder care. Some employers have begun to develop policies and practices to create family-friendly workplaces, but such a shift requires a significant change in the workplace culture and necessitates "buy-in" from both employers and employees. At the public policy level, feminists have lobbied for a national childcare program and improvements in maternity/parental benefits under Employment Insurance (EI). At the same, the tightening of eligibility requirements for EI has made it more difficult for unemployed individuals, particularly those engaged in non-standard forms of work, to meet these requirements. In addition, feminists have used various legislative measures to enforce pay equity (equal pay for equal work) and to work toward employment equity (equal pay for work of equal value) (for more detail, see Benoit 2000: 92–107).

More generally, what can be done to expand women's job opportunities beyond the "pink collar ghetto"? Does the answer lie in changing the ways in which we educate girls or in providing mentorship programs that encourage young women to enter into non-traditional professions? Or do we encourage employers to develop workplace cultures that are friendly to women? And what's wrong with caring work anyway? How do we promote a shift in attitudes that recognizes the value of women's contributions and compensates them accordingly? These are the kind of questions that underlie the chapters in this section.

Writing from a Marxist-feminist perspective, Elaine Coburn provides an introduction to globalization by arguing that "World capitalism is the context for unequal gender relationships… women around the world are linked, but not always or even typically by bonds of solidarity." Globalization is not new in the sense that over 500 hundred years ago, many European nation-states sought new commodities and cheap labour (often slave labour), through imperial and mercantile capitalist ventures. What is new is that the new information technologies, the relative ease in transporting goods, and new production strategies allow transnational corporations and international institutions to move capital across national borders and around the world at lightning speed. The result is that corporations have been able to demand concessions from workers under the threat that otherwise they will move their businesses to countries where workers are still paid very low wages. According to Coburn, "This enhanced power relative to the working class and the state-created conditions for a new political (class) compromise, often summarized as neoliberalism."

Neoliberalism is based on free market principles — "free" for a few, not the many — that include "the privatization of formerly public goods and services"; "the explicit or de facto weakening of health, safety, and environmental legislation costly to capital"; "the liberalization of financial transactions and trade"; and "the 'warfare' state's expansion." The difference between neoliberal capitalism and earlier capitalist modes of production is that neoliberal ideas, policies, and practices have gained a foothold worldwide, but like earlier forms of capitalism, neoliberalism is being implemented mostly by men, and "not just any men," as Coburn notes, "rather neoliberal institutions [are] dominated by white, bourgeois men, often from, or educated in, the world's most powerful nations, notably the United States."

The effects of neoliberalism are uneven. The biggest beneficiaries are capitalist and professional class men and women across the world capitalist system while "both working-class women and working-class men lose." However, working-class men's and women's experience of neoliberal globalization differ in terms of the kind of work they do and where they work. As a result, "Too many women, like too many working-class men, are engaged in struggles for basic survival"; these shared experiences provide opportunities for women's solidarity around the world, but past experience shows people are unlikely to cross class lines.

Most of us who live in a city have very little contact with the producers of our food — except perhaps in the case of local markets, which have been growing in popularity over the last fifteen years. Moreover, media stories decry children's knowledge of food sources. For example, *The Farmer's Guardian* (2007) reported on a study that found in Britain "thousands of eight-year-olds [believe] that cows lay eggs and that bacon comes from cattle or sheep." Migration to the cities, the industrialization of food production, the desire for cheaper food-stuffs, the creation of food as a commodity rather than a basic necessity, and the demand for certain types of food that don't grow in Canada all year round — if at all — have contributed to the increased social, as well as geographic, distance between the food that we eat and the people who produce it; many of course live in the global South.

Deborah Barndt's story of the movement of tomatoes from the field to the table pro-vides an excellent example of the globalization of the food industry. In her chapter, Barndt examines the experiences of two groups of female workers: Mexican women who work in an agribusiness and Canadian women who work in a supermarket as part-time cashiers. Their stories, as Barndt demonstrates, reveal the ways in which southern countries have an increasing role in producing food for export while northern countries have become consum-ers of food. In many ways, the experience of southern and northern female workers in this production-consumption nexus differ significantly by the kinds of work that they do, the gender narratives that help organize the work, the location of their work, as well as their race/ethnicity, and their familial relations. But despite their differences Mexican and Canadian workers share some of the same issues: most are struggling to survive financially and jug-gling familial responsibilities, domestic labour, and paid labour; and both groups of women work for employers who want to maximize their profits to the detriment of these workers.

These shared conditions of work, as Barndt observes, are providing the basis for women in the North and South to organize for change by creating alternative models for the produc-tion and exchange of food stuffs (e.g., cooperatives); exchanging knowledge about biodiversity and the threat that monocultural food production poses to food production in the long term; and organizing around issues that connect food production to health and environmental issues. In building and connecting with communities, we can, Barndt argues, take small and big steps to create food that is nutritious, yet doesn't depend upon the exploitation of workers, nor have a harmful impact on the environment. The rise of agribusiness has led to the decline of the family farm, but until the 1970s, family farms fed the world. Family and work are inextricably bound up in a gendered division of labour on the family farm, a theme which Aritha Van Herk explores in her prose poem "First the Chores, and Then the Dishes." This refrain probably is very familiar to many of us who come from a farming background, and have performed such jobs as cleaning barns, milking cows, shovelling manure, or weeding vegetable gardens. In most cases, after we have done our work, we can anticipate some kind of reward —whether it be a treat (which for me is chocolate!) or having leisure time; doing the dishes just doesn't seem to fall into this category! What does the distinction between chores and dishes point to, and how do they relate to paid work, and gender relations?

Writing from the perspective of a daughter — "Visible difference. Daw: a jackdaw, a simpleton" — and sister — "Her brothers resist, de/sister her with their easy contempt," — Van Herk reflects on "the double discourse" of family, "its duplicitous side, the side you'd rather not admit… [the one] that you are supposed to admire, applaud, never doubt." In this Dutch Reform, Calvinist, post-World War II, immigrant family living on the prairies in the 1950s, "work was an open secret; working constant, an on-going presence." And yet despite the omnipresence of work and the disjunction between work and word play, Van Herk finds in the latter "a kind of perverse pleasure. She is in love with the word's tool, with its potential for deflection." She discovers that work can be used as an excuse to do other things ("Go away, I have work to do."), and that some kinds of work, like bringing the cows home, offer freedom "Because [this work] is unclassified, a space for acts of imagination. Illicit acts."

This family is deeply patriarchal, more out of practicality than intention, muses Van Herk; nonetheless, it depends upon a gendered division of labour which values physical over intellectual labour: "In the old days, there was only muscle, and that was someone else's, a man's. Muscles were off-limits, off-duty for women." But in doing her chores, this daughter/sister acquires muscles that are useful, for performing unladylike tasks such as changing a tire. Moreover, she learns, while doing the dishes, that the tongue is a muscle, and "she begins to think of tongue, its wonderful freedom within the mouth, and how it cannot ache the way muscles do. And she begins to use it, her tongue, her dutiful double, her immigrant prairie tongue." She imagines other ways of being in the world and the reconfiguring of ideas about family. And then, there are the dishes!

In the 1990s, the provincial government placed a moratorium on the Newfoundland cod fishery in response to overfishing; the effects — economic, social, and psychological — were devastating for families and communities along the Newfoundland shoreline, many of whom lost their jobs and faced uncertain futures. The effects, however, were felt differently by women and men in the fishing industry because the labour force is organized, *inter alia*, by gender; women and men are situated in different occupations, and in general, women's work in the fishing industry, if recognized at all, has lower status and less pay than men's. This differential valuing of men and women's work is captured very concisely in the title of Nicole Gerrada Power's chapter, "Men Fish, Women Help."

For many fish harvesters, fishing is "in their blood"; boys learn the techniques of commercial fishing at a young age by apprenticing with a more experienced fish harvester, but "they also learn what it means to be a 'fisherman,'" the gender narratives that code this activity as masculine. Although a few women fish, they usually perform unpaid work as a "helper" to a male relative. Most women, however, who work for wages in the fishing industry, work as processing workers. However, even in processing plants, the workspace is structured by gender, with women working in production and clerical jobs, and men in the higher status and better paying jobs in fish cutting. In addition to performing paid and unpaid work associated with fishing, most women are responsible for domestic labour and childcare.

When the moratorium on cod fishing was imposed, many men and women lost their jobs, but state strategies continued to perpetuate a gendered division of labour and women's subordinate status. Since women were underrepresented in the processing plants and had lower seniority, they were more vulnerable to losing their jobs. In addition, because many women had interrupted work histories as a result of their childcare responsibilities, they did not qualify for the same level of benefits under the federally funded adjustment programs, or they were unable to take advantage of retraining programs either because they could not afford childcare (not provided for under the program), or they were unable to leave their homes and communities because as "mothers, t[hey] were not accorded the same cultural permission" as men.

Male harvesters adapted to the moratorium in different ways depending upon their employment status and available capital. Owners of boats with limited capital tended to downsize and recruited their female partners as crew members while skippers with more financial resources "invest[ed] more heavily by purchasing quotas for alternative species and buying larger vessels." Crew members were offered retraining or retirement, but the state's overall strategy was to reduce the number of workers in the fishing industry while, at the same, professionalizing the harvesting workforce by classifying fish harvesters into "core/non-core categories" that were/are used to determine who gets what fisheries resources, with core fish harvesters having privileged access to licenses, quotas, and vessels." The results, as Power demonstrates, are the transformation of the fishing industry and the reconstitution of the gendered division of labour.

In which country were the clothes that you wear made? Check the label, and you will most likely find that they were made in China, Bangladesh, or Vietnam. The garment industry was one of the biggest employers in the U.S. and provided work for many Canadians for many years, but over the last few decades, much of the production work in the garment industry has been outsourced to countries where workers are paid low wages, are often exploited, and have few rights. With the introduction of new technologies, improved distribution and transportation systems, and international trade agreements, the Canadian garment industry has been transformed, resulting in the closure or downsizing of plants, and the reintroduction of home-based workers. Roxanna Ng explores the processes that produce the gendered and racialized division of labour in garment work. How is it, Ng asks, that women, and more recently women from Asia, are at the bottom of the hierarchy? In answer to her question, Ng argues that immigrant women are a source of cheap labour due to immigration policies; the women's lack of both fluency in English and "proper" educational credentials; the definition of sew as unskilled women's work, while cutting is seen as skilled men's work; and the piece-rate system, which actually penalizes productivity. Reducing this exploitation of immigrant women, Ng argues, requires a social movement of unions, labour rights groups, and concerned citizens.

Although women have made significant strides in breaking down the barriers to "some venerable bastions of male turf, like medicine and law," the same cannot be said of engineering. In 2008, women represented 12.2 percent of all engineers, which is less than the percentage of women enrolled in undergraduate engineering programs (17 percent), and even less than the number of women who practice as lawyers or doctors. In her chapter, Gillian Ranson confronts the problem of retention rates in engineering. In her view, "motherhood is a critical watershed." Female engineers experience what Ranson calls "the dual-earner disadvantage": female engineers are trying to juggle full-time careers and be a mother, while male engineers who are fathers are relatively freed from family responsibilities since the majority of their wives are stay-at-home mothers. Ranson raises the question: "Should women enter engineering on men's terms or should engineering accommodate the needs of women as mothers?"

"Unions are sites of both struggle and vehicles of resistance," says Linda Briskin in her chapter on unions and women workers. Although making up 50 percent of union members, women faced significant barriers to participation in union activities. But in the 1970s, women unionists "began to organize to resist and reconfigure the gender order of unions." They have been successful in improving women's representation in leadership positions and addressing issues of concern to women both within the union itself and at the bargaining table. In part, the success of union women can be attributed to the strategies of separate organizing and constituency building, strategies that have been adopted by other marginalized groups within the union movement.

Many of us live from paycheque to paycheque, and if we lost our jobs and didn't find another in short order, we would be facing significant financial, as well as social and psychological, consequences. The distance, however, between financial security and poverty is obviously mediated by class/occupation, education, race, gender, age, language, and ability. However, women, particularly Aboriginal and immigrant women, women with disabilities, and single mothers 1.7 million in all according to Statistics Canada 2009, are consistently over-represented in income brackets below the poverty line. Finding the theme "women and poverty" a common one, M. Nourbese Philip was bothered by "how well the words went together — as if they belonged together — women and poverty — like motherhood and apple pie."

Like many postmodern feminists, Philip "[plays] with words in a very serious way in the hope of their releasing some hidden or forgotten meaning." In this case, she traces the etymology of the word "poor," and discovers that it is "the descendant of *pauper*, which in turn was a combination of two words meaning *one who produces little*." But that definition definitely does not account for "the vast amounts of work women have traditionally done." Moreover, Philip argues, if we consider the opposite of "poor," i.e., "rich," one who produces much, women should fall into this category, but they obviously don't. "If we accept that women have traditionally produced much," writes Philip, "— and the statistics exist to support this — how do we get from the state of producing much and having little, to being described as producing little?" Philip's answer: "Theft." Women's work has been stolen by others! The word "*poverty*," Philip argues, "really only describe[s] the end result, omitting the process, the pattern and series of actions which, over the centuries, have resulted in the inevitable link between women and poverty."

Drawing on Hannah Arendt's work, Philip argues that the almost seamless pairing of "women and poverty" is not accidental. Traditionally, European languages have distinguished between *work* — "an activity which produces new objects" — and *to labour* — "meant to do work whose products or results were consumed immediately." Because women's "unproductive" labour is consumed, it is not seen as having value, and is therefore appropriated by others. Ironically, however, without women's labour, men traditionally could not engage in productive work. But, as Philip says, we know all about patriarchy and women's oppression, why do we have to research this issue? As a Black woman, Philip is keenly aware of the impact of colonialism on Black and Native women and men — the theft of their labour, spouses, children, culture, and languages. Rather than blaming the poor for *their* poverty, Philip argues, "we have to start asking questions like who did the stealing (and in some cases women stole from women as well), and what was stolen. In some instances theft of material possessions, or of remuneration for one's labour, was the least of the crimes committed." By asking these questions, we are able to reframe our understanding of poverty, shifting the responsibility away from individual blame and solutions toward an analysis of those who benefit from structured inequalities.

Living in poverty has many repercussions; the poorer you are, the more likely that you will become ill, experience higher rates of chronic illnesses, distress, low esteem, and earlier mortality. The poorer you are, the more likely that your children will suffer; poor children are more likely to experience intellectual, cognitive, and language delays, and engage in anti-social behaviours as they get older. Poverty certainly hurts individuals who live in poverty, but in one way or another, poverty affects us all. As Denise Spitzer observes in her chapter, "Poverty disrupts social cohesion in Canada and contributes to social and financial costs, putting pressure on our health, social services, and criminal justice systems."

Determining who is poor is dependent upon a number of variables: income, family status (whether single or part of a household), the number of dependants and their ages, place of residence, age, and ability status. Intuitively, you would think that measuring poverty would not be a difficult problem; it would seem "obvious" that people who live in poverty don't have enough money to make ends meet. But, in Canada, different organiza-tions within government, as well as non-governmental organizations, use different measures to determine the poverty line as a way of providing baseline data for policy development, which ultimately will lead to the provision (or not) of programs that subsidize the incomes of the poor.[4] Calculating the poverty line is a political act since the measure determines who is eligible for programs and who is not.

Spitzer identifies two models that have been used to explain women's overall economic disadvantage. The first model, Human Capital Theory, centers on the "choices" that individu-als make. If, for example, you decided not to finish high school, or forewent a post-secondary education, that is your "choice," or put more directly, "it is your fault if you don't have a well-paying job." The model does not take into account the conditions that structure those "choices," for example, parents' income, number of other siblings, and parental/familial support. In cases in which families do not have enough money to send their kids to school, the "rational choice" for a young adult is to get a job.

The second model used to explain women's position in the labour market, and preferred by feminists, is the Job Segregation Model, which argues that women "choose" jobs that fit with their responsibilities for caring for others — jobs in which women can move in and out of the labour market according to the demands of family life; or women "choose" jobs that are perceived as "naturally female," and therefore, they become clerical workers, teachers, or nurses. In this model, women's choices are made within a narrow set of parameters; that is, they are structured by gendered ideologies. These push-pull factors segregate the job market occupationally and racially, so many women end up working in part-time jobs that pay less and are less secure than the jobs of their male counterparts. In the event that women lose the income of a second earner, or they experience increase in family size, the more likely these women are to face a downward spiral into poverty.

In 1986, Philip decried the seemingly natural pairing of "women and poverty," finding it instead socially created. Now, as Spitzer notes, "the feminization of poverty is an acknowl-edged social trend in Canadian society." We know that how things are named has enormous consequences for how situations are understood and acted upon, or not. Thinking in Philip's terms, what would be the logical linguistic and material consequences of this relatively new language popularized by various United Nations documents in the 1990s? Does "the feminization of poverty" represent a move toward addressing the disproportionate number of women who live in poverty the world over, or does the term continue to naturalize the impoverishment of women?

1. Goods-producing industries include agriculture; resource-based industries such as mining, forestry, and fishing; manufacturing and construction; and utilities.
2. Service industries include finance, insurance and real estate; business, education, health and social services; accommodation, food and beverage services; other services; public administration; transportation; and communications.
3. Earnings refer to income derived from wages and salaries, which represents 72 percent and 81 percent of women's and men's total incomes respectively. Other sources of income include government transfer programs, investments, private retirement programs, alimony and child support programs, superannuation, and scholarships.
4. Statistics Canada defines those with low incomes as families or individuals who spend, on average, at least 20 percentage points more of their pre-tax income than the Canadian average on food, shelter, and clothing. Using 1992 as the base year, families and individuals with incomes below the Low Income Cutoffs usually spend more than 54.7 percent of their income on these items and are considered to be in straightened circumstances. For more details, see Statistics Canada 2009. Note that changes to this measure have been introduced as of 2010 (Murphy, Zhang and Dionne 2011).

Benoit, Cecilia. 2000. *Women, Work and Social Rights: Canada in Historical and Comparative Perspective.* Scarborough, ON: Prentice-Hall.

Bowlby, Geoff. 2008. "Studies in 'Non-standard' Employment." Ottawa: Statistics Canada. At: wiego. org/reports/statistics/nov-2008/bowlby_presentation_2008.pdf.

Canada, Royal Commission on the Status of Women. 1970. *Report.* Ottawa: Information Canada.

Farmer's Guardian. 2007. "Gap In Children's Food Knowledge" (March 2). At: farmersguardian. com/gap-in-children%92s-food-knowledge/7089.article.

Ferraro, Vincent. 2010. "Women in Canada: A Gender-Based Statistical Report: Paid Work." Ottawa: Statistics Canada. Cat. No. 89-503-X. At: statcan.gc.ca/pub/89-503-x/89-503-x2010001-eng. htm.

Hollander, Nicole. 1982. *Mercy, It's a Revolution, and I'm Still in My Bathrobe.* New York: St. Martin's Press.

Lindsay, Colin. 2008. "Are Women Spending More Time on Unpaid Domestic Work than Men in Canada?" Ottawa: Statistics Canada. Cat. No. 89-630-X (September). At: statcan.gc.ca/pub/89-630-x/2008001/ article/10705-eng.htm.

Murphy, Brian, Xuelin Zhang and Claude Dionne. 2010. *Revising Canada's Low-Income Measure (LIM).* Ottawa: Statistics Canada. Cat. No. 75F0002M. At: statcan.gc.ca/ pub/75f0002m/75f0002m2010004-eng.htm.

Statistics Canada. 2009. *Income in Canada.* Ottawa: Statistics Canada. Cat. No. 75-202-X. At: statcan. gc.ca/pub/75-202-x/2009000/analysis-analyses-eng.htm.

Williams, Cara. 2010. "Women in Canada: A Gender-Based Statistical Report. Economic Well-being." Ottawa: Statistics Canada. Cat. No. 89-503-X. At: statcan.gc.ca/pub/89-503-x/2010001/ article/11388-eng.htm.

Wilson, Susannah. 2001. "Paid Work, Jobs, and the Illusion of Economic Security." In Nancy Mandell (ed.), *Feminist Issues: Race, Class, and Sexuality.* Fourth edition. Toronto: Pearson Prentice-Hall.

Compiled by C. Lesley Biggs

- Percentage change in world Gross Domestic Product (real growth rate)[2] in 2007: +5
- Percentage change in world Gross Domestic Product (real growth rate) in 2009: -0.7[3]
- Percentage change in global trade from 2008 to 2009: -25[4]
- Percentage change in the global industrial production growth rate in 2009: -2.7
- Percentage change in Gross Domestic Product in Russia in 2009: -7.9[5]
- Percentage change in Gross Domestic Product in China in 2009: +9.1[6]
- Percentage change in global per capita income in 2009: -2[7]
- Estimated global public debt[8] in 2009 as a percentage of the Global Domestic Product: 56
- Estimated global public debt in 2007 as a percentage of the Global Domestic Product: 48.9
- Estimated world external debt in 2009: $56 trillion[9]
- Estimated total world labour force in 2009: 3.179 billion
- Percentage of world's population that was unemployed in 2009: 9
- Percentage of world's population that was unemployed in 2008: 7
- Decline in number of people between 1990 and 2004 living in extreme poverty (less than $1.00 a day): 278 million
- Decline in number of people between 1999 and 2004 living in extreme poverty (less than $1.00 per day): 150 million.
- Number of people living in extreme poverty in 2005: 1.4 billion[10]
- Poverty rate (percent of the population) in Vietnam in 1993: 58
- Poverty rate (percent of the population) in Vietnam in 2006: 16[11]
- Number of women who joined the global work force between 1997 and 2007: 200 million[12]
- Number of women in the global work force in 2007: 1.2 billion
- Number of men in the global work force in 2007: 1.8 billion
- Percentage in 2007 by which women globally are paid less than men: 17[13]
- Percentage of men in sub-Sahara Africa in 2007 who were waged and salaried workers: 35.6
- Percentage of women in sub-Sahara Africa in 2007 who were waged and salaried workers: 19.5
- Percentage of men in Latin America and the Caribbean in 2007 who were waged and salaried workers: 66.4
- Percentage of women in Latin America and the Caribbean in 2007 who were waged and salaried workers: 68.2
- Percentage of men in the developed world in 2007 who were waged and salaried workers: 91
- Percentage of women in the developed world in 2007 who were waged and salaried workers: 92.9
- Percentage of men worldwide in 2007 who were employed in agriculture: 29.6
- Percentage of women worldwide in 2007 who were employed in agriculture: 33.6
- Percentage of men in sub-Sahara Africa in 2007 who were employed in agriculture: 63.1
- Percentage of women in sub-Sahara Africa in 2007 who were employed in agriculture: 67.3
- Percentage of men in developed regions in 2007 who were employed in agriculture: 3.5
- Percentage of women in developed regions in 2007 who were employed in agriculture: 2.1

- Percentage of men worldwide in 2007 who were employed in services: 44.2
- Percentage of women worldwide in 2007 who were employed in services: 51.6
- Percentage of men in sub-Sahara Africa in 2007 who were employed in services: 24.8
- Percentage of women in sub-Sahara Africa in 2007 who were employed in services: 25.3
- Percentage of men in developed regions in 2007 who were employed in services: 62.8
- Percentage of women in developed regions in 2007 who were employed in services: 86.4
- Percentage of women with tertiary education levels who migrated from Africa in 2007: 27.7
- Percentage of men with tertiary education levels who migrated from Africa in 2007: 17.1
- Percentage of women with tertiary education levels who migrated from North America in 2007: 3.5
- Percentage of men with tertiary education levels who migrated from America in 2007: 4.1
- Number of countries in 2007 which have ratified the *United Nations' International Convention on the Protection of the Rights of All Migrant Workers and Members of their Families*: 44[14]
- Percentage of the world's labour force that was unionized in 2007: <40
- Percentage of female workers worldwide who were unionized in 2007: 19
- Ratio of women to men worldwide who held senior management positions in 2007: 1/9[15]
- Percentage of membership on management boards in Norwegian companies as of 2008 that must be women: at least 40[16]
- Percentage of women who were employed in the paid labour force in Canada in 1976: 41.9[17]
- Percentage of men who were employed in the paid labour force in Canada in 1976: 72.7
- Percentage of women who were employed in the paid labour force in Canada in 2009: 58.3
- Percentage of men who were employed in the paid labour force in Canada in 2009: 65.2
- Percentage of Aboriginal identified women who were employed in the paid labour force in Canada in 2009: 53.7
- Percentage of Aboriginal identified men who were employed in the paid labour force in Canada in 2009: 60.6
- Percentage of foreign-born women who were employed in the paid labour force in Canada in 2009: 51.0
- Percentage of foreign-born men who were employed in the paid labour force in Canada in 2009: 61.4
- Percentage of very recent (less than five years) foreign-born women who were employed in the paid labour force in Canada in 2009: 49.1
- Percentage of very recent (less than five years) foreign-born men who were employed in the paid labour force in Canada in 2009: 61.4
- Labour force participation rate for women in Canada in 1976: 37.1[18]
- Labour force participation rate for women in Canada in 2009: 47.9
- Percentage of women in Canada in 1976 who were in the paid labour force and whose youngest child was less than three years old: 27.6
- Percentage of women in Canada in 2009 who were in the paid labour force and whose youngest child was less than three years old: 64.4
- Percentage of female lone parents in Canada in 2009 who were in the paid labour force and whose youngest child was less than three years old: 45.9
- Percentage of women with partners in Canada in 2009 who were in the paid labour force and whose youngest child was less than three years old: 66.5

- Percentage of women in Canada between the ages of 25 to 44 who worked part-time in the paid labour force in 2009: 19.5
- Percentage of men in Canada between the ages of 25 to 44 who worked part-time in the paid labour force in 2009: 5.8
- Unemployment rate for women in Canada in 2009: 7
- Unemployment rate for men in Canada in 2009: 9.4
- Unemployment rate for Aboriginal identified women in Canada in 2009: 12.7
- Unemployment rate for Aboriginal identified men in Canada in 2009: 15.1
- Unemployment rate for very recent (less than five years) foreign-born women aged 15 and over in Canada in 2009: 15.9
- Unemployment rate for very recent (less than five years) foreign-born men aged 15 and over in Canada in 2009: 14.3
- Percentage of the labour force that was women who were multiple job holders in Canada in 2009: 56.2
- Percentage of women who are in unionized jobs in Canada in 1976: 22.3
- Percentage of men who are in unionized jobs in Canada in 1976: 39
- Percentage of women who are in unionized jobs in Canada in 2009: 32.6
- Percentage of men who are in unionized jobs in Canada in 2009: 30.3
- Percentage of all employed women who were working in teaching, nursing and related health occupations, clerical or other administrative positions, or sales and service occupations in Canada in 2009: 67
- Percentage of all employed men who were working in teaching, nursing and related health occupations, clerical or other administrative positions, or sales and service occupations in Canada in 2009: 31
- Percentage increase from 1987 to 2009 of women who comprised business and financial professionals in 2009: 12.9[19]
- Percentage of women who work as doctors, dentists or other health occupations in Canada in 2009: 55.2
- Percentage of women who were senior managers in Canada in 2009: 31.6
- Percentage of women who were professionals in the natural sciences, engineering and mathematics in Canada in 2009: 22.3
- Average total income for women in Canada in 2008: $30,100[20]
- Average total income for men in Canada in 2008: $47,000
- Average total income for female lone-parent families in Canada in 2008: $42,300.
- Average total income for male lone-parent families in Canada in 2008: $60,000
- Average total income for two parent families in Canada in 2008: $100,200
- Average total income for unattached females aged 16 to 64 in Canada in 2008: $33,500
- Average total income for unattached males aged 16 to 64 in Canada in 2008: $42,100
- Average total income for unattached females aged 65 and over in Canada in 2008: $29,500
- Average total income for unattached females aged 65 and over in Canada in 2008: $37,500
- Percentage of earnings[21] made by women who have graduated from high school compared to men with the same educational level in Canada in 2008: 70.4[22]
- Percentage of earnings made by women who have a university degree compared to men with the same educational level in Canada in 2008: 68.3
- Percentage of wives in dual-earner families who earned more than their husbands in Canada in 1976: 12

- Percentage of wives in dual-earner families who earned more than their husbands in Canada in 2008: 29
- Percentage of the female population in Canada in low income situations[23] in 2008: 14.4
- Percentage of the male population in Canada in low income situations in 2008: 12.2
- Percentage of women in Canada aged 65 and over who were classified as low income in 1976: 34.3
- Percentage of men in Canada aged 65 and over who were classified as low income in 1976: 26
- Percentage of women in Canada aged 65 and over who were classified as low income in 2008: 15.7
- Percentage of men in Canada aged 65 and over who were classified as low income in 2008: 8.2
- Estimated percentage of immigrants who were in low income situations in Canada in 2005: 22[24]
- Percentage chance that immigrants have higher low-income rates than the Canadian-born in 2005: 60
- Ratio of the after-transfer/before-taxes low-income among very recent (within five years) immigrants to that of the Canadian-born in 2005: 2.7:1
- Ratio of employment income for recently immigrated men to that of Canadian born men in Canada in 1980: 0.85 to $1.00[25]
- Ratio of employment income for recently immigrated men to that of Canadian born men in Canada in 2005: 0.63 to $1.00
- Ratio of employment income for recently immigrated women to that of Canadian born women in Canada in 1980: 0.85 to $1.00
- Ratio of employment income for recently immigrated women to that of Canadian born women in Canada in 2005: 0.56: $1.00
- Percentage of women in Canada with disabilities who were employed throughout the year in 2006: 46[26] [27]
- Percentage of men in Canada with disabilities who were employed throughout the year in 2006: 56
- Percentage of women in Canada with disabilities who had a postsecondary education in 2006: 45[28]
- Percentage of men in Canada with disabilities who had a postsecondary education in 2006: 46
- Percentage difference in hourly wages between women with disabilities and those without disabilities in Canada in 2006: -10
- Percentage difference in hourly wages between men with disabilities and those without in Canada in 2006: -12
- Percentage of men in Canada with a disability who also were a member of a visible minority in 2006: 88
- Risk of men in Canada who have been disabled for six years having a lower income than men without disabilities: 8:1
- Risk of women in Canada who have been disabled for six years having a lower income than women without disabilities in 2006: 4:1
- Average employment income for Aboriginal identified women in Canada in 2005: $21,791[29]
- Average employment income for Aboriginal identified men in Canada in 2005: $30,153
- Percentage of First Nations women aged 25 to 64 who had completed some form of

postsecondary education in 2006: 44[30]

- Percentage of First Nations women aged 25 to 64 who had trade credentials in 2006: 9
- Percentage of First Nations men aged 25 to 64 who had trade credentials in 2006: 18
- Percentage of First Nations women aged 25 to 64 who had completed a university degree in 2006: 21
- Percentage of First Nations men aged 25 to 64 who had completed a university degree in 2006:14

NOTES

1. The original Hypatia Index was compiled by Pamela Downe, with the assistance of Ellen Whiteman. Except when otherwise indicated in the main text, the sources cited in this Index apply to the line where first referenced and then to all those that follow until another endnote appears.
2. The Gross Domestic Product U.S. dollar estimates for countries are adjusted for inflation and report both on an official exchange rate (OER) and on a purchasing power parity (PPP) basis. Source: CIA, *The World Fact Book, Economy Overview*. At: cia.gov/library/publications/the-world-factbook/geos/xx.html. This site was changed as of August 2, 2011. As a result not all of the data that I cited in the Hypatia Index is on the new page.
3. "The decline in the GDP in 2009 marked the first year in the post-World War II era that global output — and per capita income — declined. World output contracted nearly 1 percent year-over-year, compared with average increases of about 3.5 percent per year since 1946" (CIA *World Fact Book*).
4. This figure represents the largest single year drop since World War II.
5. In 2009, Russia experienced the largest decline in GDP, followed by Mexico (-6.5 percent), Japan (-5.3 percent), Italy (-5.1 percent), Germany (-4.9 percent), and United Kingdom (-4.9 percent).
6. China experienced the largest GDP gains in 2009, followed by India (+7.4 percent) and Indonesia (+4.5 percent).
7. Average per capita income globally in 2009 was $10,400 (U.S.).
8. Public debt "records the cumulative total of all government borrowings less repayments that are denominated in a country's home currency. Public debt should not be confused with external debt, which reflects the foreign currency liabilities of both the private and public sector and must be financed out of foreign exchange earnings." Source: CIA, *The World Fact Book*. At: cia.gov/library/publications/the-world-factbook/geos/xx.html.
9. External debt refers to "the total public and private debt owed to nonresidents repayable in internationally accepted currencies, goods, or services." Source: CIA, *The World Fact Book*. At: cia.gov/library/publications/the-world-factbook/geos/xx.html.
10. If the poverty rate statistics exclude China, we can say that the world's extreme poverty rate between 1990 and 2004 declined by 32 million.
11. The income poverty rates in Vietnam represent one of the fastest declines in the world.
12. UNIFEM, 2009, *Who Answers to Women? Gender and Accountability, Progress on the World's Women, 2008–2009*. At: unifem.org/progress/2008/media/English-PoWW-ExecutiveSummary.pdf.
13. Estimates collected by the International Trade Union Confederation (ITUC) range from 3 percent to 51 percent. Information is available only for selected countries. UNIFEM, 2009, *Who Answers to Women? Gender and Accountability, Progress on the World's Women, 2008–2009*. At: unifem.org/progress/2008/media/English-PoWW-ExecutiveSummary.pdf.
14. This U.N. *Convention* came into force in 2003, and is the most comprehensive instrument for protecting migrant workers' rights. None of the top ten migrant-receiving countries in the world, including Canada, have ratified the *Convention*.
15. The percentage of women worldwide in senior management positions ranges from 3 to 12 percent.
16. This requirement came into law on January 1, 2008. Publicly listed firms that fail to comply could be closed down.
17. All figures are for labour force participants aged fifteen years or older unless otherwise specified. These figures represent the female and male *participation rates* respectively; i.e., the number of

women/men participating in the labour force as a percentage of all females/males respectively. Vincent Ferraro, 2010, *Women in Canada: A Gender-Based Statistical Report: Paid Work* (December), Statistics Canada, Ottawa: Ministry of Industry, Cat. No. 89-503-X. At: statcan.gc.ca/pub/89-503-x/89-503-x2010001-eng.htm.

18. These figures represent the participation of female/male workers as a percentage of the total labour force (Ferraro 2010).

19. Women represent 51.2 percent of business and financial professionals in Canada in 2009 (Ferraro 2010).

20. Women's income in Canada grew by 13 percent from 2000 to 2008 while men's income grew by 7 percent. Income from all sources includes wages, salaries, investments, retirement income and government transfers. Cara Williams, 2010, *Women in Canada: A Gender-Based Statistical Report, Economic Well-being* (December), Statistics Canada, Ottawa: Ministry of Industry, Cat. No. 89-503-X. At: statcan.gc.ca/pub/89-503-x/2010001/article/11388-eng.htmber 28, 2010.

21. Earnings refers to income derived from wages and salaries. These ratios refer to only full-time, full-year workers (Williams 2010).

22. Williams (2010: 32) argues that average annual earnings female to male ratio may not be as accurate as comparing hourly wages, since she found that men work on average 3.7 hours longer per week than women in the full-year, full-time, jobs. Comparing the average hourly wages of women and men, the ratio was 83.3 percent in 2008 — up from 75.7 percent in 1988.

23. These data refer to income after tax. Very low income refers to household income below the low-income cut-off. "Low income cut-offs (LICOs) — more commonly known as Canada's 'unofficial' poverty lines — are established by Statistics Canada using data from the Family Expenditure Survey (now known as the Survey of Household Spending). LICOs indicate the level of income at which a family may be in "straitened circumstances" because it spends a greater proportion of its income — 20 percentage points more — on necessities of food, shelter and clothing than does the average family of a similar size." Canadian Council on Social Development, "A Profile of Economic Security in Canada, Economic Security Fact Sheet #2: Poverty." At: ccsd.ca/factsheets/economic_security/poverty/index.htm.

24. Garnett Picot, Yuqian Lu and Feng Hou, 2009, "Immigrant Low-Income Rates: The Role of Market Income and Government Transfers," *Perspectives on Labour and Income*, Statistics Canada, Cat. No. 75-00X (December). At: statcan.gc.ca/pub/75-001-x/2009112/article/11055-eng.htm#a1.

25. Statistics Canada, 2006, "Gap in Earnings Widens Between Recent Immigrants and Canadian-Born Workers," *Earnings and Incomes of Canadians Over the Past Quarter Century, 2006 Census: Earnings*. At: statcan.gc.ca/census-recensement/2006/as-sa/97-563/p13-eng.cfm.

26. Diane Galarneau and Marian Radulescu, 2009, "Employment among the Disabled," *Perspectives on Labour and Income*, Statistics Canada, Cat. No. 75-00X (May). At: statcan.gc.ca/pub/75-001-x/2009105/article/10865-eng.htm. NB: The negative differentials for all indicators, both for women and men, increase with each year of disability.

27. In 1999, the proportion of men and women with a disability employed throughout the year was 48 percent and 39 percent respectively. Men and women with disabilities work fewer hours (thirteen and eleven weeks respectively) than men and women without disabilities (Galarneau and Radulescu 2009).

28. Fourteen percent of women and men with disabilities had a university degree (Galarneau and Radulescu 2009).

29. Statistics Canada, 2010, "Aboriginal Statistics at a Glance." At: statcan.gc.ca/pub/89-645-x/89-645-x2010001-eng.htm.

30. Of First Nations women, 21 percent had obtained a college diploma, 9 percent had a university degree, 9 percent had a trades certificate, and 5 percent had a university certificate or diploma below the bachelor's level. Shelly Milligan and Evelyne Bougie, 2009, "First Nations Women and Postsecondary Education in Canada: Snapshots from the (2006) Census," Statistics Canada, Cat. No. 89-634-X - No. 001. At: statcan.gc.ca/pub/81-004-x/2009004/article/11017-eng.htm.

Globalization and Women
A Marxist Feminist Introduction
Elaine Coburn

Describing the world capitalist system might seem a roundabout way of addressing the topic of globalization and women. Yet, for Marxist feminists, world capitalism is the context for unequal gender relationships. From this perspective, women around the world are linked, but not always or even typically by bonds of solidarity. This chapter explores the world political economic context of women's relationships, emphasizing their historical and class-specific character. This approach has political implications: freedom and justice for the vast majority of the world's women does not depend upon sexual equality within the world as it is today. Rather, genuine liberation depends upon a global transformation beyond a centuries-old world capitalist system.

Class and Gender in the World Capitalist System

Capitalism is a centuries-old mode of production; that is, it is a specific way of organizing human relationships to produce what is necessary for human existence, including food, clothing, shelter and so on. Capitalism is based upon a relationship between formally free and equal, but materially unequal and antagonistic, classes. The capitalist class, or bourgeoisie, are owners of the means of production (factories, capital, labour power, and so on) used to make goods and services sold on the market. The working class sells their labour power for a wage or salary in order to make a living. Capitalists have a structural imperative to lower labour, environmental and other costs to maintain profits that ensure their enterprise's survival. Thus, the class relationship is fundamentally antagonistic, since better working conditions and wages for workers appear as costs and reduced profits to capitalists, who must exploit workers to stay in business.

Yet class exploitation does not adequately explain all oppressions. Traditional Marxist theory must account for the specific experiences of women and racialized minorities. Of course, like men, many women have participated in the capitalist system as workers and, to a much lesser extent, as capitalists. But historically, many women have been incorporated into capitalist relationships primarily through their reproductive labour, including paid or unpaid caring activities like childcare and elder care, as well as routine household tasks like laundry, meal preparation, and so on. At the turn of the last century, for example, wives and mothers of male coal and anthracite miners in South Wales prepared meals and baths, washed and mended laundry, looked after children, cleaned coal dirt from the house and generally maintained the household so that their husbands could return to work or union activities, fed, clothed and more or less rested (Bruley 2007: 59–60). Whether paid or, as in this case, unpaid, women's reproductive labour is essential to the ongoing functioning of capitalism, notably enabling others' (men's) participation in the paid work sector.

Some feminists understand this typically female experience of reproductive labour as one aspect of the worldwide patriarchal system that oppresses women, who share a dominated or subaltern status. In contrast, Marxist feminists maintain that the concept of "woman" is not a universal and homogenous one, but is differentiated by class and other social distinctions, such as those between white collar and blue collar workers, and between white and racialized women. In contrast with working-class women, many bourgeois women perform very little direct reproductive labour; instead they employ and manage racialized working-class women and men for such domestic labour. Women's experiences, including their roles in reproductive labour, differ by class, race, age, disability and other social relations.

What is New in the World Capitalist System?
Continuity and Change in an Era of Globalization

Arguably, world capitalism dates back 500 years to the incorporation of the "new world" into the imperial centres in Europe. As a global enterprise, capitalism began with the genocide of Indigenous peoples whose presence and ways of life were obstacles to the incorporation of lands and resources by what would now be called transnational corporations, like the Hudson's Bay Company. These corporations were backed by imperial state power, including military might, and by scholarly expertise, which "scientifically" proved the inferior nature of Indigenous peoples, and thus justified their extermination or assimilation: North, Latin, and South American, African and South Asian Indigenous peoples and lands were progressively incorporated into global markets. Of course, this incorporation has been uneven, resisted and challenged by Indigenous peoples. In this sense, globalization as well as resistance to global forms of capitalism, can be traced back over hundreds of years.

If the world capitalist system is centuries old, why speak of a new phase of globalization? For Marxist feminists, the major characteristic of the new, global phase of capitalism, which began in the 1970s following a worldwide economic crisis, is the enhanced relative global power of capitalists. Enabled by new communications and transport technologies developed, in part, to reorganize production and so recapture declining profits associated with the 1970s crisis, capitalists can move more easily around the world than in the past. Thus, capital may respond to workers' demands by threatening to relocate to parts of the globe with more "flexible" working-class populations and less stringent and costly environmental, health and safety regulations. This enhanced power relative to the working class and the state created conditions for a new political (class) compromise, often summarized as neoliberalism.

Neoliberal policies may be pursued "autonomously" in the developed world by national governments, or they may be required as a condition of International Monetary Fund and World Bank loans for debt repayment in the nations on the global periphery, and, since 1989, in the former Communist countries. These policies vary worldwide but typically include

a. the privatization of formerly public goods and services (for example, treating water and DNA as goods that can be bought and sold on the market), or shifting from public to privately funded health care;
b. the explicit or *de facto* weakening of health, safety and environmental legislation costly to capital; for example, by depriving enforcement ministries of resources necessary to identify and sanction health, safety and environmental violations;
c. the liberalization of financial transactions and trade (or "free trade"), frequently formalized in international investment and trade agreements negotiated through institutions like the World Trade Organization;
d. the "warfare" state's expansion: this involves spending shifts from social services, health, education, and welfare to war-related endeavours, often aimed at securing favourable conditions for domestic capital abroad, while punitive institutions that discipline working-class populations domestically, like prisons, are expanded.

A second major feature of the world capitalist system's new global era is neoliberalism's worldwide ideological success. Following the Soviet Union's collapse in 1989, capitalism generically, and neoliberalism specifically, became the only system of political and economic action in the world. Francis Fukuyama (1992), a philosopher and advisor to Ronald Reagan, famously captured this ideological triumph when he declared the "end of history": all possible human futures would be played out within the framework of liberal capitalism and liberal democracy. Even the current economic crisis, beginning in the United States in 2008 with the so-called credit crisis (actually a crisis of under-consumption linked to increasing inequality), has not shaken capitalism's worldwide ideological dominance. Rather, the emphasis has been on developing measures to save capitalism from its own excesses; for example, by spending billions in state funds to save failed banks, rather than looking for alternatives beyond capitalism.

A third major characteristic of neoliberal globalization is that it is overwhelmingly the achievement of a small minority of men. Despite cross-national variation, worldwide, men dominate

- national parliaments, especially in the powerful economics, finance, industry and trade ministries;
- positions as "technical" experts in trade, economics and finance, whether as state bureaucrats or economic advisors in international financial institutions like the International Monetary Fund;
- economics and business departments training such technical experts, especially the most secure, senior faculty positions;
- computer science and engineering fields, responsible for innovations that make globally mobile capital and new weapons and security systems possible;
- employment as white-collar financial capitalists and speculators;
- the specialist media, like *The Financial Times* and *The Economist*, as well as the mass media's business sections, which provide ideological support for neoliberal policies.

Thus, the neoliberal phase of the worldwide capitalism system is largely the product of men, but not just any men. Rather, it is dominated by white, bourgeois men, often from, or educated in, the world's most powerful nations, notably the United States.

Neoliberal Globalization:
Consequences for Bourgeois and Working-Class Women and Men

The capitalist class and its policy-makers and ideologues are also overwhelmingly male. However, capitalists' relative increased strength under globalization is not a victory for men, as a generic, universal category, since men are no more a unified group than women. Rather, it is specifically bourgeois men and bourgeois women across the world capitalist system who benefit from neoliberal policies that expand the market's reach, while both working-class women and working-class men lose. Indeed, one striking effect of the worldwide export of neoliberal models of capitalism is increasing inequality: the rich today may be wealthier than at any time in human history. For example, a 2006 study finds that the wealthiest 2 percent of households own over 50 percent of the world's wealth, while the poorer half owns about 1 percent (Walker 2006). A single billionaire, like Bill Gates, overdetermines political and economic policy, not least through charitable initiatives like the Gates Foundation, which set health priorities for the majority of people in Africa. The initiatives developed with the help of these charities respond to donors' priorities and concerns, but are not bound by the democratic will of those they aim to help. Meanwhile, the poor suffer the consequences. For example, the wealthy benefit more from recent improvements in health, enjoying increased longevity and lower infant mortality compared to poorer fractions of the population (Coburn 2009). At the same time that neoliberalism reinforces capital's political-economic power, it has negative effects on the working-class majority, especially the least-well-off, both women and men.

Yet the relative decreased power of working-class women and men under neoliberalism translates into different experiences, based partly on gender. Take the experience of working-class migrant workers, for example. Under neoliberal globalization, both are subject to legislated vulnerability, typically deprived of the right to vote, thus having no political voice in the country in which they work. Yet the kind of labour such global migrants do differs significantly by gender, with "men in arms, women in service" (Falquet 2006). Men are employed in the expanding war-related and security industries. Thus, in the United States, over 30,000 non-American citizens, mostly men, serve in the American military in exchange for financial support for a university education and the chance to apply for permanent resident status (Meyer 2007). Likewise, privatized military services operating in Iraq, Afghanistan, and the Balkans are overwhelmingly male-dominated. Women provide services, including domestic labour and caregiving, but also prostitution or other sex work — and they do so increasingly in the private sector, as relatively better-paying and secure public-sector service employment in areas like health and education is privatized. In Canada, the mainly Filipina women who enter Canada as live-in caregivers, cannot leave the family to which they are assigned for three years without risking the loss of their work visa and, ultimately, the right to apply for permanent Canadian residency and citizenship. As a consequence of these work- and residence- conditions, such caregivers are particularly vulnerable to employer abuse. Ironically, their employers are often women, who turn to private sector care because of diminished access to good quality public sector services. Neoliberal capitalism's characteristic dynamics, including an expanding warfare state and shrinking public service sector, translate into different experiences for men and for women in a globally mobile migrant working class.

Export-processing zones (EPZs) symbolize and proliferate under the neoliberal order, facilitating international capital flows by creating geographically defined areas that offer special exemptions for capital, including reduced tariffs and taxes and infrastructure subsidies designed to attract investors as well as low-paid workers, with few labour rights. The majority of EPZs, now numbering over 5000 compared to a few hundred a decade ago, are in China and Asia, and are often concentrated in textiles and electronics (Singa Boyenge 2007). EPZs are strongly feminized, with women constituting up to 90 percent of the labour force. These poorly paid women there are classified as "unskilled" labour because of their weak educational credentials. Yet, under neoliberal privatization policies, school fees escalate, and working-class families privilege sons' education, since they are seen as more likely to join the paid workforce and help with household income. Thus, neoliberal policies that make education less accessible to working-class families combine with gender norms that direct limited working-class family resources towards male children, contributing to women's lesser schooling and justifying women workers' ongoing "superexploitation" in EPZs and other workplaces. Of course, working-class men lose through such arrangements as well, since their own wages may be driven down by the competition by women working for low pay in neighbouring EPZs. Working-class female and male workers both suffer from neoliberal globalization, but they do so in gender-distinct ways.

For Marxist feminists, neoliberal globalization links women across the world, but not always or even typically in emancipatory ways. As in previous phases of the world capitalist system, working-class women do not share interests with bourgeois women. Canadian women executives like Christine Day, the CEO of Lululemon, the Vancouver-based firm selling "yoga-inspired" fitness clothing, share only the social attribute of "woman" with the workers in Thailand, China, and Indonesia that produce Lululemon textiles, but, because higher wages for the women workers in Asia mean lower profits for Lululemon, their interests are fundamentally opposed. Furthermore, Christine Day has a broad structural interest in supporting a capitalist system that justifies the expropriation of these women's labour as a source of profit for her company. The political implication is that, in contemporary capitalist globalization, women's solidarity can extend around the globe — but not, except in a temporary, strategic way, across class lines.

For Marxist feminists, democratic political debate can only begin to take place within the context of broader political economic equality. Too many women, like too many working-class men, are engaged in struggles for basic survival: they spend most of their waking hours as "slaves to the machine," producing ephemeral goods that are not really needed or even wanted, or doing service work that is divorced from genuine caring and has simply become mass drudgery. At the same time, a very few have so much wealth that they cannot spend it in a thousand lifetimes. In this context, the aim is not to increase the number of women in the global bourgeoisie. The goal is nothing less than to transcend the world capitalist system, with its promises of equality and freedom and its realities of inequality and exploitation.

REFERENCES

Bruley, Susan. 2007. "The Politics of Food: Gender, Family, Community and Collective Feeding in South Wales in the General Strike and Miners' Lockout of 1926." *Twentieth Century British History* 18,1.

Coburn, David. 2009. "Inequality and Ill-health." In Colin Leys and Leo Panitch (eds.), *Socialist Register 2010: Health Under Capitalism: Morbid Symptoms*. Halifax and Winnipeg: Fernwood Publishing.

Falquet, Jules. 2006. "Hommes en armes et femmes 'de services': tendances néolibérales dans l'évolution de la division sexuelle et internationale du travail." *Cahiers du Genre* 40.

Fukuyama, Francis. 1992. *The End of History and the Last Man*. New York: Free Press.

Meyer, Cordula. 2007. "Fighting for a New Homeland: U.S. Army Lures Foreigners with Promise of Citizenship," Spiegel Online. At: spiegel.de/international/world/0,1518,512384,00.html.

Singa Boyenge, Jean-Pierre. 2007. *ILO Database on Export Processing Zones: Working Paper*. Geneva: International Labour Office. At: ilo.org/public/english/dialogue/sector/themes/epz/epz-db.pdf.

Walker, Andrew. 2006. "The Richest 2% Own 'Half the Wealth.'" *The BBC*. At: <http://news.bbc.co.uk/2/hi/business/6211250.stm>.

75

Stories from Field to Table
Women in the Global Food System
Deborah Barndt

Food History and My Story

As a child, I created hideaways with my friends in barns and pastures of the small farming community where I grew up. While I played, my mother tended our large garden and canned vegetables for the winter. Each fall, she joined other women around a big caldron in a park, stirring up an enormous communal batch of apple butter over an open fire. Fresh milk came from my friends' cows, and their chickens and pigs often found their way to our table.

Today as I visit my old hometown, I find the farms abandoned, the general store boarded up, and most townspeople travelling up the road to the cluster of fast food restaurants around the exit of the superhighway that now runs through the fields we once roamed. The food they eat comes from unknown origins, though you would probably recognize it as the standard fare that is fast becoming a global homogenized diet. Women still prepare it; the ingredients are usually frozen and precut which they fry or whip up in record speed, responding to our expectation of quick and convenient service.

Meanwhile, immense refrigerated trucks whiz by on the adjacent highway, carrying fresh and processed produce from southern fields or northern factories to big food retailers and consumers around North America. These foodstuffs also have stories behind them, of women who are central to the planting, picking, and packing of fruits and vegetables, to the cutting, cooking, and canning in food processing plants, to the scanning, selling, and serving of food products in supermarkets and restaurants. But these women are usually invisible to us; their stories rarely told.

My lifetime, which began as the Second World War ended, has paralleled the development of the post-war global food system, through the industrialization of agriculture, the dependence on monocultural and chemicalized production, the proliferation of "value-added" highly processed food which increase profits while endangering health. The increasingly corporatized system is characterized by a "distancing" (Kneen 1993) of production from consumption, the "uniformity" (Shiva 1993) and commercialization of food as market "commodities" (Winson 1993), an emphasis on efficiency and labour "flexibility" (Lara 1998), and increasing threats to "ecological and human health" (Griffin 1995). Women are still central to this process, but as part of a corporate flexible labour force who primarily work seasonally and part-time producing and preparing *our* food in order to feed *their* families.

Food Workers' Stories and the Tomato's Journey

My story is only one, unfolding in a small corner of this increasingly interconnected globe. As the market has moved into the home, and women have increasingly moved out of the home into the workforce (Reiter 1996), they are playing other roles in moving our food from field to table.

Let's consider, for example, women workers in two ends of the continental food system, in particular the tomato food chain: a Mexican agribusiness where women plant, prune, harvest, sort, and pack tomatoes; and a Canadian supermarket, where women part-time cashiers punch the tomato's code into the computer and pack it in your bag. In the late 1990s, I followed the journey of a corporate tomato from Mexican field to Canadian table, gathering the stories of the women whose hands move it along the way (Barndt 2002). Their experiences are shaped not only by gender, but by interlocking factors such as class, race/ethnicity, rural/urban contexts, and family intergenerational roles.

Santa Rosa Agribusiness: Picking and Packing for the North

Since the North American Free Trade Agreement (NAFTA) was implemented in 1994, the Mexican economy has become increasingly dependent on exporting agricultural products, given its comparative advantage of easy access to land, sun, and cheap labour. In fact, Empaque Santa Rosa, the second largest domestic tomato producer in Mexico, now produces 85 percent for export. In turn, it depends on a primarily female labour force, in the fields and greenhouses, and particularly in the sorting and packing of tomatoes.

Juana[1] is one of the more privileged workers, part of a 'moving maquila'[2] of skilled workers moved by the company to work in the packing plants:

I'm thirty-seven years old now. I've been following the harvests for twenty-three years. We are brought from Sinaloa with all expenses paid; the company covers the costs of transport, food, and once here, we get a house with a stove, beds, and mattresses.

NORTH

Class

Race/Ethnicity

Rural/Urban

Age/Family

SOUTH

Santa Rosa prefers women as packers because, according to the Vice President of Production: "Women can 'see' better than men... and they treat the product more gently. They can put up with more than men in all aspects: the routine and the monotony. Men are more restless and won't put up with it."

This gender ideology does not recognize that women learn to handle food from an early age, and will more readily make sacrifices to support their families. Since North American Free Trade Agreement and a subsequent peso crisis, in fact, poor Mexican families require at least five family members working in order to cover basic survival needs (Kopinak 1997).

Tomasa, a sixty-eight-year-old field worker, works with her husband Pablo at Santa Rosa. But, like most Mexican families, they depend on the migration of their kids *al norte*: "Two of my sons have gone to work in the U.S. and send money back." Like many rural Mexican women, Tomasa works a triple day: as a salaried worker for agribusiness, as the cook and caretaker of her family, and as a subsistence farmer on the family *milpa*, or cornfield. During a typical workday, she's up before dawn preparing tortillas for lunch, is picked up at 6 a.m. by a truck that delivers her to the tomato fields by 7 a.m. After seven hours of gruelling work under a hot sun, rushing to fill her forty pail daily quota, Tomasa returns to her village, and to the family plot to tend to the corn, squash and beans that are the staples in her family's diet. Her low wage (just over $5 a day) is based on an assumption that she will grow her own food, while the plantation tomatoes she picks are rushed to the border for northern consumers.

Reyna, an Indigenous farmworker, does not even have the luxury of growing her own food: "In Guerrero, we grew our own vegetables at home. But not here." Reflecting a historical racism, Indigenous workers are brought by the company from the poorer southern states and housed in horrific camps with makeshift huts, without electricity, or water, or sewage. While they work in the tomato fields, they must buy their own food, often from company-run stores.

Families like Reyna's have often been forced to migrate because their land has become wasted by intensive agrochemical use, and/or because they have become indebted by the high costs of fertilizers promoted by industrial agriculture. While paid the same, they barely eke out a living as they move from harvest to harvest. Women carry their babies on their backs as they work (both exposed to pesticides), and bear the brunt of the housework and ill health engendered by poor living conditions.

While Juana, Tomasa, and Reyna reflect some of the diversity among women agricultural workers, they play a common role as the flexible labour of global food producers, as they struggle to feed their families through work that ultimately feeds ours.

Loblaws Supermarket: Fast and Friendly Cashiers

At the consumption end of the tomato chain, women cashiers are "on the front line," so to speak, as their jobs have been transformed by similar corporate labour strategies and new technologies. While the flexibility of Mexican field workers is dependent on agricultural cycles, the flexibility of Canadian service workers is determined by consumer demand and the corporate drive for profit in the name of efficiency.

At my neighbourhood Loblaws, for example, all of the cashiers are women and almost all of them are part-timers. In the mid-1990s, Loblaws' negotiations with United Food and Commercial Workers led to a two-tiered wage structure, buyouts, and an elimination of full-time jobs. While the union negotiated wage freezes for current employees, they agreed to lower ceilings for new hires (for part-timers from $15/hour to $12.50; by 2010, there was a new minimum rate of $10.25). The proliferation of part-time work is a trend in the service sector, exempting managers from paying certain benefits and allowing them to respond to "just-in-time production," by rationalizing schedules according to demand. Companies like Loblaws justify these cutbacks by arguing that the large non-unionized discount stores (No Frills, Costco) have created crippling competition (with $9/hour wages; by 2009, this rate had not increased).

Cashiers usually fall into one of two categories: older women like Marissa who started a part-time job twenty-five years ago and kept the job to have more time for her children, and students like Carol who sees retail work as temporary job to pay her way through law school.[3] Both, however, must succumb to the pressure to be "fast and friendly," to deal politely with customers (assumed to be a "natural" women's skill) as the public face of the business, while also scanning and bagging items accurately and efficiently. The same computer technology that controls inventory also monitors cashiers' productivity, a kind of "all-seeing eye," ensuring that they meet their quota of scanning 500 items per hour. And if agrochemicals endanger Mexican fieldworkers' health, it's these new technologies that affect Canadian women cashiers, generating both physical and emotional stress (Menzies 1996).

With seniority, Marissa sets her own schedule, while more recently hired Carol may be called in at the unpopular times, such as evenings or weekends. Marissa chooses to work when her former husband can take her daughters: "I work three weekends out of four, which Loblaws loves because they've got a senior girl for their busiest period and it works out for me because I'm not paying for daycare."

But this "choice" is based on the fact that neither employers nor the state provide adequate childcare for working parents. And women's wages and working conditions still often assume a working husband who can also help out at home. Besides an increase in single mothers, and despite efforts by the women's movement to address housework, pay inequities, and childcare, working women aged 25 to 54 averaged almost two hours more per day on unpaid work activities in 2005.[4] Cashiers like Marissa are on a single mom express, juggling a part-time job with unpaid domestic labour as well as work in the informal economy.

Against tremendous odds, however, women are organizing.

Food Activism: Women Creating Alternatives

The stories above have been framed by two primary axes — production/consumption and biodiversity/cultural diversity — and by two secondary axes — work/technology and health/environment. The relationship between production and consumption, is reflected in the two contexts, with Mexicans Tomasa and Reyna representing the increasing role of southern countries in producing food for export, while Marissa, the Canadian supermarket cashier, symbolizes the consumption end of the chain in the north. This global food system threatens at the same time the biodiversity of the planet and the cultural diversity of peoples' growing and eating practices. Women's work within this system has been transformed by technology, and their personal health as well as environmental health has been endangered.

While women workers in the global food system, represented by two ends of the continental tomato chain, are impacted by all of these dynamics, they are also engaged in resistance, both personal and collective, organizational and international. In response to the distancing between production and consumption, diverse strategies are addressing this separation we all experience from the sources of the food we eat. Women are key leaders in local alternatives such as Metro Toronto's FoodShare, for example, promoting urban

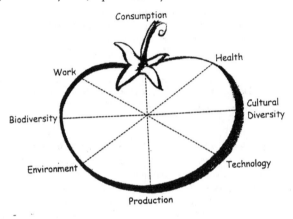

agriculture and exchanges of seeds among new immigrants, neighbourhood food box distribution, and community kitchens (Barndt 1999), reconnecting production to consumption.

Threatened by the loss of biodiversity and cultural diversity resulting from the uniformity of global food production, Indigenous populations have been defending their own genetic resources and more sustainable growing practices. A Mapuche woman in southern Chile, part of the Hemispheric Indigenous Women's Network, learned about the threats to biodiversity of monocultural production from Nettie Wiebe, Canadian farmer/activist and a founder of La Vía Campesina (an international network of peasant and Indigenous organizations). She was encouraged to keep preserving the rich variety of potato plants and has organized fairs to promote biodiversity, as well as to exchange seeds and recipes.

Relating to the shifts in work and technology, corporate flexible labour strategies have come under attack for creating job insecurity among women part-time food workers and for wreaking havoc on family eating practices. At the local level, a newly formed Organization of Contingent Workers, led by women, is addressing this issue.

Finally, the impact of the global food system on environment and health has been a major concern of women, who are key leaders in the environmental movement and in projects promoting ecological and holistic health. A Popular Health Group along with Friends of the Earth in Sayula, Mexico, have worked primarily with Indigenous women to improve the living conditions of the migrant labour camps of the tomato workers and to address poverty as a key determinant in health. In the north, ecofeminists suggest an important relationship between the exploitation of women and the exploitation of the environment, implying that perhaps women workers and tomatoes are connected after all — as commodities in a corporate food system which is being contested locally, regionally, and globally.

These stories of resistance are often even less visible than the stories of women's experiences as food workers. Perhaps this suggests another research process: seek out signs of hope among your family and community members, through local organizations and international networks. Or better yet, join or start one initiative.

NOTES

1. The quotations in this section are from interviews carried out in Sayula, Mexico, in December, 1996.
2. Maquila is the short form of the word maquiladora, and refers to the establishment of foreign-owned (mostly U.S.) assembly plants in Mexico and Central America, which are allowed to import components and raw materials duty-free and re-export the finished product to the U.S. For more information, go to en.maquilasolidarity.org.
3. The quotations in this section are from interviews carried out in Toronto, May, 1997.
4. Men aged twenty-five to fifty-four spent almost two hours more per day than women on paid work activities. Since 1986, the division between paid and unpaid labour for women and men has been converging. For more details, see Lindsay 2008.

REFERENCES

Barndt, Deborah. 2007. *Tangled Routes: Women, Work, and Globalization on the Tomato Trail.* Toronto: Rowman & Littlefield.

Barndt, Deborah (ed.). 1999. *Women Working the NAFTA Food Chain: Women, Food, and Globalization.* Toronto: Sumach Press.

Lindsay, Colin. 2008. "Are Women Spending More Time on Unpaid Domestic Work than Men in Canada?" *General Social Survey: Matter of Fact 9.* Ottawa: Statistics Canada. At: statascan.ca/english/pgdb/People/Families/famil36c.htm.

Griffin, Susan. 1995. *The Eros of Everyday Life: Essays on Ecology, Gender, and Society.* New York: Doubleday.

Kneen, Brewster. 1993. *From Land to Mouth: Understanding the Food System, Second Helping.* Toronto: NC Press.

Kopinak, Kathy. 1997. *Desert Capitalism: What are the Maquiladoras?* Montreal: Black Rose.

Lara, Sara. 1998. *Nuevas Experiencias Productivas y Nuevas Formas de Organización Flexible del Trabajo en la Agricultura Mexicana.* Mexico City: Pablos.

Menzies, Heather. 1996. *Whose Brave New World? The Information Highway and the New Economy.* Toronto: Between the Lines.

Reiter, Ester. 1996. *Making Fast Food: From the Frying Pan into the Fryer.* Kingston: McGill-Queen's University Press.

Shiva, Vandana. 1993. *Monocultures of the Mind: Perspectives on Biodiversity and Biotechnology.* Atlantic Highlands, NJ: Zed Books.

Winson, Anthony. 1993. *The Intimate Commodity: Food and the Development of the Agro-Industrial Complex in Canada.* Toronto: Garamond.

First the Chores and Then the Dishes

Aritha Van Herk

The family offers itself as a double discourse, especially in any gendered reading. What you can speculate is a halved reading of the family's doubled discourse, its duplicitous side, the side you'd rather not admit, the side you think has vanished with the onset of dishwashers and microwaves and other electrical conveniences, but a reading that still lurks under the auspices of *family* as something you are supposed to admire, applaud, never doubt.

***

In *that* family, work was an open secret; working constant, an on-going presence. It could not be finished, was never over, grew itself into a monster of extortion. Asking for attention. Gave them all the works. They had their work cut out for them just trying to keep up. There was never any question of being *finished*. The tyranny of the present participle: plowing, seeding, spraying, gardening, weeding, haying, baling, loading, stacking, unloading, swathing, combining, trucking, summer-fallowing, rounding up, milking, cleaning, chasing, separating, shovelling manure, shovelling manure, shovelling manure, spreading clean straw, trudgery, drudgery.

Nothing ever done, over, finished. The litany of the western Canadian farm family. All hands on deck, either in field or barn, working.

And then there were always the dishes.

***

Work is a word that she tries now to skew, to alter. It resists play, rather like a tin cup, merciless and utilitarian. Backwards is *krow*, and that is its only gambit, its one endearance. It refuses to flirt or even to bungle. It is an *onhandig* (Dutch for clumsy) word, bitter and direct, with the hard *k* of destination. Work. Aloud, it upstages authority, it reifies result. A process toward product, inexorable, unrelenting. Without the 'o' it is still wrk, a Siberian stalwart. And yet, she uses it herself, with a kind of perverse pleasure. She is in love with the word's tool, with its potential for deflection.

"I have work to do." (Go away, don't bother me, come back later.)

"I have to go home and do some work tonight." (The evening has an edge of boredom, the company not quite as intense as it might be. The reference to work operates as a subtle rebuke.)

"I have to work tomorrow." (I'm tired and I want to go to bed.)

"I'm working." (Ring my bell, dial my number at your own risk. I am likely to bite your head off for interrupting, that is if I bother to answer at all. I'm working, I 'm working, I am working.)

And then there are always the dishes.

***

Work is the effort required to produce one's own livelihood, an activity we have canonized through its historical development.

Gerstel and Engel offer an overview: "the Greeks regarded such effort as drudgery fit only for slaves; the Old Testament tradition believed it was punishment for original sin; Protestantism elevated work to a religious duty; and Marx argued that humans created themselves and became distinctively human through freely performed labour" (4-5).

In *that* family, work fell directly into the Protestant category: duty, with a slight edge of leftover Old Testament punishment. And, survival. The opposite end of livelihood, with its tinge of choice. Nothing so elegant or suggestive, so free. Certainly no vocation, or chosen profession. Necessary work, the necessities of work, the work of necessity. Needing to be done, a requirement. Work as a pathway to success, the immigrant drive for achievement. Work baptizing the family Canadian.

They were Calvinists, *that* family, Dutch Reformed Calvinists. Combine that with surviving occupied (for five long years) Holland, and post-war immigration to Canada. How much duty and punishment does any family need? Take it out on work, the final arbiter for all possible choices. Work as escape and justification, work as substitute for language, as its own choreography and destination. Work as an act of immigration itself, an emigrant vice, pleasure in its purity, its particular denomination. It might be called religion.

And then, there are always the dishes.

***

She tries to remember the first time in her life that she consciously undertook to work, was assigned a job. Assignation. To make illicit. That becomes her talent, the illicitation of duty.

Bringing home the cows from the pasture. Is this work? The leg-stretching hike out to the back quarter, the delicious running sorties after Jessie who wants to stand forever in the slough, the path carved through the bush of poplar and spruce, which becomes without fail the forest of Enceladus, he and all the hundred-armed giants under the green shade, the open stretch behind the bush, its kingdomed roll to the barbed wire fence that marks the edge of property (illicit, this hour for fantasy and dreaming, the open sky, the open prairie grass, the secret darkness of the woods.) And yet, the safety of that cow-worn path threaded through the trees as she follows their gently swaying backs home through duty's dereliction, and the rising knowledge that the work that offers solitude and privacy is precious. It is a job she offers to do, bringing home the cows. Because it is unclassified, a space for acts of imagination. Illicit acts. That move from fairy tales to conquerings, from delicious fears to sexual delights. Bringing home the cows teaches her to shout and sing, she has the time to test her running, she learns to taste nakedness because yes, one day it becomes necessary to take off her shirt, to let her skin into the air, the orgasm of wind. She is alone out there, she is free to learn how to love herself. This is *not* what bringing home the cows is supposed to teach her: the feel of a fairy's loaf (a round, smooth stone) against her breast, the bark of a tree under a hand that recovers every texture as sexual. She gets the docile holsteins latched into the stalls through a transparent afterwash of pleasure. Is this work? Or is the work peripheral to what really happens when her feet fly over the gopher holes and hummocks, past the tangle of chokecherry bushes and the edge of the marshy slough? In that difference she runs out of herself, out of her skin. Into freedom.

And then there are the dishes.

***

That family is more practical than hierarchical. There is so much work that it is passed along, divided up, shared around. There is always some left over, it refuses to decease itself. And the nature of *that* family? It has never occurred to them to lament their own erasure, they precede the crumbling of the institution's monolith, its nuclear effacement. They example familial disjunction, emigration as an act of distancing, as a breakage or rift. The successful evasion of cousins and maiden aunts, of dictatorial fathers. For every political and economic reason immigrants offer for their own displacement, there exists an equal number of bastard patriarchs. How do they escape the inexorable hand of the punitive father? Emigrate.

Immigrate. Free to become bastard patriarchs themselves, to establish their own dynasty.

Family as authoritative structure. Shared blood, a shared household (possession there, in the realm of hold), enforced conjunction. The hegemony of the heterosexual couple and their offspring. An economic unit. An accident. A container. A prison. A place within which to conceal crime. Misprison. Misconception, misunderstanding. Universally different; monolithically fragmented. Questions of legitimacy, illegal and surreptitious acts of love.

Breadwinnning, housekeeping, natural, biological, functional, common residence, economic co-operation, reproduction. Owned or adopted. *That* family has become its own questioned legitimacy, its own metanarrative. Relational, nurturant. And demanding. Emotional blackmail, the blood's mafia. Enforcement. A prescribed intimacy. Never permitted to escape the silent accusations of toothbrushes, the laboured rectangularity of dinner tables, the battlelines of sibling-shared bedrooms. Conjugular.

Chemical: two or more radicals acting as one. Mathematical: reciprocally related or interchangeable. Kindred in origin and meaning. Where does *that* family derive from?

Then, there are always the dishes.

***

She tries to sort it out, her place within them, the strangely morbid internalization of dutiful daughter/sister. She did not choose them, would never have chosen their particular incestuousness of purpose; and she is certain they did not choose her, convinced *she* was an accident, and accepted only out of necessity, perhaps practicality, another pair of hands to do another set of chores, some of the work that grew and grew. There can be no doubt that she is legitimate, genetically inscribed. She knows the tracing paper of feature and gesture, posture and manual extension: her hands link her self to their deliberations.

She thinks of her as *daughter*. Visible difference. Daw: a jackdaw, a simpleton. A daughter's befittment, when she wants to be as sleek and uncatchable as the otter, its plait of movement through a still-breathing pond, but somewhere in therDawe is an *ought*, a necessity, the auxiliary followed by the infinitive. There is a moral duty in ought, an obligation, propriety, expectation. The silent but waiting mouth of a dot, naught, its circular ambivalence. Open or closed? And the daughter too, open or closed. Perhaps closer to deter, fend off, ward away, discourage. The daughter: dis/couraged. Courage the insistent spirit, intrepid timidity. Properly daughterly, a harbinger of spring. Too much to bear such ardent investment in a part she plays so badly.

She thinks of herself as *sister*. Her own sister drawing a heavy, invisible line down the middle of the bed. "Don't you dare put one finger over this line." But her sister smells of lemon and honey, and if she squints at a particular angle, she can read from the page of her sister's open book, read the forbidden story, that combination of sinister and stir, their secret siblinghood, although there is not affection between them, or not much, once she begins to talk, to talk back, talk about. Both bent to the left, underhanded unpropitious. And neither one dexterous.

She thinks of herself as *sister*. Her brothers resist, de/sister her with their easy contempt, their permissive discrepancies thought and voiced. "You're just a dumb girl." (Don't worry about having an inferiority complex: you *are* inferior.) The arm twisted behind the back, the snowball out of nowhere, the locked insistence of one's word against the other's. Her brothers teacher her otherness, they pound it into her. They promise her the future: "I'll learn you —" they say.

Is this work sistering, daughtering? It feels like work, hard work. The virulence, the tyranny of blood.

And then, there are always dishes.

***

That family as its own site of development and bereavement. Family = belonging. And there is not a damn thing she can do about it, no choice about where she landed up, no choice about who she got and where, the dice of genes, and the bingo of conception. To be fami-lied, the concept and the structure verbed, verbalized, as close as the constituents can find themselves to be being damned, as close as being saved. Kept. Wrapped within.

Leona Gom: "Home is where when you go there they have to take you in" — family that is, no abnegation of the blood, a dis/own/ment. A repudiation. A name, a blood type, a tilt of cheekbones: physical facts cannot be denied. Family builds dams, dykes, walls around itself: the nuclear item privatized into its own meltdown and reaction and subsequent explo-sion. Family wars, fallouts, and pacifications.

While she goes to friends for advice, for affection, for attention, for an isolated moment, separate from guilt and obligation. The family of friends, the ones who take her as she is, without all those troublesome genes, who don't even care about the closet skeletons, the griefs and guilts she bears for too much or too little love. The extended family, its stretched tentacles of aunts and cousins, of the mysterious and inexplicable grandmother who has her name, had it first, who looks so much like her, and who started that family, before the first world war. What affectionate leavetaking of a soldier got that grandmother: a family stretched all over the world, grandchildren as alien and unrequited as that one gasp, one moment of aspiration for intimacy.

And afterwards, there are always the dishes.

***

She knows her family has given her muscles, an inheritance profoundly useful now, when muscles help her through the rough spots. She can't rely on being ladylike anymore, it won't open doors or get her tire changed, or even give her any answers to the questions that lurk around the back door of history. This is a new binary: muscle and tongue; tongue and muscle. In the old days, there was only muscle, and that was someone else's, a man's. Muscles were off-limits, off-duty for women.

And yet she grows them, easily, bending over a shovel or a pitchfork, wielding a hoe and a rake, serious, required work, not the easy jobs of rounding up cows and collecting eggs, running errands, messages from one part of the farm to the other. Chores. Clean the cow barn, clean the pig pens, shovel the chop from the truck into the bin. Her arms and legs ache, her back clenches itself under her shoulders. Separate the milk. Lifting the full pails shoulder high, so heavy, so full, having to be careful not to spill the rich thick milk full of cream. And yet, muscles or not, she does, spills enough to catch hell and has to clean it all up, then trudges up the hill to the house and starts on supper because her mother is ironing, peels potatoes and fries sausages, and boils carrots, and sets the table and then the men come in and sit down and say they're hungry, they've been working so hard, and she serves the food and can hardly lift her fork to her mouth at her corner of the family table, and they eat and eat, and shove back their chairs and stretch out their legs while she steps over them to clear the dirty dishes.

Lucky for her, dishes never need much muscle. They hone tongue, and it is there, standing at the piled sink below the window that looks out on the road, that she begins to think of tongue, its wonderful freedom within the mouth, and how it cannot ache the way muscles do. And she begins to use it, her tongue, her dutiful double, her immigrant prairie tongue.

Her older brother carries the heavy pails of chop from granary to barn, and walking behind him, she hears the wonderfully strange and innovative ribbon of words that accompany his exertion.

"Those are swears," she says to him.

"Right," he says. "I'm swearing."

"Why?"

"Cause it's hard work and I hate doing it."

Muscle and tongue, stretching themselves into new strength, and maybe her muscles aren't as good as his, but her tongue is better, she knows that. Tongue the most flexible muscle.

Replacing the dishes.

***

Does this go beyond *that* family, to the west, to prairie and sky and the infinite weather? The west as a sprawl of desire, as a gesture of abnegation, a demand for suffering/sufferance? She can't get anywhere out here unless she suffers, and the west comes between the members of a family, filters through their conjunction like the fine dust of a summer storm, the grainy snow of blizzards.

The farm family articulated to the agricultural economy? Petit-bourgeous structure? Household and enterprise under the unrelenting eye of the prairie sky? The inseparability of property from subsistence, of weather from pleasure? Of family from place? She is sure there are no families in eastern Canada, not like the ones she knows, choking, and regressive. They are a different sort, polite and well-bred, with plenty of space for circling, for stretching the rope attached to ankles. They call each other darling, a word her family would choke on. "You," her parents say, or "Hey."

Or is *that* family an immigrant delineation? All western families immigrant: if you don't come from the east you come from farther away, a boat load and a train ride across the country away. The western family as transplanted organism, a regressive trait. Coming out of the closet. The place to dare family is in the west, a specially arranged unit, suitable to weather and space. The family that prays together stays together; the family that sleeps together snores together; the family that works together —

And then, there are still the dishes.

***

To develop her tongue muscle she takes to books. If she cannot talk back, if she has to finish her chores before she can hide in the bush, she comes to rely on books. There is a lot of spade work to be done — this is the period when she digs in the garden and the orchard, in the raspberry canes and the windbreak, plants all those ghastly trees and hoes them and waters them and stamps them into the ground. But she develops a method of carrying a pail of water while she holds a book in the other hand, the crook of her arm enabling her to read while she stumbles through her chores. This earns disapproval. Reading is a leisure activity, something she is supposed to do only for fun; although studying is important, reading is heathenish, slightly unsavory, unhealthy.

She wields them both at the same time, alternatively, separately, the spade, the book, the tongue, and the muscle, interchangeable, a slow wearing away of the investment of chores in her life. Her chores are supposed to help the family, contribute to their welfare, teach her discipline, independence, responsibility. They teach her weariness, they teach her repetition, they teach her boredom. The spade stays in her hands without an answer, it falls if she lets it go. She knows that you only need to dig a ditch for an hour to know what it's like for the rest of your life. The book stays in her head, it does not fall, but invites another, more words; it is somehow entangled with the tongue, while the spade relies on muscles, and although she can do both at the same time, muscle and think, she begins to prefer the book as adjunct to chores. For the first time, she wants more dishes; she can read while she washes dishes, but she cannot read while she milks cows or shovels chop. Reading, she makes herself invisible.

And there are always more dishes.

***

That family has its own sense of decorum, its own regulations and religion. It runs itself on schedule, on immigrant time, early to bed and early to rise, history has proven that, work first and then relaxation, no stopping until the chores are done, and everybody does his/her share, outside and in, inside and out, tractors and cows and gardens and water, even the dogs must be useful, and if the cats catch no mice they die.

That family eats at particular times, the clarity of schedule, they do not drink or dance and they go to the village for mail once every two days, to the town for groceries once a week. *That* family inhabits the clear destiny of structure, of achievement within environment, the linear narrative at work. An ethic, a myth, a belief beyond religion. Moral philosophy.

That family wades its pilgrim way through the Bible, this is the justification for its relentless schedule, for its indoctrination of the easy-going prairie. From Genesis to Revelation and then all over again. A repeated story, like chores. If she does it often enough, she will never forget how, it will be ingrained on her hands and her back, a tattoo. A rampant and indelible memory, work as evangelism.

Which goes only so far. *That* family lives next door to — what can't even be called a family — those Stangs. Their story winkled out of them over time. Renters, a bad business. Ownership essential to the marrow. Strangely indolent and happy, they are, on summer days swimming in the slough, in winter sledding. You never saw *him*, he was working away. And *she* lay in bed until ten o'clock, that was discovered by the neighbourly intervention of dropping over a dozen eggs. And their suspicious hybridity, which Jeanne (a middle Stang) recited one day in *that* family's kitchen with a glibness and ease that destroyed all notions of family as nation, even preconceptions of Irish-Catholic excess.

"Susy is my little sister, but Jackie isn't my sister, she's my dad's, and Tim is my half-brother, and my dad is my step-dad but my mother is my mother, not Jackie's. And Don is Jackie's sister, and so is Clara; not mine, but Matt and Sally are."

That family squirmed in next-door anguish. The step-family, the second family, the blended family, the melded family, did not yet exist or existed unspoken in the late fifties. And it was worse that they were happy, an outrage such happiness, such cavalier cohabitation.

And their kitchen was the worst, being invited in for coffee, and the kitchen table scattered with dishes, crusted and dry, used teabags lumped on the plates like dead mice.

Mrs. Stang — was she Mrs? — flipping her hand, "The girls are supposed to do the dishes. But they never do."

There are always more dishes to be done.

***

She wonders if her version is an embittered one, if she has intervened with her own purpose. Purpose and delight. Which subjected her, narrowed her vision, even while she knew the usefulness of spade and muscle, even while they could not contravene both tongue and book. What is the real story? The subjection of girls? Domestic deprivation, economic exploitation? No. Nothing within a family is exploitive if *everyone* works hard.

Raised as a boy, able to tackle anything, drive a tractor, lift heavy pails. But delineated as girl — inside the house is only women's work, arrangements of domesticity. No matter what you do "outside," inside is always women's work, invisible it seems to the patriarchy's great lie: within the family women do not work. That dangerous source of revolution will the moment when work recognizes itself and refuses to be differentiated, when delight and purpose collide, and escape rides the imagination.

There are always dishes to be done.

***

That family — hers, still hers — believed/believe in work, product, professionalism. Too much spare time and she'd start making up stories, too much imagination affects real work. Creative work is hobby stuff, save it for Sunday afternoons. First the chores, and then the dishes, and then maybe, maybe, she can steal time to read. A ranking of work: physical work, women's work, head work, dream work. Work prevents dangerous thinking, it asks its own questions. And once she's done the chores she can start in on the ironing, the beds, the dishes.

The hierarchies of work still haunt her. She wanted a pen and she drove a tractor. A cloven life: interior/exterior. Refusing to be a woman who enters smaller and smaller rooms until she is crouched on the floor in a corner cupboard. She did the chores, her body still reflects the muscles she made as a child. She came inside and stepped over the long legs of her brothers who had finished their work outside. She did the dishes, gazing out the window at the open road with her hands in soapsuds. She dreamed a story, the story of what women want: to escape the family, to invent themselves past its boundaries and its work. To refuse the seduction of the great patriarchy, its actual and figurative incest. She made herself a construction site, and used spade and muscle and purpose to build tongue and book and delight.

The family is a prism/prison. It refracts all selves into fragments. Promising safety, warmth, comfort, it insists on its own dutiful schedule. It lives women down to the numbed level of the work it creates. It families women into that old position of blood and bone and muscle. Does it dare to acknowledge the blended family and the merged family and the second family and the homosexual family and the family of friends? So far, no. Its misprision is in its refusal to be subject, to lose hold of its pretended objectivity. If it can do that, subject, it might escape the begat clauses of the Old Testament and live again, renewed and positive.

When she was twelve her mother hung a mirror in her room. This may seem a slight occurrence, but in *that* family, where vanity was frowned upon and there was no money for extra furnishings, the mirror finding its way onto her wall was unusual. Was it because she was a girl, a means to reinforce her "nature"? Was it because her mother hoped the mirror would conduct sex education on her behalf and she wouldn't have to offer any explanations? Was it because the mother wanted her to see the muscles she had made doing chores? There, in that silvery reflection, she learned to dance with her double. She forgave herself her gender and the family that she had landed in. She forgave her family. She forgave the west. She even forgave the dishes and those endless hours she spent washing them.

Book and spade, tongue and muscle, delight and purpose, can come together if the body and the body's double escape the family. And in the absence of escape, its disappearing act, the family can re-fashion itself — fluid and proteus will encompass the new genders and the new blood relatives of contemporary dreaming.

***

There will always be dishes but they need not cloud the mirror of gender. They can dream us past our own devourment: the eating and the eaten western family.

NOTE

In Aritha van Herk, 1991, *Invisible Ink (crypto-fictions)*, Edmonton: NeWest Press. Reprinted with permission.

REFERENCE

Gerstel, Naomi, and Harriet Engel Gross. 1987. "Introduction and Overview." In *Families and Work*. Philadelphia: Temple University Press.

77

Men Fish, Women Help

Nicole Gerarda Power

Fisheries in Newfoundland and Labrador have undergone dramatic environmental, industrial and regulatory changes in the last few decades. By the 1990s, cod and other groundfish stocks had been overfished to near extinction. Subsequent state-imposed moratoria on declining fish stocks displaced thousands of fish harvesters and processing workers. In the years following, adjustment programs, plant closures, reclassification of fish harvesters and the professionalization movement served to cut and limit the number of individuals directly involved in the fishery. By the turn of the twenty-first century, the Newfoundland fishery had been transformed from one that combined large-scale trawlers and small, inshore vessels to harvest cod to one that relied largely on vessels measuring less than sixty-five feet in length to harvest shellfish, especially crab. In this chapter, I reflect on fisheries work spanning the last decade and a half. I focus on how such environmental, industrial and regulatory changes have reshaped fisheries work and how the effects of such changes on fisheries work have been mediated by gender. I argue that these changes and their effects have reinforced the fishery as a site of masculine privilege, both in terms of access to material resources and its meanings.

Gender and the Fishing Industry

Fisheries-related work and its workplaces, spaces and meanings have been and continue to be configured by, among other things, gender (see Power 2005). In other words, who does what and where, and what these divisions mean are in large part structured by gender. It has been customary in Newfoundland communities for boys and young men to acquire fishing know-how through apprenticeships with experienced fish harvesters, usually an older male relative, and to gain access to fishing property (e.g., boats) through patrilineal inheritance patterns (Neis 1993). Increasingly, these apprenticeships are formalized through professional certification mechanisms and standardized training. As a result, inheritance patterns now must be reconciled in terms of a new regulatory regime that limits new entries into the profession (Fisheries and Oceans 2001). Retiring harvesters are attempting to recoup some of their investment in the very expensive crab fishery, and therefore are working longer, while also preserving space for their sons (Power et al. 2006).

Through apprenticeships, boys and young men learn not only how to fish experientially, they also learn what it means to be a "fisherman." Fishing is a way to make a living, but it is also a way of life, a way of being in this world. According to harvesters, fishing is "in the blood." To put it another way, the "fisherman's" body is produced as "natural" through repeated experiences of doing mundane work, and this "feel" for doing the job is understood by harvesters as evidence of an essential self — the fisherman or more recently the professional fish harvester. At the same time, engaging in fishing produces the work identity of the "fisherman" (Power et al., forthcoming).

Women tend to be differently located in fisheries work as processing workers, or as unpaid workers in fisheries-dependent households. When women do harvest, they tend to enter through a male family member. They are expected to take up a helper role, reflecting women's exclusion from accessing fisheries resources as well as the lack of recognition for their unpaid, caring and domestic work (Power 2005: see Chapter 6). Within processing, women have been over-represented in jobs located on the production floor (e.g., packing) and in clerical work (Rowe 1991: 15, 18). Men, in contrast, have tended to hold indirect jobs in processing (e.g., in marketing and transportation) and high-status and highly paid jobs in fish cutting (Rowe 1991: 6–7, 18). Despite the fact that the majority of workers in the processing sector in the years preceding the moratorium were women and that they worked in a sex-segregated environment, filling positions deemed effeminate for men, fish processing plants have been largely regarded as masculine, dirty, smelly environments that, as one male interviewee put it, are "no place for a woman" (Power 2005). Even at the level of the body, hair-nets, overcoats, and rubber boots obscure any trace of femininity. This view of the plant as masculine is reflected in women's understandings of themselves in relation to fisheries work. In contrast to harvesters' construction of an embodied work identity, women were generally hesitant to lay claim to or invest in a fisheries-based work identity.

Because gender has structured fisheries work and its meanings, the effects of ecological, industrial and regulatory restructuring have been different for women and men (Power 2005: Chapter 6). In the period immediately following the moratorium, the processing industry's labour force was cut substantially with serious impacts on women. Because of their over-representation in processing, seniority lists that ignored their later entrance into processing work and their increased likelihood of disruptions in work histories due to childcare responsibilities, they were especially vulnerable to job loss, while being limited in their access to federally funded adjustment packages (Neis et al. 2001; Williams 1996). Compared to displaced male workers, women tended to qualify for lower incomes and for shorter periods, and were less able to participate in or benefit from retraining programs (Robinson 1995; Williams 1996). There was no accommodation of women's child-care responsibilities in terms of provision and costs in the design of retraining programs. Reduced household incomes made purchasing childcare unaffordable. In addition, beliefs about mothering limited women's options. Mothers were not accorded the same cultural permission as fathers to leave their families and communities to take part in retraining programs or to find alternative work (Power 2005: Chapter 6).

Unlike processing workers, self-employed harvesters who wish to remain in the fishery have been able to do so by adapting fishing practices (Power 2005). One's ability to remain in the industry varies according to fishing status, household needs and available resources. Skippers of vessels have been able to exercise more direct control over decisions regarding staying or leaving the industry than crew members. Harvesters lacking capital scaled back their investment and moved into smaller boats requiring fewer crew and less gear, or began to fish with their female partners, often depending on the age of children and the availability of childcare. Harvesters with access to financial resources opted to invest more heavily by purchasing quotas for alternative species and buying larger vessels.

At the same time, state adjustment initiatives in the post-moratorium period have focused on reducing capacity in the harvesting sector through retirement schemes, retraining programs and the reclassification of fish harvesters and their enterprises (Power 2005). In 1997 the Department of Fisheries and Oceans implemented a classification scheme to sort fish harvesters in the under-sixty-five-foot fleet into core and non-core categories, replacing the full-time/part-time designations (Fisheries and Oceans 2001; PFHCB 2010). The core/non-core categories are used to determine who gets what fisheries resources, with core fish harvesters having privileged access to licenses, quotas and vessels. The DFO classification scheme restricts the membership by limiting new entries to replacement of core enterprises exiting the industry and to harvesters with level II professionalization status. When the

Professional Fish Harvesters' Certification Board was initially established around the same time, it grandparented fish harvesters into the appropriate status (apprentice, level I or level II) based on criteria that included attachment to and dependency on the fishery (defined primarily in terms of years fishing and fishing income). New entrants are expected to complete formal training, to accumulate sea time under the supervision of an experienced harvester and to demonstrate a financial dependency on the fishery (PFHCB 2010).

The criteria for membership in the core fishery and professionalization status do not exclude women in principle. However, women's domestic and childcare responsibilities make it difficult to meet the criteria by constraining their access to training and by interrupting actual fishing work — these constraints translate into less annual fisheries income (Power 2005: Chapter 6). Traditional inheritance patterns and current replacement regulations that allow an exiting harvester to identify his replacement have limited women's entry into and their access to resources within harvesting. Women are underrepresented as license holders and are over-represented at the apprentice level (Grzetic 2004). Roughly 15 percent of inshore fish harvesters are women (FFAW 2010) and while this number is up from eight per cent in 1981 (Grzetic 2004: 17), the increase in the participation rate largely reflects decreased work opportunities for women and changing fishing practices (e.g., the use of new technologies, the shift in target species from cod to crab) that facilitate women's entry. This increase means that more women are working on fishing boats today, and that women and men must negotiate gendered arrangements of work.

The presence of women on vessels disrupts established gender configurations of work and space. Nevertheless, the gender divisions of labour established on the vessel and the meanings of women's presence reproduce the dominant gender arrangements in the fishing industry (Power 2005, 2008). Women harvesters tended to do jobs that reflect their work in fish processing plants. For example, in the case of crab harvesting, women worked at sorting crab on deck. Men tended to steer the vessel and operate electronic equipment, often because women simply lacked the technical knowledge required to do these tasks. The shift from harvesting cod to crab facilitated women's entrance into harvesting, yet, because there is a tendency to interpret crab harvesting as "easy," women's work could be simply "explained away" as not really fishing (Power 2008). (For example, hydraulic equipment required for crab harvesting reduces the need for physicality to manipulate gear.) In addition, harvesters describe the crab fishery as less competitive and requiring fewer skills than was demanded in the hunt for cod. The new management strategy of individual quotas mean there is no competition to catch as much crab as possible before the total allowable catch is landed. In theory, individual quotas give skippers more control over decisions about when to fish and also provide them with a general sense about how much money they will earn before leaving the wharf. There is a general sense among harvesters that crab, which, as bottom crawlers, tends to have limited mobility and is relatively easy to find using the latest fish-finding equipment.

Men Fish. Women Help

The Newfoundland fishery has undergone a major transformation in the past twenty years. The near extinction of cod and other groundfish stocks and the moratoria imposed by the government in the early 1990s has led to fundamental changes in the way in which fish are harvested (from large-scale trawlers and small, inshore vessels to smaller vessels) and the type of catch (from cod and other groundfish stocks to the harvest of shellfish, especially crab). In general, fisheries as sites of work have become increasingly feminized since they are no longer associated with the (masculine) physicality of fishing and the experiential knowledge acquired through apprenticeship. The effects of changes in the regulatory, environmental and industrial context seem to encourage the predominantly male harvesters to shift away from investing a sense of self in the work itself, toward a masculinity that values professional status and the acquisition of fishing capital (e.g., sophisticated vessels and technologies, individual quotas and licenses) (Power 2008). However, despite the feminization of the fishing industry, gender relations have been reorganized in such a way that women still remain in subordinate positions (with corresponding lower power, instability and continued primary responsibility for domestic labour). It is not surprising that, given women's lack of direct ownership of or access to fisheries resources, they identify largely as "helpers" on vessels and invested a sense of self in their connections to the household (Power 2005: Chapter 6). Men fish. Women help.

REFERENCES

FFAW (Fish, Food and Allied Workers). "Women in the FFAW." At: ffaw.nf.ca/?Content=About_Us/ Womens_Committee.

Fisheries and Oceans Canada. 2001. *Fisheries Management Policies on Canada's Atlantic Coast.* Ottawa: Fisheries and Oceans Canada. At: dfo-mpo.gc.ca/afpr-rppa/Doc_Doc/FM_Policies_e.htm.

Grzetic, B. 2004. *Women Fishes These Days.* Halifax: Fernwood Publishing.

Neis, B. 1993. "From 'Shipped Girls' to 'Brides of the State': The Transition from Familial to Social Patriarchy in the Newfoundland Fishing Industry." *Canadian Journal of Regional Science* 16, 2.

Neis, B., B. Grzetic and M. Pidgeon. 2001. "From Fishplant to Nickel Smelter: Health Determinants and the Health of Newfoundland's Women Fish and Shellfish Processors in an Environment of Restructuring." Research report. St. John's: Memorial University of Newfoundland.

Power, N. 2008. "Occupational Risks, Safety and Masculinity: Newfoundland Fish Harvesters' Experiences and Understandings of Fishery Risks." *Health, Risk & Society* 10, 6.

____. 2005. *What Do They Call a Fisherman? Men, Gender, and Restructuring in the Newfoundland Fishery.* St. John's, NF: Institute of Social and Economic Research.

Power, N., D. Howse, B. Neis, and S. Brennan. Forthcoming. "Gendered Bodies at Work: Insights from Marine and Coastal OHS Research." *Policy and Practice in Health and Safety.*

Power, N., B. Neis, S. Brennan and M. Binkley. 2006. "Newfoundland and Labrador Fish Harvesters' Perceptions of Risk." In Stephen Bornstein and Michael Murray (project leaders), *SafeCatch: Final Report.* March. Submitted to the National SAR Secretariat New Initiatives Fund. At: safetynet. mun.ca/safecatch.htm.

Professional Fish Harvesters Certification Board (PFHCB). At: pfhcb.com.

Robinson, J. 1995. "Women and Fish Plant Closure: A Case of Trepassey, Newfoundland." In C. McGrath, B. Neis and M. Porter (eds.), *Their Lives and Times: Women in Newfoundland and Labrador, A Collage.* St. John's: Killick Press.

Rowe, A. 1991. *Effect of the Crisis in the Newfoundland Fishery on Women Who Work in the Industry.* St. John's: Women's Policy Office, Government of Newfoundland and Labrador.

Williams, S. 1996. *Our Lives Are at Stake: Women and the Fishery Crisis in Newfoundland and Labrador.* St. John's: Institute of Social and Economic Research.

Immigrant Workers and Globalized Garment Production
The Convergence of Gender, Race and Class Relations

Roxana Ng

The Garment Industry: Employer of Immigrant Women

The downturn of the auto industry has received extensive media coverage and government bail-outs since 2009. Unfortunately, but not surprisingly, a peculiar silence has surrounded the demise of garment production — a female-dominated industry — in Canada. In this chapter I explore the contemporary reality of working-class, immigrant female garment workers in Canada, whose lives are emblematic of the convergence of gender, race and class relations. These relations are being transformed by globalization and work restructuring — new forces in the evolving dynamic of capitalism. But, despite the enormity of these transformations, unions, academics and activists are working with garment workers to ameliorate the negative effects of globalization.

The Changing Garment Industry

The garment industry is predominantly Canadian-owned; it was the eighth largest provider of manufacturing jobs in the country. However, since the 1980s it has experienced a rapid decline: by 2007, it had become one of the smallest industries in Canada. According to Industry Canada calculations, the size of the garment labour force dropped by 28 percent between 1989 and 1994, and by a further 28.5 percent between 1998 and 2004. Between 2004 and 2008, the labour force shrank by another 40 percent, reducing the total number of workers to 44,400. These figures are not definitive (I will explain the problem of only looking at official data later on in the chapter); they nevertheless illustrate the scale of the decline of this sector, which largely made use of and continues to employ female immigrant workers.

There are various reasons for this decline. Since the 1980s, control within the industry has shifted from manufacturers to large retail chains, such as Hudson's Bay (which owns Zellers and K Mart, and which, in turn, was bought out by a U.S. company), and increasingly to transnational chains such as Wal-Mart (the largest retail chain in the world). To keep up with global competition, the retailers' strategy is to deliver the most fashionable clothes to the market quickly: this has been made possible by at least three interlocking processes. First, technological innovations, such as electronic data interchange (EDI), have enabled retailers to gain control of the production process, allowing them to keep better records of their stock and to keep less stock on hand. Sales of garments on the rack in retail stores can be communicated to production plants almost instantaneously anywhere in the world. EDI has enabled manufacturers and retailers to reduce mass production, storage, and other overhead costs. Retailers are able to demand quicker turn-around time for production, and require suppliers (contractors and sub-contractors) to provide garments on consignment, and/or at last year's price.

Second, improved distribution and transportation systems allow garments to be delivered more quickly to stores, even from far-away places. Therefore many manufacturers can rely on off-shore production to keep labour costs low.

Third, trade agreements, such as the North American Free Trade Agreement (NAFTA), reduced tariffs on clothing produced elsewhere in North America, thereby enabling retailers to order, and large manufacturers to produce, garments from countries with lower labour costs. The 1995 Agreement of Textiles and Clothing (ATC), negotiated through the World Trade Organization (WTO), instituted a progressive lifting of quotas for importing garments produced in the developing world. The complete lifting of import quotas in 2005 saw the practical annihilation of garment production in Canada. In anticipation of the full implementation of the ATC, most large U.S. and Canadian manufacturers (e.g., Gildan, the largest Canadian T-shirt manufacturer) have moved their entire production process to cheaper production sites, notably China. Correspondingly, imports from these countries are flooding the local clothing markets, further undermining local production.

Manufacturers have responded to their loss of control in different ways. Some retired and got out of the business altogether. Some became importers or contractors to retailers: they sub-contract out work to plants in low-waged countries through a vast and expanding global production network. This network has taken advantage of trade agreements between/among governments, and the establishment of free trade zones in developing countries (Yanz et al. 1999). To lower costs and increase productivity, some have reorganized production locally by sub-contracting to smaller shops and jobbers. Employers have scaled back on their plants, retaining a couple of cutters, and using home-based workers for the bulk of their production (Ng 1999). The effects of this restructuring are job loss and the re-emergence of home-based work and sweatshop operations (Johnson 1982). The increasing concentration of ownership of the garment industry has ironically led to a more fragmented production process, organized through layers of contracting and sub-contracting, with retailers and large manufacturers at the top of the pyramid.

Immigrant Garment Workers: Gender, Race and Class Relations

What is not immediately visible in the above description is the gendered and racialized hierarchy within the garment industry. According to a Union of Needletrade and Industrial Textile Employees (UNITE) study conducted in 2000 (Gunning el al. 2000), the garment industry was comprised of about 50 percent immigrants and 76 percent women. The composition of this labour force has changed over time. In the period immediately after the war, many garment workers were immigrant men from Europe. As they acquired skills and seniority they moved up the production hierarchy (e.g., by becoming cutters who are seen to be more skilled than sewing-machine operators). Women, most recently from Asia (Hong Kong, China, India, and Vietnam), then replaced them as sewing-machine operators at the bottom of the garment production hierarchy.

Differentiation within the garment industry is produced through gendered constructions of skill. As sewing-machine operators, immigrant women use the skills that they have acquired in domestic settings (such as mending and sewing), which can be readily transferred to the industrial context; thus these workers are seen by employers as unskilled or semi-skilled (as compared to cutters who are seen to be skilled). Sewing is seen to be a women's skill; it is paid less than the work done by cutters in garment production. These skill differences are seen as an extension of the "natural" differences between men and women. The gendering process results in the devaluing of women's skills while creating and reinforcing women's inferiority socially and economically.

The Payment System

Historically and presently, the garment industry has relied on low wages for its competitive advantage, and the use of women and immigrants as a pool of inexpensive labour. In the past, working from home and sweatshop operations were integral to this sector. With the formation of the International Ladies Garment Workers' Union (ILGWU), first in the United States and then in Canada, garment workers became one of the few unionized female work forces to receive decent wages and employee benefits: they have been protected by labour legislation and rights to collective bargaining since the 1930s.

Globalization and the restructuring of the garment industry has had a negative impact on garment workers. The downsizing of plants and shift back to home-based work has disrupted the process of collective bargaining, and significantly reduced workers' ability to bargain for decent wages and working conditions. This trend is compounded by the neoliberal discourse ("letting the market decide") that has shaped state policies since the 1980s. The liberalization of provincial employment standards (for example, the extension of the work week and cutbacks in health and safety regulations) makes negotiating with employers even more difficult for workers and unions.

To obtain accurate figures on the average wages of garment workers is extremely difficult due to the nature of the piece-rate system. Workers are paid for each piece of work completed. They rarely complete a whole garment. Workers are typically paid between twenty to fifty cents for section work (for example, sewing on pockets or collars). The hourly rate therefore differs a great deal depending on the design and type of garment. Incredibly, the piece rate in the 1980s remains the same today. In her 1982 book, Laura Johnson reported a piece rate of $2 for sewing a skirt. Twenty years later, workers also make $2 for a skirt; a shirt pays around $3, and a dress $4–5. These items retail for $200 or more. In my 1999 study on homeworkers and their working conditions, I estimated the average hourly rate for homeworkers in Toronto to be between $6 and $8 based on the piece rate and number of items completed per hour (Ng 1999). The highest hourly rate reported was $17 per hour for evening gowns, and the lowest was $2 per hour. Accordingly to Statistics Canada, the average hourly rate for clothing manufacturing in early 2009 was $12.79 per hour, a slight drop from $12.92 per hour for the same period in 2008.[1] Exacerbating the low wages is the fact that most garment workers, especially homeworkers, do not receive benefits. Because of the lack of effective monitoring of employer practices, workers have little recourse, apart from discontinuing work, in disputes with their employers.

The discussion above shows concretely how garment workers have been transformed from wage workers to homeworkers. Far from being abstract concepts, globalization and work restructuring are concrete processes and practices that are observable and identifiable. We see how trade agreements enable employers to move production sites around the world in search of cheap labour. We further see how liberalization of labour standards enables employers to increase their exploitation of workers. Cutbacks on the monitoring of labour standards have made it easier for contractors and sub-contractors to violate labour standards without fear of discovery or sanction. Increasingly, garment workers in Canada share a similar fate to that of their less well-off counterparts in third world countries. From the standpoint of garment workers, the overall picture is one of decreasing protection and lower wages; that is, of deepening exploitation.

What Can Be/Is Being Done?

Giving the tremendous odds faced by garment workers in Canada and globally, it is clear that drastic measures are needed to ameliorate increasing labour rights violations. In addition to the efforts of unions and labour rights groups, concerned citizens can be involved in at least three areas: research, public education, and activism. While I have separated them for the purpose of identifying areas of action, in fact they work in concert with each other.

First, we need to do more and better research tracking the global production and organization of apparel and textiles. Due to the private nature of ownership and the secretive character of garment production, it is very difficult to trace the extensive network and chain of garment production in Canada and globally. Tracking the global interconnections and investment patterns between/among garment plants therefore requires researchers with multidisciplinary knowledge and skills. For example, statistical analysis of export and import figures of garment manufacturing, together with interviews with garment workers, illuminates the multifaceted and contradictory nature of garment production across national borders. Through collaboration and partnership among researchers in different locations (e.g., in the academy, in unions, in the community), we will begin to unravel the complex nature and organization of garment production in Canada and elsewhere.

Second, we need to raise public awareness about the complex system of exploitation of workers and the strategies used by retailers and large manufacturers to augment profit. Instead of deregulating, governments need to legislate better protection and monitoring, and improve regulation. But governments will only become more accountable if taxpayers insist on it: research and public education need to be bolstered by activism on the part of citizens. For example, as a result of lobbying by students and other concerned citizens, the University of Toronto developed, in 1999, a Code of Conduct for Trademark Licensees to ensure that the suppliers of the university's trademarked merchandise (such as T-shirts, sweatshirts, and souvenirs), meet minimum employment standards regarding such issues as wages and benefits, working hours and overtime compensation. For example, when CBC TV aired the program "Disclosure" in 2002, exposing the poor working conditions in Gildan Activewear's "southern sweatshops," the university held them accountable, asking for a response to the allegations. Such pressure can keep manufacturers and retailers and responsible as employers.

Finally, we need to develop alliances and multipronged strategies, not only with workers in Canada, but with workers and groups in the global South. Given the intimate connection of garment production between northern and southern countries, gains by one group of workers will have a ripple effect on other groups. An example of an organization that combines these three areas of action identified above is the Maquila Solidarity Network (MSN).[2] This Toronto-based non-profit network of more than 400 organizations is concerned with labour issues worldwide and has been at the forefront of research and advocacy in relation to garment production. It traces Canadian manufacturers' involvement in garment production in Mexico, Central America, the Caribbean Basin and, more recently, Asia. In addition to doing research, MSN is also collaborating with women's and labour rights organizations in the economic South, for example by advocating the development and implementation of codes of conduct governing garment production. Working in coalition with labour and other social action organizations, the network has initiated and organized campaigns in Canada to bring to light the situation of garment workers worldwide, telling Canadians what they can do to ameliorate the plight of these workers. Their latest disclosure and no-sweat campaign integrates research, public education and worker education. The disclosure campaign, mounted by the Ethical Trading Action Group, is trying to get the federal government to amend the *Textile Labelling Act* so that the "CA number" would have to appear on clothing labels. This tag would enable researchers and activists to trace the global network of garment production by Canadian manufacturers, as well as educating Canadians about the nature of garment production.

Eliminating inequity is the responsibility of us all. By working together in solidarity and cooperation, we can push back or push away the detrimental effects of globalization, and work toward a global system that would benefit the majority of the world population.

NOTES

1. Note that the averages include a wide range of employees within a sector, and may or may not reflect earnings of sewers specifically (Statistics Canada 2009).
2. For the work of the MSN, which is also the secretariat of the Ethical Trading Action Group, see their website. At: maquilasolidarity.org.

REFERENCES

Canada, Industry Canada.1996. *Clothing Industry Statistical Data*. Ottawa: Author.

Gunning, J., J. Eaton, S. Ferrier, M. Kerr, A. King and J. Maltby. 2000. *Dealing with Work-Related Musculoskeletal Disorders in the Ontario Clothing Industry*. Report submitted to the Research Advisory Council of the Workplace Safety & Insurance Board, UNITE, November 3.

Johnson, Laura. 1982. *The Seam Allowance: Industrial Home Sewing in Canada*. Toronto: Women's Press.

Marx, Karl. 1954. *Capital, Volume 1*. Moscow: Progress Books.

Ng, Roxana. 2002. "Freedom For Whom? Globalization and Trade from the Standpoint of Garment Workers." *Canadian Woman Studies* 21/22, 4&1 (Spring/Summer).

___. 1999. "Homeworking: Dream Realized or Freedom Constrained? The Globalized Reality of Immigrant Garment Workers." *Canadian Woman Studies* 19,3 (Fall).

Statistics Canada. 2009. *Employment, Earnings and Hours*. Ottawa. Catalogue no. 72-002-X. At: statcan. gc.ca/pub/72-002-x/72-002-x2010006-eng.pdf&t=Employment Earnings and Hours.

Yanz, Lynda, Bob Jeffcott, Deena Ladd and Joan Atlin. 1999. *Policy Options to Improve Standards for Garment Workers in Canada and Internationally*. Ottawa: Status of Women Canada, (January).

79

Gender among the "Guys"

Some Reflections on Work, Family Life, and Retention of Women in Engineering

Gillian Ranson

On the face of it, occupational barriers to women seem to be coming down. While the range of occupations in which men work is still far more extensive, women are entering male-dominated jobs and workplaces in increasing numbers. Indeed, some venerable bastions of male professional turf, like medicine and law, are now close to gender parity. Engineering, however, is a different story.

According to Engineers Canada (EC), the national organization of Canadian professional engineers and engineering associations, the numbers of female engineering undergraduates in Canada increased annually after 1972, until 2002, when the proportion of women in engineering programs peaked at about 20 percent. That percentage has been declining steadily ever since. Currently, says a 2008 study commissioned by EC and the Canadian Council of Technicians and Technologists, the share of women in undergraduate programs is roughly where it was in the early- to mid-1990s — about 17 percent. The proportion of women actually practising in the profession is even lower than the percentage studying engineering. Census figures for 2006 indicate women made up about 12.2 percent of engineers, a considerable increase on their 6.1 percent share in 1986, but still well behind the proportions of women lawyers (38.6 percent in 2006 compared to 21.8 percent in 1986) and women physicians (36.4 percent in 2006 compared to 22.8 percent in 1986). Given the decline in the number of women enrolled in engineering undergraduate programs since 2002, the proportion of women in engineering jobs has also likely peaked.

There is another side to the problem of attracting women into engineering: what growth there has been in the numbers of women professional engineers is among recent graduates, young women who are trying to establish careers at the age when they're also typically establishing relationships and deciding whether to have children. These life-course decisions lie at the heart of what I suspect will be major problems of retention of women in engineering.

The Engineering Study

As a sociologist whose research focus is on the interface of gender, families and paid employment, I had these retention problems in mind when, in 1997, I started a program of research on engineers and engineering work. My research base was Calgary, Alberta, the centre of the powerful oil and gas industry in Canada, and a city reputed to have one of the highest per capita populations of engineers of any city in the world.

The first phase of the study involved tracking women and men who had graduated from the Faculty of Engineering at the University of Calgary between 1980 and 1990. The second phase, carried out during 1999 and 2000, involved a similar career-tracking study of engineers within a single company — a major oil company in Calgary. Altogether, I gathered survey and interview data on work and family issues from 390 individuals who had trained as, and/or were working as, engineers. Of these, 179 were women, and 211 were men.

This rich base of information has told me a great deal about engineers' working lives, and the way their professional careers are affected by family responsibilities. I am now strongly persuaded that there are significant differences between the women and the men. But these differences don't show up right away among young, single women and men in, say, entry-level jobs. The really telling gender differences start to emerge with the arrival of children, in the way gender mediates parenthood. For women in engineering, motherhood is a critical watershed, because it positions them differently from their male colleagues. If they intend to keep working, they're usually victims of what I call the "dual-earner disadvantage" when it comes to family responsibilities. And at work, largely as a result of this disadvantage, it is much harder for them as mothers to be "one of the guys" as well.

The "Dual-Earner Disadvantage"

The phenomenon I came to call the "dual-earner disadvantage" was, for me, the most compelling finding from the first phase of the study. In order to describe it, it's necessary to provide some context. Of the 164 women and 153 men who took part in the first phase, about 86 percent of the men, and 77 percent of the women, identified themselves as married. About 71 percent of the women and 69 percent of the men had at least one child. One major difference between the mothers and the fathers was their employment status: about 97 percent of the fathers were in full-time paid work, compared to 66 percent of the mothers. About 10 percent of the mothers were working twenty to thirty hours a week, and 23 percent were working less than ten hours. But among the mothers and fathers in full-time work, another striking difference emerged. Some 92 percent of the mothers, but only 25 percent of the fathers, had spouses who *also* worked full-time. This difference meant that most of the mothers in full-time engineering jobs were juggling the demands of family life in dual-earner families. Almost all of the fathers, however, were in more traditional families in which the man was the main money-earner and the woman was mainly responsible for domestic labour.

I don't mean to suggest that there are no advantages to women in dual-earner families; for one thing, there is likely to be money for childcare and other domestic support. And women engineers in dual-earner families may be able to take career risks not possible for men whose income is the only one in the family. On the other hand, men with wives to care for the family can devote much more time and energy to their jobs, perhaps on the grounds that the job *is* the only one in the family. The outcome among engineers who are parents is that men, whose careers are privileged and who are generally free from domestic family responsibilities, work alongside women whose careers do not necessarily come first in their families, and who take on much more responsibility for their families than their male colleagues do. This is what I mean by the "dual-earner disadvantage."

Working as "One of the Guys"

The traditional family situations experienced by most of the mainly white, middle-class, Canadian-born fathers in my study may seem surprising for the late 1990s, which was when the interviews were done. But it is not so surprising for men in a resolutely male-dominated profession, working (as many of the Calgary participants were) in the equally male-dominated oil industry. Until very recently, that industry really was a man's world. But here's a very important point: without women around to provide a basis for comparison, it didn't appear as a *man's* world. It just appeared as *the* world. In workplaces full of men, gender doesn't seem to be an issue. That's why, as sociologist Joan Acker (1990) has pointed out, we continue to think of workplaces as gender-neutral spaces, and "workers" as abstract, gender-neutral beings whose lives outside of work are irrelevant. Acker contends that in the real world of actual workers, the only "worker" who comes close to this abstract image is "the male worker whose life centers on his full-time, life-long job, while his wife or another woman takes care of his personal needs and his children" (Acker 1990: 149).

For professions like engineering, particularly as practised in Calgary, Acker's description was, until recently, a good fit for most engineers. The template of the engineering professional developed out of a history of engineering as a profession with origins in military institutions (Hacker 1989) and strong links to the symbolically masculine attributes of scientific and technical rationality (Wajcman 1991). Recent initiatives to get women into engineering have usually been predicated on the assumption that "women should be modified to fit into engineering rather than the other way around" (Faulkner 2000: 93). In other words, the women who do enter engineering are expected to do so on men's terms. Initiatives to "get women in" are usually based on the liberal feminist assumption that women are, for practical purposes, the same as men.

Much research on women in engineering (e.g., Hacker 1989; Carter and Kirkup 1990; Eisenhart and Finkel 1998; Dryburgh 1999; Kvande 1999; Faulkner 2000; Jorgenson 2000, 2002, Ranson 2005; Faulkner 2007; Bastalich et al. 2008; Powell et al. 2009) indicates that many do indeed see themselves as the same as men — or at any rate see a need to be seen in this way. In the workplace, they work to be accepted as "one of the guys." Many who use this strategy "want to be 'like' their male colleagues and accent this similarity while distancing themselves from 'the majority of women'" (Kvande 1999: 311). It's very important to recognize, though, that this strategy is as much as anything else a survival strategy. In male-dominated workplaces, where the "requirements of success" are presented in male terms because that's how they've always been understood, it's very hard for women to do anything but conform. All of these situations boil down to the following propositions: women who act as "one of the guys" will probably be fine. But women who act like women may be in trouble. What happens, for example, when "one of the guys" discovers she's pregnant?

The experience of Claire, one of the women I interviewed in the first phase of my study, illustrates how this dilemma can play out. Claire worked for an energy company and had been "fast-tracked" to a position well beyond what was expected for her level of experience. She, like many of the women I interviewed, downplayed issues of gender in the workplace. As "one of the guys," she clearly distanced herself from any suggestion that gender had affected her own experience:

> I mean I've certainly never experienced any sort of, um, I don't know what to call it, but, you know, discrimination or anything like that. I've always been given, I mean, I think opportunities go to those people who are willing to work for them, and who are willing to put their nose to the grindstone.

But earlier in the interview, Claire had described how an unexpected pregnancy had played out at work:

> My manager and I had… some issues, when I first told him that I was pregnant. We went back and forth quite a bit. The first thing he said to me was, when I told him, was not "Congratulations," it was, "Well, who's going to do the annual plan?" Because he started, he goes, "Well, how long would you be taking [in maternity leave]? How much are you entitled to? Would you consider coming back early?" And we went back and forth for four or five months. And I was just miserable… We have a very good relationship, but it put, it put a lot of strain on it. It's probably taken us a good year, to get back to where we were before.

Returning to "where they were before" required Claire to become "one of the guys" again. This was possible at least in part because her partner was extremely unusual for my study in his willingness to allow her career to be privileged over his. So she was parenting rather like "one of the guys" as well, focusing on her career and delegating childcare to a nanny and her husband. Like several of the men I interviewed, she spoke wistfully about increasing her family involvement some time in the future.

For other women, trained to see engineering careers and workplace requirements in male terms, being engineers and also being mothers represents what Jorgenson (2000) calls "mutually incongruous" identities. This identity clash doesn't necessarily mean that women with children give up engineering (though many do — proportionately far more than would be the case if they were working in female-, rather than male-dominated occupations). What it does mean, very often, is that they scale back their careers. They choose carefully where they work. Large organizations with firmly established family policies are popular. So is contract or consulting work. Some women postpone having children till their careers are firmly established and they have paid their dues as "guys." Sometimes, of course, they don't have children.

Levelling the Playing Field

Perhaps concerned employers' most common response to the difficulties women encounter in balancing work and family responsibilities is the establishment of "family friendly" workplace policies and programs like flex-time and family days. Such programs are ostensibly intended to help both mothers and fathers, but in practice they are taken up mainly by women. This means that the programs do much less to "level the playing field" than might be expected because they entrench perceptions that women need "help" (while men do not), and that family responsibilities belong to women exclusively. The playing field will never be levelled as long as women's success depends on their becoming "one of the guys." What's badly needed is a change in how "guys" balance work and family responsibilities. The experiences of the fathers I interviewed for the study indicate that some men certainly want to be more involved with their children than fathers of the past (and engineers of the old school) have been. Research now suggests that rigid workplace expectations may cause men to conceal the strength of their psychological commitment to their families (Pleck 1993; Cohen 1991, 1993). It's time for workplaces to acknowledge that men, as well as women, have family responsibilities, and for men, as well as women, to make those responsibilities public.

REFERENCES

Acker, Joan. 1990. "Hierarchies, Jobs, Bodies: A Theory of Gendered Organizations." *Gender & Society* 29,2.
Bastalich, Wendy, Suzanne Franzway, Judith Gill and Rhonda Sharp. 2008. "'Oh You Must Be Very Clever!' High-Achieving Women, Professional Power and the Ongoing Negotiation of Workplace Identity." *Gender and Education* 20, 3.
Carter, A., and G. Kirkup. 1990. *Women in Engineering*. Basingstoke: Macmillan.
Cohen, T. 1993. "What Do Fathers Provide? Reconsidering the Economic and Nurturant Dimensions of Men as Parents." In J. Hood (ed.), *Men, Work and Family*. Newbury Park: Sage.
___. 1991. "Speaking with Men: Application of a Feminist Methodology to the Study of Men's Lives." *Men's Studies Review* 8,4.
Dryburgh, Heather. 1999. "Work Hard, Play Hard: Women and Professionalization in Engineering — Adapting to the Culture." *Gender & Society* 13,5.
Eisenhart, M., and E. Finkel. 1998. *Women's Science*. Chicago: University of Chicago Press.
Engineers Canada. 2008. *Engineering and Technology Labour Market Study. Achieving Diversity: Strategies That Work*. A etlms.engineerscanada.ca/media/Achieving%20Diversity-Strategies%20that%20 Work1.pdf.
Faulkner, Wendy. 2007. "'Nuts and Bolts and People': Gender-Troubled Engineering Identities." *Social*

Studies of Science 37,3.

___. 2000. "The Power *and* the Pleasure? A Research Agenda for 'Making Gender Stick' to Engineers." *Science, Technology and Human Values* 25,1.

Hacker, Sally. 1989. *Pleasure, Power and Technology.* Boston: Unwin Hyman.

Jorgenson, Jane. 2002. "Engineering Selves: Negotiating Gender and Identity in Technical Work." *Management Communication Quarterly* 15,3.

___. 2000. "Interpreting the Intersections of Work and Family: Frame Conflicts in Women's Work." *The Electronic Journal of Communication* 10,3 and 4.

Kvande, Elin. 1999. "'In the Belly of the Beast': Constructing Femininities in Engineering Organizations." *European Journal of Women's Studies* 6.

Pleck, J. 1993. "Are 'Family-Supportive' Employer Policies Relevant to Men?" In J. Hood (ed.), *Men, Work and Family*. Newbury Park: Sage.

Powell, Abigail, Barbara Bagilhole and Andrew Dainty. 2009. "How Women Engineers Do and Undo Gender: Consequences for Gender Equality." *Gender, Work and Organization* 16,4.

Ranson, Gillian. 2005. "No Longer 'One of the Boys': Negotiations with Motherhood, as Prospect or Reality, among Women in Engineering." *Canadian Review of Sociology and Anthropology* 42,2.

Wajcman, Judy. 1991. *Feminism Confronts Technology*. Cambridge: Polity Press.

80

Sites of Struggle or Vehicles of Resistance

Unions and Women Workers

Linda Briskin

Unions and Women Workers

Unions get bad press. The mainstream media, when they bother to cover issues about working people and unions, refer invariably to union *bosses* and *greedy* workers. Certainly it is true that unionized workers, especially women, make more then the non-unionized for doing the same work. In fact, in 2007, unionized women workers in Canada made 36.4 percent more than their non-unionized sisters: this is called the "union premium" (Jackson 2010). For childcare workers, almost all of whom are women, the union premium was 54.7 percent; that is, unionized childcare workers made $17.88 per hour compared to $11.56 earned by those who were not unionized. Unions also play a major role in closing the wage gap between women and men. In 2007, union women made $22.79 per hour, 93.5 percent of the wage of unionized men. Their non-unionized sisters made only $16.71 per hour, which represents 78.8 percent of the wages of non-union men (Jackson and Schellenberg 2009; Jackson 2010).[1]

But a living wage can hardly be considered a sign of greed. According to the Canadian Centre for Policy Alternatives, in 2004, the poorest 10 percent of Canadian families raising children earned less than $9,400 per year. The richest 10 percent made 82 times more — almost triple the ratio of 1976 (At: policyalternatives.ca/newsroom/news-releases/canadas-growing-gap-new-30-year-high).[2]

To add insult to injury, those with annual incomes of more than $265,000 saw their tax rate decline dramatically between 1990 and 2005 while those in the bottom 10 percent of income earners — with earnings of $13,500 or less — watched their rate rise by 5 percent (Lee 2007).

In addition to union wage advantage, unionized workers are also more likely to have full-time jobs, health and pension benefits, more control over their work, access to a formal grievance procedure and some degree of job security. All workers have the right to join unions since a 1948 United Nations Declaration; however, employers and the media continue to be hostile to unions. In a time of increasingly precarious employment, unions are essential to protect the rights of workers, especially women who face lower wages, occupational segregation, and over-representation among the part-time employees. For young women workers who are clustered in the retail and fast-food industries and suffer minimum wages, meagre benefits and unpredictable hours, unions are critical.

Young Women Organizing

In 1994, a Canadian, Sarah Inglis, was the first person to try to organize a union at a McDonald's outlet. She had started working there at fourteen and when asked why she wanted a union, she said, "For respect, dignity and job security" (Inglis 1994: 22). Over the course of a campaign, mounted with the help of the Service Employees International Union (SEIU), she and other workers faced employer hostility and threats. Sarah reported, "People... were scared of losing their jobs. People were very intimidated" (25). Although it is illegal to fire workers who lead an organizing effort, cutting the hours of part-timers or assigning them the worst shifts and jobs is relatively easy. The intimidation was successful and the campaign to unionize failed.

However, two years later, in 1996, women workers at Suzy Shier organized two re-tail stores in Canada, despite threats from management. Like Sarah Inglis, Deborah De Angelis, who initiated the unionization campaign, said, "My fight isn't about money: it's about dignity" (1998: 26). Although it took a year to negotiate a first contract, De Angelis reported that having a voice is the biggest gain: "Before, they could fire you, no problem. They had nobody to answer to. Before, if the manager didn't like what you were saying, she just wouldn't put you on the schedule. And if you were not on the schedule for four weeks, you were automatically terminated. That policy is now gone, thanks to the collective agree-ment…. That is so much power" (29). In response to the pressure of young workers, many unions now have youth committees, youth representation on leadership bodies and special polices about youth workers. For example, the Communications, Energy and Paperworkers Union of Canada (CEP) is striving to improve the place of young workers in society and in their union: in 2008 it passed a special policy which includes calls for higher minimum wages; the removal of all discriminatory youth or student minimum wages; special employment programs for unemployed youth; and a dramatic lowering of tuition fees in all post-secondary and vocational education programs.[3]

Labour Market Restructuring

Labour market restructuring and globalization are transforming work in Canada. Employers have increased their calls for labour flexibility; created more part-time, part-year service work, often referred to as precarious or casual labour; and endorsed more contracting-out and homework. Employers are also moving their factories to countries with no minimum wages, no health and safety legislation and little access to unions, resulting in serious job losses in Canada's heavily unionized, male-dominated manufacturing industries. Men are now com-peting for what have traditionally been women's jobs in the less-unionized service industries and the few professions where women have dominated, such as nursing and teaching. These changes have significantly reduced union membership, and made unionization more difficult.

Yet, in the current context, workers, especially women, need unions more than ever. Union activity fosters personal empowerment, political awareness and collective solidarity. Unions provide a vehicle for struggling around fundamental issues affecting the household and the workplace, issues such as economic independence, the right to secure employment, childcare, and harassment- and violence-free environments. Unions also lobby to influence government policy and legislation on equality issues. And unionization clearly offers women material benefits.

Unions and Male Domination

Unions are often pictured as male-dominated institutions run by tough, even ruthless, working-class men, yet about half of Canadian union members are women, most working in public sector jobs. Despite almost reaching numerical equality, women continue to face four major barriers to union participation (Braithwaite and Byrne 1995). First, women already face a "double day," working for wages and doing the vast majority of unpaid household work. To be a union activist means a "triple day," often impossible for women with children. Second, women's segregation in low-paid work with unrecognized skills and little flexibility means they may not be encouraged or chosen to be union leaders. Third, inside unions, the validation of dominant forms of masculinity have reinforced some men's resistance to the participation of women. Finally traditional gender stereotypes, for example, the view that women are overly emotional, when internalized by women, weakens their confidence in their capacity to organize and lead. When such stereotypes are externalized by men, they result in discrimination against women. Once elected, women union leaders may face a lack of respect and social punishments such as laughter and negative labelling for raising women's issues (Briskin 2006b).

Resisting the Gender Order of Unions

Like all social institutions, unions are organized by gender. Gender practices in unions have most often been about exclusion and power. However, in the 1970s, women began to organize to resist and reconfigure the gender order of unions. Union women have challenged the traditional gender order of unions through a range of initiatives.

Representation in Elected Positions

In order to address women's under-representation in top elected positions, many unions and federations have enacted affirmative action policies that designate or add seats on leadership bodies for women. The increased awareness of representational issues has led to employment equity for union staff, and affirmative action seats on union executive boards for racial minorities, lesbians and gays, people with disabilities, and aboriginal peoples.

Redefining Union Issues

Canadian women unionists have successfully pressured unions to take up issues of childcare, reproductive rights, harassment, pay equity and employment equity, among others. A dramatic case in point is the increasing union involvement, with active support from top leadership, in the broad issues around violence against women. These campaigns go well beyond a focus on employer harassment or even co-worker harassment: many have successfully integrated issues around racial harassment and violence.

Although some union hierarchies have questioned the relevance of such issues to unions, shifts have now occurred in both union policy and the collective bargaining agenda. By 1999, half of Canadian workers covered by major collective agreements had the protection of a formal sexual harassment clause (up from 20 percent in 1985); 60.5 percent of such agreements contained a non-discrimination clause; and 27.6 percent had pay equity (equal pay for work of equal value) clauses (up from 5.4 percent in 1985) (Jackson and Schellenberg 1999). In 1986 only 2.5 percent of collective agreements covering 5.6 percent of employees had affirmative action provisions. By 1995 the numbers had increased to almost 11 percent of agreements and 14.8 percent of employees; and by 2004 to 16.7 percent of agreements and 30.8 percent of employees (Briskin 2006a).

Gender Mainstreaming

In order to protect against the potential marginalization associated with women's issues, gendering union issues (sometimes called "gender mainstreaming") is now on union agendas. This change has meant a move from identifying a women's platform of concerns to recognizing the gender implications in all issues — such as seniority, health and safety, contracting out, privatization and precariousness. Such a shift facilitates taking account of the gender-specific concerns of male workers. Issues are also being scrutinized for their impact on diverse groups of women and men. For example, discussions of family benefits increasingly reject traditional definitions of family that exclude lesbian and gay couples. Such inclusivity helps build bridges among diverse groups of women unionists, and alliances with marginalized male workers.

For more than four decades in Canada, union women's separate organizing has promoted women's leadership, challenged traditional leaderships to be more accountable, encouraged unions to be more democratic and participatory, and pressured unions to take up women's concerns as union members and as workers — through policy initiatives as well as at the negotiating table. Separate organizing includes informal women's networks or caucuses; formal, sometimes elected, women's committees; and women-only educational conferences, activities increasingly supported by unions.

In examining separate organizing, it is useful to distinguish between separatism as a *goal* — an end in itself — and separate organizing as a *strategy* — a means to an end, in this case, the integration of women as full citizens in unions. Women's separate organizing has also provided an important precedent. Increasingly women and men of colour, lesbians and gay men, people with disabilities and Aboriginal peoples are organizing separately inside the union movement, often through Human Rights and Rainbow Committees, Pink Triangle Committees, and Aboriginal Circles. In fact, since 2000, unions have made remarkable strides in developing policy on racism, homophobia, and sexism, and more recently on transphobia and ableism (Briskin 1999a, 1993; Hunt and Rayside 2007).[4]

Coalition Building and Transnational Organizing

Since the late 1970s, the women's movement in Canada has embraced alliances and coalitions in order to bring women together from unions, political parties, and community-based groups to co-operate nationally, provincially and locally. In turn, trade union women work with community-based feminist groups, both to build coalitions around key issues, such as childcare and pay equity, and to pressure the union movement to respond to feminist challenges. In fact, the movement of union women has had an important impact on the politics and practices of the Canadian women's movement, emphasizing a class perspective and weakening the tendency towards individualistic solutions. Coalition strategies both respond to and highlight the significance of diversity; that is, they represent an organizational alternative to homogeneous organizations that tend to silence marginal voices.

The globalization of production, the mobility of capital, and competitive wage bargaining across national boundaries are putting transnational solidarity on the agenda of unions. As a result, unions are building alliances with workers in other countries. Many key initiatives have originated with women activists who emphasize the significance of gender within global capitalism. For example, at the prompting of women activists in both unions and communities, the Canadian union movement was actively involved in building the World March of Women, the goals of which were to eliminate poverty and violence in women's lives. Launched on March 8, 2000, it culminated on October 17, 2000, the International Day for the Elimination of Poverty. This worldwide march, endorsed by over 200 countries and 2200 organizations, was initiated by the Fédération des femmes du Québec.

Unions and Equity

Unions offer one of the few vehicles through which to resist the restructuring of labour markets. Unions also help to counter the ideological onslaught promoting competition and the marketplace, patriarchal values for workplaces and households, and radical individualism, which undermines citizenship rights and rejects claims made on the basis of systemic discrimination. Unions are now a decisive arena for organizing by equity-seeking groups. However, union commitment to equality initiatives, participatory democracy and coalition building did not come about without resistance. In fact, the movement of union women has struggled for more than forty years to bring about this transformation.

NOTES

1. This chapter draws freely on my previously published articles: Briskin 1999, 1999a, 2002, and 2004.
2. A video on the growing gap in Canada is available on the Internet. At policyalternatives.ca/multimedia/canadas-growing-gap-explained.
3. Information on the CEP Young Workers Committee is on the Internet. At: cep.ca/list/all/1/by-date?topic=young-workers-committee.
4. The equity-related initiatives of seven Canadian unions are profiled on the Gender and Work Database: CAW, CEP, CUPE, NUPGE, OPSEU, UFCW and USWA. At: genderwork.ca/cms/display-article.php?sid=42&aid=55. See also the website of the Canadian Labour Congress. At canadianlabour.ca/en/equality.

REFERENCES

Braithwaite, Mary, and Catherine Byrne. 1995. *Women in Decision-Making in Trade Unions.* Brussels: European Trade Union Confederation.
Briskin, Linda. 2006a. *Equity Bargaining/Bargaining Equity*. Toronto: Centre for Research on Work and Society, York University. July 2006. At: arts.yorku.ca/sosc/lbriskin/pdf/bargainingpaperFINAL3secure.pdf.
____. 2006b. "Union Leadership and Equity Representation." For the Union Module of the Gender and Work Database. At: genderwork.ca/Briskin_Leadership_Paper_April_2006.pdf.
____. 2004 "Unions: Resistance and Mobilization." In Philomena Essed, David Goldberg and Audrey Kobayashi (eds.), *Blackwell Companion to Gender Studies*. London: Blackwell Press.
____. 2002. "The Equity Project in Canadian Unions: Confronting the Challenge of Restructuring and Globalization." In Fiona Colgan and Sue Ledwith (eds.), *Gender, Diversity and Trade Unions: International Perspectives*. London: Routledge.
____. 1999. "Feminisms, Feminization and Democratization in Canadian Unions." In Karen Blackford, Marie-Luce Garceau and Sandra Kirby (eds.), *Feminist Success Stories/Célébrons nos réussites féministes*. Ottawa: University of Ottawa Press.
____. 1999a. "Autonomy, Diversity and Integration: Union Women's Separate Organizing in North America and Western Europe in the Context of Restructuring and Globalization." *Women's Studies International Forum* 22,5.
____. 1993. "Union Women and Separate Organizing." In Patricia McDermott (ed.), *Women Challenging Unions: Feminism, Democracy And Militancy*. Toronto: University of Toronto Press.
De Angelis, Deborah, as told to Jonathan Eaton. 1998. "Wake Up Little Suzy: Women Retail Workers Organize." *Our Times* 17
Hunt, Gerald, and David Rayside (eds.). 2007. *Equity, Diversity and Canadian Labour.* Toronto: University of Toronto Press.
Inglis, Sarah. 1994. "McDonald's Union Drive-thru: Sarah Inglis Tells Her Story." *Our Times* 13.
Jackson, Andrew. 2010. *Work and Labour in Canada: Critical Issues* (second ed.). Toronto: Canadian Scholars' Press.
Jackson, Andrew, and Grant Schellenberg. 1999. "Unions, Collective Bargaining and Labour Market Outcomes for Canadian Women: Past Gains and Future Challenges." In Richard Chaykowski and Lisa Powell (eds.), *Women and Work*. Kingston: McGill-Queen's University Press.
Lee, Mark. 2007. *Eroding Tax Fairness*. Ottawa: Canadian Centre for Policy Alternatives. At: LocalSettings/Temp/policyalternatives.ca/documents/National_Office_Pubs/2007/Eroding_Tax_Fairness_web.pdf.

81

Women and Theft

M. NourbeSe Philip[1]

In 1986, I was asked to take part in a panel discussion at the Arts Against Apartheid Festival — the theme: "Women and Poverty." I don't know what it must be like to be truly poor — having no options as well as having no money (I can only imagine it). Since I stopped practising law at a legal clinic many years ago, my contact with poor people has been limited. So what could I say about women and poverty that would be new and not a repetition of old and hackneyed platitudes? What bothered me about the theme — "women and poverty" — was how well the words went together — as if they belonged together — women and poverty — like motherhood and apple pie.

I went to Rabbi Klein's *Dictionary of Etymology* for help. "Poverty," he told me, came from the word "pauper," meaning "poor." Next I checked with Oxford, and they — all men undoubtedly — told me that poor was the state of having few or no material possessions — *that*, I could identify with; the opposite of rich — we were getting a little closer to the meat of the issue here. I went back to the Rabbi, and he told me "poor" was also the descendant of "pauper," which in turn was a combination of two words meaning "one who produces little." One who produces little. Women? Women produce little. Women are poor because they produce little. None of that made any sense, as I thought of the vast quantities of work women have traditionally done. They are presently responsible for two-thirds of all working hours in the world.

I went back to Rabbi Klein on the subject of being rich; he told me that the origin of "rich" was to be found in being kingly — not queenly, but kingly.

Kings, paupers, and women — I was on to something here, I felt. I certainly wouldn't have said that kings were noted for producing much — if they have had a great deal of material wealth and displayed it, this has usually been as a result of others producing — much or little — and being forced to give it up to the king, or having it taken away to make kings rich. And if the opposite of rich is poor — the state of producing little — surely we're entitled to assume that one of the qualities of being rich is producing much. Surely. But logic is not something the English language is noted for, and here were those kings — who hadn't produced much — in close association with the word "rich," of which "poor" was the opposite. But I know had much more than I started out with — women, kings, and between them, poverty — the condition of being poor or producing little.

If we accept that women have traditionally produced much — and the statistics exist to support this — how do we get from the state of producing much and having little, to being described as producing little? Was there a word that could describe the process by which kings who produced little were made rich, and women who produced much became poor? I came at it another way — if women produced much and now had little, it was either because they gave it away, lost it, or had it taken away from them. I knew they hadn't lost it; in some instances they may have given it away out of love for their families, but since they were very seldom, if ever, free agents, you couldn't really call it giving; so that left the last explanation.

Theft. "Women and Theft" became the subject of my presentation. The word "poverty,"

I argued, really only described the end result, omitting the process, the pattern and series of actions which, over the centuries, has resulted in the inevitable link between women and poverty.

I was, as I often do, playing with words in a very serious way in the hope of their releasing some hidden or forgotten meaning. What I hadn't known at the time was that there was very good reason, with a long and distinguished pedigree, why the words "women" and "poverty" belonged together. It lay in the distinction, traditionally unacknowledged, as Hannah Arendt argues, between labour and work.

This distinction, according to Arendt, has been largely ignored in political thought and modern labour theories, yet is reflected in all European languages, in the existence of different words for these two activities — *labour* and *work* — although these words are used interchangeably and almost synonymously.

Traditionally, "work" has referred to that activity which produces new objects — objects that added to the world of things, and often outlasted the humans that made them. "To labour" meant to do work whose products or results were consumed immediately; objects, if produced, were produced only incidentally. The distinguishing mark of labour lay in the immediate consumption of its products; its significance in its essentiality; without labour, life was not liveable. Under the general rubric of labour we can include cooking, cleaning and general caretaking, all of which are indispensable to living. Despite its essential quality, however, or probably *because* of it, every attempt was made to keep this type of work and those who did it — women and slaves — hidden and away from public life. "Women were hidden away," writes Arendt, "not only because they were somebody else's property, but because their life was laborious, devoted to bodily functions" (Arendt 1958: 72). A classic case of blaming the victim.

Labour or non-productive work didn't enrich the world, reasoned those early thinkers; it resulted in nothing because its results were consumed immediately, leaving nothing behind — except, of course, more labour. These men were appropriately contemptuous of this type of work and those carrying it out. They were wrong, of course. Labour did produce something of value — of inestimable value: the freedom and potential productivity of masters and men; freedom to pursue whatever public activity they were engaged upon. It would take Marx to recognize the surplus value in the labouring activity itself, and to articulate how the labour of some would suffice for the life of all. But in the history of Western thought — reflected in the language — labour and poverty belonged together, since "the activity corresponding to the status of poverty was labouring."

All of which takes us right back to kings — the rich — and paupers who produce little. The contradiction at the heart of the word "poor" is patent, if we follow Arendt's argument, for poor people have not only produced much, or laboured much, but they have had much taken away from them and were then described as producing little. The word itself now encapsulates, reflects, perpetuates and so magnifies the theft. And within the traditional category of the poor were women, whose work was laborious. So the words "women" and "poverty" did belong together after all. Historically. Socially. Politically. Etymologically.

So what? We know about the oppression of women — by men, by the patriarchy — and am I not just stating the obvious? Perhaps, but the obvious is still not received opinion, and the statistics that appear in Robin Morgan's *Sisterhood is Global* help buttress my argument that what we ought to be talking about is women and theft: "women represent one half the global population, one third of the labour force, yet they receive only one tenth of the world income and own less than one tenth of world property."[2]

But there is more to it than that. What I'm interested in is how language continues to betray itself, its sources and its context — how it continues to imprison us. My question is this: is there anything to be gained by talking of women and theft, rather than women and poverty? I believe so. Poverty describes a state — a rather passive state, and most public discussion on the issue of poverty pays little attention to how the state of poverty is brought about — how integrally related it is to our own system.

As a Black woman, when I think of women and theft, I make the immediate association with even more blatant forms of theft that Black women — and men — in the New World were subject to — not only theft of their labour, but of their spouses, their children, their religion, their culture, and their languages. So too the Native peoples of the New World. In the universally tragic contact of the West with other cultures, the leitmotif of theft and impoverishment will always be found.

Maybe it's my errant belief in the power of the word, but it seems to me that if we start talking about women — Black and non-Black women — and theft, we have to start asking questions like who did the stealing (and in some cases women stole from women as well), and what was stolen. In some instances theft of material possessions, or of remuneration for one's labour, was the least of the crimes committed. Maybe we can even start taking about reparations for women, instead of affirmative action. What are we affirming? That women have been victims of theft for centuries, or men's overwhelming generosity in recognizing themselves as thieves? Strong language? Perhaps. But what I am most interested in revealing is that even when we believe we are being objectively descriptive by using a word like "poverty," or "poor," we continue the myth that poor people are poor because they are poor — they produce little; we have all, I'm sure, heard the variation of that argument about Blacks, Native people and women.

So let's really start reconstructing the language that surrounds us — here's a start; instead of aid to Africa, let's start talking about reparations to Africa (the first word suggests hand-outs, the latter acknowledges the existence of a wrong); instead of women and poverty, let's talk about women and theft — then let's talk some more about compensation for that theft.

A tall order? Undoubtedly. But as a writer nurtured on the bile of a colonial language, whose only intent was imperialistic, I see no way around the language, only through it, challenging the mystification and half-truths at its core.

NOTES

M. NourbeSe Philip, 1992, "Women and Theft," in M. Nourbese Philip, *Frontiers: Selected Essays and Writings on Racism and Culture, 1984–1992*, Toronto: Mercury Press. Adapted and reprinted with permission.

1. The unusual form of Philip's second name needs to be understood in the context of people of African ancestry in the Black diaspora often re-spelling their names in order to dispel(1) the colonizing effects of Imperial English and its re-namings.

2. Editor's note: According to UNICEF, as of 2007, "women perform two-thirds of the world's work, they only earn one tenth of the income, and own less than one per cent of the world's property." Source: UNICEF, 2007, "Gender Equality — The Big Picture." At: unicef.org/gender/index_big-picture.html.

REFERENCES

Arendt, Hannah. 1958. *The Human Condition*. Chicago: University of Chicago Press.

Morgan, Robin (ed.). 1984. *Sisterhood Is Global*. New York: Feminist Press.

Women and Poverty

Denise Spitzer

Gia is coming home from a tough shift at the local café. Ever since the plant closed, there are few customers, fewer shifts, and even fewer tips. Gia thinks about Lauren's abrupt departure last week. Her wages were barely covering the cost of childcare so, when the fees went up, she had to quit. Gia is thinking about a similar move. She likes her work, chatting with customers, and joking with the other servers, but the cost of childcare is using up all of her income. "At least if I were on social assistance, the cost of Louis' prescriptions would be covered," she thinks. "And with this recession who knows when those folks in the plant will get back to work — and back to leaving those tips!"

In Canada, over 1.7 million low-income women like Gia face decisions like these each day as they struggle to earn sufficient income to take care of themselves and their families (Townson 2009). Poverty is not, however, just an individual problem; it has implications for Canadian society as a whole. Links between poverty and poor health are well-established. Low-income individuals report higher rates of chronic disease, distress and low-self esteem (Lightman, Mitchell and Wilson 2008). Children are also deeply affected by growing up in poverty. Poor children are more likely to exhibit anti-social behaviour, learning disabilities and language delay (Ross, Scott and Smith 2000). Poverty disrupts social cohesion in Canada and contributes to social and financial costs, putting pressure on our health, social services and criminal justice systems, yet poverty is a fact of life for many Canadians — especially women and children.

What Is Poverty?

Gia does not need a statistician to tell her she is living in poverty. For her, poverty means visiting the food bank, arriving late to a job interview because the bus was not on schedule, hoping her children do not need more school supplies and skipping meals to keep the kids fed.

Government programs and policies, however, require quantitative data to understand the breadth and depth of the problem and to inform decision-making. Statistics Canada uses three indicators to describe low-income status. The first, Low-Income Cut-Off (LICO), is a measure that identifies low-income households as those that spend 20 percent more on basic shelter, food and clothing than the local average, based on family size and geography (Statistics Canada 2008). The second measure, Low-Income Measure (LIM), is calculated as 50 percent of median after-tax income, accounting for family size. The third is the Market Basket Measure (MBM), which examines the ability of households to purchase a specific array of goods and services deemed essential for survival (HRSDC 2008).

Poverty in Canada: Women and Children First

The face of poverty in Canada is disproportionately female (Lindsay and Almey 2006a). In fact the term "feminization of poverty" has come into common parlance as it reflects the reality that women face greater likelihood of being poor than men. Factors such as age, family structure, health status, immigration status and ethnicity may further contribute to women's vulnerability to poverty (Lindsay and Almey 2006a).

For example, 36 percent of Aboriginal women are classified as low-income as compared to 17 percent of non-Aboriginal women and 32 percent of Aboriginal men (O'Donnell 2006). Immigrants are at greater risk of being poor than Canadian-born individuals: visible minority status increases the likelihood of living in poverty even more dramatically (Kazemipur and Halli 2001), while nearly a quarter of foreign-born women live in poverty (Lindsay and Almey 2006c). In addition, while Canadians with disabilities are more likely to experience poverty than the average citizen, the rates of poverty among women with disabilities are even higher than those of men (Fournier-Savard 2006).

While these groups have been identified as poor, women's poverty may be masked by the status of their partners. For years, economists presumed that members of a household shared equally in resources such as income and would therefore share in socioeconomic status. Evidence suggests, however, that members of a household may have disparate access to resources depending on their ability to exercise power within the family, thus women and children may still be poor despite the affluence of male partners (Phipps and Burton 1995).

Why Are Women Poor?

Clearly, women, in particular those who live with disabilities, are lone parents, immigrants, indigenous and women of colour, are over-represented among the ranks of the poor. Yet the question remains — why? Access to the labour market, concentration in low-waged employment, the proliferation of part-time work, the demands of caregiving and the consequences of divorce all appear to contribute to women's poverty (Ross, Scott and Smith 2000; Townson 2009).

Of course, not all women are poor; individual women may earn as much or more than individual men, but when we view aggregate statistical data, we find significant wage disparities between women and men. However, these findings may mask inequities within categories of men and women. For example, men and women of colour are disadvantaged not only with regard to the population as a whole, but also in relation to Euro-Canadian women (Lindsey and Almey 2006c). The gender wage gap, however, persists and is largely due to an overwhelming concentration of women in low-waged positions in service, sales and manufacturing industries; the result is that women may be employed in the marketplace — but may still be poor.

Two major explanations have been offered for women's overall economic disadvantage. The first model, Human Capital Theory, asserts that, when individuals make rational choices to invest in certain opportunities, such as education and additional skills training, and when they demonstrate greater allegiance to employers by remaining in positions longer, they are the recipients of appropriate financial reward (Johnson 2000). Accordingly, Gia's disadvantaged economic situation could be perceived as a result of the poor choices she made: choosing to forego further education in order to raise her daughter or changing jobs in order to follow her ex-husband to a different city.

Feminists have critiqued the explanatory power of this approach. First, education is not as potent a predictor of income for women as it is for men (Krieger et al. 1993). In Canada, women with university educations earn 30 percent less than their male counterparts (Lindsay and Almey 2006a). Furthermore, women are constrained in their efforts to attain further skills training because of the financial cost, the demands of family obligations, and by the fact that employers are less likely to offer additional training to female employees. Women like Gia do appear to hold more discontinuous employment records than men, making them appear less committed to their employer: however, childbearing, caregiving responsibilities and the expectation that they will follow male partners in their career paths contributes to this phenomenon (Ollenburger and Moore 1998).

The second model, Job Segregation Theory, asserts that women and men occupy different echelons of the work force with women filling positions that are less remunerative (Lorber 1994). According to this theory, women are either drawn to positions that are poorly waged because they tend to offer more flexible working conditions, which are compatible with family responsibilities, or they are attracted to labour that reflects "female" traits, such as caring, which are less valued in our society. Conversely, occupations may become devalued as more women enter the field, as has occurred in office work and academia. According to this model, women who work part-time so they can care for an elderly parent in addition to their children will be economically disadvantaged by virtue of their decision and/or obligation to fulfill these familial duties. Still others who have opted to work in home care or childcare are penalized financially due to the low value placed on these occupations. Gia's high school girl friends who went on to work in office management or as teaching aids have found that these positions are not as lucrative as the ones their male schoolmates secured after they completed a similar number of years of trade or technical training.

The Job Segregation Model complements Marxist perspectives that focus on the use of women (and children) as a reserve army of labour whose efforts can be harnessed to occupy temporarily lower-waged positions when required, while men are paid a family wage meant to cover the cost of their labour and the domestic labour of women and children. In capitalist societies, work of so-called exchange value — work in the marketplace for commodities — commands financial rewards and is traditionally associated with men. It is more highly valued than domestic labour, which is regarded as work of use-value — the socially necessary, generally female labour associated with household and family (Benston 1969). Hence, the notion of men as breadwinners is naturalized. These differences also contribute to unequal relations and economic statuses within the household (Ollenburger and Moore 1998).

While voluntary migrants are selected to enter Canada based upon a set of criteria that include education and demand for their skills, foreign-born workers still face considerable challenges in finding acceptance for their credentials and experience. Consequently, immigrants — women in particular — tend to be under-employed (Haan 2008). While most migrants recover their former socioeconomic status in the following generation, that does not hold true for visible minority migrants even with equivalent education and skills, indicating that racism plays a significant role in hindering upward mobility (Kazemipur and Halli 2001; Haan 2008). Similarly, women with disabilities face considerable barriers in obtaining remunerative work. Myths about disabilities, as well as the lack of incentives to adapt workplaces to accommodate workers with disabilities, create roadblocks to inclusivity (Fawcett 2000).

In the current context of globalization and the subsequent loss of full-time industrial jobs in Canada, women's labour has been increasingly directed towards part-time work that is low-waged and unlikely to be unionized (Armstrong 1996). Part-time labour is viewed as more compatible with women's familial responsibilities, in particular family caregiving. Commonly, women are expected to forfeit other activities in favour of caring for children, the elderly or the infirm. These demands may compel women to give up jobs or select part-time work to enable them to carry out these tasks particularly in the absence of universal daycare programs or adequate home care services (Luxton and Corman 2001).

Women's association with lower wages is critical to our understanding of the distribution of poverty in Canada. Changes in household configuration — whether due to an increase in family size or loss of household income earners through death or desertion — is a major factor driving women into poverty (Lochhead and Scott 2000). Once in poverty, women's economic mobility is limited.

Gender Ideologies, Gender Roles and the Feminization of Poverty

The feminization of poverty is an acknowledged social trend in Canadian society. Immigration status, ethnicity and disability are among the factors that can constrain women's access to remunerative employment that is commensurate with their skills and education. While men's socioeconomic status is also influenced by these factors, women remain the most vulnerable to poverty. Not surprisingly, a lifetime of poorly waged labour and the increased probability that women will outlive male partners contribute to diminished circumstances among a significant proportion of senior women — although, currently, fewer live in poverty than in the 1990s (Lindsay and Almey 2006a). In addition, gender ideologies and gender roles further shape and reinforce the relative impoverishment of women. Occupations that employ large numbers of women, or are associated with labour regarded as "naturally" female such as care work, are devalued both socially and economically. Moreover, women's caregiving responsibilities may mean that women are often under greater pressure to juggle the demands of family and employment, resulting in higher percentages of women in part-time employment.

Gender ideologies also play into the popular image of the "welfare mother" — the passive victim awaiting a government handout who embodies the feminization of poverty. Despite the stereotype, women who contend with poverty are not passive victims awaiting the next government handout. Women in poverty are often resourceful, designing ingenious ways to survive in difficult circumstances through building networks of reciprocity that may share childcare, offer material assistance and other forms of social support (Turner and Grieco 2000). Such women have also organized themselves in local and national groups to raise awareness about the realities of living in poverty and to find ways to alleviate the current situation and eliminate the conditions that perpetuate poverty in Canada.

REFERENCES

Armstrong, Pat. 1996. "The Feminization of the Labour Force: Harmonizing Down in a Global Economy." In I. Bakker (ed.), *Rethinking Restructuring: Gender and Change in Canada.* Toronto: University of Toronto Press.

Benston, Margaret. 1969. "The Political Economy of Women's Liberation." *Monthly Review* 21 (September).

Fawcett, Gail. 2000. *Bringing Down the Barriers: The Labour Market and Women with Disabilities in Ontario.* At: ccsd.ca/pubs/2000/wd/intro.htm.

Fournier-Savard, Patric. 2006. "Women with Disabilities." *Women in Canada: A Gender-Based Statistical Report.* Ottawa: Statistics Canada. At: dsp-psd.pwgsc.gc.ca/Collection-R/Statcan/89-503-X/0010589-503-XIE.pdf.

Haan, Michael. 2008. "The Place of Place: Location and Immigrant Economic Well-Being in Canada." *Population Research and Policy Review* 27.

HRSDC (Human Resources and Skills Development Canada). 2008. "Low Income in Canada: Using the Market Basket Measure." At: hrsdc.gc.ca/eng/publications_resources/research/categories/inclusion/2008/sp-864-10-2008.

Johnson, Colleen. 2000. "Racial Disparities and Neoclassical Economics: The Poverty of Human Capital Explanations." *The Social Science Journal* 37,3.

Kazemipur, Abdolmohammad, and Shiva Halli. 2001. "The Changing Colour of Poverty in Canada." *CRSA/RCSA* 38,2.

Krieger, Nancy, et al. 1993. "Racism, Sexism and Social Class: Implications for Studies of Health, Disease and Well-Being." *American Journal of Preventative Medicine* 9,6.

Lightman, Ernie, Andrew Mitchell and Beth Wilson. 2008. *Poverty Is Making Us Sick: A Comprehensive*

Survey of Income and Health in Canada. Toronto: Wellesley Institute.

Lindsay, Colin, and Marcia Almey. 2006a. "Income and Earnings." *Women in Canada*. Ottawa: Statistics Canada.

___. 2006b. "Paid and Unpaid Work." *Women in Canada*. Ottawa: Statistics Canada.

___. 2006c. "Immigrant Women." *Women in Canada*. Ottawa: Statistics Canada.

Lochhead, Clarence, and Scott, Katherine. 2000. *The Dynamics of Women's Poverty.* Ottawa: Status of Women Canada.

Lorber, Judith. 1994. *Paradoxes of Gender.* New Haven: Yale University Press.

Luxton, Meg, and June Corman. 2001. *Getting By in Hard Times: Gendered Labour at Home and on the Job.* Toronto: University of Toronto Press.

O'Donnell, Vivian. 2006. "Aboriginal Women in Canada." *Women in Canada.* Ottawa: Statistics Canada.

Ollenburger, Jane, and Helen Moore. 1998. *A Sociology of Women: The Intersections of Patriarchy, Capitalism and Colonization.* Upper Saddle River, NJ: Prentice Hall.

Phipps, Shelly, and Peter Burton. 1995. "Sharing within Families: Implications for the Measurement of Poverty Among Individuals in Canada." *The Canadian Journal of Economics* 28,1.

Ross, David P., Katherine Scott and Peter J. Smith. 2000. *The Canadian Fact Book on Poverty.* Ottawa: Canadian Council on Social Development.

Schechter, Stephen, and Bernard Paquet. 1999. "Contested Approaches in the Study of Poverty: The Canadian Case and the Argument for Inclusion." *Current Sociology* 47,3.

Statistics Canada. 2008. *Low Income Definitions.* At: statcan.gc.ca/pub/13f0022x/00003/notedef/5801174-eng.htm.

Townson, Monica. 2009. *Women's Poverty and the Recession.* Ottawa: Canadian Centre for Policy Alternatives.

Turner, J., and M. Grieco. 2000. "Gender and Time Poverty: The Neglected Social Policy Implications of Gendered Time, Transport and Travel." *Time & Society* 9,1.

Law, Governance, Politics and Public Policy

C. Lesley Biggs

The "Public" and the "Private"

In my introductory Women's and Gender Studies classes, I often distinguish between what I call "big 'P' politics" and "small 'p' politics." "Big 'P' politics" are those events and decisions that take place in the political arena that we tend to associate with provincial legislatures and Parliament, and are debated within and among political parties. "Small 'p' politics" are the everyday power relations that shape our lives, including the ways in which we "do gender" and are gendered by others, and the ways we perform our racialized identities, our blackness or whiteness, for example, and are racialized by others. In part, I use this distinction to demonstrate that social change is not synonymous with changes in legislation. Far from it! Often the legal changes take place only after public opinion has shifted on an issue, and usually only after a long period of debate and lobbying, processes that can sometimes take decades to achieve. Legislatures are not outside gender relations and other hierarchies of power; and in fact, given the identities of our elected representatives, who are mostly white men drawn from the middle and upper classes, it is not surprising that they are not leaders of change despite claims to be acting in the "public interest."

My intent in making the distinction between "big 'P'" and "small 'p' politics is to demonstrate that, with awareness, we can make small changes in our lives and affect the lives of others, even though we may be operating within a narrow range of "choices." Our choices matter, and when we fear being ridiculed or treated with hostility, those choices can take courage because most of us would like to "fit in." "Small 'p'" politics may include trying to raise your child in a non-sexist environment, refusing to laugh at a racist joke, fundraising for a women's shelter, or wearing a *hijab* or other clothing and fashions that signal difference; "small 'p'" politics may also include challenging a school policy that prohibits gay teens from attending their graduation celebrations as couples, or getting a male hockey team to allow your daughter to play. Many of these issues often can be negotiated quietly and easily resolved (if people are reasonable and rational), but they also can and have become a source of public controversy. And herein lies the limits of my distinction between "big 'P'" and "small 'p'" politics because what may begin as a "private matter" quickly can become a "public issue," as C. Wright Mills (1959 [1976]) noted over fifty years ago. Moreover, raising public awareness about an issue does not necessarily need to translate into lobbying for legislative change. For example, the movements for environmental sustainability have focused on educating the public about the ways in which creating a greener planet can be achieved through conserving energy or recycling, as well as lobbying governments for changes in the regulation of industries that pollute the earth.

The distinction between "big 'P'" and "small 'p'" politics overlaps in many ways with the distinction between "the public" and "private" sphere, a binary which was fully articulated in the debate over "the woman question" in Canada, Britain, and the United States. The inheritors of Enlightenment ideas such as "equality, fraternity, and liberty," were faced with the paradox of calling for enfranchisement for all (well, actually initially that meant men with landed property) while excluding women and minority groups. Of course, the term "fraternity" signals who is in the voters' club — i.e., members of the brotherhood — while erasing everybody else. This conundrum is captured ironically in a February 1915 statement by May Clendenan, a Western Canadian Women's rights advocate: "If democracy is a right, women should have it; if it isn't, men shouldn't have it" (Munroe 2009).

Early twentieth-century feminists in Canada were well aware that women and their families were affected by what happened in the public sphere, and they were particularly concerned about the impact of poverty, white slavery (prostitution), alcoholism, and Venus' curse (venereal disease). As a result, these feminists used the rhetoric of women's proper sphere to make a claim for women's rights, including the rights to vote and run for political office. For example, Janice Fiamengo (2008) argues that Western Canadian feminist Nellie McClung, one of the "Famous Five," brilliantly recasts "the meaning of housekeeping to encompass the whole territory of domestic and public."In her book *In Times Like These*, McClung wrote:

> Women have cleaned up things since time began; and if women ever get into politics there will be a cleaning-out of pigeon-holes and forgotten corners, on which the dust of years has fallen, and the sound of the political carpet-beater will be heard in the land (cited in Fiamengo 2008: 201).

Reference to the federal Parliament as the "House" has great subversive potential when we apply McClung's formidable wit!

From early feminist formulations to the present, the public/private divide has been subjected to scrutiny, particularly since the institution of the family often straddles the divide. Our laws define what constitutes a family, and, until recently when same-sex marriage was legally recognized in Canada, the family was comprised of a husband and wife, and any children. Particular constructions of the family are evident in our tax laws, too, in terms of who gets to claim whom as "dependants." Divorce laws determine the conditions under which a marriage can end, the division of property, and the amount of support for an ex-spouse and children. Similarly in the past, pension plans applied strict definitions of family when deciding beneficiaries. In the collection of statistical data, the term "head of household" referred to the husband/father, who was the main source of financial support, but the term had the effect of subordinating women's monetary and domestic contributions to the family (Thomas 2010; Statistics Canada 2011). In keeping with the times, Statistics Canada dropped the "head of household" designation in 1976 (see Thomas 2010).

Our laws define age of consent for sexual behaviour, eligibility for voting, alcohol consumption, and the prosecution of offenses and jail time. Until 1988, the law determined if a woman was eligible for an abortion; laws also prescribe rules for adoption and the transactions for the transfer of embryos and sperm. On almost any form, you are asked to provide information about your sex: "Are you male or female?" But what if you are transsexual? Where do you fit? (One of my pet peeves on such forms is "marital status," defined as single, married, co-habiting, or divorced. I have been divorced for almost thirty years; when do I stop being "divorced" and become "single?" I check "single.") The examples above are just some of the ways in which the state regulates families, and many of these laws are deeply gendered.

Thinking About Human Rights

Central to liberal-democratic discourse is the concept of rights. The Oxford English Dictionary (OED) identifies three distinct denotations of "right." First, a right can refer to "that which is considered proper, correct, or consonant with justice, and related uses." Second, a right can refer to "the legal, moral, or natural entitlement, and related uses," and third, a right can refer to "that which is straight." This latter definition is not employed in legal discourse, but given the binary between "straight" and "gay" people, the meaning of "straight" in this context recalls the ways in which heteronormativity was embedded in law, and was considered "proper" and "correct," despite not being "consonant with justice."

The term "rights" is often paired with an adjective. For example, the OED defines human rights as "rights possessed by humans, especially the set of entitlements held to belong to every person as a condition of being human." This definition of rights would seem to be unambiguous since it suggests that everyone — every human — should have "a set of entitlements." However, it is a sad commentary on the human community that not everybody is considered fully human — full humanity is often defined in practice as male, white, able-bodied, or heterosexual — so that various forms of oppression, including murder of the so-called "sub-human" group, are then justified. If we look at the phrase "women's rights," which the OED defines as "rights possessed by women, especially, as considered to be equal with those of men," we again realize that this pairing has been necessary only because women have had to struggle for their rights in order to be considered equal to men. If women were equal, there would be no need for the phrase "women's rights"; rather these rights would be covered under the general rubric of "human rights."

We often take our rights for granted; they are seen as "universal" and "obvious," and therefore they are "unambiguous" and "uncontroversial." But, as Marie-Bénédicte Dembour (2010: 2) argues, "different people hold different concepts of human rights." She identifies four schools of thought regarding human rights, each with implications for the understanding of human rights law, the foundation of human rights, the realization of human rights, the universality of human rights, and overall faith in human rights (Dembour 2010: 5–10). According to Dembour, natural rights scholars believe in rights and embrace the most taken-for-granted view (as expressed in the OED's definition): "human rights as those rights one possesses simply by being a human being"; natural rights are based, then, on species entitlements. These scholars have faith in human rights law because rights are "natural"; that is, people *have* rights by virtue of being human, which for some scholars is directly connected to concepts such as the Divine, or God, or to some other metaphysical connection. In the absence of this link, natural rights scholars argue that rights are foundational as a result of legal consensus.

Unlike the natural school of human rights, the deliberative school does not believe in rights existing by virtue of being human. Deliberative scholars "conceive of human rights as political values that liberal societies *choose* to adopt... human rights come into existence through societal agreement" (Dembour 2010: 3, emphasis in the original). As a result, deliberative scholars recognize that human rights are not held universally; rather, deliberative rights are ideal rights for which societies should strive. Despite this contextual understanding of human rights, the deliberative school has faith in law to realize the goal of human rights. In contrast, the protest school of human rights has little faith in the law, believing that the agendas of human rights laws and institutions can be high-jacked by social/political elite or become mired in bureaucratization. (Here, I would add that the effectiveness of institutions like human rights commissions is undermined by underfunding — one form of elite high-jacking). "The protest school," according to Dembour, "is concerned first and foremost with redressing injustice. For protest scholars, human rights articulate rightful claims made by or on behalf of the poor, the unprivileged, and the oppressed" (Dembour 2010: 3). Protest scholars are able to point to the myriad of human rights abuses that demonstrate that the law has not protected individuals, and in some cases, it has been used as an instrument of oppression and discrimination.

Discourse scholars are different from the three previous schools of thought because, according to Dembour, they do not believe in human rights. Instead discourse scholars argue that "human rights exist only because people talk about them" (Dembour 2010: 4). That is, human rights are not "natural," "inalienable," or "universal," but are central to liberal democratic discourse, which draws on the idea of meritocracy (i.e., individuals are rewarded with monetary success and status that spring from their achievements and the "choices" that they have made). Those who believe in meritocracy do not generally examine the factors that have structured success and individual decision making, thus justifying the inequitable distribution of power and resources. Nonetheless, discourse scholars acknowledge the power of language to shape our world; the discourse of rights is so embedded in our language that "rights" seem "natural." But these scholars maintain that the dominance of individualistic human rights in liberal democratic discourse privileges individual autonomy and freedom and private property while limiting the possibility of developing more imaginative approaches to addressing social injustice.

Each school of thought in its own way addresses the difference between formal and substantive equality. Formal equality is said to be achieved when everybody is treated the same before and under the law regardless of race, gender, ability, etc. The problem with this application of the rule of law is that individuals are not identically situated. For example, some individuals and groups have more power and resources in making their voices heard when legislation is being enacted, or when individuals and groups come into conflict with the law, or are seeking redress for injustices experienced by them. "The formal equality model," as the Centre for Equality Rights in Accommodation (CERA n.d.) observes, "tends to perpetuate discrimination and inequality because it cannot address *real inequality in circumstances*" (emphasis in the original). In order to achieve substantive equality, the discriminatory effects of the laws, policies, and practices need to be identified and the barriers removed. In this case, according to CERA, individuals and groups will achieve "equality of opportunity," but this mechanism is not the same as "equality of results," or outcome. For example, legal aid societies, which are publicly funded and publicly accountable non-profit organizations, provide legal assistance to low-income people who cannot otherwise afford the services of a lawyer. Thus legal aid levels the playing field for low income individuals by providing similar resources to those available to other, higher income individuals. As a result, low-income people may have adequate representation in the legal system (as opposed to the situation in which low-income individuals might represent themselves because they cannot afford a lawyer, thereby significantly enhancing their chances of conviction and severe penalty). What the legal aid societies cannot do is address the over-representation of low-income, particularly Aboriginal, people who come into conflict with the law in Canada. To achieve equality of effect in this case would require addressing the sources of structural inequality, as well as the legacy of colonialism in the case of Aboriginal people.

Mary Wollstonecraft's *A Vindication of the Rights of Women* is often heralded as the first book in liberal-democratic countries to argue for women's rights based as natural rights — God-given in this case. Since then, of course, feminists have advocated for women's rights utilizing "natural" rights arguments to demand the right to vote and to equal pay. However, as Janice McLaughlin (2003) points out, feminists have also developed three other strategies. The first is the pursuit of gendered rights, which take into account the specific position of women who traditionally have been located in the domestic sphere. "Rights," McLaughlin argues, "have been formulated through placing the private sphere outside of its remit" (McLaughlin 2003: 34). One example of gendered rights entails the recognition of women's contribution to the household through unpaid labour. Although this work is supposed to be calculated in the division of property when a couple divorces, women have not necessarily been accorded their share.[1]

A third strategy for women's rights advocates is the notion of concrete rights, which are akin to the deliberative model of human rights discussed above. In this framework, the context or concrete situations of women are taken into account in order to achieve a universal and fair outcome. According to McLaughlin (2003: 35), concrete rights "[bring] together the subject of liberalism — *the generalized other* — with the subject of difference — *the concrete other*" (emphasis in the original). McLaughlin goes on to say that "Supplementing the principle of valuing the generalized other with knowledge of the concrete other is compatible with liberalism because impartial justice requires knowledge of the particularity of the individual." An example of concrete rights is the principle of equal-pay-for-work-of-equal-value. Under traditional liberalism, men and women should be paid the same if they are doing the same jobs (although note that women's entry into some job categories was a hard won right when achieved, as well as an ongoing struggle in other situations!). The fact that women overall make less money than men also would be deemed "fair" since women and men work in different occupations and sectors of the economy. However, the principle of equal pay for work of equal value argues that jobs can be evaluated according to four criteria: skill, responsibility, effort, and working conditions. According to the Canadian Human Rights Commission (2010a), "Job evaluation plans are used to determine the value of each job in a consistent, equitable manner." Thus individuals doing very different jobs could end up with the same scores, thereby allowing women's work to be valued in the same way as men's work.

The final strategy for attaining women's rights identified by McLaughlin (2003) is to work for group or collective rights. Drawing on the work of philosopher Iris Marion Young, McLaughlin (2003: 37) argues that "certain individuals do not benefit from universal rights because it is their membership in, and association with, groups that are systematically discriminated against in Western society, which leads to their rights being denied." Class action suits in general represent the pursuit of group rights; it is a proactive strategy that seeks to redress a wrong. The most poignant example of the pursuit of group rights in Canada is the class actions taken by Aboriginal peoples to redress the injustices inflicted by the residential school system (Canadian Human Rights Commission 2010b). Other successful pursuits of group rights include ensuring access to telephone services for the deaf and hearing-impaired (Canadian Human Rights Commission 2010c); making reparations to Japanese Canadians for property seized in World War II; American women agitating for the Equal Rights Amendment (which was passed in 1972, but failed to be ratified by all fifty states by the 1982 deadline); and women who suffered autoimmune disease from their silicone breast implants securing a $3.4 billion settlement in 1994 from the major implant manufacturers. In most cases, these victories came after many years of litigation to have the litigants' claims of injustice redressed; most groups are not successful.

During the United Nations' Decade of Women (1975-1985), the concept of women's human rights gained currency among women across the world, and was popularized by Hilary Rodham Clinton's address "Women's Rights Are Human Rights" at the United Nations 4th World Conference on Women in Beijing, China, in 1995.[2] As a result of coming together through these conferences sponsored by the United Nations, "women's movements around the world formed networks and coalitions to give greater visibility both to the problems that women face every day and to the centrality of women's experiences in economic, social, political and environmental issues" (Bunch and Frost 2000: 1). Women's rights could not be simply equated with political rights (important as they are), but women's human rights were connected to personal security (freedom from violence), economic security (freedom from poverty brought about in part by improving women's access to education), and food security, which encompasses access to a safe and an adequate food and water supply, and environmental sustainability. Moreover, the fusion of women's rights and human rights represents a move to destabilize the perception that women's rights are a sub-category of human rights and therefore not as important as other rights. (For example, in many nationalist resistance movements and within unions, women have/are often asked to put aside their aspirations for equality until the "main" goal of self-determination has been achieved. I'm sure that you can guess what the outcome was/is for women when they agreed to do so.) Finally, linking women's rights with human rights indicates women's ownership of human's rights.

In Charlotte Bunch and Samantha Frost's view, the concept "women's human rights" has been successful because "it is simultaneously both prosaic and revolutionary" (Bunch and Frost 2000: 1). Who could deny that women are human? "So in many ways," write Bunch and Frost, "the claim that women have human rights seems quite ordinary." At the same time, they argue "the insistence that women's rights are human rights [has] profound transformative potential… [because it recognizes] the dismal failure of countries worldwide to accord women the human dignity and respect that they deserve — simply as human beings" (Bunch and Frost 2000: 1). Adopting a human rights framework involves rethinking theory — human rights theory, that is — and practice — the reality of women's lives. First, Bunch and Frost contend that applying a gender lens to human rights reveals the ways in which "current human rights definitions and practices fail to account for the ways in which already recognized human rights abuses often affect women differently because of their gender" (Bunch and Frost 2000: 4). Second, bringing a gender lens to human rights "draw[s] attention to human rights that are specific to women that heretofore have been seen as women's rights but not recognized as "human" rights" (Bunch and Frost 2000:4). As a case in point, Bunch and Frost cite the example of freedom from violence against women, a violence that often takes on gender-specific forms, but because it is most often directed at women, it is not seen as a violation of human rights. Until 1998, "war rape" (including sexual assault, sexual enslavement, forced sterilization, forced prostitution, and forced pregnancy) was not considered a crime against humanity. However, as a result of the systematic rape of Muslim women by Bosnian Serbs in the former Yugoslavia, the United Nations established the International Criminal Court under the Rome Statute in 1998, which enables the Court to prosecute crimes of sexual violence committed during war (see Part 1 of the Rome Statute for more details [United Nations 2003]). Women can no longer be treated as "the spoils of war." The Rome Statute has been ratified by 108 states as of 2008.

Rights Then and Now

Many of us have difficulty imagining that our grandmothers and great-grandmothers did not enjoy the same rights that most of us take for granted today. There was a time when Canadian women (and many other women) lost their property when they married a man; when married women could not legally enter into contracts without their husband's consent, keep their earnings from paid work, or have separate bank accounts from their husbands. For years, women and minorities could not vote in federal, provincial, or municipal elections, and when the federal vote was extended to women in 1920, Aboriginal people, Asians, and Hindus were excluded. A woman could not get a divorce on the same grounds (simple adultery) as her husband until 1925; women were not considered "persons" under the law until 1929, which, among other things, allowed women to be appointed to the senate; equal-pay-for-equal-work legislation was not enacted until the 1950s; birth control was not legally available until 1969; and gender-neutral laws concerning sexual assault were not passed until 1983.

Not all women in Canada benefitted equally or at the same time from the extension of legal rights to women; many experienced discrimination based on Aboriginal or minority status, disability, religious belief, or sexual orientation. For example, until 1960, Aboriginal women and men were forced to give up their treaty rights if they wanted to vote in the federal election; not until 1985, did Aboriginal women win the right to keep their Indian status if they married a non-Aboriginal man; in 1928, Alberta passed legislation that permitted forced sterilization of the "feeble-minded" and "inmates" in mental hospitals. Black women and men were refused service in bars, and were required to sit in designated seating in movie theatres; Hutterites and Doukohbors were denied the right to purchase land in Alberta; Japanese-Canadians were interned during World War II; homosexual behaviour between consenting adults was illegal until 1969. Many minorities experienced discrimination in the job and housing markets throughout the twentieth century and continue to do so today.

This list of legal inequalities, which is expanded upon in Chapter 13, "So You Think That You Know Canadian Women's/Gender History?" is among countless other acts of discrimination that particular groups have experienced over much of the course of Canada's history causing untold and unnecessary hardship and suffering for individuals and their families. The denial of human rights and indifference to the idea of universal equality based on human dignity can be understood in part as the legacy of nineteenth-century conservative liberalism. Adam Smith in *The Wealth of Nations* famously wrote about "the invisible hand of the market," which represented the belief that economic markets would be self-correcting, and therefore Smith (and many others) promoted the view that governments should not intervene in the marketplace and that individuals should be "free" to pursue their own self-interests. (Actually, Smith was wrong about the invisibility — the greedy paws of nineteenth-century capitalists were clearly seen by workers, many of whom barely made a subsistence living and laboured in horrendous working conditions.)

This free market philosophy was compatible with ideas of Reverend Thomas Robert Malthus (1976 [1778]), exemplified in his *An Essay on the Principle of Population*. Malthus feared that unchecked population growth endangered the well-being of a society and prevented it from reaching its utopian state. In his view, war, famine, and epidemics represented positive corrections to population growth since they limited population growth through high mortality rates (Nice guy?!). Malthus also believed that poverty served as a negative correction since it would encourage the poor to have fewer children (presumably by abstinence or abortion since no other reliable methods were available), thereby reducing the birth rate. Malthus' ideas were controversial at the time, but nonetheless gained further momentum with the publication, in 1859, of Charles Darwin's (2006 [1859]) *The Origin of the Species*, in which Darwin proposed his theory of "natural selection" and "the survival of the fittest" in the animal world. These ideas were then picked up by others who promoted the philosophy and science of "social Darwinism," justifying social inequalities based on race, class, and gender, since these groups were believed not to have the same intellectual capabilities as white Europeans and North Americans.

Events after World War I challenged these nineteenth-century ideas. Canada, like many countries, had not been prepared for the return of soldiers from the European front, so some remained in England for two years after the war before they could be repatriated. The resulting unrest, which was heightened by the stock market crash in 1929, forced policy makers and politicians to begin to rethink the role of the state in the market and in providing a social safety net for its citizens (Moscovitch 2011). The experiences of the First World War and the Great Depression have remained part of the Canadian collective consciousness ever since. Thus, during World War II, reconstruction plans began in earnest in 1943 with the release of Leonard Marsh's *Report on Social Security for Canada*, which was followed by W.A. Marshall's *White Paper on Employment and Income* in 1945 (cited in Moscovitch 2011). With the threat of a new political competitor — Co-operative Commonwealth Federation (CCF), MacKenzie King, then Prime Minister, announced a broad range of social programs in his Speech from the Throne in 1944. However, only the *Family Allowance Act*, which gave mothers a "baby bonus" for each child, was passed in 1944. The rest of the reforms came in the 1960s during the Pearson minority government, when the Liberals were dependent upon and pushed hard by the New Democratic Party. Drawing on the ideas of British writers J.M. Keynes and William Beveridge, the economic and social policies that emerged provided a new framework and ethos which called for state intervention in the market and in the provision of social services (Moscovitch 2011). "The welfare state," as it is often called, was born.

In the context of a booming economy, Tom Kent's 1962 document *Social Policy for Canada* set the stage for the dramatic transformation of the social landscape in Canada. Pearson's minority Liberal government oversaw the introduction of the Canada Pension Plan; the Canada Assistance Plan, which provided social assistance to persons with disabilities and to single parents; Medicare, a universal health insurance plan for hospital and medical care; the Guaranteed Income Supplement for seniors on low incomes; an increase in post-secondary education funding; amendments to *The National Housing Act*; and a parallel system of social assistance for Aboriginal people (Moscovitch 2011). In 1962, the minority Pearson government introduced a new immigration act which virtually eliminated racial discrimination. Under Pierre Trudeau's majority Liberal government, a federal *Divorce Act* was passed for the first time, which enabled divorce without having to prove adultery or mental cruelty; accessing contraceptives and birth control information became no longer illegal; and homosexuality was decriminalized.

The world had changed after the Second World War: women had played an extensive role in the wartime factories and many were no longer as willing to accept their subordinate status. After the war, many single women could anticipate working in the paid labour force for part of their lifetime, but married women were expected to give up their jobs to returning servicemen, and childcare facilities were closed, making it difficult for women to stay in the paid labour force. But, by the 1960s, the participation rate of married women in the labour force had skyrocketed; they made up one-third of the labour force and represented 55 percent of the labour-force growth (Anderson 2011). In addition, women played an extensive role in the peace movements that emerged in response to the Cold War and the threat of nuclear annihilation. Women were also actively involved in the Co-operative Commonwealth Federation (CCF), the precursor of the New Democratic Party, which positioned itself as the voice of working people and farmers. Quebec's Quiet Revolution, which represented an end to the Roman Catholic hold over the political, social, and economic life of Quebecers, also led to greater freedom for women in that province. Aboriginal groups successfully challenged the *Indian Act* in 1960, allowing them to vote in federal elections without losing their Indian status. Throughout the 1960s, aware of the actions in the American Indian Movement (AIM), Canadian Aboriginal groups began to coalesce into a social movement that demanded greater control over the lives of Aboriginal people, and better access to housing, education, jobs, and health care. Finally, the Stonewall Riots, which took place in New York's Greenwich Village in 1969, signalled the beginning of gay pride and "coming out of the closet" by lesbians and gay men — not just in the U.S., but in Canada and elsewhere, too.

These events and policy decisions throughout the 1950s, 1960s, and 1970s are the context for understanding many of the subsequent successes and failures of equality-seeking groups in the 1980s through to the present. Rather than understand "context" as simply background, we can analyze the welfare state as a set of interwoven policies (texts) and practices that were enacted to create this particular configuration of the state, which continue to influence, albeit to a much lesser degree, contemporary ideas about the role of the state in the economy and in the provision of a social safety net. In her earlier work, Janine Brodie describes "the welfare state" as one expression of a political rationality — "a particular way of seeing the social and political terrain [which] privileges certain vocabularies, styles of truth-telling and truth-tellers" (Brodie 2008: 147). In the post-war period until the early 1980s, "the welfare state" represented a dominant political rationality, becoming embedded in the social life of Canada, Britain, and other Western industrialized countries. A seeming consensus existed that the state should intervene in the economy and provide for those who are underprivileged or poor, as well as providing universal services such as Medicare.

By the 1980s, in response in part to the oil crisis throughout the 1970s, the political discourse had shifted, embracing what is often known as "Thatcherism" in Britain and "Reaganonmics" in the United States — both philosophies represented a return to a "free" market economy and a right-wing social agenda. A similar shift happened in Canada in 1984 with the election of a Progressive Conservative government, which subsequently passed the North American Free Trade Agreement (NAFTA) and the Goods and Services Tax (GST). Neoliberalism emerged as the dominant political rationality (see Chapter 73 for more detail), and as Brodie (2008: 147–48) observes, shifts in rationality require changes in identity formation (personal and national narratives), cultural identities, political consensus, and political practices. The philosophy of the "welfare state" remains a "residual rationality" — a cultural trace best exemplified by Canadians' overwhelming support for universal health care,[3] despite persistent efforts by federal and provincial governments to privatize this program. Thus, political space can be thought of as "zones of conflict" where "dominant, residual and emergent rationalities cohabitate the political space in dynamic tension with each other" (Brodie 2008: 148). As a result, a gap between policies and practices often exists as dominant and residual rationalities clash and contradict one another, constrained by older institutional structures and identities as new ones emerge.

Equity-seeking groups continue to advocate for redress to past injustices or to maintain elements of the social "safety net," but they do so in a new environment, one that is considerably less receptive than in the past. The shift to neoliberalism has had a profound impact on women and women's issues. In their chapter, Brodie and Bakker argue that "the policy goal of achieving gender equality [has] been systematically displaced through the prioritization of child- and family-centred initiatives, market principles, and individual self-reliance." Before the 1980s, the Canadian federal government had established "a network of gender-based policy machinery within the federal government — one of the most elaborate in the world at the time." Some provincial governments did the same. Through state feminism, i.e., "the advocacy of women's movement within the state" (Lovenduski 2005: 4), feminist bureaucrats (sometimes referred to as "femocrats") sought, as Brodie and Bakker observe, "the development of policies and agencies designed to enhance the status of women in all sectors of society, and provide them with points of entry into the policy-making process."

The 1984 election of the Progressive Conservatives (PC), as noted above, signalled the end of an era because the PCs sought "to de-legitimize gender-based claims on the state," first by disparaging feminism within political debates; second, by dismantling or curbing the autonomy of feminist agencies within the state apparatus; and finally, by removing women "as an analytic category in social policy development, and in turn, eroding women's equality as a central goal in Canadian public policy." In its place, the federal government reframed its social policy agendas placing the child, "the most vulnerable member of society," as the main focus of its social policy agenda. You may wonder "what is wrong with focussing on children?" and the answer, is of course, nothing. In fact, such an emphasis was long overdue, according to Bakker and Brodie, but the "poor child" was presented in political discourse as a disembodied subject, separate from poor mothers. The root cause of child poverty, as has been pointed out time and time again by anti-poverty activists, is the feminization of poverty, but gendered structural inequalities that women experience in the job market were not only not addressed by Conservative governments, but such inequalities were also erased from the government's social policy platforms. Given the experience of Canadian feminists' relationship to the state, the question as to whether state institutions are viable mechanisms to advance women's agenda now arises. What do you think?

The *Canadian Charter of Rights and Freedoms* marked "a significant political and legal victory" for women across Canada since it encoded equality rights in the *Constitution Act, 1982*. But like most legal reforms affecting women, the provision of a gender-specific clause did not happen without a fight. In her chapter, lawyer and constitutional activist Marilou McPhederan describes the role of the Ad Hoc Committee of Canadian Women on the Constitution (of which she was a member) in ensuring that the equality clauses (section 15) became part of the *Charter*. Far from being a "slam-dunk," (you would think that it would be obvious that equality clauses would be included in the *Charter*), the inclusion of section 15 was mired in controversy. First Prime Minister Jean Chrétien reneged on the Liberal government's promise to include section 15 in the *Charter*, and then his government introduced the famous "notwithstanding clause,"[4] which could override section 15. Keenly aware of American women's attempt to have the Equal Rights Amendment ratified in their constitution, women across Canada lobbied furiously for the inclusion of the equality clauses, and ultimately they were successful. However, a moratorium was placed on section 15 for three years, and when it was lifted on April 17, 1985, the "Ad Hockers" set up a women's legal defence fund so that the *Charter* could be used to support equality rights for women. Legal Education and Action Fund (LEAF) was born! Since then LEAF has intervened in 150 cases with many successes (see leaf.ca for more detail).

The *Indian Act*, which was passed by the Government of Canada in 1876, was the legal embodiment of colonial relations at that time, and in its current configuration, combined with the policies and practices that developed from the original *Act*, continues to influence the lives of Aboriginal peoples across Canada. "The objective [of the 1876 *Act*]," as Pamela Downe observes in her chapter, "was to promote an agenda of assimilation whereby culturally distinct Aboriginal communities would be eliminated and integrated into the larger and emerging European-based society of colonial Canada." The *Act* had a profound impact on the identities of Aboriginal peoples, since in part, one goal of the *Act* was to try to define who was an Indian. The *Act* also sought to impose Anglo patriarchal relations within Aboriginal communities; as a result, Aboriginal women were not allowed to vote in band council elections, a right that some had held previously. If an Aboriginal woman's husband died without a will, the decision to allow her to inherit his property was left to the discretion of the Superintendent General of Indian Affairs; and if a woman married a man without Indian status, she lost hers.

The *Indian Act* has been amended many times, sometimes moving forward the First Nations' agenda for self-determination while simultaneously perpetuating the federal government's assimilationist agenda. The status of Aboriginal women is a case in point: not until the 1985 passage of Bill C-31, a bill to bring the *Indian Act* into line with the provisions of the *Canadian Charter of Rights and Freedoms*, did Aboriginal women win the right to retain their Indian status and that of their children if they married a man without Indian status.

Moreover, Aboriginal women and children who had lost their status before 1985 had their full Indian status reinstated at this time. However, so-called C-31 women were not able to confer status on their grandchildren even though women without Indian status who married Aboriginal men had this right. As Downe comments, "rather than repealing the patriarchal assumptions that inform this policy, Bill C-31 only displaces them by two generations." While the inequality between Aboriginal women and men would seem obvious, Aboriginal women fought a long and arduous battle with the federal government, the resolution of which (Bill C-31) was forced upon the government by a decision of the United Nations Human Rights Commission. In addition, Aboriginal women faced opposition within Aboriginal communities both before and after the passage of Bill C-31 in part because membership in a band is tied to funding for housing, education, and social assistance; and funding was not increased after the amendment to accommodate increased numbers drawing on social services (Native Women's Association of Canada 2007).

As these legal and quasi-legal battles demonstrate, Aboriginal men and women are not outside of "a colonial and patriarchal mindset." "Colonization," as Anna Hunter writes in her chapter, "has taken its toll on all Aboriginal peoples but perhaps their greatest toll on women." In order for Aboriginal men and women to achieve their personal and collective self-determination, they must undergo a "decolonizing of the mind," a lifelong process which is not easily undone without personal and collective struggles for self-awareness. One way to achieve decolonization, argues Hunter, is to include a gender-based analysis of Aboriginal self-government, which unites theory of self-government with practice. Gender-based analysis is both an analytical tool and "a process, a way of thinking, to understand how the experiences of women and men are different and how they are the same" (Prairie Women's Health Centre of Excellence [PWHCE] 2011). A gender-based analysis incorporates "a diversity analysis and considers, wherever possible, how income, age, culture, ethnicity, sexual orientation, ability and geographic location and other factors interact with sex and with gender roles, within different groups of people" (PWHCE 2011).

Self-government is generally understood as "the right of Aboriginal peoples to be recognized as autonomous political communities with the authority and resources to decide the course of their individual and collective futures." This is the theory, but how does it work in practice if Aboriginal women are not in leadership roles in national Aboriginal organizations and women's issues are not represented in policies and program development? Male bias, Hunter argues, is not necessarily deliberate or malicious, but its effect is to marginalize the concerns and needs of Aboriginal women. As Hunter demonstrates, a gender-based analysis can go a long way in revealing the ways in which male bias has impacted, for example, Aboriginal child welfare policies and funding arrangements, as well as suggesting corrective measures that do not further marginalize Aboriginal women and their children.

Gender-based analysis is part of the larger, global strategy of gender-mainstreaming, which as United Nations Women (2011) argues, "involves gender perspectives and attention to the goal of gender equality... central to all activities — policy development, research, advocacy/dialogue, legislation, resource allocation, and planning, implementation and monitoring of programmes and projects." The uptake of gender-mainstreaming varies by country. For example, in their comparison of gender-streaming strategies in Canada and the Netherlands, Joan Eveline and Carol Bacchi (2005) found that these countries drew upon different understandings of gender, resulting in different reform approaches. In Canada, gender-mainstreaming has focussed on the differences between women and men, thereby relying on gender disaggregated statistics to demonstrate these differences. According to Eveline and Bacchi, the problem with the Canadian approach is twofold. First, it is based on the assumption that women's needs should be addressed so that women can participate on equal terms with men in Canadian society, a position which is akin to the "add-and-stir" approach of liberal feminism. Second, the Canadian mainstreaming approach is based on the assumption that gender is something that people *have* rather than something that they *do*. As a result, this strategy "does not draw attention to the unequal power relations between men and women" (Eveline and Bacchi 2005: 503), and the strategy itself may have a gendering effect by reinforcing the view of differences between women and men.

In contrast, the gender-mainstreaming approach in the Netherlands "makes the key point that women's lives will not change until men's lives change" (Eveline and Bacchi 2005: 506). Rather than focus on gender, the Dutch methodology is based on an environmental impact assessment of *gender relations*. "A Gender Impact Assessment," according to Eveline and Bacchi (2005: 507) comprises three elements: "a) locating the structurally unequal power relations between women and men; b) highlighting the processes or mechanisms that produce and reproduce those unequal power relations; and c) providing criteria for evaluating the data which allow for the inclusion of 'unequal power' — namely equality, autonomy, and diversity/pluriformity." Thus, unlike the Canadian model, the Dutch approach refuses to accept that the primary goal of gender-mainstreaming is the inclusion of women in the status quo.

Gender-mainstreaming is not without its critics, and Stephen Lewis, former United Nations' Special Envoy for HIV/AIDS in Africa, is one of the fiercest. Women are "barely represented" in the high-ranking positions within the United Nations' organization, Lewis points out, "despite the fact that every one of the United Nation's major human rights policies includes a non-discrimination clause based on sex and a declaration of equality between women and men." According to Lewis, "Instead of bona fide, specialized programs, women get 'gender mainstreaming,'" and "gender mainstreaming is a pox for women. The worst thing you can do for women is to fold their concerns into the mandates of U.N. agencies, or bury them under the activities of government ministries. Once you've mainstreamed gender, it's everybody's business and nobody's business. Everyone's accountable and no one's accountable." Lewis says, "the ongoing struggle to embrace gender equality was most poignantly brought home to me in confronting the pandemic of HIV/AIDS." In graphic detail, Lewis describes the devastating impact of HIV/AIDS on women and their children living in Zimbabwe, Malawi, Zambia, and Lesotho. Lewis and his colleague James Morris, the executive director of the World Food Programme, found that the HIV/AIDS crisis was "wreaking havoc with agricultural productivity" since time once spent on walking to distant fields and growing a variety of foods had been given over to caring for the sick. AIDS leads to hunger; hunger exacerbates AIDS." Lewis places much of the responsibility on African governments, which are, in his view, "deficient" in protecting women. But "[these governments] would not be allowed to indulge in such asinine and/or negligent behaviour if there were a watchdog, a full-fledged agency or institution as part of the United Nations, whose job it was to ride herd on the recalcitrants." Lewis was named one of the "100 Most Influential People in the World" by *Time* magazine in 2005. Listen up!

"The law is an ass," is a common complaint, often made in reference to anachronisms in the law. The original source of this famous quotation is a statement by Mr. Bumble in Charles Dickens' novel *Oliver Twist*. Having learned that his wife had pawned stolen property, Mr. Bumble is informed that "the law supposes that your wife acts under your direction." In response, Mr. Bumble argues that "If the law supposes that… the law is a ass — a idiot. If that's the eye of the law, the law is a bachelor; and the worst I wish the law is, that his eye may be opened by experience — by experience." Several gendered assumptions characteristic of nineteenth-century ideas about gender relations operate in this exchange, of course; men are responsible for women's actions since the latter are not considered competent in the eyes of the law; and the law itself is gendered as denoted by the pronoun "he." But Bumble's experience of being married tells him that his wife exercises power within the relationship — a situation that would be unknown if the law was "a bachelor," having no experience of married life.

Mary Nyquist reworks this famous phrase by stating, "The law is *not* an ass if you are behind it" (emphasis added). In her poem "Without the Law," Nyquist demonstrates the ways in which a man of privilege, "a well-heeled white man has been tailor-/made to slip right through, effortlessly." With all of the trappings of being civilized — "in the face of solid house, nicely/turned-out wife, frank, upstanding gaze," this seemingly upstanding man is above suspicion, and yet he commits the most heinous of crimes.

In most of the history of women's legal struggles for equality rights, it is women who are seeking redress for injustices usually perpetrated by men. However, as our understanding of gender has become more complicated, taking into account the ways in which gender intersects with other forms of oppression, there is a much greater probability of feminists clashing with one another. In her chapter, Joanna Harris examines the legal arguments presented in the case of *Nixon v. Vancouver Rape Relief Society* (hereafter referred to as *Nixon*) in which transsexual rights came into conflict with women's substantive equality. Kimberly Nixon was a post-operative male-to-female transsexual, who, having sought the services of the Battered Women's Support Services after ending an abusive relationship, wished to train as a volunteer with the Vancouver Rape Relief Society. Upon discovery that Nixon had once been a male, the Society asked her to end her training program, to which Nixon immediately responded by filing a complaint with the British Columbia Human Rights Commission stating that she had been discriminated against on the basis of sex. As Harris argues, the case turned on the definition of discrimination in the *British Columbia Human Rights Code* and the concept of human dignity defined in the *Charter of Rights and Freedoms*. Both Nixon and the Vancouver Rape Relief Society agreed that gender existed on a continuum, but the Vancouver Rape Relief Society argued that "lifelong experience as a woman was a bona fide occupational requirement for peer counsellors" and that non-transexual women were entitled to form an identifiable group to protect its welfare and interests. "What happened?" you may ask. Well, of course, you will have to read the chapter to find out the final outcome of the courts' decision. Read carefully! The legal arguments are complicated!

Why do women come into conflict with the law? This question informs the work of Elizabeth Comack, who examines in her chapter the androcentric bias within criminology and the need for a gender lens in understanding criminalized women. Like most of us studying in the 1970s, Comack did not realize until many years later how male-centred her education was. The texts that Comack studied were mostly written by male academics who developed theories about criminal behaviour based on the experiences of men, and then presented those theories as general explanations for criminal behaviour, for men and women alike. More often than not, women in conflict with the law were virtually invisible in the criminological literature, in part because they have lower crime and incarceration rates. But when women did come into view, Comack argues that "they were understood in relation to a male standard or measuring rod, and typically judged to be lacking." Women's experiences were not evaluated on their own merit.

Comack had one of those "aha" moments while driving home one day following a difficult set of interviews with women who were incarcerated. She realized that many women who were in jail had histories of physical and sexual abuse, and that the "malestream" thought which had informed criminological theory could not explain adequately women's criminal behaviour. Inspired by the work of the women's movement in the area of violence against women (another area that had been unexamined in male-centred criminology), Comack and other feminist criminologists began to look more closely at the lives of women who were in conflict with the law.

Drawing on a woman-centred approach, in which knowledge is produced about and for women, Comack and other feminist sociologists indeed confirmed the frequent connection between a history of abuse and women who violate the law. Sometimes these women ended up in prison for resisting their abusers; others were unable to cope with the trauma of the abuse while still others ended up on the streets in order to escape abuse, where they stole, prostituted themselves in order to survive, and suffered more abuse at the hands of pimps and drug dealers. In addition to uncovering a link between women's abuse and criminal behaviour, Comack and other feminist sociologists found strong associations with women's violation of the law, the feminization of poverty, and racial discrimination — particularly as it affects Aboriginal women, who have much higher rates of incarceration than non-Aboriginal women.

The work of feminist criminologists like Comack has transformed the discipline of criminology, bringing a much needed gender lens to research in this area. In addition, feminist research into women who are in conflict with the law has contributed substantially to organizations like the Elizabeth Fry Societies across Canada, which seek to "ensure substantive equality in the delivery and development of services and programs through public education, research, legislative and administrative reform, regionally, nationally, and internationally" (Canadian Association of Elizabeth Fry Societies 2011).

NOTES

1. In *Murdoch v. Murdoch* [1975] 1 S.C.R. 423, the Supreme Court of Canada ruled that Irene Murdoch, an abused wife, was not entitled to her share of the ranch when she and her husband divorced, even though she had contributed to labour on the farm, invested an inheritance in the farm, and performed the domestic duties, while her husband was away from the farm for five months out of the year. The public outcry resulted in significant changes to property laws.
2. For the full text of the speech, see Clinton (1995).
3. A 2009 poll conducted by Nanos Research found that 86.2 percent of Canadians support Medicare (Canadian Health Care Coalition 2009).
4. According to Johansen and Rosen (2008) section 33 (1) of the *Charter of Rights and Freedoms* provides for Parliament and a provincial legislature to override Sections 2, and 7 to 15 of the *Charter*. By invoking section 33(1), section 33(2) is put into motion, and "the overriding legislation renders the relevant Charter right or rights 'not entrenched' for the purposes of that legislation. In effect, parliamentary sovereignty is revived by the exercise of the override power in that specific legislative context. Section 33(3) provides that each exercise of the notwithstanding power has a lifespan of five years or less, after which it expires, unless Parliament or the legislature re-enacts it under section 33(4) for a further period of five years or less" (Johansen and Rosen 2008). Sections 3-6, 16-22, 23, 28, 24, 27, 29 are not subject to recourse to section 33 by Parliament or a legislature.

REFERENCES

Anderson, Doris. 2011. "The Status of Women." *Canadian Encyclopedia*. At: thecanadianencyclopedia. com/index.cfm?Params=A1ARTA0007673&PgNm=TCE.

Brodie, Janine. 2008. "We Are All Equal Now: Contemporary Gender Politics In Canada." *Feminist Theory* 9,2.

Bunch, Charlotte, and Samantha Frost. 2000. "Women's Human Rights: An Introduction." In Cheris Kramarae and Dale Spender (eds.), *Routledge International Encyclopedia of Women: Global Women's Issues and Knowledge*. Routledge. At: cwgl.rutgers.edu/globalcenter/whr.html.

Canadian Association of Elizabeth Fry Societies. 2011. "Mission Statement." At: elizabethfry.ca.

Canadian Human Rights Commission. 2010a. "Resources: Equal Pay For Work of Equal Value: Employer's Guide." At: chrc-ccdp.ca/publications/employers_responsibility-eng.aspx.

___. 2010b. "Overview: Expanding Knowledge: Strategic Initiatives: Aboriginal Rights and Human Rights." At: chrc-ccdp.ca/proactive_initiatives/ section_67/page4-eng.aspx.

___. 2010c. "Overview: Expanding Knowledge: Strategic Initiatives: Telephone Access for the Deaf and Hearing Impaired." At: chrc-ccdp.ca/proactive_initiatives/recentreports_rapportrecents-eng.aspx#2.

Canada, House of Commons, Special Committee on Social Security. 1943. "Report On Social Security For Canada." Prepared by Dr. L.C. Marsh for the Advisory Committee on Reconstruction. Ottawa: King's Printer.

Canadian Health Care Coalition. 2009. *Newsroom.* "New Poll Shows Overwhelming Support for Public Health Care: CMA President out of Touch with Most Canadians." At: medicare.ca/new-poll-shows-overwhelming-support-for-public-health-care.

CERA (Centre for Equality Rights in Accommodation). n.d. "Fundamentals of Human Rights." At: equalityrights.org/cera/?page_id=72

Clinton, Hilary Rodham. "Remarks to the U.N. 4th World Conference on Women Plenary Session Delivered 5 September 1995, Beijing, China." At: americanrhetoric.com/speeches/ hillaryclintonbeijingspeech.htm.

Darwin, Charles. 2006 [1859]. *On the Origin of Species: By Means of Natural Selection.* Mineola, NY: Dover Publications.

Dembour, Marie-Bénédicte. 2010. "What Are Human Rights? Four Schools of Thought." *Human Rights Quarterly* 32,1.

Eveline, Joan, and Carol Bacchi. 2005. "What Are We Mainstreaming when We Mainstream Gender?" *International Feminist Journal of Politics* 7,4.

Fiamengo, Janice. 2008. *The Woman's Page: Journalism and Rhetoric in Early Canada.* Toronto: University of Toronto Press.

Johansen, David, and Philip Rosen. 2008. "The Notwithstanding Clause of the Charter." *Parliament of Canada.* At: parl.gc.ca/Content/LOP/researchpublications/bp194-e.htm.

Kent, Tom. 1962. *Social Policy for Canada: Towards a Philosophy of Social Security.* Ottawa: Policy Press.

Lovenduski, Joni. 2005. "Introduction: State Feminism and the Political Representation of Women." In Joni Lovenduski (ed.), *State Feminism and Political Representation.* Cambridge: University of Cambridge Press.

Malthus, Thomas Robert, and Philip Appleman (ed.). c1976 [1778]. *An Essay on the Principle of Population: Text, Sources and Background, Critics.* New York: Norton.

McLaughlin, Janet. 2003. *Feminist Social and Political Theory.* Houndsmills, Basingstoke, Hamshire, England, and New York: Palgrave MacMillan.

Mills, C. Wright. 1959 [1976]. *The Sociological Imagination.* New York: Oxford University Press.

Moscovitch, Allan. 2011. "The Welfare State." *The Canadian Encyclopedia.* Historica Dominion. At: thecanadianencyclopedia.com/index.cfm?PgNm=TCE&Params=A1ARTA0008518

Munroe, Dawn. 2009. *Famous Women Quotes.* "On Politics." At: famouscanadianwomen.com/quotes/ quotes page.htm#politics.

Native Women's Association of Canada. 2007. "Aboriginal Women and Bill C-31: An Issue Paper." At: laa.gov.nl.ca/laa/naws/pdf/nwac-billc-31.pdf

Smith, Adam. 2002 [1776]. *The Glasgow Edition of the Works and Correspondence of Adam Smith* [Electronic Resource]. Charlottesville, VA: InteLex Corporation.

PWHCE (Prairie Women's Health Centre of Excellence). 2011. "Training: What Is Gender-Based Analysis?" At: pwhce.ca/training.htm.

Statistics Canada. 2011. "Canadian Census History." At: census2011.gc.ca/ccr03/ccr03_005-eng.htm.

Thomas, Derrick. 2010. "The Census and the Evolution of Gender Roles in Early 20th Century Canada." Ottawa: Ministry of Industry. At: statcan.gc.ca/pub/11-008-x/2010001/article/11125-eng.htm.

Thomas, Mark. 2004. "Setting the Minimum: Ontario's Employment Standards in the Postwar Years, 1944–1968." *Labour/Le Travail* 54. At: historycooperative.org/journals/llt/54/thomas.html.

United Nations. 2003. *Rome Statute of the International Court.* At: untreaty.un.org/cod/icc/statute/ romefra.htm.

United Nations Women. 2011. "Gender Mainstreaming." At: un.org/womenwatch/osagi/gender-mainstreaming.htm.

Wollenstonecraft, Mary, and Janet Todd (ed.). 1993 [1792]. *A Vindication of the Rights of Women.* London: Penguin Classics.

- Date when the Fourth World Conference on Women, Action for Equality, Development and Peace in Beijing was organized by the United Nations' (U.N.) Commission on the Status of Women, with the U.N. Division for the Advancement of Women (DAW) United Nations: 1995
- Number of states[2] that endorsed the Beijing Declaration and Platform for Action passed by the U.N.: 189 (by consensus)
- Percentage of women worldwide in 2008 who served as elected representatives in their national assemblies: 18.4[3]
- Number of countries in 2008 where women have exceeded 30 percent of representatives in national assemblies: 22
- Percentage of women who served as elected representatives in the Rwanda *Inteko Ishinga Amategeko* (national parliament) in 2008, which has the highest number of female representatives of all countries in the world: 48.8
- Percentage of women who were elected representatives in the Swedish *Riksdag* (national parliament) in 2008: 47
- Percentage of women who were elected representatives in the Canadian parliament in 2008: 21.3
- Percentage of women who held ministerial positions in the Canadian parliament in 2008: 16
- Date by which female elected representatives in national assemblies in developed countries would reach 40 percent given current rates: 2029
- Date by which female elected representatives in national assemblies in developing countries would reach 40percent given current rates: 2047
- Date by which female representatives in national assemblies could reach a critical mass of 30 percent if quotas were used: 2015
- Date when the U.N. *Universal Declaration on Human Rights*, affirming "respect for human rights and for fundamental freedoms for all without distinction as to... sex," was passed: 1945
- Proportion of parties in 2008 that have ratified the U.N. 1979 *Convention on the Elimination of All Forms of Discrimination Against Women* (CEDAW)[4]: 185/189
- Number of developed countries in 2008 that have registered formal reservations[5] about CEDAW: 8
- Number of countries in Central and Eastern Europe and the Commonwealth of Independent States (CEE/CIS) that have registered formal reservations about CEDAW (the lowest number): 3
- Number of countries in the Middle East and North Africa that have registered formal reservations about CEDAW (the highest number): 14
- Number of decisions handed down by the CEDAW Complaints Committee since it was established in 1999: 5
- Net disbursements of Official Development Assistance[6] (ODA) from donor to recipient countries in 2006: $103.9 billion (U.S.)
- Percentage of Official Development Assistance (ODA) allocated to gender equality

as either a principal or significant objective by countries using the Gender Equality Marker (GEM) reporting system: 27

- Percentage of ODA allocated by Canada in 2006 to gender equality as a principal objective: 11
- Percentage of ODA allocated by Canada in 2006 to gender equality as a significant objective: 47
- Percentage of ODA allocated to gender-focused aid for health, education and other social infrastructure in 2006: 75.7
- Percentage of ODA allocated to gender-focused aid for economic infrastructure in 2006: 5.1
- World Bank estimates of global costs in 2006 for "interventions directly aimed at promoting gender equality": $7 to $13 per capita (U.S.)
- Percentage of the World Bank's lending in 2008 to projects in social development, gender and inclusion: 5.1
- Percentage of the World Bank's lending in 2008 to projects in public sector governance with a gender focus: 4
- Amount allocated by the World Bank in 2008 to projects in public sector governance: $52,303,000 (U.S.)
- Ratio of women's organizations worldwide that had annual budgets in 2006 whose budgets were of less than $50,000 (U.S.): 2/3[7]
- Total income of 729 women's rights organizations worldwide in 2005: $79 million (U.S.)
- Percentage of income from bi/multilateral development assistance to 729 women's rights organizations in 2005: 23
- Percentage of income from private or public foundations, non-government organizations and private donors to 729 women's rights organizations in 2005: 37
- Percentage of income from national/local governments to 729 women's rights organizations in 2005: 11
- Total income of World Vision International,[8] the world's largest Christian international development organization, in 2005: $2 billion (U.S.)
- Number of countries in 2003 that had specific or non-specific legislation in place regarding rape and sexual assault: 144/188[9]
- Number of countries in 2003 that had specific or non-specific legislation in place regarding domestic violence: 89/188
- Number of countries in 2003 that had specific or non-specific legislation in place regarding sexual harassment: 59/186
- Number of countries in 2003 that had specific or non-specific legislation in place regarding marital rape: 43/185
- Ratio of selected countries in 2005 that had Supreme Court benches on which fewer than 25 percent of judges are women: 2/3
- Number of female judges in the International Criminal Court[10] as of 2010: 11/19[11]
- Number of female judges in the Supreme Court of Canada as of December 2010: 4/9[12]
- Number of female police officers sent to Liberia by Government of India in 2007, becoming the first all-female Formed Police Unit in the U.N.'s peacekeeping history: 100[13]
- Percentage of convictions for cases of rape that had been referred by the Gender-Based Violence Desk at the Rwandan National Police Headquarters in 2006: 45 (803/1777)

- Number of women who served as U.N. peacekeepers between 1957 and 1989: 20[14]
- Percentage of women serving as military and police personnel in U.N. peacekeeping missions in 2010: 2.42 and 8.7 respectively
- Date by which the U.N. would like member states to raise the number of female police officers serving in peacekeeping missions to 20 percent: 2014
- Percentage of female officers in the South African police force in 2006: 29
- Percentage of female constables in Canadian police forces in 2009: 21[15]
- Percentage of female officers in senior ranks in Canadian polices forces in 2004: 9
- Percentage of female officers in senior ranks in Canadian polices forces in 2009: 14
- Percentage of sworn female officers in the Australian federal police forces in 2010: 33[16]
- Ratio of females aged 12 and older in 2005 of all who were accused by police services of committing a violation against the Canadian *Criminal Code*: 1/5[17]
- Percentage of females aged 12 and older in 2005 who were accused by police of committing property crime, of all women who were accused of violations against the Canadian *Criminal Code*: 47
- Percentage of males aged 12 and older in 2005 who were accused by police services of committing property crimes, of all men who were accused of violations against the Canadian *Criminal Code*: 39
- Percentage of females aged 12 and older in 2005 who were accused by police services of committing a violation against a person, of all women who were accused of violations against the Canadian *Criminal Code*: 28
- Percentage of males aged 12 and older in 2005 who were accused by police services of committing a violation against a person, of all men who were accused of violations against the Canadian *Criminal Code*: 34
- Percentage of females in 2005 who were in conflict with police for violations against the administration of justice, such as bail violations and failure to appear in court, of all women who were accused of violations against the Canadian *Criminal Code*: 17
- Rate in Canada in 2005 at which males committed fraud and property crimes (other than motor vehicle) compared to females: 2:1
- Ratio of adult females to males who were charged in Canada in 2005 for violent offences: 1:5
- Ratio of adult females to males who were charged in Canada in 1986 for violent offences: 1:9
- Number of adults in custody for every 100,000 adults in the population in Canada 2008/2009: 141[18]
- Percentage of female offenders of the total custody (federal and provincial) population in 2008/2009: 10
- Percentage of Aboriginal offenders of the total custody (federal and provincial) population in 2008/2009: 27
- Percentage of Aboriginal women of all women remanded and admitted to sentenced custody in 2008/2009: 28 and 37 respectively
- Percentage of Aboriginal men of all men remanded and admitted to sentenced custody in 2008/2009: 20 and 25 respectively

- Percentage of Aboriginal people of the total population in Canada in 2008/2009: 3
- Percentage change in adults in the incarceration rate in Canada from 2007–2008 to 2008–2009: +1[19]
- Percentage change in the number of Aboriginal people in sentenced custody in Canada from 2004–2005 to 2008–2009: +2
- Percentage change in the number of Aboriginal women in sentenced custody and in remand in Canada from 2004–2005 to 2008–2009: +6 and +2 respectively
- Percentage change in the number of Aboriginal men in sentenced custody and in remand in Canada from 2004–2005 to 2008–2009: +2 and +1 respectively
- Percentage of adults in provincial custody in Canada in 2008–2009 who have some secondary education or less: 44.9
- Percentage of adults in provincial custody in Canada in 2008–2009 who were unemployed (but able to work): 47.3
- Percentage change from 2007–2008 to 2008–2009 in the total operating costs (controlling for information) to provide correctional services in Canada: +7
- Amount allocated to the budget of Correctional Services Canada in 2008 to build new prisons and finance their infrastructure from 2010–2011 to 2012–2013: $478.8 million (+27 percent)[20]
- Number of prisons in Canada that have been closed in the past two hundred years: 2
- Percentage of inmates in Canadian federal prisons in 2009 who had a significant mental illness (e.g., schizophrenia): 11[21]
- Percentage of inmates in Canadian federal prisons in 2009 who were taking pre-scription medication for a psychiatric condition: 20
- Ratio of female inmates in Canadian federal prisons in 2009 who had previously been hospitalized for psychiatric reasons: 1:3
- Estimated number of prisoners in Canadian federal prisons in 2009 who were in segregation and who were mentally ill: 1/3
- Number of mental health beds in federal prisons across Canada in 2009: 600
- Estimated percentage that Correctional Services Canada spent in 2009 on the security side of its mandate: 97[22]
- Estimated percentage that Correctional Services Canada spent in 2009 on the timely and safe reintegration of offenders; i.e., programs and interventions designed to deal with, among other things, violence prevention and drug abuse: 3
- Percentage change in federal funding to the Status of Women budget in the 2006 federal budget: -20 (or $5 million)[23]
- Federal funding to the Law Reform Commission and the Court Challenges Program[24] (CCP) in the 2006 federal budget: $00
- Federal funding allocated in 2010 for the Canadian national strategy on missing and murdered Aboriginal women: $10 million[25]
- Federal funding allocated in 2010 from the Canadian national strategy on missing and murdered Aboriginal women to the RCMP's Canadian Police Centre for Missing and Exploited Children: $4/$10 million[26]
- Federal funding allocated in 2010 from the Canadian national strategy on missing and murdered Aboriginal women to *Sisters in Spirit*, the project of the National Aboriginal Women's Association that spearheaded research into missing Aboriginal women: 0

1. The original Hypatia Index was compiled by Pamela Downe, with the assistance of Ellen Whiteman. Except when otherwise indicated in the main text, the sources cited in this Index apply to the line where first referenced and then to all those that follow until another endnote appears.

2. "The term "Parties" refers to states and other entities with treaty-making capacity which have expressed their consent to be bound by a treaty and where the treaty is in force for such states and entities. There are 192 member states in the United Nations and 195 countries worldwide. The latter include Vatican City, Kosovo and Taiwan, which are considered countries but are not member states of the U.N. Source: United Nations Treaty Collection, 2011, "Definitions." At: treaties.un.org/Pages/Overview.aspx?path=overview/definition/page1_en.xml.

3. UNIFEM, 2009, *Who Answers to Women? Gender and Accountability. Progress on the World's Women, 2008–2009*. At: unifem.org/progress/2008/ media/English-PoWW-ExecutiveSummary.pdf.

4. "The Convention on the Elimination of All Forms of Discrimination Against Women (CEDAW), adopted in 1979… sets out the measures required for its elimination and the achievement of gender equality. CEDAW is a binding source of international law for those states that have become parties" (UNIFEM 2009: 75). Canada ratified CEDAW on December 10, 1981.

5. The categories of reservations include international arbitration, rights in marriage and guardianship, compatibility with traditional codes, equality and employment, and other (which includes multiple reservations or a general reservation to the treaty).

6. The bulk of ODA is delivered through bilateral agreements between individual donor countries and a recipient country; 30 percent is delivered through organizations such as the U.N., the World Bank and global funds. ODA represents 0.3 percent of developed countries' combined national income.

7. Association for Women's Rights in Development, 2007, "The Second Fund*her* Report: Financial Sustainability for Women's Movements Worldwide." At: awid.org/eng/Issues-and-Analysis/ Library/Financial-Sustainability-for-Women-s-Movement-s-Worldwide-Second-FundHer-Report.

8. World Vision has no mandate to support emergency contraception and abortion.

9. UNIFEM, 2009, *Who Answers to Women? Gender and Accountability*, op. cit., see note 3.

10. "The International Criminal Court (ICC) is an independent, permanent court that tries persons accused of the most serious crimes of international concern, namely genocide, crimes against humanity and war crimes. The ICC is based on a treaty, joined by 114 countries." At: icc-cpi.int/ Menus/ICC/About+the+Court/Frequently+asked+Questions.

11. Women's Initiatives for Justice, 2010, *Gender Report 2010: International Criminal Court*. At: iccwomen. org/news/docs/GRC10-WEB-11-10-v4_Final-version-Dec.pdf.

12. Supreme Court of Canada, "*About the Court: Current Judges*." At: scc-csc.gc.ca/court-cour/ju/ cju-jua-eng.asp.

13. UNIFEM, 2009, *Who Answers to Women? Gender and Accountability*, op. cit., see note 3.

14. United Nations Peacekeeping. At: org/en/peacekeeping/women.shtml.

15. Statistics Canada, 2009, "Police Resources in Canada, 2009." At: statcan.gc.ca/pub/85-225-x/2009000/part-partie1-eng.htm.

16. Australian Federal Police, 2010, "AFP Staff Statistics-Gender." At: afp.gov.au/media-centre/ facts-stats/afp-staff-statistics.aspx.

17. Statistics Canada, 2008, "Study: Female Offenders," *The Daily* (January 24). At: statcan.gc.ca/ daily-quotidien/080124/dq080124a-eng.htm. For the full study, see Rebecca Kong and Kathy AuCoin, 2008, "Female Offenders in Canada," *Juristat* 28 (1), Statistics Canada, Cat. no. 85-002-XIE. At: statcan.gc.ca/pub/85-002-x/2008001/article/10509-eng.htm.

18. Donna Calverley, 2010, "Adult Correctional Services in Canada, 2008/2009." *Juristat* (Fall) 30 (3), Statistics Canada. At: statcan.gc.ca/pub/85-002-x/2010003/article/11353-eng.pdf.

19. "This 1% increase in the number of adults admitted to remand is a change from the overall longer-term trend which saw admissions to remand generally increasing from 1999–2000 to 2007–2008 and admissions to sentenced custody declining" (Calverley 2010: 7).

20. Michael Jackson and Graham Stewart, 2010, "Fear-Driven Policy: Ottawa's Harsh New Penal

Proposals Won't Make Us Safer, Just Poorer — and Less Humane," *The Literary Review of Canada* (May). At: johnhoward.ca/media/Fear-Driven PolicyLTCMay2010.pdf.

21. Kate Lunau, 2010, "The Wrong Fix: We Put the Mentally Ill in Jail. Now They're Ending up in Solitary," *Macleans.ca* (January 21). At: macleans.ca/2010/01/21/the-wrong-fix.

22. Kate Lunau, 2010, "What's the Agenda Behind the Tory Prison Budget Boost? Prison Ombudsman Howard Sapers Makes Sense of the Proposed Influx of Money," *Macleans.ca* (March 30). At: macleans.ca/2010/03/30/whats-the-agenda-behind-the-tory-prison-budget-boost.

23. Canadian Association of University Teachers, 2006, "Commentary on the Sept. 26th Announcement of $1 Billion Funding Cuts." At: dawn.thot.net/cuts.html. Numerous other responses from equity-seeking groups can be found on this site.

24. "The Court Challenges Program of Canada is a national non-profit organization which was set up in 1985 to provide financial assistance for important court cases that advance language and equality rights guaranteed under Canada's Constitution" (ccppcj.ca/e/ccp.shtml). The CCP was funded first by the Mulroney government, but the funding was withdrawn in 1992 and re-established under the Chretien government in 1994. In 2008, the Harper government restored $1.5 million annually to the CCP, but the fund can be accessed only by linguistic minorities to defend their charter rights before the courts. See CanWest Media Publications, 2008, "Tories Restore Parts of Scrapped Court Challenges Program," *Montreal Gazette* (June 19). At: canada.com/vancouversun/story.html ?id=c826456d-22c3-425f-9491-7f5dc65776bc.

25. APTN National News, 2010, "Native Women's Association Felt 'Betrayed' by Conservative Government" (October 29). At: aptn.ca/pages/news/2010/11/08/native-womens-association-betrayed-by-conservative-government.

26. As of October 2010, $6 million had not been allocated.

Why I Fought for the
Charter and LEAF

Marilou McPhedran

When I was growing up in rural Manitoba, I had never heard of the "Famous Five" who litigated the "Persons Case" of 1929, nor was I aware of what a raw deal Canadian women were getting when they turned to our legal system for justice. Constitutional equality rights for Canadian women and other fundamental rights and freedoms were first "guaranteed" in the text of the *Canadian Charter of Rights and Freedoms*, entrenched within the *Constitution Act*, 1982, proclaimed on April 17, 1982 — and this is why we decided to launch Women's Legal Education and Action Fund (LEAF) on that same date in 1985. I look back now, in LEAF's twenty-fifth anniversary year, and know that without the mobilization of women by the "Ad Hoc Committee of Canadian Women on the Constitution" to fight for women's rights in the early 1980s (the largest in Canadian history), law students today might well be learning much the same kind of unjust case law as I did.

I was in law school in 1975 when "ranch wife," Irene Murdoch, fought through the courts and failed in trying to use the *Canadian Bill of Rights* to get her fair share of matrimonial property following her divorce. Mrs. Murdoch had put part of her inheritance into farm land, and had run the ranch for months each year by herself. There was also evidence that Mrs. Murdoch had had her jaw broken by her husband. Nonetheless in dismissal of her twenty-five years as a ranch wife, the Supreme Court of Canada denied her claim, agreeing with the trial judge that she had only done the "routine" work of "any ranch wife." Women — living ordinary lives — identified with Irene's humiliating loss, including my irate mother, who called me from rural Manitoba to demand to know what her daughter, the Toronto law student, was going to do about it! Women of my mother's generation across the country mobilized to demand their property rights, resulting in a national logroll of family law reform, which demonstrated the value of flexing political muscle to many Canadian women who had pressured their governments.

I was just starting out as a lawyer in the fall of 1980, when Prime Minister Trudeau surprised many, just after the Quebec referendum, by proposing an entrenched rights charter as part of his constitutional patriation process. But his draft charter mimicked the *Canadian Bill of Rights*: the same law under which Irene Murdoch, and every other woman who tried to use it to gain equality, had already lost.

In January 1981, Attorney General of Canada, Jean Chrétien, announced significant improvements to section 15 of the *Charter*, including changing its title to "equality rights," giving much of the credit to the Canadian Advisory Council on the Status of Women (CACSW), including legal counsel Mary Eberts, (who became a LEAF founder). Yet, barely a week later, Doris Anderson resigned as President of CACSW, alleging that government insiders had cancelled the CACSW women's constitutional conference. Within days, I'd been dispatched to Ottawa by the new grassroots alliance of the Ad Hoc Committee of Canadian Women on the Constitution to help organize a replacement constitutional conference on Valentine's Day 1981. More than 1,300 women came to Parliament Hill to push for even stronger equality rights provisions in the draft constitution.

I volunteered to lobby on Parliament Hill, while crowds of angry women confronted political leaders at home, right up to the steps of their legislative buildings, laying claim to a place in Canadian constitutional history in headlines of the time, largely lost in subsequent historical accounts of that period. For example, by the time the *Globe and Mail* issued a special educational supplement on the *Charter* a year later, the impact of the women's lobby was not acknowledged. In April 1981, amendments to the *Charter*, including a last-minute, unanimously approved insertion of the section 28 "Equal Rights Amendment" (ERA), passed the House of Commons and the Senate.

During this period, our sense of the importance of an ERA was heightened by concern that American women were fighting for, but seemed likely to lose (and did), their years-long campaign for an ERA to the American constitution. By the end of 1981, the national and provincial governments had responded to the Supreme Court of Canada's constitutional reference decision by agreeing on a new *non obstante* (notwithstanding) override clause, destined to become section 33. Thousands of women, who had mobilized across Canada through Ad Hoc lobbying, were shocked when what they thought was their significant political and legal victory came up for grabs. When the Prime Minister announced that it was only logical for a section 33 to override *both* section 15 and section 28, women constitutional activists described the override as a "surtax" on their hard-won constitutional rights — and successfully remobilized to free section 28 — which states, "Notwithstanding anything in this *Charter*, the rights and freedom referred to in it are guaranteed equally to male and female persons."

The Ad Hoc alliance stopped the "taking of twenty eight." The section 33 override was lifted from the section 28, but not from section 15, and during the three-year moratorium on section 15, some of us "Ad Hockers" focused on setting up a women's legal defence fund so we'd be ready to use the *Charter* for women — as soon as the moratorium ended on April 17, 1985 — and that's how we came to found LEAF, to turn rights on paper into lived rights.

Canadian Charter of Rights and Freedoms[1]
[Note: bolding and underlining as it appears in the legislation.]
PART I OF THE CONSTITUTION ACT, 1982
Assented to March 29th, 1982

Equality Rights
Equality before and under law and equal protection and benefit of law

15. (1) Every individual is equal before and under the law and has the right to the equal protection and equal benefit of the law without discrimination and, in particular, without discrimination based on race, national or ethnic origin, colour, religion, sex, age or mental or physical disability.

Affirmative action programs

(2) Subsection (1) does not preclude any law, program or activity that has as its object the amelioration of conditions of disadvantaged individuals or groups including those that are disadvantaged because of race, national or ethnic origin, colour, religion, sex, age or mental or physical disability.

NOTES

Marilou McPhedran. 2010. "Why I Fought for the Charter and Leaf." *LEAFLines* 16,1. Adapted and reprinted with permission.
1. At: laws.justice.gc.ca/en/charter.

84

Policies of Discrimination

The Canadian *Indian Act*

Pamela Downe

In 1876, the Government of Canada passed the first *Indian Act* in an attempt to define who was an "Indian" and to control the mobility, economy and culture of Canada's diverse Aboriginal peoples. The objective was to promote an agenda of assimilation whereby culturally distinct Aboriginal communities would be eliminated and integrated into the larger and emerging European-based society of colonial Canada. The impact of this legislation on Aboriginal women, men and children cannot be overstated. As Bonita Lawrence (2000: 76) argues, "The *Indian Act*... is much more than a set of regulations that have controlled every aspect of Indian life for over a century. It provides a way of understanding Native identity." The *Indian Act* of 1876 consolidated policies dealing with the "protection, civilization and assimilation" of Aboriginal peoples. The colonial racism that informs this legislation is clear. In a 1920 presentation to parliament, Duncan Campbell Scott, former Superintendent General of Indian Affairs, stated: "Our object is to continue until there is not a single Indian in Canada that has not been absorbed into the body politic and there is no Indian Question" (cited in Arnot 2000: 256).

The 1876 *Act* stipulated under what conditions someone could be defined as "Indian" and under what conditions Aboriginal people could be "enfranchised," losing Indian status. The discriminatory policies set forth in this *Act* had far-reaching implications. If an Aboriginal man or woman decided to pursue state-recognized and professional education, the *Indian Act* stipulated that s/he would lose Indian status (the racist logic being that there could be no formally recognized Indian educated in the same way as a Euro-Canadian citizen). Some traditional ceremonies were banned by the *Indian Act*: a paternalistic system of supervision was established through the creation of a federal Department of Indian Affairs, expressed most forcefully through the appointed "Indian Agents."

For "Indian" women, the Indian Act was extremely problematic for it denied them the right to vote in band elections or to participate in decisions about reserve land surrenders. If her husband died without leaving a will, a woman was required to be of "good moral character" (as judged by the Superintendent General of Indian affairs) in order to receive any of her husband's property. And if a woman married a man without Indian status, she lost her own official status as did her children. It was thought that a woman was to be subsumed in the identity of her husband, for when a non-Indian woman married an officially recognized "Indian" man, his status was then conferred to her and all subsequent children (see RCAP 1996).

The *Act* went through many revisions and permutations; each marked with specific gains towards First Nations self-determination as well as certain drawbacks that perpetuated the federal government's assimilationist agenda. The 1951 *Act*, for example, increased the imposition of provincial laws and standards on status Indians but it also removed cultural prohibitions banning certain ceremonies (Bartlett 1988). In 1985, the watershed Bill C-31 amendment repealed the policies that required "Indian" women and their children to lose status when those women married a non-status man. While this was an important victory, it is equally important to note that the Bill only reinstates "Indian" status to the enfranchised women and their children. Legal status is still not conferred to the grandchildren of enfranchised women. Therefore, rather than repealing the patriarchal assumptions that inform this policy, Bill C-31 only displaces them by two generations (RCAP 1996). It is also important to note that some women who regained status through Bill C-31 experienced tremendous discrimination by Aboriginal and non-Aboriginal communities alike. The legacy of their enfranchisement was stigmatizing and these women had to overcome many obstacles to reclaim a place for themselves as recognized "Status Indians." However, despite its limitations, Bill C-31 repeals all policies of enfranchisement, guaranteeing status to those First Nations people who may have once feared that it would be taken from them.

In April 2001, the Minister of Indian Affairs and Northern Development introduced the First Nations Governance Initiative (FNGI). In theory, the FNGI is an interim step towards self-governance putting "the power to handle community governance affairs where it belongs, in the hands of First Nations people themselves" (Indian and Northern Affairs 2002). However, as Anna Hunter explains so well in chapter 85, the FNGI does not adequately consider the specific gender- or class-based needs of those people it hopes to benefit. Moreover, there is a lack of "cultural fit" between the template of governance established by the federal government and the daily decision-making dynamics that characterize many First Nations communities.

As students and scholars of Women's and Gender Studies, we are faced with the important and necessary task of examining how influential policies discriminate against those most intimately affected by a collective colonial past. What follows are excerpts from two versions of the *Indian Act of Canada* as well as from Bill C-31. The language that is used and the context that is established reveals a great deal about the cultural assumptions held by policy-makers towards Aboriginal peoples, Aboriginal women and the power of the Euro-Canadian state.

I. The Indian Act, 1876

[…]

Terms

3.   The following terms contained in this Act shall be held to have the meaning hereinafter assigned to them…:

(1)   The term "band" means any tribe, band or body of Indians who own or are interested in a reserve or in Indian lands in common, of which the legal tide is vested in the Crown […]

(3)   The term "Indian" means

First. Any person of Indian blood reputed to belong to a particular band;

Secondly. Any legitimate child of such person;

Thirdly. Any woman who is or was lawfully married to such person.

(a)   Provided that any illegitimate child, unless having shared with the consent of the band in the distribution moneys of such band for a period exceeding two years, may, at any time, be excluded from the membership thereof by the band, if […] sanctioned by the Superintendent-General:

[…]

(c)   Provided that any Indian woman marrying any other than an Indian or non-treaty Indian shall cease to be an Indian in any respect within the meaning of this Act

[…]

(d) Provided that any Indian woman marrying an Indian of any other band shall cease to be a member of the band to which she formerly belonged, and become a member of the band [...] of which her husband is a member:

(e) Provided also that no half-breed in Manitoba who has shared in the distribution of half-breed lands shall be accounted an Indian; and that no half-breed head of family (except the widow of an Indian, or a half-breed who has already been admitted into a treaty), shall [...] be accounted an Indian, or entitled to be admitted into any Indian treaty.

[...]

(5) The term "reserve" means any tract or tracts of land set apart by treaty or otherwise for the use of benefit of or granted to a particular band of Indians, of which the legal title is the Crown, but which is unsurrendered, and includes all the trees, wood, timber, soil, stone, minerals, metals or other valuables thereon or therein.

[...]

Protection of Reserves

11. No person [...] other than an Indian of the band, shall settle, reside or hunt upon, occupy or use any land or marsh, or shall settle, reside upon or occupy any road, or allowance for roads running through any reserve belonging to [...] such a band;

[...]

Privileges of Indians

64. No Indian or non-treaty Indian shall be liable to be taxed for any real or personal property, unless he holds real estate under lease or in fee simple, or personal property, outside of the reserve or special reserve, in which case he shall be liable to be taxed for such real or personal property at the same rate as other persons in the locality in which it is situate.

[...]

Disabilities and Penalties

72. The Superintendent-General shall have power to stop the payment of the annuity and interest money of any Indian who may be proved, to the satisfaction of the Superintendent-General, to have been guilty of deserting his family, and the said Superintendent-General may apply the same towards the support of any family, woman or child so deserted; also to stop the payment of the annuity and interest money of any woman having no children, who deserts her husband and lives immorally with another man.

[...]

Enfranchisement

86. Whenever any Indian man, or unmarried woman, of the full age of twenty-one years, obtains the consent of the band of which he or she is a member to become enfranchised [...] the local agent shall report [...] the name of the applicant to the Superintendent-General; whereupon the Superintendent-General [...] shall authorize some competent person to report whether the applicant is an Indian who, from the degree of civilization to which he attained, and the character for integrity, morality and sobriety which he bears, appears to be qualified to be [enfranchised]:

(1) Any Indian who may be admitted to the degree of Doctor of Medicine, or to any other degree by any University of Learning, or who may be admitted in any Province of the Dominion to practice law [...], or who may enter Holy Orders or who may be licensed by any denomination of Christians as a Minister of the Gospel, shall *ipso facto* become and be enfranchised under this Act.

Assented to 12 April 1876

Administration

3. (1) This Act shall be administered by the Minister of Indian Affairs and Northern Development, who shall be the superintendent-general of Indian affairs.

[...]

Definition and Registration of Indians

5. An Indian Register shall be maintained in the Department [of Indian Affairs], which shall consist of Band Lists and General Lists and in which shall be recorded the name of every person who is entitled to be registered as an Indian.

[...]

> 11. Subject to section 12, a person is entitled to be registered if that person
> (a) [is] entitled to hold, use or enjoy the lands and other immovable property belonging to the various tribes, bands or bodies of Indians in Canada;
> (b) is a member of a band [...]
> (c) is a male person who is a direct descendant in the male line of a male person described in paragraph (a) or (b);
> (d) is the legitimate child of
> (i) a male person described in paragraph (a) or (b), or
> (ii) a person described in paragraph (c);
> (e) is the illegitimate child of a female person described in paragraph (a), (b) or (d); or
> (f) is the wife or widow of a person who is entitled to be registered by virtue of paragraph (a), (b), (c), (d), or (e).
>
> [...]
>
> 12. (1) The following persons are not entitled to be registered [...]:
> (a) a person who
> (i) has received or has been allotted half-breed lands or money scrip,
> (ii) is a descendant of a person described in subparagraph (i),
> (iii) is enfranchised
>
> [....]

(b) a woman who married a person who is not an Indian, unless that woman is subsequently the wife or widow of a person described in section 11.

[...]

14. A woman who is a member of a band ceases to be a member of that band if she marries a person who is not a member of that band, but if she marries a member of another band, she thereupon becomes a member of the band of which her husband is a member.

Enfranchisement

[Previous Sections pertaining to enfranchisement are replaced by Sections 109 – 112]

> 109. (1) On the report of the Minister that an Indian has applied for enfranchisement and that in his opinion the Indian
> (a) is of the full age of twenty-one years,
> (b) is capable of assuming duties and responsibilities of citizenship, and
> (c) when enfranchised, will be capable of supporting himself and his dependents, the Governor in Council may by order declare that the Indian and his wife and minor unmarried children are enfranchised.

[...]

(2) On the report of the Minister that an Indian woman married a person who is not an Indian, the Governor in Council may by order declare that the woman is enfranchised as of the date of her marriage and, on the recommendation of the Minister may by order declare that all or any of her children are enfranchised as of the date of the marriage or such other date as the order may specify.

[…]

III. *Bill C-31: An Act to Amend The Indian Act, 1985*

Clause 4: This amendment would substitute for the existing scheme of band membership […].

It would also eliminate provisions relating to entitlement to registration that discriminate on the basis of sex and would replace them with non-discriminatory rules for determining entitlement. As well, it would eliminate the distinction between 'legitimate' and 'illegitimate' children and provide for the reinstatement of persons who have lost their entitlement to registration under discriminatory provisions or, in certain cases, through enfranchisement.

The proposed sections 5 to 7 would deal with registration in the Indian Register, sections 6 and 7 replacing the present sections 11 and 12.

[…]

6. (1) Subject to section 7, a person is entitled to be registered if

[…]

(c) the name of that person was omitted or deleted from the Indian Register, or from a band list […] under subparagraph […] 12(1)(b), subsection 12(2) or subsection 109(2) […] or under any former provision of this Act relating to the same subject matter as any of those provisions.

[…]

Clause 12: The amendment to subsection 68(1) and the repeal of subsection 68(2) [based on section 72 in the 1876 Indian Act] would establish the same rule for male and female Indians with respect to support payments in circumstances such as desertion. The repeal of subsection 68(3) would remove a special rule for "illegitimate" children.

[…]

Clause 14: The repeal of sections 109 to 113 would remove the concept of enfranchisement from the Indian Act.

REFERENCES

Arnot, David M. 2000 [1998]. "The Five Treaties in Saskatchewan: An Historical Overview." In Ron. Laliberte et al. (eds.), *Expressions in Canadian Native Studies*. Saskatoon: University of Saskatchewan Extension Press.

Bartlett, Richard. 1988. *The Indian Act of Canada* second edition. Saskatoon: University of Saskatchewan Native Law Centre.

Indian and Northern Affairs Canada. 2002. "Minister Introduces First Nations Governance Legislation." *News Release Communiqué*, June 14. Ottawa: Government of Canada.

Lawrence, Bonita. 2000. "Mixed-Race Urban Native People: Surviving a Legacy of Policies of Genocide." In Ron. Laliberte et al. (eds.), *Expressions in Canadian Native Studies*. Saskatoon: University of Saskatchewan Extension Press.

RCAP (Royal Commission on Aboriginal Peoples). 1996. *Report of the Royal Commission on Aboriginal Peoples*. Ottawa: Canada Communication Group.

For and by Men
Colony, Gender and Aboriginal Self-Government

Anna Hunter

The inherent right of Aboriginal self-government is a topic that figures centrally in Canada's political culture and, as such, elicits strong opinions about its merits and feasibility. Interestingly, though, there is a notable lack of consideration of underlying and unequal power relations that shape the discourse of Aboriginal self-government. In particular, its colonial and gendered implications are routinely ignored by Aboriginal and non-Aboriginal people. As a result, the construction and implementation of the policies and programs of Aboriginal self-government remain confined by a colonial and patriarchal mindset that limits its potential. In order to address this situation, I propose a re-conceptualization of Aboriginal self-government that unites the theory of self-government with the practice, in order to support indigenous women and men in their personal and collective journeys towards self-determination. This re-conceptualization focuses upon ensuring that the concerns and issues of the members of Aboriginal communities are placed onto the agendas of those developing and implementing the programs and policies of Aboriginal self-government. The overall intention is to demonstrate the necessity of considering policy and program developments in terms of the interconnections among race, culture,[1] gender, power and structural oppression.

What is Aboriginal Self-Government?

In its most basic sense, Aboriginal self-government expresses the desire of Aboriginal peoples to control their own destiny. More specifically, it is the right of Aboriginal peoples to be recognized as autonomous political communities with the authority and resources to decide the course of their individual and collective futures (Murphy 2001: 109). Aboriginal self-government includes the capacity to take responsibility for the education, health and welfare of community members within its jurisdiction. Aboriginal self-government includes the right to make economic and social policy, administer taxes, pass laws, manage land and natural resources and negotiate with other governments.

Aboriginal self-government is an inherent right that originates in the original occupation and use of the land prior to European contact. It cannot be delegated or unilaterally extinguished because its source lies within the Aboriginal peoples rather than external sources such as international law, the common law or the Canadian Constitution (RCAP 1996: 110). However, Aboriginal self-government is still about choice. It cannot be foisted on those Aboriginal communities that are not ready or willing to undertake it. Nor can self-government be handed down in a template fashion. In order to maximize its probability of success, it needs to be negotiated between the Aboriginal government and the federal and provincial governments in a manner that respects the distinct cultural norms and practices of the Aboriginal people (Cornell and Kalt 1998).

Within the past thirty years, Aboriginal peoples have made significant positive strides towards fulfilling this agenda of self-government. Numerous Aboriginal self-government agreements have been negotiated, ratified and accorded constitutional protection, including the 1993 *Nunavut Land Claims Agreement* and the 1998 *Nisga'a Final Agreement*. In addition to these comprehensive agreements, many Aboriginal groups have entered into smaller scale negotiations to assume administrative responsibility and control over key areas of tribal life such as child welfare, education and health services delivery. Each example of self-government has cumulatively increased its overall potential and viability. As Wayne Warry explains: "self-government is an emergent, iterative process — its meaning and validity become clearer with its practice" (Warry 2000: 49).

The prevalence and variety of Aboriginal self-government models in operation throughout the country should serve to recognize the many benefits of this policy approach. However, vigilance must be taken to ensure that its full potential is realized in the face of external and internal pressures. It is imperative that Aboriginal peoples are equipped with the appropriate level of authority and resources to direct and participate in the government processes that affect their communities. Only in this way can we move away from unequal and imbalanced power relations and not inadvertently expanding and strengthening them.

Situating the Role of Gender-Based Analysis in Aboriginal Relations

When working and writing in the field of Aboriginal relations, it is extremely important to include a gender-based analysis. As Emma LaRoque (1996: 11) explains, colonization processes have taken their toll on all Aboriginal peoples but perhaps their greatest toll on women. Aboriginal women face the double discrimination of racism and sexism, which are fostered and perpetuated through statutory mechanisms such as the *Indian Act*. As a result, Aboriginal women continue to be routinely dispossessed of their inherited rights, lands, identities and families. In comparison to the larger Canadian society, Aboriginal women remain disadvantaged in terms of high unemployment rates, low-income levels, single-parent families and low formal education levels. On top of this, Aboriginal women deal with excessively high rates of physical, sexual and psychological abuse (Green 2000: 333–34) and disproportionately high rates of incarceration (Monture-Angus 1992).

Aboriginal women also face exclusion from leadership roles, which has promoted a definite male bias in terms of policy and program development in Aboriginal communities. Although many Aboriginal women have assumed positions of leadership within the community at the grassroots level, they are generally under-represented in the more powerful, agenda setting and decision-making positions of umbrella organizations (such as the Assembly of First Nations, the Métis National Council, the Federated Saskatchewan Indian Nations, the Union of B.C. Indian Chiefs) and large bureaucracies. Not only are women absent from high ranking political offices, gender issues (which dovetail with cultural issues) also tend to be absent. Economic issues related to lands and resources take up the majority of time and energy of community and government leaders, while community-based initiatives such as health, education and child welfare are negotiated outside of the actual treaty process.[2] Leaving these sociocultural issues without the protection of treaty status is a pattern repeated in our political and governing institutions across the country. As such, the potential new policies and programs of Aboriginal self-government are dramatically reduced.

This is a structural and systemic problem. A gender-based analysis, however, can help to clarify the interconnections between culture and gender in understandings of the promise and purpose of Aboriginal self-government. It can provide a strategy to offset the continued practice of implementing shortsighted policies and programs that generate dependency and despair, not empowerment and self-sufficiency. The federal and provincial governments have maintained their colonial legacy of policies and programs directed at controlling and assimilating all spheres of Aboriginal life and community within their reach. Many Aboriginal governments have internalized this legacy by incorporating template protocols and agreements that serve external needs and traditions before addressing internal needs and traditions.

Child welfare policies and practices demonstrate male bias and its implications. Child welfare policy is an important example because it is a core area of Aboriginal jurisdiction (RCAP 1996: 215–23); there are a number of related legislative initiatives directed to ensuring that Aboriginal people are involved in the planning and delivery of services to Aboriginal families and their children.[3] Furthermore, we can all relate to meeting the needs of children and families. Finally, child welfare services are typically used by people at an extremely vulnerable point in their lives, and therefore they require special consideration.

Aboriginal people have faced a long line of destructive and assimilationist child welfare policies (Fournier and Crey 1997). As a First Nations woman, I have personally witnessed the intergenerational effects of these policies. In my grandparents' generation, First Nation peoples endured residential school policies that removed children from their communities and placed them in boarding schools that were designed to assimilate the children into western practices. In my mother's generation, First Nations communities faced the "Sixties Scoop," the practice of the mainstream governments removing children from Native homes and placing them into non-Native ones. In my generation, Aboriginal communities were provided with legislation that gives priority to keeping children-in-care within Native homes. In my children's generation, First Nations governments are engaging in child welfare negotiations to assume the authority to develop and implement their own child welfare systems.

On the surface, it appears that significant strides have been made to address the colonial legacy of assimilationist policies that have worked to separate Aboriginal children from their families. The new policy directions, in line with First Nations' right to self-government, recognize that the best interests of an Aboriginal child and community are served by ensuring tribal participation in proceedings involving Aboriginal children. These policies also allow First Nations communities to re-establish cultural continuity for the children of their community. Thus, it is easy to understand why the new policies are typically considered as a progressive improvement in this fundamentally important area of tribal life.

However, a deeper examination uncovers many underlying structural and systemic problems. Because those political power-brokers who negotiated the new policies operate within the confines of a colonial and patriarchal mindset, the specific ramifications of the policy to women were not considered. For example, due consideration was not given to the women who had escaped communities that they felt were unsafe and unhealthy, only to be told that their children would have to return there if they needed to enter into care or to be adopted. Similarly, due consideration was not given to the bond between a mother and child that continues beyond legal agreements. A woman who decided to stay in her home community and who, for whatever reason, had a child enter into care or into adoption proceedings would surely find the close proximity of that child particularly hard to deal with in small reserve communities where everyone is connected through kinship. Finally, due consideration was not given to alternatives to the colonial nuclear family, nor was the assumption that this family model represents what is best for children questioned. Why was the colonial ideal of a small, heterosexual and generally two-generational family given primacy over traditional forms of extended and community-based kin? What about short-term arrangements within the larger family network that could help connect both the parents and child to the community? How can implementing the mainstream models of child protection without tailoring the programs and policies to the particular needs of the community and its members be considered progressive? By now it should be well understood that in order for policies and programs to be successful in Aboriginal communities, there must be a cultural "match" (Cornell and Kalt 1998: 196), yet this has not been built into the new agreements.

The shortcomings in the legislation are not necessarily the result of deliberate or malicious intent on the part of individual negotiators on either side of the table. Rather, they stem from the unexamined male bias that operates to marginalize women's needs. This marginalization is exacerbated by funding arrangements that are mired in colonial structures that strain Aboriginal communities. These funding arrangements include: (1) those that are based on the number of on-reserve status members and that strain already under-resourced reserves to provide housing, education, health care, employment opportunities, family services and so on to current residents as well as returning children and adults; and (2) those that favour the short-term and reactive practice of apprehending children rather than long term and proactive solutions based on adequate financial and cultural support. Such funding arrangements reflect an internalized colonial mindset that incorporates mainstream policies instead of working to recover, reinstate and when necessary creatively construct cultural and traditional Aboriginal models. This combination of colonial practice and patriarchal bias has led to a situation in which policy development and implementation lack sensitivity to gender, culture, community dynamics and to the differential impacts on the lives of women and men.

Aboriginal Self-Government and Gender

The interconnections between culture and gender can have a deep impact on the potential of programs and policies of Aboriginal self-government. As a solution, it is important to pay particular attention to how the acts and ideologies of colonialism, oppression and patriarchy can adversely influence even well-intentioned policies. Devoting attention to the underlying power dynamics that are often left unexamined will allow us to realize the purpose and promise of Aboriginal self-government in ways that benefit all community members. I also believe that this kind of critical inquiry is one of the best ways to avoid "ghettoizing" women's issues. What are too often dismissed as women's issues are the responsibility of the community as a whole and can no longer be relegated to the sidelines. Incorporating these issues centrally in ways that challenge existing sexist and colonial strategies will redress the male bias that has heretofore dramatically limited our visions of traditional forms of governance.

It should now be apparent that gender is a critical consideration in the development of the policies and programs of Aboriginal self-government and that gendered implications need to be considered in tandem with other forms of colonial oppressions. The inter-generational pattern of pain that is so common to many Aboriginal people is more than coincidence; it is the result of systemic and structural imbalances that have fostered dependency and despair. We cannot continue to allow the development and implementation of shortsighted policies and programs that do not address these underlying imbalances. We need individually and collectively to challenge the status quo to ensure that the implementation of Aboriginal self-government incorporates traditional beliefs, values, identities and ways of life. In doing so, we will be closer to a truly inclusive form of self-government that fully supports indigenous women and men in their personal and collective journeys.

NOTES

1. There are some people who limit indigenous identity to racial categories such as ancestry and blood quantum percentages. However I argue that it is the culture and unique ways of viewing the world of indigenous peoples that form fundamental determinants of indigenous identity.
2. For an overview of the political negotiation process, see the B.C. Treaty Commission website. At: bctreaty.net.
3. For example, see *Child, Family and Community Services Act* [RSBC 1996] Chapter 46; *Child and Family Services Act* R.S.O. 1990, Chapter C.11.

Anderson, Kim. 2000. *A Recognition of Being: Reconstructing Native Womanhood*. Toronto: Sumach Press.

Cornell, Stephen, and Joseph Kalt. 1998. "Sovereignty and Nation-Building: The Development Challenge in Indian Country Today." *American Indian Culture and Research Journal* 22,4.

Fournier, Suzanne, and Ernie Crey. 1997. *Stolen From Our Embrace*. Vancouver: Douglas and McIntyre.

Government of Canada. 1996. Royal Commission on Aboriginal Peoples, *Restructuring the Relationship*. Volume 2: Part One. Ottawa.

Green, Joyce. 2000. "Constitutionalizing the Patriarchy: Aboriginal Women and Aboriginal Government." In Ron Laliberte et al. (eds.), *Expressions in Canadian Native Studies*. Saskatoon: University of Saskatchewan Extension Press.

LaRoque, Emma. 1996. "The Colonization of a Native Woman Scholar." In Christine Miller and Patricia Chuchryk (eds.), *Women of the First Nations: Power, Wisdom, and Strength*. Winnipeg: University of Manitoba Press.

Monture-Angus, Patricia. 1992. "The Violence We Women Do." In Constance Backhouse and David Flaherty (eds.), *Challenging Times: The Women's Movement in Canada and the United States*. Montreal: McGill-Queen's University Press.

____ 1999. *Journeying Forward: Dreaming First Nations' Independence*. Halifax: Fernwood Publishing.

Murphy, Michael. 2001. "Culture and the Courts: A New Direction in Canadian Jurisprudence on Aboriginal Rights?" *Canadian Journal of Political Science* 34,1.

Warry, Wayne. 2000. *Unfinished Dreams*. Toronto: University of Toronto Press.

86

Women
Half The World, Barely Represented

Stephen Lewis

On the wall of my study at home, there hangs a picture which I value highly, albeit in a somewhat perverse fashion. It's a stunning photograph of the entire leadership of the United Nations (U.N.) secretariat in 1985. The Secretary-General of the time was Javier Pérez de Cuéllar: in the photo, he is surrounded by all of his Under-Secretaries-General and all of his Secretaries-General. They're standing in a resplendent, unbroken row on the podium of the General Assembly, immediately beneath the huge and ornate representation of the logo of the United Nations.

There are thirty-two of them in all. Not one woman. Not one. It was 1985, a mere [twenty-five] years ago. That just says everything there is to say about multilateralism and gender. I was Canada's ambassador to the U.N. at the time, and with the full encouragement of the Canadian Ministry of Foreign Affairs, I pursued a very tough line on discrimination against women within the U.N. system, as well as worldwide gender discrimination on every front.

Fundamentally, the U.N. should be driving the gender agenda. It's the world body with the greatest reach, and everything that underpins its legitimacy speaks to equality. *The Charter of the United Nations, the Universal Declaration of Human Rights, the Convention on the Elimination of All Forms of Discrimination Against Women, the Covenant on Economic, Social and Cultural Rights, the Covenant on Political and Civil Rights* — they all speak to equality.

Every one of these landmark human rights instruments contains explicit clauses affirming non-discrimination on the basis of sex and declaring equality between men and women. If they were followed, this would be a different world.

Undoubtedly, the covenant with the greatest potential influence is the *Convention on the Elimination of All Forms of Discrimination Against Women* (CEDAW), which was promulgated on December 18, 1979. It's as though it were the Magna Carta for women. No other convention is quite so powerfully worded. It's also the second most highly ratified convention in the history of international covenants: 181 out of 191 countries have ratified it. Only *the Convention on the Rights of the Child* has a larger number of ratifications, at 189. It should also be remembered that when a country ratifies a convention, it effectively becomes an instrument of binding international law in that country. It speaks volumes that so many countries feel they can ignore the prescriptions of CEDAW with impunity; there are simply no enforcement mechanisms, and when it's inconvenient to uphold the convention, countries are blithely negligent.

In addition to the exemplary covenants of equality, it's also useful to invoke the substance of the great international conferences which were held throughout the 1990s, and actually form the basis for the agencies of the United Nations in the twenty-first century, including the MDGs (Millennium Development Goals). It is sometimes forgotten that the world gathered in a successive series of conferences that laboriously etched the mandate for social progress for decades to come.

These were not vast conclaves of disputation and negotiation with little relevance to the real world. These were international conferences which gave rise to cadres of women activists, in one country after another, who then spent the better part of their lives advocating for equality. The global became local with a vengeance. What is not often realized is the way in which these conferences became hotbeds of consciousness-raising for women from all over the developing world. The experience is transforming. Everyone returns home determined to light the fires of change. The paucity of progress following these global meetings has had little to do with the women; it has everything to do with the monolithic walls of male authority, and how indescribably tough it is to bring those walls down.

Despite all the lip service paid by the U.N. member states to the importance of gender equality, only eleven of the 191 ambassadors, or 5.7 percent, are women. Worse still, the make-up of the workforce of the U.N. agencies — a balance over which the powers-that-be within the secretariat has some control — is similarly distorted. The funds, programs, and agencies will tell you, proudly, that up to 33 percent of their professional staff are women, but, quite aside from asking why it should be only 33 percent (it's both embarrassing and indefensible, the way in which we've consigned 50 percent to some unattainable fantasy), a closer scrutiny will show that the concentration of women is invariably at the lower professional categories, but inevitably, in the absence of rigorous affirmative action, their movement upwards is halting and incremental.

But that's just the half of it, and the lesser half. The other aspect of multilateralism, astonishing and offensive in equal measure, is the absence of any single, powerful agency with the U.N. system to represent women. Women constitute more than half the world's population, and in the extensive labyrinth of the U.N. organizations, they are barely represented.

I say "barely" because there is the United Nations Development Fund for Women, or UNIFEM. But UNIFEM is little known beyond U.N. circles, and is not taken seriously by the hierarchy within. How could it be? Apart from the miniscule budget,[1] neither the executive director of UNIFEM, or UNIFEM itself, is senior on the U.N. grid… to be at the level of the head of UNIFEM — a D2, it's called — has no greater status than, say, a person who heads up a UNICEF office in one large country.

But this isn't a large country we're talking about. We're talking about more than half the world's population. And it's rank, really rank, to treat women's issues in such a scandalous manner. Let me make it clear: in my over twenty years working directly or indirectly with the United Nations, I can safely say that only a tiny cadre of voices speaks strongly for women.

Instead of bona fide, specialized programs, women get "gender mainstreaming," and gender mainstreaming is a pox for women. The worst thing you can do for women is to fold their concerns into the mandates of U.N. agencies, or bury them under the activities of government ministries. Once you've mainstreamed gender, it's everybody's business and nobody's business. Everyone's accountable and no one's accountable.

Gender mainstreaming might work if we had what the sports and financial enthusiasts call a "level playing field"; that is to say, if there were real equality and equality between women and men. Then gender mainstreaming becomes a way of maintaining that equality. But when you start from such gross inequality, mainstreaming entrenches the disparities. So the only way to deal with these issues is to preserve for them a pride of place — to construct for women an edifice, an institution, an agency whose sole preoccupation is to advance the position of women. Or more accurately, to support women to create their own such entity. Then you couldn't mainstream, mute, or dilute it any way because it would be separate — separately responsible, separately accountable. Its voice would always be heard because it wouldn't be subsumed into the miasma of uniformity.

When all is said and done, the ongoing struggle to embrace gender equality was most poignantly brought home to me in confronting the pandemic of HIV/AIDS. And in particular, one specific memorable experience.

In January 2003, I travelled with James Morris, the executive director of the World Food Programme, to four countries in southern Africa: Zimbabwe, Malawi, Zambia, and Lesotho. Southern Africa was then (as now) in the grip of a brutal food shortage, and the combination of hunger and AIDS was something we wanted to investigate. Apart from the reports of the U.N. representatives in the field, there was also a newly current academic thesis called "New Variant Famine." The name had been coined by Alex de Waal, a gifted and knowledgeable Africanist, who, upon close study, had evolved the argument that food shortages were the result of illness caused by AIDS as much as they were the result of climate.

We were interested, if skeptical. It seemed far more likely that the driving force would be erratic rainfall and drought.

I had been in the region only the month before, and experienced a kind of renewable shock, but James Morris, on his first extensive trip to the region, was absolutely stunned by what we encountered. There were hunger and starvation everywhere, and while the actual famine or near-famine was clearly influenced by successive droughts, there was no question that AIDS was playing havoc with agricultural productivity.

The state of the health of the women in the villages was ghastly. Household income was ransacked, and time once spent on walking to distant fields and growing a variety of foods had been given over to caring for the sick. AIDS leads to hunger; hunger exacerbates AIDS. It's a merciless interaction. The numbers of orphan children are beyond belief; in fact, so beyond belief that when we drafted our report, we actually said, "The situation of orphans represents a humanitarian catastrophe and a violation of the rights of children. The apparent inability of the United Nations system and the international community to adequately support national governments in their response to the needs of the huge numbers of orphans in the region is unacceptable." That's U.N.-speak for saying, "You've failed lamentably: for God's sake get your act together."

We travelled with eighteen colleagues from eight different U.N. agencies and the Southern African Development Community (SADC), and I vividly remember the repetitive sense of numbed incomprehension as we boarded the plane to fly to yet another country.

Let me quote the key passage [from the report] at some length.

The mission was struck in particular by how food shortages appear to aggravate the impact of HIV/AIDS by accelerating the progress of the disease in HIV-positive individuals…. Perhaps the most disturbing realization came with a better understanding of the impact that this crisis is having on the region's women. It was evident to the mission that although the prevalence of HIV infection is highest among women and girls — who also take on nearly all the responsibilities of caring for the sick and orphaned, in addition to their regular obligations such as providing food for their households — very little is being done to reduce women's risks, to protect them from sexual aggression and violence, to ease their burdens, or to support their coping and caring efforts. The apparent lack of urgency, leadership, direction, and responsibility in the response of the United Nations, national governments, and the international community to the pandemic's effects on women and girls is deeply troubling. For example, the early adoption of mainstreaming approaches to gender within United Nations agencies, funds, and programs has made gender issues everyone's concern but no one's responsibility. Whereas gender policies and principles are widely discussed by the United Nations, governments and NGOs, the urgent actions flowing from those discussions must be implemented. So far, that does not appear to have happened.[2]

I never feel more agitated than in the face of what's happening to women. The atmosphere of benign neglect, compounded by the rooted gender inequality, all adds up to a death sentence for countless millions of women in the developing world. For whatever reason, we can't break the monolith of indifference and paralysis.

I have tried to give you a glimpse, experienced or discerned on a personal basis, of the struggle for women's human rights. I can't pretend that it's more than a glimpse, and it doesn't begin to approximate the frustrations and heroism, tenacity and despair, progress and setbacks faced by the leaders of the women's movement itself. I've concentrated on Africa because it's the continent I know best, and because it yields such vivid examples.

Governments in Africa do not do well in the protection of women's rights. In fact, as I shall momentarily demonstrate, they are profoundly deficient. I've been completely taken aback, on more than one occasion, by the wall of indifference thrown up by cabinet ministers when I raise, for example, the plight of women in the era of AIDS. At one point, in the case of Angola, a very senior member of the administration lapsed into locker-room smirking at the mere mention of women. My argument is quite simple: they would not be allowed to indulge in such asinine and/or negligent behaviour if there were a watchdog, a full-fledged agency or institution as part of the United Nations, whose job it was to ride herd on the recalcitrants. Governments get away with it because no one cares enough to prevent governments from getting away with it.

And what is the upshot? In the UNDP Human Development Report for 2003, there is a gender-related development index which rates most of the countries of the world according to a number of economic and social indices, taking into account, in particular, performance on the overall status of women. Let me identify the twenty countries at the bottom of the list of 145 which are ranked for gender, starting with the country right at the bottom and working up: Sierra Leone, Niger, Burkina Faso, Mali, Burundi, Mozambique, Ethiopia, Central African Republic, Guinea-Bissau, Democratic Republic of the Congo, Angola, Côte d'Ivoire, Chad, Zambia, Malawi, Benin, Tanzania, Rwanda, Senegal, Eritrea.

Twenty countries: all are African. While it is appalling that Africa occupies a place of such dishonour, showing how so many leaders are beyond redemption on issues of gender, it should also give everyone pause about the role of multilaterialism. It's not possible for the U.N. family in any of these twenty countries to grab the heads of state by the scruff of the neck and shake them into equality. But it would be the role of the U.N. family to shame, blame, and propose solutions, all the while yelling from the rooftops that inequality is obscene. Only then will change have a chance.

NOTES

Stephen Lewis, 2005, CBC Massey Lectures: *The Race Against Time*, Toronto: House of Anansi Press. Adapted and reprinted by permission.

1. Editor's Note: In 2004, the annual budget for UNIFEM was $45 million; 2.25 percent of UNICEF's $2 billion total budget (Lewis 2005: 123).

2. Editor's Note: In the original lecture/essay, Stephen Lewis credits Paula Donovan, who at the time was regional advisor for UNICEF's AIDS in East and southern Africa, for writing the sections of the report pertaining to women. Lewis describes these sections as "tough and trenchant" and wouldn't have happened without Donovan's presence on the mission (Lewis 2005: 135). In the original lecture/essay, Lewis describes three responses, in 2002, 2003, and 2004 respectively, in which the U.N. charged committees to develop plans for addressing the impact of AIDS on women and children. At the time of writing, Lewis stated that "very little [had] come of the [2004 report]" (Lewis 2005: 142).

87

Without the Law

Mary Nyquist

For Carole and Nanni

The law's not an ass if you're behind it.
No camel struggling to exit a needle's eye,
a well-heeled white man has been tailor-
made to slip right through, effortlessly.

In the wide eyes of the law grounds for
suspicion settle at the bottom of the cup
set aside in the face of solid house, nicely
turned-out wife, frank, upstanding gaze.

Yet even the priest had it tough compared
to you, regarded so highly for skilful prosecution of justice that, unobserved, you
overleapt the bar to which you'd been called.

Whether above or, ergo, securely outside
the law, with the same, practised dexterity
you took both it and each one of your
daughters into your own, assured hands.

Long after they'd grown and left home
you would sit rubbing, counting every
year that settled the violations beyond
what the Statute of Limitations allowed,

thereby making you a law unto yourself.

Propter hoc

giving you a hearty slap on the back,
the long arm of the law reached out,
you assumed, to hold them down, stifle
any protests, cradle them safely within.

Competing Claims from Disadvantaged Groups
Nixon v. Vancouver Rape Relief Society

Joanna Harris

The complex relationship between trans rights and women's substantive equality is exemplified by the case of *Nixon v. Vancouver Rape Relief Society* (hereafter referred to as *Nixon*) — a clear example of the dilemma caused when two concepts come into conflict.

Anti-Discrimination Law in Canada

In Canada, discrimination is addressed using various legal instruments: the *Charter of Rights and Freedoms* (part of Canada's Constitution) and federal, provincial or territorial human rights codes.[1]

Under the *Charter*, specifically section 15, a mere distinction drawn between two people does not in itself constitute discrimination. The distinction must be based on a specified or analogous ground; the grounds specified in the *Charter* are race, national or ethnic origin, colour, religion, sex, age and mental or physical disability. Analogous grounds have also been held to include, for example, sexual orientation. In subsequent case law, the Supreme Court of Canada established another overarching principle, namely, the prevention of violations of human dignity: they established a three-part test in order to determine whether discrimination occurred (*Law v. Canada* [*Minister of Employment and Immigration*] 1999, hereafter referred to as *Law v. Canada* or *Law*). The Court first considers if there is a formal distinction drawn, based on personal characteristics; second, if the law or action on the part of the government fails to take into account the claimant's already disadvantaged position within Canada based on an enumerated or analogous ground; and third, if this differential treatment discriminates in a substantive sense, which would defy the purpose of remedying prejudice, stereotyping and historical disadvantage.

The final step helps the Court consider whether a claimant's dignity has been infringed. Mr. Justice Frank Iacobucci, in the significant 1999 decision *Law v. Canada* defines human dignity in the context of section 15:

> Human dignity means that an individual or group feels self-respect and self-worth. It is concerned with physical and psychological integrity and empowerment. Human dignity is harmed by unfair treatment and premised upon personal traits or circumstances which do not relate to individual needs, capacities or merits. (*Law v. Canada* 1999: 53)

In contrast to the *Charter* provisions, a finding of discrimination in the federal, provincial and territorial human rights legislation has not, at least historically, depended upon infringement of human dignity. While the human rights codes refer generally, by way of their preambles or statement of objectives, to the concept of preservation of human dignity (Tarnopolsky 2001: 4-100.3), the legal analysis has been analytically distinct from that laid out by Justice Iacobucci in the *Law* decision. The relevant test for a finding of discrimination in Canadian human rights codes was decided in *Meiorin* decision (*British Columbia* [*Public Service Employee Relations Commission*] v. *B.C.G.E.U* 1997): when a distinction in treatment between two people is made directly, or by the effect of seemingly neutral requirement, discrimination is considered to have occurred prima facie (on its face), and the finding of discrimination will prevail until contradicted and overcome by other evidence. Therefore, the onus shifts to the alleged perpetrator who must defend their conduct based on a bona fide (genuine) occupational requirement that requires an employee to be accommodated to the point of undue hardship.

The distinction between the *Charter* dignity analysis and the *B.C. Human Rights Code* was at the crux of Vancouver Rape Relief's appeal to the Supreme Court of British Columbia on December 19, 2003, in the *Nixon* case. The B.C. Human Rights Tribunal decision of January 17, 2002, did not adopt the *Charter* analysis, which considers the element of human dignity. Subsequently, the B.C. Supreme Court overturned this decision, holding that the *Charter* analysis should apply. However, the B.C. Court of Appeal reviewed this case and determined on July 12, 2005 that the "broad application of the *Law* framework in a case without governmental overtones" is inappropriate (*Vancouver Rape Relief Society v. Nixon* 2005: at para 39).

The *Nixon* Case

Kimberly Nixon is a post-operative male-to-female transsexual. In 1987, at age thirty, she attended the Gender Disorder Clinic at the Vancouver General Hospital. Three years later, she had sex-reassignment surgery and her birth certificate was subsequently amended to change the sex designation of birth from male to female. In 1992 and 1993, Kimberly experienced physical and emotional abuse in a relationship with a male partner. When this relationship ended she was referred to the services of Battered Women's Support Services (BWSS). In August 1995, she responded to a Vancouver Rape Relief Society advertisement calling for volunteers. All potential volunteers are pre-screened to ensure that they agree with Rape Relief's views as a feminist, pro-choice and lesbian-positive organization. Rape Relief also requires that volunteer peer counsellors be women. Men interested in volunteering at Rape Relief are offered positions on the fundraising committee.

After passing the pre-screening interview, Kimberly was invited to attend the peer-counsellor training session. When she attended the first night of her training, she was immediately recognized by the training facilitator as an individual who had not always been physically female. During the first break the facilitator, Ms. Cormier, approached Kimberly and asked to speak with her in private. Their conversation confirmed that Kimberly had not been a woman since birth. Ms. Cormier asked that Kimberly leave the training group, and she complied.

The next day, Kimberly filed a complaint with the British Columbia Council of Human Rights. Following her removal from the Rape Relief training program, she testified that, due to the distress she felt, she returned to the support group at BWSS. In the fall of 1996, she applied and was accepted into the BWSS training program for volunteers. Kimberly ended her involvement with BWSS after she discovered that the members circulated what she considered to be "hate" literature about transsexuals. She worked briefly for Peggy's Place, a transition house for women who, in addition to dealing with male violence or battering, have mental-health issues. Kimberly was considered a very capable volunteer in her subsequent positions.

Judicial History

The B.C. Human Rights Tribunal heard Kimberly's arguments that Rape Relief had discriminated against her on the basis of sex,[2] by denying her a service (a training program in counselling women who have experienced violence) and an employment opportunity (*Vancouver Rape Relief Society v. British Columbia [Human Rights Commission]* 2002). The tribunal ruled that the relationship between Rape Relief and its volunteers fell within the definition of employment and found that there had been prima facie discrimination — discrimination had occurred without having to provide any further evidence — against Kimberly on both accounts.

Thus, Rape Relief was required to justify this discriminatory treatment. Rape Relief argued that lifelong experience as a woman was a bona fide occupational requirement for peer counsellors and, in addition, Rape Relief had attempted to accommodate Kimberly by suggesting that she join its fundraising committee. In effect, Rape Relief argued that it had accommodated Kimberly up to the point of undue hardship for the organization. The tribunal rejected both of these claims. In addition, the tribunal rejected Rape Relief's argument based on section 41 of the *B.C. Human Rights Code*, which stipulates that it is not discrimination for a non-profit organization whose "primary purpose" is promoting the welfare and interests of the identifiable group. The tribunal ruled that the evidence did not establish that Rape Relief's primary purpose was "the promotion of women who fit their political definition of what it means to be a woman" (*Nixon v. Vancouver Rape Relief* 2002: 221). The tribunal also held that Rape Relief did not establish that it was necessary to exclude transsexuals in order to accomplish the organization's goals.

In a controversial and highly publicized decision, taken January 17, 2002, the tribunal ordered Rape Relief "to cease denying, for discriminatory reasons, to transsexual women the opportunity of participating in their training program and the opportunity, on completion of the training, for the same group of women of volunteering at Rape Relief" (*Nixon v. Vancouver Rape Relief* 2002: 231). In addition, an award in the amount of $7,500 was ordered for injury to Kimberly's dignity, feelings and self-respect. At the time of this decision, this was the highest amount in special compensation ever awarded in the tribunal's history.

Legal Issues at the Tribunal and Before the Courts

Rape Relief petitioned to the B.C. Supreme Court for judicial review of the tribunal's decision. Issues considered by the court were the effect of section 41 of the Code, discrimination under the *Law* analytical framework and "dignity" under the *Law* framework.

The B.C. Supreme Court quashed the tribunal's order. Mr. Justice Edwards held that the tribunal was incorrect in not applying the *Law* analytical framework. The tribunal's finding, that Kimberly's exclusion from Rape Relief's volunteer training was prima facie discrimination, could not stand up under the *Law* analysis. Both Rape Relief and Kimberly characterized gender as a continuum rather than a binary male/female concept. Justice Edwards accepted Rape Relief's submission that Rape Relief's community of women was located on the far end of the female continuum.

The B.C. Supreme Court decision also held, as was implicit in the tribunal's decision, that women who were born and raised as girls and women ("non-transsexual" women) are entitled to form a group protected under the exemption provisions of section 41 of the [Human Rights] Code. Justice Edwards held that the tribunal failed to correctly interpret and apply the leading Supreme Court of Canada decision on section 41 in *Caldwell v. St. Thomas Aquinas High School* (1984, hereafter referred to as *Caldwell*). The Supreme Court of Canada found that section 41 is a rights-granting provision, and as such, is not subject to the restrictive interpretation generally applicable to legislative provisions which place limitations on rights. The *Caldwell* decision also held that it was permissible to make a preference of one member of the identifiable group over another, as long as the distinction was made honestly, in good faith and in the sincerely held belief that it is imposed in the interest of the adequate performance of the work, and if it was related, in an objective sense, to the performance of employment (*Ontario Human Rights Commission v. Etobicoke* 1982). Justice Edwards followed this reasoning and allowed the preference of one member of the identifiable groups over another, as long as the distinction was made for the benefit of the members of the community served by Rape Relief. Further, Justice Edwards ruled that Rape Relief did not have to prove its primary purpose had a political dimension in light of the bona fide belief that only women born women were suitable peer counsellors for female rape victims.

The final step with the *Law* approach to section 15 is meant to be both contextual and purposeful, and its objective is to prevent the violation of human dignity. The test of whether dignity has been harmed is both subjective and objective. It is therefore necessary to consider the context of the complainant from the standpoint of a reasonable person.

Justice Edwards believed that Kimberly's exclusion from a "relatively small obscure self-defining private organization cannot have the same impact on human dignity as legislated exclusion from a statutory benefit program" (*Law v. Canada* 1999: 145). Because her exclusion didn't bear state approval, and hence some wider public acceptance, it was therefore judged not to be a public indignity. Although the court agreed that this was no less subjectively hurtful to Kimberly, the court distinguished the issue of the objective impact on human dignity, which was held to be unreasonably exaggerated. In particular, the court noted, "no reasonable male to female transsexual, standing in Ms. Nixon's shoes, could plausibly" argue that they "can no longer participate in the economic, social and cultural life of the province" (*Law v. Canada* 1999: 151). Additionally, Christine Boyle, counsel for Rape Relief, argued that a reasonable person would take into account the needs of disadvantaged groups to understand their own experience.

In essence, the court characterized the nature of Rape Relief as a political organization and the nature of the dispute, essentially a political one over membership criteria (*Vancouver Rape Relief Society v. Nixon* 2005: 114). It was not the function of the [Human Rights] Code to provide a referee and impose "state-sanctioned penalties in political disputes between private organizations." Finally, Justice Edwards held that the reason Kimberly was attracted to the peer-counsellor training program was because it would vindicate her womanhood, because it was part of a women-only organization. Her participation was held to have a political dimension.

In the end, the tribunal's conclusion that Rape Relief's exclusion of Kimberly as discriminatory was found to be unreasonable and the order for Rape Relief to pay her $7,500 in compensation was set aside. The B.C. Supreme Court's decision leaves room, as the *Law* decision suggests, for different forms of disadvantage. The decision also allows and recognizes the experience of growing up as a girl and living as a woman to be a permissible basis for a group to exclusively associate.

The decision by the B.C. Supreme Court has been substantially upheld by the B.C. Court of Appeal. On July 12, 2005, Kimberly's appeal of Justice Edward's decision was dismissed. The Court of Appeal found that the test of "discrimination" under the *B.C. Human Rights Code* was met. Rape Relief was held to be exempt from the application of the Code by virtue of section 41.

Violence Against Women

Many women's groups, sexual assault centres and women's interval houses insist on a women-only membership. It is seen as "essential to the struggle to restore dignity to disempowered women" and "necessary conditions to self-empowerment in a socio-economic and cultural context where access to and mobility within public space is still largely controlled by men and where women's roles and opportunity are frequently defined against their own interests"

(Denike and Renshaw 2003: 13). Members gathering from oppressed groups to organize against oppression is a well-recognized tactic of addressing the effects of oppression and forming strategies for change (Freire 1970: cited in Findlay 2003).

Most women's organizations, including Rape Relief, believe that gender exists along a continuum and none of the needs and desires of their groups are considered unique or exclusive to them, but given the systemic nature of such groups, identity must be a legitimate basis for organizing. "It is essential to the integrity and autonomy of these groups that they be able to define and control membership in their group." Rape Relief thus excluded Kimberly because of the unique role Rape Relief serves for women experiencing violence.

NOTES

Johanna Harris, 2006, "Competing Claims from Disadvantaged Groups: *Nixon V. Vancouver Rape Relief Society*," in Krista Scott-Dixon (ed.), *Trans/forming Feminisms: Trans/Feminist Voices Speak Out*. Toronto: Sumach Press. Adapted and reprinted with permission.

1. For non-government actors, the *Charter* does not apply. When discrimination occurs by a private actor, the complainant must seek redress under the applicable human rights code.

2. Rape Relief had applied to halt proceeding on the basis that the *B.C. Human Rights Code* did not specifically prohibit discrimination based on transsexualism or gender identity. Mr. Justice Davies disagreed and that "it would be wrong to interpret the prohibition against discrimination on the basis of sex in the *Code* as not also prohibiting discrimination against an individual merely because that person or group is not readily identifiable as being either male or female." *Vancouver Rape Relief Society v. British Columbia (Human Rights Commission)* [2002], 57.

REFERENCES

Denike, Margaret, and Sal Renshaw. 2003. "Transgender and Women's Substantive Equality." Paper prepared at the National Consultation on Transgender and Women's Substantive Equality, National Association of Women and the Law.

Findlay, Barbara. 2003. "'Real Women': Kimberly Nixon v. Vancouver Rape Relief." *University of British Columbia Law Review* 36.

Tarnopolsky, Walter Surma. 2001. *Discrimination and the Law*. Scarborough: Carswell.

LEGAL DECISIONS

British Columbia (Public Service Employee Relations Commission) v. B.C.G.E.U., 176 D.L.R. (4th) 1.35 C.H.R.R. D/257, [1997] 3 S.C.R. 3.

Caldwell v. St. Thomas Aquinas High School, [1984] 2 S.C.R. 603, (QL).

Law v. Canada (Minister of Employment and Immigration), [1999] S.C.R. 497 [Law].

Nixon v. Vancouver Rape Relief [2002] B.C.H.R.T.D. No 1 2001 B.C.H.R.T. 1 (QL).

Ontario Human Rights Commission v. Etobicoke (Borough of), [1982] 1 S.C.R. 202 (QL), 208.

Vancouver Rape Relief Society v. British Columbia (Human Rights Commission) [2002] B.C.H.R.T.D. No. 1, 57.

Vancouver Rape Relief Society v. Nixon 2005 BCCA 601 at para 39.

89

Bringing Criminalized Women into View

Elizabeth Comack

During my undergraduate studies in the 1970s, I majored in sociology with a specialization in criminology. Like thousands before me, I worked my way through the canon of criminology — the body of knowledge considered to be central to a full understanding of the discipline. In the process, I became well-versed in the theoretical explanations that criminology had to offer for why people became involved in crime. I subsequently went on to complete a doctoral degree, and secured a job as a university professor, but not until many years later did I come to appreciate fully how male-centred was my education.

In the early 1990s I was working on a project that involved interviewing women held in a provincial prison. I was interested in exploring the connections between the women's violations of the law and their histories of physical and sexual abuse — 78 percent of the women in this prison had reported victimization experiences (Comack 1996). I can clearly recall the drive home after a particularly difficult day of interviews. It was one of those "aha" moments we sometimes have. Reflecting on what the women had shared with me made all those theories of crime I'd learned seem woefully inadequate because those theories failed to capture the reality of the women's lives. That moment is fixed in my memory, and strengthens my resolve to engage in work that is rooted in women's experiences. Only then can we fully appreciate the factors that bring women into conflict with the law.

Invisible Women

For too long, women were virtually invisible in academic discourse on crime and the criminal justice system. Despite the use of generic terms — such as "criminal," "defendant," or "delinquent" — criminology has historically been about men. More often than not, criminologists simply gave no consideration to women.

Examining the official statistics on crime helps make some sense of the male-centredness of criminology. In any one year, women are charged with no more than 20 percent of Criminal Code offences in Canada, so men constitute the majority of those charged. Nevertheless, although this crime-by-sex ratio has long been recognized, most criminologists never stopped to question it. Instead, they proceeded to develop theories of crime causation that took men as their subject, and then framed a general theory of crime applicable to the whole population. As one example, Robert Merton's (1938) anomie theory was offered as a general theory explaining crime in relation to the strain that results from the disjunction between culture goals (like monetary success) and institutionalized means (education, jobs). While Merton's theory reflected a sensitivity to the class inequalities that exist in society, the same could not be said of his awareness of gender inequalities. If lower-class individuals were more likely to engage in crime because of a lack of access to the institutionalized means for achieving monetary success alone, then it follows that women — who, as a group, experience a similar lack of access — should also be found to commit an equal share of crime as a consequence of this strain. But the statistics tell us that this is not the case.

When women did come into view in mainstream criminological theories, they were understood in relation to a male standard or measuring rod, and typically judged to be lacking. Albert Cohen's (1955) subcultural theory, for instance, was premised on a male-centred conception of U.S. society. Cohen singled out values, such as ambition, individualism, achievement and emotional restraint, as constituting "the American way of life." In effect, what he describes are those traits traditionally associated with the hegemonic male role. Women — who are described by Cohen as "inactive, unambitious, uncreative, and lazy" — are simply relegated to the sidelines.

Feminist criminologists took issue with the male-centredness of the discipline, pointing out that the mainstream theories of crime were really "malestream." To remedy this bias, these scholars argued that feminist criminology would have to transgress the boundaries of traditional criminology, to start from outside criminological discourse in order to understand better the social worlds of women and girls. In carrying out this project, feminist criminologists drew inspiration from the movement to end violence against women.

Transgressing Criminology: The Issue of Male Violence against Women

At the same time as feminists were fashioning their critiques of criminology, the women's movement was breaking the silence around the issue of male violence against women. This violence was understood as a manifestation of patriarchy — the systemic and individual power that men exercise over women — and various studies revealed the violence to be a widespread and pervasive phenomenon. For instance, in 1993, Statistics Canada released the findings of the Violence Against Women (VAW) Survey. The first survey of its kind anywhere in the world, the VAW Survey included responses from 12,300 women. Using definitions of physical and sexual assault consistent with the *Criminal Code*, the survey found that one-half of Canadian women had experienced at least one incident of physical or sexual violence since the age of sixteen. The survey also found that 29 percent of ever-married women had been assaulted by a spouse.

The work of the movement to end violence against women allowed feminist criminologists to break away from mainstream criminology, which had been complicit in the social silencing of the issue of male violence against women. Official statistics suggested that crimes like rape were relatively infrequent in their occurrence. Victim surveys — which asked respondents whether they had been victimized by crime — indicated that the group most at risk of victimization was young men, not women. Most mainstream criminologists took these data sources at face value. They seldom questioned whether (and why) acts like rape might be underreported, undercharged, or under- or unsuccessfully prosecuted, or the extent to which victim surveys had been constructed in ways that excluded the behaviours women feared most. Much of traditional criminology also tended to mirror widely held cultural myths about male violence against women — myths, such as that women "ask for it" by their dress or behaviour. In these terms, the issue of violence against women pointed to significant bias and knowledge gaps in mainstream criminology: this encouraged a host of studies by feminist criminologists intent on rectifying this omission.

In revealing the widespread and pervasive nature of male violence against women, the movement also raised the issue of the impact that experiences of violence have on women who come into conflict with the law. Several quantitative studies in the 1990s began to expose the extent of abuse experienced by women caught up in the criminal justice system. In interviewing women serving federal sentences, Margaret Shaw and her colleagues (1991) found that 68 percent had been physically abused as children or adults, and 53 percent were sexually abused at some point in their lives. Among Aboriginal women, the figures were considerably higher: 90 percent said that they had been physically abused, and 61 percent reported sexual abuse (Shaw et al. 1991: vii, 31).

Influenced by these findings, as well as by the call to transgress the boundaries of criminology and discover more about the lives of women who come into conflict with the law, feminist criminologists began to engage in qualitative research.

Women in Trouble

One of the primary tasks of feminist scholarship has been to produce knowledge that is "women-centred" — knowledge that is about and for women. This task has involved placing women as knowers at the centre of the inquiry in order to produce better understandings of women and the world. In criminology, this undertaking took the form of interviewing women who were caught up in the net of the criminal justice system to find out more about their lives. A key focus of this research was the link between women's victimization and their criminal involvement.

In the United States, Mary Gilfus (1992) conducted life-history interviews with twenty incarcerated women to understand their entry into street crime. Most of these women had grown up with violence, and violence was a common feature in their relationships with men. Themes that marked the women's transitions from childhood to adulthood included repeated victimization experiences, drug addiction, involvement in the sex trade, relationships with men involved in street crime and the demands of mothering.

Working in Canada, Ellen Adelberg and Claudia Currie (1987) reported on the lives of seven women sentenced to federal terms of imprisonment. Regularly occurring themes in these women's lives include "poverty, child and wife battering, sexual assault, [and] women's conditioning to accept positions of submissiveness and dependency upon men," which led Adelberg and Currie to conclude: "The problems suffered by women offenders are similar to the problems suffered by many women in our society, only perhaps more acutely" (1987: 68, 98).

My own work, *Women in Trouble* (Comack 1996), was built around the stories of twenty-four incarcerated women. The women's stories revealed complex connections between women's law violations and their history of abuse. Sometimes the connections are direct, as in the case of women sent to prison for resisting their abusers. Janice, for instance, was serving a sentence for manslaughter. She talked about how the offence occurred at a party:

> I was at a party, and this guy, older guy, came, came on to me. He tried telling me, "Why don't you go to bed with me. I'm getting some money, you know." And I said, "No." And then he started hitting me. And then he raped me. And then [pause] I lost it. Like, I just, I went, I got very angry and I snapped. And I started hitting him. I threw a coffee table on top of his head and then I stabbed him. (Comack 1996: 96)

Sometimes the connections only become discernible after a woman's law violations are located in the context of her struggle to cope with abuse and its effects. Merideth's long history of abuse began with her father sexually assaulting her as a young child and extended to several violent relationships with men. She was imprisoned for bouncing cheques and reported writing the cheques to purchase "new things to keep her mind off the abuse": "I've never had any kind of conflict with the law. [long pause] When I started dealing with all these different things, then I started having problems. And then I took it out in the form of fraud" (Comack 1996: 86).

Sometimes the connections are even more entangled, as in the case of women who end up on the street, where abuse and law violation become enmeshed in their ongoing, everyday struggle to survive. Another woman in prison, Brenda, described her life on the street:

Street life is a, it's a power game, you know? Street life? You have to show you're tough. You have to beat up this broad or you have to shank [knife] this person, or, you know, you're always carrying guns, you always have blow [cocaine] on you, you always have drugs on you, and you're always working the streets with the pimps and the bikers, you know? That, that alone, you know, it has so much fucking abuse, it has more abuse than what you were brought up with!… I find living on the street I went through more abuse than I did at home. (Comack 1996: 105–06)

Drawing out the connections between women's experiences of victimization and their law-breaking activities had the overall benefit of locating women's law violations in a broader social context characterized by inequalities of class, race and gender.

With regard to class inequalities, feminist criminologists drew the connections between women's involvement in crime and the feminization of poverty. In recent decades, poverty has increasingly taken on a "female face" — especially in terms of the number of single-parent families headed by women. In 2003, the poverty rate for single-parent mothers in Canada was 49 percent, the highest rate for any family type (National Council of Welfare 2006). As more and more women are confronted with the task of making ends meet under dire circumstances, the link between poverty and women's lawbreaking becomes more obvi-ous. As Margaret Jackson (1999: 201) has observed: "Over 80% of all incarcerated women in Canada are in prison for poverty related offences."

In terms of racial inequalities, while Aboriginal people in Canada are disproportionately represented in crime statistics, the over-representation of Aboriginal women in Canadian prisons is even greater than that of Aboriginal men. Although Aboriginal adults only account for 3 percent of the Canadian population, they accounted for 22 percent of admissions to sentenced custody in 2007/2008; 24 percent of women serving a custodial sentence in the provincial/territorial system were Aboriginal, compared to 17 percent of men (Perreault 2009).

The figures for the Prairie region are even more troubling. According to a one-day snap-shot of persons held in provincial custody in Manitoba on September 6, 2000, 63 percent (731 of 1153) of men in custody were Aboriginal while 73 percent (41 of 56) of the women were Aboriginal (AJIC 2001). Aboriginal women are incarcerated for more violent offences (homicide, assault, robbery) than are non-Aboriginal women, and alcohol has played a role in the offences of twice as many Aboriginal women in prison as it has for Aboriginal men. Making sense of these patterns involves acknowledging how the historical forces that have shaped Aboriginal experience — colonization, residential schooling, economic and politi-cal marginalization, and forced dependency on the state — have culminated in a situation in which violence, drugging and drinking have reached epidemic proportions in many Aboriginal communities.

Attention to gender inequality — and its interconnections with race and class — has assisted in explaining some forms of sex-trade work. According to Holly Johnson and Karen Rodgers (1993: 101), women's involvement in prostitution is a reflection of their subordinate social and economic position in society: "Prostitution thrives in a society which values women more for their sexuality than for their skilled labour, and which puts women in a class of commodity to be bought and sold. Research has shown one of the major causes of prostitu-tion to be the economic plight of women, particularly young, poorly educated women who have limited *legitimate* employment records" (emphasis in the original).

In learning more about the lives of women and the troubles that have brought them into conflict with the law (problems with drugs and alcohol use, histories of violence and abuse, lack of education and job skills, and struggles to provide and care for their children), feminist criminologists have endeavoured to understand these women's lives in terms of the structured inequalities in society that have contoured and constrained their choices. In the process, feminist criminologists have contributed to the advocacy work of organizations such as the Canadian Association of Elizabeth Fry Societies in their struggle for justice and equality for criminalized women (see: elizabethfry.ca; Horri, Parkes and Pate 2006). Their work has transformed the discipline of criminology. No longer can criminologists be content to fashion theories that ignore gender. Bringing women into view has also led to the realization that women are not the only ones with a gender — men's lives too need to be situated in gendered terms.

REFERENCES

Adelberg, E., and C. Currie. 1987. "In Their Own Words: Seven Women's Stories." In E. Adelberg and C. Currie (eds.), *Too Few to Count: Canadian Women in Conflict with the Law*. Vancouver: Press Gang.

AJIC (Aboriginal Justice Implementation Commission). 2001. *Final Report*. Winnipeg, Manitoba.

Cohen, Albert. *Delinquent Boys*. Glencoe, IL: Free Press.

Comack, E. 1996. *Women in Trouble*. Halifax: Fernwood Publishing.

Gilfus, M. 1992. "From Victims to Survivors to Offenders: Women's Routes of Entry and Immersion into Street Crime." *Women and Criminal Justice* 4, 1.

Horri, G., D. Parkes and K. Pate. 2006. "Are Women's Rights Worth the Paper They're Written On? Collaborating to Enforce the Human Rights of Criminalized Women." In G. Balfour and E. Comack (eds.), *Criminalizing Women: Gender and (In)justice in Neo-liberal Times*. Halifax: Fernwood Publishing.

Jackson, M. 1999. "Canadian Aboriginal Women and Their 'Criminality': The Cycle of Violence and the Context of Difference." *The Australian and New Zealand Journal of Criminology* 32,2.

Johnson, H., and K. Rodgers. 1993. "A Statistical Overview of Women and Crime in Canada." In E. Adelberg and C. Currie (eds.), *In Conflict with the Law: Women and the Canadian Criminal Justice System*. Vancouver: Press Gang.

Merton, Robert. 1938. "Social Structure and Anomie." *American Sociological Review* 3 (October).

National Council of Welfare. 2006. "Women and Poverty." At: ncwcnbes.net.

Perreault, S. 2009. "The Incarceration of Aboriginal People in Adult Correctional Services." *Juristat* 29,3 (July).

Shaw, M., K. Rodgers, J. Blanchette, T. Hattem, L.S. Thomas and L. Tamarack. 1991. *Survey of Federally Sentenced Women: Report of the Task Force on Federally Sentenced Women*. User Report 1991-4. Ottawa: Corrections Branch, Ministry of Solicitor General of Canada.

90

Where Are the Women?
Gender Equity, Budgets and Canadian Public Policy

Janine Brodie and Isabella Bakker

Gender-Based Policy Capacity

In the past thirty years, Canadians have witnessed both a marked rise and precipitous decline in the importance attributed to gender in the development of social policy and in the pursuit of the broader social goals of gender equality and inclusive citizenship. Although gender continues to be a central factor informing policy development among international institutions, such as the United Nations, various international development agencies, and, to a lesser extent, the European Union, gender equality has progressively fallen off the political radar in many Western democracies. In Anglo-American democracies, such as Canada and Australia, where neoliberal governing assumptions have been embraced, the policy goal of achieving gender equality have been systematically displaced in the last decade through the prioritization of child- and family-centred initiatives, market principles, and individual self-reliance (Brodie 2002). The combined effect of these new currents in social policy thinking, as Anne Summers (2003: 6), a former head of the Australian Office of the Status of Women, has observed, suggests that "we have come to the end of equality."

In the early 1970s, Canada emerged as a leader among developed countries in the development of policies and agencies designed to enhance the status of women in all sectors of society, and provide them with points of entry into the policy-making process. The 1970 Report of the Royal Commission on the Status of Women (RCSW) was instrumental to this process. In all, the Commission made 167 recommendations, some 122 of which were exclusively federal responsibilities. The RCSW is widely recognized as having set much of the political and legislative agenda for the Canadian women's movement for the 1970s and beyond (Brodie 1995: 42–44).

One of the most immediate impacts of the RCSW was the elaboration of a network of gender-based policy machinery within the federal government — one of the most elaborate in the world at the time. In 1971, the Office of the Coordinator for the Status of Women was established within the Privy Council Office, and a year later the Women's Program was set up within the Citizenship Branch of the Secretary of State. Its mandate was "the development of a society in which the full potential of women as citizens is recognized and utilized" (Burt 1994: 216). This mandate reflected the prevailing governing philosophy at the time that state funding of disadvantaged groups enriched both Canadian democracy and the public policy process by making it more responsive to community needs and priorities. Guided by this commitment, federal funding for the Women's Program grew from a meager $233,000 in 1973 to $12.4 million in 1987, leaving in its wake a mosaic of national feminist organizations with the resources to generate research on women's issues, lobby government and hold it accountable, as well as a vibrant mix of grassroots women's organizations that provided education, shelters and services to women marginalized by, for example, abuse, immigrant status and poverty (Burt and Hardman 2001: 204). In 1973, this gender-based infrastructure was further developed with the establishment of the Canadian Advisory Council on the Status of Women (CACSW), an arm's-length organization designed to provide policy advice to the federal government and to liaise with the organized women's movement. In 1976, the Office of the Coordinator was moved out of the Privy Council Office and expanded into an interdepartmental co-ordinating agency — Status of Women Canada — and linked into the federal cabinet through the creation of a Minister Responsible for the Status of Women.

During these years, many Canadian provinces also followed the federal example, setting up some form of gender-based policy machinery or advisory mechanism. By the mid-1980s, most provinces had two, if not three, vehicles for policy advice. Most provinces had some form of advisory council, which generally was created through provincial legislation, consisting of appointees supported by permanent employees or civil servants, and funded by government (in the earlier years, both provincial and federal), predominantly reported either to the provincial executive office or to a minister responsible for the status of women. Most provinces, especially during the 1980s, developed policy machinery inside of provincial bureaucracies in the form of a women's bureau, directorate, or secretariat. However, almost as quickly as this policy infrastructure was set in place, broader social and political forces began to erode both the resources afforded these units to build community alliances and influence government actors, and the very saliency attributed to gender and gender equality in the policy-making process. In the current era, both the gendered focus of social policy and the broad social goal of advancing gender equality have been virtually erased from the policy agendas of Canada's governments.

The disappearance of women — both as a focus of public policy and as a distinct political constituency — began in the mid-1980s and accelerated during the 1990s. This erasure began with the *delegitimization* of women's groups, indeed of virtually all equality-seeking groups as relevant voices in the policy process. This process also eroded the legitimacy accorded to gender units inside of government. Often viewed as a backlash against second wave feminism, this phase was followed by the *dismantling* of much of the gender-based policy capacity within the federal government and in many of the provinces. Finally, women largely *disappeared* from social policy debates. Children were identified as the central, if not only legitimate objects of ameliorative social policy, and the women were re-defined, especially in social assistance policy, as genderless individuals with the obligation to be self-sufficient (Brodie 2007).

Delegitimization

The progressive delegitimization of a "women's voice" in the Canadian policy process began in the mid-1980s and coincided with the ascendancy of neoliberal governing practices, as well as a broader wave of social conservatism that swept over many Western democracies during these years. In Canada, a newly elected Progressive Conservative government (1984) rather quickly ran into political opposition from the organized women's movement, especially from its flagship, the National Action Committee on the Status of Women (NAC), which strongly objected to the new government's legislative

agenda of reducing the state, dismantling universal social programs, empowering the market, and, further into its mandate, striking a free trade deal with the United States. Later in the 1980s, feminism and feminists were regularly disparaged in political debate and in the popular media and, along with other equality-seeking groups, labelled as "special interest" groups. According to this construction, "special interests" stood outside of and in opposition to the interests of "ordinary" Canadians, while federal funding of such groups served only to skew policy priorities and to waste scarce (and undeserved) public resources (Brodie 1995). It was argued that so-called special interest organizations should be funded, not by the public, but by the private constituencies they represented (Dobrowolsky 2004:

187). In other words, equality-seeking groups were considered lobbyists, and should be treated as such.

The rhetoric of special interests, largely imported from the American social conservative movement, veiled a broader backlash against mainstream feminism and its interface with the post-war welfare state. The increasingly unchallenged construction of equality-seeking groups as "special interests" also contributed to the waning influence of gender-based agencies within the federal bureaucracy. Between 1987 and 1990, for example, the Conservative government cut funds to community groups, shelters, and targeted services, while meager injections of new funding were largely confined to the Canadian Panel on Violence Against Women (1991), as well as related educational and infrastructural initiatives following the 1990 Montreal massacre of 14 women engineering students (Burt and Hardman 2001: 205). Even in the face of this tragedy, the problem of violence against women was progressively re-named and policies reformulated as one of "family violence," and funding targeted to women's groups doing anti-violence work was cut substantially.

Dismantling

The delegitimization of gender-based citizenship claims on the state was soon followed by the dismantling of much of the federal government's gender-based policy capacity, especially after the election of the new Liberal government in 1993. The Canadian Advisory Council on the Status of Women was closed in 1995. Similarly, the federal government's Women's Program, which was charged with providing operational and project funding to women's organizations, was folded into Status of Women Canada (Dobrowolsky 2004: 176–182). In 1995, the Minister Responsible for the Status of Women was downgraded to the lower status of Secretary of State Responsible for the Status of Women, and thus a designated space for the articulation of women's interests around the federal cabinet table was lost. During these same years, the Status of Women Canada was progressively downsized and shifted to the margins of the social policy field, most recently being housed under the umbrella of Canadian Heritage. Gendered identity, it would appear, is now coded as just one of many identities that make up the Canadian multicultural mosaic, rather than as a fundamental structuring principle informing the daily lives of Canadians, and a critical component of citizenship equality.

These many changes in the organization of Canada's policy machinery coincided with the federal government's enthusiastic endorsement of gender mainstreaming and gender-based analysis (GBA) in its 1996 Federal Plan for Gender Equality. The federal plan committed the government to an encompassing implementation of gender-based analysis in the development of policies, programs, and legislation (Status of Women Canada 2002: 3). Many academics caution that there are both opportunities and constraints associated with this governing instrument. For example, GBA may not be sufficiently attentive to differences in the needs and priorities of women variously situated by family status, race, sexuality, ethnicity, or class. Neither can GBA effectively engage with the assumptions informing new policy initiatives (Burt and Hardman 2001: 208–211). Gender-based analysis can also be implemented as an in-house and technocratic exercise that erodes the link between government agencies and the broader community.

The dismantling process also can be clearly tracked at the provincial level, especially in Canada's richest provinces. In 1996 Alberta became the first province to dismantle its gender-based policy machinery when it eliminated the Alberta Advisory Council on Women's Issues. This arbitrary action met considerable resistance, both from provincial women's groups and opposition parties in the legislature (Harder 2003). The government's response to these objections was characteristic of the kinds of arguments that have been made in Canada and elsewhere by governments determined to dismantle their gender-based policy machinery. One typical response has been that women's organizations have matured and strengthened to the point where they no longer need public support to maintain their capacity to speak to government. The other typical argument rallied against women's policy agencies was that women are too diverse a constituency to be represented by a single agency.

The gender units of other provinces, which have not so sharply turned toward neoliberal governing practices, however, share a number of common experiences. First, they report that their budgetary allocations have decreased or remained virtually frozen for the past decade. Second, in many provinces, once-autonomous advisory councils now either have been folded into the permanent bureaucracy or communicate with government through actors in the permanent bureaucracy. Finally, many provincial units report the increasing tendency for provincial governments to demand business plans that effectively narrow the range of their research and consultation activities.

Disappearance

In addition to the delegitimization of a women's voice and the dismantling of gender units within the state machinery, women as an analytic category in social policy development disappeared, resulting in the erosion of women's equality as a central goal of Canadian public policy. We focus here on the elevation of the child (and family) as the priority constituency of social policy reform. This development involved what Lister (2004) called "the politics of renaming." As Dobrowolsky and Jenson (2004: 172) rightly reminded us, "Representational adjustments to the names of claimants is significant" in understanding how social policy is framed, which social actors are considered as legitimate claimants, what kinds of policy interventions are considered appropriate and by whom. However, although contemporary social problems may be framed and analyzed *as if* gender is no longer relevant, the gendered underpinning of these same social problems do not disappear. To the contrary, they tend to intensify (Bakker and Gill 2003; Brodie 2003).

The ascendancy of the child as the iconic subject of social policy reaches back to the late-1980s when the federal government, following a growing international trend, pledged to end child poverty by the turn of the millennium (McKeen 2003: 94–101). Following the ratification of the U.N.'s Convention on the Rights of the Child in 1991, the Mulroney government embarked on its "child's agenda," concentrating its energies particularly on children at risk. The federal government's almost singular concern with the child and children's poverty intensified during the Chrétien years, especially after the introduction of the Canadian Child Tax Benefit and subsequent elaborations such as the National Child Benefit and the Child Disability Benefit.

The goal of eliminating child poverty in Canada was both overdue and necessary; but, in many ways, the elevation of the abstract "poor child" as the focus of social policy reform incorrectly specified the policy problem. As poverty groups have emphasized time and again, the feminization of poverty is a root cause of child poverty, but the gendered structures of inequality in Canada's labour markets and in society do not enter into a child-centred policy frame (Dobrowolsky and Jenson 2004: 174). Rather, this "politics of naming" effectively set up an opposition between the child and other disadvantaged groups: as a dichotomy between the deserving and undeserving poor, as well as between child and parent. The federal government's agenda for children fails to acknowledge the inescapable fact that, in the vast majority of cases, poor children live with poor women who experience poverty in many different ways. In the absence of policies and programs addressing the structural basis of women's poverty, a childcare agenda is unlikely to meet its primary objective of reducing child poverty (Paterson et al. 2004: 140).

NOTE

Janine Brodie and Isabella Bakker, 2008, *Where Are The Women? Gender Equity, Budgets, and Canadian Public Policy*, Ottawa, Canadian Council for Policy Alternatives. Adapted and reprinted with permission.

REFERENCES

Bakker, Isabella, and Stephen Gill. 2003. "Global Political Economy and Social Reproduction." In Isabella Bakker and Stephen Gill (eds.), *Power, Production, and Social Reproduction*. London: Palgrave.

Brodie, Janine. 2003. "Globalization, In/Security, and the Paradoxes of the Social." In Isabella Bakker and Stephen Gill (eds.), *Power, Production, and Social Reproduction*. London: Palgrave.

Brodie, Janine. 1995. *Politics on the Margins: Restructuring and the Canadian Women's Movement*. Halifax: Fernwood Publishing.

Burt, Sandra. 1994. "The Women's Movement: Working to Transform Public Policy." In James Bickerton and Alain Gagnon (eds.), *Canadian Politics* second ed. Peterborough, ON: Broadview Press.

Burt, Sandra, and Sonya Hardman,=. 2001. "The Case of Disappearing Targets: The Liberals and Gender Equality." In Leslie Pal (ed.), *How Ottawa Spends, 2001–2002: Power in Transition*. Toronto: Oxford University Press.

Dobrowolsky, Alexandra. 2004. "The Chrétien Liberal Legacy and Women: Changing Policy Priorities with Little Cause for Celebration." *Review of Constitutional Studies* 9,1–2.

Dobrowolsky, Alexandra, and Jane Jenson. 2004. "Shifting Representations of Citizenship: Canadian Politics of Women and Children." *Social Politics* 1,2.

Harder, Lois. 2003. *States of Struggle: Feminism and Politics in Alberta*. Edmonton: University of Alberta Press.

Lister, Ruth. 2004. *Poverty*. Cambridge: Polity Press.

McKeen, Wendy. 2003. *Money in Their Own Name: The Feminist Voice in Poverty Debate in Canada*. Toronto: University of Toronto Press.

Paterson, Stephanie, Karine Levasseur and Tatyana Teplova. 2004. "I Spy with My Little Eye… Canada's National Child Benefit." In Bruce Doern (ed.), *How Ottawa Spends: Mandate Change in the Paul Martin Era*. Montreal: McGill-Queen's University Press.

Summers, Anne. 2003. *The End of Equality: Work, Babies, and Women's Choices in the 21st Century*. Sydney: Random House

Status of Women Canada. 200. "Resources: Gender Equity Consultation." At: swc-cfc.gc.ca/resources/consultations/ges09-2005/intro e.html.

Status of Women Canada. 2007. At: swc-cfc.gc.ca/newroom/news2007/0307–2_e.html.

CHANGING THE WORLD: ACTIVISM FOR EQUITY

C. Lesley Biggs

Women's rights — which we too often take for granted these days — are a relatively new development in history, and therefore still quite fragile. Which is why we must keep the torch of equality burning brightly. Let us continue to fuel the flame and ensure we pass it on, from woman to woman, mother to daughter — as well as mother to son — generation to generation. (Michäelle Jean, 2007, former Governor-General of Canada, Special Envoy to UNESCO)

Until all of us have made it, none of us have made it. (Rosemary Brown, the first black woman elected to the Canadian House of Parliament, cited in Munroe 2009)

Lessons from the Abortion Caravan

After a 3,000 mile trek from Vancouver, the Abortion Caravan, "a convoy of young women — coat hangers and a black coffin in tow," arrived on Parliament Hill in Ottawa on Mother's Day, May 12, 1970 (Ormsby 2010). According to Mary Ormsby (2010) of the *Toronto Star*, "Hundreds of women rallied for two days at Parliament and some 50 disrupted the sitting House of Commons, chaining themselves to seats and chanting 'free abortions on demand.'" The protesters were determined "to push the [abortion] issue from shameful silence into the national consciousness." Back in 1970, two thousand women Canadian women died in 1970 as a result of back alley or self-induced abortions while another 20,000 women were hospitalized for botched ones. Prior to 1969, abortion was illegal. In 1969, the Criminal Code was amended to decriminalize abortions, and a woman could get one if it was approved by a hospital Therapeutic Abortion Committee.

The Abortion Caravan was the first Canadian national-scale feminist protest. According to Judy Rebick (cited in Gallop 2007), " [The protesters] put abortion on the map; they put birth control on the map; and they put a grassroots women's movement on the map." Donning the trappings of respectability (stockings, coiffed hair, make-up, and gloves), these young women "shocked" Canadians, writes Ormsby, with their bold action, which shut down Parliament for the first time in its history. The Abortion Caravan not only signalled the birth of the national women's movement in Canada and laid the foundation for a well-organized pro-choice move-ment, but the protest also reframed our understanding of "rebellion" from bloody battles fought primarily by men (for example, the Lower and Upper Canada Rebellions of 1937–38) to include women's fight to control their reproductive labour" (Sethna cited in Gallop 2007).

Despite its importance, the Abortion Caravan has all but disappeared from history (but perhaps not herstory!), rarely making it into the textbooks. Yet *This Magazine* has dubbed the Abortion Caravan as one of the four[1] "most underrated rebellions in Canadian history" (Gallop et al. 2007); coverage of this event rarely makes it into history textbooks even though, "it has had a lasting effect on this country" (Gallop et al. 2007). Women's right to control their own fertility has had tremendous implications both for women's economic and social autonomy and freedom, and for the wellbeing of families who seek to give their children the best life possible by limiting the number of children for which they must provide.

But, the struggle for reproductive freedom is not over. Writing in 2009, Vicki Saporta reports that "access to abortion in Canada is still patchy," with services unevenly distributed throughout Canada. Although the birth rate among teenage women has declined significantly since the 1970s, the teenage pregnancy rate remains high (14.5 per 1,000 live births). The effects of this have short and long term health, social and economic consequences, and disproportionately affect women who are poor (Rotterman 2007). Finally, after not responding to the International Planned Parenthood Federation's application in the spring of 2009, the Conservative government under the leadership of Stephen Harper has not, as of April 2011, reinstated funds ($18 million) to the group, which provides sexual and reproductive health services in over 180 countries, many in the Global South (Mayeda and Warren 2011).

The brief account of the Abortion Caravan demonstrates the need to retain a collective memory of past events and practices. Remembering events like the Abortion Caravan helps "to keep the torch of equality burning brightly," a need that Michäelle Jean reminds us of in this chapter's first epigraph. Most Canadian women — all of the opinion polls confirm this view — do not want to return to the days when abortion was illegal and women paid dearly, sometimes with their lives, to end an unwanted pregnancy. That same knowledge should also enable us to empathize and connect with women in those many parts of the world where maternal mortality rates are extraordinarily high so that we can support them in their struggle for reproductive rights as they define them. Restoration of the funds for International Planned Parenthood is one way to support this goal. Knowledge of events such as the Abortion Caravan should be shared from one generation to the next, as Jean suggests — not, in my view, as a nostalgic rendering of past achievements, but rather as collective memory shedding light on the ways in which the past shapes and constrains the present. Doing so helps us understand the dilemmas posed by old and emerging rationalities.

Recounting he history of the Abortion Caravan also provides a poignant example of what Michäelle Jean so aptly referred to as "the fragility of women's rights." Despite the extraordinary efforts and gains that the women's movement here in Canada and globally have made, most of these rights remain contested, and a gap often exists between formal rights enshrined in law and women's daily lives. Moreover, as Brodie and Bakker (see Chapter 90) indicate, women have lost ground in some important areas as women-specific representation has been all but erased within the state and funding for women's non-governmental organizations has been slashed. As a result, many women's groups have been forced to re-orient their programs to projects of interest to federal or provincial governments, or to abandon advocacy for research altogether.

The academic disciplines of Women's and/or Gender Studies have also been subject to scrutiny within the academy, and in some cases, Women's Studies departments have been closed down. Moreover, this interdisciplinary field of study has also come under attack by national newspaper columnists. For example, an editorial appearing in the *National Post* (2010) argued that "The radical feminism behind these [Women's Studies] courses has done untold damage to families, our court systems, labour laws, constitutional freedoms and even the ordinary relations between men and women." In response to critics of the editorial, Barbara Kay (2010) declares, "Women's Studies are nothing more than political activism with a blackboard, not objective scholarship."

Kay has a long history attacking feminism (see her website at: barbarakay.ca), but this rant against Women's Studies was in response to the debate within the Canadian Women's Studies community about the name changes of academic departments and programs from "Women's Studies" to some combinations of "Women's Studies," "Gender Studies," "Sexuality Studies," or "Equality Studies." The loss of the name "Women's Studies" was lamented by Catherine Porter (2009) in the *Toronto Star*. Kay and Porter sparred off on the Canadian Broadcasting Corporation's morning program *The Current*, hosted by Anna-Marie Tremonti. The show itself became a site of controversy, resulting in a follow-up interview with Ann Braithwaite, a professor and Co-ordinator of Women's Studies at the University of Prince Edward Island, who co-authored *Troubling Women's Studies: Pasts, Presents and Possibilities*.

Kay, of course, is entitled to her opinion (after all, Canada is a democracy that prides itself on free speech), but her opinion is just that: an opinion that is ironically not based on systematic research, given that she accuses Women's Studies of being biased. Rather Kay seems to take delight in skewering the work of early second wave feminists, presenting them as if they were representative of all feminism, while also ignoring feminist criticism of these earlier ideas and almost any other issue. Moreover, Kay is not particularly literate about the use of statistics; she argues, for example, that men are also victims of violence, and, therefore, women can no longer claim to be the only victims. Most feminists do not dispute the fact that men/boys are victims, even though the statistics indicate that most perpetrators of violence are men. But, they also take into account the gendered and racialized nature of violence and whether it is related to sexual orientation; i.e., the type of violence, the gender/racialized status and sexual identity of the victim and offender, and under what circumstances (intimate versus stranger) the violence takes place, and where (public versus private spaces). (For more details, see the Hypatia Index at Section 4.) The result is a more complex picture, one that does not pit women/girls against men/boys.

Kay, however, is right about one thing, though: the debate over the name change signals fundamental changes taking place within "Women's and/or Gender Studies," but this shift is not just to get more people into Women's Studies or related courses and programs, as she claims, because enrolment is an issue for many disciplines in Arts and Sciences across Canada. Rather, the name change represents the acceptance of the diversity among women and between women and men, the intersections of gender, race/ethnicity, ability, sexual orientation and age. The debate is, therefore, consistent with Rosemary Brown's assertion, "Until all of us have made it, none of us have made it." However, the question, and the source of much debate within feminism as we saw in the Introduction for Section 1, is how to incorporate recognition of differences while retaining the core objectives of feminism (McLaughlin 2003: 11).

What is the future of feminism? Some — both feminists and non-feminists — would say that, like every other movement before it, feminism has outlived its usefulness, having become anachronistic, or they would say the battle for equality has been won, and Barbara Kay would applaud the end of feminism. The evidence, however, doesn't support the view that feminism is no longer relevant. Various structured inequalities persist, but the social, political, economic and cultural forces that helped to usher the second wave onto the political stage in Western industrialized countries no longer exist; the question is whether feminists can adapt to a changing world in order to advance its projects.

Other feminists worry about the future of academic feminism as opposed to feminist movements or projects. With the institutionalization of feminism in universities, the fear is that academic feminism has been or will be captured by institutional requirements (e.g., the demands of tenure and promotion, the obligation to secure outside funding and the need to attract students). As a result, academic feminists will be rewarded for what is seen as elitist theorizing that bears little or no relationship to day-to-day lives of "real" women; and/or the ties between academic feminists other equity-seeking groups advocating for social change will be strained, if not severed (McLaughlin 2003).

On a more optimistic note, the debates within feminism are also sources of innovation and creativity as they push the boundaries of knowledge. But feminism requires a new agenda, one that "acknowledges both new times and important continuities" (McLaughlin 2003: 19). Uncertain times require living with uncertainty, which can be both liberating and anxiety producing. Ahmed et al. (2000) argue that "Feminism must refuse to (re)present itself as programmatic, *as having an object which can always be successfully translated into a final end or outcome*" (cited in McLaughlin 2003: 20, emphasis in the original). For example, unlike second wave feminism, which drew firm distinctions between the sex/gender divide, third wave feminism, particularly the branch that engages in cultural production, has sought to "trouble" the naturalization of the dualistic systems of sex/gender and sexuality by eliding masculinities and femininities, and homosexualities and heterosexualities, leading to individuals who identify themselves as genderqueer and who occupy "a third space" in which all genders, regardless of their expression, are celebrated (see, for example, genderqueer-revolution.org/gqr/home.html). Even the category of sex itself has been challenged as the emergence of transsexual individuals confront not only patriarchal assumptions about biological sex, but also earlier feminist analyses that argued that sex was the substrate upon which gender identities were constructed.

One of the significant differences between second and third wave feminisms is organizing across communities. The development of the new communication technologies such as the Internet and cell phones has provided novel opportunities for networking, coalition building and creating communities that connect local activists with each other and local issues with the global. Through on-line communities, blogs and social networking sites like Facebook, a new politic has emerged that involves bringing together seemingly different communities often focussed on one issue/activity while cutting across what would have been previously seen as political divisions in order to achieve practical solutions. Sometimes these communities have a fleeting existence; having made their point, they disappear. Others develop into powerful organizations, which, with instantaneous communication, can respond quickly to new challenges.

Of course, the new information technologies are not inherently benign; the digital divide creates new ways of structuring inequality between the "haves" and the "have nots," who don't have access to computers and the Internet. This divide is deeply embedded in class, gender and racial relations, which affect not only individuals, but also groups and nations. In addition, the new social media pose significant threats to privacy; the sheer volume of information on the Internet is often overwhelming, requiring savvy and intelligent users of the Internet to sort out fact from fiction. Other groups are using information technologies to promote their ideas and interests that seek to sustain structured inequalities.

The new information technologies embody tensions and contradictions, and they are transforming our world at all levels — socially, politically, economically and culturally. Aldous Huxley, in his landmark book *Brave New World,* offered a dystopic vision of society in which technological advances, industrial capitalism and consumerism pose a threat to individual identity. In many ways, we face similar challenges with the development of technologies of all kinds, globalization and neoliberalism, and rampant consumerism. Feminism and its allies offer an alternative view in which a new brave world embraces social justice for all, so that all of us can make it!

In her chapter, Natalie Gerum asks, "What does it mean to be an activist?" Does this term conjure up images of "A red bandana, a smoke bomb and a placard for change? A blockade across a logging road, with people chained to trees as bulldozers inch closer?" This view of activism was true for Gerum, but it did not fit her self-mage, a straight A student in high school who did all of the "right" things and didn't challenge authority. And then in 2002, she went to the Pearson Seminar on Youth Leadership (PSYL) in Victoria, British Columbia, and met her first activist who had participated in protests, but who also "was articulate, thoughtful and friendly," and didn't fit exactly the stereotype of an activist. In the following three weeks, Gerum met many other activists of different sorts, but what united them was that they were well informed about political issues. At first Gerum was intimidated by these activists since she was not very knowledgeable, but in the safe space created at PSYL, Gerum "began to see how activist issues related to [her] and knew that [she] could get informed about these issues"; it is never too late to learn. Following Mahatma Gandhi's challenge to humanity, Gerum also learned "to be the change that [she] want[ed] to see in the world." While global events affected Gerum, she could also affect them. For Gerum, activism works at a personal and public level; it's about "actively leading a life that reflects the kind of world you want to live in, and it's about creating action beyond yourself and acting as an agent of change." But the message of Gerum's chapter is everyone needs to define for her or himself what it means to be an activist.

As a result of her experiences at PSYL, Gerum became involved in activities centred on environmental sustainability, an issue that many associate with women who, as a result of their connections to reproduction, are deemed to be the rightful protectors of "Mother Nature." But, as Maureen Reed points out in her chapter, very few analysts examine women who support resource exploitation — logging in this case. In the 1990s, the government of British Columbia introduced new regulations in the management of land use toward greater protection of forest ecosystems. This shift in government policy, supported by environmentalists, threatened the livelihoods of those working in the logging industry, leading workers and companies to unite in "massive protests" against these changes. Women, most of whom were partners of male workers employed in the industry, but some were also workers, played a frontline role in these protests.

Reed's chapter in part examines the politics of women's politics within feminism. For some feminists, women's involvement in politics is understood (both by the women themselves and by academics) as an extension of women's mothering and caring roles. This work, however, can be interpreted positively within radical, liberal, maternal or ecofeminist frameworks that centre on revaluing women's contributions in the domestic sphere. In some frameworks, the concept of women's work was used by feminists to justify metaphorically women's participation in public life. That is, women could use their domestic skills to "clean up" the nation as an extension of their nurturing and mothering roles. In other cases, women's contributions to the home were used by feminists to claim rights to household assets, support after divorce, incorporation into pension plans or recognition of domestic labour to the Gross National Product. However, women's involvement in politics can be interpreted negatively within feminist frameworks when this work is understood as an extension of patriarchal values and practices that uphold traditional views of womanhood and mothering. Reed argues that the situation is not so cut-and-dried.

Drawing on the concept of "embeddedness," Reed demonstrates that "women's perspectives and choices for activism [are] nested within local social and spatial contexts." In order to understand women's support for forestry workers, Reed argues that we need to examine the "local effects of restructuring the forest industry, changing ecologies, reorganization of government environmental and social policies, geographic and social isolation, the availability of physical and social infrastructure, local labour practices, community social norms, and gender ideologies and practices within households." As a result, Reed found that women's "support of workers, forestry practices, and forestry culture was not unified, conservative, progressive, or crassly material." In the case of forestry activism, Reed argues that the concept of embeddedness helps us "to [avoid] classifying activities into static dichotomies of 'pro' versus 'anti'" environmental actions. In what ways might "embeddedness" help you to understand activism in your community?

Midwives have assisted women all over the world for thousands of years. But a generation ago — my generation — the practice of midwifery was illegal in Canada; now it is considered a "profession," and most Canadian midwives attend university to obtain their credentials. What happened to the midwives of yesteryear? How do we account for the re-emergence of midwifery in the 1970s when women started to lobby for its legal recognition? In her chapter, Sheryl Nestel traces the history of midwifery in Ontario to the present. She argues that, starting in the mid- to late-nineteenth century, many factors accounted for the decline of midwifery including the rise of medical profession, which led to restrictive licensing laws, the reframing of pregnancy and childbirth as an illness that needed to be treated by specialists in hospitals rather than by midwives at home, the centralization of health care generally in hospitals, family responsibilities, language barriers, and the "failure" to see midwifery as a "profession" like other health-care professions. By the mid-1950s, midwifery care — by and for women — had been virtually erased from the health-care scene; it was now left in the hands of doctors and nurses.

However, two European doctors — Grantly Dick-Read and Fernand LaMaze — challenged the medical model of pregnancy and childbirth in which interventions (like forceps, episiotomies, analgesics and anesthetics) had become routine. By the 1960s, "natural" childbirth had become popular among many women, but this framework did not disrupt patriarchal assumptions about the role of women as wives and mothers, and "natural" childbirth was even hailed as a way of strengthening marriages! Feminists were critical of the gendered and racist assumptions underlying these views of womanhood, but they also supported the demedicalization of childbirth and the need for a woman-centred model for childbirth and infant care, including the option of home birth. Thus an uneasy alliance was born between "natural" childbirth and feminist health activists, as well as constituencies from the counterculture movement, British-trained midwives who were unable to practise in Canada, and women from marginalized religious communities. Politics sometimes makes strange bedfellows!

This coalition gained momentum throughout the 1970s and 1980s as more women learned the craft of midwifery through apprenticeship and self-directed study, and as the midwifery movement became more organized, forming a powerful lobby group. Ultimately, these midwives and their supporters achieved their goal and *The Midwifery Act* was passed in Ontario in 1993. At the time of writing, midwifery has been legally recognized (but not necessarily funded) in all provinces except Prince Edward Island. However not all women who practised midwifery before the legislation equally benefitted equally; immigrant, racialized women who practised in their home countries were excluded, and Aboriginal women sought to be excluded from the legislation so that they could retain their traditional practices and customs. Moreover, few women are able to access the services of a midwife despite reported high levels of satisfaction with the personal and humane care that they deliver. Demand outstrips the supply, and only a small group of women in Canada (8 percent) are able to get midwifery care, while the majority still labour under the medical model.

Activism is a practice that can take many forms, ranging from personal reflection to public participation in a variety of ways. Lois Keith, in her poem, "Tomorrow I'm Going to Rewrite the English Language," demonstrates the intersection of private/public activism as she reflects on and writes about the ambulist metaphors of power and success that are deeply embedded in our language, but that are dis-abling for those whose mobility is constrained. Telling a woman with a disability that she has to stand on her own two feet, or that she should stay one step ahead if she wants to succeed, or to stand up for herself when challenged has no relevance for Keith; in fact these metaphors border on the ridiculous for people like her. Keith argues that this way of speaking "is a very male way / To describe the world. / All this walking tall." Instead, Keith wants to rewrite the English language, "Creating the world in my own image. / Mine will be a gentler, more womanly way / To describe my progress. / I will wheel, cover and encircle." Now it's your turn to rewrite the English language in your own image. Give it a whirl!

By far most of the activism around women's issues has been done by women. But, you might say, "Well, if women want change, then they must make it happen." Or you might reason that "Men benefit from the status quo; it is not in their interests to fight for equality." But, in his chapter, Gerry Coulter argues that struggling for equality rights *is* in men's interest, and, in fact, there is no better time in history for men to engage in the democratic process. Why should men fight for equality rights? First, Coulter argues that when individuals or groups are oppressed, their talents and potential contributions to society also are suppressed. But when democratic citizenship rights are extended to all, everyone benefits because countries and communities are strengthened when everyone's talents can be expressed and utilized for the greater good. But "participation in a democratic society takes courage," Coulter argues, and he invites men, particularly young men, to take this traditional masculine value to heart. The challenge facing young men today, according to Coulter, is "[to fully embrace] democratic society as a courageous individual." When faced with conflicting messages about what it means to be a man today, young men should ask themselves, "How am I going to contribute to a more democratic society in a way that makes my life and my community a place where everyone's talents are valued?"

The second reason men should work to secure equality rights for all is that patriarchy is harmful to men. Coulter reminds us that patriarchy is not just about men dominating women, but also men dominating other men; not all men benefit equally from patriarchal privilege, and chances are that many young men have experienced "the law of the father" in their own homes, as well as other forms of male domination if they are gay or transgendered, negatively racialized/minoritized or have a disability. Many men, in their attempts to achieve the status of hegemonic masculinity, are often wounded in their quest. Having been taught to suppress their emotions, many men express frustration, anger and lack of emotional connection in other ways. Not surprisingly, compared to women, men have significantly higher rates of heart disease, car accidents, alcoholism, suicide and murder, as well as dying younger. These health and safety issues point to social problems that are often tied to masculine gender scripts that are oppressive to men — even if men don't realize it. Coulter doesn't absolve men of their responsibilities in equality for all; rather he understands that men's struggles are different than women's, but they are no less complex.

We began this book, with Lillian Allen's poem "Feminism 101," and we end with another of her poems, "Feminism 104." Of course, you will have to read it to find out what advanced feminism means — if you dare!

NOTE

1. The other three events were the Oka crisis in 1990, the Ford strike in 1945 and the Fraser Canyon War in British Columbia in 1858. For more detail, see Gallop et al. (2007).

REFERENCES

Braithwaite, Ann, Susan Heald, Susanne Luhmann and Sharon Rosenberg. 2005. *Troubling Women's Studies: Pasts, Presents and Possibilities*. Toronto: Sumach Press.

Gallop, Angie. 2007. "Abortion Caravan, 1970: Ladies Close the House." *This Magazine* (July–August). At: thismagazine.ca/issues/2007/07/risingup.php.

Gallop, Angie, Craig Saunders, Jim Stanford and Carla Tonelli. 2007: "Rising Up: The Stereotype Is Wrong. Our History Isn't that Peaceful. A Retrospective on Four Under-Appreciated Canadian Rebellions Whose Effects Are Still with Us." *This Magazine* (July–August). At: thismagazine.ca/issues/2007/07/risingup.php.

Harris, Anita. 2001. "Riding My Own Tidal Wave: Young Women's Feminist Work." *Canadian Woman Studies* 20/21,4(1).

Jean, Michäelle. 2007. "Leading by Example: Empowering the Next Generation of Canadian Women." September 30. Rideau Hall. *Archive of Women's Political Communication*. At: womenspeechachive.org/women/profile/speech/index.cfm?ProfileID=89&SpeechID=432.

Kay, Barbara, 2010. "Women's Studies Courses Are Political Activism, Not Academic Scholarship." *National Post* February 2. At: network.nationalpost.com/np/blogs/fullcomment/archive/2010/02/02/barbara-kay-women-s-studies-courses-are-political-activism-not-academic-scholarship.aspx#ixzz1RBPnI5Vd.

Mayeda, Andrew, and Jeremy Warren. 2011. "Tories Leave Planned Parenthood in Limbo over Funding." Postmedia News. At: canada.com/news/Tories+leave+Planned+Parenthood+limbo+over+funding/4651779/story.html.

Munroe, Dawn. 2009. "Women's Quotes: Equality." *Famous Women Canadian*. At: famouscanadianwomen.com/quotes/quotespage.htm#equality.

National Post, 2010. "Women's Studies Is Still with Us." January 26. At: network.nationalpost.com/np/blogs/fullcomment/archive/2010/01/26/national-post-editorial-board-women-s-studies-is-still-with-us.aspx.

Ormsby, Mary. 2010. "The Abortion Caravan Succeeded. Or Did It?" *Toronto Star* May 30. At: thestar.com/news/canada/article/816511--the-abortion-caravan-succeeded-or-did-it.

Porter, Catherine. 2009. "My Thoughts on 'Women's Studies.'" *Toronto Star* December 01. At: thestar.com/news/gta/article/732868-- porter- my-thoughts-on-women-s-studies.

Rotterman, Michelle. 2007. "Second or Subsequent Births to Teenagers." *Health Reports* 18,1(February). Ottawa: Ministry of Industry. Catalogue 82-003. At: statscan.gc.ca/pub/82-003-x/2006002/article/mothers-meres/9525-eng.pdf.

Saporta, Vicki. 2009. "Access to Abortion in Canada Still Patchy." *Toronto Star* January 28. At: thestar.com/comment/article/578265.

Tremonti, Anna-Marie. 2010. *The Current.* January 12. Canadian Broadcasting Corporation. At: cbc.ca/thecurrent/episode/2010/ 01/12/january-12-2010.

United Nations' Millennium Development Goals (MDG)[1]

MDG1: Eradicate Extreme Poverty and Hunger

Target: Year by which MDG1a is to reduce by half the proportion of people whose income is less than one dollar per day: 2015

Target: Year by which MDG1b is to achieve full and productive employment and decent work for all, including women and young people: 2015

Target: Year by which MDG1a is to reduce by half the proportion of people who suffer from hunger: 2015

Indicators: MDG1a: Proportion of population below U.S.$1 (PPP) per day; poverty gap ratio; share of poorest quintile in national consumption

MDG1b: Prevalence of underweight children under five years of age; proportion of population below minimum level of dietary energy consumption

MDG1c: Growth rate of GDP per person employed; employment-to-population ratio; proportion of employed people living below U.S.$1 (PPP) per day; proportion of own-account and contributing family workers in total employment

- Percentage decline in vulnerable employment[2] globally since 1997: 3
- Number of people in 2007 who were classified in the vulnerable employment category: 1.5 billion
- Percentage of people in 2007 who were classified in the vulnerable employment category and who were women: 51.7
- Ratio of women workers in sub-Saharan Africa and South Asia in 2007 who were classified in the vulnerable employment category: 8.1/10
- Ratio of men workers in sub-Saharan Africa and South Asia in 2007 who were classified in the vulnerable employment category: 6.4/10
- Ratio of women workers in developed countries in 2007 who were classified in the vulnerable employment category: .07/10
- Ratio of men workers in developed countries in 2007 who were classified in the vulnerable employment category: .09/10
- Female employment-to-population[3] ratio (expressed as a percent) in South East Asia in 2007: 34
- Male employment-to-population ratio (expressed as a percent) in South East Asia in 2007: 78
- Female employment-to-population ratio (expressed as a percent) in the Middle East and North Africa in 2007: 22
- Male employment-to-population ratio (expressed as a percent) in the Middle East and North Africa in 2007: 70
- Female employment-to-population ratio (expressed as a percent) in developed regions in 2007: 50

- Male employment-to-population ratio (expressed as a percent) in developed regions in 2007: 65

MDG2 Achieve Primary Universal Education

Target: Year by which the MDG2 goal is to ensure that children everywhere, boys and girls alike, will be able to complete a full course of primary schooling: 2015

Indicators: Net enrolment ratio in primary education; proportion of pupils starting grade one who reach last grade of primary; literacy rate of 15- to 24-year olds, women and men

- Percentage of children who were enrolled in primary education in 1991: 80
- Percentage of children who were enrolled in primary education in 2005: 88
- Percentage of the estimated 72 million in 2005 who were not in school and who were girls: 57
- Percentage of boy children in sub-Saharan Africa in 2005 who were enrolled in secondary education: 28
- Percentage of girl children in sub-Saharan Africa in 2005 who were enrolled in secondary education: 25
- Percentage of boy children in developed countries in 2005 who were enrolled in secondary education: 90
- Percentage of girl children in developed countries in 2005 who were enrolled in secondary education: 92
- Ratio of women to men in sub-Saharan Africa and South Asia in 2005 who were enrolled in tertiary education: 6.5/10
- Ratio of women to men in the Middle East and North Africa in 2005 who were enrolled in tertiary education: 1/1
- Ratio of women to men in Central and Eastern European, the Commonwealth of Independent States, and developed countries in 2005 who were enrolled in tertiary education: 1.2/1

MDG3: Promote Equality and Empower Women

Target: Year by which the MDG3[4] is to eliminate gender disparity in all levels of education: 2015

Indicators: Ratios of girls to boys in primary, secondary, and tertiary education; share of women in waged employment in the non-agricultural sector; proportion of seats held by women in national parliament

- Percentage of women's share of seats globally in national parliaments (lower or single house) as of June 2008: 18.4
- Percentage in women's share of waged non-agricultural employment globally — which brings significant benefits in terms of women's capacity to control income and decision-making — from 1990 to 2005: 3
- Ratio of women's share of waged non-agricultural employment globally in the Middle East, North Africa, and South Asia in 2005 compared to men's share globally: 1/4
- Ratio of women's share of waged non-agricultural employment globally in developed countries in 2005 compared to men's share globally: 4.6/10

MDG4: Reduce Child Mortality

Target: Year by which the MDG4 is to reduce the under-five child mortality by two-thirds: 2015

Indicators: Under-five mortality rate; infant mortality rate; proportion of one-year-olds immunized against measles

- Child mortality rate (deaths per 1,000 live births) in 1990: 106
- Child mortality rate (deaths per 1,000 live births) in 2005: 83
- Probability of a girl child dying before the age of 5 if she lived in sub-Saharan Africa in 2006: 144/1000
- Probability of a boy child dying before the age of 5 if he lived in sub-Saharan Africa in 2006: 156/1000
- Probability of a girl child dying before the age of 5 if she lived in South Asia in 2006: 80/1000
- Probability of a boy child dying before the age of 5 if he lived in South Asia in 2006: 75/1000
- Probability of a girl child dying before the age of 5 if she lived in the developed countries in 2006: 5/1000
- Probability of a boy child dying before the age of 5 if he lived in the developed countries in 2006: 6/1000
- Date by which the MDG4 to reduce child mortality will be achieved if the current rate of decline continues: 2045

MDG5: Improve Maternal Health

Target: Date by which the MDG5a is to reduce maternal mortality ratio by three quarters: 2015
Target: Date by which the MDG5b is to achieve universal access to reproductive health: 2015

Indicators: MDG5a: Maternal mortality ratio; proportion of births attended by skilled health personnel
MDG5b: contraceptive prevalence rate; adolescent birth rate; antenatal care coverage; unmet need for family planning

- Number of women globally who die every year during pregnancy and childbirth: 500,000
- Estimated percentage of deaths of women globally who die every year during pregnancy and childbirth that are preventable: 90
- Percentage change in number of maternal deaths from 1990 to 2005: +<7 (430 deaths per 100,000 live births up to 400)
- Ratio of maternal deaths in sub-Saharan Africa for all live births in 2005: 1/22[5]
- Number of maternal deaths (per 100,000 live births) in South Asia in 1990: 650
- Number of maternal deaths (per 100,000 live births) in South Asia in 2005: 500
- Risk of maternal deaths in developed regions in 2005: 1/8,000
- Percentage of births attended by skilled health personnel (doctors, nurses or mid-wives) in sub-Saharan Africa in 2006: 44
- Percentage of births attended by skilled health personnel (doctors, nurses or mid-wives) in South Asia in 2006: 47
- Percentage of births attended by skilled health personnel (doctors, nurses or mid-wives) in developed regions in 2006: 100

- Estimated number of women in the world who had an unmet need for family planning in 2005: 137 million
- Percentage of women in the world who used contraception in 1990: 55
- Percentage of women in the world who used contraception in 2005: 64
- Estimated change in the global maternal death rate in 2007 (including deaths that result from unsafe abortions) if unplanned pregnancies could be prevented: 1/4

MDG6: Combat HIV/AIDS, Malaria, and Other Diseases

Target: Year by which MDG6a is to have halted and reversed the spread of HIV/AIDS: 2015

Target: Year by which MDG6b is to achieve universal access to treatment for HIV/AIDS for all those who need it: 2010

Target: Year by which MDG6c is to have halted and reverse the incidence of malaria and other major diseases: 2015

Indicators: MDG6a: HIV prevalence among population aged 15 to 24 years; condom use at last high-risk sex; proportion of population aged 15 to 24 years with comprehensive correct knowledge of HIV/AIDS

MDG6b: ratio of school attendance of orphans to school attendance of non-orphans aged 10 to 14 years; MDG6c: incidence and death rates associated with malaria; proportion of children under 5 sleeping under insecticide-treated bed nets; proportion of children under 5 with fever who are treated with appropriate anti-malarial drugs; incidence, prevalence and death rates associated with tuberculosis; proportion of tuberculosis cases detected and cured under directly observed treatment short course; proportion of population with advanced HIV infection with access to anti-retroviral drugs

- Percentage of adults globally in 2007 who were living with HIV/AIDS and who were women: 50
- Percentage of women among adults living in sub-Saharan Africa living with HIV/AIDS in 1990: 54
- Percentage of women among adults living in sub-Saharan Africa living with HIV/AIDS in 2007: 60
- Percentage of women among adults living in the Caribbean living with HIV/AIDS in 1990: 24
- Percentage of women among adults living in the Caribbean living with HIV/AIDS in 2007: 43
- Percentage of women among adults living in developed regions living with HIV/AIDS in 2007: 30
- Ratio of females to males aged 15 to 24 living with HIV/AIDS in 2007 in selected African countries with high prevalence environments: 3:1
- Percentage of females and males aged 15 to 24 with comprehensive correct knowledge of HIV/AIDS living in the Congo in 2005–2006: 10 and 22 respectively
- Percentage of females and males aged 15 to 24 with comprehensive correct knowledge of HIV/AIDS living in Rwanda in 2005–2006: 51 and 54 respectively
- Percentage of pregnant women in low- and middle-income countries in 2005 who were HIV-positive and were receiving services to prevent the transmission of the virus to their newborns: 11
- Number of insecticide-treated mosquito nets (ITNs) delivered to sub-Saharan Africa between 2008 and 2010: 289 million[6]

- Number of people who were protected by insecticide-treated mosquito nets (ITNs) between 2008 and 2010: 578 million.
- Number of countries in sub-Saharan Africa that have adopted Intermittent Preventive Treatment (IPTp)[7] for pregnant women (IPTp) as a national policy by the end of 2008: 35/45
- Percentage of pregnant women in Angola in 2007–2008 who received the second dose of IPTp: 2.4[8]
- Percentage of pregnant women in Zambia in 2007-2008 who received the second dose of IPTp: 62
- Number of countries that have adopted a national policy of IPT for infants (IPTi): 0

MDG7: Ensure Environmental Sustainability[9]

Target: Year by which MDG7a is to integrate the principles of sustainable development into country policies and programmes and reverse the loss of environmental resources: 2015

Target: Year by which MDG7b is to achieve a significant reduction in the rate of biodiversity loss: 2010

Target: Year by which MDG7c is to halve the proportion of people without sustainable access to safe drinking water and basic sanitation: 2015

Target: Year by which MDG7d is to achieve a significant improvement in the lives of at least 100 million slum dwellers: 2020

Indicators: MDG7a: Proportion of land area covered by forest; CO_2 emissions, total, per capita and per U.S.$1 GDP (PPP); consumption of ozone-depleting substances; proportion of fish stocks within safe biological limits; proportion of total water resources used; proportion of terrestrial and marine areas protected; proportion of species threatened with extinction

MDG7b: proportion of population using an improved drinking water source; proportion of population using an improved sanitation facility

MDG7c: proportion of urban population living in slums

- Estimated number of hours every year that women and children in Africa spend fetching and carrying water: 40 billion

MDG8: Develop a Global Partnership for Development

Target 8a: Year by which MDG8a is to develop further an open, rule-based, predictable, non-discriminatory trading and financial system: 2015

Target 8b: Year by which MDG8b is to address the special needs of the least developed countries: 2015

Target 8c: Year by which MDG8c to address the special needs of landlocked developing countries and small island developing states: 2015

Target 8d: Year by which MDG8d to deal comprehensively with the debt problems of developing countries through national and international measures in order to make debt sustainable in the long term: 2015

Target 8e: Year by which MDG8e to provide, in cooperation with pharmaceutical companies, access to affordable essential drugs in developing countries: 2015

Target 8f: Year by which MDG8f to make available, in cooperation with the private sector, the benefits of new technologies, especially information and communications: 2015

(N.B. Some of the following indicators are monitored separately for the least developed countries [LDCs], Africa, landlocked developing countries and small island developing states.)

Official Development Assistance Indicators: Net ODA, total and to the least developed countries, as a percentage of OECD/DAC donors' gross national income; proportion of total bilateral, sector allocable ODA of OECD/DAC donors to basic social services (basic education, primary health care, nutrition, safe water, and sanitation); proportion of bilateral official development assistance of OECD/DAC donors that is untied; ODA received in landlocked developing countries as a proportion of their gross national incomes; ODA received in small island developing states as a proportion of their gross national incomes.

Market Access Indicators: Proportion of total developed country imports (by value and excluding arms) from developing countries and least developed countries admitted free of duty; average tariffs imposed by developed countries on agricultural products and textiles and clothing from developing countries; agricultural support estimate for OECD countries as a percentage of their gross domestic product; proportion of ODA provided to help build trade capacity.

Debt Sustainability Indicators: Total number of countries that have reached their Heavily Indebted Poor Countries (HIPC) decision points, and number that have reached their HIPC completion points (cumulative); debt relief committed under HIPC and Multilateral Debt Relief Initiatives (MDRI); debt service as a percentage of exports of goods and services.

Targets 8 e and f Indicators: Proportion of population with access to affordable essential drugs on a sustainable basis; telephone lines per 100 population; cellular subscribers per 100 population; Internet users per 100 population.

- Amount of disbursements from Organisation for Economic Co-operation and Development (OECD)[10] Official Development Assistance (ODA)[11] for gender equality in 2002: $2.5 billion (U.S.)
- Amount of disbursements from OECD Official Development Assistance (ODA) for gender equality in 2006: $7.2 billion (U.S.)
- Percentage change in overall ODA disbursements for gender equality from 2002 to 2006: +2
- Proportion of gender equality-focused bilateral aid (of donors marking for gender) to Latin America, the Caribbean, South Asia, and sub-Saharan Africa in 2006: 1/3
- Proportion of gender equality-focused bilateral aid (of donors marking for gender) to the Middle East, North Africa, East Asia, and the Pacific in 2006: 1/5

Note from the editors. A few of the statistics in this Index have been repeated from Hypatia Indexes that appeared earlier in the book, but by being presented in relation to the U.N.'s MDGs, these statistics provide a snapshot of the (slow) progress (as in the case of gender equality in enrolment in primary education, the eradication of poverty, the decline in child mortality rates, the representation of women in public office, the stabilization of the spread of HIV/AIDS and the meeting of targets for improved water) or lack of progress (as in the case of completion of primary education, the decline in employment and an increase in vulnerable employment, the failure to meet the 2010 target for biodiversity conservation and the lack of treatment for HIV/AIDS patients). For a more comprehensive list of success in meeting MDGs, see un.org/millenniumgoals/global.shtml.

These statistics in general reinforce the view that women's and children's needs are defined through social and health development rather than economic or political development, as evidenced by specified targets and gender marker indices for the former themes but not the latter. Moreover, we might critique the indices used to measure gender equality or the MDGs themselves. Perhaps most glaring is the absence of a MDG or an indicator to measure progress against violence against women. The World Health Organization (WHO) notes that "Violence against women in particular hinders progress in achieving development targets. Despite the growing recognition of violence against women as a public health and human rights concern, and of the obstacle it poses for development, this type of violence continues to have an unjustifiably low priority on the international development agenda and in planning, programming and budgeting." For a full discussion of this issue, see WHO 2005, *Addressing Violence Against Women and Achieving the Millennium Development Goals*. At: who.int/gender/documents/women_MDGs_report/en/index.html.

We invite you to think about developing MDGs for your community, province, or for Canada as a whole. What are the major issues that need to be addressed over the next ten years? What targets would you set in order to accomplish these goals? And what indices would you use to measure success?

NOTES

1. According to UNIFEM (2009), "The MDGs are the expression of a global aspiration to eliminate human suffering and promote inclusive development, and they have also become a central element of many national planning systems. The MDGs, with their clear, time-bound targets, provide the core elements of a tracking system, with indicators against which progress can be measured and monitored around the world. In this sense, they form a key element of accountability systems — they outline the outcomes expected from national and international investments in poverty reduction, education, health, and environmental protection. They provide not just shared indicators of progress, but they are reviewed in regular global events — such as the High Level Event on the MDGs in September 2008 — during which progress may be assessed, deficits subjected to scrutiny, and efforts redoubled" (2009: 116). Source: UNIFEM, 2009, *Who Answers to Women? Gender and Accountability. Progress on the World's Women, 2008–2009*. At: unifem.org/materials/item_detail.php?ProductID=134. For further information on the background of the MDGs, see un.org/millenniumgoals/bkgd.shtml.
2. "Vulnerable employment is defined as self-employed workers or those contributing to family work with little or no pay" (UNIFEM 2009: 118).
3. "The employment to population ratio is defined as the number of employed persons, calculated as a percentage of the working-age population. The employment-to-population ratio (Figure MDG1.2) indicates the extent to which economies use the productive potential of men and women" (UNIFEM 2009: 119).
4. The only target for MDG3 is to achieve educational parity. This goal is also the target for MDG2.
5. This figure has remained virtually the same since 1990.
6. WHO, 2010, *World Malaria Report*. At: un.org/millenniumgoals/pdf/World_Malaria_Report_2010.pdf.
7. According to the WHO *World Malaria Report*, "Intermittent preventive treatment in pregnancy (IPTp): All pregnant women at risk of *P. falciparum* infection in countries in sub-Saharan Africa with stable malaria transmission should receive at least two doses of sulfadoxine-pyrimethamine (SP), given at the first and second scheduled antenatal care visits (at least one month apart) after 'quickening' (the first noted movement of the fetus)" (2010: 5).
8. This data is based on households surveys conducted in eight countries for which data were available for 2007–2009 (WHO 2010: xiv).

9. According to UNIFEM, "Data is scarce on the impact of environmental degradation and climate change on poor women. However the strong correlation between the time taken by women to fetch and carry water and the availability of water on the household premises suggest that changes in climate through drought, floods, erratic rainfall and deforestation will increase women's work in water and household fuel collection" (2009: 130).

10. For more information about the OECD, see oecd.org/home/0,2987,en_2649_201185_1_1_1_1_1,00.html.

11. According to UNIFEM, "Bilateral Sector Allocable Overseas Development Aid (ODA) refers to aid from bilateral sources allocated to identifiable sectors (like education and health). Non-sector allocable aid includes budgetary support and other forms of assistance that do not target specific sectors. Total ODA includes bilateral and multilateral DAC members and is identified as sector-allocable or non sector-allocable aid" (2009: 132). UNIFEM notes that much international attention is being paid to aid effectiveness, but "the importance of addressing gender inequality through aid and governance has not been adequately recognized in the largely technical agenda of the Paris Declaration. To date, no consistent tracking system of investment on gender equality aid exists in multilateral institutions; an exception is the OECD gender marker, but less than half of the funds eligible for 'screening' use this marker" (2009: 133).

91

Finding the "I" in Action
Defining Activism to Include Me

Natalie Gerum

When I say the word "activist," what do you think of? A red bandana, a smoke bomb, and a placard for change? A blockade across a logging road, with people chained to trees as bulldozers inch closer? Or do you think of a straight-A student with a role in the school play, a seat in the jazz band, and a position on the student council? I didn't, either. The bandana and the smoke bomb — that's how I defined activism. And it wasn't how I defined myself.

Growing up in Hamilton, Ontario, I was a good student, and good students weren't activists — good students couldn't be activists. We didn't speak out against authority or go to protests or challenge policy; we followed the rules, respected our teachers and accepted the status quo. I didn't want to participate in organizations that were considered fringe and fanatical, because I knew the adults in my life would disapprove. And the actions these groups took scared me: they seemed so pushy, so aggressive. Tear gas and riot squads — those had nothing to do with me.

Environmentalism, especially, *really*, had nothing to do with me. Environmental activists were always the ones on the evening news facing off against police squads. Not only did they prompt a few disapproving headlines each week, but they also talked about issues I'd never learned about in school or at home. Of all the activist issues, I identified least with environmental concerns. Environmentalists had the bandanas plus beards and bare feet. No, I was a good student, and all I wanted was one day to become a good teacher.

Then, I kicked off my shoes. In the summer of 2002 I participated in the Pearson Seminar on Youth Leadership (PSYL) in Victoria, British Columbia. Every year PSYL brings together 120 youth from across Canada and around the globe and encourages them to explore and develop skills that will help them become future community and world leaders. At PSYL, I expected to meet presidents of student councils, food bank volunteers, and people who taught swimming lessons — people like me. I most definitely didn't expect to meet an activist on my first night there. We were all sitting on the lawn of one of the dormitories, getting to know each other and telling stories. All of a sudden, this girl started talking about protests she'd been to and what it was like to be tear-gassed and dragged away by riot squads. She used acronyms I didn't understand and talked about free trade agreements and international policies I'd never heard of. She was incredibly informed, well-spoken and knowledgeable — and I was totally intimidated. This girl fell right into my definition of activism; everything she talked about was what I avoided. Yet she was articulate, thoughtful, and friendly. I went to bed that night very anxious about the next three weeks. Did everybody else there have stories like that girl's?

I went to the opening presentation of the seminar scared that I'd stick out, that someone would realize I didn't really understand why the United States was invading Iraq, or didn't know what areas of British Columbia were being clear-cut, or couldn't list the companies that used child labour. It was one of the only times in my life I've sat in the back row, and the only time during PSYL, because after the first day, everything in my universe changed, including me.

Over the next three weeks we participated in interactive workshops, simulation exercises, and creative activities run by the program coordinators and took in a series of presentations by guest speakers from a variety of different movements for change. Lyndsay was one of our first presenters. "'The media' doesn't get it," she said when she started her workshop. She had pink hair, and started her own organization about critical thinking, media, and globalization when she was nineteen. She was so articulate, so informed — and she was an activist. I could relate to what she was saying, though — it made sense to me. Before I heard her speak, globalization was a word I heard once in a while, but I never understood what it meant or how it was relevant to me. Globalization, Lyndsay explained, affected who controlled the media and what information was made available to citizens. And the media influenced how I perceived the world. I learned that globalization, "an activist issue," mattered in my life.

I began to see that I was connected to activist issues, but I still didn't know much about them, and I was apprehensive about my ignorance. Where was I supposed to begin to learn what's wrong with the world and how to fix it? Not having the knowledge about global issues was another barrier to my becoming involved in effecting change.

But at PSYL, I learned not to be ashamed of how little I knew. In her workshop about privatization in Bolivia, Sheelagh, our coordinator, asked us, "What happens to the provision of a service once it's privatized?" That question would once have sent me running for the safety of the back row, but I felt I was in a safe space at the seminar, free to ask as many questions as I wanted and to begin becoming informed. It wasn't too late to start learning about water privatization and other global issues. It wasn't too late to become active — but I wasn't prepared to become an activist.

Even though I began to see how activist issues related to me and knew that I could get informed about these issues, I couldn't get over the negative connotations of the word "activist" or those images of belligerent protesters on the evening news. However, I soon learned that those smoke bombs and bulldozers had nothing to do with one of Canada's most well-respected activists.

Dr. Mary Wynne-Ashford is a member of Physicians for Global Survival, an anti-nuclear organization working to abolish nuclear weapons. On the anniversary of the nuclear bombing of Nagasaki in World War II, she came to PSYL to give a presentation on her involvement in the movement to abolish nuclear armaments. This incredibly educated woman didn't fit my stereotype of an activist — she was a grandmother and a doctor. But she actively demonstrated and spoke out against nuclear weapons and dedicated her life to creating a safer world. Her activism was intimidating; it was empowering, and it made me realize that there were many kinds of activism — and activists. What I had seen on the news was only one very biased portrayal of activists; the smoke bombs the media showed were really a smoke screen of prevailing anti-activist sentiment. I realized that it takes all different kinds of people to make change, and I could be one of those people. I could be an activist.

After PSYL, I could no longer accept that it was wrong to stand up and take action for what I believed in. At the seminar I'd built incredible relationships with all kinds of activists. These individuals weren't wrong — they were doing the right thing to build a better world.

Throughout PSYL, we'd taken Mahatma Gandhi's challenge to humanity: to be the change that we wanted to see in the world. At the end of those three weeks, I realized those words were a call to activism, a world that included Lyndsay and Sheelagh and Dr. Ashford — and could even include me. I learned not only that global issues affect me, but also, and more important, that *I* could affect these issues if I chose to.

I also became much better informed. Before the seminar, I wouldn't have known where to find information about contemporary global issues: PSYL afforded me an "in." After that summer I felt that by learning about these activist issues, I'd taken a first step towards making change and taking action, and the next steps came much more easily.

I have come to think of activism as twofold: it means *being* the change, actively leading a life that reflects the kind of world you want to live in, and it's about creating action beyond yourself and acting as an agent of change. It's about believing in something so passionately that you can't just contain it within your own life; you want, need, feel a responsibility to share it with others — your family, your friends, your community, your government, your world. Activism is action that happens on both a personal and a public level, and I was ready to make activism part of my life.

As I redefined activism to include myself, I also needed to redefine my life to include activism. I still wanted to be a teacher, but now I wanted to facilitate for others the kind of experience I had at PSYL, where I felt I'd received a much more relevant education than I had ever gotten at school. I realized that, for education to truly create positive change, it needed to nurture agents of change. It needed to give students an "in" to learning about global issues and affirm that activism wasn't wrong. As I searched for a chance to further develop these ideas about education, I remembered that two of our co-ordinators from PSYL, Meredith and Mark, worked for an outdoor school in B.C., and I knew that anything these two incredible individuals were involved with had to be worth checking out.

Based out of British Columbia's Sunshine Coast, Sea to Sky Outdoor School for Sustainability Education is a leader in environmental and experiential education in Canada. Recognizing the need to empower students to become conscientious actors, not only on environmental issues, but also in life, Sea to Sky welcomes school groups from across southern British Columbia each year during the spring and fall to embrace the ideals of community, leadership, and action in the hope of shifting our society towards a more sustainable future.

After just four days of volunteering on one of the school's island sites, I was overwhelmed by inspiration: students were engaged in what they were learning; the teachers, known as "Islanders," were a co-operative, creative, and committed team of educators; and the school community dynamically fused a love for learning and a love of the earth. My plans for the future shifted significantly following my time at Sea to Sky.

Environmentalism has been the final frontier of activism for me — even after PSYL, I still found it daunting. I realize now that my discomfort with it had nothing to do with beards and bare feet, and everything to do with my having no desire to incorporate environmentalism into my life. I was comfortable with my daily habits and didn't want to make sacrifices. But at Sea to Sky, we were all living in a way that was completely compatible with environmental consciousness: I was composting, stagger-showering, and eating vegetarian. And it was empowering. Just as PSYL had been my "in" to activism, Sea to Sky was my "in" to environmentalism. I came to recognize my connection to the earth; I saw how my choices affected the planet, and I realized that, although I was part of the problem, I could be part of the solution — my engagement made a difference. The Sea to Sky approach towards sustainability wasn't mainstream, but I wasn't alone in adopting it, either. I now understood, after having lived and learned beside the amazing Islander team, that I had support in my ambitions from a whole community of folks choosing to live more lightly on the earth.

I knew then that sustainability education was my kind of activism. One of the songs from Sea to Sky's "Sounds of Sustainability" repertoire sums up my journey of finding passion as a person and as an activist.

Go wild, let the wonder flow
Go wild, let the wisdom grow

And when you feel your heart go beyond your skin
And you know that's the way it's always been
Tell me what are you waiting for?
Go wild, get your self outdoors.

There were no more reasons to wait before taking action. I'd logically reasoned and thought out my definition of activism; now I *felt* it. A few years ago after that first visit to the island when I threw open the doors to activism, I'm feeling it more than ever.

I don't know yet if I want to teach in a school or work with popular education initiatives outside the classroom. However, I do know that as an educator, I don't want to be confined by curriculum or school board mandates; I don't want to constrain students' energy and enthusiasm within four walls and credit requirements; and I don't want anything to do with existing conventions — I want to replace convention with community, care, courage, and consciousness. I want to inspire passion and encourage action. I want to be an educator for activism.

When I say the word "activist," don't think about the smoke bomb and bandana, forget the chains and the bulldozers, and tune out the angry chanting. When I say the word "activist," think of the possibilities, think about your passion, and think of yourself.

NOTE

Natalie Gerum, 2007, "Finding the 'I' in Action: Defining Activism to Include Me," in Daniel Cohen, Aldana, Severn Cullis-Suzuki, Kris Frederickson, Ahmed Kayssi and Cynthia MacKenzie (eds.), *Notes from Canada's Young Activists*, Vancouver and Berkeley: Greystone Books. Adapted and reprinted with permission.

92

Husband's Wives and Other Myths of Activism by Forestry-Town Women

Maureen G. Reed

There is now a large popular and academic literature that documents and celebrates women's environmental activism, which suggests that women are moral and logistical leaders in social protest and nature protection (e.g., Berman et al. 1994; Shiva 1989; Merchant 1995; Mellor 1997; Sturgeon 1997). In contrast, there is very little work that explores the perspectives of women who appear to support resource exploitation. Previous research about rural women's activism has either considered women who organize to protect the natural environment (eco-feminism) or studied women who seek to protect rural livelihoods (labour studies). The purpose of my research was to try to understand the motivations, perspectives and actions of women who supported industrial forestry on Canada's West Coast during the 1990s (see Reed 1997, 2000, 2003). I wanted to learn more and to find a way to bridge this divide in the literature.

During the 1990s, in British Columbia, land use regulations were changing, and planning processes were underway to allocate more lands for protection from resource use. Several new acts or major policy initiatives were introduced to protect forest ecosystems. These initiatives increased the technical requirements of many types of jobs, requiring workers to gain certification to use/maintain certain equipment, or to ensure their work was in compliance with new standards. Despite the fact that historical rates of overcutting, technological, and market shifts all contributed to changes in the industry, workers and companies united against government and environmental organizations to retain their hold on remaining stands. By the mid-1990s, government-induced changes met with massive protests from men and women living in forested rural communities who argued that forestry communities and culture were now the endangered species in need of protection.

In my study, I analyzed policy documents and Census data, and undertook fifty interviews and three focus groups with women living in nine forestry communities on northern Vancouver Island where, according to one government study, 51 percent of employment income came from forestry occupations in 1996 (Horne 1999).[1] Almost 15,000 people lived in the region. I targeted women who worked in forestry-related occupations (government, industry, non-governmental organizations) and/or were partnered with men in forestry. Forty-one of the women interviewed fit into this category.[2]

Interpreting Women's Community Work

Women's politics — sometimes referred to as maternal politics or social mothering — relates to actions taken by women to protect traditional obligations without disrupting the dominant gender norms, practices and relations (Ruddick 1989).[3] Scholars of women's work in rural and resource towns have adopted this theme, attributing women's activist roles in community-based organizations to their roots in a conservative ideology related to social mothering. They have suggested that women become involved to a far greater extent than men in self-help, voluntary, community-based caring activities as an extension of traditional family values and priorities and/or to compensate for limited access to social welfare and public services (Marchak 1983; Little 1987, 2002; Seitz 1995). Such activities rarely challenge either the decision-making responsibilities within rural communities, the structure of gender relations or the division of labour (Little 1987). Feminist scholars have tended to view actions tied to supporting the "family home" as conservative ones aimed at retaining the status quo. Yet there are challenges to this interpretation.

In a conservative culture, a community may legitimate women's political participation if it is considered an extension of the patriarchal views of women as wives and mothers, particularly in places where the primary role of men has been difficult or impossible to fulfill (Murray 1995). Kathleen Murray's (1995) study of women's activism in forestry towns of Newfoundland revealed that women do not simply passively accept the boundaries of social behaviour, but they use their roles as caretakers and nurturers to actively maneuver within the boundaries of local patriarchal norms and structures. Similarly, scholars of gender/development studies and environmental justice suggest that women mobilize politically as wives and mothers, not just to support traditional gender norms but in recognition of "practical gender interests." Their efforts challenge the power relationships inherent in the gendered, classed and racialized (and possibly other) positions of women and men (for extensive discussion, see Molyneux 1985; Moser 1989; Mayoux 1995; Parpart 1995; di Chiro 1998; 2000). With these ideas in mind, where might the actions of forestry-town women fit?

Seeing the Trees Among the Stories of Forestry-Town Women

Many women in my own study undertook front-line protests in support of forestry at the B.C. Legislature, in Clayoquot Sound, and/or during local events. But these activities were not their only or most important forms of community activism. Indeed, forty of the women who were publicly active took part in seventy-four local voluntary organizations.[4] From the interviews, I generated detailed stories of individual women (Reed 2000, 2003). The stories revealed both consistency and contradiction within and across individual interviews. I found a few women who lived out the stereotype of the "traditional" family life. Some were active in Canadian Women in Timber (CWIT), a pro-industry group that supports fairly traditional interpretations of appropriate roles for women in forestry and family settings. Others who supported forestry in other ways found CWIT "too traditional" (their words).

The women in my study knew that structural changes were happening in the industry and that their communities needed to diversify if they were to survive. Some spoke openly about the huge profits and waste of the early years, the fact that the old growth is declining, and that logging companies are only grudgingly changing their practices. Women who worked as registered professional foresters spoke openly about the sexism within the forestry profession. Some spoke of ways in which influential community members had invoked an unhealthy silence about the changes before them. Yet women from all backgrounds spoke compassionately about the fears and concerns that loggers had for their jobs, for their health (physical and mental) as well as for their local environments. They spoke about the increased stress on professional foresters and waged workers, the fear of new legal sanctions if they make mistakes, the increased paper work and/or technical requirements to meet the new standards and the decreased ability to undertake proper field analysis.

Interpreting the actions and political agendas of women's community work is tricky. Where women's community work is viewed as a "natural" extension of their home responsibilities, it is frequently viewed as conservative. By engaging in community work, women who were not employed could gain some of the benefits of paid employment, such as improved social, organizational and technical skills, and greater self-esteem and a sense of place within a male-dominated community. Yet their work frequently supported the male-dominated employment structure and local culture. Women volunteers were rarely considered "local experts" either within or beyond their local communities. Instead, these women are apt to be labelled (by partners, local decision makers and academics) "good girls," because they are doing what is expected by community norms.

Even if women break out of the notion that "family" motivates their perspective, they may also be branded conservative. Those who seek to protect industrial forestry versus the environment are often classified on the right wing of these debates. Yet, many women I interviewed called themselves feminists. They worked to improve conditions for women, providing safe places for women who were subjected to violence, arguing for better health services, addressing employment disparity within their communities and working on community development issues that were particularly relevant to women. Furthermore, they contested the idea that they did not actively protect the environment. While many women protested against wilderness preservation groups, they undertook many daily activities to protect nature. One woman, for example, kept constant watch for whales to support a scientific research project, others worked with youth to restore local streams and fish populations. Their motivations were to promote family cohesion, youth well-being, environmental protection, and community development. Many women spoke of a love of nature and a regular and ongoing intimacy with the non-human environment. Some challenged urbanites to become as knowledgeable about and active in protecting their own local environments.

In short, I found that explanations that emphasized "traditional family norms" (labour studies) or "environmental sensibilities" (eco-feminism) did not account for the multiple layerings that shape women's lives or multiple forms or sites of women's political activism. For people living in these communities on northern Vancouver Island, family, place and lifestyle were intimately interwoven. As a result of these more diverse stories, I sought other theories to explain women's perspectives and actions.

The Embeddedness of Women's Activism

I began to view women's perspectives and choices for activism as nested within local social and spatial contexts. In my case, details of these contexts relate to local effects of restructuring of the forest industry, changing ecologies, reorganization of government environmental and social policies, geographic and social isolation, the availability of physical and social infrastructure, local labour practices, community social norms, and gender ideologies and practices within households. These factors inscribed women's identities and shaped their motivations for, and choices about, forestry and political activism. I found that women's support of workers, forestry practices, and forestry culture was not unified, conservative, progressive, or crassly material. Rather, women's activism, both individual and collective, could be more accurately identified as heterogeneous and contingent, complex, contradictory and *embedded*.

Drawing on embeddedness as a spatial connotation of being rooted in place and in social life, human geographers, Susan Hanson and Geraldine Pratt argued that the concept is valuable because it "opens the recognition that gendered identities, including aspirations and desires, *are fully embedded in* — and indeed inconceivable apart from — place and that different gender identities are shaped through different places" (1995: 18, emphasis added). The idea of embeddedness within specific situations of place and social relations may bridge the gap between feminists primarily concerned with women's connections to economic and social life (e.g., labour studies students), and feminists concerned with women's connections to their non-human environments (e.g., eco-feminist researchers). If gender identities are shaped by and embedded within material and cultural conditions, we might anticipate that gender practices are played out differently in forestry towns and in urban settings.

I used the notion of embeddedness because I believe it helps to explain multiple motivations, perspectives and activisms of forestry-town women, and avoids classifying activities into static dichotomies of "pro" versus "anti" environmental actions. Embeddedness may also help to maintain an engaged and sympathetic understanding of the complex and contradictory nature of women's lives that is attempted by feminist research methods (Reinharz 1992; Moss et al. 1993; England 1994). By listening and considering alternative viewpoints, feminist researchers can help build an environmental movement that goes beyond ideological positioning and invites multiple others to take standing in ongoing debates.

NOTES

Acknowledgements: This study was funded by the late Crown corporation, Forest Renewal BC. The Centre for Research in Women's Studies and Gender Relations provided a safe space to begin this research. Paul Jance, Keith Bigelow and Cathie Williamson provided technical assistance. Maija Heimo, Janice May and Mary Pullen were research assistants. I thank those from Vancouver Island who helped me in this research, including the women who agreed to share their stories. Thank you to C. Lesley Biggs and Pam Downe for including me in the fold.

1. This number was even higher for particular communities (e.g., 58 percent for Port McNeill and 84 percent for Port Alice (Horne 1999).
2. A detailed description of the methodology is available in Reed (2001).
3. Women's politics is different from feminist politics, which Sue Ruddick (1989: 234) defines as "dedicated to transforming those social and domestic arrangements that (minimally) deliberately or unwittingly penalize women because of their sex."
4. This tally excludes activities in community events, Aboriginal organizations and organizations related to children and sports (e.g., parent advisory committees, Brownies, sporting teams).

REFERENCES

Berman, T., G. Ingram, M. Gibbons, R. Hatch, L. Maignon and C. Hatch. 1994. *Clayoquot and Dissent*. Vancouver: Ronsdale Press.

Di Chiro, G. 2000. "Bearing Witness or Taking Action? Toxic Tourism and Environmental Justice." In R. Hofitcher (ed.), *Reclaiming the Environmental Debate: The Politics of Health in a Toxic Culture*. Cambridge, MA: MIT Press.

___. 1998. "Environmental Justice from the Grassroots: Reflections on History, Gender and Expertise." In D. Faber (ed.), *The Struggle For Ecological Democracy: Environmental Justice Movements in the United States*. New York: Guilford.

England, K. 1994. "Getting Personal: Reflexivity, Positionality, and Feminist Research." *Professional Geographer* 46.

Hanson, S., and G. Pratt. 1995. *Gender, Work, and Space*. London and New York: Routledge.

Horne, G. 1999. *British Columbia Local Area Economic Dependencies and Impact Ratios 1996*. Victoria, BC: Business and Economic Statistics, Ministry of Finance and Corporate Relations.

Little, J. 2002. *Gender and Rural Geography: Identity, Sexuality and Power in the Countryside*. Pearson Educational, Essex.

___. 1987. "Gender Relations in Rural Areas: The Importance of Women's Domestic Role." *Journal of Rural Studies* 3.

Marchak, P. 1983. *Green Gold: The Forest Industry in British Columbia*. Vancouver, BC: UBC Press.

Mayoux, L. 1995. "Beyond Naivety: Women, Gender Inequality and Participatory Development." *Development and Change* 26.

Mellor, M. 1997. *Feminism and Ecology*. Cambridge: Polity Press in association with Blackwell.

Merchant, C. 1995. *Earthcare: Women and the Environment*. London and New York: Routledge.

Molyneux, M. 1985. "Mobilization Without Emancipation? Women's Interests, the State and Revolution in Nicaragua." *Feminist Studies* 11.

Moser, C.O.N. 1989. "Gender Planning in the Third World: Meeting Practical and Strategic Gender Needs." *World Development* 8.

Moss, P., J. Eyles, I. Dyck and D. Rose. 1993. "Focus: Feminism as Method." *The Canadian Geographer* 37.

Murray, K. 1995. "Women's Political Strategies in a Logging Town." In L.F. Felt and P.R. Sinclair (eds.), *Living on the Edge: The Great Northern Peninsula of Newfoundland.* St. John: Institute of Social and Economic Research.

Parpart, J.L. 1995. "Deconstructing the Development 'Expert': Gender, Development and the 'Vulnerable groups.'" In M.H. Marchand and J.L. Parpart (eds.), *Feminism/Postmodernism/Development.* London and New York: Routledge.

Reed, M.G. 2003. *Taking Stands: Gender and the Social Sustainability of Rural Communities.* Vancouver: UBC Press.

___. 2001. "Reconsidering Success and Failure in Feminist Research." In P. Moss (ed.), *Doing Feminist Geography and Being Feminist in Geographic Research.* Oxford: Blackwell.

___. 2000. "Taking Stands: A Feminist Perspective on 'Other' Women's Activism in Forestry Communities of Northern Vancouver Island." *Gender, Place and Culture* 7(4).

___. 1997. "Seeing Trees: Engendering Environmental and Land Use Planning." *The Canadian Geographer* 14(4).

Reinharz, S. 1992. *Feminist Methods in Social Research.* New York and Oxford: Oxford University Press.

Ruddick, S. 1989. *Maternal Thinking: Towards a Politics of Peace.* Boston: Beacon Press.

Seitz, V.R. 1995. *Women, Development, and Communities for Empowerment in Appalachia.* Albany, NY: State University of New York Press.

Shiva, V. 1989. *Staying Alive: Women, Ecology and Development.* Delhi: Kali for Women and London: Zed Press.

Sturgeon, N. 1997. *Ecofeminist Natures: Race, Gender, Feminist Theory and Political Action.* New York and London: Routledge.

93

Midwifery Care in Canada
Looking Back, Looking Forward
Sheryl Nestel

What comes to mind when midwives and midwifery are raised as topics of discussion in relation to childbearing in Canada today? For some, it may be the hazy literary image of Sairey Gamp, the dirty crone of Charles Dickens' 1884 novel *Martin Chuzzlewit*, or maybe the witch/midwife portrayed in the infamous fifteenth-century religious tract *Malleus Maleficarum*,[1] or even the hippy midwife whose back-to-the-land philosophy includes the rejection of medicalized childbirth and of the scientific rationality upon which it is based. Many simply regard midwives as relics of a medical past in which childbirth was a much riskier event for mothers and babies; they view the transfer of maternity care to physicians as a marker of the ways in which modern medicine has improved maternal and infant health. For some, however, the term "midwife" conjures up a far more positive image. For them, the twenty-first-century midwife is a modern health-care professional, characterized not only by her extensive formal training, but also by her belief that childbirth is a normal physiological process, one endowed with social, spiritual and biological meaning. The different meanings ascribed to midwifery noted above convey, albeit crudely, the dividing lines along which recent struggles over whose definition of childbirth will prevail and whether or not there is room for multiple, and at times competing, approaches to maternity care in technologically advanced countries such as Canada. Midwives and their supporters undoubtedly challenge the dominance of the medical management of childbirth.

Where Have All the Midwives Gone?

Historians have offered a number of explanations as to how and why physicians wrested control from midwives, ultimately claiming authority over maternity care in Canada and the United States. Recent accounts ascribe the rise of medical dominance to the convergence of several factors. Historians have argued that efforts by physicians in the late nineteenth and early twentieth century promoted restrictive legislation which ultimately eliminated competition, not just from midwives but also from healers trained outside the scientific medical tradition (Biggs 1990). Protective licensing laws discouraged midwives from continuing their practice, leaving space for physicians to extend their professional reach into the area of childbirth. Geographical distances, family responsibilities, language barriers and a failure to see midwifery as a "profession" all contributed to the disappearance of midwifery in Canada (Bourgeault 2006: 50). By the middle of the twentieth century, childbirth had been transformed from an important family- and community-centred biological and social event into one whose location was the hospital and whose meaning was primarily medical. The trend to hospitalization for all women appeared unstoppable, with the figure for hospital births in Canada reaching 76 percent in 1950 (Mitchinson 2002: 175).

The Routinization of Medicalized Childbirth

The move from home to hospital and from midwife to physician attendance at childbirth has its roots in philosophical precepts that are still with us more than three centuries after their appearance. Emerging from Enlightenment philosophies that saw science as being able to free humankind from the superstitions and irrationality of medieval life, a new European worldview embraced scientific rationality and the technologies it produced as harbingers of human freedom and well-being. The role of the human body was central to this worldview. Positing the notion of a firm mind/body duality, seventeenth-century French philosopher René Descartes saw the human body as a machine that could be understood and controlled through the application of scientific principles, while the mind was knowable by God alone. Such a view has persisted and has exercised a formative influence over the practice of medicine. As feminist sociologist Barbara Katz Roth argues, in the context of this mechanized view of the body, "problems in the body are technical problems requiring technical solutions, whether it is a mechanical repair, a chemical rebalancing or a 'debugging' of the system" (Katz Rothman 1991: 34). This concept however has been applied differently to male and female bodies. As anthropologist Robbie Davis-Floyd puts the matter:

> The men who established the idea of the body as a machine also firmly established the male body as the prototype of this machine. Insofar as it deviated from the male standard, the female body was regarded as abnormal, inherently defective and dangerously under the influence of nature, which due to its unpredictability and its occasional monstrosities, was itself regarded as inherently defective and in need of constant manipulation by man. (Davis-Floyd 1992: 51)

However, gender classification must be viewed also in the context of the nineteenth-century project of racial categorization that posited the inherent inferiority and other shared characteristics of women and people of colour. Such categorization has had a profound effect on medical practice: the intertwining of the categories of race and gender is important to discern when examining scientific approaches to women's reproductive care. Indeed many important gynaecological operations were only integrated into obstetrical care after they had been practised on African-American slaves in the American South. In the racist thinking of the day, it was assumed that African-American women would suffer less pain from the medical experimentation than white women (McGregor 1998).

The Beginnings of Reform

Popularized largely by two European obstetricians, both of whom were male, challenges to the medical model of childbirth emerged as early as the 1930s. Grantly Dick-Read in Great Britain and Fernand Lamaze in France introduced methods for "natural childbirth" which were subsequently embraced, largely by white middle-class women both in Europe and North America, starting in the 1940s (Edwards and Waldorf 1984). Their approach involved specialized breathing techniques (psychoprophylaxis), the presence of partners in the birthing room, and overcoming the pain and fear that characterized "civilized" women's attitudes toward childbirth.[2] The 1950s and 1960s saw a proliferation of organizations devoted to promoting alternatives to medicalized childbirth and the "scientific" infant care practices it spawned (Apple 2006). One such organization was the La Leche League, which encouraged women to embrace breastfeeding, a practice that had declined dramatically in the post-war years. While "natural childbirth" methods signalled women's refusal to participate in medicalized childbirth, such methods largely upheld rather than challenged traditional attitudes towards motherhood, touting childbirth as an experience that strengthened marriage and the nuclear family, and promoting childrearing as a new science, which demanded a full-time maternal commitment (Ehrenreich and English 1978). While many hospitals were influenced by the call for more homelike settings and liberalized policies for partners and other birth companions, in the long run, "natural childbirth" techniques did virtually nothing to change the power balance in the birthing room, producing instead a more compliant patient. Sociologist Barbara Katz Rothman described the "natural childbirth" scenario as "mother, coached by father, behaves herself while doctor delivers the baby" (Rothman 1991: 93). Indeed, feminist theorizing of birth and motherhood burgeoned following Adrienne Rich's (1976) groundbreaking book *Of Woman Born*, which offers a scathing critique of the natural childbirth movement's reinforcement of racist and patriarchal social norms.

The Re-emergence of Midwifery in Canada

While early movements for childbirth reform may have championed traditional roles for women, they also challenged the dominance of medical knowledge, trumpeted a woman-centred model for childbirth and infant care, and helped re-introduce home birth as an alternative to medicalized hospital birth (Rothman 1991: 108). While incompatible on some levels, traditional childbirth reformers and the emerging feminist movement of the 1970s in Canada were able to join forces despite lack of consensus on issues such as abortion.

Indeed, the re-emergence of midwifery in the 1970s in Canada represented a convergence of multiple and sometimes conflicting forces. These forces included not only the feminist and traditional women's health movements mentioned above (some of which challenged the medical management of childbirth), but also counterculture lifestyle practices, and efforts by largely British-trained midwives to have their skills recognized within the health-care system. Ontario, the first province to legalize midwifery, boasts a particularly complex history of the profession's re-emergence. In the 1960s and early 1970s some Toronto women, often from marginalized religious communities, and, increasingly, women and their partners who sought birth experiences outside of the hospital setting, utilized the services of doctors willing to provide care at home births (Bourgeault 2006).

In the 1970s some women, through apprenticeship and self-directed study, acquired the skills necessary to the provision of reproductive care within a framework that promoted informed choice in the birthing process, appropriate use of technology and the recognition of birth as a psycho-social as well as a physiological event. Central to this form of midwifery has been the belief that while choice of birthplace is a fundamental right, a woman's home is the birthing venue most likely to provide the optimum conditions for the achievement of humanized childbirth.[3] By the mid-1980s, midwifery shifted from a loosely organized social movement to a tightly orchestrated political project that systematically pursued state regulation and funding for the revitalized profession.

After more than a decade of concerted political activity, the first Canadian legislation establishing midwifery as a state-regulated and state-funded health profession was passed into law in Ontario on December 31, 1993. Hailed as a "victory for women" (Martin 1992: 417), the enactment of midwifery legislation in Ontario has been viewed as a triumph of grassroots feminist organizing and as part of the ongoing struggle for gender equity and female reproductive autonomy. This important change in health care, however, has not been immune to criticism. In my earlier work (2007), I found that the process of legalization has been a racially exclusionary one because thousands of immigrant midwives of colour who might have practised were unable to qualify.[4] As a result, not all women have benefitted equally from the implementation of midwifery. First Nations women worked to have Aboriginal midwifery severed from the legislation for fear that it would render the work of some traditional practitioners illegal. At present Aboriginal women throughout Canada are striving to revive traditional Aboriginal practices and train enough practitioners to serve urban and rural First Nations women (Native Women's Association of Canada 2007).

Midwifery is currently legal (but not necessarily funded) in all provinces except Prince Edward Island.[5] Baccalaureate-granting midwifery programs exist in British Columbia, Manitoba, Ontario and Quebec, and programs are poised to open in other provinces in the future. Currently, nearly 800 midwives are registered to practice in Canada.

The Midwifery vs. the Medical Model of Care: Which Will Prevail?

As of 2009 in Canada, only a small minority of births — between 1 percent in Alberta and 8 percent in Ontario (canadianmidwives.org/british_columbia.htm) — are attended by midwives, despite midwifery clients reporting overwhelmingly high degrees of satisfaction with their care. In Ontario, for example, a recent survey by the Ministry of Health and Long-Term Care found that 98.7 percent of midwifery clients expressed satisfaction (Cameron 2005: 207). Numerous reasons exist for this disparity between satisfaction levels and the low numbers of midwife-assisted births, the most important being that the demand for midwifery care continues to outstrip the availability of midwives in most provinces and territories. When a service provides more extensive and more personalized care (including in the postpartum period) than do physicians; encourages an active decision-making role for child-bearing women in pregnancy and birthing rather than a relative loss of autonomy; costs less than half of a physician's care; and offers women the choice of home or hospital birth, it is difficult to understand why it has not become the model of care that most women choose, when it is appropriate and available. For some women, obstetrical care in hospital and access to all that contemporary medical science has to offer are essential to a healthy outcome. However, for many women, midwifery offers a form of care that emphasizes the normalcy of pregnancy and birthing, where medical resources are utilized only when absolutely necessary. Admittedly, it is difficult to accept as "normal," processes that we have been urged to treat as inherently risky and dangerous. In times when we are compelled to use our health-care resources more judiciously, we may find that the revival of a model of maternity care that was for so long distrusted may offer both midwives and physicians a template for providing more satisfying and healthier reproductive experiences for all women.

NOTES

1. For a critical examination of the witch midwife figures, see Barbara Ehrenreich and Deirdre English's influential 1973 pamphlet *Witches, Midwives, and Nurses*.
2. For a discussion of how Dick-Read's philosophy encouraged white mothers to bear more children in the face of substantial immigration of people of colour to Britain from former colonies and a subsequent tide of racism, see Nestel 1995.
3. Current research confirms that when women who were at low risk for obstetrical complications delivered with certified midwives at planned home births, lower rates of medical intervention and outcomes that were as healthy as those of women who delivered in hospital (Johnson and Daviss 2005) occurred.
4. Many factors contributed to the exclusion of racialized minority midwives from practice, including the costs of recertification as well as institutional and interpersonal racism. For a detailed discussion, see Nestel 2007.
5. See Canadian Association of Midwives at: canadianmidwives.org.

REFERENCES

Apple, Rima. 2006. *Perfect Motherhood: Science and Childrearing in America*. New Brunswick, NJ: Rutgers University Press.

Biggs, L. 2004. "Rethinking the History of Midwifery in Canada." In Ivy Lynn Bourgeault, Cecilia Benoit and Robbie Davis-Floyd (eds.), *Reconceiving Midwifery*. Montreal and Kingston: McGill-Queen's University Press.

___. 1990. "'The Case of the Missing Midwives': A History of Midwifery in Ontario from 1795–1900." In K. Arnup, A. Levesque and R.R. Pierson (eds.), *Delivering Motherhood: Maternal Ideologies and*

Practices in the 19th and 20th Centuries. London and New York: Routledge.

Bourgeault, Ivy Lynn. 2006. *Push! The Struggle for Midwifery in Ontario*. Montreal and Kingston: McGill-Queen's University Press.

Cameron, Heather. 2005. "Modern Midwifery in Ontario: An Effective Model of Health Care." *University of Toronto Medical Journal* 82.

Davis-Floyd, R.E. 1992. *Birth as an American Rite of Passage*. Berkeley and Los Angeles: University of California Press.

Edwards, Margot, and Mary Waldorf. 1984. *Reclaiming Birth: History and Heroines of American Childbirth Reform*. Trumansburg, NY: Crossing Press.

Ehrenreich, Barbara, and Deirdre English. 1978. *Witches, Midwives, and Nurses*. New York: Feminist Press.

Johnson, Kenneth C., and Betty-Anne Daviss. 2005. "Outcomes of Planned Home Births with Certified Professional Midwives: Large Prospective Study in North America." *British Medical Journal* 330.

Leavitt, Judith Walzer. 1986. *Brought to Bed: Childbearing in America 1750–1950*. New York: Oxford University Press.

Martin, D. 1992. "The Midwives Tale: Old Wisdom and a New Challenge to the Control of Reproduction." *Columbia Journal of Gender and the Law* 3(1).

McGregor, D.K. 1998. *From Midwives to Medicine: The Birth of American Gynaecology*. New Jersey: Rutgers University Press.

Mitchinson, W. 2002. *Giving Birth in Canada: 1900–1950*. Toronto: University of Toronto Press.

Native Women's Association of Canada. 2007. *Aboriginal Women, Reproductive Health, Midwifery and Birthing Centres: An Issue Paper*.

Nestel, S. 2007. *Obstructed Labour: Race and Gender in the Re-emergence of Midwifery*. Vancouver: University of British Columbia Press.

___. 1995. "'Other' Mothers: Race and Representation in Natural Childbirth Discourse." *Resources for Feminist Research* 23(4).

Rich, A. 1986 [1976]. *Of Woman Born: Motherhood as Experience and Institution*. New York: Norton.

Rothman, B.K. 1991. *In Labor: Women and Power in the Birthplace*. New York: Norton.

94

Tomorrow I'm Going to Rewrite the English Language

Lois Keith

Tomorrow I am going to rewrite the English language.
I will discard all those striving ambulist metaphors
of power and success.
And construct new ways to describe my strength.
My new, different strength.

Then I won't have to feel dependent
Because I can't stand on my own two feet.
And I'll refuse to feel a failure
When I don't stay one step ahead.
I won't feel inadequate if I can't
Stand up for myself
Or illogical when I don't
Take it one step at a time.

I will make them understand that it is a very male way
To describe the world.
All this walking tall
And making great strides.

Yes, tomorrow I am going to rewrite the English Language
Creating the world in my own image.
Mine will be a gentler, more womanly way
To describe my progress.
I will wheel, cover and encircle.
Somehow, I will learn to say it all.

NOTE

Lois Keith, 1996, "Tomorrow I'm Going to Rewrite the English Language," in Lois Keith (ed.), *What Happened To You?* New York: New Press. Reprinted with permission.

95

The Courage to Act as a Male in a Democratic Society

An Examination of the Limits Placed on Men by Patriarchy

Gerry Coulter

I begin my Communication, Gender and Culture course by asking students to write a 500-word essay on the topic: "What does it mean to be a man at the beginning of the twenty-first century?" In the many answers I receive for this assignment, there is one clear area of agreement between most males and females: it is very difficult to be man at the present time. My students write that men now face conflicting messages. On the one hand, men are told to value traditional masculine stereotypes: to be strong, unemotional, stoic and tough. On the other hand, men are told that they should re-examine traditional masculinity, learn to value their human emotions and eschew fighting and toughness in favour of well-reasoned and peaceful settlements.

I am a teacher who deeply values my students and the constant education we receive from each other. What then do I say to them, as a man, about a subject on which we seem to disagree so much? My perspective is very different from most of my students in that I firmly believe there has never been a better time to be a man than the present. I agree that being male can be a little confusing and sometimes difficult, especially in one's late teens and early twenties. I also believe that young men today possess an opportunity never before manifest in recorded history. What is this opportunity and how do young men seize it?

To fully understand what is at stake for young men today involves thinking through: what democratic citizenship means, what being an individual means and what it means to be truly courageous. Being a member of a democratic society means that one is entitled to play a role in government and to possess human rights and guarantees of one's personal dignity. Every citizen has the same rights claims. Yet we all know that there are gaps between the ideal of democracy and equity and the reality of inequality. Democracy is never finished. First Nations people and racialized minorities have been fighting long and hard for an equality that is not yet achieved in North America. Similarly, women have struggled first for universal suffrage and the right to be legally defined as citizens, and today for employment equity and the right to control their own bodies. Each time one of these basic democratic rights battles is won, such as Aboriginals stopping the removal of their children to residential schools, or gays and lesbians gaining legal rights that heterosexuals take for granted, or visible minorities winning a battle against racist actions, or women securing the right to equal pay for work of equal value, our democracy becomes stronger and one step closer to an ideal condition.

While some white males might even oppose some of these changes, they end up benefiting as much as anyone else from the freedom of living life in the best society its people could build at the time. It is also a reassuring aspect of history that many of those who fought against a proposed democratic reform come to realize after it is achieved that their country or community has actually been strengthened by the change. Think for example of the New York Yankees, who have won four of the past six World Series as I write. If we imposed a "whites only" rule on baseball, as existed to the middle of the twentieth century, we would have to remove one third of the team. What is true of sports franchises is true of professional offices and university faculties. Think how much talent we repress when we stand obstacles in the way of the achievement of equality of condition for groups of people.

Think of how many more talented people remain in the wings awaiting North American society to learn to value more fully Aboriginals, gays, lesbians, bi-sexuals, visible minorities, people with disabilities and women, to name only a few undervalued groups. The promise of the democratic victories yet to be won is the promise that we may all benefit from a society with as few barriers as possible to everyone's participation.

The opportunity awaiting young men today is the task of fully embracing democratic society as courageous individuals. This means that young men have to approach those conflicting messages they receive while asking themselves an important question: how am I going to contribute to a more democratic society in a way that makes my life and my community a place where everyone's talents are valued? If young men guide themselves in this way, it will provide them with a strong tool to sort out the messages that may actually limit their lives from the messages that will allow them to enhance their lives.

What I am suggesting is that men today should value one aspect of traditional masculinity that we have always been taught to value: courage. Democratic society is the result of the courageous activity of many people. Indeed, courage is the essential ingredient of citizenship. It is the key to an individual's ability to express their power to act in the world. When we consider that the Latin root of courage is "cor" or heart, we understand that courage is the ability to act on behalf of a prior-felt commitment to do what is right. The enemy of courage is fear. If young men today feel confused or that they should be doing more than they are about equality, it is likely that they are feeling a courageous desire to act, limited by the fear of offending the traditions of patriarchy. Participation in democracy takes courage, just as it takes courage to go out onto any field of play where one may suffer injury. Young men have been taught to overcome fear of the playing field. In the same way, our late teens and early twenties confront us with the challenge of participating in democratic society. To all young men the questions are posed: Do you wish to remain on the bench of life or enter the field of play? Will fear limit your courage to participate in progressive causes?

I would also suggest that if men carefully examine the problem of patriarchy they will find that it is not simply a system in which men dominate women, but rather a system whereby certain men dominate women and other men. As fear is the enemy of the courage to act for a more democratic society, it is also the sustaining force of patriarchal inequality. Among the first things that young men should consider is that patriarchy limits their ability to act as responsible democratic citizens. Commitments to sexism, to racism, to exclusion of any kind limit the individual citizen almost as much as the lives of the excluded are limited. A simple example is the issue of pay equity. While men should support pay equity as a moral principle, we can also consider that an important argument in its favour is that it limits the lives of men in heterosexual partnerships. If the person with whom you share your overall household income is underpaid by her employer, then it is your joint household that is subsidizing the government office or private sector company discriminating against her. In a similar manner, as members of a society rich in diversity, commitments to any kind of inequality and the lack of freedom all forms of it support make us all poorer as social citizens. Men who complain about equity policies and hiring practices seem to forget that a system of "affirmative action" has existed for centuries in western society — affirming of those who were white and male. Why do we never hear "he got that job because he is a man," when it's been going on since time immemorial?

The collection of articles in this book demonstrates very well the problem of patriarchy from the perspective of women. While it is very important for men to support and participate in the equity struggles of women, it is also important to realize that patriarchy also poses devastating limitations for men. Aside from the ability to fully participate in democratic society, commitment to patriarchal conceptions of masculinity also limits the individual male in profound ways.

One of the ways in which traditional conceptions of masculinity hurt men is in terms of health and safety. Often framed as "women's issues," which they clearly are, health and safety concerns are also very important "men's issues." Traditional conceptions of masculinity pose the male body as a weapon and an object to the human being who inhabits it. We are told to be tough, to stand up and fight for ourselves, to hide our tears from public view, to "suck up" pain, to value professional success over family and happiness and to take physical risks. Commitment to this ideal of manhood has given us a world in which we are almost twice as likely to die of heart disease than women, more than two and a half times as likely to die from accidents and their adverse affects, more than twice as likely to die from chronic liver disease and cirrhosis, three and a half times as likely to be a victim of homicide and four times as likely to die from suicide (Sabo 2001: 347). Joining the effort of women's movements committed to safer, healthier communities simply makes good sense when we realize that patriarchy is also killing men.

Our campuses must be made places where any woman can walk without fear, night and day, and also where men do not live in fear of other men. Our roadways and our workplaces should not be places where male commitment to inhuman conceptions of bravado and overwork shorten our lives. Our communities should be places where we can openly discuss our problems, express our sexualities and admit that we have difficulties that require the support of others. Our communities can be made true communities of support and enrichment, not places where men feel their ultimate recourse is self-annihilation. Without the concerted and continued efforts of the current generation of young men, our communities will not become these kinds of places. Being a young man today presents one with an enormous opportunity to expand the efforts of women to build safer communities and to construct a humane definition of what it means to be a man.

An especially problematic aspect of traditional definitions of maleness is the notion that a real man deals with his own problems and difficulties. He is a rock; an emotional island. In my younger years this socialization manifested itself in me in terms of going into periods of several days of distracted brooding while I worked out a problem on my own. After about three days my old self would emerge, ready to tell everyone what I had decided. The process of decision-making was clearly understood as a matter of my own efforts in solitude. Perhaps that is why I made so many poor decisions in my youth. While it may be possible to continue this pattern of solitary decision-making into adulthood, it is not advised, especially if one plans to share one's life with someone else. Among the most important things I have learned from the woman I married is how much less difficult, and painful, it is to discuss my problems with her and my friends, and to consult with others when an important decision arises. I consider the ability to rely on trusted friends and intimates for advice an important aspect of emotional maturity. It is also the basis of a healthy relationship with another person.

One of the things that most separates men and women in intimate relationships is the former's inability to talk intimately. Few things frustrate the typical female more than an uncommunicative male. While our silence may be interpreted as a strength by traditional patriarchs, those patriarchs do not understand the kind of young women with whom young men are seeking partnerships today. To be a man in a successful relationship today requires an openness to communicate about intimate issues. Adherence to the traditional masculine norm of incommunicative problem solving will continue to foster emotional immaturity in adulthood. Today the opportunities for personal emotive development are boundless for men, especially in contrast to previous generations, who suffered alone in silence.

It may seem trite to quote the well worn dictum that "we have nothing to fear but fear itself," but the remark does contain a good deal of truth for young men who are feeling confused today. Fear involves a state of paralysis, an inability to act toward what you know to be the right and just course of action. Overcoming fear will involve supporting female friends, co-workers and colleagues through difficult times. It will mean participating actively in the struggle for more equitable workplaces. It will mean finding words for feelings that are difficult to express. Yet, men who carefully examine the issues will soon discover that they are also fighting important battles for themselves. They will find themselves acting on the impulse of courage to make the world they live in not only a more equitable place for others but a more humane and livable place for themselves. They will be participating in the construction of a society in which it is not at all difficult to be male, to live lives as people without the limits of patriarchy on our democracy, our workplaces and our lives at home. By taking equity seriously, including the re-evaluation of what it means to be a man, young men today also take important steps toward personal and professional success and fulfillment in their broadest meaning. Those who do not are not only missing out in the moral, spiritual and democratic sense, they are being left behind by better possible futures in a material sense as well.

There was never a time in history when it was better to be young and male for those with the courage to act. We are rapidly reaching a place in history when doing the right thing for democracy is also doing the right thing for ourselves, but has it not always been so for those who truly succeed in life and were truly happy with themselves?

REFERENCE

Sabo, Don. 2001. "Masculinity and Men's Health: Moving toward Post-Superman Era Prevention." In Michael Kimmel and Michael Messner (eds.), *Men's Lives* fifth edition. Needham Heights, MA: Allyn and Bacon.

96

Feminism 104

Lillian Allen

revolution

NOTE

Lillian Allen, 1993, "revolution," in Lillian Allen *Women Do This Every Day*, Toronto: Women's Press. Reprinted with permission.